Conflict and Consensus
in American History

Conflict and Consensus

in American History

Volume I

Ninth Edition

Edited by

Allen F. Davis

Temple University

Harold D. Woodman

Purdue University

Houghton Mifflin Company   Boston   New York

For Gregory and Paul
&
Allan and David

Senior Sponsoring Editor: Patricia A. Coryell
Assistant Editor: Jeanne Herring
Associate Project Editor: Elena Di Cesare
Editorial Assistant: Angela Schoenherr
Senior Designer: Henry Rachlin
Associate Production Coordinator: Deb Frydman
Director of Manufacturing: Michael O'Dea
Marketing Manager: Clint Crockett

Cover image and design by Minko Dimov.

Photo Credits

Chapter 1: © North Wind Picture Archives; Chapter 2: © The Massachusetts Historical Society; Chapter 3: © 1993 North Wind Picture Archives; Chapter 4: © Library of Congress (image of Hamilton), © Virginia State Chamber of Commerce (image of Jefferson); Chapter 5: From the Art Collection of The Boatmen's National Bank of St. Louis; Chapter 6: © The Bettman Archive; Chapter 7: © Corbis-Bettmann; Chapter 8: © Brown Brothers; Chapter 9: © The Granger Collection; Chapter 10: © Archive Photos.

Printed in the U.S.A.

Library of Congress Catalog Card Number: 96-76888

ISBN: 0-669-41696-7

23456789-DOH-00 99 98 97

Contents

Preface

We are pleased that the continued success of *Conflict and Consensus in American History* has warranted publication of this ninth edition. Those familiar with earlier editions will note that we have not changed the basic organization. We seek to keep the book useful for the introductory course and, therefore, have retained the traditional periodization found in most of the popular survey texts. But, like the best of these texts, we have given considerable attention to social history, to the history of women and minorities, and to the contributions of ordinary people to the history of the United States. Our goal has been to suggest, whenever possible, how events that have been traditionally viewed from the elite white male perspective often take on new and richer meaning when women, blacks, and common folk are integrated into the story.

In this latest edition, we have also retained our emphasis on the theme of conflict and consensus. Our experience and the experiences of those who have used the book have persuaded us that the presentation of conflicting views of particular periods and problems, when shown within the context of general interpretations, allows students to deepen their understanding of the historical details and provides them with the means to interpret the broad sweep of the country's history. We remain convinced that the theme of conflict and consensus remains viable and valuable more than a generation after the first so-called consensus historians challenged prevailing views. If the issues are not always as starkly presented as they once were, they nevertheless remain important sources of disagreement among historians, as the selections in this volume make clear.

In this edition, as in the previous ones, we have avoided presenting only two extreme positions on each problem raised. Such an either/or approach is artificial, and forces students to choose between extremes or to conclude, without adequate evidence, that the truth must be midway between the two extremes. We have, therefore, included three selections dealing with each problem and have chosen selections that illustrate the subtleties of interpretation rather than stark and rigid presentations of either point of view. Although we have sought to be up to date by choosing selections illustrating the most recent scholarship, we reject the idea that the newest is always the best and therefore have retained older work we deemed important, influential, and of high quality.

In the third edition we added a general introduction designed to help the beginning student understand why historians disagree. We found that students were often confused rather than enlightened when presented with conflicting interpretations of the same events. Too often they lacked the skills needed to discern the bases of disagreements. Perhaps because of their experience in memorizing details and answering multiple-choice questions, they concluded that when historians disagreed, one must be right and the others wrong. Instead of seeing a variety of interpretations as a means to enrich and broaden their understanding of the nation's past, many students concluded that the inclusion of a variety of interpretations was a little trick designed to force them to discover the "right" answer. Because of the favorable response to this brief introduction to historical methods and philosophy, we have retained it with some revisions, including a brief discussion of the most recent developments in historical scholarship. As a further aid to students, we have provided a brief introduction to each chapter in which we set the general historical context, discuss the particular selections included in the chapter, and raise a series of questions and suggestions to help readers understand the evidence, the arguments, and the methods the authors use.

Our main concern has not been with historiography, although we do direct interested students to relevant historiographical discussions. Beginning students are not especially interested in tracing shifting interpretations, nor should they be at this stage. They should be stimulated to learn *what* happened and *why* it happened by seeing how different historians, viewing the same event, have attempted to answer these questions. We have therefore concentrated not on the evolution of historical writing but on the historical problems themselves. We hope to leave students with a heightened understanding of how various issues in American history are interpreted and at the same time to provide the ammunition for thoughtful and spirited discussions. The brief, annotated bibliographies provided at the end of each chapter are not designed to be exhaustive, but they will help those who might wish to do further reading on a particular interpretation.

A. F. D.
H. D. W.

Acknowledgments

We wish to thank the various publishers and authors for permission to reprint copyrighted material. This book had its origin in our introductory course in American history at the University of Missouri; our former teaching assistants and students will recognize many of the ideas, as will those with whom we have worked at Temple University and Purdue University. We are grateful for their aid and recognize that in a real sense they have been collaborators.

We would also like to thank the many teachers and students who have made useful comments on this and earlier editions. Their candid evaluations and suggestions have been invaluable. We are especially grateful to Maria A. Brown of El Camino College; Luis Flores of Longview Community College; Thomas L. Powers of the University of South Carolina, Sumter; Harry Hewitt of Midwestern State University; Roger D. Launius of Louisiana State University; Robert C. McMath, Jr., of the Georgia Institute of Technology; William E. Pemberton of the University of Wisconsin—La Crosse; Thomas L. Powers of the University of South Carolina—Sumter; Don Hansdorff of the College of Staten Island, City University of New York; Gerald R. Gill of Tufts University; Bennett H. Wall of the University of Georgia; S. J. Adams of Lake Tahoe Community College; Hyman Berman of the University of Minnesota; C. Yuan of Worcester State College; Steven R. Boyd of the University of Texas at San Antonio; Robert L. Branyan and Lawrence H. Larsen of the University of Missouri, Kansas City; Franklin Mitchell of the University of Southern California; Lyle Dorsett of Wheaton College; James F. Watts of the City College of the City University of New York; John Burnham of Ohio State University; J. Stanley Lemons of Rhode Island College; William Cutler, Herbert Ershkowitz, and Howard Ohline of Temple University; Richard S. Kirkendall of the University of Washington; Alonzo Hamby of Ohio University; William O. Wagnon, Jr., of Washburn University of Topeka; Alice Kessler-Harris of Rutgers University; Kenneth Wayne Mixon and Henry R. Warnock of Mercer University; Ross Webb of Winthrop College; Joe P. Dunn of Converse College; Alton Hornsby of Morehouse College; Juliet Walker of the University of Illinois at Urbana-Champaign; Anita Goodstein of the University of the South; Sharon Alter of William Rainey Harper College; Jess Flemion of San Diego State University; Ruth W. Towne of Northeast Missouri State University; Jean S. Hunt of Loop College; James M. Morris of Christopher Newport College; S. L. Silberman of Connecticut College; Michel Dahlin of the University of Colorado at Colorado Springs; Bryan LeBeau of Creighton University; Gerald W. Wolff of the University of South Dakota; Cynthia K. Morrongiello of Garden City Senior High School, Garden City, New York; Mark Pittenger of Grand Valley State College; Roger P. Davis of the University of Nevada/Las Vegas; and Charles Hardy of West Chester State University.

A. F. D.
H. D. W.

Conflict and Consensus
in American History

Introduction:
History and Historians

Most students are usually introduced to the study of history by way of a fat textbook and become quickly immersed in a vast sea of names, dates, events, and statistics. The students' skills are then tested by examinations that require them to show how much of the data they remember; the more they remember, the higher their grades. From this experience a number of conclusions seem obvious: the study of history is the study of "facts" about the past; the more "facts" you know, the better you are as a student of history. The professional historian, whether teacher or textbook writer, is simply one who brings together a very large number of "facts."

Of course, only the most naive of students fail to see that the data of history, the "facts," are presented in an organized manner. Textbooks describe not only what happened, but also why it happened. For example, students learn that Puritans began coming from England to the Massachusetts Bay Colony in the New World in 1630, but they also learn why the Puritans came when they read about the religious persecutions in seventeenth-century England. Similarly, they read of the steady trek of people westward during the nineteenth century; however, at the same time they learn details that explain this movement of people—the availability of fertile lands in the West, the discovery of gold in California, the improvement of roads and other transportation facilities.

But beginning students, even as they come to recognize that their teacher and their textbook are explaining as well as describing events in the past, still have no reason to alter their notion of what history is all about. They are still working in the realm of "fact." The "fact" of the movement of people into Ohio is explained by the "fact" that fertile land was available there. They may learn more details about the event—how many people went to Ohio, when they arrived, where they settled—and about the explanation—the cost of land in Ohio, the availability of credit, the exhaustion of soils in the eastern states. Or they may be introduced to a fuller explanation when they read that some people came to Ohio to escape their creditors or to seek adventure or to speculate in land. In either case, they are simply learning more "facts." An advanced course in American history in high school differs from the sixth-grade course in American history in that it gives more detail; the older students must remember more "facts."

Students who have been introduced to history in this way may become confused upon discovering in a book like this one that historians often disagree sharply. To be sure, historians present their material in familiar ways; they tell us what happened and why it happened by presenting a mass of historical data. But students soon discover that two or three or more historians dealing with the same event may come to quite different conclusions about it. Sometimes two historians will use two very different sets of "facts" in describing an event, and this leads them to different conclusions. At other times, however, the same "facts" are given different meanings by different historians, and their conclusions therefore differ.

Experience and common sense might lead students to conclude that when historians disagree, one must be right while the others must be wrong. Just as students remember being marked down on their exams when they presented incorrect or inadequate information, they conclude that some historians are wrong because they have their "facts" wrong. But in this case, both common sense and experience can be profoundly misleading. Not only do students find that all historians argue reasonably and persuasively, but they also discover that the "facts" historians present—the names, dates, events, figures—usually turn out to be correct. Moreover, complicating matters even further, they often find that contending historians often agree on the facts and that they regularly use much the same data to come to different conclusions. To state that all are right when they say different things seems irrational; in any case, such an approach is often unacceptable to teachers who expect their students to take a position. The only way out for the baffled students is to choose one point of view for reasons they cannot fully explain. History, which had seemed to be a cut-and-dried matter of memorizing "facts," now becomes a matter of choosing one good interpretation from among many. Historical truth becomes a matter of personal preference, like the choice of one brand-name item over another in a supermarket.

This position is hardly satisfying. And when their teachers inform them that the controversy over historical interpretations is what lends excitement to the study of history, students can only respond that they feel more confusion than excitement. They cannot help but feel that two diametrically opposed points of view about an event cannot both be right; yet they lack the ability to decide between them.

Obviously, there is no easy solution to this problem. Historians do not disagree in order to spread confusion or to provide the raw material for "problems" books such as this one. Historians disagree because they view the past from different perspectives and because they ask different questions and therefore get different answers. Once students grasp this, they have taken the first step toward being able to evaluate the work of various historians. But before pursuing this matter, we must consider a problem that we have more or less taken for granted: What is history?

The word *history* has several meanings. In its broadest sense, it denotes the whole of the human past. More restricted is the notion that history is the *recorded* past, that is, that part of human life which has left some sort of record such as folk tales, artifacts, or written documents. Finally, history may be defined as that which historians write about the past.

Of course, the three meanings are related. Historians writing about the past base their accounts on the remains of the past, on the artifacts and documents left by people. Obviously they cannot know everything for the simple reason that not every event, every happening, was fully and completely recorded. And the further back one goes in time, the fewer are the records that remain. In this sense, then, the historian can only approximate history in the first meaning above—that is, history as the entire human past.

But this does not say enough. If historians cannot know everything because not everything was recorded, neither do they use all the records that are available to them. Rather, historians *select* from the total those records they deem most significant. Moreover, to complicate matters a bit more, they also recreate parts of the past for which they have no recorded evidence. Like detectives, they piece together evidence to fill in the gaps in the available records.

Historians are able to select evidence and to create evidence by using some theory or idea of human motivation and behavior. Sometimes this appears to be easy, requiring very little sophistication and subtlety. Thus, for example, historians investigating America's entry into World War I would probably find that the sinking of American merchant ships on the high seas by German submarines was relevant to their discussion. At the same time, they would most likely not use evidence that President Woodrow Wilson was dissatisfied with a new hat he bought during the first months of 1917. The choice as to which fact to use is based on a theory—admittedly, in this case a rather crude theory, but a theory nonetheless. It would go something like this: National leaders contemplating war are more likely to be influenced by belligerent acts against their countries than by their unhappiness with their haberdashers.

The choice, of course, is not always so obvious. But, before pursuing the problem further, it is important to note that a choice must be made. Historians do not just present facts; they present *some* facts and not others. They choose those facts that seem significant and reject others. This is one of the reasons that historians disagree: they have different views or different theories concerning human behavior and therefore find different kinds of information significant.

Perhaps it might appear that the subject matter being investigated, rather than any theory held by the historian, dictates which facts are significant. But this is not really so. With a little imagination—and poetic license—one could conceive of a psychological explanation for Wilson's actions that would include mounting frustration and anger fed in part, at least, by his strong disappointment with his new hat. In this case the purchase of a new hat would be a relevant fact in explaining Wilson's decision to ask Congress for a declaration of war. If readers find this outlandish, it is only because their notions of presidential motivation do not include this kind of personal reaction as an influence in determining matters of state.

If the choices were always as simple as choosing between German submarines and President Wilson's new hat, the problem would be easily resolved. But usually the choices are not so easy to make. Historians investigating the United States's entry into World War I will find in addition to German submarine warfare a whole series of other facts that could be relevant to the event under study. For instance, they will find that the British government had a propaganda machine at work in the United States that did its best to win public support for the British cause. They will discover that American bankers had made large loans to the British, loans that would not be repaid in the event of a British defeat.

They will read of the interception of the "Zimmermann Note," in which the German foreign secretary ordered the German minister in Mexico, in the event of war, to suggest an alliance between Germany and Mexico whereby Mexico, with German support, could win back territory taken from Mexico by the United States in the Mexican War. They will also find among many American political leaders a deep concern over the balance of power in Europe, a balance that would be destroyed—to America's disadvantage—if the Germans were able to defeat the French and the British and thereby emerge as the sole major power in Europe.

What, then, are the historians investigating America's entry into World War I to make of these facts? One group could simply conclude that America entered the war for several reasons and then list the facts they have discovered. By doing so, they would be making two important assumptions: (1) those facts they put on their list—in this case, German submarine warfare, British propaganda, American loans, the Zimmermann Note, and concern over the balance of power—are the main reasons, while those they do not list are not important; and (2) those things they put on their list are of equal importance in explaining the United States's role. But another group of historians might argue that the list is incomplete in that it does not take into account the generally pro-British views of Woodrow Wilson, views that stemmed from the President's background and education. The result will be a disagreement among the historians. Moreover, because the second group raise the question of Wilson's views, they will find a number of relevant facts that the first group would ignore. They will concern themselves with Wilson's education, with the influence of his teachers, with the books he read, and with the books he wrote. In short, although both groups of historians are dealing with the same subject—America's entry into World War I—they will come to different conclusions and use different facts to support their points of view. The facts selected, and those ignored, will depend not on the problem studied but on the points of view of the historians.

Similarly, a third group of historians might maintain that the various items on the list should not be given equal weight, that one of the reasons listed—say bankers' loans—was most important and that the others seemed to be significant only because of the overwhelming power of the bankers to influence American policy. The theory here would be that economic matters are the key to human motivation and that a small number of wealthy bankers have a disproportionate ability to influence government. Again, these historians will disagree with the first two groups, and they will find relevant certain facts that the others overlook—for example, bankers' opinions, the lobbying activities of bankers, financial and political connections between bankers and politicians, and the like.

In the examples given, historians disagree and use different facts or give different emphasis to the same facts because they begin from different premises; in other words, they have different theories of human motivation. But to put the matter in this way is somewhat misleading. It makes it appear that historical scholarship is merely a matter of deduction, as in Euclidean geometry, where conclusions are deduced from a set of given premises termed axioms and postulates. If this were so, historians would have it very easy. They would begin with a premise—for example, human beings are primarily motivated by selfish economic interests—and then they would seek whatever evidence they could find that showed people acting in that manner. They would ignore contrary evidence as unimportant or explain it away as being mere rhetoric designed to hide real motivations. The results of such efforts would be foreordained; the actors and the details might be different, but in the end the explanations would always be the same.

Historians term this approach or method "determinism," and most modern historians reject it. They argue that the premises cannot be merely assumed but must be proved or at least supported by concrete historical information. Nevertheless, historians cannot even begin their investigations without adopting some theory, even if it is expressed vaguely and held tentatively. In the course of their investigations they might alter or refine the original theory or replace it with another. But their final product will always rest upon some kind of theoretical base. Thus, if two historians become convinced by their evidence that different factors motivated the behavior of the people involved in a particular event, they will disagree, presenting different facts and giving different meanings to the same facts.

But there is still another realm of disagreement that, although it often appears similar to that just discussed, in fact stems from something rather different. Historians sometimes disagree because they are not really discussing the same thing. Often they are merely considering different levels of cause and effect. A few examples will illustrate this point.

The simplest level of analysis of cause and effect is to recognize what may be called proximate cause. "I was late for class," you explain, "because I overslept." Or, to use a historical example, "The Civil War began because South Carolina shore batteries under the command of General Beauregard opened fire on the federal garrison at Fort Sumter on April 12, 1861." Neither statement can be faulted on the grounds that it is inaccurate; at the same time, however, neither is sufficient as an explanation of the event being considered. The next question is obvious: Why did you oversleep, or why did relations between one state and the federal government reach the point where differences had to be settled by war? To this you may answer that you were out very late last night at a party, and the historian may respond that the authorities in South Carolina concluded that the election of Abraham Lincoln and his subsequent actions in threatening to supply the federal garrison at Fort Sumter were a clear menace to the well-being of South Carolina.

We have now dug more deeply into the problems, but the answers may still not be sufficient to satisfy us. Again we ask the question why and the answer takes us more deeply into the causes of the events under consideration. As we probe further, of course, the answers become more difficult and more complex. The problems discussed earlier—a theory of motivation and the selection of facts—begin to become increasingly important, and disagreements among historians will begin to emerge. But the potential for another kind of disagreement also arises. The further back or the deeper the historian goes, the more factors there are to be considered and the more tenuous the connection between cause and effect becomes. Historians may disagree about the point at which to begin their analysis—that is, about the location of a point beyond which the causal connection becomes so tenuous as to be meaningless. You might argue that the ultimate cause of your being late to class was the fact that you were born, but obviously this goes back too far to be meaningful. That you were born is, of course, a *necessary* factor—unless that had happened, you could not have been late—but is not a *sufficient* factor; it does not really tell enough to explain your behavior today. Similarly, we could trace the cause of the Civil War back to the discovery of America, but again, this is a necessary but not a sufficient cause.

The point at which causes are both necessary and sufficient is not self-evident. In part, the point is determined by the theoretical stance of historians. If they decide that slavery is the key to understanding the coming of the Civil War, the point will be located somewhere along the continuum of the history of slavery in the United States. But even those historians who agree that slavery is the key to the war will not necessarily agree at what point slavery becomes both necessary and sufficient. The historians who believe that slavery was a constant irritant driving the North and South apart might begin their discussion with the introduction of blacks into Virginia in 1619. They would find relevant the antislavery attitudes of Northerners during the colonial period, the conflict over slavery in the Constitutional Convention, the Missouri Compromise, the militant abolitionist movement of the 1830s, and the Compromise of 1850. But other historians might argue that the slavery issue did not become really significant until it was associated with the settlement of the western lands. They would probably begin their discussion with the Missouri Compromise, and the facts they would find most relevant would be those that illustrated the fear many people had of the expansion of slavery into the new western lands.

Ostensibly, both groups of historians would be discussing the role of slavery in the coming of the Civil War, but actually they would be discussing two different things. For the first group, the expansion of slavery to the West would be only part of a longer and more complex story; for the second group, slavery and the West would be the whole story. Sometimes the same facts would be used by both, with each giving them different weight and significance; at other times one group would find some facts relevant that the other would not.

An important variant of this kind of disagreement among historians may be illustrated by returning to our earlier example of the causes of American entry into World War I. Some historians might set out to discover the effects of British propaganda efforts in molding public and official views toward the war. German submarine warfare, the Zimmermann Note, bankers' loans, and other matters would enter the discussion, but they would all be seen from the perspective of the ways in which the British propaganda machine used them to win American support for the British side.

Historians emphasizing the role of British propaganda would disagree with those emphasizing the influential role of bankers, although both groups of historians would be using many of the same facts to support their points of view. In reality, of course, the disagreement arises at least in part from the fact that the two groups of historians are not really discussing the same things.

The reader should now be in a position to understand something of the sources of disagreement among historians. Historians arrive at different conclusions because they have different notions about human motivation and different ideas about what constitutes necessary and sufficient cause, and because they seek to investigate different aspects of the same problems. All supply their readers with data and information—that is, with "facts"—to support their arguments. And, with rare exceptions, all of the facts presented are accurate.

Clearly, then, historical facts as such have no intrinsic meaning; they take on meaning and significance only when they are organized and presented by historians with a particular point of view. The well-used phrase "let the facts speak for themselves" therefore has no real meaning. The facts do *not* speak for themselves; historians use the facts in a particular way and therefore they, and not the facts, are doing the speaking. In other words, historians give meaning to facts by assessing their significance and by presenting them in a particular manner. In short, they *interpret*. Because different historians use different facts or use the same facts in different ways, their interpretations differ.

Once we understand the sources of differences among historians we are in a better position to evaluate their work. To be sure, our ability to understand why historians disagree will not make it possible to eliminate all disagreement. Only if we could devise a model of unquestioned validity that completely explained human behavior would it be possible for us to end disagreement. Any analysis that began by assuming a different model or explanation would be wrong.*

But we do not have such a complete and foolproof explanatory model. Nor can we expect to find one. Human life is too complicated to be so completely modeled; different problems require different explanatory models or theories. And because historians cannot agree as to which is the best model to employ for any given problem and because they are constantly devising new models, disagreements are destined to remain.

For the readers who have been patient enough to follow the argument to this point, the conclusions stated here may appear somewhat dismal and unrewarding. In convincing them that evaluating a historical interpretation is not like picking an item off a supermarket shelf, have we done more than move them to another store with a different stock on its shelves? If there are many explanatory models to choose from, and if no one of them is complete, foolproof, and guaranteed true, then it would appear that we are simply in another store with different merchandise on display.

Such a conclusion is unwarranted. In the first place, students who are able to understand the premises from which historians begin will be able to comprehend the way historians work and the process by which they fashion interpretation. Moreover, this understanding will enable them to evaluate the work of the historians. For at this stage students are no longer simply memorizing details; nor are they attempting to evaluate a historical essay by trying to discover whether each of the facts presented is true. They can now ask more important questions of the material before them. Are the premises from which historians begin adequate

---

*It should be noted in passing that even if we had such a theory, there would be much room for disagreement because we would often lack the required data. Some essential information would be lost through deliberate or accidental destruction. Other information might leave no record. Records of births, deaths, income, and so forth are now required by law, but in earlier days these records were not kept or were kept only sporadically. And telephone and personal conversations might leave no concrete record even though they could have a profound influence on behavior.

explanations of human behavior? Do the facts they present really flow from their premises and support their conclusions? Are there other data that would tend to undermine their arguments and throw doubt on the adequacy of their premises?

As students attempt to answer these questions, they begin to learn history by thinking and acting like historians; they begin to accumulate knowledge, understanding, and insight in much the same ways that historians do. And they begin to understand more fully how historians gain new information, how they reassess information others have used, and how they come to new and different conclusions.

Historians are constantly getting new information that had been unavailable to their predecessors. Diaries, letters, business records, and family Bibles are always being found in attics, in basements, and even in remote corners of large research libraries; and government agencies, private organizations, and individuals regularly make their letters, reports, and other papers available to historians. This new information sometimes supports and enriches earlier interpretations by providing more concrete details about matters that earlier writers merely suggested or surmised because they lacked the newly available information. Often, however, the new information leads historians to revise earlier interpretations by revealing actions, thoughts, and behavior that were unknown to earlier historians because the documents were unavailable to them.

But the availability of new information does not fully explain the sources of disagreement among historians and the regular process of revision of older interpretations. Much of the "new" information that later writers use is not new in the sense of being newly discovered or made available. The information was in the archives and libraries all the time, but historians did not use it, or they used it in very different ways. In short, the "facts" were there, but until historians asked different questions, the facts had no meaning or relevance, and historians ignored them.

Historians ask new questions and therefore seek new facts to answer the questions for a variety of reasons. They often gain new insights from the research of social scientists such as economists, political scientists, sociologists, and psychologists. Investigations by these scholars into such problems as family relationships, the influence of propaganda on behavior, the effects of the money supply on economic change, the relationship between voting patterns and racial and ethnic origin, and the psychological effects of racism all suggest new questions that historians might find valuable in investigating the past and in turn new kinds of data—facts—that they should seek in answering the new questions. In seeking such answers, historians also master and use new techniques and methods. For example, modern statistical methods and the computer permit the historian to handle huge masses of data quickly and accurately.

Historians also learn from one another. For example, when one historian discovers the existence of certain political, social, and economic relationships in a given city at a certain time, he or she provides other historians studying other cities, either at the same or different times, with what may be important and enlightening insights. International comparisons of similar events and institutions can also reveal important features that will be invisible or obscure when these events and institutions are viewed from the perspective of a single nation's history.

Finally, and perhaps most important, their own experiences often help historians to relate the past to the present; that is, they interpret the past through a frame of reference that is influenced by the world in which they live. During World War II, for instance, historians reexamined the causes and consequences of World War I, just as the war in Vietnam provided a new perspective on the Cold War years. The civil rights movement and black radicalism in the 1960s inspired a number of historians to reinterpret the role of abolitionists in the events leading up to the Civil War and to give more attention to race and racism in American life. In a similar way the feminist movement spurred them to reexamine the role of women and the family in the American past, while urban violence, the black revolution, and increasing ethnic identity led them to reassess the importance of violence, slavery, and ethnicity in American history.

When historians use the insights and techniques of the social scientists and when they make comparisons over time and place, the results may be enlightening and valuable. But they may also be misleading. By mechanically applying one or another theory of human behavior taken from the social sciences or by using behavior patterns in one place or time to explain behavior in another place or time, historians run the twin risks of determinism and anachronism. The attitudes, perceptions, and outlooks of people in one area or time in the past may differ considerably from those of another area or time. Therefore, for example, evidence that would explain certain kinds of behavior in the United States in the 1990s would not necessarily explain similar behavior in an earlier time.

A concrete example will illustrate the point. In recent years, some historians have provided evidence that in the pre–Civil War decades Southerners who owned slaves and grew cotton earned a rate of profit that equaled or exceeded that of investments in other enterprises elsewhere in the nation. From this evidence, some conclude that Southerners continued to invest primarily in slaves and cotton production (rather than in commerce and industry) because of the high rate of return earned in such investment. Others add that Southerners were willing to go to war to protect this profitable enterprise. A crucial assumption concerning behavior underlies this reasoning: Southerners acted like modern businessmen, making their investment decisions based upon the highest expected rate of return. That assumption may indeed be valid, but students should be aware first, that it *is* an assumption, and second, that the assumption is not necessarily supported by the evidence that Southerners continued to invest in slaves and cotton production. Southerners might have continued to buy slaves and grow cotton for reasons other than expected high rates of profit; social or political benefits that came with being a slaveowning cotton planter may have been their primary motivation.

In short, then, insights from the social sciences as well as those from other times and places are invaluable—indeed, essential—for historians. But they must be used with care, because they carry assumptions about behavior that may not be appropriate when applied to other times and places. By recognizing the theories and assumptions that guide historians when they formulate questions to investigate and then gather, evaluate, and present the evidence to answer these questions, students may more readily understand how historians work and why they disagree, and will thus be able to evaluate more accurately the work of the historians they read.

At first it may seem frustrating to realize that there is no one easy answer to the problems historians raise and that "truth" is but an elusive yet intriguing goal in a never-ending quest. But when students realize this, they have *begun* their education. At that point, they will find the study of history to be a significant, exhilarating, and useful part of their education. For coming to grips with conflicting interpretations of the past is more than an interesting classroom game; it is part of a larger process of coming to terms with the world around us. Every day we are asked to evaluate articles in newspapers and magazines or reports of events provided by friends or media commentators. A knowledge of history provides a background for interpreting these accounts; but more than that, the past and the present are so interconnected that one's interpretation of the American Revolution, slavery, the progressive movement, or American foreign policy after World War II is intimately related to one's views toward civil rights and domestic and foreign policy today.

The discussion thus far has emphasized the element of disagreement among historians and has attempted to show beginning students how these disagreements arise and how they should deal with them. But if disagreements arise because historians often start their analyses from different perspectives, it does not follow that there is no agreement at all among historians. On the contrary, groups of historians have tended to assume similar theoretical postures, and the result has been the emergence of "schools" of historical writing. All differences among members of a particular school do not disappear, but their approaches remain similar enough to differentiate them from members of other schools.

Identifying schools and placing historians in them is seldom easy and is always somewhat arbitrary. The reasons are obvious enough: the amount and complexity of work about America's past are so great that it is possible to identify a large number of schools. Moreover, because few historians begin with an explicit ideology or philosophy of history, their work may fit into a number of possible schools. Finally, most good historians do not cling dogmatically to a particular approach. As their research and writing proceeds, as they learn more, or as contemporary events alter their perspectives, their interpretations tend to change.

In organizing this book we have chosen two recurrent and important schools, or interpretive themes, in the writings on American history: conflict and consensus. Admittedly, the choice, in one sense at least, is arbitrary; we could have chosen from a number of other unifying themes. On the other hand, the choice has not been completely arbitrary in that these themes—conflict and consensus—expressed either explicitly or implicitly, may be found in virtually all major interpretations of our country's past. The student who reads the following pages and attempts to evaluate the arguments presented will be faced with two real and meaningful ways to understand the American past and, indeed, to judge the contemporary American scene.

Stripped to its essentials, the task of historians is to deal with change. And nowhere do historians find change more manifest than when they study the United States. Almost in the twinkling of an eye, a vast, scarcely populated continent was transformed into a major industrial power of phenomenal complexity. Overnight, virgin forests became fertile farms; Indian trails became roads, highways, and railroads; and empty spaces became bustling cities. Matching this transformation of the physical face of the continent were equally momentous changes in politics, social relations, ideas, and attitudes. For most Americans, constant and rapid change was inevitable if only because it was so obvious. "Ten years in America are like a century in Spain," wrote the German immigrant Francis Leiber soon after his arrival in the United States early in the nineteenth century. "The United States really changes in some respects more within ten years than a country like Spain has within a hundred."

But who could argue that Europe was static and unchanging? True enough, Europe had little in the way of trackless wilderness to be discovered, settled, and transformed; and, true also, Europe was crowded with the remnants of what might appear to be an unchanging past—cathedrals and monuments, aristocratic and royal institutions, and ways of doing things that seemed to have existed time out of mind. But at the same time, Europe periodically exploded into change. Indeed, time after time, Americans saw Europe swept by rebellion and war as one group after another sought, often successfully, to revolutionize European lives and institutions.

Generations of American historians have tried to describe and to explain the vast alterations that have taken place on the North American continent. As they did so, many kept one eye on the changes in European institutions, seeking to compare and to contrast the nature of changes in Europe with those of North America. But even as they read the historical documents, often in the light of European history and experience, the historians themselves were living through vast and rapid changes taking place around them in the United States, changes that often influenced their historical scholarship. From the rich and varied work by American historians two rather distinct traditions or interpretive themes have emerged, each of which has sought to provide a general explanation for American historical development.

One tradition stresses conflict, finding American history to be similar in this respect to that of Europe. Historians within this tradition often speak of revolutionary changes and emphasize the importance of conflict in bringing these changes. They stress the class, ethnic, racial, and political *differences* among Americans and the fundamental nature of the conflicts these differences created: democrats versus aristocrats, debtors versus creditors, workers versus businessmen, North versus South, farmers versus railroads, blacks versus whites. Change, they argue, is a result of this never-ending conflict; it arises from the efforts of particular groups and classes to impose their hegemony over American society, or at least to increase their influence over that society.

The other tradition stresses the uniqueness of the American experience by finding a basic consensus in American society. According to this tradition, all Americans of whatever class or station shared what was essentially a common outlook. To be sure, Americans did not all live alike nor did they always agree with one another. But their disagreements, especially when compared with the dissensions that divided European society, were not fundamental. Consensus historians do not ignore class and sectional differences, and they do not deny conflicts between groups such as workers and employers; but they do deny that these conflicts were basic. Americans, they argue, achieved a consensus on fundamentals; if they disagreed, their disagreements were minor differences within an underlying consensus. Change, then, is the result of a fundamental agreement that change is required and does not arise from a struggle for power.

Although both these themes can be found in the earliest writings on American history, they became dominant interpretive themes only during the twentieth century. The theme of conflict was central to the writings of those Richard Hofstadter has called the "Progressive Historians": Frederick Jackson Turner, Charles A. Beard, and Vernon L. Parrington. Growing up in the midst of the nation's rapid industrialization and living in a time of increasing protest against the problems created by that industrialization, these historians saw the past in terms of bitter conflict. Their influence, as the reader of the following pages will discover, was profound.

The theme of consensus, with its roots in the nationalistic histories of the nineteenth century, became especially important beginning in the early 1950s, in part as a reaction to what some considered to be the overstatements of the conflict school and in part as a reaction to world conditions. For many American historians at the time, European revolutionary and ideological conflicts seemed strangely alien to the United States, making historical interpretations cast in the European mold completely inappropriate. Looking at the past, these historians discovered that America had always been different from Europe. For the most part, the United States had been spared the bitter conflicts that divided European countries, because Americans from the beginning had agreed on fundamentals. Consensus historians therefore stressed the uniqueness of the American experience and sought to explain the origins of this uniqueness.

Like the conflict historians of an earlier generation, the new consensus historians had a great influence on American historical thought. An especially important part of the consensus school was the American Studies movement, an interdisciplinary effort to combine history, literature, and the social sciences to describe and explain the special and unique American experience and to define an American "character" that was molded by that experience.

But the consensus historians were not without their critics. John Higham argued that they were "homogenizing" American history; he accused them of "carrying out a massive grading operation to smooth over America's social convulsions." He and other critics did not simply call for a return to the history of the progressive historians. They argued that the consensus historians had made the American past bland and meaningless because they ignored real and significant differences that produced sharp conflicts. Even some of the consensus historians began to have second thoughts about the interpretation. Richard Hofstadter, who had been a sharp critic of the conflict historians, felt that the consensus interpretation had gone too far. "Americans may not have quarreled over profound ideological matters, as these are formulated in the history of political thought, but they quarreled consistently enough over issues that had real pith and moment," he wrote in 1967 in a new introduction to his book *The American Political Tradition*. He added that "an obsessive fixation on the elements of consensus that do undoubtedly exist strips the story of the drama and the interest it has."

The responses to the concern over the seeming domination of the consensus school and the homogenization of American history were not long in coming. Indeed, many were already under way. Sometimes the responses became little more than arguments over the meaning given to the words *conflict* and *consensus* or were simply reassertions of the old conflict interpretations. Most historians, however, did far more. They used new techniques, often drawing upon the scholarship of other disciplines. They adopted fresh approaches, asking new questions that led to the discovery of new sources and the reevaluation of existing evidence. The result was not only new interpretations of the nation's past but also a considerable redefinition of what constituted that past, that is, a redefinition of what kinds of questions historians should ask about the past.

Quantitative historians, aided by the computer and modern statistical methods and using theories borrowed from economics, sociology, political science, linguistics, anthropology, and psychology, conducted massive investigations of such matters as economic growth patterns, voting behavior, family life, social mobility, changes in standards of living, and fashions. Social historians, using both quantitative and more traditional methods, attempted to write what they called history "from the bottom up," seeking to investigate and even emphasize the lives of ordinary people rather than members of the political and economic elite. Labor historians who had traditionally concentrated on organized labor gave increasing attention to the culture and ideology of workers in unorganized shops and factories. Many social historians as well as political and economic historians argued that most Americans, especially in the years before the changes in technology allowed for the rapid dissemination of news and information, experienced history on a local level. Hence they studied local developments in great detail, concerning themselves with small communities, villages and towns, and neighborhoods within larger cities; they also gave considerable attention to local religious and political institutions.

Intellectual and cultural historians, investigating ideology and the use of language to discover how people perceived and made sense of the world in which they lived, described what they called "republican" and "liberal" syntheses. The republican synthesis, essentially a consensus interpretation with its emphasis on all Americans united in a quest for republican virtue, was sharply challenged by historians who found that many Americans, even as they mouthed the words of republicanism, gave these words very different meanings. Indeed, some Americans used republican language to attack republicanism. Other historians argued that the republican synthesis was never universal, that it always found itself challenged by liberalism, that is, by the ideas and practices of the modern free market. Some intellectual and cultural historians began to give increasing attention to popular culture, insisting that the concentration on the study of "high culture" was elitist, unrepresentative, and therefore misleading.

Another sign of change came with the appearance of a group calling themselves "new western historians." These historians broke sharply with Frederick Jackson Turner, arguing that the frontier experience was not the whole of American western history and that even the frontier experience was more diverse and complicated than Turner had argued. Indians and Mexicans, miners and environmentalists, ranchers and urbanites, and women along with men were some of the diverse groups of people who became important actors in the new western history.

The work of the new western historians reveals what perhaps has been the most significant change in the writing of American history: the increasing attention historians began to give to gender, race, and ethnicity.

Fueled in part by the feminist movement and in part by the belated recognition of the absence of women in so much of the writings on American history, historians began to investigate the parts played by women in events and areas—for example, the Revolution, the Civil War, and the West—that they had traditionally studied as male dominated. This added a new dimension to the study of traditional subjects by showing that the role of women was often an important part of the story. Sometimes such investigations led historians to challenge the traditional periodization of history as marked by wars, elections, and political movements. While some historians sought to overcome the neglect of women's voices in traditionally studied areas, others began to look into matters involving women—for example, courtship, the family, and the household economy—that had received little or no attention previously, but that, their studies showed, were important factors in historical development.

Another area experiencing a rush of new and innovative scholarship was that of African-American history. In addition to more subtle and meaningful discussions of traditional areas of race relations, racism, and race conflict, the new work dealt with the development of a distinctive African-American culture and ideology. Much of this new work in such diverse areas as, for example, slavery, the transition from slavery to freedom after the Civil War, the fight for integration, black political action, and South to North migration told the story from the black perspective and stressed the importance of blacks as actors rather than as powerless victims.

Much of the same perspective marked the new studies of other racial and ethnic groups. Historians no longer viewed Indian history as simply the story of wars, defeat, and historical oblivion on the reservations as told from the perspective of the victorious and "civilized" whites; new work emphasized Indian culture and indigenous religious and social practices. Historians studying other racial and ethnic groups gave similar emphasis to cultural persistences as well as to changes over time, sharply calling into question older notions of the melting pot and providing evidence of significant differences among ethnic groups that earlier historians had ignored.

What much of this new work has in common is its emphasis on diversity, on differences among Americans that usually led to conflict rather than consensus. Americans, it suggests, have always been divided by race, class, gender, and ethnicity, and these differences are significant enough to mean that it is wrong and misleading to speak of an American history that is shared by all who reside within the nation's borders. There is not *an* American mind or *an* American culture, but many American minds and cultures, and this diversity has often—indeed, has usually—led to significant conflicts.

This new work, which mounts a strenuous attack on the consensus history that critics such as John Higham charged had homogenized American history, has not been universally accepted. Critics, although they do not deny the differences among Americans, nevertheless argue that those who emphasize diversity, that is, the differences among Americans, create a history without a central synthesis, without a general unifying theme that would give meaning to American history. Those who emphasize diversity usually find the lack of a general synthesis to be a virtue, not a problem; diversity aims at inclusiveness, they insist, and inclusiveness is closer to reality than a general synthesis that could only be artificial. But their opponents insist with equal vigor that recognition of diversity and inclusiveness does not preclude the existence of a general synthesis; indeed, they argue, giving exclusive attention to differences hides underlying themes and cultural features that unite Americans within their diversity.

In sum, then, new work has enriched historical writing and has often provided a more subtle and complex story of the nation's past. Nevertheless, the themes of conflict and consensus, although significantly altered in emphasis and content, continue to be relevant and therefore continue to be important ways to view the complexities of American history.

The lines that divide the conflict from the consensus historians are not as sharp as they once were. If many contemporary historians draw from both in their analyses of America's past, the emphasis on one or the other remains, both in studies of particular movements and periods as well as in general assessments of the course of American history. Differences in interpretation will persist even as historians continue their work, and, although their efforts will never end the debate, they will give us a richer understanding of our nation's past. This ongoing quest for understanding gives historical scholarship its interest and excitement. The readings that follow, by introducing students to the two traditions of conflict and consensus and their variations through the words of some of their most able proponents, will also introduce students to some of that interest and excitement.

SUGGESTIONS FOR FURTHER READING

When historians seek to determine how to evaluate evidence, they are really attempting to answer a whole set of very complicated questions. Is their goal to achieve fairness, objectivity, and balance? If so, what exactly do these words mean when applied to historical scholarship? Is it possible to find truth in history? Can the study of the past be made scientific? Are all conclusions by historians relative because historians cannot escape bias and because they make assumptions that they cannot support with adequate evidence? A few volumes on the theory and practice of history have been written specifically for the beginning student; examples are Walter T. K. Nugent, *Creative History* (Philadelphia, 1967), and Allan J. Lichtman and Valerie French, *Historians and the Living Past* (Arlington Heights, Ill., 1978). More sophisticated but eminently readable are four classic studies: Marc Bloch, *The Historian's Craft* (New York, 1953); Allan Nevins, *The Gateway to History* (Garden City, N.Y., 1962); Louis Gottschalk, *Understanding History* (New York, 1963); and E. H. Carr, *What Is History?* (New York, 1964). Several more recent studies deserve attention. Joyce Appleby, Lynn Hunt, and Margaret Jacob, *Telling the Truth About History* (New York, 1994) is a clearly written and sensible survey that

---

*Available in paperback edition.

provides a fine review of current debates about "history's relationship to scientific truth, objectivity, postmodernism and the politics of identity." Gene Wise, *American Historical Explanations* (Minneapolis, 1980) is also a very valuable discussion of these and other matters. Peter Novick, *That Noble Dream: The "Objectivity Question" and the American Historical Profession* (New York, 1988) is a fascinating and valuable account of history writing in the United States. An illuminating and superbly written guide to historical research and writing is Jacques Barzun and Henry F. Graff, *The Modern Researcher*, 5th ed. (Fort Worth, 1992).

For an introduction to the controversy over the value of quantitative history, see Robert William Fogel and G. R. Elton, *Which Road to the Past? Two Views of History* (New Haven, Conn., 1983), a friendly, but sharp, debate between a "new" and a "traditional" historian. Quantitative history is difficult for the uninitiated, but for those who want a taste of it, a good introduction is William O. Adydelotte, Allan G. Bogue, and Robert William Fogel, eds., *The Dimensions of Quantitative Research in History* (Princeton, N.J., 1972).

A brief, very accessible introduction to the postmodern approach to history, or at least one historian's view of this approach, is Keith Jenkins, *Re-thinking History* (New York, 1991). For those interested in going further into exploring the mysteries of postmodernism as well as the new historicism, deconstructionism, and other concepts that are influencing some historians, good places to start are the following: Madan Sarup, *An Introductory Guide to Post-Structuralism and Postmodernism* (Athens, Ga., 1989); Bryan D. Palmer, *Descent into Discourse: The Reification of Language and the Writing of Social History* (Philadelphia, 1990); and John E. Toews, "Intellectual History After the Linguistic Turn," *American Historical Review,* 92 (October 1987), 879–907.

Students wishing to pursue the historiography (that is, the history of historical writing) of the conflict-consensus theme should begin with the progressive historians. Charles A. Beard was a prolific writer, but the best approach to him is through Charles and Mary Beard, *The Rise of American Civilization* (New York, 1927, 1930), a lively and interesting interpretation of the whole course of American history, with an emphasis on class and economic conflict. Beard's *An Economic Interpretation of the Constitution* (New York, 1913, 1935) must be read by any serious student. Vernon Parrington's three-volume *Main Currents in American Thought* (New York, 1927, 1930) complements Beard's work and deals with the relationship of literature and ideas to society and social movements. Frederick Jackson Turner's essays may be found in *The Frontier in American History* (New York, 1920) and *The Significance of Sections in American History* (New York, 1932). There are many discussions of the work and influence of these historians; the reader can do no better than to begin with Richard Hofstadter, *The Progressive Historians* (New York, 1968), the work of a perceptive and sensitive critic. This book's great value is enhanced by an outstanding "bibliographical essay" that will lead the student deep into the literature on the subject.

Any serious student of the consensus historians must read and study Louis Hartz, *The Liberal Tradition in America* (New York, 1955) and the key works of Daniel J. Boorstin: *The Genius of American Politics* (Chicago, 1953); *The Americans: The Colonial Experience* (New York, 1958); *The Americans: The Democratic Experience* (New York, 1973); and *The Americans: The National Experience* (New York, 1965). A perceptive discussion of these books as well as of the entire consensus school along with good bibliographical information may be found in the Hofstadter volume cited above. An important and provocative critique of the consensus approach is John Higham, "The Cult of the American Consensus," *Commentary,* 27 (February 1959), 93–100. See also Gene Wise, "Political 'Reality' in Recent American Scholarship: Progressives Versus Symbolists," *American Quarterly,* 22, Part 2 (Summer 1967), 303–28.

John Higham, *History: Professional Scholarship in America* (Baltimore, 1983) is a concise overview of American historiography that places the conflict-consensus debate in perspective. Ernst A. Breisach, *American Progressive History: An Experiment in Modernization* (Chicago, 1993) is a useful summary that describes the rise and decline of the progressive "conflict" interpretation and places the story in the context of European historiography. David W. Noble, *The End of American History* (Minneapolis, 1985) is especially interested in the theory and meaning of historical scholarship after the "collapse of the Progressive paradigm." Bernard Sternsher, *Consensus, Conflict and American Historians* (Bloomington, Ind., 1975) examines the theme in great detail.

The literature on women's history is vast; a good place to start is Gerda Lerner, *The Majority Finds Its Past: Placing Women in History* (New York, 1979). There are many collections of articles on women's history that include valuable bibliographies. See, for examples, Linda K. Kerber and Jane Sherron DeHart, eds., *Women's America*, 3rd ed. (New York, 1991); Jean E. Friedman and William G. Shade, eds., *Our American Sisters: Women in American Life and Thought*, 2nd ed. (Boston, 1976); and Berenice A. Carroll, ed., *Liberating Women's History: Theoretical and Critical Essays* (Urbana, Ill., 1976).

Drew Gilpin Faust, *Mothers of Invention: Women of the Slaveholding South in the American Civil War* (Chapel Hill, N.C., 1996) is a recent example of how our understanding of traditional subjects such as the Confederacy, the Civil War, and Southern slavery is enhanced by a consideration of the role of women. Work on women's history has spurred an interest in men's history—or, more accurately, in the history of masculinity in America. A good recent survey is Michael Kimmel, *Manhood in America: A Cultural History* (New York, 1995).

Important and influential examples of the American Studies approach are Henry Nash Smith, *Virgin Land* (Cambridge, Mass., 1950); R. W. B. Lewis, *The American Adam* (Chicago, 1955); and Leo Marx, *The Machine in the Garden: Technology and the Pastoral Idea in America* (New York, 1964). A study of the American Studies approach is Cecil F. Tate, *The Search for a Method in American Studies* (Minneapolis, 1973). Changing emphases in American Studies may be followed in the articles in the *American Quarterly*, the journal of the American Studies Association.

Good general introductions to the new western history by two of its leading practitioners are Patricia Nelson Limerick, *The Legacy of Conquest: The Unbroken Past of the American West* (New York, 1987); and Richard White, *'It's Your Misfortune and None of My Own': A New History of the American West* (Norman, Okla., 1991). A very brief discussion of recent trends in Indian history along with a good introductory bibliography is Donald Parman, "Twentieth Century Indian History: Achievements, Needs, and Problems," *OAH Magazine of History* (Fall 1994), 9, 10–16.

Important contributions to the republican synthesis are Bernard Bailyn, *The Ideological Origins of the American Revolution* (Cambridge, Mass., 1967); J. G. A. Pocock, "Machiavelli, Harrington, and English Political Ideologies in the Eighteenth Century," *William and Mary Quarterly*, 3rd series, 22 (October 1965), 549–83; and Gordon Wood, *The Creation of the American Republic, 1776–1787* (Chapel Hill, N.C., 1969). Critics of republicanism are Isaac Kramnick, "Republican Revisionism Revisited," *American Historical Review*, 87 (June 1982), 629–64; Joyce Appleby, *Capitalism and a New Social Order: The Republican Vision of the 1790s* (New York, 1984); and John Patrick Diggins, *The Lost Soul of American Politics: Virtue, Self-Interest and the Foundations of Liberalism* (New York, 1985). These and other works on the republican synthesis are reviewed in two articles by Robert E. Shalhope, "Toward a Republican Synthesis: The Emergence of an Understanding of Republicanism in American Historiography," *William and Mary Quarterly*, 3rd series, 29 (January 1972), 49–80; and "Republicanism and Early American Historiography," *William and Mary Quarterly*, 3rd series, 39 (April 1982), 334–56. A special issue of the *American Quarterly,* 37 (Fall 1985), contains a half-dozen articles on "Republicanism in the History and Historiography of the United States." *Reviews in American History,* 10 (December 1982), contains articles surveying the state of scholarship in some twenty subdisciplines in American history. A more recent survey and evaluation of the new histories is Eric Foner, ed., *The New American History* (Philadelphia, 1990), a collection of thirteen essays on the scholarship of the last twenty years that "shattered the 'consensus' vision that had dominated historical writing."

The debate over diversity has created lively controversy. In December 1988 at a meeting of the American Historical Association, five historians with varying points of view concerning the state of historical scholarship presented papers that illustrated some of the sharp differences that divide the profession. These papers, which were published in the *American Historical Review,* 94 (June 1989), 654–98, under the general title "The Old History and the New," provide a convenient introduction to the debate: Theodore S. Hamerow, "The Bureaucratization of History"; Gertrude Himmelfarb, "Some Reflections on the New History"; Lawrence W. Levine, "The Unpredictable Past: Reflections on Recent American Historiography"; Joan Wallach Scott, "History in Crisis? The Others' Side of the Story"; and John E. Toews, "Perspectives on 'The Old History and the New': A Comment." Lawrence W. Levine, who welcomes the emphasis on diversity because of what he considers to be the need for inclusiveness, expanded on his argument in the *American Historical Review* in a volume of essays, *The Unpredictable Past: Explorations in American Cultural History* (New York, 1993). Gertrude Himmelfarb, a sharp critic of those who emphasize diversity and see no unifying synthesis in American history, presents her views in more detail in her book *The New History and the Old: Critical Essays and Reappraisals* (Cambridge, Mass., 1987). John Higham, who earlier had been critical of the consensus historians, has more recently raised some doubts about the later emphasis on diversity in his essay "Multiculturalism and Universalism: A History and a Critique," *American Quarterly,* 45 (1993), 195–219. In light of the debate, Michael Kammen finds an old interpretation worthy of refinement and reconsideration in "The Problem of American Exceptionalism: A Reconsideration," *American Quarterly,* 45 (March 1993), 1–43.

1

Power, Politics, and Wealth in Colonial America

In the spring of 1607 three small ships, the Susan Constant, the Godspeed, and the Discovery, sailed up Chesapeake Bay. In May a small group of travel-weary colonists disembarked at what they thought was a suitable site and founded Jamestown, which was to be the first permanent English settlement in the New World. The decades that followed witnessed the establishment of other English colonies—the Pilgrims at Plymouth, a group including many Catholics at Maryland, and the Puritans at Massachusetts Bay. In these and other early settlements the colonists' first task became simple survival in an often inhospitable and always unfamiliar environment. Survival required more than clearing the land, planting crops, and building shelters.

19

The settlers left behind not only their homes and fields but also the institutions and laws that had governed their lives. They carried with them memories of the past and visions of the future that they would build, but these were merely ideas that had to be given substance if they were to become real in the New World. The settlers had to work out rules and regulations to govern their relationships with one another and with the authorities back home in the Old World.

In the early years the colonists had little trouble agreeing with one another. Survival in the wilderness was the main concern of the small and relatively homogeneous population. But problems quickly appeared. Later arrivals often did not share the ideas of the first settlers, and sometimes even those who did agree (or thought they did) in principle found that they sharply disagreed when it came time to put principles into practice. Differences arose over such matters as the distribution of land, church doctrine, the manner in which leaders were to be chosen, and, once chosen, the powers such leaders should have. Moreover, successful expansion helped create social classes and divisions as some colonials grew wealthier than their neighbors by amassing more land, by buying slaves and indentured servants to increase their production, and by engaging in trade and commerce.

These differences affected political life in the colonies. Each colony had a representative assembly, a council, and a governor as well as other local governing agencies such as town meetings, county administrators, and church assemblies. Because the actions of these governing bodies were so important in dealing with differences among them, the colonists naturally concerned themselves with such matters as how representatives should be chosen, who could hold office, and how different regions and interests should be represented. Leaders of various groups used newspapers and pamphlets to mobilize opinion, to pressure political leaders, and to influence elections. Sometimes angry words led to mob actions or even to organized armed intervention in the political process, as in Bacon's Rebellion in Virginia.

By the 1770s, the handful of settlers at Jamestown had swelled to more than two million people who lived in an area stretching from present-day Maine to southern Georgia. The farming population—more than 90 percent of the total—ranged from tobacco planters and grain growers with hundreds (or even thousands) of acres and hundreds of slaves or indentured servants working the land to farmers working small plots with their own labor and that of their families. The colonies also boasted a number of thriving cities such as Boston, New York, and Philadelphia, with a population of prosperous merchants, skilled artisans, and propertyless laborers.

Each colony, therefore, was divided economically and socially by class, status, wealth, and religion. Moreover, no intercolonial agency existed to deal with common problems or to provide a unified voice in dealing with the authorities in London. Although some intercolonial trade and exchange of population meant that the colonies were never completely isolated from one another, each was a separate political unit, dealing in its own way with internal affairs and with the authorities in the mother country. Therefore, the ability of the colonists to establish social cohesion and unity within each colony and the achievement in the mid-

1760s of the intercolonial unity necessary to engage Britain in a long and successful war for independence were remarkable feats.

Historians have attempted to describe and explain the sources of this unity
and to assess its depth. Some argue that despite variations over time and by region, most Americans were united by common experiences in the New World. Although these shared experiences did not erase social and economic differences,
they did give most Americans enough in common to set them apart from Old
World societies and to create a basic consensus within. Other historians, however, insist that colonial economic and political life was marked by sharp and bitter conflicts arising from differences in wealth and status. Unity, some of these
historians note, resulted less from consensus within than from common grievances, at least by the mid-eighteenth century, against Britain. But others, even as
they stress conflicts within colonial society, argue that Americans gradually developed institutions that, although they did not end conflict, provided the means
to resolve these conflicts in a manner that created basic social consensus within
colonies and enough intercolonial consensus to create the unity necessary to confront the British. The following selections illustrate some of these differences
among historians.

Stephen Foster, in the first selection, describes politics in the Puritan commonwealth founded in New England in the early seventeenth century. The Puritans, armed with firm religious and political convictions, came to America determined to found "a city upon a hill" that would be a model for all people. That
model was not, as some have argued, one of democracy and equality; on the contrary, the Puritans rejected both. They believed in a hierarchical society marked
by social inequality in which the lesser folk regularly consented to their own inequality and deferred to their betters. Foster notes that the Puritans who remained in England developed notions of equality as a means to protect themselves from the bitter opposition they faced. But the American Puritans, he
argues, living without this opposition, felt no pressures to become radical: "they
had no need to grow revolutionary; they never had anything to revolt against."
In the end, however, the Puritans became both revolutionary and committed to
principles that led to increased democracy and equality, but Foster insists that
these developments were not an inevitable result of Puritan ideas.

In evaluating Foster's discussion, readers should be aware that dissent did
arise in the Puritan colony and that Puritan leaders sought to maintain consensus
by silencing dissenters by punishment, banishment, or even execution. But coercion could not silence dissent. As Foster notes, contradictions within the Puritan
ideology itself helped to undermine the very consensus that the ideology strove to
create.

In the second selection, James A. Henretta, adopting a broader perspective
that considers all of the colonies, seeks to show how social and economic change
both undermined earlier consensus and created a new unity. He points to growing class divisions based upon unequal wealth that carried the potential—and
sometimes the reality—of sharp conflict within each colony. But he also notes the
development of new forms of unity along sectional lines, which made for significant sectional differences with the potential for sectional conflicts. He argues

that the evolution of an aristocratic society in the South and an entrepreneurial society in the North molded personality types and created institutional structures that mitigated the conflicts arising from class differences and differences over political authority in each section. Like Foster, Henretta stresses the unique experiences in the New World in the formation of New World institutions. At the same time, however, Henretta implies that some of the class differences in the New World began to resemble those of the Old.

In the final selection, Gary B. Nash considers some of these class differences and assesses their significance. Nash emphasizes conflicts arising from sharp differences in wealth in colonial cities during the eighteenth century, finding deep resentment and the beginnings of a "radical ideology" among the poor. The economic maturation of the colonies led some urban dwellers at least to question "some of the most fundamental tenets of colonial thought." It would seem to follow that unless the opposition could be destroyed, compromise or accommodation would radically change society and politics in the colonies. Nash notes that the revolutionary ferment provided added opportunities for urban radicals to achieve the reforms they sought.

As the American colonies grew in size and wealth, did they become more unstable and prone to conflict? Did the growing division between rich and poor and between east and west, north and south create fundamental class and sectional conflicts? Or did the colonial experience create peculiarly American social and political institutions that unified rather than divided Americans?

The thirteen mainland English colonies certainly agreed enough to be able to unite and fight a successful war for independence. But did this unity reveal an underlying consensus in the midst of diversity, or did it merely indicate agreement on opposition to a common enemy that papered over fundamental differences that divided Americans?

STEPHEN FOSTER

Puritanism and Democracy:
A Mixed Legacy

In the beginning God created the heaven and the earth and in the end he created New England. This was the course of human history from Genesis I: 1 to 5 *Carolus Rex* as viewed from the quarterdeck of the *Arbella* one June day in 1630 when the coast of the New World came into sight for the first time. On board the ship were Governor John Winthrop and his company, a group of English men and women now denominated "Puritans," though in their own estimation they were simply the most important body of people since the Apostles. The latter had brought true Christianity to the Old Israel, the Puritans would recreate it in a new.

Winthrop and the others on the *Arbella* would not have used the label "Puritan," but they did admit to advocating a thoroughgoing reformation of the church and society of their native England, the purging from both of their popish and "humane" corruptions, and their reorganization according to the Word of God. For the church this meant congregational polity and "Calvinist" doctrine, for society a strange mixture of some of the most commonplace of European ideals, and some of the most extraordinary.

In their homeland any kind of change except for the worse seemed impossible. King Charles I and his ecclesiastical advisor William Laud had just suspended Parliament and inaugurated the "Eleven Years Tyranny" that would end only with the Civil War and death on the scaffold for both men. But in 1630 the bloody and violent conclusion to the King's Peace lay years in the future: for many English Puritans the only alternative to Charles and Laud seemed to lie in following the lead of a company of English Separatists from Scrooby, men so dissatisfied with the Church of England that they had broken with it entirely, going into exile at Leyden and then in 1620 forsaking even the relative comfort of

Holland for the arduous but unrestricted life of pilgrims in the "wilderness" of New Plymouth Colony. A new land, separated from king and bishops by three thousand miles of Atlantic Ocean, offered Winthrop's company their only chance of creating the kind of world they wanted.

The thousands of settlers who poured into New England after 1630 founded not one colony there but four, in addition to the earlier settlement at New Plymouth. Winthrop himself established Massachusetts Bay, the largest of the five, which grew so steadily in population that some of its settlers, under the leadership of the Rev. Thomas Hooker, found themselves overcrowded and moved south to found Connecticut in 1636. Two years later Theophilus Eaton and the Rev. John Davenport, skeptical even of the godliness of the Bay colony, established New Haven to the south of Hooker's settlements and maintained a separate existence from the rest of Connecticut until 1664. Rhode Island, the fifth colony, grew out of four separate towns built by a variety of heretics expelled from Massachusetts between 1636 and 1643. All told, the combined policies of Charles I and Laud had made England seem unattractive enough for over fifteen thousand of their Puritan countrymen to emigrate to the more congenial environment of New England in the decade 1630 to 1640. . . .

They had crossed an ocean and come to a strange and unsettled land, but they founded a society designed to benefit England and all Christendom by serving as a model for the reformation of other churches and other states in what Puritans and non-Puritans alike commonly considered "these last times" before the Second Coming of Christ. While the *Arbella* still rode the Atlantic midway between the Old World and the New, Winthrop composed and delivered his *Model of Christian Charity,* concluding with a warning quoted in whole or part many times afterwards:

we must Consider that wee shall be as a Citty upon a Hill, the eies of all people are uppon us; soe that if wee shall deale falsely with our god in this worke wee have undertaken and soe cause him to withdrawe his present help from us, wee shall be made a story and a by-word through the world, wee shall open the mouthes of enemies to speake evill of the wayes of god and all professours for Gods sake; we shall shame the faces of many of gods worthy servants, and cause theire prayers to be turned into Cursses upon us till wee be consumed out of the good land whether wee are going. . . .

They could scarcely have picked a better time or place in which to try it. Distracted by internal conflicts, the English government had to allow the Puritan colonists to rule themselves as they pleased for over half a century, while the new land itself presented equally few obstacles to the Lord's work. In coming to America, the Puritans not only escaped a tyrannous king and meddling bishops, they escaped every European institution whatsoever, except such as they chose to resurrect in a form suitable to their purposes. As Englishmen reacting to new circumstances they often used traditional English techniques, but they could not and would not try to recreate English society in its entirety: if they had been happy with life in England they never would have left in the first place. In the New World they could build as God had commanded without having to accommodate social theory to any preexisting social reality; they had brought their reality with them. . . .

Puritan social values called not just for good bookkeeping, but for subordination, inequality, authority, unity, suppression of the individual will for the good of the whole, and any number of other concepts that have a distinctly sinister sound today. We would prefer in our discomfort to ignore the grip these ideas had on the mass of seventeenth-century society everywhere and to point instead to the instances where men flouted them as proof positive that Man seeks freedom and individualism—or at least he does once he receives a few acres of free land in fee simple. Unfortunately, the experience of several millennia have shown man's nature to be distressingly malleable whatever the system of land tenure in which he may function. In New England in the seventeenth century a dominant elite did not have to force a constantly insurgent majority into obedience; social distinctions were part of a set of assumptions held in common by all ranks of society. Some men certainly did rebel and rail against authority until it silenced them with stocks or whipping post, just as some men today rebel and rail against the fates on Saturday nights, smashing plate-glass windows and bar-room furniture until they too earn the same reward as their predecessors (suitably modernized). In Winthrop's company the meaner sort as well as the better believed in inequality, and the few who refused to accept it did so only in the same sense as we refuse to accept sickness and death.

The real danger to the Puritan social ethic came from within, from the institutions it created, or at least permitted to be created. New England society lacked the range of its English equivalent: it had no nobility and few poor cottagers. The church too had lost its official hierarchy, nor could its ministers hold civil office and—thanks to a restrictive admissions policy—they had no disciplinary authority over a large segment of the population. Finally, in a country largely engaged in farming, there were relatively few tenants and no manors or manorial dues to symbolize the landlord's authority.

Puritan doctrine itself tended to contradict its own social ideal. Advocates of political hierarchy would do well to base their franchise on something other than church membership; governors who rule by God's ordinance should not make their offices dependent on popular elections; ministers who preach that every man should remain in his calling should not call upon every man to increase his estate; above all, anyone who maintains traditional concepts of social relationships should not found them on voluntary contracts. The drama of Puritan society in New England lies in the extent to which the force of ideological commitment alone could maintain a system of political and social subordination for which the traditional material and institutional bases were lacking and which was undermined by many tendencies within the very ideology which supported it. . . .

By seventeenth-century standards Puritan society had little chance of surviving in the New World. Lacking most of the traditional means through which Europeans ordinarily established social cohesion and maintained order, the New England colonies should, in theory, have quickly disintegrated from internal disunion or collapsed at the first blow from a foreign or savage enemy. Stability would have to wait on the development of a landed aristocracy approximating the familiar upper stratum of European societies: a class of men who combined in the same hands economic, social, and political power, monopolized all pretensions of education, and claimed public service as their exclusive right and duty.

The early history of the Chesapeake region confirmed this gloomy prediction: peace and order could come only in the eighteenth century with the multiplication of large plantations and the great planters who owned them. Seventeenth-century New England, suffering from the same defects as its neighbors to the south with a few disabilities of its own making thrown in, should have fared even worse; instead, it enjoyed what unsympathetic contemporaries must have regarded as an unseemly success. Facing a bleak environment and the necessity of instituting unprecedented ways of life, New Englanders still managed to preserve a high degree of unity and a respectable capacity for resisting external pressure. Potentially explosive issues like the Antinomian crisis passed without too much breach of the peace, and even the massive mortality and economic dislocation following King Philip's War left the New England colonies still in one piece, while a much milder Indian threat in Virginia at the same time precipitated Bacon's Rebellion and the virtual collapse of that colony's governing institutions.

Safety in early America seemed to lie in being Puritan. The organization of the New England town and the clearly articulated goals of the Puritan experiment made for a tighter, more homogeneous society that knew what it was and where it was going and had a host of devices, from public schools to printed sermons, to remind it of that fact. Most important of all, the terms of the Puritan experiment demanded that every morally capable adult give his positive and knowing assent to the imperatives issued by pulpit and press. Though it sounds strange to say it, few societies in Western culture have ever depended more thoroughly or more self-consciously on the consent of their members than the allegedly repressive "theocracies" of early New England.

The state's last resort, force, rested in the hands of a militia embracing all able-bodied males, and every aspect of public life in New England demanded the formal assent of the public. Church members elected their ministers, town meetings their selectmen, freemen their deputies and magistrates, and militiamen their officers. Not even full membership in the visible church came automatically: only those explicitly willing to could sign the church covenant and take communion. The temptation to find the genesis of modern democracy in New England or Puritanism or both seems irresistible; indeed, there have been many unable to resist it from the time of the founding of New England to the present day.

American Puritanism did substitute a radical voluntarism for most of the customary engines of social coercion of early modern Europe. In the place of a hereditary monarch, a titled nobility, a church hierarchy, and a landlord class stood the characteristic Puritan covenants, written and unwritten, that legitimated the civil and ecclesiastical politics of New England. And yet the leader of the Puritan colonies hoped to achieve through this least traditional and most "modern" of means, the most traditional and ancient of ends: peace, order, unity, and love. God was not glorified by division, by diversity, by social conflict, by all that is the strength and weakness of liberal, pluralistic democracy. Holiness as much as statecraft called for every man in his place, bound to every other by the rights and obligations appropriate to his position in an organic social hierarchy. But holiness as much as statecraft also demanded that every man actively and repeatedly consent to his own inequality, that by covenant and ballot he confirm his adherence to the Lord's unitary truth and the small group of laymen and clergy who were its executors. Such a formula would have struck any prudent European as quixotic if not subversive; but, considering the stormy history of seventeenth-century Europe, the New England states did obtain far more unity and order than most European governments with similar goals and (in traditional terms) much more formidable instruments for achieving them.

Present-day sensibilities, conditioned by three centuries of contrary experience, find it difficult to understand subordination by consent of the subordinated. It is easier to identify the voluntaristic elements in Puritan society with more modern aspirations or to seize on every instance of lawbreaking as proof positive that so ridiculous an ethic did not influence anyone aside from a few callow writers of sermons. Believing in no one way ourselves, we forget that men who did could cast their votes, less as an expression of their individual preferences than as a sign of their collective union with the established interpreters and custodians of God's eternal law. Winthrop's "civil liberty," the "liberty to that only which is good, just and honest," accurately embodied the ideals of an age that understood freedom only as a voluntary acquiescence in a divinely ordained system of authority and deference. Annual elections failed to convince Winthrop that he owed an accounting of the ordinary course of his government to anyone but God. He told the electorate as much in his Hingham militia speech of 1645—and, justly rebuked, they promptly reelected him governor once a year every year for the rest of his life.

"Civil liberty" may have been a Puritan peculiarity, but it received powerful reinforcement from social assumptions that New Englanders held in common with the rest of Western civilization. Hierarchy seemed natural, equality glaringly abnormal. The deputies, the most representative part of the Bay Colony's polity, represented their constituents by repeatedly voting for sumptuary laws that would deny to a large portion of the men who elected them the finery deemed suitable only to richer and more honorable citizens. The God of order, graded social order, did not deprive himself of his basic nature in endowing his people with the ballot.

For all their penchant for voting, New Englanders seemed unable to pass over so much as a list of names without arranging them in an order of precedence. Every Sunday morning a fair number of Puritan congregations came face to face with their God decently and in order, taking seats in the meeting house assigned according to formulas based on arcane combinations of age, wealth, and social standing. Ranking of students at Harvard and Yale according to the status of their parents testified to the same faith in inequality, as did the assorted honorifics from "esquire" down to "goodman" affected by men of local prominence.

Inconsistency in the use of titles was the rule, while the noisy protests of churchgoers and college students slighted by assignments below their dignity became a depressingly regular feature of ecclesiastical and academic life. Outside of a rigid caste system social distinctions always tend to blur, but such imprecision hardly constitutes a creeping egalitarianism. The violence and frequency of protests over inaccurate assignments in themselves demonstrate that New Englanders took the existence of hierarchy seriously even if they could not agree over their respective places within it. A New England freeholder of middling size might quarrel with his neighbor over a seat in the meeting house, and his town clerk might give him a "goodman" on one tax list and no distinction at all on another, yet freeholder, neighbor, and clerk all knew where they stood in relation to a Winthrop or a Bradstreet.

Admittedly, for every instance of respect cited, a counter instance of disrespect could probably also be adduced. The sumptuary laws, like all legislation, may be taken as a sign of the weakness of social ideals as well as of their strength, and a criminal brought to justice serves at one and the same time to show that standards were flouted and that they were enforced. Even the absence of criminal prosecutions can be made to show either that laws were obeyed or that they were ignored. The double edge on every bit of evidence makes it impossible to prove that New Englanders or anyone else habitually deferred to their superiors; laws, court cases, and all the rest establish only what the American Puritans thought they *ought* to do, whether they actually did it or not.

If *ought* is a subtler prison than *is*, it is nonetheless a prison. To defy Puritan norms was merely to continue to take them as a point of reference; they could be escaped only by being completely replaced. But any new set of imperatives would need more of a foundation than apathy and defiance, and despite extensive male suffrage and a relatively equal distribution of wealth, despite town meetings and a public school system, seventeenth-century New Englanders had no positive ideological justification for egalitarianism. The *"Levelling Spirit"* that the ministers like to flay was not a coherent social philosophy but the sporadic, directionless, and doomed spirit of revolt that prompted some men more desperate than most to defy values they themselves really felt to be true. New England's levellers were not Lieutenant Colonel John Lilburne and Colonel Thomas Rainborough, they were the servant who justified bashing in his master's head by claiming to be as good a man as he, and Peter Bussaker, who hoped to meet some of the members of the church in hell and did not question but that he should. The servant died on the gallows, and Bussaker was more drunkard than democrat.

It is difficult to connect the men who punished Bussaker for contempt of authority with the Englishmen of the same religious persuasion who beheaded Charles I in the name of contractual government and fundamental law. New England not only had no John Lilburne, it lacked even a John Milton, who would have at least imposed some sort of equality among the saints even if he had little interest in the rights of the unregenerate. After his triumphant Hingham militia speech of 1645, John Winthrop would probably have choked on Milton's assertion of 1649 that the people might remove their magistrates whenever they chose, with or without cause:

It follows lastly—that since the King or Magistrate holds his authoritie of the people, both originally and naturally for their good in the first place, and not his owne, then may the people as oft as they shall judge it for the best, either choose him or reject him, retaine him or depose him though no Tyrant, meerly by the libertie and right of free born men, to be govern'd as seems to them best.

For a moment one can almost forget that Winthrop owed his magistracy to annual elections in which a majority of the Bay Colony's adult males could participate, while Milton's great protagonist, Oliver Cromwell, could claim his power only by the exercise of naked force. Apparently Puritans had to be in a minority before they could come out with anything resembling a doctrine of popular rights. When they enjoyed majority support, as in America, they had no need to grow revolutionary; they never had anything to revolt against.

Political radicalism, democratic or otherwise, appeared mainly in Puritanism Militant, not Puritanism Triumphant. In New England for the first and last time Puritans engaged in legitimating a new and unprecedented order rather than in tearing down an old and traditional one. Their chief spokesmen not surprisingly had much to say about the duties of obedience and submission that would have sounded odd to their comrades on the bullet-torn fields of Naseby and Marston Moor. But such emphasis on the lack of "democratic" elements in the New Englanders' thought obscures their real relationship with the English Independents and the extent to which they actually put into practice the Independents' most visionary and apparently unachievable goals. Insistence on the rule of the saints, on government of and by the regenerate, ultimately poisoned the concept of liberty held by men like Milton and turned their beloved commonwealth into Paradise Lost, but Massachusetts managed to base its franchise successfully on just such a basis for half a century. In their election of magistrates New Englanders even achieved what the foremost cynic of the seventeenth century, Thomas Hobbes, declared to be impossible, the voluntary submission of the majority of the people to a small minority considered the wise and the virtuous.

Milton's and Cromwell's insoluble dilemma, the reconciliation of the twin goals of reformation and liberty, never existed for their New World brethren because New Englanders did use their liberty to achieve reformation in a way contemporary Englishmen would not. America was really a kind of intellectual Australia, where ideas long extinct elsewhere lived on far beyond their allotted time, sheltered in their isolation from the cataclysms that transformed the same species on the mainland into completely new forms. The main settlement of New England occurred prior to the English Civil War, and Puritan social theory in the New World remained for a century and more much as it had been in the England of the 1630s, the England of the Great Migration, long after the strains of war, the Interregnum, and the Restoration had fragmented and radicalized the parent faith. Lilburne and Prynne had stood together in 1638 and they stood so symbolically ever after, for those of their coreligionists who left England before the great falling out.

American Puritanism nevertheless shared in revolutionary potentials common to reformed Protestantism in general. Everywhere except in a few out-of-the-way corners like New England the radical wing of the Protestant cause found itself in the opposition; and under those circumstances principle and necessity together combined to force it to appeal, over the heads of the powers that were, to the individual consciences of the true believers.

As early as the 1550s the Marian exiles John Ponet and Christopher Goodman had gone far beyond any of the contemporary Protestant writers of the Continent by assigning the duty of overthrowing an ungodly monarch to the "multitude," collectively or even individually. The law of nature was plain enough, and the duty of enforcing it general enough, for every man who failed to stop the execution of an unjust law to share in the sin of those who had made it. Goodman had no comfort for any who would excuse themselves on the grounds that they were private persons unconnected with affairs of state:

But they will peradventure excuse theselves, as thogh God had no thing to do with them, because they be not Apostels; nor Prophets. Nevertheless they may be assured, they shall be as they ever have bene, subjects to his plages and punishmentes: and so Will he have a do with them, thogh they would have nought to do with hym.

The special standard of behavior the Lord required of New Englanders only increased the vital material interest each member of the covenanted community had in the conduct of every other member, for a breach of the natural law in Roxbury or a sin left unpunished in Watertown would also bring fire and brimstone to Dedham. When one Tryal Pore confessed to the sin of fornication before the Middlesex County Court, in 1656, she admitted that "by this sinn I have not only donn what I can to Poull doune Judgmente from the lord on my selve but allso apon the place where I live." Public misconduct by the Bay Colony's government would hardly have been less provoking than Tryal Pore's periodic misdemeanors.

Nor could exposition of the fundamental law always remain the exclusive vocation of authorized interpreters acting without reference to the ignorant multitude while the authorities openly disagreed with each other and appealed to the public as a whole. The Marian exiles had fallen back on the people so much sooner than other European Protestants in part because they had no one else to fall back upon—no pope, no provincial parliaments, no *Untere Obrigkeit.* "We must obey the preachers onely when they bring Gods word," Goodman informed his readers, assuming they had sense enough to realize that their preachers currently were bringing nothing of the sort. Whatever the prerogatives of the educated and the highly placed, when it came time to draw swords each individual would have to decide for himself whom to follow, Bishop Ponet or Bishop Gardiner, John Milton or Sir Robert Filmer.

For a time the early unity of the New England colonists did enable their ministry to reassert the rights of the privileged few: "if it be in matters of Religion, there is the Priest; if in matters civil, there is the Magistrate." Yet when the Rev. John Norton made that statement he conveniently overlooked that fact that he was not a priest of the Holy Roman Catholic Church but of the single most disorganized and anarchic ecclesiastical organization in Christendom. The issue which prompted his declaration, the dispute over the half-way covenant, indicated clearly enough that even in the New World the teachers of God's word might occasionally preach against each other, just as the magistrates could not always keep from airing their disputes in public, in effect referring them to the freemen for decision at the next election.

Three thousand miles of Atlantic Ocean did not deprive the inhabitants of New England of all similarities with their English counterparts. There was more than a little foretaste of the Banqueting Hall on that January day of 1649 in Thomas Shepard's warning of 1638 that if the bramble should reign over Massachusetts, the freemen had best arm themselves with hatchets to cut it down. There was more than a little reminder of John Hampden in Samuel Symond's decision of 1657 declaring void and unenforceable any positive statute violating the "fundamental law of mine and thine." Had there been a bit more interference from England in the 1630s, the New World Puritans too might have discovered, like John Bradshaw, that resistance to tyranny was obedience to God. But Bradshaw's declaration fell short of another one: that all men are created equal and endowed by their creator with certain unalienable rights. Revolution was acceptable to Puritans only because their state existed to enforce a positive pattern of virtue laid down by revealed and natural law. A ruler who diverted the state from that end might be overthrown by an expression of the popular will—a popular will conceived of as the unanimous voice of all right-thinking men, not the sum of the particular opinions of the majority. The question of majorities did not arise in an ideology which presumed that all uncorrupted intellects agreed on the same basic truths. As for minorities, American Puritans consigned them to Rhode Island in this world and the devil in the next. "I dare take upon me, to be the Haerauld of *New-England,* so farre, as to proclaime to the world, in the name of our Colony, that all Familist, Antinomians, Anabaptists and other Enthusiasts, shall have free Liberty to keep away from us, and such as will come to be gone as fast as they can, the sooner the better."

In its original form radical Protestantism all too easily passed over into a millenarianism that led to the dictatorship of the regenerate. The Marian exiles would not have balked at a Protestant minority overthrowing a Catholic majority in the name of the law of nature, nor did Milton see anything wrong in asserting that only those whose natural capabilities had been in some part restored by grace could claim their natural liberties. Only they could read the law of nature written on the hearts of all but obscured by sin for most. If Milton made much of reason, it was right reason, reason illuminated by grace.

If men within themselves would be govern'd by reason, and not generally give up their understanding to a double tyrannie, of Custom from without, and blind affections within, they would discerne better, what it is to favour and uphold the Tyrant of a Nation. But being slaves within doors, no wonder they strive so much to have the public state conformably govern'd to the inward vitious rule by which they govern themselves. For indeed none can love freedom heartilie, but good men; the rest love not freedom, but license; which never hath more scope or more indulgence than under Tyrants.

Before *The Tenure of Kings and Magistrates* became *The Declaration of Independence,* Puritans would have to stop distinguishing between regenerate and unregenerate for political purposes, which meant abandoning many of the central assumptions on which New England politics was based. Seventeenth-century doctrine could be made to yield eighteenth-century republicanism only by a very selective accentuation of individual elements within it, without regard to the logic that bound together the whole.

The components of the original synthesis were disparate enough to begin with. Puritans had painted a black picture of what was largely because they had such a high ideal of what ought to be: natural man's will and intellect seemed so depraved because unfallen man's faculties had been so magnificent. The rub came in deciding just how many of these former powers grace actually restored. On the one hand, a regenerate people could establish a "popular state" in both their civil and ecclesiastical polity; that is, they could elect their governors, lay and clerical. On the other hand, they were not quite regenerate enough to govern themselves, but must elect only the wise and virtuous and leave government up to them. Yet even the wise and virtuous had enough of the Old Man in them to require frequent elections, carefully prescribed bounds to governmental power, and a deliberately fragmented polity.

John Cotton's defense of the New England church system was especially ambiguous, and consequently especially pregnant with implication for the future. Critics found the Congregational Way "democratical" and therefore anarchic. Cotton replied by denying it was any such thing, pointing out that while the multitude might elect the church officers they still did not rule themselves, but "are governed by the Elders so long as they rule a right, to wit, while they hold forth the word and voyce of Christ, which the sheep of Christ are want to heare." All well and good, except that he could not stop with that assertion. He had to go on and argue that, even if the churches *were* "democratical," nevertheless the membership, all regenerate, could follow God's laws by itself:

Though the government were democraticall (as it is not) yet here is no tumultuous disordere, where not the will *of each man beareth the sway, but the* voyce of Christ *alone is heard, who is the Head and Monarch of the Church.*

The seventeenth century found New England's church polity more interesting than its civil government, but New Englanders never denied that as the scriptures guided church affairs, so an equally clear law of nature determined civil concerns. Unfallen man had always been able to follow this law, and to the extent that eighteenth-century writers began (in John Wise's phrase) to "wave the Consideration of Mans Moral Turpitude," that is, to consider all men as unfallen, to that extent they began to lay the basis for a democratic ideology. By 1794 a president of Yale, Ezra Stiles, could digress from an apology for the judges of Charles I long enough to announce that the common people could govern themselves according to the rules of reason, and still think himself the legitimate intellectual heir of the regicides he defended:

The charm and unintelligible mysteries wrapt up in the name of a King being done away, the way would be open for all nations to a rational government and policy, on such plain and obvious general principles, as would be intelligible to the plainest rustic, to the substantial yeomanry, or men of landed estates, which ought to be the body of the population. Every one could understand it plain as a Locke or a Camden. And whatever the Filmers and Acherlys may say, the common people are abundantly capable and susceptible of such a polity.

Generalizing the rights of the elect by identifying the regenerate intellect with the rational faculties common to all men still might produce a kind of majority authoritarianism. If the truth were all that obvious, then all men of good will should agree on it, and any dissent from their consensus would have to come from men of very ill will indeed. The elective dictatorship of the wise and virtuous could give way to the still more formidable dictatorship of the many. Stiles himself was saved from these consequences by his steadfast faith in the ability of the public as a whole to recognize the truth when it was presented. Error in a popular state generally sprang from misinformation, not the incompetence of the people. "The common people will generally judge right, when duly informed. The general liberty is safe and secure in their hands. It is not from deficiency of abilities to judge, but from want of information, if they at any time as a body go wrong." The best way to keep them well informed was to allow the circulation of the widest possible variety of opinions. "Factionary societies," even those begun "with the primary and direct desire of overthrowing the government," ought to be tolerated, for they could ultimately do a popular state little harm and might do it much good, encouraging "extensive discussions which enlighten the public; defeat insidious and partial cunning, and bring forward an open and firm support of good and acceptable government."

Substitution of natural reason for grace provided only one route from Puritanism to equality. A diametrically opposite process could yield almost the same result: instead of universalizing grace, the heirs of the Puritan tradition could also deny it altogether and democratize depravity. From the very founding of the Puritan colonies most New Englanders preferred to put their faith in written laws and detailed limitations on government rather than in men, however wise or gracious. John Cotton spoke for Puritans generally in his often quoted remarks on human nature and power:

There is a straine in a mans heart that will sometime or other runne out to excess, unless the Lord restraine it, but it is not good to venture it: It is necessary therefore, that all power that is on earth be limited, Church-power or other: If there be power given to speak great things, then look for great blasphemies, look for a licentious abuse of it.

A preoccupation with internal corruption has come down to modern times as the Puritans' least agreeable attribute, though oddly enough it had much to do with creating those features of the Bay Colony's government now considered most democratic. Because even magistrates, the most saintly of the saints, had a sizable residue of natural lust left in them, their power had to be limited by a codified body of laws, frequent elections, and the popular element in the "mixt" polity. These devices originally functioned only as emergency safeguards against the occasional aberrations of usually trustworthy rulers, but the moment New Englanders admitted that no man could read the law of nature aright, that all men were equally corrupt, that no faith could be placed in internal self-discipline (call it grace or virtue, piety or learning), then bills of rights and fragmented polity became the sum and substance of sound politics.

In a world without clear and uncorrupted minds the only safety lay in numbers. Delivering the Massachusetts election sermon in that most significant of years, 1776, the Rev. Samuel West denied that since the Fall any man could understand the law of nature. "We have a law in our members, which is constantly warring against the law of the mind," he announced, neglecting to exempt saints and cultivated gentlemen. But if no special group could claim access to the truth, if there was no grace on which to found dominion, then ultimate authority had to rest with the people as a whole. Given the universal prevalence of self-interest and "the strong propensities of our animal nature" only the consent of the whole of society would guarantee a disinterested decision.

It is true that the publick may be imposed upon by a misrepresentation of facts; but this may be said of the publick, which can't always be said of individuals, viz. that the publick is always willing to be rightly informed, and when it has proper matter of conviction laid before it, its judgment is always right.

Belief in a law of nature did not necessarily guarantee a liberal or egalitarian society. In seventeenth-century New England natural law had provided a good part of that one unalterable way that the votes of the freemen could only assent to, never shape, and that could be interpreted only by the learned few versed in the esoteric skills essential to statecraft. John Winthrop had left the determination of what was good, just, and honest to a small body of magistrates and ministers relying on the "light of nature (especially where the image of God in man is in parte renewed by Christ)." For Winthrop, "the best part is always the least, and of the best part the wiser part is always the lesser. The old law was choose ye out judges, etc., and thou shalt bring the matter to the judge, etc."

Winthrop's more wary contemporaries insisted on laying down the rule for the judges to judge by and on tempering their authority with some participation by the people, but they left the preponderant power with the wisest and best. A positive ideal of majority rule could come only on the day when even the judges lost faith in wisdom and virtue, when even the chief ideologue of the Essex Junto, Theophilus Parsons, could declare that the "morals of all people in all ages, have been shockingly corrupted" and answer negatively his own query, "shall we alone boast an exemption from the general fate of mankind?" Sharing Winthrop's low estimate of human nature without Winthrop's exceptions, Parsons declined to define civil liberty, liberty under government, as the right to follow certain eternal principles. Liberty was nothing more than "the right every man in the state has, to do whatever is not prohibited by laws, TO WHICH HE HAS GIVEN HIS CONSENT."

Comparisons of this sort indicate how far men like Parsons and Stiles had come from the ethic of Cotton and Winthrop as much as the ˠubstantial debt they owed to it. It takes a peculiar measure of desperation to make the first New Englanders into democrats: one must be either an unsympathetic seventeenth-century controversialist or a very sympathetic twentieth-century historian. American Puritanism in its heyday was neither democratic nor undemocratic as moderns understand the term; it was sui generis. If it must be assimilated to a twentieth-century model, it could quite plausibly be to one of our postdemocratic political nightmares. In retrospect Puritan voluntarism seems almost plebiscitarian, and its ideal of civil liberty comes horribly close to "democratic centrism."

Any such analogy, of course, would do violence to the intellectual universe of another time; it would seem safer to draw no modern analogies at all. The witches' brew that went under the name of Puritan social thought could have spawned almost anything. Abolishing the law of nature might have led to the Leviathan state; universalizing grace might have only substituted the majority for the elect as the executors of God's unchanging decrees. There was nothing inevitable about the transformation the original doctrine would undergo in America, either in 1630 or 1760 or at any point in between. A whole range of individuals from John Locke to Lord North had each his contribution to make before John Winthrop's colony became the Massachusetts of Samuel Adams, let alone the America of George Bancroft.

Seventeenth-century New Englanders would not have found our search for modern facsimiles for their institutions very relevant or very meaningful. Their minds set on other things, they went their way apparently oblivious to the tensions inherent in the tightly knit set of paradoxes that would be their legacy to the future. Professing a faith that preached subordination by consent, ruled by the superiors in a land where physical conditions permitted relatively little material superiority, they dedicated themselves to the establishment of a model society for the reformation of a humanity they considered hopelessly corrupt. Their social ethic stands as a monument to the proposition that the contradictory is not the irreconcilable.

JAMES A. HENRETTA

Wealth, Authority, and Power

The Evolution of the Southern Aristocracy

The presence of black slaves at the bottom of the social scale had a large, perhaps even a determinative, effect on the nature of white society. Before 1670 there had been relatively few blacks resident in the Chesapeake region, certainly not more than 5 percent of the total population, and not all of them were bound to hereditary lifetime service. From the very first, Africans had been perceived by whites as racially distinct and culturally different; but initially they had been treated in law in much the same manner as indentured servants from Europe. Then, rather suddenly, their status was completely undermined. A series of laws passed between 1667 and 1671 stated that conversion to Christianity did not relieve a black of his bondage. At the same time it became clear that Africans, and their children, served for life rather than for a specific period of years; and that color was the single defining feature of their status as slaves. By the end of the seventeenth century all of the southern American colonies had outlawed miscegenation: to be black or brown was to be a chattel slave, the personal property of one who was white and free.

Just at the time that this general debasement of blacks was taking place, the lines of class and status in white society were taking on a more coherent and a more permanent form. The high prices paid for Chesapeake tobacco during the first half-century of settlement had brought quick fortunes to those privileged colonists, many of them the younger sons of London merchants and bureaucrats, with large land grants and many indentured servants. The growing economic cleavages in Chesapeake society were accentuated by the falling price of tobacco after 1660, which struck particularly hard at the small yeoman farmers with limited capital resources, and by the attempts of certain leading families to appropriate control of government on the local and provincial levels.

In 1675 social discontent helped to precipitate an armed uprising led by Nathaniel Bacon, an ambitious planter of good connections and considerable means. The laws passed by Bacon's Assembly sought to limit the political power of important families on the county level by broadening the suffrage to include tenants and by creating elective posts to offset the power of appointed magistrates. Other laws, conceived and supported by the very families whose local predominance was under attack from below, attempted to combat the growing influence of the provincial council and its domination by a few families favored by the royal governor. The appointive powers of the governor were drastically limited while provincial councillors were excluded from the county courts and their tax exemptions were revoked.

Bacon's Assembly was ousted within a year, and the reform programs (especially on the local level) were as abortive as the revolt itself. Within a few decades it became generally accepted that certain established families were destined to be preeminent in wealth and power. During these same years the once-prevalent fear among the landed classes that white and black servants would rise together in rebellion gradually vanished; the fastening of a subordinate status on Africans had ensured that all white men would stand together. Subsequently, the social distance between black and white was to appear far greater than the social or economic inequalities among the classes of the white population.

The reasons for the simultaneous emergence of a caste and a class society in the Chesapeake are not completely clear, but this much is certain: In 1700, as throughout southern history, the extensive ownership of slaves and the expropriation of the produce of their labor was the prerogative of a privileged minority. There were about 3,000 slaves in Maryland at the beginning of the eighteenth century, but they were owned by only about 1,000 to 1,250 whites—less than one-fourth of the 5,000–6,000 white households in the province. The probate records in Maryland during the 1690s reveal that 75 percent of the planters whose wills were probated held property assessed at less than £100 sterling. Not only were these men too poor to own a slave or an indentured servant, but over one-third of them were landless and had to lease the very soil they worked. Shipping 1,200 to 3,000 pounds of tobacco each year (worth £6 to £15 sterling), this tarnished residue of the once-proud yeoman class scraped along at a subsistence level, often deeply in debt to the local storekeeper or moneylender.

A second distinct group in the white population was that 20 percent whose estates at probate were valued at £100 to £500 sterling. During their lifetimes most of these men had owned slaves—usually from one to five—and so had a vested interest in the perpetuation of the system. The labor of their black workers or, less often, investment in land or in a store had lifted these families above the majority of poor white planters. But social prestige and political power eluded these men as well. These honors were reserved, in the main, for the wealthiest 5 percent of the white population, the members of the 250 households who owned from a quarter to a third of all the slaves and who controlled the bulk of the wealth of the society.

During the first half of the eighteenth century the proportion of slaves in the total population increased dramatically (from 20 to 40 percent in Virginia and from 11 to 30 percent in Maryland). This development, the result of high rates of natural increase and of a significant increase in slave importation, had an important effect on the social structure of the white community. A greater proportion of whites employed slave labor. By the 1730s only 55 percent of the probated estates were assessed at less than £100 sterling as compared to 75 percent a generation before. Nearly half of the white planters now had sufficient resources to own a slave (although not this many actually did). Even taking into account the rise in prices—which meant that £100 sterling was worth less in actual purchasing power—there had been a significant increase in the prosperity of the white population, but (interestingly enough) this general improvement had not resulted in greater equality within the white community.

Indeed, just the opposite, for the dimensions of the upper class expanded—in numbers and in wealth. In the 1690s the Great Planters of Maryland, those who at their deaths had estates worth £1,000 or more, constituted only 1.5 percent of those whose wills were probated. This proportion rose steadily: to 2.2 percent during the 1720s; to 3.6 percent during the 1730s; and to 3.9 percent of the total sample during the 1750s. The white population of Maryland had increased fourfold during these six decades, but the number of Great Planters had grown by a factor of ten. The wealth generated by the use of more slaves and the expansion of the tobacco industry had not been diffused equally among the members of the white community but had helped to create a relatively large class of wealthy planters.

Many of the members of this elite group were related by blood or marriage to those Great Planters who had established their predominance during the last quarter of the seventeenth century. The unique feature of the landed aristocracy of the Chesapeake was its ability to perpetuate its control over a society that was rapidly expanding, both in numbers and in geographic area. The total number of white households in Virginia increased from about 6,000 in 1700 to 80,000 in 1790, but economic wealth and political power resided in the hands of the same family clans at the end of this period as at the beginning. In the decades preceding the war for independence no less than 70 percent of the 110 leaders of the Virginia House of Burgesses were drawn from families resident in Virginia before 1690.

The remarkable success of the Great Planters of Virginia in preserving and extending the power of their families was the result of high rates of reproduction (which provided an ample supply of sons to take over family lands and of daughters to marry into established or rapidly rising families) and also of the system by which the resources of the family were transmitted from one generation to the next. The estate of the father did not pass to the eldest son (as among the aristocracy of eighteenth century England) leaving younger sons to find their fortunes in law, government, or the church. It was, instead, distributed among all of his male and female offspring. . . .

As these sons and daughters took up residence on the lands accumulated for them by the economic success and political acumen of their father, the family extended its influence into new localities. And this expansion more than matched the numerical and geographical growth of the colony as a whole. In the end, the weight of these established families came to press, like the atmosphere itself, evenly over the whole face of Virginia. (A similar proliferation of the upper classes had taken place in England during the sixteenth century, also during a period of rapid population growth.) Of the 100 wealthiest men in the state in 1787, all except four owned lands in at least two counties, and more than half had estates in at least four counties. There was a certain irony in this development; for the practice of partible inheritance had produced both a greater equality within the ranks of the wealthy families and a greater disparity between the resources of these clans and the rest of the population. Seven members of the Carter family, the richest of all of the clans, owned a total of 170,000 acres of land and 2,300 slaves scattered over seven different counties. They were joined, as members of the privileged one hundred, by nine members of the Cocke family, eight Fitzhughs, seven Harrisons, eight Lees, seven Randolphs, and eight Washingtons.

It was this small homogeneous elite—English by descent, Anglican in religion, and linked to one another by ties of kinship and bonds of economic interest—which monopolized the political life of Virginia during the eighteenth century. There were seven members of the Lee family, all of the same generation, sitting in the Virginia assembly in the 1750s and representing five different counties. And the majority of all of the leaders of the House of Burgesses between 1720 and 1775, the men who sat on the important committees and dominated the debates, were related by blood or marriage to one or another of the dozen or so great family clans. That 60 percent of the white adult males had sufficient property to vote and that 45 percent of them regularly exercised the franchise was irrelevant given this concentration of hereditary power. In this deferential society the mass of poor white planters acquiesced in the decisions of their betters and submitted meekly to their rule. . . .

The children of the poor white planter sensed what their parents knew all too well: that they occupied an inferior place in the social hierarchy and should act accordingly. "We were accustomed to look upon, what were called *gentle folks*, as beings of a superior order," recalled the Reverend Devereux Jarratt, the son of a carpenter who eventually rose to a position of authority within the Church of England. . . . The consciousness of social inferiority, inculcated in childhood to such an extent that it induced physical fear, became an enduring part of the behavior patterns (and perhaps even the personalities) of thousands of poor whites. Wherever they went, in the town or in the fields, in public or private, these men and women carried the stigma of subordinate rank with them: in their halting speech, gnarled hands, and emaciated faces. They were deferential to those above them and—especially when emboldened by drink or by numbers—harshly demanded respect from slaves and servants, whom they could consider as their social inferiors.

A hierarchical and authoritarian pattern of personal relationships had come to characterize southern colonial society by 1700, and it persisted for more than a century and a half because the conduct it sanctioned corresponded to the actual distribution of power and influence in the community. The existence of these established role expectations, these shared experiences and assumptions, also helped to perpetuate that system. The "difference between gentle and simple" which Jaratt testified was "universal among all of my age and rank," had become part of the social environment, accepted by the inhabitants as immutable and correct. Anchored in the child-training and socialization process and solidified by the institutionalized roles of adult life, this pattern of relationships came to form an integral part of the sense of identity of thousands of adult individuals. The congruence between the social structure and the personalities of those who composed it was not exact; in this, as in any society, there was a great deal of "slippage," as the mobility achieved by Jaratt himself clearly demonstrated. And, yet, the strength and pervasiveness of these role expectations and values worked constantly to inhibit any widespread intellectual or personal challenge to the existing system. They became, in a very real sense, the social chains which bound this stratified society together. The shackles of psychological dependence and subordination had come to bind the minds of poor whites as tightly as iron chains bound the limbs of blacks.

Entrepreneurial Capitalism and Social Differentiation

It is not inequality itself, but its extent and the mode of its institutionalization, that differentiates one society from another. In the northern colonies women were placed in a position legally, socially, and economically inferior to men. The male population itself was divided by age, abilities, and accomplishments. Yet the spectrum of wealth and power in the agricultural sector of the North was much narrower than in the South and the hierarchy of social prestige was not based on the ownership of other men and women. The relative parity among the rural inhabitants of Pennsylvania, Benjamin Franklin suggested in 1759, arose

first from a more equal distribution of land by the assemblies . . . and secondly, from the nature of their occupation; husbandmen with small tracts of land, though they may by industry maintain themselves and families in mediocrity, [have] few means of acquiring great wealth. . . .

"The hopes of having land of their own and becoming independent of Landlords," observed another writer, "is what chiefly induces people into America."

This commitment to independence as a prime social value had an important effect on the political life of the local community. Only those who were not dependent on others—in practical terms, those who controlled property—could hope to have a voice in the affairs of the town. This sharp line of demarcation excluded all married women, whose real and personal possessions belonged to their husbands. It also severely restricted the rights of children and of servants, who were the dependents of the male parent in the household in which they lived and worked.

During the seventeenth century the institution of bonded servitude had functioned as a means of introducing children into adult society, training them for their life's work on the farms or in the shops of others, or exposing them to good manners (and a steady diet) in the homes of the well-to-do. The system of indenture also served as a means of providing employment for adult immigrants who did not have resources sufficient to support themselves. In either case, bonded servitude was a step on the bottom of the social or agricultural ladder. . . .

By the middle of the eighteenth century the system of indentured servitude was breaking down as a method of social control. The family unit was unable to assimilate or control the culturally distinct groups which now composed the servant class. Moreover, in the large colonial cities, the majority of the dependent white population was no longer encompassed within the bounds of family government. In Boston in 1771, 29 percent of the adult male population were neither property owners nor the dependents of taxpaying members of the community.

These propertyless men, mostly laborers, seamen, or journeymen artisans who bargained their services for wages, introduced an element of instability into the bottom of the urban social order. Apart from the economic sanctions exercised by employers during the hours of work, there was no institutional method for controlling the activities of these men and their families, many of whom moved from town to town in search of economic subsistence. Of the 188 propertyless men resident in Boston in 1687, only 64 (or 35 percent) were resident in the town eight years later. This rate of persistence was less than half of that of the wealthiest portion of the population, those who were tied to the community by bonds of kinship and of economic investment. A century later the relationship between occupational status and permanence of residence was much the same; of the 546 proletarians in Boston in 1780 only 228 (or 42 percent) remained a decade later.

Given the differing material condition and life style of this floating population of workers, an increase in social disorder was only to be expected. Until the agitation against British rule gave an ideological edge to the antiauthoritarian and unruly activities of this lumpenproletariat, most of its violent energies were directed at other members of the class or against the black population. . . .

The members of this turbulent section of the population were not, as a rule, master mechanics or master craftsmen with established business or even the less affluent but stable and respected workingmen who were members of the dozens of private clubs and societies which had appeared among the urban lower classes. They were, rather, the drifters, the undesirables, the part-time workers, the unfortunate men who lacked the family background or class advantages or individual psychological resources to compete successfully in the harsh and impersonal world of a market economy. To survive, prosper, and thrive in a system based on commercial exchange demanded a very different set of moral and mental attitudes from those required in a culture founded on personal dependence. Life in a contractual society necessitated more calculating behavior than that in a community divided along the lines of inherited or ascribed status; sociability was suddenly less important than self-reliance. The way was open here for a man of great ambition and exceptional abilities to rise in his own lifetime to a position of great wealth. And yet, both individual initiative and the opportunity to exploit it were socially determined; the same opportunities were simply not open to all men.

The career of Thomas Hancock was a prime example of the cumulative advantages bestowed by social class and childhood training. Born in Lexington, Massachusetts, in 1703, Hancock was the third son of a Congregationalist minister. Although his two older brothers had been sent to Harvard, Thomas was apprenticed at the age of fourteen to a bookseller. This was a relatively humble, but not an insignificant, beginning. His father's status and educational background had given the young man expectations and aspirations which went far beyond those of most children in the community. The accident of birth gave him greater opportunities as well. . . . After setting up his own business at the end of his seven-year indenture, he made a "good" marriage to the daughter of an established dealer in books and general merchandise.

The solid advantages bestowed by his class background explain only a part of Hancock's subsequent career. The traits of character fashioned during his childhood and young adult years also played a crucial role. He did not—indeed could not—rest content as an ordinary shopkeeper; his ambition was too strong, always prompting him to expand and to diversify his activities. Within a few years he was trading molasses for fish in Newfoundland; importing Dutch tea through St. Eustatius in the West Indies; working on a commission basis for English merchants with interests in Boston; investing in trading ventures; and accumulating his own fleet of merchant ships. Only in 1737, when his fortune was well established, did Hancock pause to erect a testimonial to his success in the form of a mansion on Beacon Hill.

The acquisitive mentality and the capitalistic activities which raised Hancock far above his already substantial origins were, to some extent, merely the latest manifestation of an ethos characteristic of the commercial classes in European society for hundreds of years. The only unique feature of the appearance of these values in America was in the extent of their influence and in the relative absence of a countervailing (if not predominant) ethic of aristocratic leisure and gentility. "The only principle of life propagated among the young people is to get money," Cadwallader Colden reported from New York in 1748, "and men are only esteemed according to what they are worth—that is, the money they are possessed of.". . .

The existence of these values and these patterns of behavior had a profound meaning. They hinted at the existence, on an extensive scale, of a new type of modal personality in the northern areas of colonial America. This was the dynamic character structure of the rational entrepreneur, an individual who is at once intensely ambitious, compulsively motivated, and yet cautious and calculating in his business activities.

The roots of this personality structure extended backward to an earlier phase of American (and English) history, to the religious upheavals in the mother country which, during the seventeenth century, led to the migration of dissenting Protestants to the new world. There was, in the communities formed in the American wilderness, a strange blend of old and new ideas, values, and institutions—an accurate reflection of the fact that Puritanism itself represented a key transitional phase in the long and slow evolution from a traditional to a modern conception of life, authority, and personality.

Initially, the transplantation of Puritanism to American soil accentuated the more traditional and conservative elements of this complex and contradictory social movement. In the small isolated agricultural settlements of seventeenth century New England, the father stood at the head of the family, exacting obedience from all those dependent on him; the village leaders, men dignified by age and experience, filled the offices of government and dominated political affairs; the minister directed the spiritual lives of his congregation, arranging their seating in church to reflect before God their standing among men. The pattern of authority and the institutions that gave it expression were one and the same. The key to the Puritan character as it developed in this environment "can be found in the responses of individuals to the series of stern fathers who stood over them in the homes of their childhood, in the church, in society, and in the state.". . . .

Children raised in this type of home developed a hyperactive conscience. Charged with personal responsibility for their actions and deeply concerned to avoid offense, they were forced to discriminate for themselves between what their parents would approve or disapprove, between what was "right" and what was "wrong." With the development of full moral autonomy, this process of discrimination became divorced from the system of reinforcement that had engendered it: The individual's conscience (or superego) warned him against moral transgression and urged him on to a continual reform of himself.

This inner psychological dynamic pushed men and women onward in the pursuit of higher standards and demanded excellence and achievement, however those terms were defined. . . . Here then in the childtraining practices and the social values of certain dissenting Protestant sects (and perhaps also a certain class within those religious groups) was an important source of the entrepreneurial character structure. Here also was the threat of boundless discontent—a compulsiveness which could be harnessed only by a strict organization of activity. "The order which the Quakers are accustomed from childhood to apply to the distribution of their tasks, their thoughts, and every moment of their lives," a percipient French visitor to Philadelphia observed, "economizes time, activity and money."

There were many differences between the Congregational creed of Thomas Hancock's father and the Quakerism of the Philadelphia Friends, but their members practiced a similar method of childtraining: a middle path which kept well clear of the extremes of authoritarian repression and parental neglect. Not all of their children became self-reliant adults imbued with a deep need for achievement. Sex roles, birth order, and the wider environment also affected the socialization process; and, in any event, inherited propensities could only be influenced within certain limits. Nonetheless, the results were impressive. Quakers constituted less than one-seventh of the population of Philadelphia in 1769, but they accounted for more than half of those who paid taxes in excess of £100. Of the seventeen wealthiest men in the city, twelve had been raised as Friends. . . .

The new entrepreneurial personality was most prevalent in urban centers and among particular classes and religious groups, but the economic behavior patterns and materialistic values which accompanied (and/or reinforced) it knew no geographic or social limits. . . .

The key elements, in rural and urban areas alike, were the growing scarcity of certain factors of production (which increased the economic leverage of those who controlled them) and the opportunities offered to merchants and creditors to provide processed goods and financial services to an expanding population. In Chester County, for example, the number of taxpayers tripled in the half-century following 1730. By 1782 between 25 percent and 35 percent of all taxpayers were either tenant farmers or "inmates"—married artisans or laborers living in dwellings owned by others—who, each month, paid a part of their income in rent to the land- and house-owning members of the community, and yet another part to storekeepers and other creditors in return for services. The established property owners and middlemen thus amassed a disproportionate share of the growing wealth of the county. Because of their position they were able to secure—through rents, commission and interest charges, retail markups, and the like—a part of the income of many others.

This method of accumulating wealth was different from that practiced in the slave colonies, where the *entire* surplus product of the black slave was expropriated by his master. It was, rather, a system of agrarian and commercial capitalism in which a *part* of the output of many free men was funneled into the hands of a few. By 1774 the poorest 50 percent of all the adults who were potential wealth holders in the colonies of New Jersey, Delaware, and Pennsylvania owned only 13 percent of the total wealth of this region, as against the 40 percent held by the richest tenth of the population. But because of the general increase in prosperity (the result, in part, of the entrepreneurial activities of the affluent taxpayers), the standard of living of many members of the poorer half of the society was higher than that of their parents or grandparents. Concealed behind the increase in inequality (but part of the same process of economic development and social differentiation) was a significant rise in the absolute wealth of the community.

Indeed, it was this facet of the total evolutionary process that was the subject of most contemporary comment. "One half of the wealth of this city is owned by men who wear leather aprons," a contributor to a Philadelphia newspaper claimed in the 1770s, "and the other half by those whose fathers or grandfathers wore leather aprons." However, valid as a statement of personal belief, the logic was deceptive and the remark misleading. Those who had benefited substantially from the labor of their parents numbered only 10 percent of the population, and this small group of wealthy taxpayers controlled 54 percent of the city's wealth in 1774. Moreover, even the present generation of artisans and shopkeepers constituted only half of the residents of the community. Below both of these relatively privileged groups were 40 percent of the free adult inhabitants; the members of this sizeable fraction of the society owned a pitiful 4 percent of the total wealth.

It was not this depressed section of the population, however, who controlled the development of Philadelphia or who conceived its myths and values. This was the prerogative of the successful, those long-time residents who saw about them only those craftsmen and storekeepers who had succeeded and not the great numbers who had failed and floated away to other settlements. The descriptions of social reality composed by the members of this literate and articulate section of the community were optimistic not only because of the actual growth and prosperity of the city but also because they assumed that their own experience reflected that of the society as a whole. As always, the myths of the ruling class propagated a distorted, if attractive, version of social existence.

However skewed in their depiction of reality, these myths of social mobility and economic affluence were of crucial importance. They expressed, in an intangible, abstract form, the values and aspirations of the leading part of the community. Grudgingly acquiesced in by ordinary laborers; tacitly accepted by tenant farmers; and wholeheartedly embraced by small landowners, newly arrived indentured servants, hardworking artisans, and ambitious storekeepers, they constituted a set of shared beliefs which obscured (or perhaps justified) the acute differences in their respective material conditions.

Insofar as these elite and entrepreneurial values were internalized by the populace at large or assumed institutionalized form as role expectations of the adult members of the society, they bound this stratified community together and facilitated its continued economic expansion. Thus the White Oaks of Philadelphia—a society of relatively poor if respectable ship carpenters—instituted, as the high point of their year's social activity, an Annual Fishery which was modeled directly on the more elaborate and more prestigious festival celebrated by the gentry of the town. This conscious emulation of the social habits of their betters, this cultural mimesis, testified to the hold exercised on the minds and emotions of the lower status groups by the values and way of life of the wealthy merchants and gentry. Freer than the black slave, more prosperous than the poor white planter, blessed with a genuine opportunity for social mobility, the urban mechanic was, nevertheless, encompassed in a mental world not entirely of his own making.

The Social Basis of Provincial Politics

There were several levels of political activity in the colonies, each concerned with a different array of problems and each subject to a separate constituency. On the highest plane, the politics of empire were conducted primarily in London by aristocratic Englishmen and imperial bureaucrats with little personal knowledge of American affairs and by merchants and commercial groups with interests of their own to defend. Through their agents or allies in England the colonists in America had a voice in the deliberations that took place in the Palace, in Parliament, and in the Plantation Office, but it was weak and not often heard.

Local politics in America was equally impervious to imperial direction. In hundreds of towns, townships, and counties officials were elected and taxes levied by the resident inhabitants without direction or interference from London. These essentially autonomous systems of political power intersected on the provincial level: in the clash between the royal governor and the representative assemblies of the various colonies. The governor's task was to secure local support for imperial edicts and parliamentary legislation, if possible by persuasion but by patronage, threat, or bribery if necessary. All too often the weapons at his disposal (a few offices and military contracts, his own personal prestige and political abilities) were inadequate to the task.

These difficulties increased over time. No comprehensive and coherent colonial policy was conceived in London for implementation in America, and the patronage at the disposal of the governors was gradually appropriated by English ministers anxious to reward their own friends and supporters. An even more important factor in bringing about a slow decline in imperial authority was the appearance of an indigenous political elite. In the first generations of settlement most of the colonies lacked a distinct governing class or group of political leaders at the provincial level. Successful families might predominate in a given locality and royal governors might gather a small clique of supporters, but the ingredients of a functioning political system—a complex web of interest groups, family alliances, and regional factions—was completely lacking. Thus there was a period of "chaotic" factionalism in which there was "a ruthless competition for dominance, power, and economic advantage among rival groups of leading men, groups which were largely ad hoc and impermanent."

This type of political activity—uncertain, constantly shifting, based on temporary alliances over specific issues—was the mark of a polity in which there was no sure center of social gravity. This chaotic state was characteristic of government throughout the colonies, except in the special circumstances created by the existence of the Puritan oligarchy in New England, during the first decades of settlement. It was true in Virginia until 1660 and in Maryland until 1689; it appeared as well upon the colonization of Pennsylvania, New Hampshire, and the Carolinas lasting, in each instance, for thirty or forty years. These conditions magnified the importance of the royal or proprietary governors, giving them effective authority out of proportion to the inherent powers of their office. This kaleidoscopic system of politics mirrored, on the governmental level, the unsettled social and economic structure of the community.

As social fluidity crystallized into coherent form, atomistic factionalism gave way to more stable and more predictable types of political activity. This evolution took two forms. In Virginia after 1720 and in South Carolina after 1740 the monopolization of wealth by a group of interrelated families with similar social interests and cultural values brought about the creation of a powerful political elite. . . . There were differences of opinion among individuals and struggles for power among families, but these contests were muted in tone and essentially superficial in character. They hinged on personal differences among men and not on deep economic, social, or religious cleavages in society.

The second, and more common, evolutionary political form was the emergence of a polity characterized by "stable" factionalism, with two or more relatively permanent interest groups contending for power. The classic case of this process of development was Rhode Island. Until the 1750s provincial politics in this small corporate colony had been virtually nonexistent, in part because of the absence of a strong executive branch of government. Each year the men selected by local communities of farmers predominated in the General Assembly and, in conjunction with the representatives from mercantile Newport, passed the few tax laws and general ordinances that were required. On nine occasions between 1710 and 1751 the agricultural interest enacted paper money bills designed to stimulate trade and relieve agrarian indebtedness; but apart from this particular schism between Newport and its hinterland, there were few permanent divisions within the assembly.

The emergence of Providence as a port city in competition with Newport effected a realignment of economic ties and created a system of factional politics based on sectional advantage. The spread of credit facilities and market contacts inward from the two urban centers prompted an intense civic rivalry which took political form in a bitter contest for control of the elective governorship. In 1755 the post was won by Stephen Hopkins, a merchant of Providence; this victory inaugurated a struggle for the governorship between the Hopkins family and the Ward family of Newport which lasted until the outbreak of the war for independence. The two family factions were agreed on questions of financial policy (succeeding finally in 1763 in winning assembly approval for a bill to control the value of currency) but differed sharply over the grant of monopolies, the apportionment of taxes, the bestowal of patronage, and other governmental actions which could be turned to sectional advantage. It was the prevailing strength of the Hopkins faction, guaranteed finally in the election of 1767, which resulted in the establishment of the College of Rhode Island (Brown University) in Providence rather than in Newport.

Thus the atomistic factionalism of provincial government in Rhode Island, based on the autonomy of small farming communities, had given way under the pressure of economic development to a more coherent political system dominated by merchants, lawyers, and their commercial allies resident in the urban centers. There were similar centralizing and stabilizing forces at work in other colonies as successful families translated their wealth and social prestige into political power on the provincial level. In New York a faction led by the Livingston family and based on support from the Hudson River aristocracy and dissenting religious sects battled for political hegemony with the Delanceys—Episcopalian in religion, mercantile in sympathy, and allied to the landowners of Westchester County. In the absence of political "parties," these family alliances based on social and religious interest groups had come to constitute the structural basis of provincial politics. Here also the diversity of the population made political activity open, competitive, and abusive—not at all conducive to the inculcation of habits of deference among the mass of the voters.

This emergence of an indigenous American polity, based solidly on the accumulated wealth and achieved status of a native-born elite, undermined the power of the royal governor. The deflation of imperial authority was greatest in those colonies, such as Virginia, where there were few differences among the representatives which could be exploited to the advantage of the Crown, but the process was everywhere the same. Only the socially and politically underdeveloped colonies could be easily managed in the interest of the mother country. . . .

As old families and established groups tightened their grip on the institutions of government during the first three-quarters of the eighteenth century, American politics became more elitist and oligarchic. Fewer and fewer settlers could justly observe, with Cadwallader Colden, that "the most opulent families, in our own memory, have risen from the lowest ranks of the people." Even in relatively democratic Connecticut the 600 offices above town level were filled by only 400 different men (because of plural officeholding) in the 1750s; and in any one year over half of these officials were members of the one hundred most prominent families. A few decades later, John Adams remarked:

Go into every village in New England and you will find that the office of justice of the peace, and even the place of representative, which has ever depended only on the freest election of the people, have generally descended from generation to generation, in three or four families at most.

Politics had become predictable. The great mass of ordinary men voted for the members of those families who had proved their astuteness in economic affairs and whose large houses and social prestige clearly marked them out for the management of the affairs of state.

The difference between the politics of the northern colonies and those in the South did not lie primarily in the extent of the franchise, but rather in the proportion of men who were genuinely eligible for office. In Virginia, Maryland, and much of South Carolina all of the black population and 75 percent of the white inhabitants were automatically excluded, by color or condition, from an active role in the decision making process. Political life was the prerogative of the privileged members of this quasi-aristocratic society: capable, well-read men who were, in a very real sense, born to rule. In these regions of colonial America a place in the county court or the legislature was effectively limited to nominees chosen from among the top 10 percent of the total adult male population.

The social spectrum of political representation and active participation in the North was about twice as large. The absence of a large slave population and a cultural heritage of independence had resulted in a less highly stratified society; and the greater diversity of economic activities had brought moderate affluence to a greater proportion of the total population, especially in the predominant rural sector. There were the glimmerings of an established oligarchy in New York, with its mass of tenant farmers presided over by members of the Livingston, Van Courtland, or Van Rensselaer families—and even in Massachusetts, where 40 percent of the top officials in thirteen towns were drawn from their four leading families. But there was also more competition for office among men of considerable property and less deference paid to them by those of ordinary means, especially in the heterogeneous middle colonies. If its abusive tone, open character, and social, religious, and sectional diversity occasionally gave the royal or proprietary governor greater leverage and more room to maneuver, the emphasis on local autonomy and the democratic thrust of the provincial politics of the North rendered it as impervious to imperial direction and control as that of the less internally divided colonies to the south.

Conflict and Consensus

Common allegiance to the British Crown produced similarities in language, culture, and political institutions in the various American colonies, but it could not prevent (or conceal) their fundamental divergences in social development. The economic base and the composition of the population varied from one region to another; and so also did the value systems, behavior patterns, and character structures of their inhabitants. Within each area, however, the fragments, or facets, of social life formed a coherent and interdependent whole. Each of these social systems had a number of functionally critical qualities; and these can be isolated, as a set of abstractions, for comparison and contrast. . . .

Despite reliance on force and a strict caste division between the races, the society of the southern American colonies was not plural in character. The widely dispersed black population was unable to maintain a viable religion and culture of its own. Moreover, the gradual acculturization of native-born slaves through the total-institution of slavery gradually lessened the crude dependence on force. As time passed, elements of "consensus" and of moral persuasion began to infuse the system of social control. This was especially the case among the poor white planters who quickly learned to accept their subordinate place in the social hierarchy. Thus, although sharply divided along the lines of race and class, this society (except in the backcountry) was relatively stable; conflict was latent, not manifest.

By contrast, New England society was a model of the consensus made possible by homogeneity. British troops were never stationed in these settlements until 1768 and their presence then was an important factor in bringing about armed revolt by the xenophobic resident population. There had been previous outbreaks of violence against customs officials and other royal bureaucrats, likewise the agents of an alien and external power. There had also been a good many uprisings which were extrainstitutional in character: "mobs" composed of a fair cross-section of the population took action, for example, against deviant elements (such as prostitutes, carriers of contagious diseases, and those who sought to hoard food or manipulate its price) who seemed to constitute a danger to the moral or physical health of the community. As a rule these mass police actions received the tacit support of the local officials. Lacking a powerful constabulary and overwhelmingly white, Anglo-Saxon, and dissenting Protestant in composition, these communities mobilized the entire body politic for the task of preserving order.

This system of social self-control was possible because of the relative uniformity of thought and condition among the members of these towns. Access to many communities in New England was strictly regulated by the resident population, and undesirable aliens were constantly "warned out." These rigid standards of social (and often religious) selection were designed to insure that these settlements remained restricted to like-minded inhabitants. This quest for unanimity was bolstered by a religious ideology which stressed self-restraint and selflessness in dealings with others; by a system of childtraining which fostered a strong moral conscience and an acute sense of right and wrong; and by cultural habits and social expectations which placed a high value on conformity to accepted standards. Once the members of a town meeting had achieved consensus on a given issue, their decision assumed an ethical significance all were bound to respect.

Those who would not heed the voice of the community were encouraged to leave or, upon occasion, actually expelled. There was no toleration of diversity in this homogeneous region; no philosophical commitment to the rule of the majority. "The major part of those who were present were [farmers]," the merchants of Salem, Massachusetts, argued when protesting against a tax schedule which imposed high rates on their financial assets, "and the vote then passed was properly their vote and not the vote of the whole body of the town." The metaphor—with its implication of a mutually dependent and interconnected polity in which the well-being of one member affected the condition of all—was completely appropriate. It reflected the social and cultural homogeneity of most of rural New England and the intuitive rejection by most of its inhabitants of a world in which there was a diversity of value systems; they had no historical experience of such complexity.

The cultural difference between the original Dutch settlers and their English conquerors had helped to provoke Leisler's rebellion in New York in 1689; and the result had been permanent stationing of a detachment of British troops in the colony. Subsequent migration of thousands of Germans and Scotch-Irish Presbyterians into Dutch New York (and the neighboring provinces of New Jersey and Pennsylvania, which were already the home of a sizable Quaker population) introduced even more diversity into the social complexity of this region. And yet these colonies never degenerated into plural societies ruled only by naked force.

New England democracy, a "democracy devoid of legitimate difference, dissent, and conflict," had a very different character from that developed by the more heterogeneous society of the middle colonies. A political system based on compromise and accommodation gradually (and grudgingly) emerged in this area during the course of the eighteenth century, giving institutional legitimacy and an encompassing constitutional form to its cultural diversity. Political factionalism was rife in these provinces—was perhaps more intense here than anywhere in the British empire—but these legislative struggles served to prevent a resort to physical force and political coercion. All religious and cultural factions, even eventually the rough Scotch-Irish Presbyterians of the frontier regions, were accepted into the polity on the basis of equality. Consensus was limited to representation and participation; not, as in New England, to the substance of politics. But this was sufficient to preserve social stability while generating a competitive type of politics which eventually produced (in the persons of Aaron Burr, De Witt Clinton, and Martin Van Buren) the first really professional politicians in American history.

If the middle colonies lacked the homogeneous solidarity of New England or the enforced stability of southern slave society during the eighteenth century, these provinces were also spared their rigorous psychological or martial systems of social control. The internal coherence of the middle colonies did not derive from the existence of dependent personalities created by huge disparities in wealth and status or from the institutionalized violence of slavery; nor did it rely on invocation of a conformity in thought and action which stultified individual self-expression by channeling it into accepted forms. It was not completely accidental that the freedom of the press to criticize government officials was first clearly enunciated in New York—in the Zenger case of 1735. And the grounds of defense, which admitted the libel but justified it as being true, adumbrated a new principle of law. Forced by the contingencies of history to deal with diversity, the inhabitants of the middle colonies were slowly accommodating their laws, political systems, and personal mental outlooks to their unpredictable new world of social and cultural complexity.

At midcentury these problems had assumed a new sense of urgency, not only in the middle colonies, but also in areas less well-equipped by experience or inclination to deal with them. Beginning in 1740 there were a series of interrelated crises in American society as the inherent tendencies of two generations of rapid population growth, extensive economic development, and increased social diversity rushed forward to fulfillment. In more than one colony these new tensions were to pull the inherited web of social authority and political power to the breaking point.

GARY B. NASH

Social Change and the Growth of Prerevolutionary Urban Radicalism

I

The most generally recognized alteration in eighteenth-century urban social structures is the long-range trend toward a less even distribution of wealth. Tax lists for Boston, Philadelphia, and New York, ranging over nearly a century prior to the Revolution, make this clear. By the early 1770s the top 5 percent of Boston's taxpayers controlled 49 percent of the taxable assets of the community, whereas they had held only 30 percent in 1687. In Philadelphia the top twentieth increased its share of wealth from 33 to 55 percent between 1693 and 1774. Those in the lower half of society, who in Boston in 1687 had commanded 9 percent of the taxable wealth, were left collectively with a mere 5 percent in 1771. In Philadelphia, those in the lower half of the wealth spectrum saw their share of wealth drop from 10.1 to 3.3 percent in the same period. It is now evident that the concentration of wealth had proceeded very far in the eighteenth-century cities.

Though city dwellers from the middle and lower ranks could not measure this redistribution of economic resources with statistical precision, they could readily discern the general trend. No one could doubt that upper-class merchants were amassing fortunes when four-wheeled coaches, manned by liveried Negro slaves, appeared in Boston's crooked streets, or when urban mansions, lavishly furnished in imitation of the English aristocracy, rose in Philadelphia and New York. Colonial probate records reveal that personal estates of £5,000 sterling were rare in the northern cities before 1730, but by 1750 the wealthiest town dwellers were frequently leaving assets of £20,000 sterling, exclusive of real

Gary B. Nash, "Social Change and the Growth of Prerevolutionary Urban Radicalism" from *The American Revolution: Explorations in the History of American Radicalism*, edited by Alfred F. Young (1976), pp. 7–18, 30–32. Reprinted by permission.

estate, and sometimes fortunes of more than £50,000 sterling—equivalent in purchasing power to about 2.5 million dollars today. Wealth of this magnitude was not disguised in cities with populations ranging from about 16,000 in Boston to about 25,000 in New York and Philadelphia and with geographical expanses half as large as public university campuses today.

While urban growth produced a genuinely wealthy upper class, it simultaneously created a large class of impoverished city dwellers. All of the cities built almshouses in the 1730s in order to house under one roof as many of the growing number of poor as possible. This was the beginning of a long trend toward substituting confinement in workhouses and almshouses for the older familial system of direct payments to the poor at home. The new system was designed to reduce the cost of caring for a growing number of marginal persons—people who, after the 1730s, were no longer simply the aged, widowed, crippled, incurably ill, or orphaned members of society, but also the seasonally unemployed, war veterans, new immigrants, and migrants from inland areas seeking employment in the cities. These persons, whose numbers grew impressively in the 1750s and 1760s, were now expected to contribute to their own support through cloth weaving, shoemaking, and oakum picking in city workhouses.

Beginning in Boston in the 1740s and in New York and Philadelphia somewhat later, poverty scarred the lives of a growing part of the urban populations. Among its causes were periodic unemployment, rising prices that outstripped wage increases, and war taxes which fell with unusual severity on the lower classes. In Boston, where the Overseers of the Poor had expended only £25–35 sterling per thousand inhabitants in the 1720s and 1730s, per capita expenditures for the poor more than doubled in the 1740s and 1750s, and then doubled again in the last fifteen years of the colonial period. Poor relief rose similarly in Philadelphia and New York after 1750.

In the third quarter of the eighteenth century poverty struck even harder at Boston's population and then blighted the lives of the New York and Philadelphia laboring classes to a degree unparalleled in the first half of the century. In New York, the wartime boom of 1755–1760 was followed by postwar depression. High rents and unemployment brought hundreds of families to the edge of indigency. The incidence of poverty jumped more than fourfold between 1750 and 1775. By 1772 a total of 425 persons jostled for space in the city's almshouse, which had been built to accommodate about 100 indigents. In Philadelphia, in the decade before the Revolution, more than 900 persons each year were admitted to the city's institutions for the impoverished—the almshouse, workhouse, and Hospital for the Sick Poor. The data on poor relief leaves little room for doubt that the third quarter of the eighteenth century was an era of severe economic and social dislocation in the cities, and that by the end of the colonial period a large number of urban dwellers were without property, without opportunity, and, except for public aid, without the means of obtaining the necessities of life.

The economic changes that redistributed wealth, filled the almshouses to overflowing, and drove up poor rates, also hit hard at the lower part of the middle class in the generation before the Revolution. These people—master artisans rather than laborers, skilled shipwrights rather than merchant seamen, shopkeepers rather than peddlers—were financially humbled in substantial numbers in Boston beginning in the 1740s and in Philadelphia and New York a dozen years later.

In Boston, this crumbling of middle-class economic security can be traced in individual cases through the probate records and in aggregate form in the declining number of "taxables." In that city, where the population remained nearly static, at about 15,500 from 1735 to the Revolution, the number of "rateable polls" declined from a high of more than 3,600 in 1735, when the city's economy was at its peak, to a low of about 2,500 around mid-century. By 1771, Boston's taxables still numbered less than 2,600. This decline of more than a thousand taxable adults was not caused by loss of population but by the sagging fortunes of more than 1,000 householders—almost one third of the city's taxpaying population. Boston's selectmen made this clear in 1757 when they pointed out that "besides a great Number of Poor . . . who are either wholly or in part maintained by the Town, & so are exempt from being Taxed, there are many who are Rateable according to Law . . . who are yet in such poor Circumstances that Considering how little business there is to be done in Boston they can scarcely procure from day to day daily Bread for themselves & Families."

In Philadelphia, the decay of a substantial part of the "middling sort" similarly altered the urban scene, though the trend began later and did not proceed as far as in Boston. City tax collectors reported the names of each taxable inhabitant from whom they were unable to extract a tax, and the survival of their records allows for some precision in tracing this phenomenon. Taxpayers dropped from the rolls because of poverty represented less than 3 percent of the taxables in the period before 1740, but they increased to about 6 to 7 percent in the two decades beginning in 1740, and then to one in every ten taxpayers in the fifteen years before the Revolution.

The probate records of Boston and Philadelphia tell a similar tale of economic insecurity hovering over the middle ranges of urban society. Among these people in Boston, median wealth at death dropped sharply between 1685 and 1735 and then made a partial but uneven recovery as the Revolution approached. The average carpenter, baker, shopkeeper, shipwright, or tavernkeeper dying in Boston between 1735 and 1765 had less to show for a lifetime's work than his counterpart of a half century before. In Philadelphia, those in the lower ranges of the middle class also saw the value of their assets, accumulated over a lifetime's labor, slowly decline during the first half of the eighteenth century, though not so severely as in Boston. The startling conclusion that must be drawn from a study of nearly 4,500 Boston and Philadelphia inventories of estates at probate is that population growth and economic development in the colonial cities did not raise the standard of living and broaden opportunities for the vast majority of people, but instead conferred benefits primarily upon those at the top of the social pyramid. The long-range effect of growth was to erode the personal assets held at death by those in the lower 75 percent of Boston society and the lower 60 percent of Philadelphia society. Though many city dwellers had made spectacular individual ascents from the bottom, in the manner of Benjamin Franklin of Philadelphia or Isaac Sears of New York, the statistical chances of success for those beginning beneath the upper class were considerably less after the first quarter of the eighteenth century than before. The dominating fact of late colonial life for many middle-class as well as most lower-class city folk was not economic achievement but economic frustration.

II

Understanding that the cities were becoming centers of frustrated ambition, propertylessness, genuine distress for those in the lower strata, and stagnating fortunes for many in the middle class makes comprehensible much of the violence, protest, and impassioned rhetoric that occurred in the half-generation before the colonial challenge to British regulations began in 1764. Upper-class colonists typically condemned these verbal attacks and civil disorders as the work of the "rabble," the "mob," the "canaille," or individuals "of turbulent disposition." These labels were used to discredit crowd activity, and historians have only recently recognized that the "rabble" often included a broad range of city dwellers, from slaves and servants through laborers and seamen to artisans and shopkeepers—all of whom were directly or indirectly expressing grievances. Cutting across class lines, and often unified by economic conditions that struck at the welfare of both the lower and middle classes, these crowds began to play a larger role in a political process that grew more heated as the colonial period came to an end. This developing consciousness and political sophistication of ordinary city dwellers came rapidly to fruition in the early 1760s and thereafter played a major role in the advent of the Revolution.

Alienation and protest had been present in the northern cities, especially during periods of economic difficulty, since the early eighteenth century. In Boston, between 1709 and 1713, townspeople protested vigorously and then took extralegal action when Andrew Belcher, a wealthy merchant, refused to stop exporting grain during a bread shortage in the city. Belcher had grown fat on war contracts during Queen Anne's War, and when he chose to export grain to the Caribbean, at a handsome profit, rather than sell it for a smaller profit to hungry townspeople, his ships were attacked and his warehouses emptied by an angry crowd. Rank had no privileges, as even the lieutenant-governor was shot when he tried to intervene. Bostonians of meagre means learned that through concerted action, the powerless could become powerful, if only for the moment. Wealthy merchants who would not listen to pleas from the community could be forced through collective action to subordinate profits to the public need.

After the end of Queen Anne's War, in 1713, Boston was troubled by postwar recession and inflation, which cut into the wages of working people. Attempts to organize a land bank in order to increase the scarce circulating medium in Boston were opposed by wealthy men, many of them former war contractors. Gathering around the unpopular governor, Paul Dudley, these fiscal conservatives blamed the hard times on the extravagant habits of "the Ordinary sort" of people, who squandered their money on a "foolish fondness of Forreign Commodities & Fashions" and on too frequent tippling in the town's taverns. But such explanations did not deceive returning war veterans, the unemployed, or those caught in an inflationary squeeze. They protested openly against men who made their fortunes "by grinding the poor," as one writer expressed it, and who studied "how to oppress, cheat, and overreach their neighbours." "The Rich, Great, and Potent," stormed this angry spokesman, "with rapacious violence bear down all before them, who have not wealth, or strength to encounter or avoid their fury." Although the land bank movement failed in 1720, it was out of this defeat that the Boston Caucus, the political organization designed to mobilize the middle- and lower-class electorate in the decades to come, arose.

In Philadelphia, economic issues also set the mechanic and laborer against the rich as early as the 1720s. When a business recession brought unemployment and a severe shortage of specie (the only legal circulating medium), leading merchant-politicians argued that the problem was moral in nature. If the poor were unemployed or hungry, they had their own lack of industry and prudence to thank, wrote James Logan, a thriving merchant and land speculator. "The Sot, the Rambler, the Spendthrift, and the Slip Season," he charged, were at the heart of the slump. Schemes for reviving the economy with emissions of paper money were reckless attempts to cheat those who worked for their money instead of drinking their time away.

But, as in Boston, the majority of people were not fooled by such high-toned arguments. Angry tracts appeared on both sides of the debate concerning the causes and cure for recession. Those who favored paper money and called for restrictions on land speculators and monopolizers of the money market made an attack on wealth itself an important theme. Logan found bricks flying through his windows and a crowd threatening to level his house. Meanwhile, he looked on in disgust as Governor William Keith organized a political caucus, encouraged laboring men to participate in politics, and conducted a campaign aimed at discrediting Logan and other wealthy merchants. "It is neither the Great, the Rich, nor the Learned, that compose the Body of any People, and . . . civil Government ought carefully to protect the poor, laborious and industrious Part of Mankind," Keith cautioned the Assembly in 1723. Logan, formerly respected as William Penn's chief proprietary officeholder, a member of council, a judge of the colony's highest court, and Pennsylvania's most educated man, now found himself reviled in widely distributed tracts as "Pedagogus Mathematicus"—an ambitious, ruthless elitist. He and his henchmen, cried the pamphleteers, deserved to be called "petty Tyrants of this Province," "Serpents in the Grass," "Rich Misers," "Phenomena of Aristocracy," "Infringers of our Priviledges," and "Understrappers of Government."

In a striking inversion of the conventional eighteenth-century thinking that only the rich and educated were equipped to hold high political offices, the Keithian faction urged the voters to recognize that "a mean Man, of small Interest, devoted to the faithful Discharge of his Trust and Duty to the Government" was far more to be valued than rich and learned men. For the rest of the decade the anti-Logan forces, organized into political clubs in Philadelphia, held sway at the annual elections and passed legislation to relieve the distress of the lower-class unemployed and middle-class debtors. Members of the Philadelphia elite, such as Logan and merchant Isaac Norris, hated the "new vile people [who] may be truly called a mob," and deplored Keith's "doctrine of reducing all to a level." But they could no longer manage politics from the top. The "moral economy of the crowd," as E. P. Thompson has called it—the people's sense that basic rules of equity in social relations had been breached—had intervened when the rich would do nothing to relieve suffering in a period of economic decline.

When an economic slump beset New York in the 1730s, causing unemployment and an increase in suits for debt, the reaction was much the same as in the other cities. The John Peter Zenger trial of this era is best remembered as a chapter in the history of the freedom of the press. But central to the campaign organized by Zenger's supporters were the indictment of the rich and the mobilization of the artisanry against them. A 1734 election tract reminded the New York electorate that the city's strength—and its future—lay with the fortunes of "Shuttle" the weaver, "Plane" the joiner, "Drive" the carter, "Mortar" the mason, "Tar" the mariner, "Snip" the tailor, "Smallrent" the fair-minded landlord, and "John Poor" the tenant. Pitted against them were "Gripe the Merchant, Squeeze the Shopkeeper, Spintext and Quible the Lawyer." In arguments reminiscent of those in Philadelphia a decade before, the Lewis Morris faction counseled the people that "A poor honest Man [is] preferable to a rich Knave." Only by electing men responsive to the needs of the whole community, the Morrisites advised, could New Yorkers arrest the forces that were impoverishing the artisan class while fattening the purses of merchants and moneylenders. The conservative clergy of the city advised working people to pray harder in difficult times, but the Morrisite pamphleteers urged the electorate to throw out of office those "people in Exalted Stations" who looked with disdain upon "those they call the Vulgar, the Mob, the herd of Mechanicks."

Attacks on wealth and concentrated power continued in New York through 1737. The opulent and educated of the city were exposed as self-interested and oppressive men, not the public-minded community servants that conventional political philosophy prescribed. Though the leaders of the Morris faction were themselves men of substantial wealth, and though they never advocated a truly popular form of politics, their attacks on the rich and their organization of artisan voters became imbedded in the structure and ideology of politics.

A decade later, political contention broke out again in New York City and attacks on the wealthy and well-born were revived. To some extent the political factionalism in the period from 1747 to 1755 represented a competition for power and profit between different elements of the elite. DeLanceys were pitted against Coldens, and Alexanders against Bayards, in a game where the stakes were control of land in neighboring New Jersey, the profits of the Iroquois fur trade, and the power of the assembly in opposition to the governor and his clique of officeholders. But as in earlier decades, the success of these intra-elite struggles depended upon gaining support from below. In appealing to the artisans and tradesmen, especially during periods of economic decline, bitter charges surfaced about the selfishness of wealthy men and the social inequities in society which they promoted. Cadwallader Colden's *Address to the Freeholders* in 1747 inveighed against the rich, who did not build their fortunes "by the honestest means" and who had no genuine concern for the "publick spirit." Colden attacked the wealthy, among whose ranks he figured importantly, as tax dodgers who indulged in wanton displays of wealth and gave little thought to the welfare of those below them. "The midling rank of mankind," argued Colden, was far more honest, dependable, sober, and public spirited "in all Countries," and it was therefore best to trust "our Liberty & Property" to them rather than to New York's "rich jolly or swaggering companions."

In Boston, resentment against the rich, focusing on specific economic grievances, continued to find voice in the middle third of the century. Moreover, since the forming of the caucus a generation before, well-coordinated street action channeled the wrath of townspeople against those who were thought to act against the interest of the commonality. In the 1730s an extended debate erupted on establishing a public market where prices and marketing conditions would be controlled. Many Bostonians in the lower and middle strata regarded a regulated public market as a device of merchants and fiscal conservatives to drive small retailers from the field and reap the profits of victualing Boston themselves. Though they lost their cause after a number of bitter debates and close votes at the town meeting in the mid-1730s, these humbler people, who probably included many without a vote, ultimately prevailed by demolishing the public market on Dock Square in 1737. The attack was accompanied by much "murmuring agt the Government & the rich people," lamented Benjamin Colman, an advocate of the regulated market and a member of the conservative faction. Worse yet, "none of the Rioters or Mutineers" could be discovered. Their support was so broad that they promised that any attempt to arrest or arraign the saboteurs would be met by "Five Hundred Men in Solemn League and Covenant," who would resist the sheriff and destroy any other markets erected by wealthy merchants. The timbers of the public market which fell before the night raiders in 1737 showed how widely held was the conviction that only this kind of civil disobedience would "deliver the poor oppressed and distressed People out of the Hands of the Rich and Mighty."

The Land Bank controversy from 1740 to 1742 further inflamed a wide segment of Boston society. Most of the colony, including Boston, favored a land bank which would relieve the economic distress of the period by issuing more paper money and thus continuing the inflationist policies of the last twenty years. In opposition stood a group of Boston merchants, who "had railed against the evils of paper money" for years and now "damned the Bank as merely a more invidious form of the soft money panacea typically favored by the province's poor and unsuccessful." One of their spokesmen, William Douglass, reflected the elitist view by characterizing the dispute as a struggle between the "Idle & Extravagant who want to borrow money at any bad lay" and "our considerable Foreign Traders and rich Men."

Even though the inflationists swept the Massachusetts assembly elections of 1740 and 1741, they could not overcome the combined opposition of Governor Jonathan Belcher, a group of wealthy merchants, and officials in England. In the end, the Land Bank movement was thwarted. The defeat was not lightly accepted or quickly forgotten by debtors and Bostonians of modest means. Three years later, a committee of the Boston town meeting, which had consistently promoted inflated paper currency as a means of relief for Boston's numerous debtors, exploded with angry words at another deflationist proposal of the mercantile elite: "We cannot suppose, because in some extraordinary Times when a Party Spirit has run high there have been some Abuses of Our Liberties and Priviledges, that therefore We should in a Servile Manner give them all up. And have our Bread & Water measured out to Us by those Who Riot in Luxury & Wantonness on Our Sweat & Toil and be told by them that we are too happy, because we are not reduced to Eat Grass with the Cattle."

The crowning blow to ordinary Bostonians came in 1748 when Thomas Hutchinson, the principal architect of the monetary policy favored by the wealthiest merchants, engineered a merciless devaluation of Massachusetts currency as a cure to the continuing inflation, which by now had reduced the value of paper money to a fraction of its face value. With many persons unemployed, with poverty afflicting hundreds of families, and with Hutchinson personifying the military contractors who had reaped fortunes from King George's War (1739–1747) while common people suffered, popular sentiment exploded. The newspapers carried a rancorous debate on the proposed devaluation, street fights broke out when the new policy was instituted, and Hutchinson was personally threatened on several occasions. An anonymous pamphleteer put into words the sentiment óf many in the city who had watched the gap widen between rich and poor during hard times. "Poverty and Discontent appear in every Face, (except the Countenances of the Rich), and dwell upon every Tongue." A few men, fed by "Lust of Power, Lust of Fame, Lust of Money," had grown rich by supplying military expeditions during the last war and had now cornered the paper money market and manipulated the rates of exchange for English sterling to their own profit. "No Wonder such Men can build Ships, Houses, buy Farms, set up their Coaches, Chariots, live very splendidly, purchase Fame, Posts of Honour," railed the pamphleteer. But such "Birds of prey . . . are Enemies to all Communities— wherever they live."

The growing sentiment in the cities against the wealthy was nourished by the Great Awakening—the outbreak of religious enthusiasm throughout the colonies beginning in the late 1730s. Although this eruption of evangelical fervor is primarily identified as a rural phenomenon, it also had powerful effects in the cities, where fiery preachers such as George Whitefield and Gilbert Tennant had their greatest successes. We have no study as yet of the Great Awakening in the cities, but clues abound that one important reason for its urban appeal was the fact that the evangelists took as one of their primary targets the growth of wealth and extravagance, accompanied by a dwindling of social concern in colonial America. Nowhere was this manifested more noticeably than in the cities.

The urban dwellers who thronged to hear George Whitefield in Philadelphia in 1739 and 1741 and those who crowded the Common in Boston to hear Whitefield and the vituperative James Davenport in the early 1740s were overwhelmingly from the "lower orders," so far as we can tell. What accounts for their "awakening" is the evangelists' presentation of a personal religion where humble folk might find succor from debt, daily toil, sickness, and want, and might express deeply felt emotions in an equality of fellowship. At the same time, the revivalist preachers spread a radical message concerning established authority. City dwellers were urged to partake in mass revivals, where the social distance be-

tween clergyman and parishioner and among worshippers themselves was oblit-
erated. They were exhorted to be skeptical toward dogma and to participate in
ecclesiastical affairs rather than bow passively to established hierarchy.

Through the Great Awakening, doctrinal controversy and attacks on religious leaders became widely accepted in the 1740s. In Boston the itinerant
preacher James Davenport hotly indicted the rich and powerful and advised ordinary people to break through the crust of tradition in order to right the wrongs
of a decaying society. It was the spectre of unlearned artisans and laborers assuming authority in this manner that frightened many upper-class city dwellers and
led them to charge the revivalists with preaching levelism and anarchy. "It is . . .
an exceedingly difficult, gloomy time with us . . . ," wrote one conservative clergyman from Boston. "Such an enthusiastic, factious, censorious Spirit was never
known here. . . . Every low-bred, illiterate Person can resolve Cases of Conscience and settle the most difficult Points of Divinity better than the most
learned Divines."

Such charges were heard repeatedly during the Great Awakening, revealing
the fears of those who trembled to see the "unthinking multitude" invested with
a new dignity and importance. Nor could the passing of the Awakening reverse
the tide, for this new sense of power remained a part of the social outlook of ordinary people. In fact, the radical transformation of religious feeling overflowed
into civil affairs. The new feeling of autonomy and importance was bred in the
churches, but now it was carried into the streets. Laboring people in the city
learned "to identify the millennium with the establishment of governments which
derived their power from the people, and which were free from the great disparities of wealth which characterized the old world."

III

The crescendo of urban protest and extralegal activity in the prerevolutionary
decades cannot be separated from the condition of people's lives. Of course those
who authored attacks on the growing concentration of wealth and power were
rarely artisans or laborers; usually they were men who occupied the middle or
upper echelons of society, and sometimes they were men who sought their own
gain—installment in office, or the defeat of a competitor for government favors.
But whatever their motives, their sharp criticisms of the changes in urban society
were widely shared among humbler townspeople. It is impossible to say how
much they shaped rather than reflected the views of those in the lower half of the
social structure—urban dwellers whose opportunities and daily existence had
been most adversely affected by the structural changes overtaking the colonial
cities. But the willingness of broad segments of urban society to participate in attacks on narrowly concentrated wealth and power—both at the polls where the
poor and propertyless were excluded, and in the streets where everyone, including women, apprentices, indentured servants, and slaves, could engage in action—should remind us that a rising tide of class antagonism and political consciousness, paralleling important economic changes, was a distinguishing feature
of the cities at the end of the colonial period. . . .

IV

The growing resentment of wealth, the rejection of an elitist conception of politics, and the articulation of artisan- and laboring-class interests also gained momentum after 1765. These were vital developments in the revolutionary period. Indeed, it was the extraordinary new vigor of urban laboring people in defining and pursuing their goals that raised the frightening spectre of a radicalized form of politics and a radically changed society in the minds of many upper-class city dwellers, who later abandoned the resistance movement against England that they had initially supported and led.

That no full-fledged proletarian radical ideology emerged in the decade before the Revolution should not surprise us, for this was a preindustrial society in which no proletariat yet existed. Instead, we can best understand the long movement of protest against concentrated wealth and power, building powerfully as social and economic conditions changed in the cities, as a reflection of the disillusionment of laborers, artisans, and many middle-class city dwellers against a system that no longer delivered equitable rewards to the industrious. "Is it equitable that 99, rather 999, should suffer for the Extravagance or Grandeur of one," asked a New Yorker in 1765, "especially when it is considered that Men frequently owe their Wealth to the impoverishment of their Neighbors?" Such thoughts, cutting across class lines, were gaining force among large parts of the urban population in the late colonial period. They were directed squarely at outmoded notions that only the idle and profligate could fail in America and that only the educated and wealthy were entitled to manage political affairs.

But the absence of clearly identifiable class consciousness and of organized proletarian radicalism does not mean that a radical ideology, nurtured within the matrix of preindustrial values and modes of thought, failed to emerge during the Revolution. Though this chapter in the history of the Revolution is largely unwritten, current scholarship is making it clear that the radicalization of thought in the cities, set in motion by economic and social change, advanced very rapidly once the barriers of traditional thought were broken down. A storm of demands, often accompanied by crowd action to insure their implementation, rose from the urban "tradesmen" and "mechanicks": for the end of closed assembly debates and the erection of public galleries in the legislative houses; for published roll-call votes which would indicate how faithfully elected legislators followed the wishes of their constituents; for open-air meetings where laboring men could help devise and implement public policy; for more equitable laying of taxes; for price controls instituted by and for the laboring classes to shield them from avaricious men of wealth; and for the election of mechanics and other ordinary people at all levels of government.

How rapidly politics and political ideology could be transformed, as colonists debated the issue of rebellion, is well illustrated by the case of Philadelphia. In one brief decade preceding the Revolution the artisanry and laboring poor of the city moved from a position of clear political inferiority to a position of political control. They took over the political machinery of the city, pushed through the most radical state constitution of the period, and articulated concepts of society and political economy that would have stunned their predecessors. By mid-1776, laborers, artisans, and small tradesmen, employing extralegal measures when electoral politics failed, were in clear command in Philadelphia. Working with middle-class leaders such as James Cannon, Timothy Matlack, Thomas Young, and Thomas Paine, they launched a full-scale attack on wealth and even on the right to acquire unlimited private property. By the summer of 1776 the militant Privates Committee, which probably represented the poorest workers, became the foremost carrier of radical ideology in Pennsylvania. It urged the voters, in electing delegates for the constitutional convention, to shun "great and overgrown rich men [who] will be improper to be trusted, [for] they will be too apt to be framing distinctions in society, because they will reap the benefits of all such distinctions." Going even further, they drew up a bill of rights for consideration by the convention, which included the proposition that "an enormous proportion of property vested in a few individuals is dangerous to the rights, and destructive of the common happiness, of mankind; and therefore every free state hath a right by its laws to discourage the possession of such property." For four years, in an extremely fluid political scene, a radicalized artisanry shaped—and sometimes dominated—city and state politics, while setting forth the most fully articulated ideology of reform yet heard in America.

These calls for reform varied from city to city, depending on differing conditions, past politics, and the qualities of particular leaders. Not all the reforms were implemented, especially those that went to the heart of the structural problems in the economy. Pennsylvania, for example, did not adopt the radical limitation on property holding. But that we know from hindsight that the most radical challenges to the existing system were thwarted, or enjoyed only a short period of success, does not mean that they are not a vital part of the revolutionary story. At the time, the disaffected in the cities were questioning some of the most fundamental tenets of colonial thought. Ordinary people, in bold opposition to their superiors, to whom custom required that they defer, were creating power and suggesting solutions to problems affecting their daily lives. . . . How far these calls for radical reform extended and the success they achieved are matters that historians have begun to investigate only lately. But this much is clear: even though many reforms were defeated or instituted briefly and then abandoned, political thought and behavior would never again be the same in America.

SUGGESTIONS FOR FURTHER READING

A brief general survey of the colonial period is Clarence L. Ver Steeg, *The Formative Years, 1607–1763* (New York, 1964). Ver Steeg argues that the growth and expansion of the colonies led to great instability and even armed conflict in the late seventeenth and early eighteenth centuries. This conflict was a sign of the disruptiveness of change as "English colonies became American provinces." But the result was a new, American consensus. Wesley Frank Craven, *The Southern Colonies in the Seventeenth Century, 1607–1689* (Baton Rouge, La., 1949) finds conflict in the form of an attack on economic

---

*Available in paperback edition.

and political abuses. He calls Nathaniel Bacon, who led an uprising in Virginia in 1676, one of the many "who have shaped the long tradition of political liberalism in America." Daniel J. Boorstin, *The Americans: The Colonial Experience (New York, 1958) perceptively traces the evolution of a peculiarly American society in the New World. On this point see also Sigmund Diamond, "From Organization to Society: Virginia in the Seventeenth Century," American Journal of Sociology, 63 (March 1958), 457–75.

Curtis P. Nettels, The Roots of American Civilization (New York, 1963) puts far more emphasis on class conflict, which, he says, arose from the unequal distribution of wealth and power in the colonies. The nature and extent of class differences are surveyed in Jackson Turner Main, *The Social Structure of Revolutionary America (Princeton, 1965).

John J. McCusker and Russell R. Menard, *The Economy of British America, 1607–1789 (Chapel Hill, N.C., 1985) surveys colonial economic change and considers such questions as the growth and distribution of wealth and the place of the colonies in the Atlantic economic community. D. W. Meinig, The Shaping of America (New Haven, Conn., 1986) is a brilliant work by a historical geographer.

The tensions and conflicts that settlers in the New World brought from Europe, the new tensions and conflicts that arose in the new conditions, and the nature of the adjustments are considered in a number of important studies. Carl Bridenbaugh, *Vexed and Troubled Englishmen, 1590–1642 (New York, 1968), surveys the English background, and T. H. Breen, *Puritans and Adventurers (New York, 1980), examines some of the ways in which English values were transferred and changed in the colonies. Thomas C. Cochran in Part I of his *Business in American Life: A History (New York, 1972) discusses the development of a business mentality in the colonies. Richard Hofstadter, *America at 1750: A Social Portrait (New York, 1971) describes the colonies in the mideighteenth century as a "middle-class world" that developed from the modernizing tendencies already evident in the Old World. Bernard Bailyn, *The New England Merchants in the Seventeenth Century (Cambridge, Mass., 1955) traces the conflict between merchants and religious leaders for political hegemony, a conflict that ended with merchant victory. Edmund Morgan, *The Puritan Dilemma: The Story of John Winthrop (Boston, 1958) shows how Winthrop attempted to balance the Puritan notions of independence with the need for unity in New England. In *American Slavery, American Freedom: The Ordeal of Colonial Virginia (New York, 1975), Morgan finds conflict resolution of a different kind; he argues that the growth of freedom (for whites) and the blunting of class conflict (among whites) were the result of the enslavement and debasement of blacks. Allan Kulikoff, Tobacco and Slaves: The Development of Southern Cultures in the Chesapeake, 1680–1800 (Chapel Hill, N.C., 1986) considers how economic change affected family life, the position of women, and race relations. A more general study of slavery and the colonial attitudes toward blacks is Winthrop Jordan, *White over Black: American Attitudes Toward the Negro, 1550–1812 (Chapel Hill, N.C., 1968). A good introduction to Indian, black, and white relations during the colonial period is Gary B. Nash, *Red, White, and Black: The Peoples of Early America (Englewood Cliffs, N.J., 1982).

A number of studies shed considerable light on the political and social structure of individual towns. Among these are Charles S. Grant, Democracy in the Connecticut Frontier Town of Kent (New York, 1961); Sumner Chilton Powell, *Puritan Village: The Formation of a New Town (Middletown, Conn., 1963); Kenneth A. Lockridge, *A New England Town: The First Hundred Years, Dedham, Massachusetts, 1636–1736 (New York, 1970); G. B. Warden, Boston, 1689–1776 (Boston, 1970); Michael Zuckerman, *Peaceable Kingdoms: New England Towns in the Eighteenth Century (New York, 1970); Christine Leigh Heyrman, Commerce and Culture: The Maritime Communities of Colonial Massachusetts, 1690–1750 (New York, 1984); and Barry Levy, Quakers and the

American Family: British Settlement in the Delaware Valley, 1650–1765 (New York, 1988).

Three recent ambitious books find many of the differences and conflicts in colonial America rooted in British region, class, and status differences that were transported to the New World: Bernard Bailyn, *Voyagers to the West: A Passage in the Peopling of America on the Eve of the Revolution* (New York, 1986); David Hackett Fischer, *Albion's Seed: Four British Folkways in America* (New York, 1989); and Jack P. Greene, *Pursuits of Happiness: The Social Development of Early Modern British Colonies and the Formation of American Culture* (Chapel Hill, N.C., 1988).

Some historians find the colonial opposition to the British tax and trade restrictions to be an effort to protect and encourage a modernizing commercial economy (see John W. Tyler, *Smugglers and Patriots: Boston Merchants and the Advent of the American Revolution* [Boston, 1986]); others, however, see it as an attempt to restrain the growing commercialization (see J. E. Crowley, *This SHEBA, Self: The Conceptualization of Economic Life in Eighteenth-Century America* [Baltimore, 1974]).

2

The American Revolution

When the representatives of the American colonies agreed in 1776 to end their allegiance to the British crown, they used their Declaration of Independence to explain and justify their action: "a decent respect to the opinions of mankind requires that they should declare the causes which impel them to the separation." They began their discussion of the "causes" of the revolution by presenting a general philosophy of government, a philosophy based upon a set of "self-evident" truths: "that all men are created equal, that they are endowed by their Creator with certain unalienable Rights, that among these are Life, Liberty and the pursuit of Happiness." Governments, they continued, are created "to secure these rights," and if they fail to do so, the people have the "right" and the "duty" to abolish them. Most of the remainder of the Declaration consists of a long list of "repeated injuries and usurpations" by the king, all designed to establish "an absolute Tyranny over these States." Such abuses by a "Tyrant" who was "unfit to be the ruler of a free people" left the colonists no choice but to declare their independence.

Thus, for the revolutionaries—at least, as they explained their actions in the Declaration of Independence—the causes of the revolution were primarily political and constitutional. The colonists broke their ties with Great Britain because the king had undermined their governments, had taxed them without their consent, and in numerous other ways had become a tyrant seeking to create an "absolute Despotism" over the people. From this perspective, then, it appeared that the revolutionaries did not consider their Revolution to be revolutionary. On the contrary, they seemed to be insisting that their decision to separate from the mother country was conservative; they were merely seeking to protect—to conserve—their established and just rights from the attempted usurpations by the king. The real revolutionary was the king, for he, not the colonists, sought change. The colonists had long accepted the king's actions with "patient sufferance," but finally his "long train of abuses" left them no choice but to resist by declaring their independence.

Although few historians accept all of the reasons the colonists gave to explain their actions, many accept the general argument in the Declaration. In a variety of ways, they argue, the experience in the New World had created a new people with new ideas who built new institutions of government and social relations. Although the colonists sometimes disputed and disagreed in elections or about the wisdom of particular policies concerning such matters as paper money or land distribution, they agreed on fundamentals. They became revolutionaries only because they felt it necessary to fight to maintain what they already had and generally accepted. The Revolution was not revolutionary at all, concludes historian Daniel J. Boorstin; it was merely a "conservative colonial rebellion." Obviously, the theme of such interpretations is consensus, not conflict.

Other historians sharply disagree. Writing in 1909, the historian Carl Becker argued that the American Revolution was really a dual revolution: "The American Revolution was the result of two general movements: the contests for home-rule and independence, and the democratization of American politics and society. Of these movements, the latter was fundamental." Thus for Becker and others who agree with him, Americans were not united. On the contrary, sharp class cleavages in American society created conflicts among Americans that significantly influenced the course of the Revolution. The Revolution, then, arose from the desire to reform the British empire—by separating from it—and from the desire to reform society at home—by instituting democratic and libertarian reforms and by undermining the power of the local aristocracy. Conflict, not consensus, is the theme of these interpretations.

Some historians have argued that the interpretation stressing ideological differences with Britain and the interpretation stressing internal class conflict are not mutually exclusive. Americans, they insist, could believe that the British government was oppressive, thereby justifying separation, and at the same time believe that independence should bring extensive political, economic, and social reform at home. The talk of freedom, liberty, and equality that were a part of the revolutionary agitation could simultaneously unite the colonists in their opposition to the British and stimulate reformist actions by groups with grievances at home. Indeed, the disruption of ordinary political processes, along with the need to agitate, organize, and involve the masses of the people during the Revolution, helped to stimulate internal demands for reform.

The debate among historians concerning the Revolution therefore involves both causes and results and the possible connections between the two. In the selections that follow, the reader is introduced to important contributions to this debate.

In the first selection, Gordon S. Wood argues that the American Revolution should not be compared to the French Revolution or the Russian Revolution, but that it was a radical revolution nonetheless. The American Revolution, he maintains, fundamentally transformed American society as well as American politics and culture. It changed the personal and social relationship of people to each other and altered the course of history.

Historians usually discuss wars and revolutions as strictly the work of men, but Mary Beth Norton, in the second selection, considers how women responded to the revolutionary ideas of liberty and equality and to their experiences in the war itself. She argues that the Revolution had a profound effect on American women—white and black, patriot and loyalist. She shows that women were not merely responding to the actions of men but were also actively involved in revolutionary activities, although the Revolution looked quite different from the women's perspective. Women were often the victims of war, but for some the war meant opportunity, as well. In the end, Norton insists, the revolutionary experiences brought a significant change in the role of women in American society by dissolving some of the social distinctions between men and women.

In the final selection, Edmund S. Morgan finds class conflicts within the colonies, but, he argues, among whites, a combination of opportunities for social mobility and general agreement to keep the black "laborers in chains" mitigated the disruptive force of class conflict during the Revolution. Far sharper and more important were sectional conflicts in the colonies, and the Revolution "aggravated" this divisive sectionalism. But despite these conflicts, Americans achieved a consensus because they accepted what a British minister called "the absurd notion that all men are equal." Acceptance of this creed, Morgan concludes, created a consensus not by ending all conflicts but rather by providing a new means to resolve them.

Obviously, the American Revolution was a successful colonial rebellion resulting in the independence of thirteen of the English colonies in the New World. But was that revolution the result of generations of gradual change that created a consensus among Americans that culminated in revolt when the British government sought to deprive Americans of rights they deemed theirs? If so, then perhaps the greatest significance of the American Revolution was that it was not revolutionary and therefore differed fundamentally from later revolutions such as those in France in 1789 and in Russia in 1917, which brought significant social change.

If, however, the colonial experience created class, gender, and sectional differences that helped cause the revolution and then transformed the colonial rebellion into a social revolution, then the American Revolution seems far more radical. But how radical were the changes? Was there a significant shift in social relations? Did the oppressed achieve an improvement in their status, wealth, or power as a result of the Revolution?

Perhaps the most significant change brought by the Revolution came with the revolutionary ideas and the behavior that these ideas engendered. Did the stirring principles enunciated in the Declaration of Independence reflect and help to create a new consensus based on the ideas of democracy and equality? If so, then what made the colonial rebellion revolutionary was not simply the political separation from England but rather the ideological separation from English ideas and social relations.

GORDON S. WOOD

The Radicalism of
the American Revolution

We Americans like to think of our revolution as not being radical; indeed, most of the time we consider it downright conservative. It certainly does not appear to resemble the revolutions of other nations in which people were killed, property was destroyed, and everything was turned upside down. The American revolutionary leaders do not fit our conventional image of revolutionaries—angry, passionate, reckless, maybe even bloodthirsty for the sake of a cause. We can think of Robespierre, Lenin, and Mao Zedong as revolutionaries, but not George Washington, Thomas Jefferson, and John Adams. They seem too stuffy, too solemn, too cautious, too much the gentlemen. We cannot quite conceive of revolutionaries in powdered hair and knee breeches. The American revolutionaries seem to belong in drawing rooms or legislative halls, not in cellars or in the streets. They made speeches, not bombs; they wrote learned pamphlets, not manifestos. They were not abstract theorists and they were not social levelers. They did not kill one another; they did not devour themselves. There was no reign of terror in the American Revolution and no resultant dictator—no Cromwell, no Bonaparte. The American Revolution does not seem to have the same kinds of causes—the social wrongs, the class conflict, the impoverishment, the grossly inequitable distributions of wealth—that presumably lie behind other revolutions. There were no peasant uprisings, no jacqueries, no burning of châteaux, no storming of prisons.

Of course, there have been many historians—Progressive or neo-Progressive historians, as they have been called—who have sought, as Hannah Arendt put it, "to interpret the American Revolution in the light of the French Revolution," and to look for the same kinds of internal violence, class conflict, and social deprivation that presumably lay behind the French Revolution and other modern revolutions. Since the beginning of the twentieth century these Progressive historians have formulated various social interpretations of the American Revolution essentially designed to show that the Revolution, in Carl Becker's famous words, was not only about "home rule" but also about "who was to rule at home." They have tried to describe the Revolution essentially as a social struggle by deprived and underprivileged groups against entrenched elites. But, it has been correctly pointed out, despite an extraordinary amount of research and writing during a good part of this century, the purposes of these Progressive and neo-Progressive historians—"to portray the origins and goals of the Revolution as in some significant measure expressions of a peculiar economic malaise or of the social protests and aspirations of an impoverished or threatened mass population—have not been fulfilled." They have not been fulfilled because the social conditions that generically are supposed to lie behind all revolutions—poverty and economic deprivation—were not present in colonial America. There should no longer be any doubt about it: the white American colonists were not an oppressed people; they had no crushing imperial chains to throw off. In fact, the colonists knew they were freer, more equal, more prosperous, and less burdened with cumbersome feudal and monarchical restraints than any other part of mankind in the eighteenth century. Such a situation, however, does not mean that colonial society was not susceptible to revolution.

Precisely because the impulses to revolution in eighteenth-century America bear little or no resemblance to the impulses that presumably account for modern social protests and revolutions, we have tended to think of the American Revolution as having no social character, as having virtually nothing to do with the society, as having no social causes and no social consequences. It has therefore often been considered to be essentially an intellectual event, a constitutional defense of American rights against British encroachments ("no taxation without representation"), undertaken not to change the existing structure of society but to preserve it. For some historians the Revolution seems to be little more than a colonial rebellion or a war for independence. Even when we have recognized the radicalism of the Revolution, we admit only a political, not a social radicalism. The revolutionary leaders, it is said, were peculiar "eighteenth-century radicals concerned, like the eighteenth-century British radicals, not with the need to recast the social order nor with the problems of the economic inequality and the injustices of stratified societies but with the need to purify a corrupt constitution and fight off the apparent growth of prerogative power." Consequently, we have generally described the Revolution as an unusually conservative affair, concerned almost exclusively with politics and constitutional rights, and, in comparison with the social radicalism of the other great revolutions of history, hardly a revolution at all.

If we measure the radicalism of revolutions by the degree of social misery or economic deprivation suffered, or by the number of people killed or manor houses burned, then this conventional emphasis on the conservatism of the American Revolution becomes true enough. But if we measure the radicalism by the amount of social change that actually took place—by transformations in the relationships that bound people to each other—then the American Revolution was not conservative at all; on the contrary: it was as radical and as revolutionary as any in history. Of course, the American Revolution was very different from other revolutions. But it was no less radical and no less social for being different. In fact, it was one of the greatest revolutions the world has known, a momentous upheaval that not only fundamentally altered the character of American society but decisively affected the course of subsequent history.

It was as radical and social as any revolution in history, but it was radical and social in a very special eighteenth-century sense. No doubt many of the concerns and much of the language of that premodern, pre-Marxian eighteenth century were almost entirely political. That was because most people in that very different distant world could not as yet conceive of society apart from government. The social distinctions and economic deprivations that we today think of as the consequence of class divisions, business exploitation, or various isms—capitalism, racism, etc.—were in the eighteenth century usually thought to be caused by the abuses of government. Social honors, social distinctions, perquisites of office, business contracts, privileges and monopolies, even excessive property and wealth of various sorts—all social evils and social deprivations—in fact seemed to flow from connections to government, in the end from connections to monarchical authority. So that when Anglo-American radicals talked in what seems to be only political terms—purifying a corrupt constitution, eliminating courtiers, fighting off crown power, and, most important, becoming republicans—they nevertheless had a decidedly social message. In our eyes the American revolutionaries appear to be absorbed in changing only their governments, not their society. But in destroying monarchy and establishing republics they were changing their society as well as their governments, and they knew it. Only they did not know— they could scarcely have imagined—how much of their society they would change. J. Franklin Jameson, who more than two generations ago described the Revolution as a social movement only to be roundly criticized by a succeeding generation of historians, was at least right about one thing: "the stream of revolution, once started, could not be confined within narrow banks, but spread abroad upon the land."

By the time the Revolution had run its course in the early nineteenth century, American society had been radically and thoroughly transformed. One class did not overthrow another; the poor did not supplant the rich. But social relationships—the way people were connected one to another—were changed, and decisively so. By the early years of the nineteenth century the Revolution had created a society fundamentally different from the colonial society of the eighteenth century. It was in fact a new society unlike any that had ever existed anywhere in the world.

Of course, there were complexities and variations in early American society and culture—local, regional, sectional, ethnic, and class differences that historians are uncovering every day—that make difficult any generalizations about Americans as a whole. This study is written in spite of these complexities and variations, not in ignorance of them. There is a time for understanding the particular, and there is a time for understanding the whole. Not only is it important that we periodically attempt to bring the many monographic studies of eighteenth-century America together to see the patterns they compose, but it is essential that we do so—if we are to extend our still meager understanding of an event as significant as the American Revolution.

That revolution did more than legally create the United States; it transformed American society. Because the story of America has turned out the way it has, because the United States in the twentieth century has become the great power that it is, it is difficult, if not impossible, to appreciate and recover fully the insignificant and puny origins of the country. In 1760 America was only a collection of disparate colonies huddled along a narrow strip of the Atlantic coast—economically underdeveloped outposts existing on the very edges of the civilized world. The less than two million monarchical subjects who lived in these colonies still took for granted that society was and ought to be a hierarchy of ranks and degrees of dependency and that most people were bound together by personal ties of one sort or another. Yet scarcely fifty years later these insignificant borderland provinces had become a giant, almost continent-wide republic of nearly ten million egalitarian-minded bustling citizens who not only had thrust themselves into the vanguard of history but had fundamentally altered their society and their social relationships. Far from remaining monarchical, hierarchy-ridden subjects on the margin of civilization, Americans had become, almost overnight, the most liberal, the most democratic, the most commercially minded, and the most modern people in the world.

And this astonishing transformation took place without industrialization, without urbanization, without railroads, without the aid of any of the great forces we usually invoke to explain "modernization." It was the Revolution that was crucial to this transformation. It was the Revolution, more than any other single event, that made America into the most liberal, democratic, and modern nation in the world.

Of course, some nations of Western Europe likewise experienced great social transformations and "democratic revolutions" in these same years. The American Revolution was not unique; it was only different. Because of this shared Western-wide experience in democratization, it has been argued by more than one historian that the broader social transformation that carried Americans from one century and one kind of society to another was "inevitable" and "would have been completed with or without the American Revolution." Therefore, this broader social revolution should not be confused with the American Revolution. America, it is said, would have emerged into the modern world as a liberal, democratic, and capitalistic society even without the Revolution. One could, of course, say the same thing about the relationship between the French Revolution and the emergence of France in the nineteenth century as a liberal, democratic, and capitalistic society; and indeed, much of the current revisionist historical writing on the French Revolution is based on just such a distinction. But in America, no more than in France, that was not the way it happened: the American Revolution and the social transformation of America between 1760 and the early years of the nineteenth century were inextricably bound together. Perhaps the social transformation would have happened "in any case," but we will never know. It was in fact linked to the Revolution; they occurred together. The American Revolution was integral to the changes occurring in American society, politics, and culture at the end of the eighteenth century.

These changes were radical, and they were extensive. To focus, as we are today apt to do, on what the Revolution did not accomplish—highlighting and lamenting its failure to abolish slavery and change fundamentally the lot of women—is to miss the great significance of what it did accomplish; indeed, the Revolution made possible the anti-slavery and women's rights movements of the nineteenth century and in fact all our current egalitarian thinking. The Revolution not only radically changed the personal and social relationships of people, including the position of women, but also destroyed aristocracy as it had been understood in the Western world for at least two millennia. The Revolution brought respectability and even dominance to ordinary people long held in contempt and gave dignity to their menial labor in a manner unprecedented in history and to a degree not equaled elsewhere in the world. The Revolution did not just eliminate monarchy and create republics; it actually reconstituted what Americans meant by public or state power and brought about an entirely new kind of popular politics and a new kind of democratic officeholder. The Revolution not only changed the culture of Americans—making over their art, architecture, and iconography—but even altered their understanding of history, knowledge, and truth. Most important, it made the interests and prosperity of ordinary people—their pursuits of happiness—the goal of society and government. The Revolution did not merely create a political and legal environment conducive to economic expansion; it also released powerful popular entrepreneurial and commercial energies that few realized existed and transformed the economic landscape of the country. In short, the Revolution was the most radical and most far-reaching event in American history. . . .

The Revolution brought to the surface the republican tendencies of American life. The "Suddenness" of the change from monarchy to republicanism was "astonishing." "Idolatry to Monarchs, and servility to Aristocratical Pride," said John Adams in the summer of 1776, "was never so totally eradicated from so many Minds in so short a Time." Probably Adams should not have been astonished, for the truncated nature of American society with its high proportion of freeholders seemed naturally made for republicanism. Yet adopting republicanism was not simply a matter of bringing American culture more into line with the society. It meant as well an opportunity to abolish what remained of monarchy and to create once and for all new, enlightened republican relationships among people.

Such a change marked a real and radical revolution, a change of society, not just of government. People were to be "changed," said the South Carolina physician and historian David Ramsay, "from subjects to citizens," and "the difference is immense. Subject is derived from the Latin words, *sub* and *jacio,* and means one who is under the power of another; but a citizen is a unit of a mass of free people, who, collectively, possess sovereignty. Subjects look up to a master, but citizens are so far equal, that none have hereditary rights superior to others. Each citizen of a free state contains, within himself, by nature and the constitution, as much of the common sovereignty as another." Such a republican society assumed very different sorts of human relationships from that of a monarchy.

By the late 1760s and early 1770s a potentially revolutionary situation existed in many of the colonies. There was little evidence of those social conditions we often associate with revolution (and some historians have desperately sought to find): no mass poverty, no seething social discontent, no grinding oppression. For most white Americans there was greater prosperity than anywhere else in the world; in fact, the experience of that growing prosperity contributed to the unprecedented eighteenth-century sense that people here and now were capable of ordering their own reality. Consequently, there was a great deal of jealousy and touchiness everywhere, for what could be made could be unmade; the people were acutely nervous about their prosperity and the liberty that seemed to make it possible. With the erosion of much of what remained of traditional social relationships, more and more individuals had broken away from their families, communities, and patrons and were experiencing the anxiety of freedom and independence. Social changes, particularly since the 1740s, multiplied rapidly, and many Americans struggled to make sense of what was happening. These social changes were complicated, and they are easily misinterpreted. Luxury and conspicuous consumption by very ordinary people were increasing. So, too, was religious dissent of all sorts. The rich became richer, and aristocratic gentry everywhere became more conspicuous and self-conscious; and the numbers of poor in some cities and the numbers of landless in some areas increased. But social classes based on occupation or wealth did not set themselves against one another, for no classes in this modern sense yet existed. The society was becoming more unequal, but its inequalities were not the source of the instability and anxiety. . . .

By the middle of the century these social changes were being expressed in politics. Americans everywhere complained of "a Scramble for Wealth and Power" by men of "worldly Spirits." Indeed, there were by the early 1760s "so many jarring and opposite Interests and Systems" that no one in authority could relax, no magistrate, no ruler, could long remain unchallenged. More and more ordinary people were participating in electoral politics, and in many of the colonies the number of contested elections for assembly seats markedly increased. This expansion of popular politics originated not because the mass of people pressed upward from below with new demands but because competing gentry, for their own parochial and tactical purposes, courted the people and bid for their support by invoking popular whig rhetoric. Opposition factions in the colonial assemblies made repeated appeals to the people as counterweights to the use of royal authority by the governors, especially as the older personal avenues of appeal over the heads of the governors to interests in England became clogged and unusable. But popular principles and popular participation in politics, once aroused, could not be easily put down; and by the eve of the Revolution, without anyone's intending or even being clearly aware of what was happening, traditional monarchical ways of governing through kin and patronage were transformed under the impact of the imperial crisis. "Family-Interests," like the Livingstons and De Lanceys in New York, or the Pinckneys and Leighs of South Carolina, observed one prescient British official in 1776, "have been long in a gradual Decay; and perhaps a new arrangement of political affairs may leave them wholly extinct." Those who were used to seeing politics as essentially a squabble among gentlemen were bewildered by the "strange metamorphosis or other" that was taking place.

With the weakening of family connections and the further fragmentation of colonial interests, crown officials and other conservatives made strenuous efforts to lessen popular participation in politics and to control the "democratic" part of the colonists' mixed constitutions. Some royal governors attempted to restrict the expansion of popular representation in the assemblies, to limit the meetings of the assemblies, and to veto the laws passed by the assemblies. Other officials toyed with plans for remodeling the colonial governments, for making the salaries of royal officials independent of the colonial legislatures, and for strengthening the royal councils or upper houses in the legislatures. Some even suggested introducing a titled nobility into America in order to stabilize colonial society. But most royal officials relied on whatever traditional monarchical instruments of political patronage and influence they had available to them to curb popular disorder and popular pressure—using intricate maneuvering and personal manipulation of important men in place of whig and republican appeals to the people.

After 1763 all these efforts became hopelessly entangled in the British government's attempts to reform its awkwardly structured empire and to extract revenue from the colonists. All parts of British policy came together to threaten each colonist's expanding republican expectations of liberty and independence. In the emotionally charged atmosphere of the 1760s and 1770s, all the imperial efforts at reform seemed to be an evil extension of what was destroying liberty in England itself. Through the manipulation of puppets or placemen in the House of Commons, the crown—since 1760 in the hands of a new young king, George III—was sapping the strength of popular representation in Parliament and unbalancing the English constitution. Events seemed to show that the crown, with the aid of a pliant Parliament, was trying to reach across the Atlantic to corrupt Americans in the same way.

Americans steeped in the radical whig and republican ideology of opposition to the court regarded these monarchical techniques of personal influence and patronage as "corruption," as attempts by great men and their power-hungry minions to promote their private interests at the expense of the public good and to destroy the colonists' balanced constitutions and their popular liberty. This corruption had created pockets of royal influence throughout America and had made the crown itself, said John Adams, nothing but a "private interest." Such corruption had turned the colonies into a dumping ground for worthless place-seekers from Britain, "strangers *ignorant* of the interests and laws of the Colonies . . . sent over," complained William Henry Drayton of South Carolina, "to fill offices of 200£ or 300£ per annum, as their only subsistence in life." Americans were warned that they could no longer trust those "who either hold or expect to hold certain advantages by setting examples of servility to their countrymen." Men who themselves were tied to patrons simply "serve as decoys, for drawing the innocent and unwary into snares." Such corruption had allowed even distinguished Americans like Thomas Hutchinson and his clan in Massachusetts to pile up offices to the exclusion of those who John Adams and James Otis felt were better men. The hatred of Hutchinson was so great that sometimes it could scarcely be contained. "Good God!" declared Josiah Quincy in 1770. "What must be the distress, the sentiments, and feelings of a people, legislated, condemned and governed, by a creature so mercenary, so dependent, and so—but I forbear: my anguish is too exquisite—my heart is too full!" The term "pensioner," Hutchinson ruefully noted, was one "which among Americans conveys a very odious Idea."

By adopting the language of the radical whig opposition and by attacking the monarchical abuse of family influence and patronage, however, the American revolutionaries were not simply expressing their resentment of corrupt political practices that had denied some of them the highest offices of colonial government. They actually were tearing at the bonds holding the traditional monarchical society together. Their assault necessarily was as much social as it was political.

But this social assault was not the sort we are used to today in describing revolutions. The great social antagonists of the American Revolution were not poor vs. rich, workers vs. employers, or even democrats vs. aristocrats. They were patriots vs. courtiers—categories appropriate to the monarchical world in which the colonists had been reared. Courtiers were persons whose position or rank came artificially from above—from hereditary or personal connections that ultimately flowed from the crown or court. Courtiers, said John Adams, were those who applied themselves "to the Passions and Prejudices, the Follies and Vices of Great Men in order to obtain their Smiles, Esteem, and Patronage and consequently their favors and Preferments." Patriots, on the other hand, were those who not only loved their country but were free of dependent connections and influence; their position or rank came naturally from their talent and from below, from recognition by the people. "A real patriot," declared one American in 1776, was "the most illustrious character in human life. Is not the interest and happiness of his fellow creatures his care?"

Only by understanding the hierarchical structure of monarchical society and taking the patriots' assault on courtiers seriously can we begin to appreciate the significance of the displacement of the loyalists—that is, of those who maintained their allegiance to the British crown. The loyalists may have numbered close to half a million, or 20 percent of white Americans. As many as 80,000 of them are estimated to have left the thirteen colonies during the American Revolution, over six times as many émigrés per 1,000 of population as fled France during the French Revolution. Although many of these American émigrés, unlike the French émigrés, did not have to abandon their nation and could remain as much British subjects in Canada or the West Indies or Britain itself as they had been in one of the thirteen colonies, nevertheless, the emigration of the loyalists had significant effects on American society.

It was not how many loyalists who were displaced that was important; it was who they were. A disproportionate number of them were well-to-do gentry operating at the pinnacles of power and patronage—royal or proprietary officeholders, big overseas dry-goods merchants, and rich landowners. Because they commanded important chains of influence, their removal disrupted colonial society to a degree far in excess of their numbers. The emigration of members of the De Lancey, De Peyster, Walton, and Cruger families of New York, who, one historian has said, were related "by blood and marriage to more than half the aristocracy of the Hudson Valley," collapsed the connections and interests holding together large clusters of New York society. Similar ramifying disruptions were felt in Pennsylvania from the departure of members of the Penns, Allens, Chews, Hamiltons, and Shippens, who formed particularly prominent, cohesive, and influential groups. Young James Allen realized only too well what the Revolution was doing. "Private friendships are broken off," he wrote in his diary, and his distinguished family and its important connections were "totally unhinged."

It was the same everywhere. The removal of the loyalist heads of these chains of interest had destructive effects on the society out of all proportion to the actual numbers involved. Only forty-six Boston merchants were named in Massachusetts's banishment act of 1778, yet among these were some of the wealthiest families—the Ervings, Winslows, Clarks, and Lloyds—whose connections of kin, friends, and clients ramified throughout the society. True, the vacancies in Boston created by their removal were quickly filled by ambitious north shore merchants, including the Cabots, Lees, Jacksons, Lowells, Grays, Higginsons, and Gerrys. But the bases of the newcomers' positions were necessarily different, and the very recency of their arrival opened them to resentment and further challenge. As early as 1779 James Warren was complaining that in Boston "fellows who would have cleaned my shoes five years ago, have amassed fortunes, and are riding in chariots."

Many of the loyalists' networks of kin and patronage were, of course, extensive enough to protect some of them from patriot persecution and confiscation of their property and to allow others to return quietly to the United States at the end of the war. Some departing loyalists even left members of their families in America to look after their interests. Yet neither the returning loyalists nor the patriots who took many of their places were able to re-create precisely the old prewar chains of family and patronage. Post-revolutionary society was inevitably put together on new republican terms. Social and business links formed during the war and after were thinner and more precarious, less emotional and more calculating than they had been. The lines of interest and influence created by the Revolution were looser and less personal, based less on kin and more on devotion to the patriot cause or on wealth alone. The Revolution effectively weakened or severed those loyalties of the *ancien régime* that had enabled men like William Allen or James De Lancey to form their extensive webs of personal and familial influence.

To eliminate those clusters of personal and familial influence and transform the society became the idealistic goal of the revolutionaries. Any position that came from any source but talent and the will of the people now seemed undeserved and dependent. Patrimonialism, plural officeholding, and patronage of all sorts—practices that had usually been taken for granted in a monarchical society—came under attack. It might have been possible earlier for a royal governor like Jonathan Belcher of Massachusetts to brag that "I never lost any thing I could get in an honest way." But after mid-century the piling up of offices and fees and the open exploitation of them ceased to be tolerable. "A multiplicity of public trusts" in a few persons, wrote Oxenbridge Thacher of Massachusetts in 1763, was indeed the practice "in the *infancy* of the country." It was necessary then when "gentlemen of education and ability could not be found . . . to fill up every place in government." But now "the case is very much alter'd."

The prevailing revulsion against corruption and the use of patronage spilled over to affect even those who were unconnected with royal authority. Despite their stands against royal government, the self-perpetuating oligarchies of the Virginia county courts were not free from criticism. Spread of republican sentiments explains some of the anger of Virginians such as Jefferson, Patrick Henry, and Richard Henry Lee against the older clique of Tidewater planters who tended to look after one another and to restrain the entry of others into their inner circle. The scandal in 1766 involving John Robinson, speaker of the House of Burgesses and colony treasurer, who had lent to his friends paper money he was supposed to destroy, together with the easygoing way the Virginia General Court in the same year treated the murder charge against Colonel John Chiswell, smacked of corruption. Such events, one gentleman told Richard Henry Lee, fully justified Lee's "opposition to the confederacy of the great in places, family connections, and that more to be dreaded foe to public virtue, warm and private friendship."

It is in this context that we can best understand the revolutionaries' appeal to independence, not just the independence of the country from Great Britain, but, more important, the independence of individuals from personal influence and "warm and private friendship." The purpose of the Virginia constitution of 1776, one Virginian recalled, was "to prevent the undue and overwhelming influence of great landholders in elections." This was to be done by disfranchising the landless "tenants and retainers" who depended "on the breath and varying will" of these great men and by ensuring that only men who owned their own land could vote.

A republic presumed, as the Virginia declaration of rights put it, that men in the new republic would be "equally free and independent," and property would make them so. Property in a republic was still conceived of traditionally—in proprietary terms—not as a means of personal profit or aggrandizement but rather as a source of personal authority or independence. It was regarded not merely as a material possession but also as an attribute of a man's personality that defined him and protected him from outside pressure. A carpenter's skill, for example, was his property. Jefferson feared the rabble of the cities precisely because they were without property and were thus dependent.

All dependents without property, such as women and young men, could be denied the vote because, as a convention of Essex County, Massachusetts, declared in 1778, they were "so situated as to have no wills of their own." Jefferson was so keen on this equation of property with citizenship that he proposed in 1776 that the new state of Virginia grant fifty acres of land to every man that did not have that many. Without having property and a will of his own—without having independence—a man could have no public spirit; and there could be no republic. For, as Jefferson put it, "dependence begets subservience and venality, suffocates the germ of virtue, and prepares fit tools for the designs of ambition."

In a monarchical world of numerous patron-client relations and multiple degrees of dependency, nothing could be more radical than this attempt to make every man independent. What was an ideal in the English-speaking world now became for Americans an ideological imperative. Suddenly, in the eyes of the revolutionaries, all the fine calibrations of rank and degrees of unfreedom of the traditional monarchical society became absurd and degrading. The Revolution became a full-scale assault on dependency.

At the beginning of the eighteenth century the English radical whig and deist John Toland had divided all society into those who were free and those who were dependent. "By *Freeman,*" wrote Toland, "I understand men of property, or persons that are able to live of themselves; and those who cannot subsist in this independence, I call *Servants.*" In such a simple division everyone who was not free was presumed to be a servant. Anyone tied to someone else, who was someone's client or dependent, was servile. The American revolutionary movement now brought to the surface this latent logic in eighteenth-century radical whig thinking.

Dependency was now equated with slavery, and slavery in the American world had a conspicuous significance. "What is a slave," asked a New Jersey writer in 1765, "but one who depends upon the will of another for the enjoyment of his life and property?" "Liberty," said Stephen Hopkins of Rhode Island, quoting Algernon Sidney, "solely consists in an independency upon the will of another; and by the name of slave we understand a man who can neither dispose of his person or goods, but enjoys all at the will of his master." It was left to John Adams in 1775 to draw the ultimate conclusion and to destroy in a single sentence the entire conception of society as a hierarchy of graded ranks and degrees. "There are," said Adams simply, "but two *sorts* of men in the world, freemen and slaves." Such a stark dichotomy collapsed all the delicate distinctions and dependencies of a monarchical society and created radical and momentous implications for Americans.

Independence, declared David Ramsay in a memorable Fourth of July oration in 1778, would free Americans from that monarchical world where "favor is the source of preferment," and where "he that can best please his superiors, by the low arts of fawning and adulation, is most likely to obtain favor." The revolutionaries wanted to create a new republican world in which "all offices lie open to men of merit, of whatever rank or condition." They believed that "even the reins of state may be held by the son of the poorest men, if possessed of abilities equal to the important station." They were "no more to look up for the blessings of government to hungry courtiers, or the needy dependents of British nobility"; but they had now to educate their "own children for these exalted purposes." Like Stephen Burroughs, the author of an extraordinary memoir of these years, the revolutionaries believed they were "so far . . . republican" that they considered "a man's merit to rest entirely with himself, without any regard to family, blood, or connection." We can never fully appreciate the emotional meaning these commonplace statements had for the revolutionaries until we take seriously their passionate antagonism to the prevalence of patronage and family influence in the *ancien régime.*

Of course, the revolutionary leaders did not expect poor, humble men—farmers, artisans, or tradesmen—themselves to gain high political office. Rather, they expected that the sons of such humble or ungenteel men, if they had abilities, would, as they had, acquire liberal and genteel republican attributes, perhaps by attending Harvard or the College of New Jersey at Princeton, and would thereby rise into the ranks of gentlemen and become eligible for high political office. The sparks of genius that they hoped republicanism would fan and kindle into flame belonged to men like themselves—men "drawn from obscurity" by the new opportunities of republican competition and emulation into becoming "illustrious characters, which will dazzle the world with the splendor of their names." Honor, interest, and patriotism together called them to qualify themselves and posterity "for the bench, the army, the navy, the learned professions, and all the departments of civil government." They would become what Jefferson called the "natural aristocracy"—liberally educated, enlightened gentlemen of character. For many of the revolutionary leaders this was the emotional significance of republicanism—a vindication of frustrated talent at the expense of birth and blood. For too long, they felt, merit had been denied. In a monarchical world only the arts and sciences had recognized talent as the sole criterion of leadership. Which is why even the eighteenth-century *ancien régime* called the world of the arts and sciences "the republic of letters." Who, it was asked, remembered the fathers or sons of Homer and Euclid? Such a question was a republican dagger driven into the heart of the old hereditary order. "Virtue," said Thomas Paine simply, "is not hereditary."

Because the revolutionaries are so different from us, so seemingly aristocratic themselves, it is hard for us today to appreciate the anger and resentment they felt toward hereditary aristocracy. We tend to ignore or forget the degree to which family and monarchical values dominated colonial America. But the revolutionaries knew only too well what kin and patrimonial officeholding had meant in their lives. Up and down the continent colonial gentry like Charles Carroll of Maryland had voiced their fears that "all power might center in *one family*" and that offices of government "like a precious jewel will be handed down from *father* to *son*." Everywhere men expressed their anger over the exclusive and unresponsive governments that had distributed offices, land, and privileges to favorites. Real emotion lay behind their constitutional statements, like that of the New Hampshire constitution, which declared that "no office or place whatsoever in government, shall be hereditary—the abilities and integrity requisite in all, not being transmissible to posterity or relations"; or that of the 1776 Virginia declaration of rights drawn up by George Mason, which stated that

no Man, or Set of Men are entitled to exclusive or separate Emoluments or Privileges from the Community, but in Consideration of public Services; which not being descendible, or hereditary, the Ideal of Man born a Magistrate, a Legislator, or a Judge is unnatural and absurd.

More perhaps than any other revolutionary leader Mason remained preoccupied by the social implications of this republican assault on patrimonialism. A decade later in the Philadelphia Convention he warned his colleagues that they must not forget the meaning of republicanism. The new federal Constitution of 1787 seemed to suggest that the "superior classes of society" were becoming indifferent to the rights of the "lowest classes." This was foolish, he said, because "our own children will in a short time be among the general mass." Such downward mobility was inevitable in the present circumstances of America, said the younger Charles Carroll. "In a commercial nation," he said, "the glory of illustrious progenitors will not screen their needy posterity from obscurity and want." Despite these occasional premonitions, however, few of the revolutionaries realized just how devastating republicanism would be to their children and grandchildren.

All of the founding fathers remained fascinated with the power of lineage and what William Livingston called "the Vanity of Birth and Titles." To his dying day John Adams was haunted by the veneration for family that existed in New England. Jefferson, too, always felt the power of genealogy. He, unlike Adams, was not one to let his feelings show, but even today we can sense the emotion lying beneath the placid surface of his autobiography written in 1821 at the age of seventy-seven. There he described his efforts in 1776 in Virginia to bring down that "distinct set of families" who had used the legal devices of primogeniture and entail to form themselves "into a Patrician order, distinguished by the splendor and luxury of their establishments." The privileges of this "aristocracy of wealth," wrote Jefferson, needed to be destroyed in order "to make an opening for the aristocracy of virtue and talent," of which he considered himself a prime example.

Jefferson has often been thought to have exaggerated the power of primogeniture and entail and this "Patrician order." Not only was the docking of entails very common in Virginia, but the "Patrician order" does not appear to us all that different from its challengers. But Jefferson obviously saw a difference, and it rankled him. In the opening pages of his autobiography Jefferson tells us that the lineage of his Welsh father was lost in obscurity: he was able to find in Wales only two references to his father's family. His mother, on the other hand, was a Randolph, one of the distinguished families of the "Patrician order." The Randolphs, he said with about as much derision as he ever allowed himself, "trace their pedigree far back in England & Scotland, to which let every one ascribe the faith & merit he chooses. . . ."

Benjamin Franklin likewise began his autobiography with a survey of his ancestors, concluding ruefully that he was "the youngest Son of the youngest Son for 5 Generations back"—a powerful indictment of the way primogeniture had worked to deny him through five generations. In the last year of his life, the bitterness was still there. In a codicil to his will written in June 1789 Franklin observed that most people, having received an estate from their ancestors, assumed they were obliged to pass on something to their posterity. "This obligation," he declared with emotion, "does not lie on me, who never inherited a shilling from any ancestor or relation."

In their revolutionary state constitutions and laws the revolutionaries struck out at the power of family and hereditary privilege. In the decades following the Revolution all the new states abolished the legal devices of primogeniture and entail where they existed, either by statute or by writing the abolition into their constitutions. These legal devices, as the North Carolina statute of 1784 stated, had tended "only to raise the wealth and importance of particular families and individuals, giving them an unequal and undue influence in a republic, and prove in manifold instances the source of great contention and injustice." Their abolition would therefore "tend to promote that equality of property which is of the spirit and principle of a genuine republic. . . ."

Women and children no doubt remained largely dependent on their husbands and fathers, but the revolutionary attack on patriarchal monarchy made all other dependencies in the society suspect. Indeed, once the revolutionaries collapsed all the different distinctions and dependencies of a monarchical society into either freemen or slaves, white males found it increasingly impossible to accept any dependent status whatsoever. Servitude of any sort suddenly became anomalous and anachronistic. In 1784 in New York, a group believing that indentured servitude was "contrary to . . . the idea of liberty this country has so happily established" released a shipload of immigrant servants and arranged for public subscriptions to pay for their passage. As early as 1775 in Philadelphia the proportion of the work force that was unfree—composed of servants and slaves—had already declined to 13 percent from the 40 to 50 percent that it had been at mid-century. By 1800 less than 2 percent of the city's labor force remained unfree. Before long indentured servitude virtually disappeared.

With the post-revolutionary republican culture talking of nothing but liberty, equality, and independence, even hired servants eventually became hard to come by or to control. White servants refused to call their employers "master" or "mistress"; for many the term "boss," derived from the Dutch word for master, became a euphemistic substitute. The servants themselves would not be called anything but "help," or "waiter," which was the term the character Jonathan, in Royall Tyler's 1787 play *The Contrast,* preferred in place of "servant." "The white servants generally stipulate that they shall sit at table with their masters and mistresses," declared astonished foreigners. When questioned, the servants explained that this was "a free country," that they were as good as anyone, and "that it was a sin and a shame for a free-born American to be treated like a servant." Samuel Breck, a sometime senator from Pennsylvania, thought his life would be "perfectly happy" if only he had good servants. "But so easy is a livelihood obtained that fickleness, drunkenness, and not infrequently insolence, mark the character of our domestics." In one year alone Breck hired seven different cooks and five different waiters.

When one English immigrant in the 1790s reported that "the worst circumstance of living" in Newark, New Jersey, was "the difficulty of getting domestic servants," then we know things were bad. Desperate would-be masters in several cities were eventually compelled to form organizations for the encouragement of faithful domestic servants. Some Northerners even concluded that the practice of keeping servants was "highly anti-republican." Consequently, in time Americans built hotels as public residences that were unlike anything existing in Europe. These hotels, combining both eating and lodging, prohibited tipping and were often occupied by permanent boarders. Many found living in these hotels cheaper than setting up a household with servants who were so hard to find. Foreigners found such hotels and boardinghouses to be peculiarly American institutions.

By the early nineteenth century what remained of patriarchy was in disarray. No longer were apprentices dependents within a family; they became trainees within a business that was more and more conducted outside the household. Artisans did less "bespoke" or "order" work for patrons; instead they increasingly produced for impersonal markets. This in turn meant that the master craftsmen had to hire labor and organize the sale of the products of their shops. Masters became less patriarchs and more employers, retail merchants, or businessmen. Cash payments of wages increasingly replaced the older paternalistic relationship between masters and journeymen. These free wage earners now came and went with astonishing frequency, moving not only from job to job but from city to city.

This "fluctuating" mobility of workers bewildered some employers: "while you were taking an inventory of their property," sighed one Rhode Islander, "they would sling their packs and be off."

Although both masters and journeymen often tried to maintain the traditional fiction that they were bound together for the "good of the trade," increasingly they saw themselves as employers and employees with different interests. Although observers applauded the fact that apprentices, journeymen, and masters of each craft marched together in the federal procession in Philadelphia on July 4, 1788, the tensions and divergence of interests were already visible. Before long journeymen in various crafts organized themselves against their masters' organizations, banned their employers from their meetings, and declared that "the interests of the journeymen are separate and in some respects opposite of those of their employers.". Between 1786 and 1816 at least twelve major strikes by various journeymen craftsmen occurred—the first major strikes by employees against employers in American history.

One obvious dependency the revolutionaries did not completely abolish was that of nearly a half million Afro-American slaves, and their failure to do so, amidst all their high-blown talk of liberty, makes them seem inconsistent and hypocritical in our eyes. Yet it is important to realize that the Revolution suddenly and effectively ended the cultural climate that had allowed black slavery, as well as other forms of bondage and unfreedom, to exist throughout the colonial period without serious challenge. With the revolutionary movement, black slavery became excruciatingly conspicuous in a way that it had not been in the older monarchical society with its many calibrations and degrees of unfreedom; and Americans in 1775–76 began attacking it with a vehemence that was inconceivable earlier.

For a century or more the colonists had taken slavery more or less for granted as the most base and dependent status in a hierarchy of dependencies and a world of laborers. Rarely had they felt the need either to criticize black slavery or to defend it. Now, however, the republican attack on dependency compelled Americans to see the deviant character of slavery and to confront the institution as they never had to before. It was no accident that Americans in Philadelphia in 1775 formed the first anti-slavery society in the world. As long as most people had to work merely out of poverty and the need to provide for a living, slavery and other forms of enforced labor did not seem all that different from free labor. But the growing recognition that labor was not simply a common necessity of the poor but was in fact a source of increased wealth and prosperity for ordinary workers made slavery seem more and more anomalous. Americans now recognized that slavery in a republic of workers was an aberration, "a peculiar institution," and that if any Americans were to retain it, as southern Americans eventually did, they would have to explain and justify it in new racial and anthropological ways that their former monarchical society had never needed. The Revolution in effect set in motion ideological and social forces that doomed the institution of slavery in the North and led inexorably to the Civil War.

With all men now considered to be equally free citizens, the way was prepared as well for a radical change in the conception of state power. Almost at a stroke the Revolution destroyed all the earlier talk of paternal or maternal government, filial allegiance, and mutual contractual obligations between rulers and ruled. The familial image of government now lost all its previous relevance, and the state in America emerged as something very different from what it had been.

Overnight modern conceptions of public power replaced older archaic ideas of personal monarchical government. No longer could government be seen as the king's private authority or as a bundle of prerogative rights. Rulers suddenly lost their traditional personal rights to rule, and personal allegiance as a civic bond became meaningless. The revolutionary state constitutions eliminated the crown's prerogatives outright or regranted them to the state legislatures. Popular consent now became the exclusive justification for the exercise of authority by all parts of the government—not just the houses of representatives but senates, governors, and even judges. As sovereign expressions of the popular will, these new republican governments acquired an autonomous public power that their monarchical predecessors had never possessed or even claimed. In republican America government would no longer be merely private property and private interests writ large as it had been in the colonial period. Public and private spheres that earlier had been mingled were now to be separated. Although the state legislatures, to the chagrin of many leaders, often continued to act in a traditional courtlike manner—interfering with and reversing judicial decisions, probating wills rejected by the courts, and passing private legislation affecting individuals—they now became as well sovereign embodiments of the people with a responsibility to promote a unitary public interest that was to be clearly distinguishable from the many private interests of the society.

From the outset the new republican states thus tended to view with suspicion the traditional monarchical practice of enlisting private wealth and energy for public purposes by issuing corporate privileges and licenses to private persons. In a republic no person should be allowed to exploit the public's authority for private gain. Indeed, several of the states wrote into their revolutionary constitutions declarations against any man or group of men receiving special privileges from the community. "Government," said the New Hampshire constitution, was "instituted for the common benefits, protection, and security of the whole community, and not for the private interest or emolument of any one man, family, or class of men." The North Carolina constitution stated that "perpetuities and monopolies are contrary to the genius of a State, and ought not to be allowed."

Consequently, the republican state governments sought to assert their newly enhanced public power in direct and unprecedented ways—doing for themselves what they had earlier commissioned private persons to do. They carved out exclusively public spheres of action and responsibility where none had existed before. They now drew up plans for improving everything from trade and commerce to roads and waterworks and helped to create a science of political economy for Americans. And they formed their own public organizations with paid professional staffs supported by tax money, not private labor. For many Americans the Revolution had made the "self-management of self-concerns . . . the vital part of government." The city of New York, for example, working under the authority of the state legislature, set up its own public work force to clean its streets and wharves instead of relying, as in the past, on the private residents to do these tasks. By the early nineteenth century the city of New York had become a public institution financed primarily by public taxation and concerned with particularly public concerns. It acquired what it had not had before—the power of eminent domain—and the authority to make decisions without worrying about "whose property is benefited . . . or is not benefited." The power of the state to take private property was now viewed as virtually unlimited—as long as the property was taken for exclusively public purposes.

Many concluded that the state legislatures could now do for the public whatever the people entrusted them to do. "A community must always remain competent to the superintendence of its concerns," wrote James Cheetham in 1802. "These general powers of superintendence must be entrusted somewhere. They can be no where more safely deposited than with the legislature. Subject to the constitution, all the rights and privileges of the citizen are entrusted with them." The people under monarchy, of course, had possessed long-standing rights and privileges immune from tampering by the prerogative powers and privileges of the king. But under republicanism could such popular rights continue to be set against the government? In the new republics, where there were no more crown powers and no more prerogative rights, it was questionable whether the people's personal rights could meaningfully exist apart from the people's sovereign power—the general will—expressed in their assemblies. In other words, did it any longer make sense to speak of negative liberty where the people's positive liberty was complete and supreme? To be sure, as the Pennsylvania constitution together with other revolutionary constitutions declared, "no part of man's property can be justly taken from him, or applied to public uses, without his own consent," but this consent, in 1776 at least, meant "that of his legal representatives."

Such assertions that all power to superintend and improve the society belonged to the people and was embodied in the popular state legislatures flowed naturally from republican doctrine. But well before 1800 many Americans had come to challenge the belief that such a monopoly of public power ought to be entrusted to any governmental institution whatsoever, however representative and popularly elected. Indeed, limiting popular government and protecting property and minority rights without at the same time denying the sovereign public power of the people became the great dilemma of political leaders in the new republic; indeed, it remains the great dilemma of America's constitutional democracy.

MARY BETH NORTON

Women in the Revolution

Most narratives of the Revolutionary War concentrate upon describing a series of pitched battles between uniformed armies. Yet the impact of the conflict can more accurately be assessed if it is interpreted as a civil war with profound consequences for the entire population. Every movement of troops through the American countryside brought a corresponding flight of refugees, an invasion of epidemic disease, the expropriation of foodstuffs, firewood, and livestock, widespread plundering or destruction of personal property, and occasional incidents of rape. In addition to bearing these common burdens of warfare, Americans who remained loyal to the Crown had to contend with persecution, property confiscation, and forced exile, as did patriots who lived in areas controlled by the British, although for them such reverses were only temporary.

The disruption of normal patterns of life that resulted from all these seldom-studied aspects of the conflict had an especially noticeable effect upon women, whose prewar experiences had been confined largely to the domestic realm. With their menfolk away serving in the armies for varying lengths of time, white female Americans had to venture into new fields of endeavor. In the midst of wartime trials, they alone had to make crucial decisions involving not only household and family but also the "outdoor affairs" from which they had formerly been excluded. After initially expressing hesitation about their ability to assume these new responsibilities, many white women gained a new appreciation of their own capacity and of the capability of their sex in general as they learned to handle unfamiliar tasks.

For black women, too, the war brought changes. Most notably, the British policy of offering freedom to runaway slaves encouraged a significant percentage of them to abandon their home plantation in order to seek refuge with the redcoats. In times of peace, the vast majority of runaways were youthful males, but ready access to the British army in the South during the later years of the war enabled even mothers encumbered with many children to take advantage of the opportunity to win freedom for themselves and their offspring. Of the many ironies of black-white relations in the revolutionary era, one of the most striking was the fact that while American whites were struggling against British attempts to "enslave" them, American blacks correctly regarded those same redcoats as liberators.

I

White women's experiences with wartime disruptions varied according to the region in which they lived, for the war did not affect all Americans equally at all times. New Englanders had to cope with turmoil first, but after the British evacuated Boston in 1776, the northern section of the country was relatively free of armed conflict, with the exception of coastal areas, which remained continually open to attack from the sea. In the middle states, by contrast, the continuing presence of the British army in New York City and environs from July 1776 to November 1783 and the redcoats' brief occupation of Philadelphia in 1777–1778 meant that many families had no respite from the dangers of warfare for a period of years. Although the South, on the other hand, was little touched by the war before 1778, subsequent British army movements and the internecine guerrilla conflict that raged incessantly through the backcountry had a devastating impact on the economy and society. Each of these regional patterns had different consequences for the female population.

Yet there was also similarity among women's experiences. Northerners and southerners responded alike to such stimuli as the looming threat of invasion by enemy troops, the incidence of disease, or the opportunity to accompany their husbands to the army. . . .

When news of the British sortie from Boston spread rapidly through New England towns on April 19, 1775, panic struck a civilian population awakened from "benign Slumbers" by the "beat of drum and ringing of Bell." Sixty-seven years later, Susan Mason Smith, who was thirteen in 1775, still vividly remembered that night of terror. Although her family decided not to leave their Salem home because they did not know where to find safety, she did not remove her shoes for several days thereafter, afraid to be unprepared for the next alarm. Many other families made the opposite choice, for on the morning of April 20 an observer found the roads around Boston "filld with frighted women and children, some in carts with their tattered furniture, others on foot fleeing into the woods." In the months that followed such scenes became commonplace in New England. After the battle of Bunker Hill, during which much of Charlestown was destroyed by fire, James Warren reported from Watertown that "it is Impossible to describe the Confusion in this place, Women and Children flying into the Country, armed Men Going to the field, and wounded Men returning from there fill the Streets."

Even though no other major clashes occurred in the area, life did not soon return to normal, especially for those who resided near the coast. "We live in continual Expectation of Hostilities," Abigail Adams told her husband shortly after the destruction of Charlestown. A month earlier four British ships had dropped anchor nearby in search of forage, creating another panic. "People women children from the Iron Works flocking down this way—every woman and child above or from below my Fathers," she wrote then, conveying a sense of distraction even in her prose. "My Fathers family flying, the Drs. in great distress, . . . my Aunt had her Bed thrown into a cart, into which she got herself, and ordered the boy to drive her of[f]."

The same images of disorder reverberated through later descriptions of similar scenes. "I arrived here late last night and found people in the utmost confusion, Familys, Women, Children, & Luggage all along the road as I came, mooving different ways," reported a Georgian in 1776 after an Indian raid. Rumors that the British were sailing up the Chesapeake that same year elicited an identical reaction in Annapolis, "what with the darkness of the night, thunder, lightning, and rain, cries of women and children, people hurrying their effects into the country, drums beating to arms, etc." Many of the refugees must have felt like Helena Kortwright Brasher, who, when she and her family fled the British attack on Esopus, New York, asked, "Where God can we fly from danger? All places appear equally precarious," or like Ann Eliza Bleecker of Tomhanick, New York, whose friends and relatives "scattered like a flock of frighted birds" before the "hurricane" of Burgoyne's invasion in the fall of 1777. Mrs. Bleecker, who never recovered her emotional equilibrium after the death of her baby daughter on that wild flight, wrote of how she and her children had wandered "solitary through the dark woods, expecting every moment to meet the bloody ally of *Britain* [the Indians]," before reaching the safety of Albany. Over two years later Mrs. Bleecker told a friend, "Alas! the wilderness is within: I muse so long on the dead until I am unfit for the company of the living." The eighty-six-year-old widow of a revolutionary soldier obviously spoke for many when she observed in 1840, "There was so much Suffering, and so many alarms in our neighborhood in those hard times, that it has always been painful for me to dwell upon them."

Faced with the uncertain dangers of flight, some, like the Mason family of Salem before them, decided to remain where they were. In 1777 a Pennsylvanian told John Adams resolutely that "if the two opposite Armys were to come here alternately ten times, she would stand by her Property until she should be kill'd. If she must be a Beggar, it should be where she was known." Hannah Iredell's sister Jean Blair made the same choice in 1781 when the redcoats neared her North Carolina home. "The English are certainly at Halifax but I suppose they will be every where & I will fix myself here it is as safe as any where else & I can be no longer tossed about," she declared. The Philadelphian Elizabeth Farmer also decided to stay in her house, despite the fact that it lay between the lines during the occupation of the city in 1777–1778. As a result, she, her husband, and their daughter were endangered by frequent gunfire, had difficulty obtaining adequate food supplies, and suffered "manny cold days" that winter because the British confiscated their firewood. "Notwithstanding we thought ourselves well of[f] in comparison to some," she remarked in 1783. "Most of the houses near us have been either burnt or pulled down as would have been the case with us if we had not stayd in it even at the hasard of our lives.". . .

Even after the redcoats' long-awaited departure, Boston, said one resident, was not "that agreable place it once was—Almost every thing here, appears Gloomy & Mallancholy." One of the chief reasons for the Bostonians' gloom was the presence of epidemic disease in their midst. The unhealthy conditions in the besieged city had helped to incubate both smallpox and dysentery, and an epidemic of the latter had already swept the Massachusetts countryside the preceding fall, killing Abigail Adams's mother and niece, among many others. "The desolation of War is not so distressing as the Havock made by the pestilence," Abigail remarked then. She could do nothing to prevent the deaths from dysentery, but smallpox was another matter. After it became clear that the disease would probably spread across New England, carried by soldiers returning from the army that had invaded Canada as well as by Bostonians, she began making arrangements to have herself and her children inoculated.

Abigail Adams and other eighteenth-century Americans could not reach such a decision lightly, for inoculation required being deliberately infected with the disease. Waiting to take smallpox "in the natural way" was to court death, yet no parents wanted to place their children knowingly into mortal danger or to risk their serious disfigurement. Accordingly, adults usually postponed inoculation for themselves and their offspring as long as possible. The war forced them to face the issue directly, since smallpox followed the armies so inevitably that some Americans charged the British with the "hellish Pollicy" of intentionally spreading the disease. Therefore, whenever a large number of soldiers from either side arrived in a given area, parents had to make life-or-death decisions. Indeed, like Abigail Adams, many wives were forced to reach those decisions on their own in the absence of their husbands. . . .

In addition to carrying smallpox, the armies brought a specific terror to American women: the fear of rape. The only female New Englanders who personally confronted this problem on a large scale were residents of Fairfield and New Haven, the Connecticut towns raided by English and Hessian troops in early July 1779. Shortly after the raid, the Continental Congress collected depositions from women who had been attacked by the redcoats. Two local residents declared that they had fought off sexual assaults with the help of passersby, but Christiana Gatter was not so fortunate. Her husband, who had been severely beaten by the British earlier in the day, ran away when a group of soldiers broke into their home at half past two in the morning. "Two of them laid hold of me and threw me on the Bed and swore if I made any noise or Resistance they would kill me in a moment," Mrs. Gatter testified, so "I was obliged to Submit" to each of them in turn. Her fate was hardly enviable, yet far worse were the circumstances of girls living on Staten Island and in New Jersey, who during the fall and winter of 1776 were subjected to repeated rapes by British troops stationed in the area. Whereas the Connecticut incidents and other similar occurrences took place in the context of brief excursions in search of plunder, the 1776 rapes were both systematic and especially brutal. . . .

Depositions collected by the Continental Congress gave the most vivid accounts of the experiences of women in New Jersey in late 1776. Particularly revealing are those that pertain to a series of incidents at the home of Edmund Palmer, an elderly Hunterdon County farmer. One December day, a number of

British soldiers from a nearby camp came to the house. One of them dragged Palmer's thirteen-year-old granddaughter, Abigail, into a back room. She "Scream'd & beged of him to let her alone, but some of Said Soldiers said they wou'd knock her Eyes out if she did not hold her Tongue." Over the ineffectual pleas of her grandfather and her aunt Mary Phillips, Abigail was raped three times. Abigail testified that "for three Days successively, Divers Soldiers wou'd come to the House & Treat her in the Same manner." On one of those days, her aunt Mary was raped in the barn and her friend Sarah Cain, who had come to comfort her, was also assaulted. Finally, on the evening of the third day two soldiers demanded that Abigail and Sarah's younger sister Elisabeth, who was fifteen, accompany them to their camp. "One of them Said he had come for his Girl, & Swore he wou'd have her, & Seiz'd hold of her Hand & told her to Bundle up her Cloaths for she shou'd go with them," Abigail recounted. She and Elisabeth were then forced into another room despite the efforts of Edmund Palmer and Elisabeth's father, Thomas. Elisabeth recalled that "the said Soldiers Ravished them both and then took them away to their Camp, where they was both Treated by some others of the Soldiers in the same cruel manner," until they were rescued by an officer. After spending the night at a nearby farmhouse, the girls went home—not to Palmer's, but to Thomas Cain's. And there they were evidently safe, for they told the investigators of no further attacks. . . .

What distinguished the war in Virginia, Georgia, and the Carolinas from that in the North was its length and ferocious intensity. From the invasion of Georgia in 1778 to the ratification of the peace treaty in 1783, the South was the main theater of war, and there battles were not confined to the formal clashes between armies that had characterized the northern phase of the conflict. A prolonged guerrilla war, coupled with sporadic nonpartisan plundering and the wanderings of the British army through North Carolina and Virginia in 1780–1781, left much of the South devastated. David Ramsay's assessment of South Carolina can accurately be applied to the entire region: "[T]here was scarcely an inhabitant of the State, however obscure in character or remote in situation, whether he remained firm to one party or changed with the times, who did not partake of the general distress."

Thus Georgians and South Carolinians universally complained of the "Banditti" who raided, pillaged, and looted through their states. "Property of every kind has been taken from its Inhabitants, their Negroes, Horses & Cattle drove & carried away," declared a Georgian in 1779. That same year a South Carolinian commented that the "Havoc" caused by the robbers "is not to be described. Great Numbers of Women and Children have been left without a 2nd Shift of Clothes. The furniture which they could not carry off they wantonly broke, burnt, and destroyed." Fifteen months later Eliza Lucas Pinckney observed that "the plantations have been some quite, some nearly ruind and all with very few exceptions great sufferers[. T]heir Crops, stock, boats, Carts etc. all gone taken or destroyd and the Crops made this year must be very small by the desertion of the Negroes in planting and hoeing time." Virginia was not so seriously affected as its neighboring states to the south, but there too the distress was great in the months before the American victory at Yorktown.

Eliza Wilkinson's account of her life in the South Carolina sea islands during the 1780 British invasion dramatically conveys the sense of fear and uncertainty she felt. The area was completely at the mercy of the redcoats, she noted, with "nothing but women, a few aged gentlemen, and (shame to tell) some skulking varlets" to oppose them. On one "day of terror" in early June, she recounted, a British troop accompanied by armed blacks robbed her home of clothes and jewelry, using "the most abusive language imaginable, while making as if to hew us to pieces with their swords." After the looters had left, "I trembled so with terror, that I could not support myself," she wrote two years later, recalling that she had "indulged in the most melancholy reflections. The whole world appeared to me as a theatre, where nothing was acted but cruelty, bloodshed, and oppression; where neither age nor sex escaped the horrors of injustice and violence; where the lives and property of the innocent and inoffensive were in continual danger, and the lawless power ranged at large." In the aftermath of the attack, Mrs. Wilkinson revealed, "[W]e could neither eat, drink, nor sleep in peace; for as we lay in our clothes every night, we could not enjoy the little sleep we got. . . . Our nights were wearisome and painful; our days spent in anxiety and melancholy."

But what to Eliza Wilkinson and her fellow whites was a time of trouble and distress was for their slaves a period of unprecedented opportunity. The continuing presence of the British army in the South held out to black men and women alike the prospect of winning their freedom from bondage, for in an attempt to disrupt the Americans' labor supply and acquire additional manpower, British commanders offered liberty to slaves who would flock to the royal standard. No sex or age restrictions limited the offer to adult men alone, and so women fled to the redcoat encampments, often taking their children with them.

The detailed plantation records kept by Thomas Jefferson and John Ball make it possible to identify the family relationships of runaways from their lands. Among the twenty-three slaves who abandoned Jefferson's Virginia holdings were ten adult women and three girls. Of the five female adults who can be traced with certainty, two left with their husbands, one of them accompanied by children as well; another fled with three of her four offspring; and the remaining two, one of whom was married, ventured forth by themselves. The fifty-three blacks who fled John Ball's plantation in 1780 included eighteen women, among them eight mothers with children, some of the latter still infants. Charlotte, a childless woman whose family connections are unknown, probably led a mass escape from Ball's Kensington quarter. She originally left the plantation on May 10, in company with Bessy and her three children, but she was soon recaptured. A week later she ran away again, this time along with (and perhaps as a guide for) what Ball termed "Pino's gang." This fifteen-member group, which escaped via Ball's flatboat, was composed of Pino, his wife, their youngest daughter, and one of their two granddaughters; their daughter, Jewel, her husband, Dicky, and son, Little Pino; Dicky's sister, her husband, and their daughter; and Eleanor Lawrence, her husband, Brutus, and their two daughters. Although it is not clear whether Eleanor was related to the Pino clan, her sister Flora had also absconded to the British, along with an infant son, two weeks previously.

The impressions one receives from such fragmentary evidence—both of large numbers of female runaways and of families leaving together—are confirmed by an examination of records kept at the evacuation of New York City. Each time the British left an American port in the later years of the war, they carried large numbers of former slaves away with them, approximately ten thousand from Savannah and Charleston alone. Because the preliminary peace terms accepted in November 1782 included a clause requiring the British to return slaves to American owners, Sir Guy Carleton, the British commander, ordered the enumeration of all blacks who claimed the protection of the army. Crude biographical details were obtained from former slaves then within the lines in order to ascertain whether they should be allowed to embark with the troops for England and Nova Scotia. Blacks who had belonged to loyalists were excluded from the promise of freedom offered by the British during the war, as were any who had joined the British after November 1782. But Carleton believed himself obliged to ensure the liberty of all the others.

Of the 2,863 persons whose sex is specified on the surviving embarkation lists (119 small children were not differentiated by sex), 1,211 (or 42.3 percent) were female and 1,652 (57.7 percent) were male. The substantial proportion of female runaways reflects the ease with which even a woman with children could seek freedom when the British army was encamped only a few miles from her home. Further, the analysis of the age structure of those on the New York City lists indicates that women often brought children with them into the lines. Nearly 17 percent of the refugees were nine years of age or younger, and fully 32 percent were under twenty. Slightly more than a quarter of the mature women were explicitly identified as being accompanied by children, and the addition of other likely cases brings that proportion to 40 percent. Disregarding the 96 children who had been born free in British-held territory, each mature woman who joined the royal forces had an average of 1.6 children at her side.

An examination of familial relationships from the standpoint of 605 children (503 of them nine years old or under) listed on the embarkation rolls shows that 3 percent were accompanied solely by fathers, 17 percent were with both parents, 56.2 percent with mothers alone, and 24.3 percent with other relatives, some of whom may have been parents but who are not explicitly noted as such on the occasionally incomplete records. These families included such groups as Prince Princes, aged fifty-three, his forty-year-old wife, Margaret, their twenty-year-old daughter, Elizabeth, and her "small child," and their son, Erick, who was eleven; "Jane Thompson 70 worn out wt a grand child 5 y[r] old"; and Hannah Whitten, thirty, with her five children, ages eight, seven, six, five, and one. The five-member Sawyer clan of Norfolk, Virginia, evidently used the opportunity to seek freedom with the British as a means of reuniting. Before they all ran away in 1776, the family was divided among three owners: the mother and a child in one location, two children in another, and the father in a third. In all, despite the preponderance among the refugees of young, single adults, 40 percent of the total, like the Sawyers and the others just noted, appear to have been accompanied by relatives of some kind.

To arrive at New York City, the blacks listed on the British records had had to survive many dangers and hardships, not the least of which was the prevalence of epidemic diseases in the encampments to which they had fled. Yet they were not entirely safe even in British-occupied Manhattan. The minutes of the joint

Anglo-American board established to adjudicate claims under the peace treaty reveal liberty lost on legal technicalities important to the presiding officers but of little meaning to the blacks involved. Mercy and her three children were returned to her master because, as a resident of Westchester County, New York, she had not lived outside the British lines and so could not have come within them voluntarily to earn the protection of the freedom proclamation. Elizabeth Truant remained the property of a New Jerseyite because she had not joined the British until April 1783, after the signing of the preliminary peace terms. And, tragically, Samuel Doson, who in 1778 had kidnapped his two children from the house of their owner in order to bring them with him into New York, lost them to that same man in 1783, after he and his youngsters had already boarded a ship bound for Nova Scotia. He himself was likewise reclaimed by his loyalist master.

When enslaved men and women decided whether to run away they could not see into the future and understand the full implications of British policy for their ultimate fate. But many undoubtedly heard the tales of disease in the refugee camps, and others (like some belonging to Eliza Lucas Pinckney) were undoubtedly so "attatched to their homes and the little they have there [that they] have refused to remove." Indeed, amid the chaos of war, plantation life sometimes bore little resemblance to that of peacetime. Remaining at home in a known environment, surrounded by friends and relatives, could seem an attractive alternate to an uncertain future as a refugee, especially when white owners and overseers could no longer control the situation. For her part, Mrs. Pinckney simply surrendered to the inevitable. Speaking of her slaves, she observed to her son Thomas in the spring of 1779 that "they all do now what they please every where." The blacks on Thomas's Ashepoo plantation were no less troublesome. They "pay no Attention" to the overseer's orders, he told his mother; and the pregnant women and small children were "now perfectly free & live upon the best produce of the Plantation."

If black women chose to run away to the redcoats, they risked their lives and those of their children, but they gained the possibility of freedom in Canada, the United States, or even Africa as a reward. If they decided to stay at home, they continued in bondage but kept all their family ties intact. It must have been a wrenching decision, regardless of which choice they made. The Revolutionary War brought blacks a full share of heartbreak and pain, even as it provided them with an unprecedented opportunity to free themselves from servitude.

II

The experiences of white women during the Revolutionary War were affected by the extent of their husbands' political activism as well as by the region in which their families lived. Wives of ardent patriots and loyalists alike were left alone for varying lengths of time while their spouses served in the army or, in the case of loyalists, took refuge behind the British lines. Although women could stay with their soldier husbands and earn their own keep by serving as army cooks, nurses, or laundresses, most did not find this an attractive alternative. Life in the military camps was hard, and army commanders, while recognizing that female laborers did essential work, tended to regard them as a hindrance rather than an asset.

Only in rare cases—such as the time when the laundresses attached to General Anthony Wayne's regiment staged a strike in order to ensure that they would be adequately paid—were camp followers able to ameliorate their living and working conditions. Consequently, most women who joined the army probably did so from necessity, lacking any other means of support during their husbands' absence.

At least, though, patriot women had a choice. For the most part, loyalists were not so fortunate. From the day they and their spouses revealed their loyalty to the Crown, their fate was sealed. Like other eighteenth-century women, their lives had focused on their homes, but because of their political beliefs they lost not only those homes but also most of their possessions, and they had to flee to alien lands as well. Understandably, they often had difficulty coping with their problems. Only those women who had had some experience beyond the household prior to the war were able to manage their affairs in exile in England, Canada, or the West Indies with more than a modicum of success. . . .

The women who found it easiest to adjust to their new circumstances were those few who had previously engaged in business. Elizabeth Murray Smith Inman provides a case in point. She and her third husband, Ralph, were separated by the unexpected start of the war, for he was paying a visit to friends in Boston on April 19. With him trapped in the besieged city, Elizabeth set to work managing their farms, dismissing her anxiety "with a laugh," telling friends, "[W]e could die but once, and I was a predestinarian, therefore had no personal fear." It was consequently with astonishment and anger that she learned Ralph had panicked and intended to depart alone for London, without leaving her a power of attorney so she could act on his behalf in his absence. Is this a proper return "for the many anxious and fatigueing days I have had"? she asked him bitterly. "Believe me, Mr. Inman, I am not anxious about a mentinence [*sic*]," Elizabeth declared self-assuredly. "Experience has taught me, water-gruel and salt for supper and breakfast, with a bit of meat, a few greens or roots, are enough for me." Indeed, experience had taught her more than that: one of the reasons she was reluctant to leave Cambridge was the fact that she had just harvested a good crop of hay, a commodity much in demand by the rebel army, and she anticipated sizable profits. In the end, Ralph Inman did not emigrate, but his wife never forgave him for his cowardice. As one of her female friends commented, Elizabeth Murray Inman was "above the little fears and weaknesses which are the inseparable companions of most of our sex," and she had no patience with those who did not meet her high standards. Ten years later, when she wrote her will, she left Ralph only a tiny proportion of her large fortune.

Another loyalist woman who had little difficulty in adjusting to her spouse's absence was Grace Growden Galloway, but for very different reasons. The unhappily married Mrs. Galloway found that she welcomed Joseph's exile. "Ye Liberty of doing as I please Makes even poverty more agreeable than any time I ever spent since I married," she wrote in her diary five months after his departure; "his Unkind treatment makes me easey Nay happy not to be with him & if he is safe I want not to be kept so like a slave as he allways Made Me in preventing every wish of my heart." As a result, she resisted his attempts to persuade her to join him and their daughter Betsy in England, partly because she wanted to try to preserve the property she had inherited from her father for Betsy, but also because she distrusted Joseph, having realized that he had mismanaged that same property. With unusual insight into her own psyche, she confided to her journal in August 1779 that her frequent tirades against the British were in fact aimed at her husband: "as his ill conduct has ruin'd me & as I cannot tell ye world I abuse the English Army for their base & treacherous conduct," she disclosed.

Most women, of course, did not feel such relief when their husbands left home during the war. Quite the contrary: like a New Englander, they discovered that "every trouble however triffling I feel with double weight in your absence." Nevertheless, as time passed they learned to rely increasingly on their own judgment and ability, for they had no alternative. . . .

After months and sometimes years of controlling their own affairs, women tended to reply testily when their husbands persisted in assuming their subservience. In the summer of 1776, for instance, Sally Cobb Paine—who had been on her own since the fall of 1774—chided her husband, Robert, for not giving her adequate directions about what she should do with some legal papers. She ignored the financial arrangements he had made for her support and informed him flatly, "[W]e have sow'd our oats as you desired had I been master I should have planted it to Corn." Finally, she decided to pursue a court case against his express wishes. "[I]f it had been Let alone till your return their [*sic*] would have been nothing Left for us." Mrs. Paine had clearly become accustomed to making her own decisions, and if her husband gave orders contrary to her inclinations, she either ignored him or let him know that she disagreed with his judgment. . . .

Previous colonial wars and the obligations of business, religion, or politics had occasionally separated some American couples in the nearly two centuries that preceded the Revolution. But those separations had been sporadic and isolated, the experiences of individuals rather than of an entire society. By contrast, the disruptions of the revolutionary years affected all Americans, to a greater or lesser degree. The cumulative result was the partial breakdown and reinterpretation of the gender roles that had hitherto remained unexamined.

III

"Imitate your husbands fortitude, it is as much a female, as a masculine virtue, and we stand in as much need of it to act our part properly," Eliza Lucas Pinckney instructed her daughter-in-law in 1780. The following year William Hooper proudly proclaimed that his wife, Anne, had shown "a masculine patriotism and virtue." Thomas Cushing, a Massachusetts congressman, described to his wife, Deborah, how John Dickinson, seeing the "patriotic, calm & undaunted spirit" displayed in her letters, declared that "if it was customary to choose Women into the Assembly, he should be heartily for choosing you Speaker of the House." In short, as a New Englander remarked with respect to the wives of American diplomats, both men and women came to realize that female patriots "deserve as much reputation as their husbands and posterity will thicken laurels on their monuments."

The war, in other words, dissolved some of the distinctions between masculine and feminine traits. Women who would previously have risked criticism if they abandoned their "natural" feminine timidity now found themselves praised for doing just that. The line between male and female behavior, once apparently so impenetrable, became less well defined. It by no means disappeared, but requisite adjustments to wartime conditions brought a new recognition of the fact that traditional sex roles did not provide adequate guidelines for conduct under all circumstances. When Betsy Ambler Brent looked back on her youth from the perspective of 1810, she observed, "[N]ecessity taught us to use exertions which our girls of the present day know nothing of. We Were forced to industry to appear genteely, to study Manners to supply the place of Education, and to endeavor by amiable and agreeable conduct to make amends for the loss of fortune."

The realization that they had been equally affected by the war led some women to expect equal treatment thereafter and, on occasion, to apply to their own circumstances the general principles promulgated by the revolutionaries. "I have Don as much to Carrey on the warr as meney that Sett Now at ye healm of government & No Notice taken of me," complained the New Jersey widow Rachel Wells as she protested to the Continental Congress in 1786 about a technicality that deprived her of interest payments on the money she had invested in state bonds during the war. "If she did not fight She throw in all her mite which bought ye Sogers food & Clothing & Let them have Blankets," she explained, asking only for the "justice" due her. "Others gits their Intrust & why then a poor old widow be put of[f]?" Mrs. Wells asked. "Now gentelmen is this Liberty?"

Mary Willing Byrd's social standing was much higher than that of Rachel Wells, but she advanced a similar argument when she contended in 1781 that Virginia had treated her unfairly. She claimed the right to redress of grievances "as a female, as the parent of eight children, as a virtuous citizen, as a friend to my Country, and as a person, who never violated the laws of her Country." Byrd's recital of her qualifications was peculiarly feminine in its attention to her sex and her role as a parent (no man would have included such items on a list describing himself), but it was also sexless in its references to her patriotism and her character as a "virtuous citizen." In developing the implications of the latter term, Byrd arrived at her most important point. "I have paid my taxes and have not been Personally, or Virtually represented," she observed. "My property is taken from me and I have no redress."

The echoes of revolutionary ideology were deliberate. Mary Byrd wanted the men she addressed to think about the issue of her status as a woman, and she adopted the revolutionaries' own language in order to make her point. The same tactic was employed by Abigail Adams in her most famous exchange with her husband.

In March 1776, after admonishing John to "Remember the Ladies" and to offer them legal protection from "the unlimited power" of their husbands, Abigail issued a warning in terms that John must have found exceedingly familiar. "If perticular care and attention is not paid to the Ladies," Abigail declared, "we are determined to foment a Rebellion, and will not hold ourselves bound by any Laws in which we have no voice, or Representation." On one level, she was speaking tongue-in-cheek; she did not mean her husband to take the threat seriously. Yet she chose to make a significant observation about women's inferior legal status by putting a standard argument to new use and by applying to the position of women striking phraseology previously employed only in the male world of politics. Like Mary Willing Byrd, Abigail Adams thus demonstrated an unusual sensitivity to the possible egalitarian resonances of revolutionary ideology and showed an awareness of implications that seem to have escaped the notice of American men.

In 1782, Mrs. Adams once again directed her attention to the role of women in the American polity. This time she made no semihumorous comments but instead considered seriously the ramifications of her sex's inferior status. "Patriotism in the female Sex is the most disinterested of all virtues," she contended, because women are "excluded from honours and from offices." Their property is controlled by their husbands, "to whom the Laws have given a sovereign Authority," and they are "deprived of a voice in Legislation, obliged to submit to those Laws which are imposed upon [them]." No levity softened the sincerity of the point she made for the second time. To Abigail, the fact that women demonstrated "patriotick virtue" despite being discriminated against validated their claims to "heroick" stature. . . .

The war necessarily broke down the barrier which seemed to insulate women from the realm of politics, for they, no less than men, were caught up in the turmoil that enveloped the entire populace. Although some Americans tried to maintain the traditional fiction that a woman was "consequently no party in the present war" or that, in one woman's words, "as a Woman I cannot or at least I will not be a Traytor to either side," most understood that the old notions had to be discarded. Abigail Adams is a case in point. In June 1776, she still adhered to the conventional formula, telling John, "I can serve my partner, my family and myself, and injoy the Satisfaction of your serving your Country," thereby indicating that she believed her contributions to the patriots' cause had to be filtered through the medium of her husband. But less than two years later, in February 1778, she described her "satisfaction in the Consciousness of having discharged *my* duty to the publick." Like others of her contemporaries, she no longer drew a sharp dividing line between the feminine sphere and the masculine realm of public responsibilities.

But to recognize that women had a role to fulfill in the wider society was not to declare that male and female roles were, or should be, the same. Not even Judith Sargent Murray conceived of an androgynous world; men's and women's functions were to be equal and complementary, not identical. And so the citizens of the republic set out to discover and define woman's public role. They found it not in the notion that women should directly participate in politics, New Jersey's brief experiment with woman suffrage to the contrary. Rather, they located woman's public role in her domestic responsibilities, in her obligation to create a supportive home life for her husband, and particularly in her duty to raise republican sons who would love their country and preserve its virtuous character.

The ironies of this formulation were manifest. On the one hand, society had at last formally recognized women's work as valuable. No longer was domesticity denigrated; no longer was the feminine sphere subordinated to the masculine, nor were women regarded as inferior. The white women of nineteenth-century America could take pride in their sex in a way their female ancestors could not.

The importance of motherhood was admitted by all, and women could glory in the special role laid out for them in the copious literature that rhapsodized about beneficent feminine influences both inside and outside the home.

But, on the other hand, the republican definition of womanhood, which began as a marked step forward, grew ever more restrictive as the decades passed. Woman's domestic and maternal role came to be seen as so important that it was believed women sacrificed their femininity if they attempted to be more (or other) than wives and mothers. Accordingly, the women who were most successful in winning society's acceptance of their extradomestic activities were those who—like teachers, missionaries, charitable workers—managed to conceal their flouting of convention by subsuming their actions within the confines of an orthodox, if somewhat broadened, conception of womanhood and its proper functions.

In the prerevolutionary world, no one had bothered to define domesticity: the private realm seemed unimportant, and besides, women could not escape their inevitable destiny. In the postrevolutionary world, the social significance of household and family was recognized, and simultaneously women began to be able to choose different ways of conducting their lives. As a direct result, a definition of domesticity was at last required. The process of defining woman's proper role may well have stiffened the constraints that had always encircled female lives, but that definition also—by its very existence—signaled American society's growing comprehension of woman's importance within a sphere far wider than a private household or a marital relationship.

The legacy of the American Revolution for women was thus ambiguous. Republican womanhood eventually became Victorian womanhood, but at the same time the egalitarian rhetoric of the Revolution provided the women's rights movement with its earliest vocabulary, and the republican academies produced its first leaders. Few historical events can ever be assessed in absolute terms. With respect to its impact on women, the American Revolution is no exception.

Edmund S. Morgan

Conflict and Consensus in
the American Revolution

During the past fifteen or twenty years a division has emerged among historians of the American Revolution, a division between those who emphasize the consensus achieved by the revolting colonists and those who emphasize conflicts among them. The division has excited attention and perhaps been exaggerated because of the special position occupied by the Revolution in our national consciousness. As the noises of the approaching bicentennial grow louder, it is scarcely necessary to point out that most Americans, including historians, seem to think the Revolution was a good thing. If any episode in our past is enshrined in our consciousness, this is it. By consequence any group or cause that can affiliate itself with the Revolution may hope to have some goodness rub off on it. As an example, some of us can remember vividly the campaign of the 1930s to make the Revolution and its Founding Fathers rise to the support of Stalinism. Under the slogan "Communism is twentieth-century Americanism," Washington, Jefferson, and Franklin were enrolled posthumously in the popular front. We have similarly had, long since, Catholic interpretations of the Revolution and Calvinist interpretations, Massachusetts interpretations and Virginia interpretations, and a host of others, each somehow concerned with reflecting American-Revolutionary glory on Catholicism or Calvinism, on Massachusetts or Virginia, or whatever.

The alacrity with which the current division among scholars has been recognized, if not promoted, I believe, lies in this sanctifying power of the Revolution and its Founding Fathers. Those who contend that the Revolution bore few marks of social conflict or social upheaval seem to be denying the blessing of the Founding Fathers to present-day struggles against the establishment, while those who emphasize conflicts seem to be suggesting that conflicts, or ʌt least conflicts

Edmund S. Morgan from *Essays on the American Revolution,* ed. by Stephen G. Kurtz and James H. Hutson (University of North Carolina Press, 1973), pp. 289–309. Reprinted by permission of the author.

against an upper class or established system, are sponsored by the Founding Fathers, consecrated in the fires at Valley Forge. No such power attaches to other episodes in our history. The New Deal, for example, has not achieved sanctifying power in the national memory. Hence no one would think to classify as conservative those historians who deny that the New Deal achieved or aimed at radical social change. But to say that the Revolution did not achieve or aim at radical social change and lacked the conflicts that generally accompany such change is taken as a denial that radical social change is a good thing. Hence those who give the Founding Fathers failing grades as social revolutionaries are greeted, sometimes to their astonishment, as conservative.

But conservative and radical are relative terms, and so are consensus and conflict; and relative terms, if I may be allowed to follow for a moment the logic of Peter Ramus, can be understood only in relation to each other. Those impressed by the achievement of consensus among the Revolutionists can scarcely hope to understand the nature of that consensus without understanding the conflicts that had to be overcome or repressed in order to arrive at it. Nor can those who emphasize conflict gauge the force of the movements they examine without considering the kind of consensus that later grew out of those movements or that succeeded in subduing them. Therefore, in attempting to assess the meaning of the American Revolution, it may be worthwhile to survey the various points of consensus and conflict that can be discerned in the Revolutionary period, to weigh their effect on the Revolution, and then to examine the kind of consensus that emerged at the end, even if that consensus is thought to be no more than a sullen acquiescence in the measures of a ruling class.

The type of internal conflict that historians have most eagerly searched for among Americans of the Revolutionary period is class conflict. The search is handicapped by a problem of identification. With the struggle of the colonies against the mother country dominating the scene, how does one distinguish a class conflict within that larger conflict?

Not by the side a man chose to support. Although the first historians of the loyalists did assume that they represented an upper if not a ruling class, subsequent investigations have revealed that loyalists, like patriots, were drawn from all classes. That a man sided with the mother country or against her tells us little about his social position. Although it seems altogether likely on the latest evidence that a larger percentage of the well-to-do could be found among the loyalists than among the Revolutionists, the Revolution cut sharply across nearly all previous divisions, whether regional, ethnic, religious, or class. It was not a conflict in which one side was predominantly upper class and the other predominantly lower class.

If, then, we look only at one side, at the Americans who supported the Revolution, or who did not oppose it, can we there find that lower-class rebels were bent on the overthrow or reduction of ruling-class rebels? A moment's reflection on the nature of the Revolutionary War may moderate our expectations. The Revolutionary effort against Great Britain tended to suppress or encompass social conflicts. Where it did not, where hostility between social groups rose to a level of intensity approximating that of the conflict with the mother country, one group or the other would be likely to join with the loyalists. Some merchants in New York City, for example, felt that the local Revolutionary leaders threatened their interests more than the mother country did; and similarly some tenant farmers of the Hudson Valley felt more bitter toward their patriot landlords than they did toward king and Parliament. But these men, whether merchants or tenants, by joining the loyalist side deprived themselves of a part in any contest about who should rule at home. Loyalism in this way tended to absorb social groups that felt endangered or oppressed by the Revolutionary party. It operated as a safety valve to remove from the American side men who felt a high degree of social discontent. Or to change the figure, it drew off men at either end of the political spectrum, reducing the range of disagreements. It removed from the scene the intransigents, of whatever persuasion, who might have prevented the achievement of consensus.

Disputes did occur, of course, among those who remained on the Revolutionary side, but the extraordinary social mobility characteristic of eighteenth-century American society usually prevented such disputes from hardening along class lines. Although recent statistical samplings point to a narrowing of economic opportunity in the latter half of the eighteenth century, Americans still enjoyed an upward mobility unknown in other societies. In a land of rising men a political group formed along lower-class lines had little prospect of endurance.

The Revolution probably increased social mobility temporarily both upward and downward, ruining the fortunes of many established families and opening opportunities for speedy ascent by daring upstarts. This very mobility engendered, as it always has, political disputes, but seldom along class lines. An American who had moved up from the lower ranks carried with him the expectation of sharing with those who had already arrived the offices of government traditionally exercised by the economically and socially successful. If he found himself excluded, he could call upon a wide electorate of his former equals but present inferiors to help him achieve the kind of office that they, no less than he, considered proper for successful men. But the fact that the lower ranks were involved in the contest should not obscure the fact that the contest itself was generally a struggle for office and power between members of an upper class: the new against the established. We must be wary of seeing such struggles, like Patrick Henry's successful bid for power in Virginia, as a rising of the oppressed against their masters.

I do not mean to argue that hostility between classes did not exist at all among those who supported the Revolution or that it cannot be discerned or recognized. In the antirent riots of 1766, for example, New York tenant farmers expressed a hostility to their landlords that was not entirely absorbed by loyalism after 1775. More than one scholar has found clear expressions of class conflict in the conduct of the war and of politics in Revolutionary New York. But in assessing class conflict as a Revolutionary force, we shall be hard pressed to find many instances outside New York in which antagonism rose to the level of actual fighting or even to openly expressed hostility of the kind that might be expected to lead to fighting.

American social structure was so fluid that to talk about social classes at all in most colonies or states requires the use of very loose economic categories such as rich, poor, and middle class, or contemporary designations like "the better sort" or "the poorer sort," or occupational categories like merchant, planter, lawyer, farmer, artisan, and seaman. Americans were no less skilled than other peoples in measuring the degree of deference due to each of their neighbors for the host of reasons and prejudices that confer honor or contempt on the members of any community. But such distinctions were local, seldom negotiable beyond the neighborhood where a man was known, and not always easy to discern even there.

Nevertheless, one absolute, clearly defined, and easily recognized division did exist, that between freeman and slave. Half a million Americans, perhaps a fifth of the total population, were slaves, and slavery is so direct an assault by one group of men on another that it can properly be considered as a form of class conflict in itself. In the American Revolution, however, slaves were unable to mount any serious uprising against their masters. Although the armies of both sides sooner or later made use of slaves and gave some of them freedom for their services, neither side provided the help necessary for large-scale insurrection. Both felt more need to woo masters than slaves. Perhaps the possibility of insurrection was even lessened by the few efforts of the British to promote it. When Lord Dunmore invited the slaves of Virginia to desert their masters and join his forces, he probably drew off many of the bolder individuals, leaving behind those who were less likely to rise in revolt later. Again loyalism tended to absorb men who might otherwise have directed their energies more radically against a local ruling class.

That the American Revolution did not produce an uprising of the group in colonial society that was most visibly and legally oppressed, and oppressed with the explicit or tacit approval of the rest of the society, is itself an instructive comment on the nature of social conflict and consensus during the Revolution.

The absence of any massive revolt, white or black, may perhaps be put in perspective if we compare the labor force of the Revolutionary period with that a century earlier, when Bacon's Rebellion had terrorized the first families of Virginia. In the seventeenth century as in the eighteenth the greater part of the colonial labor force, that is, of men who worked for other men, was concentrated in the South and especially in Virginia. In 1676, when Bacon's Rebellion occurred, the laborers were mostly imported servants, English, Irish, Scottish, or Welsh, whose terms of service generally expired when they reached the age of twenty-four. They were imported at the rate of eight hundred to a thousand or perhaps as many as fifteen hundred or two thousand annually; they were mostly male, and they had come in expectation of a better life once their terms of service were up.

For a variety of reasons, in the ten or fifteen years before 1676, Virginia underwent a depression that severely curtailed the opportunities for a newly freed servant to make his way in the world. Tobacco prices were low. Land in the settled areas had been taken up in large quantities by earlier comers, and men either had to rent land at prices that left no room for profit or else they had to move to the frontiers, where Indians mounted guerrilla attacks on them. The officers of government lived high off the hog in spite of depression, by levying high taxes and voting each other generous fees, salaries, and sinecures. The result was the presence of a clearly distinguishable privileged class and a clearly distinguishable lower class, composed not merely of servants who made tobacco for their betters but of former servants who were trying to make it for themselves. These freedmen were likely to be single. They were likely to be without land of their own. But they were not likely to be without guns, especially those who had moved, as many had, to the frontier.

As early as 1673 Governor Berkeley recognized the dangers of this situation. At least one-third of Virginia's militia, he estimated, were single freedmen, who would have nothing to lose by turning their arms against their superiors for the sake of plunder. Three years later, goaded by Indian raids, they did it. Bacon's Rebellion swept across Virginia, starting among the penniless pioneers of the frontier counties and gathering momentum from the adherence of other men who had nothing to lose in a free-for-all scramble for the accumulated wealth of the privileged few. In the midst of it Berkeley wrote to England, understandably raising his estimate of the numbers of the disaffected. "How miserable that man is," he complained, "that Governes a People wher six parts of seaven at least are Poore Endebted Discontented and Armed."

A hundred years later the situation had changed radically in at least one important respect. In the South, where a large labor force still furnished the way to wealth for plantation owners, the laborers were not continually emerging into the status of independent, poverty-stricken, discontented freedmen trying to make a start against heavy odds. By the middle of the eighteenth century the majority of the entire labor force in the plantation colonies was held in permanent slavery. The development of slavery is perhaps the key to the consensus that prevailed in colonial America, for slavery meant the substitution of a helpless, closely guarded lower class for a dangerous, armed lower class that would fight if exploited too ruthlessly. The slave had more reason to revolt than the servant or the new freedman. But he was less able to. He had no hope, no rising expectations, and no arms. On top of that he was black. His status in the community was proclaimed by his color and maintained by a tyranny in which white men of all ranks and regions consented and approved. The consensus on which colonial society rested was a racist consensus.

Had the southern plantations not shifted from free to slave labor, had the planters continued to import masses of indentured servants and continued to pour them into their own and other colonies a few years later as indigent freedmen, then the picture of social mobility in the colonial period and of class conflict in the Revolution might have been quite different. The minutemen of 1775 might have been truly a rabble in arms, ready to turn from fighting the British to fighting their well-to-do neighbors, just as Bacon's men turned from fighting the Indians to fighting Berkeley and his crew. But in the century between 1676 and 1776 the growth of slavery had curbed the growth of a free, depressed lower class and correspondingly magnified the social and economic opportunities of whites. It is perhaps the greatest irony of a Revolution fought in the name of freedom, a Revolution that indeed advanced the cause of freedom throughout the world, that the men who carried it out were able to unite against British oppression because they had so completely and successfully oppressed the largest segment of their own laboring population.

To be sure, there were those among the Revolutionists who felt uncomfortable about rebelling against what they chose to call the threat of slavery, while they themselves held some 20 percent of their own population in slavery. But such feelings were translated into legal action only in states where slaves were few in number. Those were not the states where an enslaved labor force grew the country's principal exports. And if northerners freed their own slaves, they did not propose at this time to free their neighbors'. The racial consensus on which colonial society had rested was shaken a little but not broken by the Revolution.

There of course continued to be indentured servants and servants who worked for wages both in the plantation colonies and in the North. But the great majority of men who worked for other men were probably the slaves of the plantation colonies. The growing economy, in spite of periodic depressions like that of the 1670s, could absorb the number of indentured servants who turned free each year and could offer most of them an independent and comfortable if not affluent existence on the land. Only a small minority fell permanently into the servant class, like some of the sailors whom Jesse Lemisch has described, and even they reacted more visibly, violently, and vociferously against iniquities of the British government than against whatever oppression was visited upon them by their compatriots.

In sum, the evidence of Revolutionary class conflict is scanty, and for good reason. With a majority of laborers in chains and with the most discontented freedmen venting their discontent in loyalism, the struggle over who should rule at home was unlikely to bear many of the marks of class conflict. Class conflict was indubitably present, but it did not surface with an effective intensity until a later day, after the Revolution had built a consensus that could both nourish and contain it, and after social, political, and economic change had produced greater provocations to it.

Let us turn now to another kind of conflict that was more intense and also, I believe, more significant for the Revolution. If we examine the occasions when Americans fought with one another or came very close to fighting between 1763 and 1789, excluding battles between loyalists and patriots, we find a number of episodes, all of them involving men who had moved from the older coastal regions into the interior: the march of the Paxton Boys against Philadelphia, the Regulator movement in the Carolinas with its Battle of Alamance, the activities of the Green Mountain Boys in Vermont, the skirmishes of Pennamite and Yankee in the Wyoming Valley of Pennsylvania, and Shays's Rebellion in Massachusetts. However diverse in immediate cause and attendant circumstance, these conflicts had one thing in common: they were all manifestations of the discontent of western settlers or settlers on new lands against governments dominated by or subservient to the interests of older or eastern regions.

Americans of the Revolutionary period were less successful in repressing sectional conflicts than conflicts arising from class or race. Though this fact is obvious and though the westward movement has received its full share of attention, historians considering the Revolution as a social movement have not always borne in mind two conspicuous conditions of life in eighteenth-century America, conditions that lay at the root of East-West conflict: first, the extraordinary rate of population growth and, second, the abundance of land, unoccupied or only thinly occupied by the native Indians.

Although the rate of population growth in the colonies varied a good deal from place to place and from year to year, the overall long-range trend is clear. The total population of the thirteen colonies that participated in the Revolution more than doubled every twenty-five years during the eighteenth century. Beginning at about 250,000 in 1700, it rose to over 5,000,000 by 1800. As we learn more about the role of population growth in history, it may ultimately appear that the most significant social fact about America in the eighteenth century was this fearful growth, unlike anything that had been known in Europe in recorded history. Every twenty-five years the colonies had to absorb numbers equal to their total population. The result by the last quarter of the eighteenth century was explosive emigration out of the older settled regions into the West. Consider the westward thrust into the Kentucky-Tennessee area alone: the population there could scarcely have amounted to 10,000 in 1781; by 1790 it had soared to 110,000. If we note that this migration over the mountains in the 1780s by itself dwarfed the so-called Great Migration over the ocean in the 1630s, when probably no more than 50,000 left England for all parts of the New World, if we note also that migration was simultaneously occurring into other western areas, then we may begin to appreciate the magnitude of a western factor in the Revolutionary period.

The westward population explosion probably relieved the East from social conflicts that might have arisen from overcrowding; but it generated other conflicts potentially as dangerous. It set rival groups of speculators into contests for control of the richest western lands, contests that drew in and corrupted state governments and the national government. And it created a block of Americans who by moving west acquired different needs and interests from eastern Americans, but who by the same move lost their political ability to make their needs heard or attended to. People moved west so rapidly that even with the best of intentions a government could scarcely have kept up with them in furnishing the town or parish or county organization that formed the units of representation in the legislature. Because representation did not keep up with the expansion of population into new territory, governments remained under the domination of easterners and frequently neglected the needs of westerners. Even where representation was fairly proportioned, the location of the legislature subjected it to eastern influences that could bring it into serious conflict with the West.

Eastern insensitivity to western needs was the source of the Paxton incident, as it had been in part of Bacon's Rebellion. The prime western need in the early years of a settlement was to cope with the Indians, who gathered to attack the invaders of their land. Indian raids were no longer part of life in the East. The very existence of westerners furnished a buffer zone to easterners, enabling them to view the rights and wrongs of the situation with an objectivity that westerners could not achieve or afford. We need not assume that the Paxton Boys were righteous. Benjamin Franklin called them "Christian White Savages," and the epithet was deserved. They were armed thugs, terrorists, murderers; but they were also westerners, and as westerners they had grievances against an eastern-dominated legislature that spent its time arguing about who would pay the bills while it neglected the defense of the frontier.

The Regulator movement represents another phase of the same East-West conflict: the eastern-dominated governments of South Carolina and North Carolina failed to extend the machinery of law enforcement into the West as rapidly as the needs of the settlers required, and so the West took the law in its own hands. In Shay's Rebellion the Shaysites, who also called themselves Regulators, hoped to gain by direct action what the government in Boston had denied them. The Pennamite-Yankee conflict and the activities of the Green Mountain Boys offer a variation on the theme. In these cases two colonial governments, representing different speculative interests, were engaged in a contest for western lands, and the actual settlers fought with each other. The significance of the frontier in early American history, if we may borrow that phrase, was that it kept Americans in conflict. Movement of the exploding population into new lands was continually generating new communities with interests differing from those of the older communities that retained, or at least claimed, control over them.

This kind of internal conflict among Americans was far more visible during the Revolutionary period than was class conflict. Although there were overtones of class conflict in any contest between established eastern interests and the interests of pioneer western farmers, the contest was primarily geographical, created by the problem of stretching the social and political apparatus that bound one group of people to another in the expanding American universe.

That this form of conflict produced more active hostility in the Revolutionary period will seem no more than natural if we view the Revolution itself from the same perspective. The English colonies in America stood to England in the way that the western parts of the colonies stood to the eastern parts, but with even stronger grievances and correspondingly stronger hostility. The institutions that England devised for her overseas emigrants in the wake of the Great Migration were even more inadequate by 1776 than the institutions that they had devised for themselves. While many colonial legislatures had too few representatives from their western areas, Parliament, which could legislate for all the colonies, had not a single representative from them. When the colonists cried out that Parliament without American representatives knew nothing about their needs and had no right to tax them, they spoke to England in the voice of westerners speaking to easterners. In the Declaration of Independence they announced that the social and political bonds that tied them to an eastern government were severed. The American Revolution was itself a revolt of settlers in a new land against a government that by its location and composition could not be properly acquainted with their needs and could not keep up with their growth.

After 1776, in seeking to sustain the new nation they had just proclaimed themselves to be, the Americans had to contain the very force that had impelled their revolt against the mother country. If the colonies could secede from England, the West could secede from the East for the same reasons. The danger was aggravated by the fact that slavery and loyalism, which helped to lower tension between classes, perversely heightened tension between East and West. Since slavery did not move westward as rapidly as freedom, the much higher concentration of slaves in the East served to emphasize the difference in sectional interests. And since loyalism had as much appeal for disaffected regions as for disaffected individuals, it could become a catastrophic ingredient in sectional conflicts. If an entire region became sufficiently hostile to a government dominated by easterners, it might choose to rejoin the mother country. The result, as in the defection of individuals or groups, might be a greater harmony among those remaining. But the defection of a whole region could have jeopardized the viability of the Union; and a consensus formed by the secession of all dissident elements would scarcely deserve the name.

The British were not slow to recognize the advantages for them of sectional conflict and kept hoping for it after the war was over. In violation of the treaty they clung to the northwest trading posts, flirted with the disgruntled leaders of Vermont, and made plans for detaching the whole Northwest. Nor was Britain the only recourse for discontented westerners: Spain had eyes on the whole Southwest. She came uncomfortably close to detaching Kentucky when the Spanish minister maneuvered the Continental Congress into what appeared to westerners as a gross display of eastern indifference to western interests. If Congress had actually ratified the Jay-Gardoqui Treaty, with its seeming recognition of Spanish control of the Mississippi, the Americans who marched across the mountains into Kentucky and Tennessee in the 1780s might well have marched right into the arms of Spain.

In sum, while class conflict tended to be muted during the Revolutionary period by social mobility among whites, by the enslavement of blacks, and by loyalism, sectional conflict was aggravated. The gravest form of sectional conflict was East-West, but it was not the only form. The greater North-South conflict had already cast its ominous shadow in congressional voting alignments, in the uneasiness of both northerners and southerners over the continuance of slavery, and in steps taken toward abolition of slavery in the North, but not in the South. The most farsighted Americans sensed already that North-South differences as well as East-West differences might one day lead to secession. Indeed in the late 1780s so many sectional disagreements were festering that men who had led their states to a united independence fifteen years earlier now predicted the breakup of the American nation.

We know that it did not break up. What, then, other than the superior wisdom of the Founding Fathers, prevented the breakup? What sort of consensus enabled Americans to contain not only the immediate threats to their Union perceived in the 1780s but also the threats that grew with time from sectional and class conflict? The question in some measure answers itself. The Americans did achieve nationality during the Revolutionary period, and nationalism has proved to be the most powerful, if the least understood, social force of modern times. In the shrinking world of the twentieth century it has often been a sinister force, confining the vision of its devotees to a single country when they should be looking at the entire globe. But for Americans of the Revolutionary period the world was expanding instead of shrinking, and nationalism exerted a cohesive influence among the people of the several states, stretching instead of confining their political horizons. Even Jefferson, whose state loyalties proved particularly strong, urged his fellow Virginians to send their best young men to Congress, so that they could acquire the continental vision early. That vision extended not merely up and down the Atlantic seaboard but westward to the areas where Americans were moving so rapidly in the 1780s. It scarcely occurred to Jefferson that the United States might not one day reach to the Pacific and indeed occupy the whole of North America, and perhaps the Caribbean and South America too. If not everyone felt this way, there were enough who did to give American nationalism an expansive quality and to make her statesmen conscious of the need to retain the westward migrants within the national community.

Nationalism was in itself the strongest force binding Americans of the Revolutionary generation together. Devotion to the nation helped to keep both sides in any conflict on speaking terms, helped to make disagreements negotiable within the framework of national politics, and even make possible the creation of a new and stronger framework in 1787 when the old one proved unsatisfactory. But nationalism was not the only force disposing Americans to bury their conflicts. The racial consensus of colonial times, though challenged and diminished, still prevailed and helped to keep the North-South conflict from coming to center stage. The Revolutionists were not prepared to allow the issue of freedom for blacks to threaten the union of whites. By the consent of white Americans the American labor force, concentrated in the South, remained for the most part in slavery, outside the arena where American quarrels and conflicts were expected to take place. Contending factions, whether of class, region, or party, were agreed in not seeking or expecting the participation of men in chains.

The exclusion of most laborers meant that the participants on both sides of any conflict were men who possessed formidable powers, powers that were carefully withheld from slaves. Both sides could negotiate from strength and demand compromise. Although repression might be an effective mode of dealing with discontent or insubordination from slaves, it did not recommend itself as a way of handling men who had the means to fight back either politically or, if necessary, with force. Unlike the peasants of the Old World, Americans, or at least those Americans without black skin, possessed two palpable sources of power: most of them owned the land on which they lived, and a very large number of them owned guns. Land gave them economic and political power; and guns, we may as well admit, gave them firepower.

In the events that led up to the Revolution, England had failed to recognize the strength that these two kinds of power gave to her colonists. The colonists themselves knew at first hand that the ownership of land enabled a man to bid defiance to those who had traditionally controlled society through control of its lands. They had developed a society in which deference to birth and wealth was tempered by constant reminders to the rich and wellborn that their authority rested on the consent of ordinary property owners. Most adult male Americans owned property and could vote for the men who made the laws that affected their property. If they generally voted for a local bigwig, a man who held more property than they did, they did not hesitate to dump him if he neglected their interests. Similarly, within the legislative assemblies lesser men bowed to the leadership of bigger ones. As Robert Zemsky has shown, social status counted for more than seniority in at least one colonial assembly. But when the leaders of the assembly brought in a bill that looked oppressive to the back-benchers, they voted it down and even substituted impromptu measures of their own from the floor.

What alarmed Americans about taxation by Parliament was that they could not vote it down. The program that seemed so conventional and so reasonable from the standpoint of Whitehall appeared to the Americans as a threat to the power that enabled them to direct their own lives. If a legislature to which they elected no member could take their property in taxes, that legislature could ultimately take all their property and reduce them to the impotence of which they had such visible examples in the slaves at their feet. It was consensus on this point that enabled the colonies to unite so suddenly and so successfully against parliamentary taxation. The American reaction to parliamentary taxation seemed to England too hysterical and wicked to be genuine, and her statesmen failed to deal with it adequately, partly because they failed to recognize its existence.

The British failed also to recognize the existence of American firepower. It would perhaps be an exaggeration to say that most Americans had guns and knew how to use them. But it seems likely that nowhere else in the world at the time was there a population so well armed as the Americans. Governor Berkeley had perceived and experienced the implications of this fact in 1676, and as early as 1691 William Blathwayt, the English auditor general for the colonies, who was more conversant in colonial affairs than any other Englishman of the time, recorded with admiration the familiarity of the colonists with guns. "There is no Custom more generally to be observed among the young Virginians," he noted, "than that they all learn to keep and use a gun with a Marvellous dexterity as soon as ever they have strength enough to lift it to their heads." Had Lord North been as keenly aware as Blathwayt of the skills thus acquired, he and George III might not have underestimated so badly the American capacity for resistance.

In order to maintain themselves as a single nation, Americans had to recognize the economic power and firepower that Britain ignored. By the time of the Revolution the proportion of the population owning land in the East may have been somewhat reduced from what it had been fifty or a hundred years earlier, but the westerner by definition was a man who had broken out of the limited acreage of the East. Whether or not he held a secure title, he knew how to make his living from the land and to make life uncomfortable for anyone who tried to stop him. And he was even more likely than the easterner to be armed. The westerner in our history has always been a man with a gun. Eastern-dominated governments simply did not have sufficient power of their own in the long run to impose on the West conditions that armed westerners would not agree to, any more than the Continental Congress could have imposed its edicts on the states, as some members proposed, by the use of military force. American nationalism was obliged to start with the assumption that the population was armed and that no group within it, slaves excepted, could be pushed very hard in any direction it did not want to go.

With a population already equalized to a large degree by firepower and economic power, the United States began its independence appropriately with the declaration that all men are created equal. The immediate purpose was to affirm the equality of England's transatlantic colonists with Englishmen in England, who were taxed only by their elected representatives. But the simplicity of the declaration of equality endowed it with a resonance that was momentous for the whole subsequent history of the nation whose existence it announced.

It could not have been predicted at the time that this would become a national creed. The men who adopted the declaration in 1776 would scarcely have been unanimous if they had been obliged to state precisely what they meant by "created equal." Many of them, including the author of the phrase, held slaves. If the preceding analysis is correct, the fact that they were able to unite at all depended in part on their denial of equality to black Americans. Even when applied only to white Americans, the meaning of equality was hardly as self-evident as Congress declared the proposition itself to be. The equality promulgated by the Congress at Philadelphia had no power to dissolve at once the conflicts and tensions in American society. Westerners were obliged for several years to flirt with Spain and England, while eastern speculators, many of them in Congress, quarreled over the profits they hoped to gain from western settlement if the West could be kept under eastern domination. James Madison tried in vain to secure a guarantee in the Federal Constitution of the equality of western states. Instead the principle was precariously acknowledged only as a result of a shady bargain during the last weeks of the expiring Continental Congress.

But acknowledged it was in the end. The Northwest Ordinance, by stipulating that western states should be admitted to the Union on equal terms with the existing states, saved the nation from future attempts to make subordinate colonists out of its western emigrants. As the Revolutionists gradually became aware of the implications of the creed to which they had committed themselves, they also whittled down, albeit even more gradually, the inequities in their laws governing religion, representation, and inheritance. And as the social structure of the nation changed in subsequent generations, Americans probed further into the meaning of equality.

It has generally taken more than the chanting of the creed to bring about the social justice that it promises. Our history is not the chronicle of steady and continuous application of the principle of equality to match the continuous expansion of the population. The reluctance of easterners to grant equal rights to westerners was prophetic of later contests. Those who have claimed the benefits of equality in America have usually had to press their own claims against stubborn opposition. Men with power over other men have often affirmed their dedication to the principle while denying it by their actions, masters denying it to slaves, employers to workmen, natives to immigrants, whites to blacks, men to women.

Is it fair, then, to call this a point of consensus? Was it not mere rhetoric? Perhaps, if by rhetoric is meant the terms on which men can agree to speak together. An alternative rhetoric and an alternative social creed prevailed before the Revolution both in America and Europe and continued to prevail in most of Europe. That creed also offered a way to consensus, but of a quite different sort. It affirmed divine sanction for a social hierarchy in which every man knew his place and was expected to keep it. The old creed was designed to suppress the aspirations of lower classes, to make them content with their lot. Redress of grievances was not impossible, if superiors failed in their acknowledged obligations to inferiors; but the likelihood was much greater that oppression would go unchecked and that resentment would build into an explosive, revolutionary situation before redress could be obtained. The American Revolution itself was brought on by a British minister who had rejected what he called "the absurd opinion that all men are equal." That absurd opinion became the basis of the American consensus that grew out of the Revolution.

It may indeed seem an absurd sort of consensus that rests upon an invitation to conflict. The creed of equality did not give men equality, but invited them to claim it, invited them, not to know their place and keep it, but to seek and demand a better place. Yet the conflicts resulting from such demands have generally, though not always, stopped short of large-scale violence and have generally eventuated in a greater degree of actual equality. After each side has felt out the other's strengths and weaknesses, some bargain, some equivalent to a Northwest Ordinance, is agreed upon, leaving demands not quite fulfilled, leaving the most radical still discontented with remaining inequalities, but keeping the nation still committed to the creed of equality and bound to move, if haltingly, in the direction it signals.

While the creed invites resistance by the oppressed, it also enjoins accommodation by the oppressor. If it is mere rhetoric, it is a rhetoric that has kept conservatism in America on the defensive. The power that the consensus of equality has wielded over the minds of Americans ever since the Revolution is in fact nowhere more clearly exhibited than in the posture it has imposed on conservatism. To Europeans it may seem odd for conservatism to be garbed in the language of human equality, but conservatives in America quickly learned that this was the only acceptable dress in which they could appear in public. In order to argue for special privilege in the United States it was necessary to show—and it sometimes required considerable legerdemain—that special privilege was somehow the outcome of equality or a device to protect equality. John Adams, for example, contended that Americans should reserve a special place in their governments for the rich, the talented, and the well-born, on the grounds that it was necessary to isolate and thus ostracize and disarm these dangerous men in order to preserve equality. A century later William Graham Sumner argued against every kind of social legislation on the grounds that all Americans were created equal, so that every American who attained wealth and position had done so by his own efforts and therefore deserved to keep what he had earned, while the poor equally deserved their poverty. To aid the poor would threaten equality.

If these arguments today seem ludicrous, it is because conservatism in the United States has often been reduced to the ludicrous by the national commitment to equality. A conservatism based on a more congenial premise can make little headway. When the South, long after the Revolution, attempted to defend slavery on another premise, the attempt generated the greatest crisis American nationality has faced. The resulting conflict did not really destroy the racial consensus among whites and did not achieve equality for Negroes, but it did destroy slavery and it did preserve the national commitment to equality. That commitment is gradually eroding racism. And it continues to serve the oppressed, both black and white, in their efforts to attain what the nation has promised them, just as it also serves to keep most of the oppressed from totally rejecting a society that admits their right to an equal treatment not yet received.

If, then, the American Revolution produced a consensus among the victorious Americans, it was not a static consensus but one with the genius to serve changing times and needs. It was a consensus that invited conflicts and still invites them, a consensus peculiarly adapted to a growing people, a people on the move both geographically and socially. It could not have contained, but it did not produce, the kind of conflict that gave Charles I his Cromwell. It made instead for a society where a Hamilton had his Jefferson, a Hoover his Roosevelt, and a Nixon—might profit by their example. If this be conservatism, it is radicals who have made the most of it.

SUGGESTIONS FOR FURTHER READING

Carl Becker's argument that the American Revolution was a conflict within the colonies as well as a struggle against England may be found in his *History of Political Parties in the Province of New York, 1760–1776* (Madison, 1909). Arthur M. Schlesinger, *Colonial Merchants and the American Revolution* (New York, 1918) gives support to Becker's position by showing how merchants sought to protect their interests against both England and other groups in colonial society. A classic little study showing the social upheaval resulting from the revolutionary struggle is J. Franklin Jameson, *The American Revolution Considered as a Social Movement* (Princeton, N.J., 1926). These views are generally upheld by Elisha P. Douglass, *Rebels and Democrats* (Chapel Hill, N.C., 1955). Gordon S. Wood, *The Radicalism of the American Revolution* (New York, 1992), a portion of which is reprinted above, is a recent contribution to the argument that the American Revolution created profound changes in American society. Michael Kammen, *A Season of Youth: The American Revolution and the Historical Imagination* (New York, 1978) traces the meaning of the Revolution over two hundred years.

Edmund S. Morgan, *The Birth of the Republic, 1773–89*, rev. ed. (Chicago, 1977) disputes the contention that there were sharp divisions among the colonists and instead finds a basic consensus among the revolutionaries. A different emphasis emerges in a study of many of the same events in Merrill Jensen, *The Founding of a Nation: A History of the American Revolution, 1763–1776* (New York, 1968). Louis Hartz, "Democracy Without a Democratic Revolution," *American Political Science Review*, 46 (June 1952), 321–42, argues that because in America there was no aristocratic or feudal tradition to overthrow, the Revolution was no revolution at all. In Chapter 3 of his *Genius of American Politics* (Chicago, 1953), Daniel J. Boorstin uses very different evidence to come to conclusions similar to those of Louis Hartz.

Bernard Bailyn, *The Ideological Origins of the American Revolution* (Cambridge, Mass., 1967) rejects the concept of a social or internal revolution, suggesting instead that revolutionary ideas, accepted by the colonists for more than a century before the actual conflict, are what made the American Revolution truly revolutionary. On this point see also Gordon S. Wood, *The Creation of the American Republic, 1776–1787* (Chapel Hill, N.C., 1969). In his "A Note on Mobs in the American Revolution," *William and Mary Quarterly*, 23 (October 1966), 635–42, Wood compares American and European revolutionary mobs. Jesse Lemisch, "Jack Tar in the Streets: Merchant Seamen in the Politics of Revolutionary America," *William and Mary Quarterly*, 3rd ser., 25 (July 1968), 371–407, arguing that the Revolution should be seen from the point of view of the common man,

---

*Available in paperback edition.

gives support to the conflict interpretation and adds another dimension to the discussion of the mob in revolutionary America. Pauline Maier, *From Resistance to Revolution: Colonial Radicals and the Development of American Opposition to Britain, 1765–1776* (New York, 1972) describes popular uprisings and violence as the path to the Revolution. Alfred F. Young, ed., *The American Revolution: Explorations in the History of American Radicalism* (DeKalb, Ill., 1976) includes many essays that support the conflict interpretation. Additional interpretive essays, some of which support variants of the consensus interpretation, may be found in Stephen G. Kurtz and James H. Hutson, eds., *Essays on the American Revolution* (Chapel Hill, N.C., 1973). The nature of the differences that divided Americans (as well as differences that divide historians) may be found in the following studies of a loyalist, Thomas Hutchinson, and a radical, Thomas Paine: Bernard Bailyn, *The Ordeal of Thomas Hutchinson* (Cambridge, Mass., 1974); and Eric Foner, *Tom Paine and Revolutionary America* (New York, 1976).

Jay Fliegelman, *Prodigals and Pilgrims: The American Revolution Against Patriarchial Authority, 1750–1800* (New York, 1982) traces the broad cultural transformations that were in part the cause and in part the result of the American Revolution. Gary B. Nash, *The Urban Crucible: Social Change, Political Consciousness, and the Origins of the American Revolution* (Cambridge, Mass., 1979) considers the role of the urban population in the Revolution. Bernard Bailyn discusses other revolutionary leaders in *Faces of Revolution: Personalities and Themes in the Struggle for American Independence* (New York, 1990).

On women in the Revolution see Mary Beth Norton, *Liberty's Daughters: The Revolutionary Experience of American Women, 1750–1800* (Boston, 1980), from which the second selection here is taken, and Linda K. Kerber, *Women of the Republic: Intellect and Ideology in Revolutionary America* (Chapel Hill, N.C., 1980). A series of essays examining the varying effects of the Revolution on the status of women is Ronald Hoffman and Peter L. Albert, eds., *Women in the Age of the American Revolution* (Charlottesville, Va., 1989).

Important essays that survey the conflict-consensus debate and attempt to resolve it are Jack P. Greene, "The Flight from Determinism: A Review of Recent Literature on the Coming of the American Revolution," *South Atlantic Quarterly,* 61 (Spring 1962), 235–59; Jack P. Greene, "The Social Origins of the American Revolution: An Evaluation and an Interpretation," *Political Science Quarterly,* 88 (March 1973), 1–22; and Gordon S. Wood, "Rhetoric and Reality in the American Revolution," *William and Mary Quarterly,* 3rd ser., 13 (January 1966), 3–32.

Studies that place the American Revolution in a wider, world context are R. R. Palmer, *The Age of the Democratic Revolution: A Political History of Europe and America, 1760–1800,* 2 vols. (Princeton, N.J., 1959, 1964) and David Brion Davis, *Revolutions: Reflections on the American Equality and Foreign Liberations* (Cambridge, 1990).

3

The Constitution

issatisfaction with the government under the Articles of Confederation was widespread. Many charged that the government lacked the necessary power and authority to hold the new nation together and to negotiate effectively with foreign powers; they feared that the state and regional differences and jealousies and the machinations of foreign powers, particularly England, might lead to the destruction of the United States. An economic depression following the Revolutionary War precipitated an event that seemed to illustrate the dangers the new nation faced. In the summer of 1786 a group of farmers in western Massachusetts, hard hit by depression and angered by the state legislature's failure to heed their demands for a paper money issue and debtors' stay laws, took matters into their own hands. Led by Daniel Shays, they organized an army, marched on several courthouses, and threatened to take over the government. The governor called out the militia, which easily crushed the uprising; but the specter of rebellion remained and had a significant influence on those who wanted a stronger, more centralized national government, one that could maintain order and protect private property.

Even as rebellion raged in Massachusetts, a small group of delegates met at Annapolis to discuss the conflicting regulations regarding interstate commerce. The Annapolis convention went beyond problems of trade, however, issuing a call for another convention to meet the following year in Philadelphia to consider remedies for the defects in the Articles of Confederation. Delegates to the Philadelphia convention quickly scrapped the idea of revising the Articles and instead drafted a new Constitution of the United States.

The American people have come to venerate, indeed, almost to worship their constitution. For many, the founding fathers are godlike, their handiwork almost divine. Students of history, however, quickly discover that the Constitution was very controversial at the time it was drafted and that its ratification was hotly contested. They also discover that there has been a lively controversy among historians regarding the meaning and significance of the Constitution.

Some scholars have argued that the Constitution was the work of a political and economic minority striving to create a government that would limit the power of the majority. This was the view of Charles A. Beard, who in his enormously influential 1913 book, *An Economic Interpretation of the Constitution,* argued that the founding fathers were men of wealth who sought to create a government that would promote and protect their economic interests and limit the power of the small farmers and debtors. More recent scholarship in the conflict school has given less emphasis to class differences and has stressed instead sectional differences that led to sharp conflicts over such economic matters as trade and taxation policies and, most important, over slavery and states' rights.

Other historians have strongly disputed these conflict interpretations of the Constitution. Disputes at the Philadelphia convention and during ratification, they maintain, did not represent basic differences among the American people based upon property owning, class, or section. Most Americans agreed on fundamentals. They knew why they had fought the Revolution and what kind of government they wanted. But they had no precedents to follow; they were feeling their way, searching for the best means to institutionalize the goals for which they had fought. Differences over means rested on the solid foundation of a basic consensus on ends. Variations on these two interpretations are illustrated in the selections that follow.

Forrest McDonald, in the first selection, argues that the founding fathers wrote a constitution that was both conservative and radical—conservative because the framers sought to create a strong government that could secure the rights of the people and protect them from internal and external enemies, and radical because to meet these goals they created federalism, a form of government hitherto unknown. McDonald notes that the founders often disagreed about what to include in the new constitution and about the meaning of certain provisions that were included. In the end, experience, common sense, and a spirit of compromise prevailed, indicating that on basic principles a widespread consensus existed. McDonald also argues that many of the founding fathers had remarkable insights into the future needs of a new nation; these insights—along with a measure of good luck—produced a constitution that not only solved immediate problems but also provided the means to solve new problems in the future.

Peter S. Onuf, in the second selection, argues that sharp sectional or regional differences divided the new nation and posed the real danger that the new United States could not remain united. Some argued that the only alternatives available were division of the nation into several separate states or the creation of a monarchy to impose unity. The great achievement of the founding fathers was to create a new consensus that recognized, accepted, and even promoted and protected sectional differences. The compromises necessary to create the new constitution became possible once there was acceptance of the notion of states' rights via equal representation in the Senate, an arrangement that served "to secure sectional interests without directly acknowledging their legitimacy and durability." But this concession, Onuf concludes, if it made a new consensus possible, was "fundamentally flawed," for it justified the divisions that led to the Civil War.

Edward J. Erler, in the last selection, agrees that the Constitution was the result of compromises made by the delegates in Philadelphia, but he argues that the founding fathers had no need to build a new consensus. Compromises came easily at the Philadelphia convention because an underlying philosophical agreement or consensus united the delegates, a consensus, he implies, that the delegates shared with the American people. All agreed on the principles enunciated in the Declaration of Independence, and this agreement on fundamentals made compromise on details easy. "I think there can be little doubt that the Framers were attempting to put into practice the principles of the Declaration of Independence," Erler argues.

Few historians would deny that many of the founding fathers were brilliant men; the Philadelphia convention brought together one of the most remarkable groups of men ever assembled. Yet when they probe further, historians begin to disagree. Whom did these men represent, and what were they trying to accomplish? Did the men who gathered in Philadelphia in the summer of 1787 represent a cross-section of the American people, or did they represent particular classes or property interests? There were sharp differences among the founding fathers themselves, and even sharper differences divided them from other political leaders in the new nation. What was the nature of these differences? And how important were they? Did the compromises that produced the Constitution in 1789 really end the conflicts that arose during the convention? Or did the convention compromises merely paper over sharp divisions concerning such matters as states' rights and slavery and leave them to produce later political and social conflicts?

Students attempting to answer these questions and evaluate the three interpretations that follow should be aware that they deal with two related but different questions: the views and goals of the founding fathers and the results of their handiwork.

FORREST McDONALD

Powers, Principles, and Consequences

In the truest sense of the terms, the reformation of the Constitution was simultaneously a conservative and a radical act. The word *conservative* derives from the Latin *conservare*, meaning "to guard, defend, preserve." *Radical* derives from the Latin *radix*, meaning "root, base, foundation"; to be radical is to get at the root of a matter. No abstract speculative doctrines could inform such an undertaking, and both for that reason and because of the incompatibilities amongst the doctrines themselves, the political theories and ideologies at the command of the Framers were, as we have seen, of limited practical use. Those theories and ideologies helped to shape the political perspectives of the Framers and helped to define their goals, to be sure; but as Dickinson said, experience, both their own and that of the mother country, provided the surer guide.

Moreover, restructuring the central authority from a simple unicameral Congress into a complex, self-balancing, four-branched institution was only part of the genius of what the Framers did. Quite as important in their efforts to attain their goals—cementing the Union, providing for the common defense, ensuring domestic tranquility, promoting the general welfare, and securing the citizenry in its rights of life, liberty, and property—were the allocations of powers among the branches of the central government and between it and the state governments. In this portion of their work, theory was even less relevant, and experience itself was inadequate: they could rely ultimately only on common sense, their collective wisdom, and their willingness to compromise.

So it was that the Framers brought a vast knowledge of history and the whole long tradition of civic humanism with them to Philadelphia in May of 1787, and that they departed four months later having fashioned a frame of government that necessitated a redefinition of most of the terms in which the theory and ideology of civic humanism had been discussed. Into the bargain, they intro-

---

duced an entirely new concept to the discourse, that of federalism, and in the doing, created a *novus ordo seclorum:* a new order of the ages.

It is easy to forget that the convention did not start from scratch, but was
building upon an existing constitution. Under the Articles of Confederation,
Congress had been vested with a variety of powers. One set concerned the military: Congress could appoint and commission officers in the armed services,
build and equip a navy, make rules for governing the armed forces, direct their
operations, and issue letters of marque and reprisal. In the matter of international relations, it could declare war and make peace, send and receive ambassadors, make treaties and alliances, prescribe rules for captures, and punish pira-
cies and felonies on the high seas. To enforce its admiralty powers, it could
establish courts. In domestic affairs, Congress was empowered to regulate the
value of coin, to fix uniform standards of weights and measures, to regulate trade
and manage all affairs with Indians who were "not members of any of the
states," to establish and regulate post offices, to borrow money on the credit of
the United States, and to establish courts for settling disputes between states.

Under the Constitution, Congress retained all those powers (though now
sharing, as noted, some of them with the president) and was vested with ten additional powers. Five of these were of relatively minor importance: the powers to
establish uniform naturalization and bankruptcy laws, to punish counterfeiting
of United States currency or securities, to grant copyrights and patents, to punish
offenses against the law of nations, and to acquire and exercise exclusive jurisdiction over a seat of government and other property of the Untied States. One was
important but conditional: the power to protect the several states against domestic violence, on request of the state legislature or, "when the Legislature cannot
be convened," on request of the state's chief executive.

The other new powers—taxation, regulation of commerce, regulation of the
militias, and the powers implicit in the necessary and proper clause—want closer
scrutiny. The taxing power was obviously the most important, for it gave substance and energy to the others. At the convention there was no serious resistance
to vesting Congress with broad powers of taxation, though delegates from the
southern states, jealously guarding their particular interests, saw to the insertion
of certain restrictions. One was that duties on exports were forbidden: against
the arguments of Wilson, Gouverneur Morris, Dickinson, and Madison, southerners insisted that their staples be thus exempted, and with the support of the
Massachusetts and Connecticut delegations, they carried the point. Another restriction was that "all Duties, Imports and Excises shall be uniform throughout
the United States." On August 25 James McHenry and other Marylanders, concerned lest Congress might favor the ports of other states over those of their own,
proposed the restriction as part of a larger restriction on the regulation of commerce. The proposal was committed, separated from the commercial restriction,
reported out, and, on August 31, passed without dissent. But then the committee
of style, whether intentionally or inadvertently, omitted the clause from its draft
of a constitution. The oversight was noticed and, on September 14, the restriction was restored.

Still another restriction on the taxing power was that "no Capitation or other direct Tax shall be laid except in proportion to the number of Inhabitants," in which slaves were to be reckoned by the three-fifths rule. As the North Carolina delegates reported to Governor Richard Caswell, that meant not only that slaves would not be fully taxed if Congress should resort to head taxes but also that taxes on land would be the same in the southern states as in the "Eastern States," even though "we certainly have, one with another, land of twice the value that they Possess." Indeed, this restriction was so inequitable that, for practical purposes, it virtually denied Congress the power to levy direct taxes altogether. Southerners were able to win such an advantage because they demanded much more and thus could compromise with a position that still favored them. That is, some of them had adamantly insisted upon counting slaves fully in allocating seats in the House of Representatives, upon prohibiting interference in the slave trade, and upon exempting imported slaves from import duties. When they accepted less than what they had demanded in regard to these three points, the tax advantages seemed to be a fair compensation.

The most important limitation upon the taxing power had a strange history. This was the qualification that taxes could be levied only "to pay the Debts and provide for the common Defense and general Welfare of the United States." The phraseology was derived from the language of the Articles of Confederation and was understood as prohibiting the expenditure of money for such "internal improvements" as roads and canals, since those must, of necessity, promote the particular welfare of specific states rather than the "general" welfare. Gouverneur Morris, however, had other ideas. In a private conversation with James McHenry and Nathaniel Gorham, he casually remarked that the general-welfare clause would authorize the construction of piers. McHenry was horrified by the implications of so broad an interpretation of the clause, but Morris made a clever attempt to ensure that it would in fact be so interpreted. In drafting article 1, section 8 (as principal penman for the committee of style), Morris itemized the powers of Congress in clauses, separating the clauses by semicolons. He inserted a semicolon between "To lay and collect taxes, duties, imposts and excises" and the qualifying "to pay the debts and provide for the common defense and general welfare." Given the form of the whole section, that would have made the clause a positive grant of power rather than a limitation on the taxing power. Roger Sherman, however, noticed the semicolon and called it to the attention of the other delegates, whereupon a comma was put in its place.

Two final points about taxing power need be made. One is that the states were prohibited from levying duties on imports, though they continued to be free to collect all other forms of taxes. Because import duties were by far the most bountiful source of tax revenues, this tipped the federal-state balance of power considerably in the federal direction and all but assured that Congress would find it necessary to assume responsibility for the Revolutionary War debts of the states. The other point is that except for the restrictions noted above, the taxing power of Congress was unlimited. This meant, among other things, that Congress could promote manufacturing through protective tariffs and could even create a full-fledged mercantilistic system if it so desired. Thus, as far as systems of political economy were concerned, the Constitution gave Congress a blank check.

The statement is no sooner made than it wants qualification because of the restrictions attached to the second great new power vested in Congress, the power to regulate interstate and foreign commerce. As has been noted, many southern delegates in the convention insisted upon a provision that Congress not be allowed to pass "navigation acts" except by a two-thirds majority in both houses. Several New Englanders struck an agreement with South Carolina and Georgia planters, whereby the planters helped to defeat the proposed two-thirds clause and New Englanders supported the arrangements noted earlier concerning slavery and taxation. The delegates from Maryland, who were most militantly concerned in regard to commercial regulation, then sponsored a limitation on the regulatory power, which was incorporated in article 1, section 9: "No Preference shall be given by any Regulation of Commerce or Revenue to the Ports of one State over those of another: nor shall Vessels bound to, or from, one State, be obliged to enter, clear, or pay Duties in another." That clause, together with certain restrictions on the powers of the states, ensured that no matter what system of political economy was adopted, internally the United States would be the largest area of free trade in the world.

The third important new power, regulation of the militias, was fraught with ideological overtones. The republican ideologues in the convention, expressing a view that would be echoed by many opponents of the Constitution, objected that congressional control over the militias would result in tyranny. The Connecticut federalists Ellsworth and Sherman likewise objected to such control, as did Dickinson, on the ground that the states needed to be able to defend themselves. The ranks of the federalists were divided, however, for the South Carolina delegates (like those of Georgia and New Hampshire) were acutely concerned about their military vulnerability and wanted even stronger national control of the militias than the Constitution provided. Moreover, the archrepublicans from Virginia had little fear of such control, the discipline of the Virginia militia being notoriously lax. And thus, though the anti-Federalist Richard Henry Lee could declare that "the militia are the people," in the same sense that the Greek army had been the *polis,* provision for congressional power to organize, arm, and discipline the militias and to employ them to enforce the laws of the Union, as well as to suppress insurrections and repel invasions, found its way into the Constitution. Discontent with the provision, however, would later lead to the adoption of the Second Amendment.

The fourth significant new grant of power was the power "to make all Laws which shall be necessary and proper for carrying into execution" the enumerated powers. Some such clause was indispensable, given the decision to itemize the powers of Congress; and in the convention only Gerry, Randolph, and Mason expressed objections to it. In the contests over ratification, however, opponents of the Constitution would repeatedly charge that the clause amounted to an unlimited grant of power to Congress; but then, after ratification, they reversed themselves and, to justify a narrow interpretation of the powers of Congress, insisted that the word "necessary" meant indispensably and absolutely required, which was a test of constitutionality that almost no enactment would be able to pass.

In addition to allocating powers, the Framers restricted or prohibited the exercise of certain powers, as regarded both the central authority and the states. Of the specific limitations on the powers of the national/federal government, six concerned property rights in one fashion or another: the prohibition against interference in the slave trade before 1808, the ban on export duties, the restriction regarding direct taxes, the prohibition against preferential treatment of ports, the ban on taxation of interstate commerce, and the prohibition of corruption of the blood. Six more were protective of liberty: the prohibition of the suspension of the writ of habeas corpus except in times of rebellion or invasion, the prohibition of bills of attainder and ex post facto laws, the provision for impeachment of all civil officers, the provision for jury trials in criminal cases, the narrow definition of treason, and the prohibition of religious qualifications for officeholding. Five more restrictive provisions may be regarded as gestures toward adhering to republican maxims: that money bills must originate in the House of Representatives, that no money be spent except by appropriations voted by Congress, that military appropriations be limited to two years, and that dual officeholding and titles of nobility be forbidden.

None of these elicited much discussion in the convention, except for those already mentioned and the prohibitions against bills of attainder and ex post facto laws. Gerry and McHenry proposed that pair of prohibitions on August 22. There was general agreement about bills of attainder, but Gouverneur Morris and Ellsworth said it was unnecessary to prohibit ex post facto laws, since every lawyer would agree that they were "void of themselves." Wilson added that to mention ex post facto would "proclaim that we are ignorant of the first principles of Legislation." Daniel Carroll retorted that whatever the light in which ex post facto laws might be viewed by lawyers, "the State Legislatures had passed them, and they had taken effect." Williamson added that a provision against them in the North Carolina constitution had been violated, but that a prohibition was useful anyway because "the Judges can take hold of it." The prohibition was then passed by a comfortable margin.

In placing any such restrictions in the Constitution, the Framers were introducing an element of ambiguity and were opening the door for the charge that they were being inconsistent. They deliberately refrained from putting a bill of rights in the instrument, on the logical grounds that the document established a government of limited, enumerated powers, and thus, as Hamilton put it, that there was no point in declaring "that things shall not be done which there is no power to do." This argument was criticized by pointing to the prohibition against granting titles of nobility, against suspension of habeas corpus, and the like. Yet all the constitutional prohibitions were of actions that, as British history had shown, could in fact have been legitimately taken in the absence of a specific denial of the authority.

The placing of constitutional restrictions upon the powers of the states was qualitatively a different matter. The powers of the state legislatures, within the confines of their territorial jurisdictions, were quite as unlimited as those of the

British Parliament, except for a few specific restrictions contained in the state constitutions. As James Wilson put it, in the state constitutions the people did not delegate enumerated powers but rather "invested their representatives with every right and authority which they did not in explicit terms reserve." The legislatures had further limited their own powers by adopting the Articles of Confederation. Thenceforth they could not, without the consent of Congress, send or receive ambassadors or otherwise treat with foreign crowns or states, establish treaties among themselves, maintain armies or ships of war, or engage in war except if invaded; they could not grant letters of marque and reprisal except after Congress had declared war; they could not lay imposts or other duties contrary to treaties negotiated and ratified by Congress; and they could not grant titles of nobility.

The Constitution reaffirmed those restrictions—in most instances making them absolute or nearly so—and added a number of others. The states were, for practical purposes, forbidden to tax or restrain interstate or foreign commerce, which brought about a fundamental shift of power. Like the national/federal government, the states were prohibited from passing ex post facto laws and bills of attainder; in regard to the states, however, these prohibitions were aimed more at protecting property rights (recall the wartime confiscations) than at protecting liberty. The other new restrictions were designed exclusively to prevent infringement upon property rights by the legislatures. Specifically, the states were forbidden to coin money, to emit bills of credit, to make anything but gold or silver coin legal tender in payment of debts, and to pass any law impairing the obligation of contracts.

Few delegates contested any of these restrictions but one, and several wanted in addition to forbid Congress the power to issue paper money. The exception is the contract clause, whose history is shrouded in mystery. The first proposal regarding it arose late in the convention. On August 28 the delegates voted to amend an article of the committee of detail's report to read, "No state shall coin money, nor emit bills of credit, nor make any thing but gold & silver coin a tender in payment of debts." King then moved to add, "in the words used in the Ordinance of Congs establishing new States, a prohibition on the States to interfere in private contracts." The language of the Northwest Ordinance to which King referred is significant: "And, in the just preservation of rights and property, it is understood and declared, that no law ought ever to be made, or have force in the said territory, that shall, in any manner whatever, interfere with or affect private contracts or engagements, *bona fide,* and without fraud, previously formed." It is to be observed that the use of the words *"bona fide,* and without fraud" would have left abundant room for preserving the fair-value and just-price theories of contract.

The proposal met with a generally negative reaction, though not at all for that reason. Gouverneur Morris objected that "this would be going too far." The federal courts would prevent abuses within their jurisdiction, he said, but within a state "a majority must rule, whatever may be the mischief done among themselves." Mason agreed with Morris. Madison expressed mixed feelings. Wilson supported the motion but stressed that only *retrospective* interferences were to be banned. Madison responded with a question, "Is not that already done by the prohibition of ex post facto laws." Rutledge picked up on the suggestion and offered as a substitute for King's motion the words "nor pass bills of attainder or ex post facto laws." This was approved by a seven to three vote, and thus the proposed contract clause was dropped. On the next day, John Dickinson announced that he had looked up "ex post facto" in Blackstone and had found that the term "related to criminal cases only; that they would not consequently restrain the States from retrospective laws in civil cases, and that some further provision for this purpose would be requisite."

The convention, however, did not get around to making "some further provision" or even to considering the subject again. Instead, disregarding the rejection of King's motion, the committee of style inserted it into the Constitution. That the committee would presume to include in the finished document features that the convention had either not approved or had expressly rejected can be explained by two circumstances. First, the delegates had no list of what they had agreed to: they had only a general record of the votes and proceedings, which made detailed checking on the committee of style tedious and difficult. Second, by the time the committee had finished its draft, the delegates were tired, harassed and eager to finish the work and go home. In any event, the contract clause was apparently the work of the five members of the committee of style rather than of the body of the convention.

But there are other mysteries about the clause. Morris did most of the work of the draftsmanship, and one might thus assume that he was the author of the contract clause; he was obviously audacious enough to do such a thing. But Morris had outspokenly opposed the contract clause that King had proposed, and the ground of his objection applied with equal or greater force to the final version of the clause. That leaves, as possible originators, the other four members of the committee: Madison, Johnson, King, and Hamilton. The recorded speeches and extant writings of Madison and Johnson contain nothing that would suggest that either of them regarded the contract clause as other than a redundancy, a reemphasis of the constitutional prohibitions against paper money and tender laws; and thus there is no reason to suppose that either would have proposed that it be added. King had proposed the original clause, but as indicated, the qualifications he had placed on it would greatly have reduced its potency. That leaves Hamilton as a possible source.

Hamilton's earlier career as a lawyer, his later conduct as secretary of the treasury, his reasoning in his great reports, and his avid participation in a movement to modernize the law of contractual relationships all accord with an inference that he would have advocated the enshrining in fundamental law of a broad, modern conception of contracts. He had experienced firsthand the advantages of regarding corporate charters as contracts, for he had represented stockholders after Pennsylvania had revoked the charter of the Bank of North America in 1785. Later, in an advisory opinion regarding the Yazoo land purchases, he would formulate the first thoroughly reasoned argument that the contract clause was intended to apply to public grants and charters as well as to private agreements. Hamilton was the only member of the committee who thought along such lines, except insofar as he could persuade the others. He could be persuasive, and in addition to his gifts for argument, he was a long-time intimate friend of Gouverneur Morris's, he held King almost in a hypnotic spell, and he was on intimate political (though not personal) terms with Madison. But to suggest that Hamilton was the source of the contract clause is only a suggestion; we cannot know.

In the public debates on the Constitution, two interpretations of the contract clause were advanced, and neither was the one that Hamilton would offer in his advisory opinion (and that Chief Justice John Marshall would confirm in *Fletcher* v. *Peck*). The most common view was that the prohibition against legislative impairment of contractual obligations was simply a catchall extension of the bans on paper money and legal-tender laws. As James Wilson put it during the Pennsylvania ratifying convention, "There are other ways of avoiding payment of debts," such as "installment acts, and other acts of a similar effect." Madison regarded the clause in a similar, though somewhat broader, light in *Federalist* number 44. He treated it together with the other restrictions in article 1, section 10, as being designed to stop "the fluctuating policy which has directed the public councils." Madison attributed "legislative interferences, in cases affecting personal rights," to "enterprising and influential speculators" whose activities gained profit for themselves at the expense of "the more-industrious and less-informed part of the community." Luther Martin, himself an enterprising and influential speculator who opposed ratification, interpreted the contract clause in essentially the same way that Wilson and Madison did, but he painted the implications in different colors. The clause, Martin said, would prevent the states from stopping "the wealthy creditor and the moneyed man from totally destroying the poor, though industrious debtor."

Quite a different construction of the contract clause was advanced by opponents of the Constitution in Virginia and North Carolina. In Virginia, George Mason and Patrick Henry interpreted the clause as applying to public as well as private obligations, and they objected that it would necessitate the redemption of old continental bills of credit, which had depreciated to a thousand for one and had long since ceased to circulate. The face value of those bills had been over $200 million, and Mason and Henry argued that the resulting tax burden would be crushing. Madison and other defenders of the Constitution insisted, not to the satisfaction of their opponents, that article 5 (making public debts "as valid" under the Constitution as under the Confederation) covered the continental paper and that it was unaffected by article 1, section 10. In North Carolina, opponents of the Constitution reiterated the argument of Henry and Mason but added a twist of their own. North Carolina, like several other states, had issued paper currency and had made it legal tender, and obligations payable in that paper had formed the basis of a large number of contracts. The ban on paper money, anti-Federalists pointed out, would outlaw that currency, and the legal-tender clause would alter those contracts; and yet the contract clause itself prohibited them from being impaired. Champions of ratification could offer no satisfactory rebuttal, for the last-minute insertion of the clause had in fact created a temporary contradiction.

One more point about the restrictions on the powers of the states wants making. Madison's interpretation of the general purpose of article 1, section 10—that it was intended as a check upon "the fluctuating policy which has directed the public councils"—accords with the evidence contained in the records of the Constitutional Convention. That being so, it is possible to regard the supreme-law clause as vesting the judiciary, both federal and state, with the veto power over state legislation which Madison had wanted to vest in Congress or jointly in Congress and the Supreme Court. In other words, article 1, section 10, taken together with the supreme-law clause in article 6, can be interpreted as having been designed to give to the courts the power to review state laws but not acts of Congress. Such an interpretation, to be sure, is contrary to Hamilton's argument in *Federalist* number 78 and to almost all constitutional scholarship. And yet, when the supreme-law clause was introduced in the convention, it was expressly offered as a substitute for the proposed congressional veto on state legislation; and shortly after the convention had adjourned, Madison tacitly confirmed this interpretation in a letter to Jefferson and repeated his conviction that the substitution would prove to be inadequate. Moreover, the belief that the supreme-law clause established the power of judicial review over state laws but not over acts of Congress obviously had widespread currency, as is attested by the intensely hostile reaction in the Congress and in the press on the two occasions on which, before the Civil War, the Supreme Court dared to declare an act of Congress unconstitutional.

The constitutional reallocation of powers created a new form of government, unprecedented under the sun. Every previous national authority either had been centralized or else had been a confederation of sovereign constituent states. The new American system was neither one nor the other: it was a mixture of both. Madison developed the variations on this theme in *Federalist* number 39. After first calling attention to the checks inherent in having officials in the several branches be elected for periods of differing lengths, he analyzed the Constitution in respect to "the foundation on which it is to be established; to the sources from which its ordinary powers are to be drawn; to the operation of those powers; to the extent of them; and to the authority by which future changes in the government are to be introduced." He concluded that the Constitution was federal in regard to the first and fourth of these criteria, mixed in regard to the second and fifth, and national only in regard to the third. In sum, it was partly national, partly federal—not the purely national form that Madison himself had championed during the convention.

If Madison found it expedient not to divulge that he had opposed the very system he was now defending—and it seems probable that a purely national system would never have been ratified—John Dickinson similarly found it prudent not to repeat out of doors his arguments in favor of a mixed system. In his "Letters of Fabius" (notice the pseudonym, which suggested to his readers that the Constitution was a slow, cautious, conservative undertaking), Dickinson made no comments about using the states as structural substitutes for the English baronies or about fashioning the Senate in the mold of the House of Lords, which was indeed the subject of charges made by many opponents of ratification. Rather, he offered another justification of the partly national, partly federal system. The principle underlying it, he wrote, was "that a territory of such extent as that of United America, could not be safely and advantageously governed, but by a combination of republics, each retaining all the rights of supreme sovereignty, excepting such as ought to be contributed to the union." To enable these republics to preserve those sovereignties, they were "represented in a body by themselves, and with equal suffrage."

In defending these arrangements, the Framers had to work their way around a knotty theoretical problem. Blackstone and many other commentators had insisted that sovereignty, the supreme law-making power, was by definition indivisible; the cliché, repeated both in England and in America, was that it was "a solecism in politics for two coordinate sovereignties to exist together," for that would be "*imperium* in *imperio*." Hamilton had advanced the same idea at the convention, declaring flatly that "Two Sovereignties can not co-exist within the same limits." Yet in *Federalist* number 34 he asserted that in the Roman republic sovereignty had in fact been divided between the Comitia centuriata, in which voting "was so arranged as to give a superiority to the patrician interest," and the Comitia tributa, in which "the plebian interest had an entire predominancy." These were not branches of the same legislature, Hamilton said, but were "distinct and independent legislatures, . . . each having power to *annul* or *repeal* the acts of the other. . . . And yet these two legislatures coexisted for ages, and the Roman republic attained to the utmost height of human greatness."

Hamilton was able to reverse himself in that manner because he—along with Wilson, Ellsworth, and various others—had conceived of a means of attacking the problem in an ingenious way. The key to the new approach was the proposition that sovereignty embraced a large number and a wide variety of different specific powers: obviously these specific powers could be assigned to different governments, to different branches of the same government, or to different persons serving within the same branch of a government. Hamilton spelled out the implications in his opinion on the constitutionality of the Bank of the United States. "The powers of sovereignty," Hamilton wrote, "are in this country divided between the National and State Governments," and "each of the *portions* of powers delegated to the one or to the other . . . is . . . sovereign *with regard to its proper objects.*" It followed from this "that each has sovereign power as to *certain things,* and not as to *other things.* To deny that the Government of the United States has sovereign power as to its declared purposes & trusts, because its power does not extend to all cases," Hamilton continued, would also be to deny that the states retained sovereignty "in any case," because they were forbidden to do a number of things. "And thus the United States would furnish the singular spectacle of a *political society* without *sovereignty,* or of a people *governed* without *government.*"

There was one crucial feature of the scheme of things which, since it lay beyond the argument he was making on that occasion, Hamilton declined to address. Sovereignty, in its eighteenth-century signification, was absolute: sovereignty comprehended the power to command anything and everything that was naturally possible. No one contended that the combined powers of the state and federal governments were absolute, for there were some powers that remained beyond the reach of both. Logically, those powers must reside somewhere else.

The Framers made clear where that was—and incidentally pointed to where sovereignty had devolved upon independence—in the procedure they prescribed for ratification of the Constitution.

Article 7 provided that the "Ratification of the Conventions of nine States, shall be sufficient for the Establishment of this Constitution between the States so ratifying the Same." That provision by-passed the prescribed method for amending the Articles of Confederation, which required that amendments be proposed by Congress and be approved by the legislatures of all thirteen states. It was not, however, as many enemies of the Constitution charged and as some scholars have asserted, either "illegal" or a usurpation. In a resolution appended to the Constitution and "laid before Congress," the convention recommended that Congress forward the document to the states and that "it should afterwards be submitted to a Convention of Delegates, chosen in each State by the People thereof, under the Recommendation of its Legislature, for their Assent and Ratification." Congress unanimously resolved to follow that recommendation, and the legislatures of all thirteen states voted to abide by it. In so doing, Congress and the legislatures approved article 7 of the Constitution and thereby constructively amended the Articles of Confederation in regard to the amendment process; and they did so in accordance with the stipulations in the Articles themselves.

The Constitution was submitted to state conventions for several reasons. One was political: the revised procedure simplified ratification. Another was theoretical: as Madison pointed out during the first week of the convention, a constitution that was ratified by the legislatures could be construed as being only a treaty "among the Governments of Independent States," and thus it could be held that "a breach of any one article, by any of the parties, absolved the other parties" from any further obligation. Accordingly, Madison urged that the Constitution be submitted to "the supreme authority of the people themselves." But it could not be submitted to the people of the United States *as* people of the United States because of two prior commitments, one theoretical and one legal. The theoretical commitment was that no matter how Locke is read, the states as political societies, as opposed to the governments thereof, had not ceased to exist upon the declaring of independence. The legal commitment was that each of the states already had a constitution. The Constitution amended each of the state constitutions in a number of ways, and if it were adopted by a majority vote of the whole people, the people in some states would be altering both the political societies and the constitutions of other states. This, in the nature of things, they could not have the authority to do. The Constitution must, then, be submitted for ratification by each of the thirteen political societies, which is to say by the people of the several states in their capacities as people of the several states. This unmistakably implied that the source of sovereignty was the people of the states and that the residue of sovereignty that was committed neither to the national/federal nor to the state governments remained in them—an implication that was subsequently made explicit by the Tenth Amendment.

Such a compact was also something new. It was not Lockean, for the Lockean compact was between the people, on one side, and the prince, sovereign, or rulers on the other. Nor was it a compact among the people to govern themselves, as some modern scholars have contended. Rather, it was a compact among political societies, which were themselves, according to a Lockean principle, indissoluble—a principle that is explicitly confirmed in the Constitution itself by the provision in article 4, section 3, which prevents the states from being divided without their consent, and is implicitly confirmed by article 5, which exempts equal suffrage by states in the Senate from the possibility of amendment.

Because it was a new kind of compact, there were no guidelines, either in theory or in history, as to whether the compact could be dissolved, and if so, on what conditions. The Supreme Court would rule in *Texas* v. *White,* almost a century later, that the Constitution "looks to an indestructible Union, composed of indestructible states." No less important a Framer than Gouverneur Morris, however, argued to the contrary: during the War of 1812 he contended that secession, under certain circumstances, was entirely constitutional. So, too, did the southern states in 1860–1861; significantly, those states declared their secession from the constitutional Union by means of precisely the same instrumentality as that by which they had entered it, namely, conventions elected for the purpose. Closer to the founding era, many a public figure during the 1790s declared that the states could interpose their power between their citizens and the power of the federal government, and talk of secession was not unknown.

But such a question, like the earlier question of independence, could be settled only by the arbitrament of force, and the Framers' whole purpose was to establish a government based upon consent. Having been through one Machiavellian return to first principles and having seen the havoc it had wrought, they were anxious to avoid another. It was toward that end that they addressed such careful attention to the niceties of legitimizing the Constitution, and it was toward the same end that they specified the legitimate means for constitutional change in future. In that sense, the establishment of the Constitution completed and perfected the Revolution.

Another question about the nature of the constitutional Union is likewise problematical. The compact was among previously existing political societies, but it was expressly provided that new political societies might be formed and admitted to the Union. In contemplation were the creation of new states in the Northwest Territory and in what would become Kentucky and Tennessee. That is clear both from the debates in the convention and from the first paragraph of article 4, section 3 (though working out that section had involved considerable rancor and a movement, led by Luther Martin, to permit Congress to break up the larger states without their consent). But the new states thus provided for would be within the existing territorial confines of the United States, and there was an unspoken assumption among most Americans, including the Framers, that some day the United States would acquire Canada, Louisiana, and the Floridas. Some of the Framers, most influentially Gouverneur Morris, wanted to discourage the expansion of the population into that "remote wilderness," partly because expansion would retard intensive economic development in the older areas and partly because experience had convinced them that frontiersmen were the least desirable and least governable of citizens. Accordingly, Morris proposed that territory acquired in future be forever governed as provinces, with no prospect of statehood. He was unable to carry the point directly, but he deliberately phrased the first clause of the second paragraph of article 4, section 3, in such a way as to make possible permanent central control of new territories: "The Congress shall have Power to dispose of and make all needful Rules and Regulations respecting the Territory or other Property belonging to the United States."

Morris's position was entirely contrary to the tenet of agrarian republicanism which held that territorial expansion was essential so as to keep agriculture paramount to other forms of economic activity; but the clause went unnoticed in the contests over ratification of the Constitution. When it at last became relevant, upon the occasion of the Louisiana Purchase, shifts in constitutional positions became necessary. Until that time, agrarian republicans, under the leadership of Jefferson and Madison, had carried the compact-among-states doctrine of the origins of the Constitution far beyond what could be justified historically or logically. To combat various Federalist measures that they regarded as pernicious and to justify state resistance to those measures, they insisted that the Constitution was not merely a compact among members of different political societies but, rather, was one between sovereign states as sovereign states, as the Articles of Confederation had been. When the United States acquired Louisiana, however—which was constitutionally justifiable under the treaty-making power—the Republicans faced a dilemma. Their ideology told them to provide for dividing the Louisiana Territory into states, so as to make settlement attractive. Their theory of the nature of the Union told them to interpret article 4, section 3, as Morris had intended for it to be interpreted, because otherwise the Union would ultimately consist of more states than had been parties to the original compact, and their theory would be reduced to rubble. They followed the dictates of agrarianism over those of constitutional scruples; and when they did so, Federalists reversed themselves and took up the compact-among-states doctrine in resistance.

Federalists and Republicans. It was not entirely true that, as Jefferson would aver in his Inaugural Address, all Americans were simultaneously federalists and republicans, with the lower-case "f" and "r"; but it was nearly so. Both terms, however, with their variants, acquired new meanings upon the establishment of the Constitution. Earlier, *federal*—as well as *foederal, federation, federalist*—had been used in two principal ways in America, one being neutral and nonideological, the other expressing a political stance. The neutral usage was interchangeable with confederation; it was descriptive of a league of otherwise autonomous states for purposes of mutual defense, trade, or any other shared objective. The nonneutral usage was more or less interchangeable with *nationalist* or *continentalist* or *unionist;* as the Pennsylvania anti-Federalist George Bryan wrote, "The name of Federalists, or Federal men, grew up at New York and the eastern states, some time before the calling of the Convention, to denominate such as were attached to the general support of the United States, in opposition to those who preferred local and particular advantage." In that sense it was appropriate for champions of the Constitution to designate themselves as Federalists and to call their opponents anti-Federalists—though it was equally appropriate, in light of the neutral definition and of the transfers of power inherent in ratification of the Constitution, that some anti-Federalists should insist that they were acting on "true *foederal principles*" and that Federalists might properly be called consolidationists. In any event, after the adoption of the Constitution, a federal system meant one in which sovereignty was divided; thenceforth, only *confederation* was used to describe a league of sovereign entities.

As for *republic* and *republican,* we have surveyed various understandings of those terms; and it should be obvious that none of them is applicable to the national/federal government established by the Constitution. Anti-Federalists repeatedly attacked the Constitution on that ground, in two interrelated ways. One was that history and theory alike thought that republican forms of government were suitable only to small territories and among relatively homogeneous peoples. Only a small republic could maintain the voluntary attachment of the people and a voluntary obedience to its laws, make government responsible to the people, and inculcate the people with republican virtue. In addition, anti-Federalists pointed out that the Constitution violated contemporary republican principles in an assortment of particulars, ranging from an improper mixture of legislative and executive powers to the lack of a bill of rights; and they charged that in the absence of voluntary obedience to the laws, the national government would be compelled to force obedience by means of large standing armies.

Federalists sought to counter such arguments; but to do so, they must coin new definitions of what a republic was. Hamilton faced the issue in *Federalist* number 9. Had it been necessary for the United States to have copied directly from the ancient models, Hamilton wrote, he would have preferred to abandon the republican experiment altogether, for "the petty republics of Greece and Italy . . . were kept in a state of perpetual vibration between the extremes of tyranny and anarchy." Over the centuries, however, "the science of politics . . . has received great improvement." The ancients knew nothing, or knew but imperfectly, about "various principles . . . now well understood," such as the separation of powers, checks and balances, "courts composed of judges holding their offices during good behavior," and the "representation of the people in the legislature by deputies of their own election." These "wholly new discoveries," Hamilton contended, were "powerful means, by which the excellences of republican government may be retained and its imperfections lessened or avoided." In actuality, those "new discoveries" had excellent moderating effects upon mixed governments, but they had nothing whatever to do with the question, whether the American national/federal government was or was not republican. Hamilton was able to go part of the way toward connecting republicanism with constitutional order by pointing out similarities between the American system and the ancient Lycian confederacy, which Montesquieu had regarded as the best of the confederated Greek republics. After that, however, Hamilton abandoned the subject; to him the whole question was one of speculative theory, not "science."

Madison was more persistent. In *Federalist* number 14 he attempted a baldfaced redefinition of terms. One must distinguish between a republic and a democracy, he wrote. "In a democracy, the people meet and exercise the government in person; in a republic, they assemble and administer it by their representatives and agents. A democracy, consequently, will be confined to a small spot. A republic may be extended over a large region." It was a mistake, propagated by "subjects either of an absolute or limited monarchy," to cite as specimens of republics "the turbulent democracies of ancient Greece and modern Italy." Most "of the popular governments of antiquity were of the democratic species,"

Madison insisted. Knowing full well (and doubtless recognizing that his readers also knew full well) that his argument would not wash—because some of the "popular governments" to which he referred were aristocracies or oligarchies, some employed the representative principle, and some had elective monarchs—Madison temporarily left the subject there.

He picked it up again and made a second effort in *Federalist* number 39. In seeking to determine "the distinctive characters of the republican form," Madison wrote in that essay, one must disregard "the application of the term by political writers." Holland, "in which no particle of the supreme authority is derived from the people, has passed almost universally under the denomination of a republic." The same was true of Venice, where "a small body of hereditary nobles" exercised "absolute power over the great body of the people." Even Poland, "a mixture of aristocracy and of monarchy in their worst forms, has been dignified with the same appellation." And England, with a mixture of republican, monarchical, and aristocratic principles, had likewise erroneously been so called. All previous writers on politics had been wrong, Madison asserted. A republic, he declared, was nothing more and nothing less than "a government which derives all its powers directly or indirectly from the great body of the people, and is administered by persons holding their offices during pleasure, for a limited period, or during good behavior."

It can be maintained that in setting aside every political writer from Plato to Montesquieu, Madison was, in these two essays, being more than a little presumptuous, even arrogant. But in truth, because the Framers had devised a *novus ordo seclorum,* they had rendered all previous political vocabulary obsolete as it pertained to the government of the United States. That government defied categorization by any existing nomenclature: it was not a monarchy, nor an aristocracy, nor a democracy, neither yet was it a mixed form of government, nor yet a confederated republic. It was what it was, and if Madison was presumptuous in appropriating the word *republic* to describe it, he was also a prophet, for thenceforth *republic* would mean precisely what Madison said it meant.

To treat of republicanism as it pertains to the national/federal government, however, does not exhaust the subject, for there remained the state governments. Article 4, section 4, provides that "The United States shall guarantee to every State in this Union a Republican Form of Government." The document offers no hints as to what the operative words mean; indeed, the clause contains the Constitution's only reference to republicanism. But it was understood by all that the "Republican Form of Government" clause neither mandated any structural changes in the state governments nor limited their powers. The only limitations are those in article 1, section 10.

Broadly speaking, the powers that the states retained fell under the rubric "internal police," or simply the police power: the states had the powers of the *polis.* These included not only the definition and punishment of crimes and the administration of justice but also all matters concerning the health, manners, morals, safety, and welfare of the citizenry. Despite the assertions of some anti-Federalists, the states retained the police powers exclusively. These powers were nearly unlimited, and they were not affected by the subsequent adoption of the bill of rights. For example, the states could still, in the interest of public morality, establish the mode and manner of religious worship and instruction, and they could levy taxes for the support of religion—as Connecticut and Massachusetts continued to do for many years. They could stifle dissent, stifle freedom of the press, of speech, of inquiry. They could regulate food, drink, and clothing. They could do all these things and more, in the name of the common weal. They were, in sum, the American republics in the traditional meaning of that term.

But there is a flaw in that description of things. As we have seen, both theory and tradition indicated that republics could be viable only in limited territories with homogeneous populations. Anti-Federalists criticized the Constitution on that ground, arguing that only a confederation was suitable for an area so large as the United States. In rebuttal, Hamilton, Madison, Wilson, Dickinson and other Federalists developed the idea of the extended republic and recited its advantages over earlier forms; and they also pointed out that the states themselves were far too large to be governed as traditional republics.

Their arguments were sound as far as they went, but they tended to overlook the fact that the constitutional order, in the circumstances, confirmed that the country was not to be one republic or even thirteen, but a multitude of them. For the United States was a nation composed of several thousand insular communities, each of which exercised virtually absolute powers over its members through two traditional institutions, the militias and the juries. On a day-to-day basis, it was the militias, not the army of the United States, that protected the public safety; it was the juries, not the president or the state governors, who enforced the law; and it was the juries, and not either judges or legislators, who spoke authoritatively as to what the law was.

Anti-Federalists feared, or professed to fear, that the Constitution would undermine these insular republics by vesting the national/federal government with control over both the militias and the juries. Their arguments regarding the militias were hyperbolic and riddled with self-contradictions, and Federalists had no difficulty in rebutting them—as, for example, Hamilton did in *Federalist* number 29. Criticism of the Constitution in regard to juries, however, rested on more solid foundations. One ground of objection was that though trial by jury in criminal cases was provided for, the Supreme Court's "appellate Jurisdiction, both as to Law and Fact," effectively nullified the power of juries in such cases. The other ground was that the Constitution did not make any provision for jury trials in civil cases at all. Hamilton attempted to answer the anti-Federalists on both counts in *Federalist* number 81, but his arguments were highly technical and not especially convincing. The first objection was at least partially overcome by the double-jeopardy clause of the Fifth Amendment and by the procedural rights guaranteed in that and in the Sixth Amendment. The second was met with the Seventh Amendment, but the language of that amendment provided means by which the unchecked powers of juries would ultimately be brought under control: it provided that in civil cases, "the right of trial by jury shall be preserved, and no fact tried by a jury, shall be otherwise re-examined in any Court of the United States, than according to the rules of the common law." Limiting the restriction to reexamination of facts effectively confirmed the power of appellate courts to set aside jury findings in matters of law—a striking example of the truth of Hamilton's warning, in *Federalist* number 84, that a bill of rights "would afford a colorable pretext" for "the doctrine of constructive powers." Within a generation after the adoption of the Constitution, the process of "Mansfieldizing" American juries would be well under way, and within another generation, their power to rule on matters of law would be almost entirely gone.

But the curtailment of the juries, in their capacity as a multiplicity of small republics, came about not as a consequence of legal niceties but because they had, in that capacity, become anachronistic. They were barriers to the rule of law, in the sense of uniform and predictable rules of conduct within a jurisdiction; they were barriers to the expression of the general will, as voiced through legislative assemblies; and they were barriers to the onward flow of history, for a new world of competitive, acquisitive individualism was beginning to replace the old world of communitarian consensualism which the jury system symbolized and embodied.

On the last two counts the Constitution itself was somewhat anachronistic. That it thwarted the general will was a matter of design. To be sure, the precise blend of powers at the national/federal level, the distribution of powers among different levels of government, and the provisions for choosing officials in different branches for different periods of time were products of negotiation and compromise; but they also reflected the Framers' goal of preventing self-government from degenerating into majoritarian tyranny. The constitutional order could be described as republican only by employing a new definition of a term that had always been broad and imprecise. It could not be described as *democratic* except through a violent distortion of the language, for that term had a more specific meaning; nor could it be properly described even as a *representative democracy,* for parts of it represented nobody and other parts did not represent the *demos.*

From the perspective of what had gone before, the Constitution marked the culmination of a tradition of civic humanism that dated back more than two millennia and of a common-law tradition that dated back many centuries. But the order from which it sprang was already crumbling, and soon it was to be destroyed by a host of minor currents and events and by three developments of monumental force: the adoption of the Hamiltonian financial system, the French Revolution, and the enormous commercial expansion that accompanied the long succession of international wars which began in 1792. Together, these ushered in the Age of Liberalism, the Age of Capitalism and Democracy. The ensuing society of acquisitive individualists had neither room for nor need of the kind of virtuous public servants who so abundantly graced the public councils during the Founding Era.

Nevertheless, the Framers looked forward in time as well as backwards. For one thing, their plans and hopes that the *Optimates* might be recruited for national service materialized. For the better part of four decades—except during the late 1790s, when the scurrilousness of partisan politics temporarily made positions in government unattractive—the men who served the nation were of a quality not far beneath that of the Framers themselves. After that, the *Populares* took over, and a race of pygmies came to infest the public councils. By that time, however, it made little difference. The order was firmly established and self-maintaining: constitutional government had become part of the second nature of *homo politicus Americanus.*

That the Framers were able to achieve so mightily may be explained in terms of a model that Adam Smith posited in his *Theory of Moral Sentiments.* In times of civil discontent and disorder, Smith wrote, two kinds of leaders tend to arise. One kind of leader, infected with the "spirit of system," tends to "hold out some plausible plan of reformation," which he pretends "will not only remove the inconveniences and relieve the distresses immediately complained of" but will also prevent such from ever arising again. To that end he proposes "to new-model the constitution" and becomes "so enamoured with the supposed beauty of his own ideal plan of government" that he insists upon establishing it "completely and in all its parts, without any regard either to the great interests or to the strong prejudices which may oppose it: he seems to imagine that he can arrange the different members of a great society . . . as the hand arranges the different pieces upon a chessboard."

The other kind of leader acts "with proper temper and moderation," and will "respect the established powers and privileges even of individuals, and still more those of the great orders and societies into which the state is divided." He will accommodate "his public arrangements to the confirmed habits and prejudices of the people" and thereby will become able to "assume the greatest and noblest of all characters, that of the reformer and legislator of a great state; and, by the wisdom of his institutions, secure the internal tranquility and happiness of his fellow-citizens for many succeeding generations."

Both kinds of leaders were there in Philadelphia during the summer of 1787, and the second kind prevailed. They devised a new order out of materials prescribed by the ages, and they were wise enough to institutionalize the pluralism with which they worked and to draw their Constitution loosely enough so that it might live and breathe and change with time.

But perhaps that was not it at all. Perhaps, as Bismarck is reported to have said, a special Providence takes care of fools, drunks, and the United States of America. Surely the Founders believed the last of these.

Peter S. Onuf

Constitutional Politics: States, Sections, and the National Interest

Ideally the federal Constitution would create "a more perfect Union." But was a stronger central government compatible with the "Union" most Americans cherished? Federalists insisted that the union was more than a league of distinct, sovereign states, dedicated simply to collective security. As long as the states continued to control the central government, the union would remain radically imperfect and all efforts to amend the Articles of Confederation were bound to fail. Under the existing, "imbecilic" system, they argued, the true national interest could never be effectively promoted—or even recognized.

But proponents of constitutional reform had to overcome formidable obstacles. It was easy enough for them to demonstrate the defects of the Confederation Congress; it was much more difficult to redefine "union" in a way that would rationalize the new regime's redistribution of power. Federalists had to persuade skeptical voters that a transcendent national interest really existed, while reassuring them that the price of a more "energetic" government would not be the loss of individual liberties or states rights.

The authors of the Articles that were sent out to the states in 1777 and finally ratified in 1781 had been determined not to recreate the tyrannical central authority that had driven the colonists to revolution. According to Article II, "Each state retains its sovereignty, freedom, and independence": this union would be based on consent, not coercion. During the war, the states cooperated effectively, recognizing the central role of Congress and the Continental Army in vindicating American rights and securing the benefits of self-government. For enthusiastic Revolutionaries, union as means converged with union as end: because republican citizens and states were naturally drawn to each other, the elimination of Britain's corrupting rule would usher in a millennium of harmony and peace.

Reprinted from *Toward a More Perfect Union* by Neil L. York, ed. by permission of the State University of New York Press. From Neil L. York, ed., *Toward a More Perfect Union: Six Essays on the Constitution* (Provo, Utah: Brigham Young University, 1988), pp. 29–57.

134

Yet, proponents of the new Constitution insisted, such a voluntaristic and consensual "union" had proven inadequate to the exigencies of the postwar period. Furthermore, the tendency to think of union in these terms worked against the institution of a more energetic government, capable of enforcing its will across the continent. Any real or imagined threat to particular rights or interests could be resisted on principled grounds for violating the true spirit of the union. The challenge to reformers was to show that their proposed system was compatible with the genius of American politics: they had to convince voters that the American union would not be destroyed, but would instead be made more "perfect" under the Constitution. Without abandoning the revolutionary commitment to republican liberty, reformers promoted a new conception of the union grounded in a more substantial idea of the national interest.

Enlightened Self-Interest

In April 1787 a Boston writer lamented the disjointed state of the union:

We are no longer United States, because we are not under any form of energetic compact. The breath of jealousy has blown the cobweb of our confederacy asunder. Every link of the chain of union is separated from its companion. We live it is true under the appearance of friendship, but we secretly hate and envy, and endeavour to thwart the interest of each other.

As this writer saw it, the nation had been reduced to the tattered remnants of a defensive league, held together more by "a principle of fear" than by a common commitment to republican liberty. Now that the war was over, he continued, many Americans believed that elaborate collective security arrangements were unnecessary. Congress, as a result, was on the verge of collapse. But Americans would be foolish to rely on the spontaneous revival of union in the event of future attacks, even if external threats, by enforcing union, had thus far kept the states from despoiling one another. Were "it not for the British colonies and garrisons that surround us," the Boston writer concluded, "we should probably very soon contend in the field for empire."

The crucial rhetorical move in this essay was to suggest that the existing union was artificial, that it had been imposed on the states by the exigencies of the war. The union, another writer suggested, had been British, not American: "the English army" took the place of an American "executive" by forcing unified action; meanwhile "the zeal and fears of the people kept them in tolerable subordination" to Congress. Even as American arms triumphed, the states remained dependent on Britain for whatever unity they enjoyed. British commentators recognized the reactive character of the American union, concluding that Britain would sooner achieve its goals of keeping the new nation weak by avoiding the battlefield and letting the Americans destroy one another. Although the anticipated bloodbath had not yet occurred—and counterrevolution was thus delayed—many Americans were convinced by 1787 that the new nation's independence was jeopardized by the lack of an "energetic" central government. The challenge was to create an authentically American union that could hold its own in a hostile world while enabling enterprising American citizens to pursue and achieve happiness.

Reformers advanced the paradoxical argument that a weak union had been sufficient during wartime but woefully inadequate since the peace. The "positive injunction of the law" was not necessary during the war, because the "interests" and "passions" of the people were easily mobilized "in the pursuit of an important object." But the *"acquisition"* and *"preservation"* of American independence were two different things. "Such was the fervour of liberty and such the ready obedience of the people to slight recommendations," a New York essayist told the "Political Freethinkers of America," that Congress had "formed a set of *faint rules*"—the Articles of Confederation—"which seemed rather to anticipate than to cement a federal combination." In the postwar period, however, as "America sat down in peace among the governors of the earth," the debilities of the union became increasingly obvious. As Thomas Pownall, the former royal governor of Massachusetts, told his American friends in 1783, the American "Sovereign must now come forward amongst the Nations, as an active existing Agent." Otherwise, the great gains of the Revolution would soon be forfeited as the new nation collapsed into disunion, anarchy, and counterrevolution.

Reformers portrayed the weak union under the Articles as unnatural. They emphasized the discrepancy between a general, popular commitment to national unity and political structures that effectively subverted it. Commenting on the "settlement of so many great Controversies" between the states, despite these inadequate structures, John Adams concluded that "the Union has great weight in the Minds of the People." This attachment was not merely sentimental: the people identified their own interests with the interests of the nation as a whole. They recognized, a proponent of the new Constitution insisted, that the "true interests of the several parts of the Confederation are the same." Federalists contrasted the naturalness of a more perfect union with the artificial state interests that now made the formulation of national policy—not to mention its execution—virtually impossible. In short, the nation was not represented in the present union. The result was the "novel" spectacle of a "numerous and increasing people, and a boundless territory governed by a *committee of ways and means*," a potentially powerful and prosperous nation without a true government.

Constitutional reformers mixed counsels of prudence—asserting that victory in the Revolution had not secured perpetual peace and that Americans must be ever ready to defend their independence—with paeans to the new nation's vast potential for economic development. An Albany writer thus proclaimed that the Constitution "will unite under one head, and bring to one point, the resources, strength and commerce of this country, and subsequently serve to render us wealthy, respectable, and powerful, as a mercantile as well as a warlike people."

The Federalists' appeal to enlightened self-interest performed several important functions. First, they suggested that there was a positive, substantial national interest shared by all Americans, not just the small class of merchants, military men, and politicians who had taken such a prominent role in earlier efforts to strengthen the central government. The deterioration of national authority under the Articles thwarted enterprising Americans generally. The prospective interests of myriad citizens clearly transcended state boundaries, thus enabling Federalists to portray state sovereignty as an artificial barrier to popular enterprise. But most importantly, evocations of boundless prosperity enabled Federalists to develop a new conception of union and proclaim that its promise could only be fulfilled if a suitably effective national government was instituted.

The Federalist appeal to interest did not necessarily reflect a waning attachment to republican ideals, although this is what Antifederalists concluded. Constitutional reformers had long argued that the habitual identification of narrow, selfish interests with republican principles gave both "principle" and "interest" a bad name. In fact, the pursuit of individual interest should serve the national interest, wrote "Lycurgus"—provided "the sentiments of mind bear some proportion to the objects surrounding it." True patriots, he suggested, were both visionary and practical enough to exploit nature's gifts: "The works of nature are certainly much superior in this country to those in any other that has yet been discovered." "Cato" also emphasized the importance of developing the continent's natural advantages for "national happiness and respectability." Unfortunately, too many Americans were "influenced by partial and incomplete notions of civil and political liberty," and believed that "our deliverance from Britain" was a sufficient guarantee of the nation's welfare. Their mistake, "Cato" explained, was to juxtapose private interest and public good, thus rendering "liberty" a principle of mutual suspicion rather than collective enterprise. But "private happiness" and the "glory and security" of society were reciprocal:

The idea that union is the assurance of private security, has induced [individuals] not only to unite, but to feel a most sensible interest in the safety of the state, its dignity, its capacity and power. It is a general principle that this concern, this attachment to one's country, results from an ardent and active desire of private safety and happiness: If this be not true, Patriotism is an inexplicable affection, founded on no human principles, and embracing a visionary and fantastical object.

Misguided republicans who preached austerity and self-denial rejected nature's gifts and undermined the foundations of social union. This false opposition of liberty and union obstructed every effort to resuscitate the feeble Congress, dividing and impoverishing the states and jeopardizing their independence.

Reformers sought to discredit the "partial and incomplete" notions of republican liberty that threatened to betray the new nation's dazzling promise. Always assuming the worst about each other and therefore unable to formulate effective national policies, Americans so far had squandered their natural advantages. As a result, "Observator" wrote, "our public, political interests, and with them individual interests (for they will stand or fall together) cannot be promoted, but must be neglected, and in the end inevitably ruined." "Motives of self-interest" and "patriotism" thus converged, another writer agreed, in recommending the "radical cure" of a more powerful Congress that could regulate trade in the national interest and "counteract those illiberal and impolitic systems, whose influence, like that of a malignant comet, has operated so banefully throughout the states." Only with the institution of an effective national government, "Observator" concluded, would it be possible to unite the states in "one consistent plan of measures," and so "unite all the streams of water on the continent, and confine them in one channel."

Nationalism and Sectionalism

Appeals to enlightened self-interest suggested an attractive new conception of union. But, as Federalists acknowledged when they distinguished "real" from "apparent" interests, different definitions of interest could lead in different directions. Antifederalists were not convinced that "the people of the United States have one common interest" or that the integrated development of the continent's resources was somehow decreed by nature. If "interest is the band of social union," Timothy Bloodworth told the North Carolina ratifying convention, the American union could not long survive. Dismissing fanciful visions of future harmony and boundless prosperity, Bloodworth drew attention to the existing array of "jarring interests"—the differences in "soil, climate, produce, and every thing"—that divided "the Eastern, Southern, and the Middle States." In view of such differences, any augmentation of national power was bound to benefit one section at the others' expense.

In the years leading up to the Philadelphia Convention, advocates of regional interests pushed for more effective national regulation and joined in disparaging state particularism. Discordant state policies subverted the effective defense or promotion of sectional interests. At the same time, however, intersectional conflict raised concern about the potential abuse of national power should one section or another gain control of Congress. Thus, although many leading politicians throughout the country were apparently united in bemoaning the excesses of the states, their growing awareness of distinctive regional interests threatened to preclude any coordinated response to the looming "crisis." Because the present government could not counter these centrifugal tendencies, the union was in danger of collapsing.

Impasse in Congress meant inaction, a Philadelphian wrote in 1785, even though "the necessities and opposite interests of the constituent states, brook no delay nor doubt." If Congress failed to respond to these demands, he warned, southerners, westerners, and northerners would undoubtedly take matters into their own hands and the union would be destroyed.

Will the southern provinces, when in proper cultivation, wait the finger of Congress to point out markets for them?—Will the back settlers, adventurers and traders wait and languish upon a Spanish negociation, to give them the use of the Mississippi's stream, that washes their plantations? Will the eastern and northern states listen to the restrictions and prohibitions of Congress . . . ?

The problem, many Americans began to fear, was that Congress could not help one set of interests without hurting another. The result was a deepening ambivalence about the desirability of a strong national government; the crucial question was whether or not sectional interests could be both protected and promoted in a more energetic union.

Because of the problematic relationship between conceptions of the national interest and this emerging sectional consciousness, agitation for constitutional reform threatened to destroy the union even as reformers promised to perfect it. When nationalists derided the present "imbecilic" system, they inevitably conflated their own interests with the national interest. But frustration with congressional impotence led some of these "nationalists" to betray their sectional biases. A Boston correspondent, for example, wondered how long we are "to continue in our present inglorious acquiescence in the shameful resistance that some of the states persist in, against federal and national measures?" He chafed at the "paltry politics, weak jealousy," and "local interests" of the middle states, concluding with a widely reprinted proposal that New England form a "new and stronger union" of its own.

The great achievement of the Philadelphia Convention was to establish a framework for national politics that would accommodate these powerful sectionalist tendencies. It was easy enough to discredit the Articles of Confederation and lay the nation's troubles at the feet of state particularism; but the institution of a more powerful continental regime was not the only, or necessarily the most compelling, solution. In 1786 and early 1787, many commentators—articulating some of the same concerns that prompted national constitutional reform—had seriously considered the possibility of disunion. The controversy, contrary to later Federalist claims, did not pit benighted localists with their narrow conceptions of interest against cosmopolitans who could comprehend the new nation's magnificent prospects. Instead, proponents of radical constitutional change promoted ambiguous and contradictory conceptions of the national interest—and even of distinct national interests.

By the time of the Constitutional Convention, the belief that the United States might ultimately divide into three or more separate confederacies was widespread. The conventional projection was that the northern, middle, and southern states would form separate unions—and some saw the new states to the west constituting yet another union. In 1781 Alexander Hamilton predicted such a division in his *Continentalist* series: the "vanity and self importance" of "some of the larger states" might lead them "to place themselves at the head of particular confederacies independent of the general one." Many British writers were convinced that the union would collapse after the war, including Richard Champion, who anticipated that "three great Republicks" eventually would emerge. But it was only in 1786, in the wake of the Mississippi controversy, that American politicians seriously began to consider disunion. Writing from New York, Congressman James Monroe told his Virginia correspondents that northerners "have even sought a dismemberm[en]t to the Potowmack." Although several division proposals did appear in northern papers at this time, northerners were not alone in considering the idea. Many southerners blamed northern commercial interests for John Jay's ill-fated treaty and became convinced that their states would be better off on their own. During the ratification controversy, Monroe and his Antifederalist allies argued that disunion was preferable to a system that could easily "sacrifice the dearest interests of the Southern States."

Northerners and southerners who threatened each other with the destruction of the union reflected a pervasive sense that sectional differences were intractable. At the same time, constitutional reformers were becoming increasingly despondent about the prospects of ever being able to establish a more energetic continental government. As a result, the possibility of forming more perfect regional unions gained significant support. Benjamin Rush, a prominent nationalist, wrote Richard Price in England that "some of our enlightened men" had begun to "despair of a more complete union of the States in Congress" and were proposing to divide the union in three. "These confederacies they say will be united by nature, by interest, and by manners, and consequently they will be safe, agreeable and durable." Clearly, Rush thought these "enlightened men" were not misled by narrow conceptions of local interest. It was precisely because they could take a broad view, considering "nature" and "manners" as well as "interests," that Rush's friends concluded that the United States included three incipient nationalities. In the event of disunion, the New Yorker "Lycurgus" wrote, "the religion, manners, customs, exports, imports and general interest" of each section would be "the same"; this "unanimity would render us secure at home, and respected abroad, and promote agriculture, manufactures, and commerce."

Why should respectable nationalists flirt with disunionism? Some may have been more concerned with restraining the "democratic despotism" of the states than with creating a powerful national government. Efforts to draft new state constitutions that could secure property and guarantee order had either been stymied or had failed to achieve the desired results. In Pennsylvania, republican opponents of the state constitution hoped a new national constitution would, as Rush later put it, "overset our state dung cart." But there was no necessary connection between restraining the excesses of the states and creating a strong national union. When Rush wrote Price, the chances of revising the Articles looked slim, making the institution of new governments on the regional level correspondingly attractive.

Not surprisingly, many of the separate confederacy proposals circulating on the eve of the Convention sought to subordinate the states to more powerful unions. While "Lycurgus" thought the states could preserve "the same sovereignty and internal jurisdiction" they now enjoyed, most disunionists recognized the need to curb state particularism. A Boston writer linked disunion with a regional redefinition of federal-state relations that he hoped would ultimately lead to national constitutional reform. He thought it high time "to form a new and stronger union," but the work would be best begun by instituting "a new Congress, as the Representative of the nation of New-England," leaving the other states "to pursue their own imbecile and disjointed ways" until they learned "experimentally" the value of supporting a properly constituted union. "Reason" had even less patience with the states: state sovereignty was the fundamental defect of American politics. Because "there can only be one sovereignty in a government," he wrote, the "notion . . . of a government by confederation between several independent States, and each retaining its sovereignty, must be abandoned, and with it every attempt to amend the present Articles of Confederation." The solution was to "distribute the States into three republics," thereby simultaneously dissolving the union and amalgamating the separate states. Separate confederations, he suggested, violated political logic as much as the existing confederation and would fall prey to the same centrifugal tendencies.

Southerners also looked to regional unions for protection against untrammeled state power. "The doctrine of three Confederacies, or great Republics, has its' advocates here," Madison learned from a Virginia correspondent in August 1787. At least one prominent Virginian who embraced this doctrine had called for the "extinction of State legislatures" within each new union. Madison himself favored neither the abolition of the states nor the breakup of the union, but—given his low esteem for the Henryite majority in the Virginia Assembly—he probably sympathized with "enlightened men" who thought new regional unions would solve their problems.

There was considerable ambiguity about what to call these proposed regional governments. The use of the word "republic," in apposition to or in lieu of "confederation," strongly suggests that disunionists generally did not contemplate creating regional replicas of the existing union. No one would have claimed that the national government under the Articles was "republican," and this defect had always given the states' defiance of Congress an aura of legitimacy. But designating the sectional confederations "republics" would clearly establish their primacy over the states they included, a usage that anticipated the Federalists' bold use of "popular sovereignty" to legitimize the radical reallocation of power between the states and the national government.

Advocacy of sectional "republics" that would subsume if not destroy the state republics also represented an important stage in the evolution of reformers' ideas about the possibility of preserving republican government over an "extended sphere." Disunionists agreed that there were limits to the size of republics, an argument Antifederalists subsequently used to great advantage. "Reason" acknowledged the "difficulty" of representing and reconciling "the national concerns of a people so numerous, with a territory so extensive," concluding that the executive arm would have to be strengthened to an extent incompatible "with the principles of a democratic form." "All political writers of eminence agree," wrote "Lycurgus"—as did many Antifederalists after him—"that a republic should not comprehend a large territory." In projecting these extended, regional republics, disunionists pushed Montesquieu's premises to their limits but did not abandon them. Certainly, the new unions would be much larger than the small republics the influential French theorist had endorsed; many of the individual states themselves were, by this standard, too large. But proponents of separate unions thought them sufficiently homogeneous and still small enough to support republican governments, while avoiding the weaknesses endemic to small states. The existence of separate states, they suggested, simply obstructed the formulation and implementation of policy on behalf of the general—regional—interest.

Separate Unions and the Extended Republic

On the eve of the Philadelphia Convention, many Americans—including future Federalists as well as Antifederalists—shared misgivings about the size of the American union. According to conventional wisdom, a large state could only be preserved by despotic authority. Suspicious republicans thus detected monarchical tendencies in efforts to reinvigorate Congress and thereby transform the union into a consolidated state.

On the eve of the Convention, republican anxieties about incipient despotism were fueled by rumors that many Americans favored the reestablishment of monarchical government. Even staunch republicans became convinced that the return of monarchy was inevitable. They only hoped that the day would be postponed as long as possible and that when it came, Americans would be able to negotiate favorable terms with a new royal line. Exasperated by repeated failures to enlarge Congress's powers, "many, very many wish to see an emperor at the head of our nation." Without an effective national government, the union would fall apart and the new nation would soon be at the mercy of foreign predators. George Washington thought there had to be "lodged somewhere a power which will pervade the whole union in as energetic manner, as the Authority of the State Governments extend over the several States." Recognizing that the union itself had to become a "state," Americans asked themselves what kind of government would be most appropriate. Many concluded that monarchy alone could sustain "energetic" government across the continent. Some "respectable characters," reported Washington, "speak of a monarchical form . . . without horror."

Historians have paid too little attention to the spread of monarchist sentiment or to proposals for the division of the union that circulated before the delegates convened in Philadelphia. By then many Americans had become convinced of the "imbecility" of the existing union as well as of the inadequacies of the states. Some, in turn, saw the creation of a continental monarchy or a division of the union as the only plausible alternatives. The Convention had to create "an efficient federal government," David Ramsay wrote Jefferson in April 1787, or "I fear that the end of the matter will be an American monarch or three or more confederacies." If forced to choose between those alternatives, many "respectable characters" would agree with an anonymous "gentleman in Virginia" who "reprobate[d] the idea of a division of the States." "My opinion is, that America would be happier under the government of France, or the present Empress of Russia, than be divided according to that malevolent suggestion." But Madison thought the "bulk of the people" would resist monarchy: they "will probably prefer the lesser evil of a partition of the Union into three more practicable and energetic governments."

Supporters of continental monarchy were not necessarily enemies of republican liberty. Monarchists could argue that the best form of government for the union was an open question; indeed, if there was a latent form in the existing system—although this might be doubted—it was probably monarchical. Congress had exercised many of the British king's prerogatives, most notably over war and peace. Furthermore, an American monarchy would be constitutionally limited and thus compatible with the preservation of republican government in the states. Monarchists suggested that what was best for the states might not be best for the continent as a whole. Even good republicans like James Wilson had to concede that the "extent" of the United States "*seems* to require the vigour of Monarchy." Hamilton simply did not think "a Republican Government could be established over so great an extent." "The British Government was the best in the world," he told the delegates at Philadelphia, and "he doubted much whether any thing short of it would do in America."

Whatever the merits of monarchical schemes, Madison and his fellow reformers knew they could not gain the broad popular approval so essential to the legitimacy of any new regime in America. The challenge was to create more energetic governments without abandoning republican forms. Perhaps this could only be done on the regional level: separate unions might avoid the dangers of large size—the tendency of large states to succumb to despotism—while curbing the democratic excesses characteristic of small states. At the same time, these unions would accommodate fundamental differences of sectional interest. Reformers might not doubt that there was true national interest but they were increasingly doubtful that other Americans could recognize it. They feared that a union that attempted to embrace such self-consciously hostile interests was doomed to factional paralysis. Regional unions would at least facilitate a harmony of interests over fairly extended spheres, while precluding the debilitating conflicts of interest that fostered anarchy and shattered the unity of small republics.

The brief flirtation of some frustrated reformers with the idea of separate unions can be seen as a crucial step toward conceptualizing the extended republic. The first task in this project was to dissociate republican government from its exclusive association with the states. While they were unable to shake off the conventional assumption that a "state" as large as the union could only be governed despotically, some reformers did suggest that the "more practicable and energetic" regional unions could still be republics. Meanwhile, reformers warned that the tendency of individual states to claim sovereign powers jeopardized their republican character. The preservation of republican government depended on instituting a more effective union that could guarantee peace among the states and protect them from foreign powers. Reforms usually had the "British Model" in mind when they advocated more energetic central administration, but they knew the "bulk" of the people had no stomach for another king. The result of this impasse—the apparently hopeless task of striking the delicate and precarious balance between monarchical and republican principles and reconciling energy and liberty on a continental scale—was to make separate unions seem a plausible alternative.

After the Constitution was drafted, reformers quickly distanced themselves from the idea of separate confederations. Federalists presented the new system as an answer to disunionist scenarios, which they attributed to their Antifederalist opponents. Federalist rhetoric suggests that the primary goal of the Convention was not so much to restrain the states from democratic excesses—the suggestion would have been impolitic—as to keep them from joining separate unions. Washington thought the *Federalist* essays an excellent "antidote" to the scribblings of those "who wish to see this Union divided into several Confederacies." Marylander Charles Carroll asserted that if voters did not endorse the new Constitution, the union would crumble "into many distinct confederacies," with "wars, devastation, rapin[e], [and] hatred" the inevitable results. Opponents of the proposed system welcomed this confusion, Federalists charged, because of the opportunities it would give "state demagogues" to seize power and promote their selfish interests.

But Federalist charges are misleading. While some Antifederalists undoubtedly did come to the conclusion that separate confederations would be preferable to a single "consolidated" union, they forthrightly denied that this was their original intent. Indeed, the notion of a voluntary, harmonious union of republics articulated by Antifederalists like James Winthrop and John Francis Mercer during the ratification controversy bore little resemblance to the sectional unions proposed in 1786 and early 1787. I am convinced that Federalists were in fact attacking—and thus disavowing—a constitutional solution that like-minded reformers had seriously considered when prospects for an effective continental scheme seemed dimmest. Their polemics disguised their own loss of faith in the union. Projecting disunionism on their opponents, Federalists proposed to resolve a crisis that, as proponents of separate confederacies, some of them may have helped precipitate.

Federalism

"Local politics & diversity of interest will undoubtedly find their way into the [Constitutional] Convention," David Humphreys wrote. As a result, he expected "a serious proposal will be made for dividing the Continent into two or three separate Governments." Madison later insisted that the delegates never discussed the possibility, but it clearly was never far from their minds. An awareness of intractable sectional differences was apparent in Edmund Randolph's early proposal for a triple executive with members "drawn from different portions of the Country"; he regarded the alternative, a unitary executive, "as the foetus of monarchy." George Mason, a later opponent of the Constitution, also favored a three-man executive:

If the Executive is vested in three persons, one chosen from the Northern, one from the Middle, and one from the Southern States, will it not contribute to quiet the minds of the people and convince them that there will be proper concern paid to their respective concerns? Will not three men so chosen bring with them, into office, a more perfect and extensive knowledge of the real interests of this great Union?

Voters must be persuaded, Mason warned, that enlarged national powers would not be exercised at their expense.

Yet such an explicit, constitutional recognition of sectional differences was more likely to arouse than to allay anxieties about the misuse of national power.

"If three or more [executives] should be taken from as many districts," Pierce Butler argued, "there would be a constant struggle for local advantages." The constitution of the executive mirrored the state of the nation. If there was a unitary, transcendent national interest, Butler suggested, a single executive was most appropriate; but if sectional interests were paramount, disunion probably made more sense than a divided executive. Later in the debates, Gouverneur Morris asked the crucial question: Was the alleged distinction between North and South "fictitious or real?" If "fictitious," he concluded, "let it be dismissed & let us proceed with due confidence"; if "real, instead of attempting to blend incompatible things, let us at once take a friendly leave of each other."

The new Constitution could not recognize the preeminence of sectional distinctions without subverting the essential premise of national unity. At the same time, however, the new national government would have to secure vital local and regional interests, most conspicuously in the case of the large slaveholding and slave-importing states. The delegates discovered an answer to these apparently contradictory requirements during their protracted debates over representation in the national legislature. Through the complex scheme that incorporated the principle of proportional representation in one house and state equality in the other, divergent interests would be protected against hostile national majorities without being explicitly recognized. Controversial sectional issues were hardly neglected at Philadelphia, but delegates early on made the crucially important decision to suppress all traces of earlier disunionist proposals. The sections would have to achieve some sort of accommodation within a federal framework that explicitly secured the rights of the states, not the sections.

The Virginia Plan set the agenda for Convention debates. Advocates of opposing principles of representation were deeply divided and, for several frustrating weeks, no satisfactory compromise seemed possible. But the debate deflected attention away from conflicting sectional interests. Both sides were committed to national union, albeit on radically different terms. The result of the controversy was to persuade delegates that the impasse between large and small states—not sectional distinctions—constituted the most momentous obstacle to a strong national government. At the same time, however, they knew that their failure to resolve the controversy over representation could well lead to disunion and the formation of separate confederacies. Madison and the large state "nationalists" were not above threatening the small states with disunion and obliteration. Madison was so frustrated by their intransigence, historian Rosemarie Zagarri shows, that he was willing to raise the spectre of sectional conflict:

The great danger to our general government *is the great southern and northern interests of the continent, being opposed to each other. Look to the votes in congress, and most of them stand divided by the geography of the country, not according to the size of the states.*

Madison tried to persuade small-state delegates that the Virginia Plan was the safest possible arrangement for their constituents; because of their antagonistic—sectional—differences, there was no "real danger" the large states would act in concert.

Although the small states remained obdurate, Madison's speech did point the way toward the remarkably forthright intersectional negotiations that dominated the second half of the Convention. Paradoxically, however, the precondition for such negotiations was an agreement on representation that did *not* reflect the "great" sectional interests but instead juxtaposed the interests of large and small states in the respective houses. Madison insisted that proportional representation was the defining principle of a truly national government. Small-state delegates replied that one section would thereby gain a dominant position in both houses, thus subverting prospects for continuing union. "Let not too much be attempted," warned Connecticut's Oliver Ellsworth, lest "all may be lost." Any representation scheme that would "deprive" the generally small northeastern states of equal suffrage in at least one house "was at once cutting the body [of America] in two."

Large-state nationalists were forced to accept Ellsworth's premise that the government of the union would have to be "partly national" and "partly federal," a formula later embraced by "Publius" in the *Federalist*. If this meant that the political power of the small states would be exaggerated, Madisonian logic suggested that the practical effects would be inconsequential: their interests were as disparate as those of the large states. At the same time, the complicated system of representation established under the "Connecticut Compromise" provided additional security for sectional interests—as well as for all the states *as states*. Coming from a large, centrally located state with strong interests in national commercial and territorial expansion, the Virginians could discount such safeguards. For them, the interests of the state, region, and nation *apparently* coincided. Opposition to the Virginia Plan exposed the limits of Virginian "nationalism," however, and, as Lance Banning shows, Madison's great achievement at the Virginia ratifying convention was to convince his countrymen that modifications of the Virginia Plan were not fatal to their interests.

Virginians might complain that the new Constitution did not adequately recognize or secure their state's preeminent position in the union, but the "partly national," "partly federal" system did serve to mitigate intersectional tensions. One important reason for this was a crucial ambiguity about which section would enjoy the immediate advantage under the new scheme. Anticipated population shifts—toward the south and west—as well as confusion about the precise limits of the sections (would New York be aligned with the New England states and did the middle states constitute a distinct section?) made the implications of union for sectional conflict exceedingly problematic. Staughton Lynd has shown that northerners and southerners alike could project expansive visions of regional development in plans for the opening of the Old Northwest. The West, in turn, was a mirror for broader conceptions of a stronger union promoting distinctive—although not necessarily mutually exclusive—regional interests. The Framers' remarkable success in neutralizing sectional interest, or, perhaps more accurately, in redirecting its tendency from disunion and separate confederacies toward a stronger national regime, is apparent in the wildly divergent and contradictory assessments of the union's dangerous tendencies by Antifederalists in different parts of the country. As opponents of the Constitution sought to coordinate their efforts, they necessarily focused on common concerns about the despotic, "consolidationist" tendency of the new federal government, implicitly conceding that it might indeed operate equally—if equally dangerously—on all parts of the union.

More immediately, once the Convention was committed to the Connecticut Compromise, delegates could begin to talk about sectional interests without directly questioning the future of the union or the presumption of a national interest. Even when they indulged in the most extravagant rhetoric, the desirability of intersectional accommodation was understood. Thus, while South Carolinian Pierce Butler asserted that the interests of the southern and eastern (northern) states were "as different as the interests of Russia and Turkey," he spoke in favor of compromise. Indeed, the articulation of distinct interests was essential for fixing the "bargain among the Northern & Southern States" described by Gouverneur Morris: A simple majority in Congress could regulate trade—a concession to northern commerce—but no duties could be laid on exports and there would be no federal interference with the slave trade for another twenty years. The Carolinians in particular engaged in a certain amount of bluster and bluff, but the delegates were clearly committed to compromise in the Convention's last weeks.

The history of intersectional negotiations at the Constitutional Convention is familiar. It is not generally recognized, however, that agreement on the representation issue provided a framework for articulating those interests that encouraged mutual concessions. In this sense, contemporary commentators were correct in emphasizing the primacy of the representation controversy. Although, as Madison noted, conflicts over other issues might have been more "important," they only became negotiable once the character of the new national legislature was established. Ellsworth, who had himself broached the possibility of disunion in response to the large-state insistence on proportional representation, became a leading advocate of compromise. The failure to reconcile sectional differences, he told the Convention in late August, would lead "probably into several confederations and not without bloodshed." Guarantees of sectional interests would, in turn, constitute powerful incentives to support the new system.

The great discovery of nationalist reformers at Philadelphia was that equal representation of the states and the recognition of state sovereignty—which many of them considered the original source of America's troubles—could provide the crucial measure of security that would reverse the tendency toward disunion expressed in proposals for separate confederacies. As Banning suggests for Madison, the Convention was a "learning process." Pragmatic reformers became aware of the limits on national consolidation set by the vast array of conflicting interests represented at Philadelphia and by the delegates' determination to uphold what they deemed their own states' critical interests. They also had to recognize limits on their own "nationalism" dictated by their distinctive regional interests. Given the imperative of reconciling those interests—and facing the awful alternative of disunion—nationalists turned toward the states. Gouverneur Morris, for instance, persisted in considering equal state voting a "vicious principle" but realized that it could provide a vital security for the northern commercial states as population shifted southward.

The genius of states' rights within the framework of a more energetic national union was to secure sectional interests without directly acknowledging their legitimacy and durability. Of course, as Paul Finkelman shows, these guarantees, particularly on slavery, were woven into the very fabric of the new system. When slavery subsequently became the leading cause of intersectional conflict, the constitutional guarantees of slave interests would foster disunion, even as they had once made union possible. The Framers of the Constitution attempted to suppress sectional tensions by creating a more perfect—if fundamentally flawed—national union. Perhaps not surprisingly, given the Framers' reliance on federalism to counteract sectionalism, southerners finally sought to vindicate their rights and protect their interests by invoking states' rights.

The National Interest

"Whether the plans of the Southern, Eastern or Middle States succeed, never, in my opinion, ought to be known," Congressman Nathan Dane wrote from New York as the Convention met behind closed doors in Philadelphia. Dane shared the perspective of delegates who saw these sectional decisions as the leading threat to union. But Federalist defenders of the new Constitution did not seek to minimize intersectional conflict; instead they emphasized the obstacles the Framers had had to overcome to secure the national interest. "A delicate and difficult contest arose," Hamilton told the New York Convention, and the delegates realized that "it was necessary that all parties should be indulged" by "compromise, or the convention must have dissolved without effecting anything." Given the "different interests of the different parts of the union," Madison added, "it was impossible to consider the degree of concord that ultimately prevailed as less than a miracle." The two ideas—"compromise" and "miracle"—were closely linked. Only an "omnipotent, omnipresent, & beneficent Ruler" could have enabled the delegates to look beyond their own narrow interests and prejudices.

Federalists insisted that the "mutual concessions" and "mutual sacrifices" that enabled the Convention to reach agreement could never be repeated. "Such an instance of unanimity upon a great national object can scarcely be paralleled." It was unlikely the states ever would be able to respond to the Antifederalist call for a second convention. If such a meeting were held, John Hay predicted, proponents of separate confederacies would gain the upper hand; in the meantime, "it will naturally be their policy rather to cherish than to prevent divisions." The Convention's great, even "miraculous," achievement was to fashion the "delicate" compromises that growing sectional tensions had made so necessary—and yet so difficult to negotiate. The Antifederalists' opposition to the new scheme only served to accentuate sectional suspicions, thereby guaranteeing the failure of any further efforts to preserve the union.

The Federalist challenge was not to conceal the Convention's compromises, but rather to show that they bore equally on all the states. How could "such heterogenous materials" be formed into an equitable union? Under the Articles, "equality" had been secured by the *weakness* of the national government: ambitious states could *not* exploit each other by gaining control of Congress. Federalists had to show that a strong national government, with authority over individual citizens as well as the states, would sustain an equitable balance of power among the states while promoting their common interests. They made their case by juxtaposing the proposed system to what they insisted would be the inevitable results of inaction. This meant, ironically, that they aimed much of their rhetoric at the alternative arrangements—notably, the division of the union into separate confederacies—that frustrated reformers had begun to consider in the dark days before the Convention met.

By insisting that voters had to choose between the proposed Constitution and the formation of separate and hostile unions, Federalists suggested a definition of the national interest. Clearly, it was in the interest of potentially belligerent sections to reach a peaceful accommodation. Preserving the peace was an inestimable benefit—provided the national union did not permit one section to gain a permanent advantage over the others. "Equality," defined as the guarantee of vital state and regional interests, depended on a more perfect union and a strong national government. To secure these benefits, concessions on less vital interests were necessary: "the new government, constructed on the broad basis of equality, mutual benefits, and national good, is *not* calculated to secure a single state all her natural advantages." A Connecticut Federalist thus disclaimed any ambition "to obtain a preeminence over one another." The states, he concluded, "are content to be established on an equal footing."

The South Carolinians, both at the Convention and during the ratification debate, were clearest about their own interests as slaveowning planters and about the necessity of intersectional compromise. David Ramsay thought that northern concessions on slavery warranted reciprocal concessions on trade regulation. "Ought we to grudge them the carrying of our produce," he asked, "especially when it is considered, that by encouraging their shipping, we increase the means of our own defence?" With their large slave population, Carolinians were not eager to abandon the union, even for a southern confederacy. "Like ourselves," Virginia's Governor Randolph wrote, "they are diminished in their real force, by the mixture of an unhappy species of population." Vulnerable internally and externally—"two or more confederacies cannot but be competitors for power"—Randolph concluded that southerners "would be compelled to rest some where or other, power approaching near to military government." The southern states "are so weak," said Charles Cotesworth Pinckney of South Carolina, "that by ourselves we could not form a union strong enough for the purpose of effectually protecting each other." Some Virginians, reported John Blair Smith, were even convinced they would have to seek "a foreign alliance."

In late 1786 and early 1787 separate confederacies might have seemed a distinctly preferable alternative to an imbecilic continental union dominated by quasi-sovereign states. After the Philadelphia Convention, however, Federalists portrayed the formation of separate unions as the awful, probably inevitable outcome of disunion. They thus suggested a crucial distinction between legitimate sectional interests that could be guaranteed in a continental union and a section's illegitimate ambition to assume a dominant position. Such ambitions reflected the same shortsighted and partial conception of "interest" that was expressed in proposals for breaking up the union. But an imbalanced union could not long survive, nor could regional unions determined to promote their separate interests coexist peacefully. It was therefore essential for all the states to forswear the illusory advantages of *dominance,* either within the union or in a destructive competition among unions. And this meant, concluded Robert Barnwell of South Carolina, that—within clearly defined constitutional limits—the divergent, sometimes conflicting interests that made up the union had to submit to the majority will. If national power was always suspect, Barnwell reasoned, "it went against uniting at all." "A majority must be somewhere, is most evident: nothing would be more completely farcical than a government completely checked."

The Federalists' major achievement was to articulate a plausible conception of the national interest that did not depend on the destruction of the states. They warned that the separate unions sure to emerge with the failure of constitutional reform represented a much greater threat to the survival of the states than a more energetic continental union. In the event of disunion, large states would no longer be inhibited from extending their power at the expense of their small neighbors; because of their conflicting interests, regional blocs would be on a hostile footing and the inevitable militarization of American politics would subvert republican government.

Counsels of prudence were balanced by promises of future prosperity and power in Federalist rhetoric. According to promoters of the new system, the different interests that now jeopardized union could be mobilized to serve the common good. The choice was between reciprocity, commercial exchange, and economic development on one hand and mutual suspicion, war, and poverty on the other. A Federalist writer elaborated on the alternatives:

every moment seems to create new matter which will be productive either of building up a great and boundless empire, or circumscribing scanty and narrow limits for the inhabitants of this country, suited only for savage chiefs or barbarous tyrants—the latter will be the consequence, should we reject the government offered for our acceptance.

Americans could balance and harmonize their interests—and extend their freedom—by embracing a stronger union; disunion was a prescription for "tyranny" and a violation of the continent's "natural" destiny.

Federalists claimed that Americans could enjoy both security and opportunity under the Constitution. That the new government would preserve states' rights ("equal justice will be administered to each state") was crucial to their argument. From the new perspective of sectional division—precipitated by the Mississippi furor and subsequent talk about separate confederacies—the excesses of state sovereignty no longer seemed to be the central problem for reformers. Instead, the debates at Philadelphia taught them that a careful balance of state and central power could provide a framework for containing and redirecting sectionalist impulses. Their new idea of federalism thus brought into view a broadly appealing conception of union and of the national interest. Indeed, Federalists concluded, Americans could only preserve their state republics, pursue their individual interests, and exploit the magnificent natural resources of the continent if they instituted a strong national government.

Americans could thus, they hoped, mitigate if not resolve the conflicts of interest that once threatened to paralyze and destroy the union. But, as Antifederalist critics of the Constitution warned, sectional distinctions would not necessarily dissolve under the new dispensation. Indeed, the issue of Southern slavery—and its constitutional guarantees—ultimately found its solution only in the terrible destruction and slaughter of the Civil War. The idea of a substantial and expanding national interest that figured so prominently in Federalist rhetoric during the ratification controversy could not be sustained in the face of such extreme sectional polarization.

EDWARD J. ERLER

The Political Philosophy
of the Constitution

*As it was more than probable we were now digesting a plan which in
its operation would decide forever the fate of Republican
Government we ought not only to provide every guard to liberty that
its preservation could require, but be equally careful to supply the
defects which our own experience had particularly pointed out.*
—James Madison

*It has been frequently remarked that it seems to have been reserved to
the people of this county, by their conduct and example, to decide the
important question, whether societies of men are really capable or
not of establishing good government from reflection and choice, or
whether they are forever destined to depend for their political
constitutions on accident and force.*
—Alexander Hamilton

On the occasion of the bicentennial of the Constitution, the nation was confronted once again with a vigorous debate about the origins of the regime.
This time the debate concerned whether the origins—the intentions of the Framers—should be the authoritative touchstone of constitutional interpretation.
Controversies about the meaning and significance of the Constitution are hardly
surprising, since they form the most characteristic—and unique—feature of our
political life. In one way or another, all our important political questions become
constitutional questions, and these questions always—explicitly or implicitly—
involve the character of the Founding. For it is the Founding that reveals the
"standard maxim" of our political life, one that did not grow from a mythical or
prehistoric past but was based on the universal principle that "all men are created equal." The origins of America thus exist in the full light of day and can be
subjected to the most precise scrutiny. In great measure, the character of our national politics has depended upon the way in which we have viewed the work of
the Founders.

The last few years have witnessed an extraordinary public debate between
the attorney general of the United States and several members of the Supreme
Court. This debate invites us once again to consider the meaning of the Constitution as an expression of first principles. Attorney General Edwin Meese advo-

cated what he called a "jurisprudence of original intention" as an antidote to increased judicial activism. He described the main outlines of this approach in the following terms: "Where the language of the Constitution is specific, it must be obeyed. Where there is a demonstrable consensus among the framers and ratifiers as to a principle stated or implied by the Constitution, it should be followed. Where there is ambiguity as to the precise meaning or reach of a constitutional provision, it should be interpreted and applied in a manner so as to at least not contradict the text of the Constitution itself." This jurisprudential stance, Meese contended, is a necessary inference from the fact of a written constitution. The Constitution is organic law and thus superior in authority to any legislative enactment or interpretation by the Supreme Court.

Justice William Brennan responded to the attorney general's call for a return to the text of the Constitution by replying that it was both impossible and undesirable to attempt to interpret the Constitution in the light of the Framers' intentions: "Those who would restrict claims of right to the values of 1789 specifically articulated in the Constitution turn a blind eye to social progress and eschew adaptation of overarching principles to changes of social circumstances." The Constitution, according to Brennan, "is a sublime oration on the dignity of man, a bold commitment by a people to the idea of libertarian dignity protected through law." But "the demands of human dignity will never cease to evolve." Thus, the "sublime oration" on human dignity must be continually reinterpreted. And, of course, the principal role in the revision of the text belongs to the judiciary because, as Brennan notes, "judicial power resides in the authority to give meaning to the Constitution."

There are some special demands of human dignity, however, that do not evolve. Being "fixed and immutable," these demands are somehow immune from social progress and evolution. The most dramatic of these, according to Brennan, relates to capital punishment. The Constitution explicitly excludes capital punishment from its proscription against "cruel and unusual punishment" by referring in the Fifth Amendment to "capital crimes" and by providing in the same amendment that "no person" can be deprived of "life, liberty, or property without due process of law." This latter provision, of course, clearly indicates that *with* due process of law, "persons" can be deprived of life. But the evolving standards of human dignity now dictate, according to Justice Brennan, that "capital punishment is under all circumstances cruel and unusual punishment prohibited by the Eighth and Fourteenth Amendments." The Eighth Amendment was, of course, passed contemporaneously with the Fifth Amendment and therefore cannot possibly have been intended to proscribe capital punishment. An adherence to the literal language of the Constitution, in Brennan's view, would thus deny the Constitution's potential for serving as the vehicle of social progress. Brennan does not, however, attempt to explain how it is possible for some "fixed and immutable" demands to exist in a universe of constant change and progress. Perhaps these exceptions to progress are demanded by progress itself! Justice Brennan is strangely silent on this crucial point.

In any case, for Brennan, the original Constitution, before the advent of the Bill of Rights and the Reconstruction amendments, did not address the issue of human dignity, being almost exclusively concerned with the abilities and disabilities of government." It was only the progressive evolution of the Constitution away from its defective origins that transformed it into "a sparkling vision of the supremacy of the human dignity of every individual." Justice Thurgood Marshall joined the fray on the side of Justice Brennan, noting that during the bicentennial we should not be celebrating the work of the Framers, but the work of those who refused to acquiesce in the Framers' "outdated notions of 'liberty,' 'justice,' and 'equality.' " The Constitution's compromise with slavery, according to Marshall, was a fatal defect that could not be remedied within the terms of the original document. "While the Union survived the civil war, the Constitution did not. In its place arose a new, more promising basis for justice and equality, the 14th Amendment, ensuring protection of the life, liberty, and property of *all* persons against deprivations without due process, and guaranteeing equal protection of the laws." Thus, Marshall views the Fourteenth Amendment not as a completion of the principles embodied in the Constitution, but as a repudiation of the original document. For both Marshall and Brennan the origins (and the intentions of the Framers) can no longer be regarded as authoritative.

This contemporary debate necessarily impels us to a consideration of first principles. For it is only through a proper understanding of the origins of the regime that we can understand the character of this controversy about the principles of constitutional interpretation. If we find that somehow the origins are defective or outmoded, then the jurisprudence that looks upon the Constitution merely as a procedural instrument to facilitate social progress would certainly make more sense than the jurisprudence of original intent. If, on the other hand, the Founding has more theoretical and principled substance than Brennan and Marshall are willing to admit, then some version of an original intent jurisprudence is demanded by political prudence.

During the course of the debate in the Massachusetts ratifying convention in 1788, Fisher Ames, a leading Federalist, remarked in his defense of the new Constitution that "legislators have at length condescended to speak the language of philosophy; and if we adopt it, we shall demonstrate to the sneering world, who deride liberty because they have lost it, that the principles of our government are as free as the spirit of our people." It seems rather curious to us today that Ames would refer to the Constitution as a philosophic document. One does not ordinarily speak of "the philosophy of the Constitution," because we know that constitutions are political, not philosophic, documents. We are more apt to view the Framers as pragmatists rather than philosophers. Indeed, we pride ourselves on being realists, able to see through what has been called "the lost language of the Enlightenment," a language replete with references to such concepts as natural rights and natural law. Our conceit is that we can understand the work of the Framers better than the Framers understood it themselves. After all, their reference to "the laws of nature and nature's God" as the ground of political right is symbolism not only of their own "romantic" self-delusions, but of the self-delusions of their age as well. Scientific realism has taught us that the eighteenth-century idea of "nature" cannot provide the standard of political justice because—in the terms of one contemporary philosopher—nature is merely a "lottery," arbitrarily dispensing benefits and disadvantages. From this point of view, the ground of justice is not, as the Framers believed, "the laws of nature," but positive laws which have as their explicit purpose the correction of the arbitrariness of nature.

The most thorough and vigorous academic attempt to expose the defects of the origins was undertaken by Charles A. Beard in his *Economic Interpretation of the Constitution of the United States* (1913). Beard's contribution was to portray the Framers as unprincipled men who created an undemocratic government designed to further their own class interests. Douglass Adair wrote that it was Beard's purpose "to expose the nature of [the] Constitution, to unmask its hidden features in order to show that it deserved no veneration, no respect, and should carry no authority to democratic Americans of the twentieth century." What Beard seemed to reveal about the proceedings of the Constitutional Convention was that under the thin veneer of public-spiritedness affected by the delegates was a sinister and self-conscious aggrandizement of their own class interests. The Constitution, while masquerading as a democratic document, is really an economic document embodying the dominant class relations of the day. This interpretation, Beard remarked, is not to be gleaned from the language of the Constitution itself; rather, "the true inwardness of the Constitution" is revealed in the examination of the class interests of those who framed it. The Constitution, therefore, is not to be viewed as a document with any theoretical or principled integrity. But as Adair cogently pointed out, this "economic interpretation" excludes the possibility of any theoretical interpretation *a priori*. After all, from the point of view of class analysis, theory or principle is only an epiphenomenon of the more basic (and more revealing) economic relationships.

The Fathers, as pictured by Beard, were "practical" men who, knowing exactly what they wanted in the way of concrete economic privileges, were willing to stage a "coup d'état" to gain their ends. Collectively they were exhibited as being adepts in the use of force, fraud, and false propaganda. Beard gives no hint, however, that political theory played any consequential role in creating the Constitution; speculation there was in plenty in the Convention, but it was land and debt speculation, not speculative thought. Indeed, if it is possible to determine an individual's political motives by cataloguing his property, the irrelevance of theory should be apparent.

While the details of Beard's economic interpretation were refuted long ago, the main thrust of his argument survives—the Framers were pragmatists who had little use for theory or principle except insofar as it was necessary to provide a gloss upon their interest-group brokering.

In 1961 John Roche published an essay entitled "The Founding Fathers: A Reform Caucus in Action." In the intervening years this article has taken on the status of a minor classic. Roche's thesis was straightforward and simple: "While the shades of Locke and Montesquieu *may* have been hovering in the background, and the delegates *may* have been unconscious instruments of a transcendent *telos,* the careful observer of the day-to-day work of the Convention finds no over-arching principles." The concerns of the Framers, Roche continues, "were highly practical . . . they spent little time canvassing abstractions." Their real business, instead, "was to hammer out a pragmatic compromise which would both bolster the 'National interest' and be acceptable to the people. What inspiration they got came from their collective experience as professional politicians in a democratic society." The Constitution was therefore a "makeshift affair." Roche's concern, unlike Beard's, is not that the Constitution was undemocratic, but that it established an unprincipled or pragmatic democracy. From this point of view—the view that has come to dominate scholarship—the Constitution is nothing more than a bundle of compromises," a pragmatic accommodation of the various competing interests that were represented at the Convention. And, like all pragmatists, the Framers valued practice above principle—indeed, principle was no part of their practical calculations.

In Roche's view it was later generations—following the lead of the authors of *The Federalist*—who falsely imported into the Constitution "a high theoretical content." Later interpreters sought to give the Convention proceedings some theoretical dignity in order to endow the Framers with the public-spirited motives they so conspicuously lacked. Perhaps those who seek a principled interpretation of the Founding are merely engaged in the necessary task of obscuring the origins of the regime by disguising the pragmatic machinations of the Framers. The Framers were hard-headed realists; it is the benefactors of their work who indulge in romantic theorizing.

According to Roche, the best example of the Framers' willingness to engage in pragmatic compromise is the "Rube Goldberg mechanism" of the electoral college: "It was merely a jerry-rigged improvisation which has subsequently been endowed with a high theoretical content." During the course of the Convention, the mode of electing the president (as well as the other branches) was dominated by considerations drawn from the *principle* of the separation of powers. James Madison adumbrated that principle at the Convention to the general approbation of the members: "If it had been a fundamental principle of free Govt. that the Legislative, Executive & Judiciary powers should be *separately* exercised; it is equally so that they be *independently* exercised." It was no simple task to provide for the independence of the various branches in a government that was intended to be "wholly popular." As Montesquieu had pointed out, it was easier to establish a constitutional separation of powers in a mixed regime because the different (and independent) interests of the classes in society would be reflected in the government itself. There had been proposals in the Convention to have the president elected by Congress. But it was quickly recognized that this would compromise the independence of the executive and vitiate his role in the separation of powers. All proposals to have the president elected directly by the people were also rejected. Although direct election did not receive much support, it would also have tended to lessen the effectiveness of the separation of powers. To serve as a proper counterweight to the legislative branch, the president would have to have a *different* connection to the people, since it would be necessary on occasion for the president to serve the people "at the peril of their displeasure." Thus, the mechanism of the electoral college was designed specifically to produce not only an independent executive, but an energetic one as well. This mode of election—described by Alexander Hamilton as "if not perfect, at least excellent"—was dictated exclusively by considerations derived from the principle of the separation of powers. It appears jerry-built only from the perspective that presupposes that considerations of principle played no role in the Convention's deliberations.

Yet it is only too obvious that the Framers were not philosophers engaged in theoretical speculation—they were indeed practical politicians and only agitated questions of principle insofar as it was necessary to make prudential judgments. In other words, they were engaged in statesmanship—the accommodation of principle to particular circumstances. Even though the debates may have been tinged from time to time with the spirit of partisanship, the Framers did not regard the crucial compromises of the Convention as unprincipled accommodations. Instead, they saw themselves as statesmen adapting principle to meet the "exigencies of Government and the preservation of the Union." As Martin Diamond rightly noted, "The mere fact of compromise is not proof that principle, theory, and consistency were abandoned. Rather, the Framers successfully balanced the rival claims of theory and practical necessity. Despite the compromises which produced it, the Constitution is an essentially logical and consistent document resting upon a political philosophy. . . . Men of principle may properly make compromises when the compromises adequately preserve fundamental principle." The crucial ingredient that is missing from Roche's account of the Convention is the element of political statesmanship. For Roche, there is no middle ground between a conclave of philosophers and an assemblage of democratic politicians who are unabashedly aggrandizing their own self-interest. In the political universe created by Roche, every compromise is ipso facto a departure from principle. But as Diamond seems to suggest, every compromise implies an agreement in principle—otherwise no compromise would be possible. It may be true that most of the delegates to the Convention "were impatient with speculations about government that were unconnected with a particular time and place." But it is not true, as Roche insists, that the Framers were merely "practical politicians in a democratic society," inspired exclusively by "their own political futures." Roche's view does not understand the statesmanship—the genuine politics—that was the real achievement of the delegates to the Convention. This is the reason he insists upon ludicrously characterizing it as "a reform caucus" when the delegates themselves knew (and stated) that they were recurring to "first principles."

Roche rightly notes that the Framers "*made* history and did it within the limits of consensus." Consensus, of course, defines the necessary limits of statesmanship in a regime that rests upon the consent of the governed. But Roche has an extremely narrow view of the limits of consensus in 1787 and the capacity of the people to respond to democratic leadership. Roche's view, however, did find some expression in the Convention—*but it was far from the prevailing opinion.* Pierce Butler, for example, warned that "we must follow the example of Solon who gave the Athenians not the best Govt. he could devise; but the best they wd. receive." William Paterson—the principal author of the New Jersey Plan—expressed a similar concern, but one which also stemmed from his skepticism about the legitimacy of the Convention's power to devise a constitution that was not strictly federal in character. "Our object," he said, "is not such a Governmt. as may be best in itself, but such a one as our Constituents have authorized us to prepare, and as they will approve."

Madison's answer to these expressions of reticence was emphatic:

If the opinions of the people were to be our guide, it wd. be difficult to say what course we ought to take. No member of the Convention could say what the opinions of his Constituents were at this time; much less could he say what they would think if possessed of the information & lights possessed by the members here; & still less what would be their way of thinking 6 or 12 months hence. We ought to consider what was right & necessary in itself for the attainment of a proper Governmt. A plan adjusted to this idea will recommend itself.

Madison, of course, was not insensitive to the role of opinion in popular government. Writing in *The Federalist,* he agreed with Butler's assessment of Solon's role in formulating the Athenian constitution. Although "according to Plutarch" Solon had "the sole and absolute power of newmodeling the constitution" of Athens, he "confessed that he had not given to his countrymen the government best suited to their happiness, but most tolerable to their prejudices." Madison demonstrated that he understood the problem perfectly when he noted that "the most rational government will not find it a superfluous advantage to have the prejudices of the community on its side." But, as Madison also knew, in undertaking "the singular and solemn . . . experiment for correcting the errors of a system by which this crisis had been produced," "it is impossible for the people spontaneously and universally to move in concert towards their object; and it is therefore essential that such changes be instituted by some *informal and unauthorized propositions,* made by some patriotic and respectable citizen or number of citizens." While the people are incapable of acting "spontaneously and universally," they are nonetheless "the only legitimate fountain of power." Indeed, Madison wrote a few years later that "a republic involves the idea of popular rights. A representative republic *chuses* the wisdom, of which hereditary aristocracy has the *chance;* whilst it excludes the oppression of that form." And the republican form of government, more than any other, presupposes the capacity of the people to make wise choices, although not necessarily in the sense of being able to formulate the choices in the first instance.

This is the precise sense in which Madison addressed the Convention on July 5:

The Convention ought to pursue a plan which would bear the test of examination, which would be espoused & supported by the enlightened and impartial part of America, & which they could themselves vindicate & urge. It should be considered that altho' at first many may judge of the system recommended, by their opinion of the Convention, yet finally all will judge of the Convention by the system. The merits of the system alone can finally & effectually obtain the public suffrage. He was not apprehensive that the people of the small States would obstinately refuse to accede to a Govt. founded on just principles, and promising them substantial protection.

This view was echoed many times during the course of the Convention. Gouverneur Morris, among others, spoke in support of Madison: "We must look forward to the effects of what we do. These alone ought to guide us. Much has been said of the sentiments of the people. They were unknown. They could not be known. All that we can infer is that if the plan we recommend be reasonable & right; all who have reasonable minds and sound intentions will embrace it, notwithstanding what had been said by some Gentlemen." What made the Convention a valuable improvement "on the ancient mode of preparing and establishing regular plans of government" was the fact that the task of formulating the Constitution was given to a deliberative body serving as the representatives of the people and that the resulting plan was to be submitted to an *enlightened* citizenry for its approval. This was a situation totally unlike the one faced by Solon. Ancient republicanism was not the model for the Convention's "select experiment" in republicanism.

The argument in the Convention was not about the necessity of working within the bonds of consensus but what the consensus was. Roche argues that "a serious case can be made that the advocates of the New Jersey Plan, far from being ideological addicts of states'-rights, intended to substitute for the Virginia Plan a system which would both retain strong national power and have a chance of adoption in the states." But there was much uncertainty expressed in the Convention about how much of a consensus existed in favor of the confederal form of government. James Wilson, for example, made the point that it was not the people so much as the state politicos who were opposed to a national government. His remark deserves to be quoted at length:

With regard to the sentiments of the people, *he conceived it difficult to know precisely what they are. Those of the particular circle in which one moved, were commonly mistaken for the general voice. He could not persuade himself that the State Govts. & sovereignties were so much the idols of the people, nor a natl. Govt. so obnoxious to them, as some supposed. . . . Where do the people look at present for relief from the evils of which they complain? Is it from an internal reform of their Govt.? No. Sir, It is from the Natl. Councils that relief is expected. For these reasons he did not fear, that the people would not follow us into a national Govt. and it will be a further recommendation of Mr. R.'s plan that it is to be submitted to them and not to the Legislatures, for ratification.*

This was a view that was frequently expressed in the Convention. It was not the people who were most likely to object to a plan that encroached upon the existing federal relationship, but those who held positions of power under that system. Apart from considerations of legitimacy, the members of the Convention were under no illusions that it was the people, not the state legislatures, who were most likely to look favorably upon the innovations contained in the new Constitution. And, as for the problem of legitimacy, this would be resolved by the acceptance of the people. Ironically, a strong case could be made that the Convention was more representative of the sentiments of the people than the various state legislatures. Later events seem to support this assertion.

Roche cites John Dickinson's oft-quoted statement of August 13 as an expression of the general attitude of the delegates. During the course of a rather desultory argument about whether the lower house should have the exclusive power of originating money bills, Dickinson remarked that "experience must be our guide. Reason may mislead us." This statement is conclusive evidence for Roche that the delegates were practical politicians, not men of theory or principle. But read in its proper context, Dickinson's statement does not support Roche's contention. In the debate over this question, *there was no principle at stake.* "It was not Reason," Dickinson proclaimed, "that discovered the singular & admirable mechanism of the English Constitution. It was not Reason that discovered or ever could have discovered the odd & in the eye of those who are governed by reason, the absurd mode of trial by Jury. Accidents probably produced these discoveries, and experience has given a sanction to them. This is then our guide." Dickinson was replying to Wilson and Madison who had earlier argued that the experience of vesting the power to initiate money bills in the lower house of the state legislatures had been a source of faction and contention. Dickinson denied that the short experience of the state legislatures outweighed the long experience of Great Britain. "Shall we oppose to this long experience," he mused, "the short experience of 11 years which we had ourselves, on this subject." In this argument *both* sides appealed to experience; but the question could not be resolved on the basis of experience alone. Which experience was authoritative?

In *The Federalist,* Madison wrote that in considering the central problems of republican government, "theoretic reasoning, in this as in all other cases, must be qualified by the lessons of practice." Experience must always be tested in the light of some standard that is itself not a part of the historical experience. Experience, not theoretic reasoning, is the qualifier—theoretic reasoning is thus the principal ingredient in this amalgam of theory and practice that Madison understood to be statesmanship. Madison succinctly expressed the statesman's view of the matter in the notes compiled for his speech to the Convention on August 7: "We must not shut our eyes to the nature of man, nor to the light of experience." Experience is the guide only when seen or interpreted in the light of human nature—that is, in the light of political philosophy.

To concede that the Convention delegates conceived of their task in eminently practical terms is not to concede that there was no principled integrity in their deliberations. Even Roche notes that "what is striking to one who analyzes the Convention as a case-study in democratic politics is the lack of clear-cut ideological divisions in the Convention. "Indeed," Roche proclaims, "I submit that the evidence—Madison's *Notes,* the correspondence of the delegates, and debates on ratification—indicates that this was a remarkably homogeneous body on the ideological level." It is unlikely that Roche's use of the term *ideological* is meant to convey the idea of theoretical principle, but it is close enough for our present purposes. What divided the delegates at the Convention was not so much issues of ideology or principle but the practical details of implementing those principles. The famous compromises of the Convention should be understood not as a sign of a lack of principle, but in fact as attempts to accommodate constitutional principle. The Constitution may indeed be described as a "bundle of compromises," but the compromises hammered out at the Convention—every one of them seeking accommodation of a particular point of view—took place within a common theoretical horizon. And this was the theoretical horizon that had been created by the Declaration of Independence, a document that, as Thomas Jefferson explained, "was intended to be an expression of the American mind."

John Hancock, president of the Continental Congress, in his official letter transmitting the Declaration of Independence to the States remarked that "the important Consequences resulting to the American States from this Declaration of Independence, considered as the Ground and Foundation of a future Government, will naturally suggest the Propriety of proclaiming it in such a Mode, as that the People may be universally informed of it." It is significant to note that from the beginning the Declaration was considered to be the "Ground and Foundation" of any future government or governments in America. On June 19, 1787, in the course of the Convention, Luther Martin, who later left without signing the Constitution, rose to remark that "the separation from G[reat] B[ritain] placed the 13 States in a state of nature towards each other; that they would have remained in that state till this time, but for the confederation." Martin, of course, was an advocate of a strictly confederal form of government. But the question of whether the states had ever been in the state of nature with one another was not simply a metaphysical dispute. If the thirteen colonies achieved their independence of each other at the same time they gained their independence from Great Britain, then the arguments for a strong national government that entrenched upon state sovereignty could hardly be credited.

James Wilson of Pennsylvania rose to answer Martin, remarking that he "could not admit the doctrine that when the Colonies became independent of G. Britain, they became independent also of each other." As Madison recorded in his notes, Wilson "read the declaration of independence, observing thereon that the *United Colonies* were declared to be free & independent, not *Individually* but *Unitedly* and that they were confederated as they were independent, States." This speech of Wilson's was quickly seconded by Hamilton, who "denied the doctrine that the States were thrown into a State of nature." The interesting point about this colloquy is that both arguments rested "on a deeper stratum of agreement— as any disagreement which can be compromised must. The basic understanding of government and individual rights expressed in the Declaration of Independence was taken for granted. . . . But different conclusions were drawn."

Indeed, both the small and the large republic arguments were drawn from the Declaration. Both were about how best to secure the republican regime of natural rights specified in that document. Roger Sherman succinctly expressed this sentiment when he stated that "the question is not what rights naturally belong to men; but how they may be most equally & effectually guarded in Society." As Herman Belz has recently written, "Republicanism was the political philosophy of the American Revolution." The radical core of this political philosophy was the substitution of natural rights for historical rights—the natural rights of man for the historical rights of Englishmen. Harry Jaffa writes:

The preamble to the Declaration of Independence may be a succinct restatement of the theory that underlay the English Revolution of 1688, but it had little in common with the public rhetoric of that revolution. The latter explicitly accused James II only of violating a traditional constitution, not of violating natural rights. The teachings of John Locke may have served to justify revolution to Englishmen after the event; they served to justify Americans in the event. It is doubtful that many Englishmen ever would have been swayed by an appeal to universal human equality; it is undeniable that this appeal was most powerful in the American Revolution.

In short, the radical core of the American Revolution was the change from history to nature as the ground of political right. And it was this change that supplied the ground of the new Constitution.

Generally, this translated into the notion of a constitutional government that not only derived its legitimate powers from the consent of the governed but operated by means of consent. The central tenet of the Declaration of Independence—the principle that "all men are created equal"—provided the natural right foundation of American constitutionalism. For in equality the Framers found a nonarbitrary point of departure for the establishment of political right; equality, after all, is the abiding characteristic of human nature. And, because equality is grounded in human nature, it necessarily points to nature or natural right. The human species is unique in that it is the only species that has no natural rulers; human beings are free to choose—or at least have the potential to choose—their form of government, a privilege that was accorded by nature's God to no other species. The human species is therefore unique, and the regime founded on the recognition of this uniqueness will also be unique.

I think there can be little doubt that the Framers were attempting to put into practice the principles of the Declaration of Independence. It is long past the time when we could take seriously Beard's implication that the Constitution represented a Thermidorian reaction *against* the principles of the Declaration. Yet the Constitution was not totally successful. Insofar as it allowed the continued existence of slavery, it could never be a complete expression of the principles of the Declaration. It was only after the passage of the Reconstruction amendments that it could be said that the Constitution came into formal harmony with the Declaration.

But however much slavery was tolerated as an act of political expedience, its tolerance was considered by the Framers as an *exception* to the principles of the Declaration. This point was neatly expressed by Representative William A. Newell arguing for the passage of the Fourteenth Amendment before the House of Representatives in February 1866:

The combined wisdom of . . . patriotic men produced our present Constitution. It is a noble monument to their ability; but, unfortunately, like a[ll] *human instruments, it was imperfectly constructed, not because the theory was wrong, but because of the existence in the country of an institution so contrary to the genius of free government, and to the very principles upon which the Constitution was founded, that it was impossible to incorporate it into the organic law so that the latter could be preserved free from its contaminating influence. . . . The framers of the Constitution did what they considered best under the circumstances. They made freedom the rule and slavery the exception in the organization of the Government. They declared in favor of the former in language the most emphatic and sublime in history, while they placed the latter, as they fondly hoped, in a position favorable for ultimate extinction.*

The Framers treated slavery as a *necessary* evil to be expunged from the polity as soon as circumstances would allow.

The greatest force working toward the abolition of slavery would be the regime's dedication to the principle that "all men are created equal." This dedication would ensure that slavery would be considered as an exception to the principle and therefore never a legitimate part of the regime. Only a denial of the principle—a denial that would destroy the regime itself—could therefore justify slavery. But this would not be a principled justification; its only basis would be force without right. As Abraham Lincoln—surely America's profoundest explicator of the Founding—explained in 1857, the authors of the Declaration

did not mean to assert the obvious untruth, that all were then actually enjoying that equality, nor yet, that they were about to confer it immediately upon them. In fact they had no power to confer such a boon. They mean simply to declare the right, *so that the* enforcement *of it might follow as fast as circumstances should permit. They meant to set up a standard maxim for free society, which should be familiar to all, and revered by all; constantly looked to, constantly labored for, and even though never perfectly attained, constantly approximated, and thereby constantly spreading and deepening its influence. . . . The assertion that "all men are created equal" was of no practical use in effecting our separation from Great Britain; and it was placed in the Declaration, not for that, but for future use.*

The Declaration thus, in Lincoln's view, set up "a standard maxim" of political right, a maxim derived from natural human equality and therefore grounded in natural right. Stephen A. Douglas's "squatter sovereignty," which would have left the decision of whether "to vote slavery up or down" to local majorities, was simply grounded upon positivism—that is, the right of the stronger (and in democracies the stronger is the majority). And it was Douglas who insisted that the Declaration of Independence had meant only to include those of British descent. This doctrine, of course, became a leading tenet of the infamous *Dred Scott* decision. Had there been a move at the Convention to abolish slavery, the Convention would have collapsed and the Constitution would have been stillborn. As Madison and the more thoughtful Federalists realized, without a strong national government the prospects of ever abolishing slavery would be remote.

Madison pointed out in the Convention that the principal division was not between the large and small states but between the slaveholding and nonslaveholding states. The reason for this remark by Madison is evident: the division between large and small states—however much it may have agitated the Convention—did not trench directly upon the question of republican principles; the division between slaveholding and nonslaveholding states did. As Madison noted during the Convention, "Where slavery exists, the Republican Theory becomes still more fallacious." The question of federalism could reach a workable compromise without directly threatening the purity of the republican principles that informed the work of the Convention. The arguments about federalism, after all, were about what form of government, national or federal, would best *secure* republican principles. Madison and the other leading Federalists were adamant that republican liberty demanded an energetic national government, while those favoring a more confederal form of government were just as adamant that the best advantages for republican liberty were found in the state governments. But the question of slavery—while it too found its compromise in the Convention—was a compromise with republican principles. This was the tragic flaw of the Founding, a flaw that almost proved fatal to the republic in the Civil War. That it did not was due to the fact that it was still possible to rededicate the nation to those founding principles that had, by necessity, received only an incomplete expression in the Constitution. Contrary to what Justice Marshall has said, the Constitution did survive the Civil War; it was not replaced but completed by the Reconstruction amendments.

Frederick Douglass, a former slave and an abolitionist leader, understood the matter in precisely this light. In a speech delivered in February 1863, Douglass remarked that "the birth of our freedom is fixed on the day of the going forth of the Declaration of Independence." "The slaveholders," he continued, "are fighting for Slavery, and the slave system being against nature—they are fighting against the eternal laws of nature. . . . A great man once said it was useless to re-enact the laws of God, meaning thereby the laws of Nature. But a greater man than he will yet teach the world that it is useless to re-enact any other laws with any hope of their permanence." A few months later, Douglass explained the importance of the Declaration as the ground of the Constitution: "I hold that the Federal Government was never, *in its essence,* anything but an anti-slavery Government. . . . If in its origin slavery had any relation to the Government, it was only as the scaffolding to the magnificent structure, to be removed as soon as the building was completed." The essence of the Constitution, of course, found its expression in the arguments of the Declaration of Independence—those arguments derived from human nature and couched in the language of "the eternal laws of nature."

It is certain that the members of the Reconstruction Congress saw themselves as explicitly addressing the task of completing the regime of the Founding. This was the thrust of the remarks of Representative Thaddeus Stevens before the House of Representatives in May 1866:

I beg gentlemen to consider the magnitude of the task which was imposed upon the [Joint Committee on Reconstruction]. They were expected to suggest a plan for rebuilding a shattered nation—a nation which though not dissevered was yet shaken and riven . . . through four years of bloody war. It cannot be denied that this terrible struggle sprang from the vicious principles incorporated into the institutions of our country. Our fathers had been compelled to postpone the principles of their great Declaration, and wait for their full establishment till a more propitious time. That time ought to be present now.

References to the Declaration of Independence as "organic law" were so frequent throughout the debates in the thirty-ninth Congress that it can hardly be doubted that the Reconstruction Congress was, in some sense, self-consciously attempting to restore the Declaration as the authoritative source of the Constitution's principles.

A delicate question arose at the Convention with respect to its authority to propose a new Constitution. The Continental Congress had called the Convention "for the sole purpose of revising the Articles of Confederation, and reporting to Congress and the several Legislatures, such alterations and provisions therein, as shall . . . render the Federal Constitution adequate to the exigencies of Government, and the preservation of the Union." The leading Federalists in the Convention did not try to disguise the fact that they wished to scrap the Articles of Confederation and erect a "real and regular Government, as contradistinguished from the old Federal system." Madison's study of ancient and modern confederacies had convinced him that a confederacy could not be the foundation of genuine government. He told his fellow delegates that the Articles of Confederation rested on "improper principles," and that no amount of reform could transform it into a viable form of government. As Hamilton later wrote in *The Federalist,* "The great and radical vice in the construction of the existing Confederation is in the principle of LEGISLATION FOR STATES OR GOVERNMENTS, in their CORPORATE OR COLLECTIVE CAPACITIES, and as contradistinguished from the INDIVIDUALS of whom they consist." Hamilton's critique of those who still argued for the confederal principle was devastating: "They seem still to aim at things repugnant and irreconcilable; at an augmentation of federal authority without a diminution of State authority; at sovereignty in the Union and complete independence in the members. They still, in fine, seem to cherish with blind devotion the political monster of an *imperium in imperio.*" Thus, as Madison explained, the "exigencies of Government" required that the principle of Confederation must give way to the national principle, and if some believed that it was politically impossible to recommend a national government, then it was possible to recommend one that was "partly national and partly federal" in form, but national in principle.

The Convention, Madison argued, was charged with accomplishing two principal objects: revising the Articles of Confederation and rendering the federal Constitution "adequate to the exigencies of government." In Madison's view, the two charges, at bottom, were contradictory. The Convention was therefore forced to choose the more important of the two—providing for the "exigencies of government." Ultimately, however, Madison had resort to the Declaration to justify the work of the Convention. Its members, he wrote, "must have reflected that in all great changes of established governments forms ought to give way to substance; that a rigid adherence in such cases to the former would render nominal and nugatory the transcendent and precious right of the people to 'abolish or alter their governments as to them shall seem most likely to effect their safety and happiness.' " Thus Madison justified the Convention's work by an appeal to natural right, reasoning that the members of the Convention "must have borne in mind that as the plan to be framed and proposed was to be submitted to *the people themselves,* the disapprobation of this supreme authority would destroy it forever; its approbation blot out antecedent errors and irregularities."

Another question touched upon the legitimacy of the Convention's work, that is, its decision not to follow the forms prescribed for ratification by the Articles of Confederation, which required submission to the state legislatures. Instead, the Convention chose to submit the new Constitution directly to the people. This became a matter of some controversy at the Convention, and some delegates were troubled by what they regarded as the highhandedness of the proposal. On June 5 Roger Sherman argued that popular ratification was unnecessary since the Articles already provided for the assent by the state legislatures. Madison was quick to respond, revealing the importance of the mode of ratification: if the state legislatures were allowed to approve the new instrument of government, the implication would be that the states were creating the new federal government and the whole would "be considered as a Treaty only of a particular sort, among the Governments of Independent States. . . . For these reasons as well as others he thought it indispensable that the new Constitution should be ratified in the most unexceptionable form, and by the supreme authority of the people themselves."

The idea that the people were the ultimate authorities in republican government was a theme that was frequently voiced within the secret confines of the Convention proceedings. The decisive exchange on the manner of ratification occurred on August 31, near the end of the Convention's deliberations. Many delegates had come to realize that following the procedures of allowing state legislatures to pass on the new Constitution would likely spell its doom. Gouverneur Morris on this day "said he meant to facilitate the adoption of the plan, by leaving the modes approved by the several State Constitutions to be followed." Madison at this point was forced into making a very revealing speech supporting ratification by conventions chosen by the people. He noted that submitting the Constitution to the state legislatures would not succeed because "the powers given to the Genl. Govt. being taken from the State Govts the Legislatures would be more disinclined than conventions composed in part at least of other men; and if disinclined, they could devise modes apparently promoting, but really thwarting the ratification. . . . The people were in fact, the fountain of all power, and by resorting to them, all difficulties were got over." In this instance, Madison concluded, "first principles might be resorted to."

As expected, Luther Martin rose to oppose Madison, pointing out "the danger of commotions from a resort to the people & first principles in which the Governments might be on one side & the people on the other." Rufus King replied that the states "must have contemplated a recurrence to first principles before they sent deputies to this Convention." With this, the Convention consented to the "resort to first principles" by approving the proposal to submit the Constitution to conventions chosen by the people.

In his explanation of the Convention's decision in *The Federalist,* Madison was quite explicit. He called it a question "of a very delicate nature" to determine "on what principle the Confederation, which stands in the solemn form of a compact among the States, can be superseded without the unanimous consent of the parties to it." This question, he said, "is answered at once by recurring to the absolute necessity of the case; to the great principle of self-preservation; to the transcendent law of nature and of nature's God, which declares that the safety and happiness of society are the objects at which all political institutions aim and to which all such institutions must be sacrificed." Here, then, at almost the literary center of *The Federalist* is Madison's reference to "the transcendent law of nature and of nature's God" as being the object of the resort to first principles. Everyone, of course, recognized this quotation as being from the Declaration of Independence. No one could have mistaken Madison's intention in relying on the Declaration to answer this question of such "a very delicate nature." The ultimate foundation of the Constitution is the Declaration and its requirement that all legitimate government be derived from the consent of the governed. And, as Madison noted later in *The Federalist,* the central tenet of "republican theory" holds that "the people are the only legitimate fountain of power, and it is from them that the constitutional charter under which the several branches of government hold their power, is derived." This, Madison notes, is the greatest expression of the "manly spirit" of the Revolution.

I think that there can be little doubt that the Framers of the Constitution were self-consciously attempting to give practical effect to those natural rights principles that had been enunciated in the Declaration of Independence. The spirit that pervaded the Convention was one of engaging in a great republican experiment. And if there were some whose sentiments disposed them in the direction of a mixed regime—and there were some—even they recognized that the lack of a preexisting class structure and the republican "genius" of the people would make anything but a republic impossible. As Madison wrote in *The Federalist,* "The first question that offers itself is whether the general form and aspect of the government be strictly republican. It is evident that no other form would be reconcilable with the genius of the people of America; with the fundamental principles of the Revolution: or with that honorable determination which animates every votary of freedom to rest all our political experiments on the capacity of mankind for self-government. If the plan of the convention, therefore, be found to depart from the republican character, its advocates must abandon it as no longer defensible." Thus, what informs the Constitution is the "spirit of the revolution," that is, the Declaration.

Any genuine interpretation of the Constitution must therefore read the text of that document in the light of the principles of the Declaration. Neither Attorney General Meese nor Justice Brennan adopted this as a viable view of constitutional jurisprudence. Each took an extreme. Meese attempting to interpret the text without resort to principle, and Brennan resorting to principle—informed only by the vaguest notions of the "evolving demands of human dignity"—without reference to the Constitutional text. But it is only in the light of the principles of the Declaration that the text can be understood. The Fifth Amendment provides that "no person" shall "be deprived of life, liberty, or property, without due process of law." Does this clause include slaves? Are slaves to be considered as "persons" or as "property"? We know how this question was answered in *Dred Scott.* But Chief Justice Roger Brooke Taney in the *Dred Scott* opinion was forced to conclude that blacks were not included in the Declaration's phrase "all men are created equal." Here, Taney was wrong, as Lincoln many times pointed out. But what is decisive is that the question can only be settled by reference to the principles of the Declaration, not by the literal language of the Constitution. A similar analysis could be made of Brennan's view of "cruel and unusual punishment." Here Brennan ignores the *explicit* language of the Constitution in the name of evolving concepts of human dignity. This view, if it were to prevail, would simply make the idea of a written constitution absurd, to paraphrase John Marshall in *Marbury* v. *Madison* (1803).

In the last years of his life, James Madison worked on a preface to his notes on the Constitutional Convention that he wanted to be published posthumously. The preface, although never finished, was finally published in 1840, four years after his death. In the peroration, Madison, almost fifty years after the event, reflected on the spirit and the motives of the delegates.

Whatever may be the judgment pronounced on the competency of the architects of the Constitution, or whatever may be the destiny of the edifice prepared by them, I feel it a duty to express my profound & solemn conviction, derived from my intimate opportunity of observing & appreciating the views of the Convention, collectively & individually, that there never was an assembly of men, charged with a great & arduous trust, who were more pure in their motives, or more exclusively or anxiously devoted to the object committed to them, than were the members of the Federal Convention of 1787, to the object of devising and proposing a constitutional system which would best supply the defects of that which it was to replace, and best secure the permanent liberty and happiness of their country.

Madison's words sound hopelessly naive to our jaded ears. That men could act for public-spirited motives for "the permanent liberty and happiness of their country" seems incredibly superficial to an age that expects to find realistic motives in class consciousness or pragmatism. Yet I suspect we could be well served by a little naïveté in our attempt to recover the spirit of the Founding. Charles Warren characterized the attempt to interpret history in terms of economics or sociology as history that "leaves out of account the fact that a man may have an inner zeal for principles, beliefs, and ideals. . . . Those who contend, for instance, that economic causes brought about the War of the Revolution will always find it difficult to explain away the fact that the men who did the fighting thought, themselves, that they were fighting for a belief—a principle." And if we find statesmen who were attached to principles and animated by ideas, I see no need to be embarrassed by that. This does not make us less sophisticated, but it may get us nearer the truth.

SUGGESTIONS FOR FURTHER READING

Interpretations of the Constitution that stress the existence among Americans of a basic underlying consensus that led to relatively easy compromise in framing the Constitution have a long tradition in American historical scholarship. The founding fathers themselves justified their work by pointing to the problems the nation faced under the Articles of Confederation, problems that the new Constitution would solve. In an enormously influential book written in the late nineteenth century, John Fiske provided an interpretation and, in its title, a handy characterization to summarize the problems the nation faced under the Articles of Confederation: *The Critical Period of American History* (Boston, 1888). Max Farrand, who published a four-volume edition of *The Records of the Federal Convention of 1787,* wrote a history of *The Framing of the Constitution of the United States* (New Haven, 1913) that pointed to the "bundle of compromises" made by the founding fathers in their attempt to solve the problems of the "critical period."

In the same year, Charles Beard presented his very different view of the founding fathers in *An Economic Interpretation of the Constitution* (New York, 1913). Beard's influence on subsequent scholarship has been pervasive. Many historians simply accepted his class-conflict interpretation, but others sought to extend and modify his arguments while still retaining his conflict interpretation. Merrill Jensen, *The New Nation: A History of the United States During the Confederation, 1781–89* (New York, 1950) denies that the nation faced "critical" problems during the period and insists that the founders sought to curb democratic tendencies, which they feared. Jackson T. Main, *The Anti-Federalists: Critics of the Constitution* (Chapel Hill, N.C., 1961) paints a similar picture in his sympathetic description of the opponents of the new Constitution.

Another sign of Beard's influence is that critics have often cast their arguments in his terms in an attempt to undermine that influence. Forrest McDonald, *We the People: The Economic Origins of the Constitution* (Chicago, 1958); Robert E. Brown, *Charles Beard and the Constitution* (Princeton, N.J., 1956); and Henry Steele Commager, "The Constitution: Was It an Economic Document?" *American Heritage,* 10 (December 1958), 58–103, examine Beard's evidence and arguments in detail and find them wanting. Carl Van Doren, *The Great Rehearsal* (New York, 1948); Benjamin F. Wright, *Consensus and Continuity, 1776–1787* (Boston, 1958); and Edmund S. Morgan, *The Birth of the Republic, 1763–1789,* rev. ed. (Chicago, 1977) are implicit critiques of Beard that stress consensus and easy compromise rather than economic and political conflict.

If Beard's emphasis on economic differences has been subject to withering criticism, conflict interpretations are far from dead. Stanley Elkins and Eric McKitrick, "The Founding Fathers: Young Men of the Revolution," *Political Science Quarterly,* 76 (June 1961), 201–16, and Cecilia M. Kenyon, "Men of Little Faith: The Anti-Federalists on the Nature of Representative Government," *William and Mary Quarterly,* 3rd ser., 12 (January, 1955), 38–43, describe sharp differences between supporters and opponents of the Constitution that they trace to their different wartime experiences and their different visions of the future of the new nation. Jackson T. Main, *Political Parties Before the Constitution* (Chapel Hill, N.C., 1973) and Gordon S. Wood, *The Creation of the American Republic* (Chapel Hill, N.C., 1970) see conflicts stemming from differences in ideology and attitudes rather than economics and class. An insightful discussion that will carry the interested reader more deeply into the debate that Beard began and will show that it remains very much alive is John Patrick Diggins, "Power and Authority in American History: The Case of Charles A. Beard and His Critics," *American Historical Review,* 86 (October 1981), 701–30.

Staughton Lynd, in *Class Conflict, Slavery and the United States Constitution* (Indianapolis, 1967), argues that the major conflict in the Constitution Convention was not between rich and poor and small states and large, but rather between North and South over the question of slavery. On the question of slavery see also David Brion Davis, *The*

---

*Available in paperback edition.

Problem of Slavery in the Age of Revolution, 1770–1823 (Ithaca, N.Y., 1975) and Ira Berlin and Ronald Hoffman, eds., *Slavery and Freedom in the Age of the American Revolution* (Charlottesville, Va., 1983).

Collections of original essays that will provide readers with recent interpretations of the Constitution are Neil L. York, ed., *Toward a More Perfect Union: Six Essays on the Constitution* (Provo, Utah, 1988), and Herman Belz, Ronald Hoffman, and Peter J. Albert, eds., *To Form a More Perfect Union: The Critical Ideas of the Constitution* (Charlottesville, Va., 1992). Robert Gross, ed., *The Bicentennial of an Agrarian Rebellion* (Charlottesville, Va., 1993) includes a number of essays detailing the conflict that helped to stimulate a movement for a new constitution.

Michael Kammen, *A Machine That Would Go of Itself: The Constitution in American Culture* (New York, 1986) traces the ways in which the people, the politicians, and the courts have viewed the Constitution during the 200 years since its adoption. The essays in R. C. Simmons, ed., *The United States Constitution: The First 200 Years* (Manchester, Eng., 1989) consider the legacy of the Constitution, evaluating how it has developed rather than what the founding fathers had in mind. Frank Bourgin, **The Great Challenge: The Myth of Laissez-Faire in the Early Republic* (New York, 1989) insists that the founding fathers believed that the new government they created would have an important role to play in the economic development of the nation.

Once the debates in the Philadelphia Convention ended, they moved into the states during the ratification process. State-by-state discussion of these conflicts may be found in John P. Kaminski and Patrick T. Conley, *The Constitution and the States: The Role of the Original Thirteen in the Framing and the Adoption of the Federal Constitution* (Madison, Wisc., 1988), and Michael Allen Gillespie and Michael Lienesch, eds., *Ratifying the Constitution* (Lawrence, Kans., 1989).

The best way to get at the views of the participants is to read their own words. The views of the founding fathers are in the essays written in support of the new Constitution during the ratification debates by John Jay, Alexander Hamilton, and James Madison: **The Federalist Papers,* available in many editions.

Richard B. Morris, ** Witnesses at the Creation: Hamilton, Madison, Jay, and the Constitution* (New York, 1985) is a beautifully written discussion of the roles of the authors of the *Federalist Papers* as revolutionaries and founding fathers. Lance Banning, *The Sacred Fire of Liberty: James Madison and the Founding of the Federal Republic* (Ithaca, N.Y., 1995) analyzes Madison's desire for a stronger central government along with his continuing commitment to the revolutionary principles.

A useful analysis of the *Federalist Papers* is Gary Wills, *Explaining America* (New York, 1981). Herbert J. Storing, ed., **The Anti-Federalist* (Chicago, 1985) is an abridgement of his seven-volume collection of the writings of opponents of the Constitution. The multivolume *Documentary History of the Ratification of the Constitution* may be sampled in John P. Kaminski and Richard Leffler, eds., *Federalists and Antifederalists: The Debate over the Ratification of the Constitution* (Madison, Wisc., 1989).

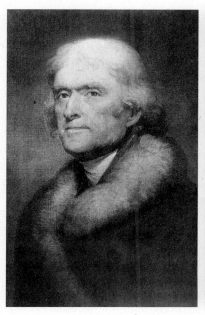

Jeffersonians
and Federalists

The ratification and general acceptance of the Constitution did not eliminate all disagreements in the new nation. Indeed, strong differences of opinion arose within George Washington's cabinet, differences that soon spread to the Congress and, through the public press, to the country at large. The economic program proposed by Washington's strong-willed secretary of the treasury, Alexander Hamilton, was soon opposed by the secretary of state, Thomas Jefferson. In less than a decade after the inauguration of the first administration under the new Constitution, disagreements had led to the formation of the nation's first organized political parties. The election of 1800 was clearly a party battle, and Jefferson's newly organized Republican party emerged victorious.

Certainly this was a time of sharp debate and furious party struggle. Yet how significant were the differences dividing the country? In his old age, looking back on the event, Thomas Jefferson called his election "the revolution of 1800," obviously an assessment that implied that vast differences separated him from his opponents. Yet in his first inaugural address, Jefferson had minimized the importance of the party conflict from which the country had just emerged. "We are all Republicans—we are all Federalists," he said.

Because Jefferson himself entertained two seemingly contradictory evaluations of his victory, later historians have been able to agree with him and still disagree among themselves. For some, Jefferson's victory was indeed a revolution; his administration is said to have ushered in a period of agrarian democracy; his victory signaled the defeat of an aristocratic and moneyed power. Others argue that Jefferson changed little of the inheritance from the Federalists he had defeated; in truth, they maintain, Jefferson continued the Federalist program.

The existence of opposing parties, then, does not by itself prove the existence of fundamental conflict during the early years of the new nation's history. Nor does the relative ease with which the Jeffersonians established their political hegemony by itself prove that they merely absorbed the program and policies of their opponents. Historians must look deeper before they can discover whether party labels revealed a major conflict in American society or merely minor differences within a basic consensus. At the same time, they must keep in mind that the country was changing rapidly during these years and that among the changes was one that opponents and supporters alike called an expansion of democracy. To see democracy and Jeffersonianism on the one side locked in a struggle with aristocracy and Federalism on the other is to recognize a fundamental conflict. But if democracy had won the day in both parties and if party conflicts had become mainly struggles for power and office, then consensus becomes the theme for the first two or three decades of the nation's history under the new Constitution.

These opposing views are revealed in the following selections. The first two focus directly on Jefferson. Morton Borden considers Jefferson to be a political compromiser, what we today would call a pragmatic politician. He denies that this means that Jefferson had no strongly held political principles or that, once in power, he abandoned his principles in order to increase his popularity. Jefferson held on to his principles and promoted promised reforms, which angered his opponents. But the differences that divided Jefferson from his opponents, while important, were not fundamental. The two sides disagreed on details but were united on fundamentals, and, therefore, Jefferson's political skills brought reforms while avoiding really significant clashes.

Lance Banning disagrees with this view. He argues that fundamental differences divided Jefferson from his opponents. He agrees that Jefferson did not go as far in his promised reforms as some of his followers desired, but he denies that Jefferson compromised his principles once in office. Jefferson and his successors created a new consensus, not because they compromised their principles but rather because their principles gathered widespread support.

To evaluate these two approaches, students might consider the nature and significance of party politics in the United States. How important are political party differences? Do Americans today agree on fundamentals and disagree merely on details? Are the differences that divide Democrats from Republicans today less important than those that divided Jeffersonians from Federalists in the early nineteenth century? Elections today are hard-fought, and candidates often charge that the election of their opponent would endanger the future well-being of the nation. Do candidates really believe this?

In the third selection, Richard Hofstadter considers the election of Jefferson in terms of such questions. He notes that neither Jefferson nor the Federalist leaders thought of their opponents as part of the legitimate, loyal opposition. Rather, each conceived of the other as an implacable enemy of the Republic, a view that certainly points to sharp and fundamental conflict. Nevertheless, he reminds the reader, the election of 1800 was the "first election in modern history which, by popular decision, resulted in the quiet and peaceful transition of national power from the hands of one of two embattled parties to another," a development that implies the existence of a widespread consensus.

The separation of Americans into different parties and factions matched by sharp and often abusive exchanges among leaders in the newspapers of the day leaves no doubt of differences among Americans during the Age of Jefferson. But how significant were these differences? Did they arise from basic economic and social cleavages in American society and reflect fundamental class conflict based on real ideological differences? Or did they reflect only minor disagreements within a general context of agreement or consensus?

Thomas Jefferson:
Political Compromiser

For twelve years the Constitution worked, after a fashion. From its inception the new document had been subjected to severe trials and divisive strains. A rebellion in Pennsylvania, a naval war with France, a demand for states' rights from Virginia and Kentucky, and various Western schemes of disunion—all had been surmounted. Had it not been for the great prestige of George Washington and the practical moderation of John Adams, America's second attempt at a federal union might have failed like the first. Partisan passions had run high in the 1790's, and any single factor on which men disagreed—Hamilton's financial plans or the French Revolution or the Sedition Act—might easily have caused a stoppage of the nation's political machinery.

The two-party system emerged during this decade, and on each important issue public opinion seemed to oscillate between Federalist and Democratic-Republican. Perhaps this was to be expected of a young nation politically adolescent. Year by year Americans were becoming more politically alert and active; if there was little room for middle ground between these two factions, yet opinions were hardly fixed and irrevocable. The culmination of partisan controversy and the test of respective strengths took place in the monumental election of 1800.

Jefferson was feared, honestly feared, by almost all Federalists. Were he to win the election, so they predicted, all the hard constructive gains of those twelve years would be dissipated. Power would be returned to the individual states; commerce would suffer; judicial power would be lessened; and the wonderful financial system of Hamilton would be dismantled and destroyed. Jefferson was an atheist, and he would attack the churches. Jefferson was a hypocrite, an aristocrat posing as democrat, appealing to the baser motives of human beings in order to obtain votes. Jefferson was a revolutionary, a Francophile and, after ruining the Army and Navy under the guise of economy measures, might very well in-

Morton Borden, "Thomas Jefferson" in *America's Eleven Greatest Presidents* ed. by Morton Borden, 2nd. ed. © 1971 by Rand McNally & Company, Chicago, pp. 52–62. Reprinted by permission.

volve the nation in a war with England. In short, it was doubtful if the Constitution could continue its successful course under such a president.

In like manner the Republicans feared another Federalist victory. To be sure, John Adams had split with Hamilton and had earned the enmity of the Essex Junto. But would he not continue Hamilton's "moneyed system"? Did not Adams share the guilt of every Federalist for the despicable Alien and Sedition Acts? Was it not true that "His Rotundity" so admired the British system that he was really a monarchist at heart? Republicans were not engaging in idle chatter, nor were they speaking solely for effect, when they predicted many dire consequences if Adams were elected. A typical rumor had Adams uniting "his house to that of his majesty of Britain" and "the bridegroom was to be king of America."

Throughout the country popular interest in the election was intense, an intensity sustained over months of balloting. When the Republicans carried New York City, Alexander Hamilton seriously suggested that the results be voided. And when the breach between Adams and Hamilton became public knowledge, Republicans nodded knowingly and quoted the maxim: "When thieves fall out, honest men come by their own."

The Federalists were narrowly defeated. But the decision was complicated by a result which many had predicted: a tied electoral vote between the two Republican candidates, Aaron Burr and Thomas Jefferson. (Indeed, the Twelfth Amendment was adopted in 1804 to avoid any such recurrence.) A choice between the two would be made by the House of Representatives. At this moment, February, 1801, the Constitution seemed on the verge of collapse. Federalist members of the lower house united in support of Burr; Republicans were just as adamant for Jefferson. After thirty-five ballots, neither side had yet obtained the necessary majority. The issue seemed hopelessly deadlocked. What would happen on March 4, inauguration day?

One representative from Maryland, sick with a high fever, was literally carried into Congress on a stretcher to maintain the tied vote of his state. The Republican governor of Pennsylvania, Thomas McKean, threatened to march on Washington with troops if the Federalists persisted in thwarting the will of the people. Hamilton was powerless; his advice that Jefferson was the lesser evil went unheeded. So great was their hatred of the Virginian that most Federalists in Congress would have opposed him regardless of the consequences. After all, they reasoned, Jefferson would dismantle the Federal government anyway. In the end, however, patriotism and common sense prevailed. For the choice was no longer Jefferson or Burr, but Jefferson or no president at all. A few Federalists, led by James A. Bayard of Delaware, could not accept the logic of their party, and threw the election to Jefferson.

What a shock it was, then, to read Jefferson's carefully chosen words in his inaugural address:

But every difference of opinion is not a difference of principle. We have called by different names brethren of the same principle. We are all republicans—we are all federalists. If there be any among us who would wish to dissolve this Union or to change its republican form, let them stand undisturbed as monuments of the safety with which error of opinion may be tolerated where reason is left free to combat it. I know, indeed, that some honest men fear that a republican government cannot be strong; that this government is not strong enough. But would the honest patriot, in the full tide of successful experiment, abandon a government which has so far kept us free and firm, on the theoretic and visionary fear that this government, the world's best hope, may by possibility want energy to preserve itself? I trust not. I believe this, on the contrary, the strongest government on earth. I believe it is the only one where every man, at the call of the laws, would fly to the standard of the law, and would meet invasions of the public order as his own personal concern. Sometimes it is said that man cannot be trusted with the government of himself. Can he, then, be trusted with the government of others? Or have we found angels in the form of kings to govern him? Let history answer this question.

The words were greeted with applause—and confusion. It was obvious that Jefferson wanted to salve the wounds of bitter factionalism. While many Federalists remained distrustful and some even regarded it as hypocritical, most men approved the tone of their new president's message.

But what did Jefferson mean? Were there no economic principles at stake in his conflicts with Hamilton? Were there no political and constitutional principles implicit in the polar views of the respective parties? And, in the last analysis, did not these differences reflect a fundamental philosophical quarrel over the nature of human beings? Was not the election of 1800 indeed a revolution? If not, then what is the meaning of Jeffersonianism?

For two terms Jefferson tried, as best he could, to apply the standards of his inaugural address. Naturally, the Alien and Sedition Acts were allowed to lapse. The new secretary of the treasury, Albert Gallatin, was instructed to devise an easily understood program to erase the public debt gradually. Internal taxes were either abolished or reduced. Frugality and economy were emphasized to an extreme. Elegant and costly social functions were replaced by simple and informal receptions. The expense of maintaining ambassadors at the courts of Portugal, Holland, and Prussia was erased by withdrawing these missions. The Army and Navy were pared down to skeleton size. To be sure, Jefferson had to reverse himself on the matter of patronage for subordinate Government posts. Originally he planned to keep these replacements to a minimum, certainly not to permit an individual's partisan opinions to be a basis for dismissal unless the man manifestly used his office for partisan purposes. This position was politically untenable, according to Jefferson's lieutenants, and they pressed him to accept a moderate number of removals. Indeed, Jefferson's handling of patronage is symbolic of what Hamilton once called his "ineradicable duplicity."

The Federalist leaders cried out in anguish at every one of these policy changes. The lowering of the nation's military strength would increase the danger of invasion. It was a rather risky gamble to assume that peace could be maintained while European war was an almost constant factor, and the United States was the major neutral carrier. The abolition of the excises, especially on distilled spirits, would force the Government to rely on tariffs, an unpredictable source of revenue depending on the wind and waves. It was charged that several foreign ambassadors were offended by Jefferson's rather affected and ultrademocratic social simplicity. Most important, the ultimate payment of the public debt would reduce national power.

This time, however, the people did not respond to the Federalist lament of impending anarchy. After all, commerce prospered throughout most of Jefferson's administration. Somehow the churches remained standing. No blood baths took place. The Bank of the United States still operated. Peace was maintained. Certainly, some Federalist judges were under attack, but the judicial power passed through this ordeal to emerge unscathed and even enhanced. Every economic indicator—urban growth, westward expansion, agricultural production, the construction of canals, turnpikes and bridges—continued to rise, undisturbed by the political bickering in Washington.

At first the Federalists were confident that they would regain power. Alexander Hamilton's elaborate scheme for an organization to espouse Christianity and the Constitution, as the "principal engine" to restore Federalist power, was rejected out of hand. He was told that "our adversaries will soon demonstrate to the world the soundness of our doctrines and the imbecility and folly of their own." But hope changed to despair as the people no longer responded; no "vibration of opinion" took place as in the 1790's. Federalism was the party of the past, an antiquated and dying philosophy. "I will fatten my pigs, and prune my trees; nor will I any longer . . . trouble to govern this country," wrote Fisher Ames: "You federalists are only lookers-on." Jefferson swept the election of 1804, capturing every state except Connecticut and Delaware from the Federalist candidate, Charles C. Pinckney. "Federalism is dead," wrote Jefferson a few years later, "without even the hope of a day of resurrection. The quondam leaders indeed retain their rancour and principles; but their followers are amalgamated with us in sentiment, if not in name."

It is the fashion of some historians to explain the Federalist demise and Republican ascendancy in terms of a great change in Jefferson. A radical natural law philosopher when he fought as minority leader, he became a first-rate utilitarian politician as president. The Virginian became an American. Revolutionary theory was cast aside when Jefferson faced the prosaic problem of having to run the country. He began to adopt some of the techniques and policies of the Federalists. Indeed, it is often observed that Jefferson "outfederalized the Federalists."

There is much to be said for this view. After all, less than three months after he assumed the presidency, Jefferson dispatched a naval squadron to the Mediterranean on a warlike mission, without asking the permission of Congress. Two members of his Cabinet, Levi Lincoln and Albert Gallatin, thought the action unconstitutional, and so advised the President. Almost from the moment of its birth the young nation had paid tribute, as did every European power, rather than risk a war with the Barbary pirates. But Jefferson could not abide such bribery. No constitutional scruples could delay for a moment his determination to force the issue. Later, Congress declared war, and in four years Barbary power was shattered. The United States under Jefferson accomplished an object that England, France, Spain, Portugal, and Holland had desired for more than a century—unfettered commerce in the Mediterranean. Here, then, in this episode, is a totally different Jefferson—not an exponent of states' rights and strict interpretation of the Constitution, but an American nationalist of the first order.

Perhaps the most frequently cited example of Jefferson's chameleon quality, however, was on the question of whether the United States should or should not purchase the Louisiana Territory from France. On this question the fundamental issue was squarely before Jefferson, and a choice could not be avoided. The purchase would more than double the size of the United States. Yet the Constitution did not specifically provide for such acquisition of foreign territory. Further, the treaty provided that this area would eventually be formed into states, full partners in the Union. Again, the Constitution did not specifically cover such incorporation. A broad interpretation of Article IV, Section III, however, might permit United States' ratification of the treaty. Should theory be sacrificed and an empire gained? Or were the means as important as the ends?

Broad or loose construction of the Constitution was the key to the growth of Federal power. Federalists had argued in this vein to justify most of their legislation in the 1790's. To Jefferson, individual liberty and governmental power were on opposite ends of a see-saw, which the Federalists had thrown off balance. He believed that government, especially the central government, must be restricted within rather narrow and essential limits. Only by continually and rigidly applying strict construction to the Constitution could this tendency to overweening power be controlled and individual liberty be safeguarded. As early as 1777, Jefferson, then governor of Virginia, had warned that constitutions must be explicit, "so as to exclude all possible doubt; . . . [lest] at some future day . . . power[s] should be assumed."

On the other hand, the purchase of Louisiana would fulfill a dream and solve a host of problems. Jefferson envisioned an American empire covering "the whole northern, if not the southern continent, with a people speaking the same language, governed in similar forms, and by similar laws." The purchase would be a giant step in the direction of democracy's inevitable growth. "Is it not better," asked Jefferson, "that the opposite bank of the Mississippi should be settled by our own brethren and children, than by strangers of another family?"

Of more immediate interest, Westerners would be able to ship their goods down the Mississippi without fear that New Orleans might be closed. Indian attacks undoubtedly would taper off without the Spanish to instigate them. Uppermost in Jefferson's mind, however, was the freedom from England that the purchase would assure. He did not fear Spanish ownership. A feeble, second-rate nation like Spain on the frontier offered little threat to America's future security. The continued possession of Louisiana by an imperialistic France led by the formidable Napoleon, however, might force the United States into an alliance with England. At first Jefferson thought a constitutional amendment specifically permitting the purchase might solve the dilemma. But Napoleon showed signs of wavering. The treaty had to be confirmed immediately, with no indication of constitutional doubt. Jefferson asked the Republican leaders in the Senate to ratify it "with as little debate as possible, and particularly so far as respects the constitutional difficulty."

In still other ways Jefferson's presidency was marked by Federalist policies which encouraged the growth of central power. Internal improvements loomed large in Jefferson's mind. While many turnpikes and canals were financed by private and state capital, he realized that Federal support would be necessary, especially in the western part of the nation. With the use of Federal money obtained from the sale of public lands, and (later) aided by direct congressional appropriations, the groundwork for the famous Cumberland road was established during Jefferson's administration. He enthusiastically supported Gallatin's plan to spend twenty million dollars of Federal funds on a network of national roads and canals. Other more pressing problems intervened, however, and it was left to later administrations to finance these local and interstate programs. If Hamilton had pressed for internal improvements in the 1790's (he suggested them in the *Report on Manufactures*), Jefferson probably would have raised constitutional objections.

Finally, is not Jefferson's change of tack further reflected in the political history of that era? Over the span of a few years it seemed as if each party had somehow reversed directions. In 1798–99 Jefferson and Madison penned the Virginia and Kentucky Resolutions as an answer to the Federalists' infamous Alien and Sedition Acts. In 1808–9 more radical but comparable rumblings of dissatisfaction emanated from some New England Federalists over Jefferson's Embargo Act. For the embargo, says one of Jefferson's biographers, was "the most arbitrary, inquisitorial, and confiscatory measure formulated in American legislation up to the period of the Civil War." Further, both parties splintered during Jefferson's administration. Many moderate Federalists, like John Quincy Adams, found themselves in closer harmony with Administration policy than with Essex Junto beliefs. And Jefferson's actions alienated old comrades, like John Randolph, Jr., whose supporters were called the Tertium Quids. It is interesting to note that there is no historical consensus of why, when, how, or what precipitated the break between Randolph and Jefferson. Randolph is always referred to as brilliant but erratic; and whatever immediate reason is alleged, the cause somehow has to do with Randolph's personality and Jefferson's betrayal of the true doctrines.

It is part of Jefferson's greatness that he could inspire a myth and project an image. But one must not confuse myth and reality, shadow and substance. Thomas Jefferson as he was, and Thomas Jefferson as people perceived him, are quite different. While both concepts of course, are of equal value in understanding our past, it is always the historian's task to make the distinction. Too often, in Jefferson's case, this has not been done. Too often the biographers have described the myth—have taken at face value the popular view of Jefferson and his enemies, contained in the vitriolic newspaper articles and pamphlets, the passionate debates and fiery speeches of that period—and missed or misconstrued the reality.

This is understandable. Even the principals inevitably became involved and helped to propagate the exaggerated images of the 1790's and thus misunderstood one another's aims and motives. Jefferson, according to his grandson, never considered Federalist fulminations "as abusing him; they had never known him. They had created an imaginary being clothed with odious attributes, to whom they gave his name; and it was against that creature of their imaginations they had levelled their anathemas." John Adams, reminiscing in a letter to Jefferson, wrote: "Both parties have excited artificial terrors and if I were summoned as a witness to say upon oath, which party had excited . . . the most terror, and which had really felt the most, I could not give a more sincere answer, than in the vulgar style 'Put them in a bag and shake them, and then see which comes out first.' "

On March 4, 1801, following a decade of verbal violence, many Americans were surprised to hear that "We are all republicans—we are all federalists." Some historians act as if they, too, are surprised. These historians then describe Jefferson's administration as if some great change took place in his thinking, and conclude that he "outfederalized the Federalists." This is a specious view, predicated on an ultraradical Jefferson of the 1790's in constant debate with an ultra-conservative Hamilton. Certainly Jefferson as president had to change. Certainly at times he had to modify, compromise, and amend his previous views. To conclude, however, that he outfederalized the Federalists is to miss the enormous consistency of Jefferson's beliefs and practices.

Jefferson was ever a national patriot second to none, not even to Hamilton. He always conceived of the United States as a unique experiment, destined for greatness so long as a sharp line isolated American civilization from European infection. Thus he strongly advised our youth to receive their education at home rather than in European schools, lest they absorb ideas and traits he considered "alarming to me as an American." From "Notes on Virginia" to his advice at the time of Monroe's doctrine, Jefferson thought of America first. It matters not that Hamilton was the better prophet; Jefferson was the better American. The French minister Adet once reported: "Although Jefferson is the friend of liberty . . . although he is an admirer of the efforts we have made to cast off our shackles . . . Jefferson, I say, is an American, and as such, he cannot sincerely be our friend. An American is the born enemy of all the peoples of Europe."

Jefferson's nature was always more practical than theoretical, more commonsensical than philosophical. Certainly the essence of his Declaration of Independence is a Lockean justification of revolution; but, said Jefferson, "It was . . . an expression of the American mind," meant "to place before mankind the common sense of the subject." Jefferson always preferred precision to "metaphysical subtleties." The Kentucky and Virginia Resolutions can be understood only as a specific rebuttal of the Sedition Act. "I can never fear that things will go far wrong," wrote Jefferson, "where common sense has fair play."

One must also remember that Hamilton's power lessened considerably in the last four years of Federalist rule. He had a strong coterie of admirers, but the vast body of Federalists sided with John Adams. Despite all Hamilton did to insure Adams' defeat, and despite the split in Federalist ranks, the fact that Jefferson's victory in 1801 was won by a narrow margin indicated Federalist approval of Adams' actions. Certainly the people at that time—Jefferson and Adams included—regarded 1801 as the year of revolution. But if historians must have a revolution, perhaps Adams' split with the Hamiltonians is a better date. "The mid-position which Adams desired to achieve," writes Manning Dauer, "was adopted, in the main, by Jefferson and his successors."

To be sure, the two men disagreed on many matters of basic importance. Jefferson placed his faith in the free election of a virtuous and talented natural aristocracy; Adams did not. Within the constitutional balance, Jefferson emphasized the power of the lower house; Adams would give greater weight to the executive and judiciary. Jefferson, as a general rule, favored a strict interpretation of the Constitution; Adams did not fear broad construction. Both believed that human beings enjoyed inalienable rights, but only Jefferson had faith in man's perfectability. Jefferson could say, "I like a little rebellion now and then. It is like a storm in the atmosphere"; Adams had grown more conservative since 1776. Jefferson always defended and befriended Thomas Paine; Adams found Edmund Burke's position on the French Revolution more palatable.

Yet, the sages of Quincy and Monticello were both moderate and practical men. Despite the obvious and basic contrasts, both Adams and Jefferson stood side by side on certain essentials: to avoid war, to quiet factionalism, to preserve republican government. Their warm friendship, renewed from 1812 to 1826 in a remarkable and masterful correspondence, was based on frankness, honesty, and respect. "About facts," Jefferson wrote, "you and I cannot differ, because truth is our mutual guide; And if any opinions you may express should be different from mine, I shall receive them with the liberality and indulgence which I ask for my own." Jefferson and Adams represent, respectively, the quintessence of the very best in American liberalism and conservatism. Their indestructible link, then, was "a keen sense of national consciousness," a realization that America's destiny was unique. This is the meaning of Jefferson's words: "We are all republicans—we are all federalists."

The Revolution of 1800 and the Principles of Ninety-Eight

I

Thomas Jefferson wrote proudly of "the revolution of 1800," calling it "as real a revolution in the principles of our government as that of 1776 was in its form." Many of his followers agreed. Today, however, most historians would probably prefer a different phrase. Too little changed—and that too slowly—to justify the connotations present in that loaded word. There were no radicals among the great triumvirate who guided the Republicans in power, as they had led them through the years of opposition. The President was bent on reconciliation with the body of his former foes. "We are all Republicans . . . all Federalists," he said. He wanted to detach the mass of Federalists from their former leaders, and he knew that this was incompatible with an abrupt reversal of the policies that had been followed for a dozen years. He had, in any case, no notion that his predecessors' work could be dismantled all at once. The Hamiltonian system might be hateful, but it had bound the nation to a contract it had no alternative except to honor. Madison and Gallatin, who were by instinct more conservative than Jefferson himself, were not disposed to disagree.

From the beginning of the new administration, nonetheless, Republicans insisted that a change of policies, not just of men, was necessary to return the state to its republican foundations. In his inaugural address, Jefferson announced commitment to "a wise and frugal government which shall restrain men from injuring one another, shall leave them otherwise free to regulate their own pursuits of industry and improvement, and shall not take from the mouth of labor the bread it has earned." This kind of government, he hinted, would be guided by a set of principles that could be readily distinguished from the policies of years before. Among them were

---

From Lance Banning, *The Jeffersonian Persuasion: Evolution of a Party Ideology*. Reprinted from Lance Banning, *The Jeffersonian Persuasion: Evolution of a Party Ideology*. Copyright © 1978 by Cornell University. Used by permission of the publisher, Cornell University Press.

Peace, commerce, and honest friendship with all nations; entangling alliances with none.

The support of the state governments in all their rights as the most competent administrations for our domestic concerns and the surest bulwarks against antirepublican tendencies. . . .

A well disciplined militia, our best reliance in peace and for the first moments of war, till regulars may relieve them. . . .

Economy in public expense, that labor may be lightly burdened.

The honest payment of our debts and sacred preservation of the public faith.

Reform began while Jefferson awaited the assembly of the first Republican Congress. Pardons were issued to the few men still affected by sedition prosecutions. The diplomatic corps, a target for its costs and for the influence it was thought to give to the executive, was cut to barest bones. A few of the most active Federalists were purged from office, while the President withheld commissions signed by Adams after his defeat was known. The evolution of a partisan appointments policy was too slow for some members of the party, who argued that "no enemy to democratic government will be provided with the means to sap and destroy any of its principles nor to profit by a government to which they are hostile in theory and practice." But even the most radical were satisfied with the administration's purpose when the President announced his program to the Seventh Congress.

Jefferson's first annual message was "an epitome of republican principles applied to practical purposes." After a review of foreign policy and Indian affairs, the President suggested abolition of all internal taxes. "The remaining sources of revenue will be sufficient," he believed, "to provide for the support of government, to pay the interest on the public debts, and to discharge the principals in shorter periods than the laws or the general expectations had contemplated. . . . Sound principles will not justify our taxing the industry of our fellow citizens to accumulate treasure for wars to happen we know not when, and which might not perhaps happen but from the temptations offered by that treasure." Burdens, he admitted, could only be reduced if expenditures fell too. But there was room to wonder "whether offices or officers have not been multiplied unnecessarily." The military, for example, was larger than required to garrison the posts, and there was no use for the surplus. "For defence against invasion, their number is as nothing; nor is it conceived needful or safe that a standing army should be kept up in time of peace." The judiciary system, packed and altered by the Federalists at the close of their regime, would naturally "present itself to the contemplation of Congress." And the laws concerning naturalization might again be liberalized.

The Seventh Congress, voting usually on party lines, did everything that Jefferson had recommended. It also gave approval to a plan prepared by Gallatin, the Secretary of the Treasury, for the complete retirement of the public debt before the end of 1817. Along with its repeal of the Judiciary Act of 1800, it reduced the army to three thousand officers and men, while lowering appropriations for the navy in the face of war with Tripoli. Of all its measures, though, the abolition of internal taxes (and four hundred revenue positions) called forth the most eloquent enunciation of the principles on which the new majority thought it should act:

The Constitution is as dear to us as to our adversaries. . . . It is by repairing the breaches that we mean to save it and to set it on a firm and lasting foundation. . . . We are yet a young nation and must learn wisdom from the experience of others. By avoiding the course which other nations have steered, we shall likewise avoid their catastrophe. Public debts, standing armies, and heavy taxes have converted the English nation into a mere machine to be used at the pleasure of the crown. . . . We have had no riot act, but we have had a Sedition Act calculated to secure the executive from free and full investigation; we have had an army and still have a small one, securing to the executive an immensity of patronage; and we have a large national debt, for the payment . . . of which it is necessary to collect "yearly millions" by means of a cloud of officers spread over the face of the country. . . . Iniquitous as we deem the manner of its settlement, we mean to discharge; but we mean not to perpetuate it; it is no part of our political creed that "a public debt is a public blessing."

Before the session ended, Jefferson could tell a friend that "some things may perhaps be left undone from motives of compromise for a time and not to alarm by too sudden a reformation," but the proceedings of the Congress gave every ground for hope that "we shall be able by degrees to introduce sound principles and make them habitual." Indeed, the session was so good a start that there was little left to recommend in 1802. The effort of the next few years would be to keep the course already set.

"Revolution" may not be the proper word to characterize the changes introduced in 1801 and early 1802. "Apostasy," however, would be worse. Yet every study of the Jeffersonian ascendency must come to terms with the magnificent and multivolumed work of Henry Adams. Though now almost a century old, the scope and literary power of this classic give it influence that has lasted to the present day. And one of Adams' major themes was the abnegation of the principles of 1798 by the Republican regime. Jefferson had hoped to put an end to parties by detaching the great body of Federalists from their irreconcilable leaders. By 1804 he seemed to have approached this end. To Adams, though, his great successes were a consequence of Jefferson's abandonment of principle and singleminded quest for popularity. If party lines were melting, it had been the Jeffersonians who had compromised their principles the most:

not a Federalist measure, not even the Alien and Sedition laws, had been expressly repudiated; . . . the national debt was larger than it had ever been before, the navy maintained and energetically employed, the national bank preserved and its operations extended; . . . the powers of the national government had been increased [in the Louisiana Purchase] to a point that made blank paper of the Constitution.

It was the Federalists, not the Republicans, who now upheld the states' rights principles of 1798.

Every part of Adams' powerful indictment could be contradicted or excused. Thus, Jefferson abandoned scruple in the case of the Louisiana Purchase with reluctance and because there seemed some danger that the Emperor of France might change his mind about a bargain that could guarantee the nation's peace while promising indefinite postponement of the day when overcrowding and development might put an end to its capacity for freedom. Jefferson continued to distrust the national bank, but would not break the public's pledge by moving to revoke its charter. The party *had* repudiated the Sedition law, explicitly refusing to renew it in the session that had also seen a relaxation of the naturalization law. The national debt *had* been considerably reduced before the purchase of Louisiana raised it once again, and it would fall much further in the years to come.

It is necessary to admit, however, that the list of Adams' charges also could be lengthened. While Jefferson himself was never reconciled, Gallatin and Madison eventually supported the Bank of the United States. While Jefferson preferred to lead by indirection, he was in fact a stronger President than either of his predecessors ever tried to be. His public messages *suggested* measures, but his hints were often taken as commands by party members in the Congress. Informally or through floor leaders in the House, the administration made its wishes known and drafted most of the important legislation. Finally, in 1808, in its progressively more stringent efforts to enforce the embargo, Jefferson's administration wielded powers over the daily life of Americans that far exceeded anything its predecessors ever sought, even using regulars to help enforce the law.

There were, without a doubt, occasions after 1801 when the warring parties came so close to switching sides that one might doubt that principle meant much to either group. The Federalists stood forth, when they could hope to profit, as defenders of states' rights. They shamelessly employed old opposition rhetoric to criticize the massive force of party loyalty and the influence of the President on Congress. Nor was Henry Adams first to charge the Jeffersonians with a surrender to the principles of their opponents. Jefferson and his successor faced a swelling discontent from a minority of purists among Republicans themselves.

In October, 1801, before the meeting of the Seventh Congress, Edmund Pendleton had published a widely read consideration of the policies that would be necessary to make the revolution of 1800 complete. Jefferson's election, he began, had "arrested a train of measures which were gradually conducting us towards ruin." But the election victory did not permit Republicans to rest content. It merely opened up an opportunity "to erect new barriers against folly, fraud, and ambition and to explain such parts of the Constitution as have been already or may be interpreted contrary to the intention of those who adopted it." Liberty, said Pendleton, is the "chief good" of government, but "if government is so constructed as to enable its administration to assail that liberty with the several weapons heretofore most fatal to it, the structure is defective: of this sort, standing armies—fleets—severe penal laws—war—and a multitude of civil officers are universally admitted to be." Union is a great good, but union can "only be preserved by confining . . . the federal government to the exercise of powers clearly required by the general interest . . . because the states exhibit such varieties of character and interests that a consolidated general government would . . .

produce civil war and dissension." A separation of powers is necessary, but the Constitution gives the Senate a part in the exercise of powers that belong to other branches "and tends to create in that body a dangerous aristocracy." Representative government must rest on the will of the people, but the people's will can "never be expressed if their representatives are corrupted or influenced by hopes of office." "Since experience has evinced that much mischief may be done under an unwise administration," it is time to consider several amendments to the Constitution. These should make the President ineligible for a second term and give the appointment of judges and ambassadors to Congress; end the Senate's role in executive functions and shorten the Senators' terms of office; make judges and legislators incapable of accepting any federal office; subject the judges to removal by the legislature; form "some check upon the abuse of public credit"; declare that treaties relating to war or peace or requiring the expenditure of money must be ratified by the whole Congress; and define the powers of the federal government in such a way as to "defy the wiles of construction."

"The Danger Not Over" was a systematic effort to define the fundamental changes that seemed to be implicit in the principles of 1798. And as the years went by without a movement to secure the constitutional amendments it had recommended, without destruction of the national bank, without complete proscription of old Federalists from places of public trust, "there were a number of people who soon thought and said to one another that Mr. Jefferson did many good things, but neglected some better things," who came to "view his policy as very like a compromise with Mr. Hamilton's, . . . a compromise between monarchy and democracy." Strongest in Virginia and including several of the most important party writers of the 1790s—George Logan and John Taylor as well as Pendleton himself—this band of "Old Republicans" soon found an eloquent, if vitriolic and eccentric, spokesman in the Congress. In 1806, John Randolph, who had led the party's forces in the Seventh Congress, broke with the administration and commenced a systematic opposition to the moral bankruptcy and "backstairs influence" of the government. As Jefferson and Madison began to face the gravest crisis of their leadership, they were persistently annoyed by a minority of vocal critics from within their former ranks. In 1808, Monroe became the unsuccessful candidate for those expressing this variety of discontent. . . .

Both [Henry] Adams and the Old Republicans identified the principles of '98 with the Virginia and Kentucky Resolutions of that year. To both, the party's creed in years of opposition centered on allegiance to states' rights. But I have tried to show that such an understanding is too narrow. Even in the crisis introduced by the repressive laws, states' rights and strict construction of the Constitution were among the means to more essential ends. The means were taken seriously, indeed, but they were never held among the absolutes. The body of the party and its most important leaders never sought, as their essential end, to hold the federal government within the narrowest of bounds. They sought, instead, a federal government that would preserve the virtues necessary to a special way of life. Their most important goal had been to check a set of policies—among them loose interpretation of the Constitution—that Republicans had seen as fundamentally destructive of the kind of government and social habits without which liberty could not survive. To judge them only on the basis of their loyalty to strict construction and states' rights is to apply a standard they had never held.

Minds changed when party leaders were confronted with responsibility. But they did not change thoroughly enough to justify the charge that they adopted principles of their opponents. The principles of the Republicans had not been Anti-federalist. Republicans had traced the evils of the 1790s to the motives of the governors, not to the government itself. With few and brief exceptions, most had thought a change of policy, without a change of structure, would effect a cure. Moreover, in the last years of the decade, the development of party thought had probably persuaded many members to believe that a simple change of men might cure more evils than they once had thought.

The Republican persuasion rose, in the beginning, under circumstances that conjoined to make a reconstruction of an ideology developed in a different time and place seem relevant for the United States. The revolutionary debt to eighteenth-century opposition thought was certainly sufficient, by itself, to have assured loud echoes of the old ideas in the first years of the new republic. But this is not the lesson of this work. Republican convictions were not simply reminiscent of the old ideas. Republicans revived the eighteenth-century ideology as a coherent structure, reconstructed it so thoroughly that the persistence of an English style of argument is easily as striking as the changes we might trace to revolutionary alterations of the American polity. At least three circumstances of the 1790s had to join with expectations prompted by the heritage of revolutionary thought to generate a reconstruction so complete. None of these circumstances persisted to the decade's end. First, popular respect for Washington and ambiguity about the nature of the new executive directed discontent at the first minister. Second, Hamiltonian finance was modeled on an English prototype. And finally, an opposition first appeared in the House of Representatives.

The Republican persuasion, in its early years, attempted to alert the nation to a ministerial conspiracy that was operating through corruption to secure the revival of a British kind of constitution. Ministerial influence would subvert the independence of the Congress, which would acquiesce in constitutional constructions leading to consolidation of the states and thence to monarchy. Meanwhile, a decay of public virtue, spread by the example of the lackeys of administration and encouraged by the shift of wealth resulting from the funding plan, would ease the way for a transition to hereditary forms. With relatively minor changes, this was just the accusation that the eighteenth-century English opposition had traditionally directed at governments in power, and, like its prototype, it was, in the beginning, the weapon of a legislative group that had to reconcile its status as minority with its commitment to majority control. Legislative blocs were fluid, and the minority could understand its own position and appeal for popular support with the assistance of traditional assumptions that the influence of the Treasury, when added to an honest difference of opinion, was sufficient to account for policies with which they disagreed.

Images of conspiracy and accusations of corruption continued to provide the starting point for Republican analyses of Federalist policies, but it was not so many years before events and circumstances pushed Republican opinion away from its original foundations. First, circumstances undermined a logical necessity of neo-opposition arguments by making the Republicans a majority in the House. Then, Hamilton resigned. Concurrently, however, Jay's Treaty and the foreign war became the major issues for dispute. In other words, just when the opposition might have savored the retirement of the archconspirator, just when their logic was endangered by their own success, events conjoined to redirect attention to the powers of the Senate and the actions of the President himself. British influence and affection for the cause of monarchy displaced attachment to the funding system as the leading explanation for administration policies. But the Republicans could see that the financial structure was dependent on the British trade, and thus the Federalists' foreign policy appeared to be a new means to old ends. In this way, the Republicans continued their conspiratorial analysis into the Adams years.

Only in the last years of the decade can we see a clearer movement of Republican concerns away from the inherited foundations of their thought and toward a style of argument that seems more native. The alteration might be traced to 1794, when the Republicans began to count on a majority of Representatives. From that point forward, we have seen, party writers focused somewhat less on the corruption of the lower house and somewhat more on dangers posed by enemies of the Republic in the several branches of the government and in the country as a whole. During the first years under Adams, critics concentrated their denunciations less on the "funding and banking gentry" or the Hamiltonian "phalanx" than on the "anglo-federal," "anglo-monarchical," or simply "tory" party. The crisis of 1798—the popular hysteria, the Quasi-War, and the Sedition Law— strengthened this trend. Such a crisis in a polity that rested on a large electorate made the administration's influence on the legislature seem less important than the efforts of a ruling party to mislead the people and destroy effective checks on Federalist abuses. Finally, the split among the Federalists confirmed the inclination to direct attacks, not at the link between the government and its dependents in the Congress—the characteristic target of the British critics of administration—but at a party that depended on its influence with the voters. During the last two years of the decade, Republican newspapers gave less space to criticism of the Congress or administration than they did to mockery of their Federalist competitors or efforts to assassinate the reputations of the leaders of the other party. The scurrility of party sheets reflected their recognition that the enemy, in the United States, was not a governmental faction of the British type, but a party with its base among the people.

When Jefferson assumed the presidential office, he and the body of his party were prepared to believe that they had wakened a majority of voters and thereby put an end to the most immediate danger to the American Republic. Removal of the enemy from power and from public trust had come to seem sufficient, by itself, to safeguard liberty while friends of freedom worked toward gradual replacement of the Hamiltonian system with one better suited to republican ways. With the conspirators deposed, the country could afford to *ease* toward change—and change would come more certainly that way. Still, change it must—change as rapidly as possible according to a very different vision of the good society. Republicans were still persuaded that the debt must be retired as rapidly as preexisting contracts would permit, without internal taxes. It should not be clung to for its broader economic uses. It would not be used as an excuse to push the federal government into revenue resources better left to separate states. Even here, fanaticism was eschewed by a majority. Jefferson's administration did not hesitate to borrow more for the Louisiana Purchase. But the Republicans were willing to subordinate almost all else to the reduction of the debt. Every year the debt existed meant, to them, another year that taxes would inflate the rich, another year of the increasing gap between the rich and poor, which was potentially destructive to free states. By 1812, Republican administrations had reduced the debt from $83 million, where it had climbed under the Federalists, to $27.5 million. They would have retired it completely in a few more years if war had not gotten in the way.

Reform did not go far enough to satisfy the Old Republicans. Change was incomplete enough—and leaders compromised enough—to make it possible for Henry Adams to support his accusation that the Jeffersonians surrendered to the principles of their opponents. Yet even Adams tried to have it several ways. Sometimes he condemned the Jeffersonians for lack of principle. Sometimes he accused them of a change of mind. At other times, however, he switched ground to level his attacks on their adherence to a set of principles that were ill-suited to the country's needs. The effort to retire the debt, he pointed out, committed the first $7.3 million of yearly revenues to payment of principal and interest. The remainder was too small to run the government and meet the costs of national defense. "The army was not large enough to hold the Indians in awe; the navy was not strong enough to watch the coasts. . . . The country was at the mercy of any Power which might choose to rob it." "Gallatin's economies turned on the question whether the national debt or the risk of foreign aggression were most dangerous to America." The Republicans assumed the former.

If we would choose among the different condemnations Adams made of the Republican regime, it would be better to prefer the last. Adherence to the principles of ninety-eight—a strikingly consistent effort to adopt and maintain policies implicit in the ideology of opposition days—is a better explanation for Republican actions during their years in power than any emphasis upon hypocrisy or change. The Old Republicans were worrisome beyond their numbers for no other reason than that they appealed to principles that still had the allegiance of large portions of the party. And, as Adams saw it, it was the party's loyalty to old ideas that brought the country to the edge of ruin in 1812.

II

The first years of the new republic were a time of unexampled prosperity and growth. The most important reason was the European war, which continued with few interruptions from 1790 to 1815. With France and Britain both preoccupied with warfare, a portion of the trade that they would normally have carried fell by default to neutrals. As the greatest trading neutral of the age, America had much to gain. It also risked involvement in the war, since both the European powers periodically attempted to deny the other neutral help.

During the 1790s, America's attempt to carry on a thriving commerce had nearly brought a war with Britain. The effort in fact resulted in a limited conflict with France. Thomas Jefferson came to the Presidency near the beginning of a brief respite in the European struggle, and the interlude of peace gave the Republicans a chance to apply their principles of governmental economy. In 1803, however, France and Britain resumed their titanic war. With Napoleon in power, Republicans had long since dropped their admiration of the French. But the commercial problems of the 1790s now returned with doubled force. After 1805, when Admiral Lord Nelson destroyed most of the French fleet in the Battle of Trafalgar, Britain was unchallengeable at sea, while Bonaparte was temporarily supreme on land. Both powers turned to economic warfare, catching the United States between.

For America the situation reached its worst in 1807. In that year Napoleon's Milan Decree completed a "continental system" under which the Emperor threatened to seize any neutral ship that had submitted to a British search or paid a duty in a British port. Britain replied with Orders-in-Council that promised to seize any neutral trading with the continent *unless* that ship had paid a British fee. The combined effect of French and British measures was to threaten any vessel engaged in the continental trade. To make the situation worse, in the summer of 1807, near the mouth of Chesapeake Bay, the British frigate "Leopard" fired upon the American warship "Chesapeake," forced it to submit to search, and impressed four sailors into British service. By any standard, "Leopard's" action was a cause for war.

War might have been an easy choice. There was a storm of patriotic outrage possibly a match for that following the revelation of the XYZ Affair ten years before. Particularly in the Old Northwest, where British officials in Canada soon began to give assistance and encouragement to Tecumseh and his efforts to unite the western tribes against the progress of new settlement, demands for war rose steadily from that point on. But the Republicans did not want war. They were determined to face the present troubles in the way that they believed the Federalists should have responded to similar problems in the 1790s.

Since the beginning of the party quarrel, Republicans had consistently expressed a fear of war and a profound distrust of normal preparations for defense. They were afraid of war's effects on civil liberties. They clung to the traditional distrust of standing armies. They had consistently opposed the frightful cost of navies. Their ideology identified high taxes, large armed forces, and the increase in executive authority that seemed inseparable from war as mortal dangers to republican society and government. Even preparations for hostilities would require abandonment of all the most important policies that they had followed since the triumph seven years before: low taxes, small armed forces, little governmental guidance of the nation's life, and quick retirement of the public debt.

In any case, Republicans had always argued that America possessed a weapon that provided an alternative to war, a weapon that had proven its effectiveness during the long struggle preceding independence. This weapon was its trade. Since opposition days, the party's leaders had maintained that the things America exported—mostly food and other raw materials—were necessities of life. The things America imported, on the other hand, were mostly manufactured goods and other "luxuries." In case of trouble, then, America could refuse to trade. Healthier than Europe, because it was not bound to large-scale manufacturing,

America would win a test of wills, creating potent discontent and dislocation in the feebler state. Trade restrictions could secure the national interest as effectively as war and without the dangers to free government and social health that war would necessarily incur. Trade was the weapon that the Madisonians had wanted to employ against the British back in 1794. It was the weapon that Republicans preferred when difficulties once again arose. Indeed, the party held to economic warfare, to its antiwar and antipreparation ideology, so long and so stubbornly that the result was nearly a disaster for the United States.

In December, 1807, Jefferson's administration responded to the French and British decrees by placing an embargo on American trade. The embargo had a measurable effect in France and Britain. Unfortunately the economic consequences for America were even worse. Under the embargo, all American sailings overseas were halted for more than a year. The country suffered a severe depression. In New England and upstate New York, noncooperation and illegal sailings rose to such proportions that the government resorted to repressive measures so severe as to endanger the Republicans' reputation as friends of limited government and guardians of civil rights. To keep the peace within the country and to safeguard their majority, the Republicans relaxed their application of the economic weapon. As Madison succeeded Jefferson, Congress started a long search for ways to hurt the Europeans more than the United States. On the surface, this looked very like a gradual retreat. Inconsistent enforcement of changing regulations meant that pressure was repeatedly relaxed just as it began to have effect, and the Republicans' persistence simply led the warring powers to conclude that America would never fight. In 1809 the embargo was replaced with a measure confining nonintercourse to trade between America and French or British ports. In 1810 restrictions were removed completely, although it was provided that nonintercourse would be resumed against one country or the other if either of the powers would agree to end its violations of neutral rights.

Since the ending of American restrictions would benefit Great Britain, Napoleon made moves that it was possible to interpret as an exemption of American shipping from the Berlin and Milan Decrees. Madison announced that nonintercourse would be imposed against the British unless the Orders-in-Council were repealed. When they were not, restrictions were resumed.

The situation quickly passed the bounds of the absurd. By the winter of 1811–1812, four years of various experiments with commercial coercion had failed to force a change in European policies. During all that time the frontier trouble had continued, and Great Britain had persisted in its arrogant, humiliating practice of impressment. Meanwhile the Republicans had lost New England and were threatened in the middle states by the revival of a party that they still considered dangerous to the survival of a democratic way. With the people growing restless under policies that damaged their prosperity without securing change, it was increasingly apparent to most members of the party that commercial weapons would not work. The choice must be between submission to the British policies and war. Neither the people's sense of national honor nor the survival of the Republican Party—a party that believed that liberty would not be safe with its opponents—would permit submission. Madison reluctantly resigned himself to war, and younger representatives from the West and South—"war hawks" to their enemies—worked a declaration through the Congress. There were defections by Clintonians and Quids, but it was basically a party vote.

III

To anyone inclined to balance gain with loss, the War of 1812 must seem a masterpiece of folly. The god who ruled its fortunes was decidedly perverse. Two days before the Senate completed a declaration of war, though not in time for news to cross the sea, the British government announced that the Orders-in-Council would be repealed. The battle at New Orleans was planned by generals who had not learned that peace had been agreed upon at Ghent on December 24, 1814, two weeks before. The slaughter on the Mississippi—nineteen months of warfare—ultimately went for naught. The Treaty of Ghent simply restored the situation that had existed before the war. Boundaries were unaltered. Disputes over neutral rights and impressment were left unresolved.

Contemporaries, however, were not disposed to make a practical calculation of this sort. After all, the war had not been fought for rational reasons alone. National honor, the reputation of republican government, and the continuing supremacy of the Republican party had seemed to be at stake.

National honor had been satisfied. Jackson's stunning victory at New Orleans more than redeemed earlier reverses in the field. And news of his triumph arrived in the East just before the news of peace. Americans celebrated the end of the struggle with a brilliant burst of national pride. They felt that they had fought a second war for independence, and had won. If little had been gained, nothing had been lost in a contest with the greatest imperial power on the earth.

Independence, of course, had never been literally at risk. For Britain the War of 1812 was an unwelcome outcome of a quarrel that had seemed a lesser evil than a relaxation of the struggle against Napoleon. Once Bonaparte was vanquished, little could be gained by further prosecution of the lesser war. British statesmen had no will whatever for the effort that would have been required to defeat, much less to subjugate, the United States. They preferred a quick renewal of the valuable American trade.

Nevertheless, a new American independence did follow the Treaty of Ghent. The American Revolution was, at least in one respect, an effort to break connections with a corrupt Old World. But withdrawal from European involvements had been far from complete. Americans could not be indifferent when the republican revolution promised to convert Europe in the years after 1789, and the new American republic had continued an oceanic trade that inevitably weighed in the power calculations of European states. Independence from European involvements could not be more complete until the new nation had proven its ability to survive the great wars of the French Revolution. The magnetic attraction of European developments would not be weakened until the United States stood once again as the preeminent republic in the world, its belief in European corruption once again confirmed. . . .

In the first years of the new federal government, Alexander Hamilton had grounded his great plans on the assumption that the world was not the kind of place where republican purists could pursue their schemes in peace. Republicans had insisted that there was an alternative to the Secretary's system, one which could secure national respectability without the unacceptable risks to revolutionary accomplishments that Hamilton's seemed to entail. In the years after 1800, they had gradually dismantled much of the foundation on which the Federalists had meant to build an America that could compete with empires such as England's on English terms. They had substituted a different vision, in which a society of independent men of virtue would appear in arms when necessary to defend America's shores, but trust their influence on the course of history, more generally, to the moral force of republican example and the necessary demand for the raw materials they would produce for trade. Jefferson and Madison had also tried a different course in foreign policy. Under the pressure of Napoleonic wars, the Republican alternative had failed.

Hamilton had been right, at least in significant part. America did not have the capacity to force the great states of Europe to accept the kind of international order within which the new nation could pursue the Republican ideal, a society in which the virtue of independent farmers and craftsmen would not be threatened by great cities, large-scale industry, professional armed forces, and a polity committed to the mysteries and dangers of English-style finance. The choice did seem to lie between greater self-sufficiency and national humiliation or war. Now, implicitly, a Republican President admitted this truth.

It was not an unconditional surrender to Hamilton's ideas. Madison could hope that vast expanses of western land and the continued leadership of genuine republicans would postpone to an indefinite future the debilitating corruption that Republicans had always feared. He still had no desire to see the land become a democratic England. Yet he did suggest that old Jeffersonian principles might be tempered with a program that would resurrect an essential portion of the Hamiltonian state. In doing so, he legitimized the other side of a debate that had held the nation's attention since 1789. He hinted that America could build on an amalgam of Republican and Federalist ideas, and the majority of his party agreed. . . .

The ancient argument did not abruptly stop. . . . As the "American System" of Henry Clay, the Hamiltonian vision of a self-sufficient republic, where industrial development would provide a domestic market for agricultural goods and federal programs would tie diverse sections into an imperial whole, remained a central topic for political division and dispute. Jacksonians attacked "aristocracy" and "corruption." Whigs condemned "King Andrew." John C. Calhoun was intensely concerned with something strongly reminiscent of corrupting influence. The new Republicans who followed Lincoln celebrated virtue and the independent man. As a consequence of revolutionary hopes and thought, proponents of American grandeur have always had to answer those who worry about a loss of innocence at home. In the years around 1815, however, the context of these controversies underwent a fundamental change. Experiments with economic coercion, followed by the War of 1812, had exposed an undeniable weakness in the principles on which the Republican party had based its rule. But the war had also made it easier to contemplate a change of course. Events destroyed one of the two great parties to the long dispute over the shaping of a society and government that could make republicanism lasting and complete. Doing this, they freed the other party to turn its attention to the needs of the future. Leadership passed increasingly to younger men, whose lives had not been molded by the great Revolution that had shaped the experience of the generation before. Arguments among the younger men would still be fierce, but the edges of hysteria grew blunt. For it was now the most appropriate means of national development that seemed to be at stake, not the very meaning of America itself.

RICHARD HOFSTADTER

The Transit of Power

I

Jefferson's ideas about parties were the conventional notions of his age. . . . No less than most of his contemporaries he was enthralled by the conviction that the sound citizen who has the public interest at heart is normally above and outside parties and the vices of partisanship. . . .

As the party battle began to take shape in the 1790's, Jefferson, though himself busy stimulating party animosities, looked upon them with some misgivings. In a letter of 1792, urging Washington to accept a second term, he argued that the President in so doing could prevent "violence or secession," which he feared might be the consequence of some of Hamilton's measures. In the same letter he also stated a notion which was to become all but obsessional in his correspondence for more than a quarter of a century, a notion which indeed colored much Republican thinking about the party battle: that the real aim of the leading Federalists was to restore monarchy on the British model, and that therefore the basic issue between the parties was monarchical versus republican principles.

Two conclusions, both fatal to the acceptance of a continuing party system, seemed to follow from this idea. The first was that the Federalists, since they harbored a goal that ran counter to the convictions of the vast majority and flouted the explicitly republican covenant of the Constitution, were simply not a legitimate party at all. And Jefferson's conviction of their un-Americanism would only have been confirmed if he had known all the details of Hamilton's uninhibited and near-treasonous intrigues with James Beckwith and George Hammond. The second, which sustained Jefferson's patient confidence in his party's ultimate victory, was that since the hard-core Federalists were monarchists and the American public was doughtily republican in its sentiments, the final triumph of his own principles, given a fair chance to assert them, was secure.

If one imagined that no less fundamental a principle than monarchy versus republicanism was at stake, one could of course waive all scruples about a strong partisan allegiance. And the justice of this course would be trebly confirmed if the opposition party, by an unmistakable squint toward England, underlined its essential foreignness. By the time of the Jay Treaty, when party lines had hardened, Jefferson had no further use for equivocal men like his fellow Virginian, Edmund Randolph, whose political conduct, he thought, had not set him on a lofty perch above parties but rather in the ignominious position of a trimmer. "Were parties here divided by a greediness for office, as in England," Jefferson explained, "to take a part with either would be unworthy of a reasonable or moral man, but where the principle of difference is as substantial and as strongly pronounced as between the republicans and Monocrats of our country, I hold it as honorable to take a firm and decided part, and as immoral to pursue a middle line, as between the parties of Honest men and Rogues, into which every country is divided." By early 1796, he was referring to the Federalists as "a faction" which "has entered in a conspiracy with the enemies of their country to chain down the legislature at the feet of both." As a conspiratorial, monarchical faction, the Federalists would have no moral claim to survival, and one can only concur with Noble Cunningham's conclusion in his careful study of Republican party history that Jefferson "never recognized the validity of the Federalist party either while Adams was in office or as an opposition party during his own administration." In the intensity of his partisan conviction, Jefferson the secularist lapsed into the language of dogma and ecclesiasticism when he spoke of the views of his foes: his letters bristle with heated digs at "apostacy," "sects," "political heresies," "conversions," "bigots," "votaries," and with invocations of "the true faith.". . .

Such, then, was Jefferson's view of the Federalists: a small faction creeping into the heart of the government under the mantle of Washington and the perverse guidance of Hamilton, addicted to false principles in politics, animated by a foreign loyalty, and given to conspiratorial schemes aiming at the consolidation of government and the return of monarchy. It was a faction which, though enjoying certain temporary advantages, would ultimately lack the power to impose its will on the great mass of loyal republicans. Here Jefferson's optimism, as always, sustained him: before long the people through their faithful representatives would take over. And at that point it would be the duty of the Republican party to annihilate the opposition—not by harsh and repressive measures like the Sedition Act, but by the more gentle means of conciliation and absorption that were available to a principled majority party. Here necessity came to fortify temperament, for the circumstances of Jefferson's election were such as to require a measure of conciliation and appeasement at the very beginning.

II

The election of 1800 was an anomalous election in a double sense: first, in that it was the first election in modern history which, by popular decision, resulted in the quiet and peaceful transition of national power from the hands of one of two embattled parties to another; second, in that it was the first of only two American elections in which, since no candidate had a majority in the Electoral College, the outcome had to be decided in the House of Representatives. The superficial circumstances of the election are quite familiar: the Constitution, written without party tickets in mind, arranged for no separate designation of presidential and vice-presidential candidates before the adoption of the Twelfth Amendment in 1804; in consequence of a lapse in party planning, the two Republican candidates, Jefferson and Burr, turned up with the same number of electoral votes, though it was clearly understood throughout the party that the Virginian was head of the ticket; when the election went to the House, where the states voted as units, the Federalists fell heir to the unhappy luxury of choosing between the two leading Republicans. The resolution of the problem is also a familiar story: how the great majority of the Federalist leaders preferred Burr; how Hamilton repeatedly pleaded that they turn from this dangerous adventurer to the more certain and predictable, as well as endurable, limitations of Jefferson; and how, in the end, under the leadership of James A. Bayard of Delaware, who swallowed Jefferson, as he wrote Adams, "so . . . as not to hazard the Constitution," the necessary portion of them abstained from voting and thus accepted Jefferson, only after an understanding, very delicate and proper and quite indirect, about the character of Jefferson's intentions had been arrived at.

Historians have spent so much effort to unravel the details of this complex election, and in particular to evaluate Burr's role and the character of the tenuous understanding or "bargain" upon which Jefferson's election depended, that some aspects of the situation which we may regard as equally significant have not yet had their due. Since the badly needed definitive account of this election remains to be written, it is necessary to proceed with caution, but it is certainly possible to examine in this event the calculations by which the two-party system in the United States took a long and decisive step forward. Here were the Federalists, many of whom, not so many months earlier, had been hoping to finish off the opposition under the pressure of a war with France and through the agency of the Alien and Sedition Acts, now quietly acquiescing in the decision of a few of their fellow partisans to put into office a man whom they had long been portraying as an atheist, a French fanatic, a libertine, a visionary, and a political incompetent. The circumstances give us a rare opportunity to look at the minds of a set of governmental leaders as they faced the loss of power, and at the interplay between the two sides as they groped for an accommodation.

Abstractly speaking, the choices opened to a defeated governmental party in a new federally organized country where the practice of legitimate opposition is still not wholly certain and where the incoming foes are profoundly suspect are three: *coup d'état*, disunion, or a resigned acceptance of their new oppositional status. Here we may begin by pointing to the central significance of something that did not happen: *violent resistance was never, at any time, discussed*. Neither was disunion discussed as a serious immediate possibility in 1801, though three years later a small but ineffectual faction of New England Federalists would lay abortive plans to bring it about. Something in the character of the American system was at work to unleash violent language but to inhibit violent solutions, and to reconcile the Federalists to the control of the government by a party they suspected of deep hostility to the Constitution. Somehow we must find a way to explain the rapid shift from the Dionysian rhetoric of American politics during the impassioned years 1795 to 1799 to the Apollonian political solution of 1800–1801.

What is observable in a wide range of Federalist letters and memoirs is a basic predisposition among the great majority of them to accept a defeat, fairly administered, even in 1800 before that defeat was a certainty. The whole historical experience of America, as well as the temperament of their class, argued against extreme or violent measures. They were conservative men, and extreme responses that might risk what they sometimes called "the public tranquillity" were not to their way of thinking. Even the instrumentalities of force were lacking in the American environment; and a class of intensely political generals, the elite corps of any *coup d'état,* was impressively absent from the American scene. Most Federalists were realistic enough to see that they were not only divided but outvoted; and none of their fulminations against democracy should blind us to the fact that they did not fancy trying to rule without a decent public mandate. Again, the federal system took some of the stream out of their frustration: in New England, where partisan feeling ran strongest among them, the Federalists were, for the time being, still in control of their own affairs at the state level. They had no reason to believe that they would be politically suppressed, and some of them thought that before very long the incompetence of the Republicans would swing the balance back to their side. Finally, the nature of the political parties and of political careers in America took some of the sting out of defeat.

The parties, for all the intensity of their passions and the bombast of their rhetoric, were new, their organization was rudimentary, and in some parts of the country partisan loyalties were thinner and more fragile than they might seem. No one, as Paul Goodman has remarked, had been born a Federalist or a Republican, and time was to show that switches from side to side were by no means unthinkable. Also, for many of the top leaders, politics was far from an exclusive concern. Political leaders were merchants, planters, lawyers, men of affairs with wide interests and with much capacity for taking pleasure in their private lives. Many of the best of them looked upon politics as a duty and not a livelihood or a pleasure. "To Bayard," his biographer pointedly observes, "the Senate was a job and not a career, a position of dignity and respectability rather than a battleground under observation by the nation." After the first flush of nationalist enthusiasm under Washington, it had become increasingly difficult to find men willing to accept positions of high responsibility and honor. Offices were refused or resigned with astonishing frequency, and Jefferson had to offer the Secretaryship of the Navy on five occasions to four different men before he had an acceptance. Professional politicians were, to be sure, emerging—fewer of them among the Federalists than among their foes—but they were somewhat looked down upon by men of eminence. And professional officeholders were the acknowledged dregs of the political world.

To some degree, the option between Jefferson and Burr distracted the Federalists from facing the full significance of their loss in 1800 and eased them into it by stages. The prevailing Federalist preference for Burr, who was widely regarded as an adventurer without fixed principles and who was even seen by many as being preferable to Jefferson precisely on this count, may certainly argue for a spirit of desperation. But here again the party was divided, and the circumstances of the affair are significant for a reading of Federalist temperature. What the Federalist leaders had to ponder was not simply the character of Burr as against that of Jefferson but also whether there was enough left of the spirit of concord or patriotism after the rancor of the preceding years to warrant thinking that they could endure Jefferson's possession of power. While it is an interesting question whether there was a firm, formally concluded "bargain" between the Virginian and some of his enemies—a question answered by most writers in the negative— it is still more interesting to note what particular assurances Hamilton suggested as necessary and that Bayard sought for when Jefferson was subtly and indirectly sounded about his intentions. Hamilton's advice and Bayard's terms shed much light on the practical differences that now separated the parties, and upon the calculations some Federalists were making about the future.

First, as to the terms: Bayard at one point approached a friend of Jefferson suggesting that if certain points of concord could be arrived at, three decisive states would withdraw their opposition to Jefferson's election. The points were enumerated: "First, . . . the subject of the public credit; secondly, the maintenance of the naval system; and, lastly, that subordinate public officers employed only in the execution of details established by law shall not be removed from office on the ground of their political character, nor without complaint against their conduct." These points were later reiterated to another intimate of Jefferson's, General Samuel Smith, who then purported to have won Jefferson's assent to them, and so gained Bayard's consent. On the second occasion the names of some of Bayard's friends were submitted, to give substance as it were, to the point about officeholders, and specific assurances involving them were offered in return. What is perhaps most interesting is that Bayard's conditions, in omitting a neutrality policy, deviate on only one count from those Hamilton proposed that the Federalists seek for: "the maintenance of the present system, especially in the cardinal articles of public credit—a navy, neutrality." Later Hamilton added patronage: "The preservation in office of our friends, except in the great departments, in respect to which and in future appointments he ought to be at liberty to appoint his friends."

One is at first disposed to conclude that despite their public ravings about Monocrats and Jacobins, American politicians were beginning to behave like politicians. The patronage question in particular argues for this point of view. But it should be realized too that for the Federalists in 1801 the question, now raised for the first time in national politics, whether an incoming party would make a wholesale sweep of public offices and install everywhere its own partisans, involved more than solicitude for the jobs and livelihoods of their friends. Jefferson's intentions as to removals and replacements were the object of a good deal of discussion in Federalist letters of 1800–1801, whose tenor suggests that, aside from the concern for loaves and fishes which was not a negligible thing for lesser party figures, the patronage issue had two further points of significance. It was, in the first instance, a symbolic matter of decisive importance: if the Federalist followers were to be swept out of all the lesser offices, the act would be a declaration of partisan warfare suggesting that the two parties were incapable of governing in concert, and that the desire of the Jeffersonians to decide the nation's policies was coupled with a gratuitous desire to retaliate and humiliate. A policy of proscription would put an end to the harmony and balance they considered essential to the republican order. Secondly, one must reckon with the Federalists' conviction that by far the larger portion of honest and able men, competent for the public business, were in their ranks; and that hence a wholesale displacement of such men might, quite aside from differences on policies, reduce the level of civic competence to a point at which the new government, established at so much effort and sacrifice, would be ruined. As Fisher Ames put it: "The success of governments depends on the selection of the men who administer them. It seems as if the ruling system would rob the country of all chance, by excluding the only classes proper to make the selection from."

Some historians have been at pains to establish that there was in fact no explicit understanding and hence no "corrupt" bargain between Jefferson and the Federalists; and certainly the way in which he was sounded out through an intermediary, who took it upon himself to tender the desired assurances after exploring Jefferson's mind, leaves Jefferson in the clear. Yet such efforts to acquit our political heroes seem to me somewhat misplaced; we would probably have reason to think less of them if they had been incapable of arriving at some kind of understanding. After all, Jefferson was morally and constitutionally entitled to the presidency, and it was the part of statesmanship, if not indeed of wisdom and morality, to offer the Federalists some assurances about his intentions. The survival of the constitutional system was at stake, and it had become necessary for both sides, in the spirit of practical men, to step back from their partisan embroilments, take a larger look at what they were doing, and try once again to make a fresh estimate of each other.

In this respect, Hamilton's appraisal of Jefferson, expressed in the course of his efforts to persuade other Federalists to accept him rather than choose Burr, becomes most illuminating. It was not many months earlier that Hamilton, trying to persuade Governor John Jay to get New York's electoral procedures changed to increase the chances of the Federalists in the forthcoming presidential election, warned Jay once again that the Republican party was a subversive and revolutionary party, and urged that his "scruples of delicacy and propriety" be set aside: "They ought not to hinder the taking of a *legal* and *constitutional step*, to prevent an *atheist* in Religion and a fanatic in politics from getting possession of the helm of the State."

But in January 1801, faced with the alternative of Burr, Hamilton was pushing this atheist and fanatic as a much safer prospective president and portraying him in quite different terms. "I admit," he wrote to Bayard in a remarkable letter, "that his politics are tinctured with fanaticism; that he is too much in earnest with his democracy; that he has been a mischievous enemy to the principal measures of our past administration; that he is crafty and persevering in his objects; that he is not scrupulous about the means of success, nor very mindful of truth, and that he is a contemptible hypocrite—" thus far as damaging an estimate as any Burrite Federalist could have wished. But, Hamilton went on, Jefferson was really not an enemy to the power of the Executive (this would prove all too true) or an advocate of putting all the powers of government in the House of Representatives. Once he found himself by way of inheriting the executive office, he would be "solicitous to come into the possession of a good estate." And then, prefatory to a long and devastating estimate of Burr's character and talents, there occurs the strategic and prophetic appraisal of Jefferson: "Nor is it true that Jefferson is zealot enough to do anything in pursuance of his principles, which will contravene his popularity or his interest. He is as likely as any man I know to temporize; to calculate what will be likely to promote his own reputation and advantage, and the probable result of such a temper is the preservation of systems, though originally opposed, which being once established, could not be overturned without danger to the person who did it. To my mind, a true estimate of Mr. Jefferson's character warrants the expectation of a temporizing, rather than a violent system." Even Jefferson's predilection for France was based more upon the popularity of France in America than upon his own sentiment, and it would cool when that popularity waned. "Add to this, that there is no fair reason to suppose him capable of being corrupted, which is a security that he will not go beyond certain limits." After his scathing dissertation upon Burr, Hamilton reverted to some partisan considerations: if the Republicans got Jefferson, they would be responsible for him; but if the Federalists should install Burr, "they adopt him, and become answerable for him." Moreover, he would doubtless win over many of them, "and the federalists will become a disorganized and contemptible party." Finally, Hamilton repeated to several correspondents his conviction that Burr could not be relied upon to keep any commitment he might make to the Federalists.

In repeated letters to Bayard and others deemed open to his waning influence, Hamilton hammered away at the contrast he had laid down between the temporizing, polite Jefferson, and the dangerous Burr, that "embryo Caesar," "the Catiline of America," the "most unfit man in the United States for the office of President"—a man who, he told Oliver Wolcott in a significant phrase, would call to his side "rogues of all parties, to overrule the good men of all parties." Jefferson would never know how much he owed to Burr for having provided such a chiaroscuro, for throwing him into such high and acceptable relief, if only to a decisive minority of Federalists. But Hamilton's sense of the situation, his implicit recognition that there were, after all, good men on both sides, casts a powerful shaft of light into the roiled and murky bottoms of Federalist rhetoric. There are moments of supreme illumination in history when the depth of men's belief in their own partisan gabble has to be submitted at last to the rigorous test of practical decision. For about eight years the Federalists had been denouncing Jefferson and his party, and in the last few years their accusations had mounted to the point at which the leader of the opposition, the Vice President of the United States, had been charged with Jacobinism, atheism, fanaticism, unscrupulousness, wanton folly, incompetence, personal treachery, and political treason. Now this atheist in religion and fanatic in politics was to be quietly installed in the new White House, by courtesy of a handful of Federalist Congressmen, and though there was still hardly a man in the Federalist party who trusted him, there was also not a man to raise a hand against him. The Federalists, having failed to install Burr, preferred to risk Jefferson rather than to risk the constitutional system that had been so laboriously built and launched, and the way in which they explained to each other this seeming change of heart deserves some attention.

III

There was, of course, nothing cheerful about Federalist acquiescence in the transit of power. The overwhelming party preference for an acknowledged adventurer like Burr in the face of the clear public mandate for Jefferson was a token of the persistence of the exacerbated party conflict of the past half-dozen years. The Federalists had not softened their view of Jefferson: they expected to have to endure grave evils from a Republican victory, and a few even took a stark apocalyptic view of it. . . .

But, with all this, the prevailing note among leading Federalists in 1800–1801 was one of short-run resignation and long-run hope, and it was only a few years later that many of them gave way to complete despair. They still had faith in their principles and confident knowledge of their influence among the dominant classes. They were entrenched in the judiciary, strong in the Senate, preponderant in New England, and at comparative strength in other states of the Union. They could hope that their continued opposition would be powerful enough to check some disasters, or, at worst, that if Jefferson did bring an exceptional train of evils, men everywhere would respond by rallying to them and bringing their party back to office, unified and perhaps stronger than ever. Hence their tactical counsel to each other during and shortly after the election and the final balloting in the House of Representatives looked not to extreme responses but to a measured judgment of the situation and to the means by which their interests could be protected and their influence best made felt. Their talk was not that of conspirators planning to react with force, but of politicians, accustomed to power, who must now learn how to play the role of a constructive constitutional opposition. They had lost only by a narrow margin, they were still free to organize opposition, and they expected that they would have an excellent chance to return to power. . . .

After violent and impassioned rhetoric of the preceding years, one is impressed, then, with the readiness of leading Federalists to adapt themselves to evils they considered inevitable, to accept the position of a legitimate opposition, and to disenthrall their practical judgment from the gaudy threats and dire predictions with which their propaganda was so free. One of Rufus King's correspondents, Joseph Hale, put it well in December 1800, when he wrote: "Men of the most judgment with us do not expect those evils to follow the adminn. of Jeff. or Burr which while they were candidates it was thought politic to predict.". . .

IV

It was characteristic of Jefferson that he perceived the keen political conflict of the years just preceding his election not as an opportunity but as a difficulty. Thanks to the efforts both of his detractors and his admirers, his historical reputation has caused us to misread him. In the Federalist tradition, later taken up by so many historians, he was a theorist, a visionary, a radical; and American liberals have praised him for the same qualities the Federalists abhorred. The modern liberal mind has been bemused by his remarks about the value of a little rebellion now and then, or watering the tree of liberty with the blood of tyrants, or having a complete constitutional revision every twenty or thirty years. But Jefferson's more provocative utterances, it has been too little noticed, were in his private correspondence. His public statements and actions were colored by a relative caution and timidity that reveal a circumspect and calculating mind—or, as so many of his contemporary foes believed, a guileful one. He was not enraptured by the drama of unrestrained political conflict; and with the very important exception of some of his views on foreign policy and war, his approach to public policy was far from utopian. He did not look forward to a vigorously innovative administration—he had seen enough of that. The most stunning achievement of his presidential years, the Louisiana Purchase, was an accident, the outcome of the collapse of Napoleon's ambitions for a Caribbean empire—the inadvertent gift of Toussaint L'Ouverture and the blacks of Haiti to this slaveholding country. Its most stunning disaster was the embargo, and the embargo itself came from Jefferson's penchant, here misapplied, for avoiding conflict. His was, as Hamilton put it in his tardy burst of pragmatic insight, a temporizing and not a violent disposition.

This disposition dictated an initial strategy of conciliation toward the Federalists, which led to a basic acceptance of the Hamiltonian fiscal system, including even the bank, to a patronage policy which Jefferson considered to be fair and compromising and hoped would appease moderate Federalists, and to an early attempt to pursue neutrality and to eschew aggravating signs of that Francophilia and Anglophobia with which the Federalists so obsessively and hyperbolically charged him. But for our concern, it is particularly important to understand that in Jefferson's mind conciliation was not a way of arriving at coexistence or of accommodating a two-party system, but a technique of absorption: he proposed to win over the major part of the amenable Federalists, leaving the intractables an impotent minority faction rather than a full-fledged opposition party. His strategy, which aimed, once again, at a party to end parties, formed another chapter in the quest for unanimity.

"The symptoms of a coalition of parties give me infinite pleasure," wrote Jefferson less than three weeks after delivering his inaugural address. "Setting aside a few only, I have been ever persuaded that the great bulk of both parties had the same principles fundamentally, and that it was only as to our foreign relations there was any division. These I hope can be so managed as to cease to be a subject of division for us. Nothing shall be spared on my part to obliterate the traces of party and consolidate the nation, if it can be done without abandonment of principle." His inaugural address itself had been designed to strike the first conciliatory note, and on the key question of party conflict it was a masterpiece of statesmanlike equivocation. It had a number of grace notes that might be calculated to appease opposition sensibilities: a prideful reference to American commerce, a strong hint about sustaining the public credit, an injunction to "pursue our own Federal and Republican principles," the memorable promise of "peace, commerce, and honest friendship with all nations, entangling alliances with none," obeisance to the memory of Washington as "our first and greatest revolutionary character," modest remarks about the fallibility of his own judgment, a promise not only to try to hold the good opinion of his supporters but also "to conciliate that of others by doing them all the good in my power," and finally, that *sine qua non* of inaugural addresses, especially necessary from one widely deemed "an atheist in religion"—an invocation of divine aid.

But it was in speaking of American conflicts that Jefferson achieved his finest subtlety. The acerbity of American political conflict, he suggested, would deceive "strangers unused to think freely and to speak and to write what they think." But now that the issue had been decided, Americans would unite for the common good. "All, too, will bear in mind this sacred principle, that though the will of the majority is in all cases to prevail, that will to be rightful must be reasonable; that the minority possess their equal rights, to violate which could be oppression." Let us restore harmony and affection to our society, he pleaded, and banish political intolerance as we have banished religious intolerance. That the agonies and agitations of Europe should have reached our shores and divided our opinions over proper measures of national safety is hardly surprising, but "every difference of opinion is not a difference of principle. We have called by different names brethren of the same principle. We are all republicans; we are all federalists."

In expressing these healing sentiments, which set a fine precedent for other chief executives taking office after acrimonious campaigns, Jefferson succeeded at a focal moment in reassuring many Federalists. Hamilton thought the address "virtually a candid retraction of past misapprehensions, and a pledge to the community that the new President will not lend himself to dangerous innovations, but in essential points tread in the steps of his predecessors." It contained some foolish but also many good ideas, George Cabot judged. "It is so conciliatory that much hope is derived from it by the Federalists," and he thought it "better liked by our party than his own." Robert Troup, who referred to its "wonderful lullaby effect" also thought it displeasing to the "most violent of the party attached to him," as did James A. Bayard. It was well calculated, Robert Goodloe Harper reported to his constituents, "to afford the hope of such an administration as may conduce to his own glory and the public good." "A fine opening," said Manasseh Cutler.

Yet the Federalists would have been much deceived if they had imagined that the striking sentence, "We are all republicans; we are all federalists," implied that Jefferson would put the principles of the two *parties,* and hence the parties themselves, on a nearly equal footing of legitimacy. The context, as well as various private utterances, showed that he meant only that almost all Americans believed both in the federal union and in the general principles of republican government, and that therefore the two parties stood close enough to be not so much reconciled as *merged,* and merged under his own standard. One can only concur here with Henry Adams's remark that Jefferson "wished to soothe the great body of his opponents, and if possible to win them over; but he had no idea of harmony or affection other than that which was to spring from his own further triumph." Jefferson's letters substantiate this interpretation. He had hardly finished the labors of the inauguration before he was writing letters to John Dickinson, James Monroe, and General Horatio Gates in which his hopes were spelled out with great clarity. Large numbers of his fellow citizens had been "hood-winked" from their principles through an extraordinary combination of circumstances, he argued, but it was now possible to enlighten them. An incorrect idea of his own views had got about, but "I am in hopes my inaugural address will in some measure set this to rights, as it will present the leading objects to be conciliation and adherence to sound principle." The leaders of the "late faction" were, of course, "incurables" and need not be courted, but "with the main body of federalists I believe it very practicable." The XYZ affair had created a political delusion among many people, but the uncertainties of the preceding month arising from the presidential election in the House of Representatives, and the alarm over a possible constitutional crisis had produced "a wonderful effect . . . on the mass of federalists." Many wanted only "a decent excuse for coming back" to a party that represented their own deepest views, and others had come over "rather than risk anarchy." Therefore Jefferson's policies, especially as to patronage, would be prudent, and would be so designed as "to give time for a perfect consolidation." In short: "if we can hit on the true line of conduct which may conciliate the honest part of those who were called federalists, and do justice to those who have so long been excluded from it, I shall hope to be able to obliterate, or rather to unite the names of federalists and republicans. The way to effect it is to preserve principle, but to treat tenderly those who have been estranged from us, and dispose their minds to view our proceedings with candour.". . .

V

It hardly needs to be said that Jefferson's middle course did not succeed in appeasing Federalist leaders. At best it can be said that it avoided goading them into violent responses for the brief period during which he consolidated his influence; and when they awoke from the relative torpor into which they receded in 1801, it was only to find, as many of them promptly concluded, that democracy was so much in the ascendant that all hopes of an early return to power had to be given up. By 1803 most of them had decided that Jefferson was as bad as they had ever expected him to be, and some of them were lamenting that the Constitution was dead. They had been infuriated by the Jeffersonian war on the judiciary, which beginning with the refusal of some of Adams's midnight appointments, went on early in 1802 to the repeal of the Judiciary Act of 1801, and was climaxed by the impeachments of Justices Pickering and Chase in 1804 and 1805. They were intensely discouraged by the Louisiana Purchase in 1803, which not only seemed to cut off all prospects of war with France but added immense western territories out of which they could foresee the Jeffersonians carving many new agrarian states and thus piling further gains on top of the already substantial Republican majorities. By 1804, when a few maddened New England conspirators tried to use Burr's candidacy for the governorship of New York as a pivot upon which to engineer an independent New England—New York confederacy, they were so far out of touch with reality that even some of the most stoutly parochial New England conservatives, whose support they had to have, hung back in discouragement and disapproval. George Cabot, speaking for Chief Justice Theophilus

Parsons, Fisher Ames, and Stephen Higginson as well as himself, warned Timothy Pickering that secession was pointless as long as democracy remained such a general creed that even New England was thoroughly infected with it. The best hope for the Federalists, he thought, would be in the public reaction to a gratuitous war with England. . . .

As renewed party strife replaced the brief testing period that followed Jefferson's inauguration, his response to the Federalist leaders was as sharp as theirs to him, and while his public stance still invoked the restoration of harmony and affection and left open his bid for the Federalist rank and file, his private correspondence was electric with flashes of impassioned hostility to opposition leaders who would "toll us back to the times when we burnt witches," to the "ravenous crew" of his foes, the "monocrats" who "wish to sap the republic by fraud," "incurables to be taken care of in a mad house," and "heroes of Billingsgate." "I wish nothing but their eternal hatred," he flared out in one of his letters. He could find nothing legitimate or useful in the Federalist opposition. "A respectable minority," he explained to Joel Barlow in May 1802, "is useful as censors," but the present minority did not qualify because it was "not respectable, being the bitterest cup of the remains of Federalism rendered desperate and furious with despair." They would not, they should not, survive at all.

If Jefferson was winning over precious few of the Federalist leaders, he had the pleasure at least of taking away much of their following and mobilizing his own to the point of nearly total party victory. To this degree his political optimism was quite justified: he had gauged public sentiment correctly and he was giving the people what they wanted—frugal government, low taxes, fiscal retrenchment, a small army and navy, peace, and the warm sentiments of democratic republicanism. And he had behind him a party far more popular and efficient than anything the Federalists could mobilize against him. He had not been in the White House as much as a year before he was reporting to Dupont de Nemours his immense satisfaction with his efforts at conciliation and unity—by which he meant Republican preponderance. If a presidential election were held a year hence, he ventured on January 18, 1802, solely on grounds of political principle and uncomplicated by personal likes or dislikes, "the federal candidate would not get the vote of a single elector in the U.S." And indeed the Congressional elections of 1802 yielded an overwhelming Republican majority, which, though somewhat weakened later by reactions to the embargo and to the War of 1812, was never substantially endangered. In May Jefferson exulted that Republican advances had reached the point at which "candid federalists acknowledge that their party can never more raise its head." In 1804 he was re-elected with the votes of all New England except Connecticut, and given a party preponderance of four to one in the Senate and five to one in the House. In his second inaugural address he congratulated the country on "the union of sentiment now manifested so generally" and anticipated among the people an "entire union of opinion." In 1807, when the Massachusetts Federalists lost even their governorship, he saw the Federalists as "completely vanquished, and never more to take the field under their own banners." The old dream of national unanimity seemed to be coming true.

As Federalism dwindled away toward virtual impotence, Jefferson seemed to fall victim to a certain inconsistency between his passion for unanimity on one side and on the other to his long-standing philosophical conviction that free men will differ and that differences will engender parties. But he was perhaps less inconsistent than he seemed: to him achieving unanimity meant not establishing a dead level of uniform thought but simply getting rid of the deep and impassioned differences which had arisen only because the extreme Federalists had foisted upon their party a preference for England and for monarchy. Unanimity did not require eliminating various low-keyed and negotiable differences of opinion between different schools of honest republicans. The chief limit to unity now indeed seemed to stem from divisions appearing in the Republican ranks in Congress and from such intrastate factionalism as disturbed the party in Pennsylvania. But none of this worried him unduly. He understood that a party which had no opposition to fight with would develop a centrifugal tendency: "We shall now be so strong that we shall split again; for freemen thinking differently and speaking and acting as they think, will form into classes of sentiment, but it must be under another name, that of federalism is to become so scouted that no party can rise under it."

On this count we can find him prophetic. Partisan victory seems finally to have brought him back to his original understanding that party differences are founded in human nature. For him the goal of unanimity was satisfied by the elimination of Federalism, the disappearance of fundamental issues; and it may not be too fanciful to see in this some likeness to Burke's satisfaction in the disappearance of "the great parties" which was the very thing Burke thought laid a foundation for moderate party differences and justifiable party loyalties. Jefferson once observed that with "the entire prostration of federalism" the remaining Federalists might form a coalition with the Republican minority; but in this he saw no danger so long as the Republican dissidents were not—here the party obsession raises its head once again—flirting with monarchy. "I had always expected," he wrote to Thomas Cooper in 1807, "that when the republicans should have put down all things under their feet, they would schismatize among themselves. I always expected, too, that whatever names the parties might bear, the real division would be into moderate and ardent republicanism. In this division there is no great evil,—not even if the minority obtain the ascendency by the accession of federal votes to their candidate; because this gives us one shade only, instead of another, of republicanism." The notion that the animating principle behind Federalism had been a passion for monarchy, however delusive it had been, led to the comforting conclusion that the last nail had now been driven into the coffin of the hereditary principle, and hence that the country had reached a unanimity deep enough. But in 1807 neither Thomas Jefferson nor George Cabot could possibly have imagined what would come in the next few years; that Jefferson would leave the presidency with a sense of failure and with diminished popularity; that Federalism, for all this, would undergo only a modest resurgence; that a war with Great Britain would finally come under the Republicans, and that, though conducted with consummate incompetence, it would lead to the complete triumph of Republicanism and the final disappearance of the Federalist party.

SUGGESTIONS FOR FURTHER READING

Henry Adams's monumental nine-volume *History of the United States During the Administrations of Jefferson and Madison* (New York, 1889–1891) is a classic that should at least be sampled by every student of American history. Adams denies that the election of 1800 could be called a revolution. He finds that Jefferson as president abandoned most of the principles and theories he advanced before his election. A recent introduction to and critical evaluation of Adams's work by a Jefferson scholar is Noble E. Cunningham, Jr., *The United States in 1800: Henry Adams Revisited* (Charlottesville, Va., 1988).

A number of studies consider the growth of political parties in the new nation. Although these studies describe the issues that divided Jeffersonian Republicans from Federalists, they implicitly or explicitly deny that the divisions were fundamental enough to make the election of 1800 a revolution. See Noble E. Cunningham, Jr., *The Jeffersonian Republicans: The Formation of Party Organization, 1789–1801* (Chapel Hill, N.C., 1957) and its sequel, *The Jeffersonian Republicans in Power: Party Operations, 1801–1809* (Chapel Hill, N.C., 1963); Richard Buel, Jr., *Securing the Revolution: Ideology in American Politics, 1789–1815* (Ithaca, N.Y., 1972); and William N. Chambers, *Political Parties in a New Nation: The American Experience, 1776–1809* (New York, 1963).

Several older studies present sharp conflict interpretations that are warmly sympathetic to Jefferson and sharply critical of Hamilton. Claude Bowers in *Jefferson and Hamilton: The Struggle for Democracy in America* (Boston, 1925) has written an interpretation of the Jefferson-Hamilton struggle as a "clear-cut fight between democracy and aristocracy." Vernon L. Parrington, in his superbly written and influential *Main Currents in American Thought* (New York, 1927), builds his analysis on the fundamental disagreements between Jefferson and Hamilton. He pictures Jefferson as the philosopher of agrarian democracy, a man who had faith in the common man's ability to rule himself. Charles A. Beard, *Economic Origins of Jeffersonian Democracy* (New York, 1915) is less emphatic about Jefferson's contribution to democracy, although he does argue that Jefferson's victory was a triumph for the agrarian interests, which, he had argued, suffered a setback with the adoption of the Constitution.

The more recent works that emphasize conflict remain sympathetic toward Jefferson but tend to be less stridently antagonistic toward Hamilton. See Lance Banning, *The Jeffersonian Persuasion: Evolution of a Party Ideology* (Ithaca, N.Y., 1978), a portion of which is reprinted here; Drew McCoy, *The Elusive Republic: Political Economy in Jeffersonian America* (Chapel Hill, N.C., 1980); and Daniel Sisson, *The American Revolution of 1800* (New York, 1974). Sisson argues that the election of 1800 was truly revolutionary in that it completed the revolution of 1776. Forrest McDonald, *The Presidency of Thomas Jefferson* (Lawrence, Kans., 1976) in a sense agrees, although for very different reasons; he argues that the Jeffersonians achieved what they promised while in opposition and their success destroyed their political influence. Richard K. Matthews, *The Radical Politics of Thomas Jefferson: A Revisionist View* (Lawrence, Kans., 1984) argues that Jefferson's political ideas provided "a humanist democratic alternative" to the market liberalism that was emerging in the early nineteenth century, views that put him into conflict with an emerging Hamiltonian-Madisonian consensus.

Hamilton is treated much more sympathetically in a number of studies that give far less emphasis to conflict. See, for example, Nathan Schachner, *The Founding Fathers* (New York, 1954) and John C. Miller, *The Federalist Era, 1789–1801* (New York,

---

*Available in paperback edition.

1960). A brief, provocative essay on Jefferson describing the consensus that united Jefferson and Hamilton may be found in Richard Hofstadter, *The American Political Tradition* (New York, 1948). Robert W. Tucker and David C. Hendrickson, *Empire of Liberty: The Statecraft of Thomas Jefferson* (New York, 1990) examines Jefferson's views on foreign policy and finds both elements of democratic isolationism and a tendency toward being a moral crusader, conflicting views that Jefferson shared with Hamilton and that have influenced American foreign policy to the present day.

Leonard Levy, *Jefferson and Civil Liberties: The Darker Side* (New York, 1973) describes a perverse kind of consensus by showing that Jefferson, the ardent opponent of the Alien and Sedition Acts, used similarly repressive measures against his opponents after he came to office. David Hackett Fischer, *The Revolution of American Conservatism: The Federalist Party in the Era of Jeffersonian Democracy* (New York, 1965) finds the emergence of a new consensus not because the Jeffersonians compromised with the Federalists but because the Federalists, once out of power, compromised with the dominant Jeffersonian ideas. Stanley Elkins and Eric McKitrick, *The Age of Federalism: The Early American Republic, 1788–1899* (New York, 1993) is a major new work that plays down the ideological conflict during the early history of the country.

The success of the Jeffersonian Republicans elicited sharp opposition within the party on a variety of issues. The "Old Republican" opposition to Jefferson from within his own party is discussed (along with many other topics) in Merrill D. Peterson, *Thomas Jefferson and the New Nation* (New York, 1970) and more fully in Norman K. Risjord, *The Old Republicans: Southern Conservatism in the Age of Jefferson* (New York, 1965). John Chester Miller, *The Wolf by the Ears: Thomas Jefferson and Slavery* (New York, 1977) describes Jefferson's ambivalent attitude towards slavery.

Recent biographies of Jefferson include Noble E. Cunningham, Jr., *In Pursuit of Reason: The Life of Thomas Jefferson* (Baton Rouge, La., 1987) and Norman K. Risjord, *Thomas Jefferson* (Madison, Wisc., 1994). Merrill D. Peterson, ed., *Thomas Jefferson: A Reference Biography* (New York, 1986) is a series of twenty-four essays by specialists on various aspects of Jefferson's life and thought followed by an annotated "Bibliographic Essay."

There is a vast literature on this subject. An introduction to some of it, along with a fascinating study of the way that Jefferson has been viewed since his death, is Merrill D. Peterson, *The Jeffersonian Image in the American Mind* (New York, 1960). A more recent bibliography is Frank Shuffelton, *Thomas Jefferson: A Comprehensive Annotated Bibliography of Writings About Him (1826–1980)* (New York, 1983), which lists 3,447 separate items.

From the Art Collection of The Boatmen's National
Bank of St. Louis

The Era of
Andrew Jackson

Some leaders seem to so dominate the age in which they live that they become symbols of that age even during their own lifetimes. Such a man was Andrew Jackson. Loved by his followers and detested by his opponents, he somehow seemed to represent both the best and the worst in America. Jackson was controversial in his own time and has since become a subject of debate among historians who seek to understand the man and the age in which he lived.

There can be no disagreement that the era of Andrew Jackson was a time of great change in America. People were moving in large numbers to the West, where they established farms and plantations and founded villages, many of which would quickly grow into thriving towns and cities. Mills and factories began to dot the landscape, especially in the East, providing an increasing supply of manufactured goods for a growing population. Steamboats, canals, and railroads linked the nation together, shrinking the vast differences that separated East and West, North and South and creating a growing market for the output of the nation's farms and shops.

The era was also marked by political changes of great significance. Universal white manhood suffrage became the norm as states dropped property and other restrictions on the right to vote. The political parties replaced the congressional caucus with the convention as the means to select presidential candidates, thereby extending popular influence on the nominating process.

Such changes provided Americans with many new opportunities. Indeed, the life of Jackson himself seemed to symbolize these opportunities. A poor Carolina back-country farm boy, he became a wealthy Tennessee planter, a popular military hero, and finally president of the United States. Yet, change also brought new problems. If some Americans, like Jackson, grew wealthy and powerful, others—indeed, most—did not. Many people felt that a new aristocracy of wealth threatened the country.

Historians differ sharply in their evaluations of the Jacksonian era. Some, emphasizing the political reforms, see it as the time of expanding democracy, the era of the common man. Jacksonianism, in this view, was the effort of the common man to expand his voice in government and defend his rights against the incursions of a new economic elite. Andrew Jackson was the charismatic leader of farmers and workers in their struggle against special privilege. Jackson's new political party, true to its name, became the party of democracy, while the Whigs—Jackson's opponents—emerged as the party of wealth and special privilege. From this perspective, Jackson's war on the Bank of the United States was a people's struggle against a powerful financial monopoly. The "spoils system" was not a cynical effort to build the party by rewarding the faithful but rather a means to bring democracy to government by replacing an entrenched aristocratic elite with ordinary men who accepted the views of the majority of the population.

Other historians disagree. They argue that in most states neither wealth nor social class distinguished Whigs from Democrats. Politicians and voters divided over local issues or, on the national level, over means rather than ends. They view Jackson's democratic stance as merely political opportunism, a clever method used by an astute politician to win political office. "Jackson never really championed the cause of the people; he only invited them to champion his," argued Thomas P. Abernethy. Moreover, others add, the Whigs quickly adopted the democratic methods of the Democrats and often much of their platform as well. The era of Jackson, some conclude, was the era of a new group of businessmen and enterpreneurs who had arisen in the wake of the nation's rapid geographic and economic expansion.

In sum, then, the first group of historians sees fundamental conflict in the era of Jackson—rich versus poor, farmers versus capitalists, employees versus employers. But the second group finds greater consensus among Americans; the violent political rhetoric, they insist, merely reflected mild disagreements over the precise way in which an essentially egalitarian, business-oriented society was to work. Some of these disagreements among historians may be seen in the following selections.

Arthur Schlesinger, Jr., describes Jacksonian democracy as a part of "that enduring struggle between the business community and the rest of society." There is no doubt in his mind that there was real and important conflict in the Age of Jackson. In the second selection, Edward Pessen examines some of the recent state studies of the Jackson period and concludes that there were no great differences between the followers of Jackson and of his opponents. He also studies the Working Men's Parties, whose members did think in terms of ideological and class conflict. But he concludes that perhaps the most important fact is how few Americans dissented from the Jacksonian consensus. Like Pessen, James Mac-Gregor Burns, in the final selection, agrees that the social and economic status of Jacksonian leaders did not differ from that of their opponents; the conflict, he argues, was between "ins" and "outs." But, Burns continues, the "outs" who rallied behind Jackson were sharply divided among themselves on major issues, and, once Jackson became president, these significant differences emerged. The Jacksonians, Burns concludes, consolidated their power by building a strong political coalition, but they did so without bringing about any radical changes.

How, then, are we to interpret the Age of Jackson? Was the period marked by the struggle of the common man to advance democracy? Was this struggle based on fundamental conflict emanating from class and sectional differences? Or did it arise from relatively minor political differences within a basic underlying consensus? Is it meaningful to talk about Jacksonian "democracy"? If so, does this mean that democracy was won in the course of a conflict with undemocratic or aristocratic forces? These questions cannot be answered without a clear understanding of what is meant by "democracy." Does democracy imply economic as well as political rights? Can there be democracy with economic and social inequality?

Students should note that the debate as summarized in this introduction and as presented in the following selections is concerned only with white males. Is it possible to speak of the expansion of democracy when women and blacks are excluded? How would the interpretation of the era of Andrew Jackson change if women and blacks were included? These questions will be considered in subsequent chapters, but readers might keep them in mind as they read and ponder the selections that follow.

Arthur M. Schlesinger, Jr.

Jacksonian Democracy Versus the Business Community

The Jacksonian revolution rested on premises which the struggles of the thirties hammered together into a kind of practical social philosophy. The outline of this way of thinking about society was clear. It was stated and re-stated, . . . on every level of political discourse from presidential messages to stump speeches, from newspaper editorials to private letters. It provided the intellectual background without which the party battles of the day cannot be understood.

I

The Jacksonians believed that there was a deep-rooted conflict in society between the "producing" and "non-producing" classes—the farmers and laborers, on the one hand, and the business community on the other. The business community was considered to hold high cards in this conflict through its network of banks and corporations, its control of education and the press, above all, its power over the state: it was therefore able to strip the working classes of the fruits of their labor. "Those who produce all wealth," said Amos Kendall, "are themselves left poor. They see principalities extending and palaces built around them, without being aware that the entire expense is a tax upon themselves."

If they wished to preserve their liberty, the producing classes would have to unite against the movement "to make the rich richer and the potent more powerful." Constitutional prescriptions and political promises afforded no sure protection. "We have heretofore been too disregardful of the fact," observed William M. Gouge, "that the social order is quite as dependent on the laws which regulate the distribution of wealth, as on political organization." The program now was to resist every attempt to concentrate wealth and power further in a single class. Since free elections do not annihilate the opposition, the fight would be unceasing. "The struggle for power," said C. C. Cambreleng, "is as eternal as the division of society. A defeat cannot destroy the boundary which perpetually separates the democracy from the aristocracy."

The specific problem was to control the power of the capitalistic groups, mainly Eastern, for the benefit of the noncapitalist groups, farmers and laboring men, East, West and South. The basic Jacksonian ideas came naturally enough from the East, which best understood the nature of business power and reacted most sharply against it. The legend that Jacksonian democracy was the explosion of the frontier, lifting into the government some violent men filled with rustic prejudices against big business, does not explain the facts, which were somewhat more complex. Jacksonian democracy was rather a second American phase of that enduring struggle between the business community and the rest of society which is the guarantee of freedom in a liberal capitalist state.

Like any social philosophy, Jacksonian democracy drew on several intellectual traditions. Basically, it was a revival of Jeffersonianism, but the Jeffersonian inheritance was strengthened by the infusion of fresh influences: notably the anti-monopolistic tradition, formulated primarily by Adam Smith and expounded in America by Gouge, Legett, Sedgwick, Cambreleng; and the pro-labor tradition, formulated primarily by William Cobbett and expounded by G. H. Evans, Ely Moore, John Ferral.

II

The inspiration of Jeffersonianism was so all-pervading and fundamental for its every aspect that Jacksonian democracy can be properly regarded as a somewhat more hard-headed and determined version of Jeffersonian democracy. But it is easy to understate the differences. Jefferson himself, though widely revered and quoted, had no personal influence on any of the leading Jacksonians save perhaps Van Buren. Madison and Monroe were accorded still more vague and perfunctory homage. The radical Jeffersonians, Taylor, Randolph and Macon, who had regarded the reign of Virginia as almost an era of betrayal, were much more vivid in the minds of the Jacksonians.

Yet even Taylor's contributions to the later period have been exaggerated. His great work, the *Inquiry into the Principles and Policy of the Government of the United States,* published in 1814 just before the Madisonian surrender, had no significant contemporary vogue except among the faithful; and its difficult style, baffling organization and interminable length prevented it ever from gaining wide currency. By Jackson's presidency it was long out of print. In 1835 it was reported unobtainable in New York and to be procured only "with great difficulty" in Virginia. There is little trace of its peculiar terminology in the Jacksonian literature.

While the *Inquiry* properly endured as the most brilliant discussion of the foundations of democracy, many of its details were in fact obsolete by 1830. It was oriented to an important degree around the use of the national debt as the mechanism of aristocracy; in Jackson's day the debt had been extinguished but the aristocracy remained. Moreover, Taylor's arguments against executive power, against the party system and for a revivified militia had lost their point for the Jacksonians. George Bancroft voiced a widely felt need when he called, in 1834, for a general work on American society. "Where doubts arise upon any point relating to the business of government," one radical wrote in response, "no dependence can be placed upon any treatise that has yet appeared which professes to discuss this subject. You must draw upon your own resources, you must think,— and think alone."

The obsolescence of Taylor was caused by the enormous change in the face of America. The period of conservative supremacy from 1816 to 1828 had irrevocably destroyed the agricultural paradise, and the Jacksonians were accommodating the insights of Jefferson to the new concrete situations. This process of readjustment involved a moderately thorough overhauling of favorite Jeffersonian doctrines.

The central Jefferson hope had been a nation of small freeholders, each acquiring thereby so much moral probity, economic security and political independence as to render unnecessary any invasion of the rights or liberties of others. The basis of such a society, as Jefferson clearly recognized, was agriculture and handicraft. What was the status of the Jeffersonian hope now that it was clear that, at best, agriculture must share the future with industry and finance?

Orestes A. Brownson exhausted one possibility in his essay on "The Laboring Classes." He reaffirmed the Jeffersonian demand: "we ask that every man become an independent proprietor, possessing enough of the goods of this world, to be able by his own moderate industry to provide for the wants of his body." But what, in practice, would this mean? As Brownson acknowledged years later, his plan would have "broken up the whole modern commercial system, prostrated the great industries, . . . and thrown the mass of the people back on the land to get their living by agricultural and mechanical pursuits." Merely to state its consequences was to prove its futility. The dominion of the small freeholder was at an end.

The new industrialism had to be accepted: banks, mills, factories, industrial capital, industrial labor. These were all distasteful realities for orthodox Jeffersonians, and, not least, the propertyless workers. "The mobs of great cities," Jefferson had said, "add just so much to the support of pure government, as sores do to the strength of the human body." The very ferocity of his images expressed the violence of his feelings. "When we get piled upon one another in large cities, as in Europe," he told Madison, "we shall become corrupt as in Europe, and go to eating one another as they do there." It was a universal sentiment among his followers. "No man should live," Nathaniel Macon used to say, "where he can hear his neighbour's dog bark."

Yet the plain political necessity of winning the labor vote obliged a change of mood. Slowly, with some embarrassment, the Jeffersonian preferences for the common man were enlarged to take in the city workers. In 1833 the *New York Evening Post,* declaring that, if anywhere, a large city of mixed population would display the evils of universal suffrage, asked if this had been the case in New York and answered: No. Amasa Walker set out the same year to prove that "great cities are not *necessarily,* as the proverb says, 'great sores,' " and looked forward cheerily to the day when they would be "great fountains and healthful moral influence, sending forth streams that shall fertilize and bless the land." The elder Theodore Sedgwick added that the cause of the bad reputation of cities was economic: "it is the sleeping in garrets and cellars; the living in holes and dens; in dirty, unpaved, unlighted streets, without the accommodations of wells, cisterns, baths, and other means of cleanliness and health"—clear up this situation, and cities will be all right.

Jackson himself never betrayed any of Jefferson's revulsion to industrialism. He was, for example, deeply interested by the mills of Lowell in 1833, and his inquiries respecting hours, wages and production showed, observers reported, "that the subject of domestic manufactures had previously engaged his attentive observation." His presidential allusions to the "producing classes" always included the workingmen of the cities. . . .

III

In several respects, then, the Jacksonians revised the Jeffersonian faith for America. They moderated that side of Jeffersonianism which talked of agricultural virtue, independent proprietors, "natural" property, abolition of industrialism, and expanded immensely that side which talked of economic equality, the laboring classes, human rights and the control of industrialism. This readjustment enabled the Jacksonians to attack economic problems which had baffled and defeated the Jeffersonians. It made for a greater realism, and was accompanied by a general toughening of the basic Jeffersonian conceptions. While the loss of "property" was serious, both symbolically and intellectually, this notion had been for most Jeffersonians somewhat submerged next to the romantic image of the free and virtuous cultivator; and the Jacksonians grew much more insistent about theories of capitalist alienation. Where, for the Jeffersonians, the tensions of class conflict tended to dissolve in vague generalizations about the democracy and the aristocracy, many Jacksonians would have agreed with A. H. Wood's remark, "It is in vain to talk of Aristocracy and Democracy—these terms are too variable and indeterminate to convey adequate ideas of the present opposing interests; the division is between the rich and the poor—the warfare is between them."

The greater realism was due, in the main, to the passage of time. The fears of Jefferson were now actualities. One handled fears by exorcism, but actualities by adjustment. For the Jeffersonians mistrust of banks and corporations was chiefly a matter of theory; for the Jacksonians it was a matter of experience. The contrast between the scintillating metaphors of John Taylor and the sober detail of William M. Gouge expressed the difference. Jefferson rejected the Industrial Revolution and sought to perpetuate the smiling society which preceded it (at least, so the philosopher; facts compelled the President toward a different policy), while Jackson, accepting industrialism as an ineradicable and even useful part of the economic landscape, sought rather to control it. Jeffersonian democracy looked wistfully back toward a past slipping further every minute into the mists of memory, while Jacksonian democracy came straightforwardly to grips with a rough and unlovely present.

The interlude saw also the gradual unfolding of certain consequences of the democratic dogma which had not been so clear to the previous generation. Though theoretically aware of the relation between political and economic power, the Jeffersonians had been occupied, chiefly, with establishing political equality. This was their mission, and they had little time to grapple with the economic questions.

But the very assertion of political equality raised inevitably the whole range of problems involved in property and class conflict. How could political equality mean anything without relative economic equality among the classes of the country? This question engaged the Jacksonians. As Orestes A. Brownson said, "A Loco-foco is a Jeffersonian Democrat, who having realized political equality, passed through one phase of the revolution, now passes on to another, and attempts the realization of social equality, so that the actual condition of men in society shall be in harmony with their acknowledged rights as citizens." This gap between Jeffersonian and Jacksonian democracy enabled men like John Quincy Adams, Henry Clay, Joseph Story and many others, who had been honest Jeffersonians, to balk at the economic extremities to which Jackson proposed to lead them.

The Jacksonians thus opened irrevocably the economic question, which the Jeffersonians had only touched halfheartedly. Yet, while they clarified these economic implications of democracy, the Jacksonians were no more successful than their predecessors in resolving certain political ambiguities. Of these, two were outstanding—the problem of the virtue of majorities, and the problem of the evil of government. . . .

IV

The radical democrats had a definite conception of their relation to history. From the Jeffersonian analysis, fortified by the insights of Adam Smith and Cobbett, they sketched out an interpretation of modern times which gave meaning and status to the Jacksonian struggles.

Power, said the Jacksonians, goes with property. In the Middle Ages the feudal nobility held power in society through its monopoly of land under feudal tenure. The overthrow of feudalism, with the rise of new forms of property, marked the first step in the long march toward freedom. The struggle was carried on by the rising business community—"commercial, or business capital, against landed capital; merchants, traders, manufacturers, artizans, against the owners of the soil, the great landed nobility." It lasted from the close of the twelfth century to the Whig Revolution of 1688 in Britain.

The aristocracy of capital thus destroyed the aristocracy of land. The business classes here performed their vital role in the drama of liberty. The victory over feudalism, as the *Democratic Review* put it, "opened the way for the entrance of the democratic principle into the Government." But the business community gained from this exploit an undeserved reputation as the champion of liberty. Its real motive had been to establish itself in power, not to free mankind; to found government on property, not on the equal rights of the people. "I know perfectly well what I am saying," cried George Bancroft, "and I assert expressly, and challenge contradiction, that in all the history of the world there is not to be found an instance of a commercial community establishing rules for self-government upon democratic principles." "It is a mistake to suppose commerce favorable to liberty," added Fenimore Cooper. "Its tendency is to a monied aristocracy." "Instead of setting man free," said Amos Kendall, it has "only increased the number of his masters."

The next great blow for liberty was the American Revolution, "effected not in favor of men in classes; . . . but in favor of men." But the work of Hamilton halted the march of democracy. "He established the money power," wrote Van Buren, "upon precisely the same foundations upon which it has been raised in England." The subsequent history of the United States was the struggle to overthrow the Hamiltonian policy and fulfill the ideals of the Revolution.

What of the future? The Jacksonians were sublimely confident: history was on their side. "It is now for the yeomanry and the mechanics to march at the head of civilization," said Bancroft. "The merchants and the lawyers, that is, the moneyed interest broke up feudalism. The day for the multitude has now dawned." "All classes, each in turn, have possessed the government," explained Brownson; "and the time has come for all predominance of class to end; for Man, the People to rule."

This was not simply a national movement. It was a movement of all people, everywhere, against their masters, and the Jacksonians watched with keen interest the stirrings of revolt abroad. Jackson and his cabinet joined in the celebrations in Washington which followed the Revolution of 1830 in France; and Van Buren, as Secretary of State, ordered the new government informed that the American people were "universally and enthusiastically in favor of that change, and of the principle upon which it was effected." (The Whigs, on the other hand, in spite of Clay's support of national revolutions in Greece and South America, remained significantly lukewarm.) Lamennais, the eloquent voice of French popular aspirations, was read in Jacksonian circles. The *Paroles d'un Croyant* influenced Orestes A. Brownson, and in 1839 *Le Livre du Peuple* was published in Boston under the title of *The People's Own Book,* translated by Nathaniel Greene, postmaster of Boston, brother of Charles Gordon Greene of the *Post* and intimate of David Henshaw.

Democrats followed with similar enthusiasm the progress of the Reform Bill in England, while the Whigs sympathized with the Tories. The Chartist uprisings at the end of the decade were greeted with delight by the Democratic press. British reformers returned this interest. Not only Cobbett and Savage Landor but the veteran radical Jeremy Bentham observed Jackson's administration with approval. Bentham, a friend of John Quincy Adams, had been disappointed at the triumph in 1828 of this military hero; but early in 1830, as he huddled by his hissing steam radiator, he heard read aloud Jackson's first message to Congress. The old man was highly pleased to discover greater agreement with the new President than with the old. Later he wrote that lengthy and cryptic memorandum entitled *Anti-Senatica,* intended to aid Jackson in the problems of his administration.

Jacksonians everywhere had this faith in the international significance of their fight. For this reason, as well as from a desire to capture their votes, Democratic leaders made special appeals to newly naturalized citizens. Where many Whigs tended to oppose immigration and demand sanctions against it, Democrats welcomed the newcomers with open arms and attacked the nativist agitation. The United States must remain a refuge from tyranny. "The capitalist class," said Samuel J. Tilden, "has banded together all over the world and organized the *modern dynasty of associated wealth,* which maintains an unquestioned ascendency over most of the civilized portions of our race." America was the proving-ground of democracy, and it was the mission of American Democrats to exhibit to the world the glories of government by the people. They were on the spearhead of history. They would not be denied. "With the friends of freedom throughout the world," declared Theophilus Fisk, "let us be co-workers." "The People of the World," cried Fanny Wright, "have but one Cause."

EDWARD PESSEN

Consensus and Ideology
in the Age of Jackson

Those who find striking contrasts in the beliefs and actions of the major parties tend to believe the Whigs and Democrats appealed to unlike constituencies. In this view, Democrats were led by plebeians, Whigs by aristocrats. The Democratic rank and file, whether in city or countryside, were allegedly much poorer than their Whig counterparts. Whiggery flourished where soils were superior. In the South it was most popular in the black belt, where plantations prevailed or where slaveownership was greatest. The religious diversity of the party memberships was also believed to reflect the social gulf dividing them. Denominations of high prestige thus aligned themselves with the party of Clay while their social inferiors chose Jacksonian Democracy. And where poor or ordinary folk voted Whig, as millions of them obviously did, a traditional interpretation explained the phenomenon in terms of an "economic dependency" that drew the lower orders to support their overlords.

According to the popular interpretation of American history that stresses the twin themes of continuity and struggle, the Jackson party took up where the Jeffersonians had left off in the never ending fight of the people against the privileged few. The Democratic party of Franklin Roosevelt's time would later fight the same good fight that had been waged a century earlier by the partisans of Old Hickory. The enemies of the people—whether Federalists, Whigs, or Liberty League—were also judged to be spiritually akin. Certainly Jacksonian campaigners regularly referred to their opponents, whether Whig, Antimason, or other, as "Federalists." There is no doubt the charge was an effective one, what with the deteriorating reputation of Washington's and Hamilton's old party after the War of 1812. What the student of history wishes to know is whether the charge was accurate. . . . The old question still stands: were the memberships of the major parties dissimilar in their social and economic backgrounds?

It is very difficult to discern any significant differences in the social composition of Democratic and Whig party leaders. Of course the situation varied from state to state. The men at the helm of the Jacksonian party in Massachusetts, for example, were outsiders, politically, and of lower status than their opposite numbers in the other party, socially, in part because the wealth of Democratic leaders was in some cases only recently come by. Yet there were Bay State Whig leaders who were also *nouveau*. The "Conscience Whigs," who emerged with the heating up of the slavery issue and who became Free Soilers after the Mexican War, were for the most part of older family and higher social status than their more expedient Whig fellows. In that state the inveterately successful Whigs reigned as the party not only of old wealth but of practically every other social stratum as well. The slight but significant differences in the social tone of major party leadership there were due essentially to the domination of state politics by one party. Whether *parvenus* or not, David Henshaw and his circle—typically bankers or members of the boards of directors of railroads and other businesses—were not poor men.

The top and "middle grade" leadership of New York State's Democratic party were not commonfolk. Rather they were men of wealth and high status, the social and economic equal of their Whig opposite numbers. New York City's Jacksonian leaders characteristically stressed their alleged plebeian backgrounds. In fact, many of them were either wealthy businessmen, merchants, and bankers, or prominent lawyers and doctors, members all of the city's "privileged aristocracy." In the other middle states the Democratic leadership was similarly in the hands of men of unusual wealth and prominence in business affairs.

In Michigan's strategic Wayne County, leaders of the two major parties, whether of the top, middle, or intermediate grades were essentially alike in their social and economic backgrounds. Lawyers and businessmen were to be found in roughly equal numbers in the Democratic and Whig top echelons. That they evidently mingled socially without regard to party suggests something of their view of the "great" party battles in their community. Differences there were in the elites of the parties but they had to do with religion, ethnic origins, the geographical backgrounds of the native-born and how long they had lived in their Michigan residences, not with wealth or occupation. In contrast to Kentucky, Democratic leaders were less footloose than their Whig counterparts. In common with other states, Michigan Whig leaders were more likely to be New Englanders and of that section's predominant Protestant denominations, less likely to be foreigners or Catholics than the Democrats. In contrast to Alabama, youth was no more a characteristic of the leadership of the one party than of the other.

The socioeconomic status of Jacksonian and Whig leaders has been most fully investigated for the southern states. Of course scholars of different persuasion will either interpret the same evidence differently or focus on different facts. Thus one study notes that Whig members of the Tennessee lower house were more than twice as likely as Democrats to be lawyers. A more recent examination of Tennessee's Congressmen finds that for all their ideological differences, the men of both parties were of roughly equal wealth and professional attainment. Despite the inevitable differences in viewpoint of the men engaged in the modern research, its most amazing feature is the essential similarity it discloses in the occupations, wealth and status of Whig and Jacksonian leaders. In Louisiana, "leaders in both parties were seemingly equal in wealth and education." North Carolina's Jacksonian leaders by the early 1830's were substantial eastern elements, rather than the frontiersmen and westerners who earlier had been influential. Mississippi's Democratic activists were for the most part successful men of affairs.

Florida's party leaders have been examined closely. The Democracy's chieftains may perhaps have owned less land and fewer slaves than their Whig colleagues. Yet the "nucleus," which constituted the original Jacksonian coalition of the early 1830's, was composed of speculators, planters, bankers, and professionals. True, many of these men later deserted the Jacksonian party for the Whigs. But the residue were not poor men. The Democratic party of 1838 to 1845 was made up of farmers and planters, large and small, with merchants, rural capitalists, and village entrepreneurs having "considerable weight" in its affairs. As in Massachusetts, newer and smaller merchants were more likely than the well-established ones to be Democrats. Yet 150 Democratic leaders in Florida, when subjected to a detailed analysis, proved to be unusually wealthy men. There were "a disproportionate number of them lawyers, relatively few yeoman farmers—fourteen percent—in contrast to planters who made up close to forty percent of the group, while merchants and manufacturers constituted twenty-five percent." For all the Whig demagogy and Democratic counter-demagogy about Jacksonian leveling and affinity for the poor, the "Democratic movement in Florida was certainly no lower-class manifestation of radicalism."

An exhaustive study of the socioeconomic and family backgrounds of the more than 1,000 Alabama Congressmen and State legislators for the period 1835 to 1856 found no important differences between Democrats and Whigs. A larger percentage of Democrats had gone to college; 47.6 percent of Democrats were planters in contrast to 34.5 percent of the Whigs. Slightly more than half of the representatives of each party were lawyers. The percentage of businessmen was about equal. A "slightly higher percentage of Whigs than Democrats" were professional men. As for religion, Methodists and Baptists abounded: there were "few Episcopalians in either party." A subsequent study of several hundred Whig and Democratic local activists in Alabama found a remarkable similarity in their situations. Occupations and religious denominations were alike while they owned equal amounts of real estate and were "strikingly similar in their pattern of slaveownership."

There is little doubt that the Whig Party in the South became increasingly preoccupied with banking and business issues or that its leadership included many wealthy merchants, bankers, and professional men. As the historians of an earlier day suggested, it was also a party dominated by the planter and slaveholder, in the language of one memorable characterization, "the broad cloth and silk stocking party." A stunning word picture of a later time depicted the typical Whig leader as the man in a silk hat nearby a Negro on a cotton bale. But the painstaking modern studies of Alabama and other southern states indicate that broadcloth and silk stockings were the badge not only of *Whig* party leadership; "the man in a silk hat nearby a Negro on a cotton bale was by no means necessarily a Whig."

In Missouri, too, the Jackson party leadership contained more slaveholders as well as the men who owned the largest numbers of slaves. Practically no Whigs owned more than 20 slaves. While Democratic leaders were wealthier and of higher status than the average Missourian, the leaders of the Whig party of that state were typically richer, more likely to be lawyers, slightly more likely to be businessmen, and while less likely to be farmers, more likely to claim large farms than the Jacksonians. Among the top leaders of the party, more than twice as many Whigs on the average had attended college—although the rate of college attendance among the Democracy's prominent figures was between 500 and 1,000 times the national average. In the city of St. Louis both parties typically put up extremely wealthy men for Mayor and middle-class persons for the Council, although Democrats did on occasion also nominate artisans to that body. On the level of "vigilance committees" or poll watchers, essentially similar patterns prevailed, although when tavern keepers and brewers are ranked as "businessmen," there is little to choose between the party faithful. The Democracy's local activists included 21 tavern keepers or brewers while the Whigs had none. Differences there were in the social and economic positions of Missouri's party leadership, but as John Vollmer Mering has observed, they were hardly those separating an "aristocracy" from a "proletariat.". . .

There seems to be a widespread assumption that a party supported overwhelmingly *by* the poor or by whatever class, is the party *of* the poor or of the class that does support it. If this is taken to mean—as I think it often is—that a so-called party of the poor either truly serves them or that it deserves their support, then I think it is a false notion. It does not take into account the power of demagogy or the gullibility of voters. To cite a drastic example, the fact that Hitler's party may have been supported by the German workers would hardly make the Nazis the party of the poor. American history, fortunately not yielding examples so dramatic as German, also affords illustrations of the point. McKinley's party would not be the party of the poor no matter how well it might do in working class electoral districts. The determination that the Democrats were the party of this or that group must finally be made not on the basis of statistics or the degree of electoral support the Democracy got from the group in question, but according to an *evaluation* of the party's behavior. . . .

The complicated New York evidence revealed "that farmers, mechanics, and 'working classes' did not form the mainstay of the Democratic party." The Jacksonians' main support came not from "low-status socioeconomic groups," but rather from "relatively high-status socioeconomic groups in the eastern counties, and relatively low-status ethnocultural and religious groups in all sections of New York." Among natives, Jacksonians won small but significant majorities from "Old British," "Old German," "Dutch" and "Penn-Jerseyite" voters, and overwhelming majorities from "Catholic Irish," "French Canadian," "French" and "New German" immigrant groups. In the Empire State the Democracy attracted gamblers, bohemians, the free thinking, the free swearing. In showing that equally prosperous communities voted differently; that economically unlike communities produced strikingly similar party percentages; and the durability of party affiliations through all manner of changing economic circumstances that overtook given communities; Benson makes a shambles of the old simplistic notion that "voters vote by class."

Other detailed studies of voting in North Carolina and New York, counties in Pennsylvania and Tennessee, and of townships in New Jersey, have also demonstrated that the relative wealth or poverty of citizens seemed to have nothing to do with their party preferences. Poorer voters divided their votes among the two major parties in almost exactly the same proportions as their wealthier neighbors. Certain counties unbelievably registered exactly the same division of votes for the parties over the course of several elections, through thick and thin, despite socioeconomic changes in their electorates.

Not that the modern findings point only in one direction. In Georgia, Whig strength did appear to be greatest "where cotton growing and attendant activities were dominant interests" and in "those counties where investment in primary types of manufacturing and commercial ventures supplemented cotton growing." But as in Alabama the response in such communities came from men of all classes. An economic interpretation failed to account for the political sympathies of the many Georgians who simply admired the good sense of Whig appeals. Maryland politics may have been unideological but Jackson electoral support at first came from the old Republican—if not necessarily poor—districts of Baltimore and the western counties. Even T. P. Abernethy, as sharp a critic of the progressive interpretation of Jacksonian Democracy as any historian of the 20th century, conceded that in the Tennessee gubernatorial election of 1839, the "focal points of Whig strength . . . tended to radiate along the lines of communication." The Whig constituency in Florida lived in the "rich, earlier-settled, plantation areas" of middle Florida, while Democrats were in the "new, frontier, small farmer region of East and South Florida." The commercial centers, however, leaned toward the Democracy.

Less than one fifth of Missouri's 108 counties consistently voted Whig in presidential elections between 1836 and 1852. The Whigs of Thomas Hart Benton's state were inveterate losers who as often as not chose not to run candidates. If one can therefore speak of characteristic Whig counties in such a state, he would note that they were relatively old or long-established, touched the Missouri or Mississippi river, contained unusually large farms, and were the more populous counties. (Of course many Democratic counties, in a state controlled by the Jacksonians, had similar traits.) That the Whig vote was high where slaveholding was great, does not substantiate the old Phillips-Cole thesis: John Mering, the modern historian of the Missouri party, cautions that "slavery and the interests it generated do not explain a Missouri county's Whiggery."

This tendency of relatively well-established, commercially active, "go ahead" communities to vote against Jackson has also been found to have been true in New Hampshire, at least in the presidential election of 1832. A "typical" Clay town in the state was old, prosperous, populous, connected to the outside world by many roads, near the ocean, possessed of a lively newspaper, great buildings, and a couple of Congregationalist churches. Jackson towns—and one had recently changed its name from Adams to Jackson!—were isolated, poor, "out of the mainstream" of New Hampshire life, sparsely populated, and had no church or perhaps one church, the Free Will Baptist. Small upland villages on poor soil worked by small farmers, with the exception of one district of 16 towns whose Clay vote has recently been interpreted as due to its relative prosperity and its proximity to the world outside and to areas of former Federalist influence, voted overwhelmingly for Old Hickory. The correlation between religious denomination and voting appears to have been greater than any other. For in addition to the "exceptional" Clay upland towns running from Sullivan to Amherst, the next to the poorest town in the state voted for Clay, while the second wealthiest went for Jackson by two to one. But the latter were exceptions to the New Hampshire pattern. For that matter any anti-Democratic voting seems to have been exceptional in a state whose "Concord Regency," led by the redoubtable Isaac Hill and Levi Woodbury, "had been electing Democratic Governors and Congressmen by wide margins since 1829."

Michigan voting late in the Jackson era, certainly in the towns and villages of Wayne County, sharply contradicts the older version of the nature of the major party electorates. Middle and lower-class persons who made up the great bulk of the electorate divided their votes, without reference to class, more or less equally among Democrats and Whigs. That towns were populated either by "rural lower classes" or by large proportions of "prosperous, middle-class farmers" was no clue to their political preferences. As in Lee Benson's New York, towns with similar social patterns differed sharply in their voting behavior while towns whose social elements were markedly unlike nevertheless exhibited similar voting patterns. No discernible correlations existed between economic status and party choice. The most striking correlations rather were to be found between ethnic identity and party, style of life and party, and above all between religion and party. Yankees, for example, tended only slightly to be Whigs, but Yankee Presbyterians, decisively. Evangelical sects were overwhelmingly Whig; Catholics, whether Irish or French, were Democrats. The ethnic patterns were also similar to New York State's, as were the relationships between life style and voting. Hedonists were Jacksonian; the God fearing, Whig.

In Kentucky, at least in 1828, Jackson seemed to do unusually well in "counties with high rates of population growth," and with men who had been active in the old Relief movement—albeit the latter movement was led by many well-to-do men who became repudiationists out of temporary need rather than compassion for poor debtors. In Virginia in 1828 both the Tidewater and Piedmont, "strongholds of conservative views," went heavily for Jackson. In North Carolina the Democratic party's social and geographical bases did not conform to the traditional ideas about them. Democratic strength in that state was not on the frontier but in "the North-Central counties and in the East." Democratic majorities were large in districts where slavery was most prominent. In a word, voting patterns were varied, sometimes contradictory, and give little support to the theory that clear-cut class lines divided Whig from Jacksonian voters. . . .

The closest thing to a classic ideological party in the entire antebellum period, the Working Men burst forth like a political meteor only to fall to earth in the space of a few years. Following the creation of the Philadelphia Working Men's party in 1828, groups sprang up all over the country. The modern discussion, focusing as it does on a few major cities, has perhaps obscured what Helen Sumner, one of the pioneer labor researchers working with John R. Commons, long ago discovered: the ubiquitousness of the movement. In fact recent investigations show it to have been even more widespread than Miss Sumner imagined. Operating under a variety of names, "Working Men's Parties," "Working Men's Republican Associations," "People's Parties," "Working Men's Societies," "Farmers' and Mechanics' Societies," "Mechanics and Other Working Men," and just plain "Working Men" appeared in most of the states of the Union. They took shape in such communities as Carlisle, Pennsylvania; Glens Falls, New York; Caldwell, New Jersey; Zanesville, Ohio; Dedham, Massachusetts; Lyme, Connecticut; and Calais, Vermont; as well as in such centers as New York City, St. Louis, Boston, Newark, and Philadelphia.

Almost every one of these organizations had its own press. These journals, most unlike the Regency's Albany *Argus* or the Whig *Columbian Centinel* in Boston, contained, in addition to accounts of Working Men's activities in their own and other cities and the usual advertisements and literary excerpts that then characterized journalism, "a spectrum of reform, from Pestallozzian educational ideas and cooperative store suggestions to the views of freethinkers and reprints from [English socialist] works." Typically edited by leaders of the new party, they provide the fullest contemporary account of what the Working Men's movement was about.

Many questions have been raised about the Working Men's party, the most important having to do with its authenticity. "Decayed Federal dandies!" not true workingmen, charged a New England journal, while at other times proto-Whig editors bitterly stamped the new organizations a mere front for the Democracy. The evidence is complicated, often contradictory, and suggests the wisdom of careful examination of the facts relating to each group before coming to conclusions as to whether they truly represented artisans and mechanics. According to Miss Sumner the issue that separated legitimate Working Men from fraudulent was the protective tariff. In some cases, she wrote, "advocates of a protective tariff assumed without warrant the popular name—'mechanics and working men.' " She suspected that these "associations of so-called workingmen which favored protection generally avoided committing themselves to the usual demands of the Working Men's party." But let the organization be silent on protection and approve the "usual demands" and her study accepted its *bona fides*. Modern scholars have been more skeptical and with good reason. For as one of them wrote, after noting the great wealth of the Philadelphia Working Men's candidates for office, "to believe that [such] a party . . . was really devoted to solving working class problems in the interests of the workers would seem to lay a heavy tax on credulity." And yet the record is clear: the Philadelphia Working Men's Party was no misnomer.

The party arose out of a decision by the city's Mechanics' Union of Trade Associations to enter into politics, in order to promote "the interests and enlightenment of the working classes." There can be no question of the authenticity of this latter group, "the first union of all the organized workmen of any city." Consisting of individual unions—or societies as they were then called—of journeymen bricklayers, painters, glaziers, typographers, house carpenters, and other craftsmen, its main purpose was to provide financial support to journeymen striking against their masters. An amendment to this Mechanics' Union's constitution, in 1828, provided that three months prior to the forthcoming elections, the membership should "nominate as candidates for public office such individuals as shall pledge themselves . . . to support and advance . . . the interests and enlightenment of the working classes." Shortly thereafter the *Mechanic's Free Press*, edited by a young Ricardian socialist, William Heighton, reported that "at a very large and respectable meeting of Journeymen House Carpenters held on Tuesday evening, July 1st . . . the Mechanics' Union of Trade Associations is entering into measures for procuring a nomination of candidates for legislative and other public offices, who will support the interest of the working classes." Thus was born the Philadelphia Working Men's party, in the promise made by journeymen workers to support at the polls individuals sympathetic to—not necessarily members of—the working class.

New York City's Working Men made their appearance in 1829 when their candidates for the State Assembly made a remarkable showing. Some contemporaries and later scholars alike explained this new party as nothing more than anti-Tammany dissidents, born out of "the bitter internal dissensions and schisms that were wrecking the Republican party of New York." The fact remains that the decision to run candidates on a separate Working Men's ticket was made at a meeting of mechanics on October 19, 1829, in agreement with the proposal by the executive body—the "Committee of Fifty." A number of journeymen's meetings held in April had created this Committee. Its purpose was to combat "all attempts to compel journeymen mechanics to work more than ten hours a day." It would seem that at least in its origins the New York Working Men's party was indubitably a response of workers to a threatened attack on their working conditions.

For Boston the evidence is not clear, for all the press unhappiness with the new party or the impressionistic recording by a journalist present at early meetings of the Working Men's party in the summer of 1830. He wrote that they were attended by large numbers of men who, "from appearance, were warm from their workshops and from other places of daily toil, but who bore on their countenances convictions of their wrongs, and a determination to use every proper means to have them redressed." Two years later New England workingmen and their friends formed the New England Association of Farmers, Mechanics, and Other Working Men, described as a "new type of labor organization, in part economic and in part political." This interesting organization was preoccupied with trying to achieve for New England's workers what remained a will-o'-the-wisp for most of the era—the 10-hour day. Its failures do not detract from its authenticity.

Logic as well as the historical record suggest the essential validity and independence from other political groupings of the Working Men's party—at least at its birth. The new party was a form of rejection by its members of both the Jacksonians and their major opponents. The Working Men stood for programs and called for changes in American society not dreamed of by the pragmatists at the helm of the major parties. And in view of the relatively small followings of the new organizations for all their idealism—or was it because of it?—it strains credulity to attribute to shrewd Jacksonian manipulators the formation of ostensibly single-class political organizations that exasperated both the business community and those many Americans of whatever class who under no circumstances wished to think of themselves as workers. . . .

The parties' real leaders are best studied not for their social and economic backgrounds, which were in fact diverse, but for their ideas and personal force, which actually accounted for their leadership. Unlike their contemporaries in the major parties these men were indeed radicals, certainly for this phase of their careers. There was nothing politic in adhering to essentially socialistic doctrines that most of the press savagely excoriated. Beliefs such as theirs, going beyond the patent demagogy of the day, could find no expression in the programs of the era's major parties. As to the party's rank and file constituency, apart from the sparkling successes achieved in Philadelphia and New York in 1829, it does not seem ever to have been very great. On the other hand, particularly in the latter city but in Boston, too, what electoral support it got did come primarily from poorer or working-class wards. In New York City its candidates got close to 50 percent of the vote of the five poorest wards while averaging only about 20 percent in the wealthier districts.

Their program was amazingly similar, with substantially the same measures advocated in most of the western and southern cities, as well as in New Jersey, Delaware, and New England, as were advocated in Philadelphia and New York. The original Philadelphia demands became the nucleus of the Working Men's program everywhere. They called above all for free, tax-supported school systems of high quality to replace the stigmatized "pauper schools." Stephen Simpson, brilliant and unreliable one-time Jacksonian, was nominated to office by the Philadelphia Working Men and became a leading figure in the movement mainly because of his advanced educational ideas. In addition, the masthead of the *Mechanic's Free Press* urged abolition of imprisonment for debt; abolition of all licensed monopolies; an entire revision or abolition of the prevailing militia system; a less expensive legal system; equal taxation on property; no legislation on religion; and a district system of elections. The paper's columns also pressed vigorously for a mechanics' lien law to assure workers first claim to the employers' payroll, shorter hours, better working conditions, and constantly urged improved housing for workers. The major parties were regularly denounced as were city fathers who administered the city by a double standard, failing either to provide sufficient "hydrant water for the accommodation of the poor" or "to clean the streets in the remote sections of the city where the workingmen reside." Political action was not considered at odds with economic, by the Working Men's leaders, for they strongly favored creation of unions. Nor does this exhaust the list even of the Philadelphia issues.

The movements in other cities added dozens of other grievances. The New York party went so far as to call for "equal property to all adults" in its early stages when the radical Thomas Skidmore was its leading figure. When he was cashiered out of the party at the end of its first year by the opportunists who had infiltrated it, with the acquiescence of the more innocent Robert Dale Owen and George Henry Evans, even the latter continued to insist, in the party's official organ, that it continued to stand for Skidmore's principles; it had only modified its tactics for achieving them. The Owen-Evans faction of the party stressed the need for a revamped educational system featured by "state guardianship" or the boarding out of working-class children in publicly-supported schools. Regional variations might call for a reform in land tenure laws or, as in the case of the New England Association, insistence on factory legislation. Abolition of capital punishment and prison reform were popular demands everywhere. In sum, Working Men's parties were champions of a great variety of political, social, economic, and educational reforms. That much of the program was not of a "bread and butter" character or that the victims of some grievances were not confined to the "laboring poor" are not valid grounds for skepticism. For it would be a most doctrinaire economic determinism indeed that insisted that authentic labor organizations confine their programs to economic issues. In that era when the diverse and youthful American labor movement was very much influenced by the radical English model, and when American workmen were as much concerned with enhanced status and educational opportunity as with material gains, organizations speaking for labor quite naturally reflected this breadth of interest. Short-term, pitifully organized affairs for the most part, a major function of the new organizations was not to win elections so much as to call attention to the gamut of abuses bearing most heavily on the nation's working people.

The Working Men were essentially independent of the majority parties although from time to time they cooperated with them. Certainly in choosing candidates they paid little attention to the previous political preferences of a nominee who was sound on an important Working Men's principle. At times, particularly during the Bank War, they cooperated closely with the Jacksonians. Stephen Simpson's refusal to issue a blanket condemnation of the "monster bank" infuriated many of his one-time admirers. The regular support given the Democracy by the Newark Working Men, their tendency, if not to hold joint nominating conventions, then to hold them on the same date and in the same town, and to approve closely similar lists of candidates, did not fail to draw the condemnation of the anti-Jacksonian press.

The New York City party broke into three pieces shortly after its 1829 success, the largest splinter supporting and subsequently being absorbed into the New York State Democratic party. New England's Working Men in 1833 threw their support in the gubernatorial campaign to Samuel Clesson Allen, champion of Andrew Jackson and enemy to Nicholas Biddle, Evidence of Working Men's collaboration with anti-Jacksonians however, as in Philadelphia, is as easily come by. When the New England Association again nominated Allen in 1834 it condemned the candidates of both major parties. Working Men of most New Jersey towns and cities typically had as little to do with Democrats as with their opponents, while even in Newark the romance was not a lasting one. It was punctuated finally by a falling out in 1836. Most of the Working Men's leaders even when cooperating with the Democrats on a particular issue, never ceased warning that the Jackson party was no different from the Clay, no more concerned with the real problems of working people.

Future studies of the Working Men's party are likely only to accentuate what previous work has disclosed: how hard it is to generalize about the movement as a whole. For as I have elsewhere noted, "there were Working Men and Working

Men. The origin of some was obscure; of others, dubious. Some arose out of economic struggles, others out of concern for status. Some came to be dominated by opportunists, other by zealots." The significant common feature of the movement as a whole was its authenticity—at least for part of its history. I regard it authentic because the parties seem to have been formed by workers and men devoted to their interests, and concerned themselves with the cause and welfare of workers, hoping to goad or influence the major parties into like concern. Of course the parties contained many men who by present standards would not qualify as workers. The definition of that day was less restrictive. George Henry Evans for example seemed to regard only "lawyers, bankers, and brokers as disqualified for membership." The equally radical William Heighton advised his Philadelphia party that "an employer [who] superintends his business" but "works with his own hands is a workingman." A movement in need of all the membership it could get would not permit a Skidmore to narrow down further its small chances for growth by establishing uncompromising standards for participation. The typical resolution of this problem was to ask few questions about the social position of any individual who in Heighton's words, was "willing to join us in obtaining our objects." But of course such an approach created additional problems.

In New York City, for example, by 1830 elements which not only were not themselves of the working class but which had little sympathy with its aspirations succeeded in taking over the party by the use of money, intrigue, and extralegal tactics that denied the floor to opposition, all the while paying lip service to the party program. There was nothing to prevent special pleaders from calling meetings designed to further their objects while masquerading under the banner of the new party. Much of the nation's press, Democratic and National Republican alike, nevertheless persisted in taking a dim view of a party whose own press constantly reminded its readers that this was a class society. "The very pretension to the necessity of such a party is a libel on the community," protested the editors of the Boston *Courier*. Shortly afterwards Edward Everett pressed home the point that rich and poor alike, all are workingmen. What need was there for a separate Working Men's party? Parties nevertheless insisted on forming, in the City of Brotherly Love obtaining the balance of power by their second electoral try, in New York winning better than 6,000 out of 21,000 votes cast in their initial effort. And yet their success was decidedly ephemeral.

Most of the Working Men's parties disappeared within five years of their birth. Among the many factors responsible for their downfall, newspaper denunciation, internal dissension in some cases introduced by infiltrators intent on taking over the party, doctrinal squabbles by party zealots, the hostility of the major parties, the increasing prosperity which, according to Miss Sumner, turned the attention of workers from "politics to trade unionism," the inexperience of their leadership, and not least the absorption of some of their program by the major parties, all played their part. Parties which sharply delineated the social and economic cleavages and disparities besetting American society on the one hand were offensive to those Americans used to more cheerful assessment, and on the other were inevitably attacked by men, newspapers, and political parties possessed of far more money, experience, and influence. And a political system which rewarded only winners of majorities or pluralities was not conducive to the perpetuation of such a movement.

Short-lived though they were the Working Men's parties were a significant phenomenon. They played an important part in the achievement of a number of the era's reforms. Particularly outstanding was their contribution to the movement for a democratic and public educational system. They agitated not only for broadened opportunities for the poor but for surprisingly sophisticated modifications in curriculum and teacher training. A final significance of the movement was its indirect testimony that even in the age of optimism, speculation, and major party demagogy, a significant number of Americans were disenchanted with their society and responsive to the voice of radical dissent. . . .

On the national level, particularly in 1844, and on the local and state levels throughout the era, a number of the third parties at times held the balance of political power. In view of the nearly equal followings of the great major parties, a minor party whose own voting support was minuscule could nevertheless manage to determine the outcome of an election. The major significance of the dissenting parties however was in other things than their occasional fateful effect on the party battles between the giants. Their very existence highlighted the nonideological nature of the Democracy and Whiggery. The absorption of parts of their program and their memberships by the major parties was one more revelation of the political knowhow of the latter. Small memberships and highly localized centers of support testified to the indifference most American voters felt toward the politics of principle and zeal. For if the very existence of third parties showed that the Jacksonian consensus was not universally subscribed to, the most revealing feature of the situation was how few Americans dissented from it.

James MacGregor Burns

The Revolt of the Outs

The simplest definition of politics is the conflict of outs versus ins. This is also the most simplistic definition, for the battle between those who hold office and those who seek it becomes enmeshed with ideological, policy, ethnic, geographical, religious, and other conflicts that may turn the contest into something more fundamental than a struggle to keep or seize power and pelf; some persons, indeed, reject office out of conviction. If ever a political contest was reduced to the simplest definition of politics, however, it was Jackson's campaign against John Quincy Adams in 1828, when a coalition of "insiders" united around a few great national issues was assailed by a coalition of outsiders agreed on hardly any issues at all.

Since the election sharpened not merely major policy issues but personal and psychological ones, it turned into the ugliest presidential contest in a generation. However divided, the outsiders were agreed on the man they wanted—Andrew Jackson—and they were united by the conviction that they had been excluded from the citadels of the political and financial system, from the centers of social status and deference. They were Westerners and Southerners incensed against the East; growers and consumers angered by abominable tariffs; mechanics and small businessmen indignant over "monopoly"; farmers hostile to middlemen and speculators.

Listen to young Congressman James K. Polk inveigh against what had come to be known as Adams' and Clay's American System: "Since 1815 the action of the Government has been . . . essentially vicious; I repeat, sir, essentially vicious." The American tripod was a "stool that stands upon three legs; first, high prices of the public lands . . . sell your lands high, prevent thereby the inducements to emigration, retain a population of paupers in the East, who may, of necessity, be driven into manufactories, to labor at low wages for their daily bread. The second branch of the system is high duties . . . first, to protect the manufacturer, by enabling him to sell his wares at higher prices, and next to produce an excess of revenue. The third branch of the system is internal improvements, which is the sponge which is to suck up the excess of revenue."

All of which sounded like the poor man against the rich, the People against the Elite, the rebels against the Establishment, until one looked to the Jacksonian leaders. They were—most of them—not mechanics or farmers or paupers but capitalists, planters, traders, landowners and speculators, slave owners, lawyers, journalists, and indeed men, like Jackson himself, who had already enjoyed the fruits of office as legislators and administrators. Still, they had acute feelings of political and psychological exclusion. And nothing had aroused both feelings as forcibly as Adams' and Clay's "deal" of January 1825—the deal that they were certain had kept Andrew Jackson out of the White House.

The campaign of 1828 began just after the "corrupt bargain" became known, when Jackson, fuming over the Judas of the West, resigned his Senate seat and started home. Neither time nor travel assuaged his feelings. He was weeping for his country's experiment in liberty, he wrote a friend, when "the rights of the people" could be bartered for promises of office. By the time he reached his Hermitage home he was talking darkly of "usurpation of power" and the "great constitutional corrective in the hands of the people" against it. Soon men in Nashville and Virginia and Washington and New York were laying plans for 1828.

A motley group was gathered behind the Old Hero—its acknowledged leader, Martin Van Buren. Small, amiable, plumpish, cautious, calculating, urbane, the New Yorker seemed almost the antithesis of the Hero, but both had made their way without much education, knew what it was to be on the outs with dominant factions in their states, and shared prejudices about bankers, entrenched federal officials, and Easterners unaware of the need to settle the western lands. Van Buren had shown himself a master political broker and coalition builder, as a leader of the "Albany Regency" and United States senator.

Jackson's old-time advisers had been mainly Westerners: Major John H. Eaton, a Florida land speculator and Tennessee politico; William B. Lewis, also of Tennessee, who had helped him as political lieutenant and fixer; Judge John Overton, an old confidant and loyalist. The most colorful by far was Thomas Hart Benton of Missouri. Expelled from the University of North Carolina for thieving from his roommates, he had moved to Tennessee, gained admission to the bar, won a seat in the state senate, served as Jackson's aide-de-camp, then moved to Missouri and within five years won election as United States senator. He and Jackson, who earlier had brawled ferociously in Tennessee, were now reconciled. A handsome, solidly built man, of considerable intellectual power, Benton had a vanity so grand and serene that friends came to accept it, like a national monument.

These men and their allies across the nation slowly worked out a simple but formidable double strategy to elect Old Hickory President. They would broaden out Jackson's personal coalition and entrench it solidly in the democratic and agrarian ranks of the old Republican party. Crucial to the first strategy was winning support from southern leaders disaffected by Adams, and the key man in this region was Vice-President Calhoun, who had broken with the President and plumped for Jackson. Although Calhoun had been elected Vice-President in 1824, he had been disturbed by the flouting of the popular will in Adams' selection by the House—and even more disturbed that two Adams terms, followed by two terms for the heir apparent, Henry Clay, would close off the presidency for sixteen years. Calhoun was already in his mid-forties. Within two years of Adams' (and his own) inauguration, having moved solidly into Jackson's camp, the dour South Carolinian was sending the Hermitage optimistic reports about 1828 prospects.

"Every indication is in our favor, or rather I should say in favor of the country's cause," he wrote Jackson in January 1827. "The whole South is safe, with a large majority of the middle states, and even in New England strong symptoms of discontent and division now appear, which must daily increase." He looked forward to the triumph of "the great principles of popular rights, which have been trampled down by the coalition." Within another year the general's lieutenants had extended their counter-coalition throughout the twenty-four states. The heart of this strategy was what Van Buren called an alliance between the "planters of the South and the plain Republicans of the North."

An even more crucial task was to build a firm foundation of popular support beneath the broadening cadre of Jackson's leaders. Van Buren & Co. decided on the bold strategy of the "substantial reorganization of the Old Republican party"—in plainer words, to build a *Jackson* party within the disheveled ranks of the cumbrous party of Monroe, Adams, and Clay. The key to this effort was unprecedented political organization. In Nashville, Jackson himself established and supervised a central committee composed of stalwarts like Lewis and Overton. In Washington, an informal caucus of members of Congress safeguarded Jackson's interests on Capitol Hill. Throughout the states, Hickory Clubs organized parades and barbecues and rallies, printed up handbills, pamphlets, and leaflets, and canvassed the voters in their homes. The Jackson men, ostentatiously taking their case "to the people," established an extraordinary number of new dailies and weeklies to combat the established newspapers that spoke for Adams and Clay. All this required money, but the Jacksonians seemed to have plenty of it. Edward Pessen estimated that the election of Jackson cost about one million dollars—a formidable sum in 1828.

The contest was largely devoid of issues, and it was meant to be. Jackson did not rally the masses by appeals to ideals of justice and equality; he stayed home and stayed quiet, except for occasional pieties and ambiguities. In vain did Adams supporters try to raise questions like the tariff and internal improvements. "The *Hurra Boys*" were all for Jackson, one Administration man sneered, but he had to admit that they constituted a "powerful host." The "National Republicans"—as the anti-Jacksonians came to be called—seemed unable to compete with a Hickory Leaf in every hat and hickory-pole raisings in every town square. Increasingly, the Jacksonians themselves were becoming known as "Democratic-Republicans," or simply "Democrats."

Slander and abuse pushed aside issues. Adams was called a monarchist, squanderer of the taxpayers' dollars on silken fripperies, Sabbath breaker, pimp. Partisans of the President in turn labeled Jackson as blasphemer, bastard, butcher, adulterer. As usual, the invective had a tiny morsel of truth. *John Quincy Adams a pimp?* Well, it seemed that in St. Petersburg, corrupted as he was by his long service in sinful foreign capitals, he had "prostituted a beautiful American girl to the carnal desires of Czar Alexander I." A fiction, of course, but a rumor to be handled only by attributing even baser acts to Jackson. The *Old Hero* an *adulterer?* Well, Jackson had indeed married Rachel Robards before she was divorced, and he may have done so knowingly, but the Jackson men had to put out sworn statements as to his innocence.

In a contest of invective and personality, no Adams could win out. Jackson beat him in the popular vote, 647,292 to 507,730. The general won the electoral college 178 to 83; Adams carried only New England and parts of the central Atlantic region. Jackson brought off a clean sweep of the rural hinterland west of New Jersey and south of the Potomac. Swept out of office by this gale of southern and "western" ballots, the National Republicans saw the results as presaging ominous changes, as their political fathers had twenty-eight years before. "Well," said an Adams backer, "a great revolution has taken place. . . ." Another wrote: "It was the howl of raving Democracy."

It was, at least, the howl of the outsiders. With the approach of Inauguration Day 1829, plain people by the hundreds descended upon Washington, crowding the lodging places and thronging the streets. They massed in front of the Capitol to hear their hero pledge reform to all and the ending of the national debt. Then they followed the new President down Pennsylvania Avenue to the White House, pushed into the mansion, and fought their way toward the punch and the ice cream. As the visitors trampled on the chairs and carpets of the house just vacated by an Adams of Boston, as they smashed china and glasses, it seemed as though a new day had dawned in Washington. Truly the outsiders were now inside the citadel of power.

A political tempest had blown in from the west. Now the nation awaited Jackson with anticipation and apprehension. Nobody knew what he would do when he arrived in Washington, Webster wrote to friends in Boston. "My opinion is, that when he comes he will bring a breeze with him. Which way it will blow, I cannot tell. . . . My fear is stronger than my *hope*." Old John Randolph of Roanoke, as passionate and apocalyptic as ever, cried that the country was ruined past redemption. "Where now could we find leaders of a revolution?"

Thousands of job seekers throughout the country had *their* idea of a good revolution: rotate the ins out of federal office, and rotate the outs in. Some stayed home in hopes of taking over as postmasters or customs collectors, but hundreds flocked to Washington, settled down in hotels and boardinghouses, and haunted the White House and the departments. . . .

Despite the furor, the number of actual removals was not large—less than 10 percent after the first eighteen months of the new administration. Probably a somewhat larger number of non-college men of lower socioeconomic station got hired. Some of the clerks and agents had been Jackson men; others had been neutral. Many other changes resulted simply from death or retirement. But a few removals were enough to put Washington in shock.

Jackson defended the removals on the ground of principle, not party. Men long in office, he said, were apt to become indifferent to the public interest: "Office is considered as a species of property, and government rather as a means of promoting individual interests than as an instrument created solely for the service of the people. . . . The duties of all public officers are, or at least admit of being made, so plain and simple that men of intelligence may readily qualify themselves for their performance. . . . In a country where offices are created solely for the benefit of the people no one man has any more intrinsic right to official station than another." Pitching his case on the level of good republicanism did not endear the President to Washington bureaucrats—or win support from old Jeffersonians like Madison, who privately criticized rotation.

The new President's inaugural address had given little concrete idea of his plans, aside from revamping of the civil service. He had straddled the issues of internal improvements, the tariff, the currency, all in a voice so low that it reminded veteran Washingtonians of Jefferson's inaudible remarks twenty-eight years before. Jackson did promise a proper regard for states' rights, economy in government, and a "just and liberal" policy toward Indians, but this was standard politicians' fare. Nor did his cabinet-building offer many clues. The two principal appointees, Van Buren as Secretary of State and Samuel D. Ingham at Treasury, came from the swing states of New York and Pennsylvania. John Eaton, Jackson's old Tennessee friend, was the new Secretary of War; other appointees came from North Carolina, Georgia, and Kentucky. Pro-South in substance, anti-Clay in sentiment, the Cabinet hardly looked like an instrument for governing. It met infrequently, usually on major occasions, but less to deliberate than to hear Jacksonian pronouncements worked up in the inner circle. Administrative policy questions were usually settled by the President and department heads in private conferences. The Cabinet rarely discussed major policy issues in the manner of a council of state.

It was the "kitchen cabinet" that both expressed and shaped the President's program. This was not a cabinet, nor of course did it meet in the kitchen; it was, rather, a shifting group of advisers on whom Jackson called as he needed them. The most influential was Amos Kendall. Born on a poor Massachusetts farm in 1789, Kendall had attended Dartmouth, taught at Groton, and studied law; unrequited by both the girl and the profession he loved, at the age of twenty-five he moved to Kentucky, where he was befriended by Mrs. Henry Clay and made tutor to the Clays' children. Later he turned to newspaper work and soon became editor of the *Argus of Western America* in Frankfort. For years a supporter of Clay and Adams, Kendall finally was caught between the Clay and Jackson factions. For reasons of both opportunism and principle he broke with Clay, moved to Washington, and was taken on as fourth auditor of the Treasury.

Another key adviser—and another former Kentuckian—was Francis Preston Blair. He looked like Kendall's political clone, having broken with Clay, embraced Jacksonian oppositionism, and succeeded Kendall as editor of the *Argus*.

He was brought to Washington to edit the new Democratic paper, the Washington *Globe,* whose columns he filled with "demonstrations of public opinion" drawn from remote country newspapers that allegedly he penned himself. Less close to Jackson was Isaac Hill, born of an impoverished New Hampshire family, a scourge of the New Hampshire squirearchy as editor of a small Concord weekly, until he moved to Washington. . . .

The great battles of Jackson's presidency began with the congressional session that got under way in December 1829. From then on, the President took on the barons of the Senate—Clay, Hayne, and the others—his own Vice-President, his own Cabinet, the opposition party, the banking elite, the Supreme Court, secessionists. At the end, Clay himself would cry out that Jackson had "swept over the Government, during the last eight years, like a tropical tornado." But if Jackson's presidency was filled with conflict, it was in large part because he embodied it, and so did the men he confronted. It was a blast out of the west that precipitated the sectional storm that would dominate the rest of Jackson's first term.

The Dance of the Factions

The chamber of the United States Senate, noon, Tuesday, January 26, 1830. An air of high expectancy hangs over the packed hall, as Washington personages push their way in from the blustery cold outside and crowd into the aisles and vestibules. A score or more fashionably dressed women, their round bonnets trimmed with drooping plumes, look down from the front row of the balcony. They are watching Senator Daniel Webster of Massachusetts, a full, almost portly figure in his old-fashioned long-tailed coat with bright gilt buttons, buff waistcoat, and large white cravat. Webster is looking toward the Vice-President of the United States, John Calhoun, in the presiding chair, erect and stern. All the Washington notables seem to be here, except for the distant man in the White House—famous senators like Hayne of South Carolina, Benton of Missouri, Woodbury of New Hampshire, celebrities of the past like John Quincy Adams and Harrison Gray Otis still haunting Washington, and so many visitors from the House that little business can be done there.

The occasion is Webster's reply to Hayne of South Carolina. A week earlier, Webster had dropped into the Senate, after finishing his legal business in the Supreme Court just a few steps away, in time to hear the South Carolina senator call for an alliance of the West and the South against the "selfish and unprincipled" East. Over the next few days, while Benton, Hayne, Webster, and other senators argued over the usual questions of national politics—public lands, internal improvements, the tariff—Webster became aware that a far more ominous set of issues was dominating the debate: those of nullification, secession, the very nature of the American Constitution. Even so, the famous orator, affluent and successful, recently remarried after the death of his first wife, might have shunned the battle except that Hayne, unusually impassioned, sarcastic, and aggressive for a young man ordinarily so moderate and courteous, had dealt him some punishing blows.

Now Webster would answer Hayne's climactic speech. Hayne's supporters were so elated by their champion's performance that Webster's own backers became apprehensive. But not Webster. When his friend Supreme Court Justice Joseph Story called on him to offer help, he replied, "Give yourself no uneasiness, Judge Story! I will grind him as fine as a pinch of snuff." And the next morning, asked on entering the Senate whether he was "well charged"—a reference to the four fingers of powder needed to charge a muzzle-loading gun—the orator replied jauntily, "*Seven* fingers!"

The long-gathering conflict now culminating in this debate was explosive enough. It had its main source in dramatic social and economic changes in the South—especially in South Carolina—which had set that section in a radically different direction from the North. A decade or two before, South Carolinians had exhibited much the same constellation of interests and attitudes as most other states in the Union. Highly nationalistic, they gloried in the fame and achievements of John Calhoun and the other southern war hawks of 1812. As consumers of products from abroad, they hated tariffs, but many South Carolinians grew or made their own products that needed protection, and they also accepted tariffs as strengthening American manufactories in the event of war.

As for slavery, most members of the South Carolinian delegation in Congress favored the compromise of 1820. To be sure, old Charles Pinckney—the same Charles Pinckney who had brought his young bride to Philadelphia in 1787 and helped write the Constitution there—warned that if Congress was ever accorded the right even to consider the subject of slavery, "there is no knowing to what length it may be carried," but most of the state's political leaders shared the moderate attitudes of nationalists like Calhoun and William Lowndes.

Then—almost overnight, it seemed later—the mood of South Carolina had altered sharply. For rice and cotton growers, the 1820s were a time of rapid economic change, price and demand instability, credit squeezes, and depression, all tending toward a rising sense of social and economic insecurity, which in turn fostered a powerful parochialism and sectionalism. The Tariff of 1828 excited the worst southern fears; it was to them literally a tariff of abominations, to be despised and shunned. In a decade of peace they could no longer accept the tariff as a defense measure. Federal policy on internal improvements and other questions also continued to antagonize South Carolinians. But behind all the old issues always loomed the specter of northern interference with slavery. An alleged slave conspiracy, led by Denmark Vesey of Charleston, along with rumors of other planned slave revolts, aroused dread over threats from inside; the stepped-up efforts of the American Colonization Society in the North aroused fears over threats from outside.

By the late 1820s the balance of South Carolina politics had changed. If the cleaving issue in the state, and in much of the South, had been nationalism versus sectionalism, that issue now was: what kind of sectionalism? to be carried how far? and how accomplished? Steadily shifting away from his old nationalism, Calhoun still had to deal more with fire eaters who wanted secession than with moderates who wished to attain South Carolina's aims within the Union. News of the abominable tariff catalyzed powerful forces already building. Calhoun wrote a brilliant tract—the South Carolina Exposition—in which he flayed national tariff policy as unconstitutional and oppressive, "calculated to corrupt the public virtue and destroy the liberty of the country"; contended that no government based on the "naked principle" of majority rule could "preserve its liberty even for a single generation"; and claimed the right of "interposition" by state governments—that is, to declare null and void "unconstitutional" acts of the national government. If the federal government did not recognize the constitutional powers of the states, South Carolina would claim the right of nullification. South Carolinians had waited through Jackson's first year, hopeful that he—a slave owner himself, after all—would redress their grievances, but in vain. Hayne's hard line in the Senate, reflecting Calhoun's arguments, showed that southern patience was running out.

So now, Webster waited to take the floor. The chamber hushed as the Vice-President recognized him. Standing majestically as he faced the chair, resting his left hand on his desk while swinging his right hand up and down, he spoke in a low but compelling tone. The orator held the floor for three hours, pausing only once or twice to consult some notes. He ridiculed Hayne's fear of federal tyranny. "Consolidation!—that perpetual cry, both of terror and delusion—consolidation!" The federal government, he declared, was the instrument not of the will of the states but of "We the People"; the national interest was the controlling one; the effort of a state to nullify a law of Congress was a revolutionary and illegal act.

As Webster warmed to the attack, his granite face seemed to come alive; his eyes burned with fervor; his "mastiff-mouth" bit off his sentences with the finality of a spring trap. A connoisseur of all the arts of oratory, he moved from exposition to argumentation to irony to banter to scorn to eloquence to pathos. When he said, "I shall enter on no encomium upon Massachusetts; she needs none," but proceeded to do so, Bay State men clustered in the gallery were said to "shed tears like girls." Webster had never felt an audience respond more eagerly and sympathetically. His peroration would soon be on New England schoolboys' lips:

When my eyes shall be turned to behold, for the last time, the sun in heaven, may I not see him shining on the broken and dishonored fragments of a once glorious Union; on States dissevered, discordant, belligerent; on a land rent with civil feuds, or drenched, it may be, in fraternal blood! Let their last feeble and lingering glance, rather, behold the gorgeous ensign of the republic, now known and honored throughout the earth, still full high advanced, its arms and trophies streaming in their original lustre, not a stripe erased or polluted, not a single star obscured, bearing for its motto no such miserable interrogatory as, What is all this worth? Nor those other words of delusion and folly, Liberty first and Union afterwards; but everywhere, spread all over in characters of living light, blazing on all its ample folds, as they float over the sea and over the land, and in every wind under the whole heavens, that other sentiment, dear to every true American heart—Liberty and Union, now and forever, one and inseparable!

A few weeks later, Calhoun & Co. received another oratorical setback. The Webster-Hayne debate had been an interparty encounter, and politically the Massachusetts senator could be dismissed as a New Englander and an old Federalist.

But what was the attitude of Andrew Jackson, a Southwesterner and a Democrat? Rather rashly, states' rights Democrats organized a celebration of Jefferson's birthday for April 13, 1830, in Washington to glorify their cause and symbolize the Democratic party alliance between East and West. Jackson and Van Buren attended, along with an array of other party leaders. The banquet in Brown's Indian Queen Hotel was hardly over and chairs pulled back from the board when the Southerners launched into speeches and toasts that evoked the Jefferson of the Alien and Sedition Acts. Defying Jackson to his face, George Troup, a Georgia planter-politician and states' rights extremist, toasted the government of the United States as more absolute than the rule of Tiberius, but as less wise than that of Augustus, and less just than that of Trajan.

All eyes turned to Jackson. Scowling at Calhoun as he signaled the crowd to rise, the old general toasted, "Our Federal Union—*it must be preserved.*" Van Buren, who had climbed up on a chair to witness the scene, saw the noisy company turn utterly silent, dumbfounded. Calhoun's hand shook, spilling a little wine down the side of his glass. But he was ready with his answering toast: "The Union—next to our liberty the most dear. . . ."

A great Virginia reel of politics was under way, as politicians chose partners and changed them, in a dance of sections and interests, issues and ideologies. Not for half a century had the nation possessed such compelling sectional leaders— the spare, consecrated Calhoun, champion of the South; the droll, sparkling, restless Clay, still "Harry of the West"; New England's hero, the imposing, magnetic Webster, "the great cannon loaded to the lips," as Emerson pictured him; the consummate politician Van Buren, keen, dexterous, opportunistic, the supple representative of New York and the other swing states. But these men were more than leaders of sections. They were statesmen with a vision of the national purpose, and they were politicians who hungered for the presidency. Hence they had to protect their standing in their state and section, while gaining national recognition and building national coalitions. They were trapped in the rising sectional feeling of Americans. And they had to deal with the unpredictable, prickly, opinionated man in the White House.

The speeches of Webster and Hayne in the Senate, the toasts of Calhoun and Jackson at Brown's Indian Queen Hotel, were the opening salvos of the 1832 presidential election campaign. Van Buren had attached his fortunes firmly to the President's, and the political foxiness of the "Little Magician," combined with the leonine presence and power of the President, made an invincible combination. Jackson struck first at Clay, his old western rival. The issue was the venerable one of internal improvements. In his December 1829 message to Congress, Jackson had questioned the constitutionality and the desirability of federal aid to roads and other projects. When Congress passed a bill authorizing government subscription of stock in a turnpike connecting Maysville and Lexington and lying wholly within Kentucky, the President vetoed it. Clay was outraged. Not only was he the author of the "American System" but only the year before he and his family had spent four days negotiating the steep curves and bottomless mud of the existing Maysville road. Still, the deliberate slap administered by Jackson helped confirm Clay as the National Republican candidate for President. Webster backed him too.

"On the whole, My Dear Sir," Webster wrote Clay two days after the veto, "I think a crisis is arriving, or rather *has arrived*. I think you cannot be kept back from the contest. The *people* will bring you out, *nolens volens. Let them do it.* . . ."

Henry Clay, John Quincy Adams' successor as head of the National Republican party, proposed to be the national candidate for President. On the eve of 1832 his party met in convention in the saloon of the Atheneum in Baltimore, with 155 delegates present from virtually all the states outside the Deep South. Former Democrat Peter Livingston of New York placed Clay's name in nomination in what was probably the first nominating speech in convention history. Clay was unanimously chosen. At another convention in Washington several months later, Clay accepted the nomination, in a speech warning that "the fate of liberty, throughout the world, mainly depends upon the maintenance of American liberty." Proudly the National Republicans presented their credo: against the spoils system, executive tyranny, and Jackson's treatment of the Indians; in favor of American capitalism in general, and in particular, of a protective tariff to foster American industry—which they defended as protecting workers as well as owners—internal improvements at federal expense, the use of public land revenues for such improvements, the maintenance of the national banking system and a stable and uniform currency.

The Democrats also met in convention in Baltimore, but the large number of delegates—334, from every state save Missouri—compelled a move to a Universalist church. The convention did not nominate Jackson; it simply "concurred," amid much enthusiasm, in a nomination already made in many states. The delegates adopted a two-thirds rule for the nomination of a Vice-President—the only real issue before the convention—and a unit rule, authorizing the majority of each delegation to cast the entire vote of the state. Van Buren easily scored far more than two-thirds of the votes on the first ballot. They did not need a positive platform; Jackson and Van Buren would run against the bank and the "aristocratic influences" favored by the National Republicans.

So the two parties confronted each other, but each was beset by factional problems. Calhoun threatened to draw votes from Jackson; and the leaders of the Webster faction, while publicly supporting Clay, were privately pessimistic about his chances and looking forward to a Webster candidacy in 1836, if not somehow in 1832. But the greatest threat to Clay lay in the strangest faction of all, a movement that called itself the Anti-Masons. For years Americans had been suspicious of secret societies, including the Masons, even though Washington and other heroes had been members. In the fall of 1826, an upstate New Yorker named William Morgan, an apostate Mason who had threatened to "expose" the secrets of Masonry, had been spirited away in a yellow carriage, driven to the Niagara frontier, and so disposed of that no trace of him was ever found.

The resulting uproar precipitated an explosive movement of moral protest, centered in New York but radiating powerfully throughout the Northeast. The movement received much of its force from antislavery and temperance New

Englanders and New Yorkers, and much of its direction from a remarkable array of leaders including William H. Seward, Thurlow Weed, and Thaddeus Stevens. Even before the National Republicans and the Democrats had convened in Baltimore, the Anti-Masons had met there, in the first presidential nominating convention in history, and chosen as their candidate William Wirt, a dignified sixty-year-old Virginia Republican of the old school. Wirt had been on his way to the National Republican convention, ready to vote for Clay; he claimed to be shocked at his nomination by the Anti-Masons, but nonetheless accepted the honor.

Which of the presidential candidates could pull enough factions and subfactions together to win a majority in the electoral college? As the campaign heated up during 1832, it became apparent that Jackson was in control. For one thing, the Democrats in the states seemed far more enthusiastic and organized than the followers of Calhoun, Clay, or Wirt. For another, the President proved himself a master in taking a moderate but clear-cut position on the issues that left other candidates appearing to be extremists. As the election campaign neared, the Administration took a more benevolent view toward reducing the tariff, lowering the cost of public lands, and even toward internal improvement.

Jackson even seemed conciliatory toward nullification, as a curious episode suggested. For years land-hungry Georgia settlers had been encroaching on Indian lands, and for years the Cherokees in particular had been resisting the tide, even to the point of setting up a kind of independent state under treaties with the federal government. Georgia refused to recognize Cherokee autonomy. Two New England missionaries were convicted and sentenced to four years at hard labor when they defied a Georgia law that compelled white residents in the Cherokee country to obtain a license and to take an oath of allegiance to the state. On the condemned men's appeal to the Supreme Court, old John Marshall, speaking for the majority, held that the national government had exclusive jurisdiction and that the Georgia law was unconstitutional. The prisoners were ordered released. When Georgia defied the decision, Jackson aided and abetted the nullifiers. "John Marshall has made his decision," he was reported to have said, "*now let him enforce it.*"

Still, mollifying nullifiers and other factions was not much of a campaign strategy. What Jackson needed was a single, compelling issue that would transcend the ordinary play of interests and sections—an issue that would mobilize an electoral majority behind his cause. And he found it, by conviction and by contingency, in Nicholas Biddle's Second National Bank of the United States.

The first and second banks had always been a staple of Republican party controversy, and few were surprised when Jackson, determined as he said to "prevent our liberties" from being "crushed by the Bank," challenged the bank's constitutionality in his first message to Congress in 1829. With the bank's charter not due to expire until 1836, the President was content to ask Congress to curb the power of the bank and thus to delay a showdown with it until the second term. He knew that Biddle was a power in the politics of Pennsylvania and other key states. Webster and Clay knew this too, and for that reason they advised Biddle to call Jackson's hand before the 1832 election by forcing him either to support the bill for recharter or to face the power of the bank at the polls. The bank chief initiated hostilities by having a recharter bill introduced in Congress, which passed it by strong majorities after a long and angry debate.

Visiting Jackson in the White House, Van Buren found the old general lying on a couch looking pale and exhausted. "The bank, Mr. Van Buren, is trying to kill me," he said, "*but I will kill it.*"

Kill it he did, with a veto and a bristling message that attacked monopoly and special privilege and boldly accepted the challenge of the "rich and power-ful" to make the bank the central issue of the campaign. His own appeal would be to the "humble members of society—the farmers, mechanics, and laborers—who have neither the time nor the means of securing like favors for themselves." Thus the people would decide. This was the first time, according to Robert Rem-ini, that a President "had taken a strong stand on an important issue, challenging the electorate to do something about it if they did not approve his position." Even Jackson was surprised by the popularity of his stand on the bank. "The veto works well," he said, "instead of crushing me as was expected and intended, it will crush the Bank."

Calhoun and his fellow nullifiers handed Jackson the other great national is-sue of the campaign. As feeling about the tariff and slavery issues boiled over in South Carolina during 1832, the nullifiers won a legislative majority in favor of a state convention that would adopt an ordinance canceling national tariff legisla-tion. Hayne prepared to resign as United States senator, to be elected governor; Calhoun would resign as Vice-President, to succeed Hayne in the Senate. Jack-son, after taking military precautions in South Carolina, prepared a "Proclama-tion to the People of South Carolina" that termed nullification an "impracticable absurdity" and ended flatly, "Disunion by armed forces is *treason.*"

The Jacksonians versus Philadelphia bankers and southern nullifiers—how could the Democrats lose? The response of the voters was decisive. Sweeping the electoral college over Clay, 219 to 49, Jackson won the electoral votes of sixteen of the twenty-four states and ran well ahead of Clay in the popular vote, 687,000 to 530,000. Jackson polled strongly in the South (except in South Carolina), well in the West, fairly well in the middle Atlantic states, and decisively in the swing states of Pennsylvania and New York. Aside from his own Kentucky, Clay's main strength lay in southern New England. Still, considering Jackson's position as national hero, and his brilliant positioning of his administration on the issues of the day, as well as the siphoning off of National Republican votes by the Anti-Masons, Clay had done well in the popular vote—a harbinger of the day when a revitalized Whig party would rise out of the ashes of the National Republicans.

Armed with his election mandate, Jackson now moved against nullification. The reaction of Carolina hotheads against his proclamation—the "mad ravings of a drivelling dotard," Congressman George McDuffie called it—only hardened his will. Although the nullifiers put up a show of resistance, enlisting 25,000 vol-unteers and even setting up a cannonball factory, it was clear that they were not eager for a military confrontation, especially after learning that the rest of the South opposed drastic action. In mid-January 1833 the President asked the Congress for a "Force" bill that would allow him to enforce the revenue laws by military action if necessary, but the bill actually tried to avert the use of force by working out procedures, including "floating customs houses" off Charleston, to avert encounters in the city.

The Force bill produced in the Senate another brilliant debate, rivaling the Hayne-Webster forensics. This time Webster took on Calhoun, who had been liberated from the silence of the presiding chair, and the remorseless logic-chopping of the new senator from South Carolina was judged to have bested the fulsome rhetoric of the New Englander. John Randolph, sitting in the gallery, found his view obscured by a lady's bonnet. "Take away that hat," he bleated, "I want to see Webster die, muscle by muscle."

A combination of forces was working now against an explosion. Calhoun was pulling back from his earlier extremism, Van Buren was restraining Jackson from exercising his dearest wish of trying and hanging the secessionist leaders, and—most important of all—Henry Clay, the old compromiser himself, was coming in with a tariff bill designed to conciliate the Carolinians. The President signed both the Force bill and the compromise tariff bill on March 2, 1833, two days before he took the oath of office for a second term. Once again he had shown a masterly ability both to manipulate factions and to rise above them, to take a national and presidential posture, and to know when to stand firm and when to compromise. . . .

In the end, the Jacksonian "wind from the west" blew noisily but left the structure of American capitalism largely intact. Nor did it move that other citadel of power, the slavocracy. Jackson and Van Buren carried the old North-South axis of the Republican party into the Democratic—the alliance built largely by Virginians and New Yorkers and devoted to Jeffersonian agrarianism, individual liberty, states' rights, and non-interference with liberty. Western leaders and voters did not upset this political balance; rather they fortified it. Thus the southern Democrats were left with a veto against any effort, gradual or radical, to curb slavery and possibly head off an explosion. Such was the price of Democratic party union, the price of national Union—a price that could not yet be calculated.

The Whigs were hardly more coherent in their own political philosophy, in part because as a party of opportunistic anti-Jacksonians they took on much of the ideological eclecticism of their Jacksonian opponents, a movement originally of opportunistic outsiders, as the two parties tangled—and became entangled—with each other. Like the Democrats, Whigs could deliver grand rhetoric through the mouths of their Websters and Clays, and like the Democrats, they advanced a spate of concrete policies. But the middle, linking level was absent here too. If the Jacksonian leaders lacked a foundation of philosophical radicalism, the Whigs lacked that of philosophical conservatism. The materials of a class system—the aristocracies, peasantries, and proletariats—that had empowered European ideologies were absent in the United States; much of the combat on the American terrain lined up entrepreneurs against entrepreneurs. No wonder Louis Hartz was reminded of "two boxers, swinging wildly, knocking each other down with accidental punches."

SUGGESTIONS FOR FURTHER READING

To place the debate in this chapter and the three that follow in context, students should be aware of the social, economic, and ideological changes taking place in the nation during the first half of the nineteenth century. A good general introduction is Douglas T. Miller, *The Birth of Modern America, 1820–1850* (New York, 1970).

Among the many discussions of economic changes taking place during this period are Stuart Bruchey, *The Roots of American Economic Growth, 1607–1861* (New York, 1968); Douglas C. North, *The Economic Growth of the United States, 1790 to 1860* (Englewood Cliffs, N.J., 1961); George Rogers Taylor, *The Transportation Revolution, 1815–1860* (New York, 1951); and Peter Temin, *The Jacksonian Economy* (New York, 1969). A sociological survey is Richard D. Brown, *Modernization: The Transformation of American Life, 1600–1865* (New York, 1976). Louis Hartz, *The Liberal Tradition in America* (New York, 1955); Joyce Appleby, *Capitalism and a New Social Order* (New York, 1984); and Sean Wilentz, *Chants Democratic: New York City and the Rise of the American Working Class* (New York, 1984) present three differing views on the evolution of liberal ideology.

Arthur M. Schlesinger, Jr., *The Age of Jackson* (Boston, 1945), a portion of which is reprinted here, deserves to be read in its entirety. Schlesinger sees Jackson as a democratic leader in a class struggle between eastern workers and business. A recent evaluation of Schlesinger's work in the light of later scholarship is Donald B. Cole, "The Age of Jackson After Forty Years," *Reviews in American History,* 14 (March 1986), 149–59. Robert V. Remini, Jackson's most recent biographer (*Andrew Jackson and the Course of American Empire, 1767–1821* [New York, 1977]; *Andrew Jackson and the Course of American Freedom, 1822–1832* [New York, 1981]; and *Andrew Jackson and the Course of American Democracy, 1833–1845* [New York, 1984]), views Jackson as the dominant figure leading the nation from the republicanism of the founding fathers to the liberal democracy of the nineteenth century. Remini emphasizes democracy and popular rights rather than liberalism and free enterprise. Remini's *The Revolutionary Age of Andrew Jackson* (New York, 1976) is a briefer version of his biography.

A number of studies develop the consensus position, but they do so from a variety of perspectives. John William Ward finds that the image of Jackson helped to define a consensus in his *Andrew Jackson: Symbol for an Age* (New York, 1955). Richard Hofstadter's chapter on Andrew Jackson in his *American Political Tradition* (New York, 1948) is a perceptive and subtle interpretation in the consensus tradition, as is, in a very different way, Marvin Meyer's use of paradox in his book *The Jacksonian Persuasion* (Stanford, 1957).

Edward Pessen in *Jacksonian America: Society, Personality, and Politics* (Homewood, Ill., 1969), from which the selection here is taken, and in *Riches, Class, and Power Before the Civil War* (Lexington, Mass., 1973) discovers a general decline rather than an advance of democracy, and he finds little difference between the wealthy leaders of the two major parties. These conditions, he argues, produced little fundamental dissent. Bray Hammond, *Banks and Politics in America from the Revolution to the Civil War* (Princeton, N.J., 1957) also finds little dividing the Jacksonians from their opponents. He argues that the era of Jackson was marked, not by an ideological struggle between business and the rest of society, but by a wild scramble of "expectant capitalists" for a place in the economic sun. Lee Benson, *The Concept of Jacksonian Democracy: New York as a Test*

---

*Available in paperback edition.

Case (Princeton, N.J., 1961) argues on the basis of considerable statistical evidence that the leaders of both the Whigs and the Democrats differed little in social and economic status, but concludes that both parties were responsible for democratic advances during the period.

That the conflict interpretation continues may be seen in Charles Grier Sellers, *The Market Revolution: Jacksonian America, 1815–1846* (New York, 1991), which locates the political struggles of the Jacksonian era in economic class conflict arising from the expansion of market capitalism. Allan Kulikoff, *The Agrarian Origins of American Capitalism* (Charlottesville, Va., 1992), painting on a wider canvas, describes the conflicts generated by the rise of capitalist economic relations in the nation.

Politics is the concern of Herbert Ershkowitz and William G. Shade, "Consensus or Conflict? Political Behavior in the State Legislatures During the Jacksonian Era," *Journal of American History,* 8 (December 1971), 591–621. They conclude that party differences "represented contrasting belief systems" and that political battles concerned far more than "the spoils of office." Similarly Lawrence Frederick Kohl, *The Politics of Individualism: Parties and the American Character in the Jacksonian Era* (New York, 1989) sees important distinctions between the Whigs and the Democrats based on different psychological profiles. These views of politics challenge, among others, Richard P. McCormick, *The Second American Party System: Party Formation in the Jacksonian Era* (Chapel Hill, N.C., 1966). Michael A. Lebowitz, "The Jacksonians: Paradox Lost?" in Barton J. Bernstein, ed., *Towards a New Past: Dissenting Essays in American History* (New York, 1968), 65–89, argues that Jacksonians looked backward, appealing to "farmers in relatively declining regions." Donald B. Cole, *The Presidency of Andrew Jackson* (Lawrence, Kans., 1993) depicts a president caught between nostalgia for the past and a fascination with the market revolution. Another recent synthesis of Jacksonian politics is Harry L. Watson, *Liberty and Power: The Politics of Jacksonian America* (New York, 1990). Merrill D. Peterson, *The Great Triumvirate: Webster, Clay, and Calhoun* (New York, 1987) discusses these leaders of the political opposition to Jackson.

Two useful historiographic essays on Jacksonian politics are Charles Grier Sellers, Jr., "Andrew Jackson Versus the Historians," *Mississippi Valley Historical Review,* 44 (March 1958), 615–34, and Ronald P. Formisano, "Toward a Reorientation of Jacksonian Politics: A Review of the Literature, 1959–1975," *Journal of American History,* 63 (June 1976), 42–65. A broader and more recent review of the state of scholarship is Sean Wilentz, "On Class and Politics in Jacksonian America," *Reviews in American History,* 10 (December 1982), 45–63.

Women in Nineteenth-Century Society

U ntil recently, women have usually been left out of American history. Historians—most often men—considered the proper subjects of history to be politics, economic change, diplomacy, and war, and therefore they considered the primary historical actors to be politicians, explorers, generals, and industrialists. Few women achieved fame, fortune, or notoriety in such areas. Most stayed at home or worked in the fields or in shops and remained anonymous and, it appeared, powerless in American society.

But, in the last few decades, the feminist movement along with a greater interest among historians in the social history of ordinary Americans has focused attention on the role and status of women in the past. Historians have discovered that although women had few formal rights and seldom attained leadership in political or economic institutions, they were not powerless; on the contrary, they

247

often played significant roles in the development of the United States. In brief, historians discovered that when they ignored women, they ignored an important part of American history.

In colonial America women had few rights (though their rights and opportunities may have been greater than those possessed by European women). Married women could not own property, could not sign contracts, had no legal right even to their own inheritances. Divorce was rarely granted and then only for the most flagrant abuses. Few women were educated beyond the elementary level, and almost all professional roles were closed to them. Woman's place was in the home; but, with the exception of a few upper-class ladies, women worked in the home and on the farm. They not only raised and prepared the food and cared for large families; they often ran a domestic factory as well, producing cloth, soap, butter, and almost all the necessities of life. Childbirth and disease made the life expectancy of a woman several years shorter than a man's. On the frontier the woman's role became even more arduous, and the slave woman, of course, faced the most difficult and hopeless life of all.

There were always a few exceptions to this pattern. Anne Hutchinson in colonial Massachusetts achieved some status (and in the eyes of most Puritan leaders, notoriety) when she challenged the Puritan leaders on matters of theology and politics, and Anne Bradstreet achieved some fame as a poet in colonial Massachusetts. Occasionally, widows of plantation owners, farmers, and merchants took over their husbands' businesses, competing successfully in what was assumed to be a man's world, and other women achieved some recognition and status as schoolteachers and midwives. But most women, in law and in practice, were subservient and subordinate to their fathers, brothers, husbands, and sons.

The American Revolution, which stimulated movements for freedom and equality in many areas of American life, had little permanent impact on the status of women. When Abigail Adams asked her husband, John Adams, in 1776 to "remember the ladies and be more generous and favorable to them than your ancestors," Adams made light of the suggestion. Neither he nor the other revolutionary leaders took action to extend the rights of women.

The period from 1800 to 1860 witnessed the consolidation of the idea that the proper sphere for a woman was in the home, and that she should be domestic, submissive, subservient, even an invalid; but this same period also saw the beginning of the women's rights movement. Women like Emma Willard, who founded the Troy Female Seminary, and Mary Lyon, who established Mount Holyoke College, pushed for equal educational opportunities for women. Women such as Margaret Fuller, writer, lecturer, and author of *Woman in the Nineteenth Century,* and Frances Wright, editor, reformer, and founder of a utopian community, were the intellectual equals of the best minds of their generation. Other women, such as Angelina and Sarah Grimké, daughters of a South Carolina slaveowner, and Harriet Tubman and Sojourner Truth, both blacks, became important leaders in the abolitionist movement. Women were active in the temperance movement, the prison reform movement, and the peace movement, and many were influenced by religious revivalism. Most of the women reformers eventually became involved in the movement for women's rights.

The beginnings of the women's rights movement in America can be dated in a number of ways. Perhaps it began at the World Anti-Slavery Convention in London in 1840 when two American delegates—Lucretia Mott, a Quaker schoolteacher, and Elizabeth Cady Stanton, a young abolitionist—were refused seats because they were women. Or perhaps the beginning was a few years later in 1848 at Seneca Falls, New York, when these two women and a few others declared their militant opposition to the powerless condition of women by holding a Woman's Rights Convention where they solemnly amended the Declaration of Independence: "We hold these truths to be self-evident: that all men and women are created equal. . . . The history of mankind is a history of repeated injuries and usurpations on the part of man toward woman, having in direct object the establishment of absolute tyranny over her." The fight was carried on by other women—lecturers like Lucy Stone, organizers and strategists like Susan B. Anthony, and many others. A few states passed married women's property laws, and it became a little less unusual to find a woman lecturer or writer. But before the Civil War the victories were rare indeed, and the movement for women's rights touched only a few.

The themes of conflict and consensus are evident when historians study the history of women. When women demanded additional rights and questioned the roles that had been assigned them, they challenged a consensus that defined their proper place. The result was often conflict between militant women and conservative men. But not all women welcomed the efforts to change their role and status; many women agreed with men and accepted the consensus that more militant women opposed. The result of this situation was conflict among women.

But the themes of conflict and consensus became more complex when historians add a consideration of gender to their analyses. If all women shared certain experiences, they were also, like men, divided from one another by class, status, region, and politics. All women, for example, lacked the franchise and were legally subordinate to men, but the effects of this inferior political and legal status and the responses of women to it were not the same for a middle- or upper-class woman and a working-class woman or, more obviously, for a slave woman and a slaveowning woman. Some of these matters, in all their complexity, are considered in the selections that follow.

In the first selection, Barbara Welter describes a popular consensus concerning the proper role and status of women in the pre–Civil War years, a consensus that she calls the "cult of true womanhood." While men built bridges and railroads and became lawyers and doctors, women, she argues, were expected to be pious, pure, submissive, and domestic. These attributes, according to the popular literature of the time, gave women special powers and responsibilities: by playing their proper role, women became the guardians of Christian virtues. But, Welter concludes, the consensus carried within it the seeds of conflict: "For if woman was so very little less than the angels, she should surely take a more active part in running the world, especially since men were making such a hash of things." Thus, by accepting the consensus—or, at least, a part of it—women could justify many activities outside of the home.

In the second selection, Gerda Lerner traces the changing status of women in the North during the nineteenth century. She shows that the cult of true womanhood was an ideological justification for defining woman's proper role as a homemaker but that professionalization and legal restrictions served to keep women out of most professional jobs even if they wanted to leave the home and work. At the same time, however, the cult proved irrelevant to the growing number of women who worked in factories and mills. The cult of true womanhood, then, described the proper role for the ladies of the middle and upper classes. Nevertheless, Lerner notes, all women had something in common: they were a part of the "largest disfranchised group in the nation's history."

In the final selection, Robert L. Griswold describes how the cult of domesticity survived but took on different meanings as women trekked west. Primitive conditions in the early frontier settlements sorely tested the cult of domesticity, and women used the ideology to challenge the male world of saloons and brothels. Sometimes the women promoted conflict as they tried to bring purity and civilization to the West, but eventually male leaders accepted the reforms promoted by the women. These women pioneers demonstrated that to accept the ideology of the cult of domesticity did not mean that women had to be powerless.

In seeking to understand the role of women in nineteenth-century America, should we emphasize those few militants who rebelled against their subservient position and took part in other reformist crusades? Or should we stress the ideology of domesticity, the view that woman's place was in the home, that she should be seen but not heard, that she should "suffer and be still"? Why did not more women join the more militant feminist movement for reform? Why were most men so vehemently opposed to it? Does equality for women lead inevitably to conflict with men?

What were the effects of the ideology of domesticity? When some women accepted it and then used it to justify their actions in reform movements, did they advance the cause of women's rights or help to fasten women's subordinate position more securely? How did class, race, and ethnicity influence attitudes toward the cult of domesticity? Did the meaning of the concept of domesticity change over time or from place to place? Were there changes in its manifestation in newly settled areas?

Answers to these questions suggest other, contemporary questions: To what extent is the nineteenth-century view that women should be pious, pure, submissive, and domestic still believed today? To what extent has the fight for equality, begun in the nineteenth century, been successful?

BARBARA WELTER

The Cult of True Womanhood:
1820–1860

The nineteenth-century American man was a busy builder of bridges and railroads, at work long hours in a materialistic society. The religious values of his forebears were neglected in practice if not in intent, and he occasionally felt some guilt that he had turned his new land, this temple of the chosen people, into one vast countinghouse. But he could salve his conscience by reflecting that he had left behind a hostage, not only to fortune, but to all the values which he held so dear and treated so lightly. Woman, in the cult of True Womanhood presented by the women's magazines, gift annuals and religious literature of the nineteenth century, was the hostage in the home. In a society where values changed frequently, where fortunes rose and fell with frightening rapidity, where social and economic mobility provided instability as well as hope, one thing at least remained the same—a true woman was a true woman wherever she was found. If anyone, male or female, dared to tamper with the complex of virtues which made up True Womanhood, he was damned immediately as an enemy of God, of civilization and of the Republic. It was a fearful obligation, a solemn responsibility, which the nineteenth-century American woman had—to uphold the pillars of the temple with her frail white hand.

The attributes of True Womanhood, by which a woman judged herself and was judged by her husband, her neighbors and society could be divided into four cardinal virtues—piety, purity, submissiveness and domesticity. Put them all together and they spell mother, daughter, sister, wife—woman. Without them, no matter whether there was fame, achievement or wealth, all was ashes. With them she was promised happiness and power.

Religion or piety was the core of woman's virtue, the source of her strength. Young men looking for a mate were cautioned to search first for piety, for if that were there, all else would follow. Religion belonged to woman by divine right, a gift of God and nature. This "peculiar susceptibility" to religion was given her for a reason: "the vestal flame of piety, lighted up by Heaven in the breast of woman" would throw its beams into the naughty world of men. So far would its candle power reach that the "Universe might be Enlightened, Improved, and Harmonized by WOMAN!!" She would be another, better Eve, working in cooperation with the Redeemer, bringing the world back "from its revolt and sin." The world would be reclaimed for God through her suffering, for "God increased the cares and sorrows of woman, that she might be sooner constrained to accept the terms of salvation." A popular poem by Mrs. Frances Osgood, "The Triumph of the Spiritual Over the Sensual" expressed just this sentiment, woman's purifying passionless love bringing an erring man back to Christ.

Dr. Charles Meigs, explaining to a graduating class of medical students why women were naturally religious, said that "hers is a pious mind. Her confiding nature leads her more readily than men to accept the proffered grace of the Gospel." Caleb Atwater, Esq., writing in *The Ladies' Repository,* saw the hand of the Lord in female piety: "Religion is exactly what a woman needs, for it gives her that dignity that best suits her dependence." And Mrs. John Sandford, who had no very high opinion of her sex, agreed thoroughly: "Religion is just what woman needs. Without it she is ever restless or unhappy. . . ." Mrs. Sandford and the others did not speak only of that restlessness of the human heart, which St. Augustine notes, that can only find its peace in God. They spoke rather of religion as a kind of tranquilizer for the many undefined longings which swept even the most pious young girl, and about which it was better to pray than to think.

One reason religion was valued was that it did not take a woman away from her "proper sphere," her home. Unlike participation in other societies or movements, church work would not make her less domestic or submissive, less a True Woman. In religious vineyards, said the *Young Ladies' Literary and Missionary Report,* "you may labor without the apprehension of detracting from the charms of feminine delicacy." Mrs. S. L. Dagg, writing from her chapter of the Society in Tuscaloosa, Alabama, was equally reassuring: "As no sensible woman will suffer her intellectual pursuits to clash with her domestic duties" she should concentrate on religious work "which promotes these very duties."

The women's seminaries aimed at aiding women to be religious, as well as accomplished. Mt. Holyoke's catalogue promised to make female education "a handmaid to the Gospel and an efficient auxiliary in the great task of renovating the world." The Young Ladies' Seminary at Bordentown, New Jersey, declared its most important function to be "the forming of a sound and virtuous character." In Keene, New Hampshire, the Seminary tried to instill a "consistent and useful character" in its students, to enable them in this life to be "a good friend, wife and mother but more important, to qualify them for "the enjoyment of Celestial Happiness in the life to come." And Joseph M' D. Mathews, Principal of Oakland Female Seminary in Hillsborough, Ohio, believed that "female education should be preeminently religious."

If religion was so vital to a woman, irreligion was almost too awful to contemplate. Women were warned not to let their literary or intellectual pursuits take them away from God. Sarah Josepha Hale spoke darkly of those who, like

Margaret Fuller, threw away the "one True Book" for others, open to error. Mrs. Hale used the unfortunate Miss Fuller as fateful proof that "the greater the intellectual force, the greater and more fatal the errors into which women fall who wander from the rock of Salvation, Christ the Saviour. . . ."

One gentleman, writing on "Female Irreligion" reminded his readers that "Man may make himself a brute, and does so very often, but can woman brutify herself to his level—the lowest level of human nature—without exerting special wonder?" Fanny Wright, because she was godless, "was no woman, mother though she be." A few years ago, he recalls, such women would have been whipped. In any case, "woman never looks lovelier than in her reverence for religion" and, conversely, "female irreligion is the most revolting feature in human character."

Purity was as essential as piety to a young woman, its absence as unnatural and unfeminine. Without it she was, in fact, no woman at all, but a member of some lower order. A "fallen woman" was a "fallen angel," unworthy of the celestial company of her sex. To contemplate the loss of purity brought tears: to be guilty of such a crime, in the women's magazines at least, brought madness or death. Even the language of the flowers had bitter words for it: a dried white rose symbolized "Death Preferable to Loss of Innocence." The marriage night was the single great event of a woman's life, when she bestowed her greatest treasure upon her husband, and from that time on was completely dependent upon him, an empty vessel, without legal or emotional existence of her own.

Therefore all True Women were urged, in the strongest possible terms, to maintain their virtue, although men, being by nature more sensual than they, would try to assault it. Thomas Branagan admitted in *The Excellency of the Female Character Vindicated* that his sex would sin and sin again, they could not help it, but woman, stronger and purer, must not give in and let man "take liberties incompatible with her delicacy." "If you do," Branagan addressed his gentle reader, "You will be left in silent sadness to bewail your credulity, imbecility, duplicity, and premature prostitution."

Mrs. Eliza Farrar, in *The Young Lady's Friend*, gave practical logistics to avoid trouble: "Sit not with another in a place that is too narrow; read not out of the same book; let not your eagerness to see anything induce you to place your head close to another person's."

If such good advice was ignored the consequences were terrible and inexorable. In *Girlhood and Womanhood: Or Sketches of My Schoolmates*, by Mrs. A. J. Graves (a kind of mid-nineteenth-century *The Group*), the bad ends of a boarding school class of girls are scrupulously recorded. The worst end of all is reserved for "Amelia Dorrington: The Lost One." Amelia died in the almshouse "the wretched victim of depravity and intemperance" and all because her mother had let her be "highspirited not prudent." These girlish high spirits had been misinterpreted by a young man, with disastrous results. Amelia's "thoughtless levity" was "followed by a total loss of virtuous principle" and Mrs. Graves editorializes that "the coldest reserve is more admirable in a woman a man wishes to make his wife, than the least approach to undue familiarity.". . .

If, however, a woman managed to withstand man's assault on her virtue, she demonstrated her superiority and her power over him. Eliza Farnham, trying to prove this female superiority, concluded smugly that "the purity of women is the everlasting barrier against which the tides of man's sensual nature surge.". . .

Men could be counted on to be grateful when women thus saved them from themselves. William Alcott, guiding young men in their relations with the opposite sex, told them that "Nothing is better calculated to preserve a young man from contamination of low pleasures and pursuits than frequent intercourse with the more refined and virtuous of the other sex." And he added, one assumes in equal innocence, that youths should "observe and learn to admire, that purity and ignorance of evil which is the characteristic of well-educated young ladies, and which, when we are near them, raises us above those sordid and sensual considerations which hold such sway over men in their intercourse with each other."

The Rev. Jonathan F. Stearns was also impressed by female chastity in the face of male passion, and warned woman never to compromise the source of her power: "Let her lay aside delicacy, and her influence over our sex is gone."

Women themselves accepted, with pride but suitable modesty, this priceless virtue. *The Ladies' Wreath*, in "Woman the Creature of God and the Manufacturer of Society" saw purity as her greatest gift and chief means of discharging her duty to save the world: "Purity is the highest beauty—the true pole-star which is to guide humanity aright in its long, varied, and perilous voyage."

Sometimes, however, a woman did not see the dangers to her treasure. In that case, they must be pointed out to her, usually by a male. In the nineteenth century any form of social change was tantamount to an attack on woman's virtue, if only it was correctly understood. For example, dress reform seemed innocuous enough and the bloomers worn by the lady of that name and her followers were certainly modest attire. Such was the reasoning only of the ignorant. In another issue of *The Ladies' Wreath* a young lady is represented in dialogue with her "Professor." The girl expresses admiration for the bloomer costume—it gives freedom of motion, is healthful and attractive. The "Professor" sets her straight. Trousers, he explains, are "only one of the many manifestations of that wild spirit of socialism and agrarian radicalism which is at present so rife in our land." The young lady recants immediately: "If this dress has any connexion with Fourierism or Socialism, or fanaticism in any shape whatever, I have no disposition to wear it at all . . . no true woman would so far compromise her delicacy as to espouse, however unwittingly, such a cause.". . .

Submission was perhaps the most feminine virtue expected of women. Men were supposed to be religious, although they rarely had time for it, and supposed to be pure, although it came awfully hard to them, but men were the movers, the doers, the actors. Women were the passive, submissive responders. The order of dialogue was, of course, fixed in Heaven. Man was "woman's superior by God's appointment, if not in intellectual dowry, at least by official decree." Therefore, as Charles Elliott argued in *The Ladies' Repository*, she should submit to him "for the sake of good order at least." In *The Ladies Companion* a young wife was quoted approvingly as saying that she did not think woman should "feel and act for herself" because "When, next to God, her husband is not the tribunal to which her heart and intellect appeals—the golden bowl of affection is broken."

Women were warned that if they tampered with this quality they tampered with the order of the Universe. . . .

"True feminine genius," said Grace Greenwood (Sara Jane Clarke) "is ever timid, doubtful, and clingingly dependent; a perpetual childhood." And she advised literary ladies in an essay on "The Intellectual Woman"—"Don't trample on the flowers while longing for the stars." A wife who submerged her own talents to work for her husband was extolled as an example of a true woman. In *Women of Worth: A Book for Girls,* Mrs. Ann Flaxman, an artist of promise herself, was praised because she "devoted herself to sustain her husband's genius and aid him in his arduous career."

Caroline Gilman's advice to the bride aimed at establishing this proper order from the beginning of a marriage: "Oh, young and lovely bride, watch well the first moments when your will conflicts with his to whom God and society have given the control. Reverence his *wishes* even when you do not his *opinions.*"

Mrs. Gilman's perfect wife in *Recollections of a Southern Matron* realizes that "the three golden threads with which domestic happiness is woven" are "to repress a harsh answer, to confess a fault, and to stop (right or wrong) in the midst of self-defense, in gentle submission." Women could do this, hard though it was, because in her heart she knew she was right and so could afford to be forgiving, even a trifle condescending. "Men are not unreasonable," averred Mrs. Gilman. "Their difficulties lie in not understanding the moral and physical nature of our sex. They often wound through ignorance, and are surprised at having offended." Wives were advised to do their best to reform men, but if they couldn't, to give up gracefully. "If any habit of his annoyed me, I spoke of it once or twice, calmly, then bore it quietly.". . .

Women then, in all her roles, accepted submission as her lot. It was a lot she had not chosen or deserved. As *Godey's* said, "the lesson of submission is forced upon woman." Without comment or criticism the writer affirms that "To suffer and to be silent under suffering seems the great command she has to obey." George Burnap referred to a woman's life as "a series of suppressed emotions." She was, as Emerson said, "more vulnerable, more infirm, more mortal than man." The death of a beautiful woman, cherished in fiction, represented woman as the innocent victim, suffering without sin, too pure and good for this world but too weak and passive to resist its evil forces. The best refuge for such a delicate creature was the warmth and safety of her home.

The true woman's place was unquestionably by her own fireside—as daughter, sister, but most of all as wife and mother. Therefore domesticity was among the virtues most prized by the women's magazines. "As society is constituted," wrote Mrs. S. E. Farley, on the "Domestic and Social Claims on Woman," the "true dignity and beauty of the female character seem to consist in a right understanding and faithful and cheerful performance of social and family duties." Sacred Scripture reenforced social pressure: "St. Paul knew what was best for women when he advised them to be domestic," said Mrs. Sandford. "There is composure at home; there is something sedative in the duties which home involves. It affords security not only from the world, but from delusions and errors of every kind.". . .

One of the most important functions of woman as comforter was her role as nurse. Her own health was probably, although regrettably, delicate. Many homes had "little sufferers," those pale children who wasted away to saintly deaths. And there were enough other illnesses of youth and age, major and minor, to give the nineteenth-century American woman nursing experience. The sickroom called for the exercise of her higher qualities of patience, mercy and gentleness as well as for her housewifely arts. She could thus fulfill her dual feminine function—beauty and usefulness.

The cookbooks of the period offer formulas for gout cordials, ointment for sore nipples, hiccough and cough remedies, opening pills and refreshing drinks for fever, along with recipes for pound cake, jumbled stewed calves head and currant wine. *The Ladies' New Book of Cookery* believed that "food prepared by the kind hand of a wife, mother, sister, friend" tasted better and had a "restorative power which money cannot purchase."

A chapter of *The Young Lady's Friend* was devoted to woman's privilege as "ministering spirit at the couch of the sick." Mrs. Farrar advised a soft voice, gentle and clean hands, and a cheerful smile. She also cautioned against an excess of female delicacy. That was all right for a young lady in the parlor, but not for bedside manners. Leeches, for example, were to be regarded as "a curious piece of mechanism . . . their ornamental stripes should recommend them even to the eye, and their valuable services to our feelings." And she went on calmly to discuss their use. Nor were women to shrink from medical terminology, since "If you cultivate right views of the wonderful structure of the body, you will be as willing to speak to a physician of the bowels as the brains of your patient."

Nursing the sick, particularly sick males, not only made a woman feel useful and accomplished, but increased her influence. In a piece of heavy-handed humor in *Godey's* a man confessed that some women were only happy when their husbands were ailing that they might have the joy of nursing him to recovery "thus gratifying their medical vanity and their love of power by making him more dependent upon them." In a similar vein a husband sometimes suspected his wife "almost wishes me dead—for the pleasure of being utterly inconsolable."

In the home women were not only the highest adornment of civilization, but they were supposed to keep busy at morally uplifting tasks. Fortunately most of housework, if looked at in true womanly fashion, could be regarded as uplifting. Mrs. Sigourney extolled its virtues: "The science of housekeeping affords exercise for the judgment and energy, ready recollection, and patient self-possession, that are the characteristics of a superior mind." According to Mrs. Farrar, making beds was good exercise, the repetitiveness of routine tasks inculcated patience and perseverance, and proper management of the home was a surprisingly complex art: "There is more to be learned about pouring out tea and coffee, than most young ladies are willing to believe." *Godey's* went so far as to suggest coyly, in "Learning vs. Housewifery" that the two were complementary, not opposed: chemistry could be utilized in cooking, geometry in dividing cloth, and phrenology in discovering talent in children. . . . The female was dangerously addicted to novels, according to the literature of the period. She should avoid them, since they interfered with "serious piety." If she simply couldn't help herself and read them anyway, she should choose edifying ones from lists of morally acceptable authors. She should study history since it "showed the depravity of the human heart and the evil nature of sin." On the whole, "religious biography was best."

The women's magazines themselves could be read without any loss of concern for the home. *Godey's* promised the husband that he would find his wife "no less assiduous for his reception, or less sincere in welcoming his return" as a result of reading their magazine. *The Lily of the Valley* won its right to be admitted to the boudoir by confessing that it was "like its namesake humble and unostentatious, but it is yet pure, and, we trust, free from moral imperfections."

No matter what later authorities claimed, the nineteenth century knew that girls *could* be ruined by a book. The seduction stories regard "exciting and dangerous books" as contributory causes of disaster. The man without honorable intentions always provides the innocent maiden with such books as a prelude to his assault on her virtue. Books which attacked or seemed to attack woman's accepted place in society were regarded as equally dangerous. A reviewer of Harriet Martineau's *Society in America* wanted it kept out of the hands of American women. They were so susceptible to persuasion, with their "gentle yielding natures" that they might listen to "the bold ravings of the hard-featured of their own sex." The frightening result: "such reading will unsettle them for their true station and pursuits, and they will throw the world back again into confusion.". . .

Marriage was seen not only in terms of service but as an increase in authority for woman. Burnap concluded that marriage improves the female character "not only because it puts her under the best possible tuition, that of the affections, and affords scope to her active energies, but because it gives her higher aims, and a more dignified position." *The Lady's Amaranth* saw it as a balance of power: "The man bears rule over his wife's person and conduct. She bears rule over his inclinations: he governs by law; she by persuasion. . . . The empire of the woman is an empire of softness . . . her commands are caresses, her menaces are tears."

Woman should marry, but not for money. She should choose only the high road of true love and not truckle to the values of a materialistic society. A story "Marrying for Money" (subtlety was not the strong point of the ladies' magazines) depicts Gertrude, the heroine, rueing the day she made her crass choice: "It is a terrible thing to live without love. . . . A woman who dares to marry for aught but the purest affection, calls down the just judgements of heaven upon her head."

The corollary to marriage, with or without true love, was motherhood, which added another dimension to her usefulness and her prestige. It also anchored her even more firmly to the home. "My Friend," wrote Mrs. Sigourney, "If in becoming a mother, you have reached the climax of your happiness, you have also taken a higher place in the scale of being . . . you have gained an increase of power." The Rev. J. N. Danforth pleaded in *The Ladies' Casket* "Oh, mother, acquit thyself well in thy humble sphere, for thou mayest affect the world." A true woman naturally loved her children; to suggest otherwise was monstrous.

America depended upon her mothers to raise up a whole generation of Christian statesmen who could say "all that I am I owe to my angel mother." The mothers must do the inculcating of virtue since the fathers, alas, were too busy chasing the dollar. Or as *The Ladies' Companion* put it more effusively, the father "weary with the heat and burden of life's summer days, or trampling with unwilling foot the decaying leaves of life's autumn, has forgotten the sympathies of life's joyous springtime. . . . The acquisition of wealth, the advancement of his children in worldly honor—these are his self-imposed tasks." It was his wife who formed "the infant mind as yet untainted by contact with evil . . . like wax beneath the plastic hand of the mother."

The Ladies' Wreath offered a fifty-dollar prize to the woman who submitted the most convincing essay on "How May An American Woman Best Show Her Patriotism." The winner was Miss Elizabeth Wetherell who provided herself with a husband in her answer. The wife in the essay of course asked her husband's opinion. He tried a few jokes first—"Call her eldest son George Washington," "Don't speak French, speak American"—but then got down to telling her in sober prize-winning truth what women could do for their country. Voting was no asset, since that would result only in "a vast increase of confusion and expense without in the smallest degree affecting the result." Besides, continued this oracle, "looking down at their child," if "we were to go a step further and let the children vote, their first act would be vote their mothers at home." There is no comment on this devastating male logic and he continues: "most women would follow the lead of their fathers and husbands," and the few who would "fly off on a tangent from the circle of home influence would cancel each other out."

The wife responds dutifully: "I see all that. I never understood so well before." Encouraged by her quick womanly perception, the master of the house resolves the question—an American woman best shows her patriotism by staying at home, where she brings her influence to bear "upon the right side of the country's weal." That woman will instinctively choose the side of right he has no doubt. Besides her "natural refinement and closeness to God" she has the "blessed advantage of a quiet life" while man is exposed to conflict and evil. She stays home with "her Bible and a well-balanced mind" and raises her sons to be good Americans. The judges rejoiced in this conclusion and paid the prize money cheerfully, remarking "they deemed it cheap at the price.". . .

The American woman had her choice—she could define her rights in the way of the women's magazines and insure them by the practice of the requisite virtues, or she could go outside the home, seeking other rewards than love. It was a decision on which, she was told, everything in her world depended. "Yours it is to determine," the Rev. Mr. Stearns solemnly warned from the pulpit, "whether the beauty and order of society . . . shall continue as it has been" or whether "society shall break up and become a chaos of disjointed and unsightly elements." If she chose to listen to other voices than those of her proper mentors, sought other rooms than those of her home, she lost both her happiness and her power—"that almost magic power, which, in her proper sphere, she now wields over the destinies of the world."

But even while the women's magazines and related literature encouraged this ideal of the perfect woman, forces were at work in the nineteenth century which impelled woman herself to change, to play a more creative role in society. The movements for social reform, westward migration, missionary activity, utopian communities, industrialism, the Civil War—all called forth responses from woman which differed from those she was trained to believe were hers by nature and divine decree. The very perfection of True Womanhood, moreover, carried within itself the seeds of its own destruction. For if woman was so very little less than the angels, she should surely take a more active part in running the world, especially since men were making such a hash of things.

Real women often felt they did not live up to the ideal of True Womanhood: some of them blamed themselves, some challenged the standard, some tried to keep the virtues and enlarge the scope of womanhood. Somehow through this mixture of challenge and acceptance, of change and continuity, the True Woman evolved into the New Woman—a transformation as startling in its way as the abolition of slavery or the coming of the machine age. And yet the stereotype, the "mystique" if you will, of what woman was and ought to be persisted, bringing guilt and confusion in the midst of opportunity.

The women's magazines and related literature had feared this very dislocation of values and blurring of roles. By careful manipulation and interpretation they sought to convince woman that she had the best of both worlds—power and virtue—and that a stable order of society depended upon her maintaining her traditional place in it. To that end she was identified with everything that was beautiful and holy.

GERDA LERNER

The Lady and the Mill Girl:
Changes in the Status of Women
in the Age of Jackson

The period 1800–1840 is one in which decisive changes occurred in the status of American women. It has remained surprisingly unexplored. With the exception of a recent, unpublished dissertation by Keith Melder and the distinctive work of Elisabeth Dexter, there is a dearth of descriptive material and an almost total absence of interpretation. Yet the period offers essential clues to an understanding of later institutional developments, particularly the shape and nature of the woman's rights movement. This analysis will consider the economic, political, and social status of women and examine the changes in each area. It will also attempt an interpretation of the ideological shifts which occurred in American society concerning the "proper" role for women.

Periodization always offers difficulties. It seemed useful here, for purposes of comparison, to group women's status before 1800 roughly under the "colonial" heading and ignore the transitional and possibly atypical shifts which occurred during the American Revolution and the early period of nationhood. Also, regional differences were ignored. The South was left out of consideration entirely because its industrial development occurred later.

The status of colonial women has been well studied and described and can briefly be summarized for comparison with the later period. Throughout the colonial period there was a marked shortage of women, which varied with the regions and always was greatest in the frontier areas. This (from the point of view of women) favorable sex ratio enhanced their status and position. The Puritan world view regarded idleness as sin; life in an underdeveloped country made it absolutely necessary that each member of the community perform an economic function. Thus work for women, married or single, was not only approved, it was regarded as a civic duty. Puritan town councils expected single girls, widows, and unattached women to be self-supporting and for a long time provided needy spinsters with parcels of land. There was no social sanction against married women working; on the contrary, wives were expected to help their husbands in their trade and won social approval for doing extra work in or out of the home. Needy children, girls as well as boys, were indentured or apprenticed and were expected to work for their keep.

The vast majority of women worked within their homes, where their labor produced most articles needed for the family. The entire colonial production of cloth and clothing and in part that of shoes was in the hands of women. In addition to these occupations, women were found in many different kinds of employment. They were butchers, silversmiths, gunsmiths, upholsterers. They ran mills, plantations, tan yards, shipyards, and every kind of shop, tavern and boarding house. They were gate keepers, jail keepers, sextons, journalists, printers, "doctoresses," apothecaries, midwives, nurses, and teachers. Women acquired their skills the same way as did the men, through apprenticeship training, frequently within their own families.

Absence of a dowry, ease of marriage and remarriage, and a more lenient attitude of the law with regard to women's property rights were manifestations of the improved position of wives in the colonies. Under British common law, marriage destroyed a woman's contractual capacity; she could not sign a contract even with the consent of her husband. But colonial authorities were more lenient toward the wife's property rights by protecting her dower rights in her husband's property, granting her personal clothing, and upholding pre-nuptial contracts between husband and wife. In the absence of the husband, colonial courts granted women "femme sole" rights, which enabled them to conduct their husband's business, sign contracts, and sue. The relative social freedom of women and the esteem in which they were held was commented upon by most early foreign travelers in America.

But economic, legal, and social status tells only part of the story. Colonial society as a whole was hierarchical, and rank and standing in society depended on the position of the men. Women did not play a determining role in ranking pattern; they took their position in society through the men of their own family or the men they married. In other words, they participated in the hierarchy only as daughters and wives, not as individuals. Similarly, their occupations were, by and large, merely auxiliary, designed to contribute to family income, enhance their husbands' business or continue it in case of widowhood. The self-supporting spinsters were certainly the exception. The underlying assumption of colonial society was that women ought to occupy an inferior and subordinate position. The settlers had brought this assumption with them from Europe; it was reflected in their legal concepts, their willingness to exclude women from political life, their discriminatory educational practices. What is remarkable is the extent to which this felt inferiority of women was constantly challenged and modified under the impact of environment, frontier conditions, and a favorable sex ratio.

By 1840 all of American society had changed. The Revolution had substituted an egalitarian ideology for the hierarchical concepts of colonial life. Privilege based on ability rather than inherited status, upward mobility for all groups of society, and unlimited opportunities for individual self-fulfillment had become ideological goals, if not always realities. For men, that is; women were, by tacit consensus, excluded from the new democracy. Indeed, their actual situation had in many respects deteriorated. While, as wives, they had benefitted from increasing wealth, urbanization, and industrialization, their role as economic producers and as political members of society differed sharply from that of men. Women's work outside of the home no longer met with social approval; on the contrary, with two notable exceptions, it was condemned. Many business and professional occupations formerly open to women were now closed, many others restricted as to training and advancement. The entry of large numbers of women into low status, low pay, and low skill industrial work had fixed such work by definition as "woman's work." Women's political status, while legally unchanged, had deteriorated relative to the advances made by men. At the same time the genteel lady of fashion had become a model of American femininity, and the definition of "woman's proper sphere" seemed narrower and more confined than ever.

Within the scope of this essay only a few of these changes can be more fully explained. The professionalization of medicine and its impact on women may serve as a typical example of what occurred in all the professions.

In colonial America there were no medical schools, no medical journals, few hospitals, and few laws pertaining to the practice of the healing arts. Clergymen and governors, barbers, quacks, apprentices, and women practiced medicine. Most practitioners acquired their credentials by reading Paracelsus and Galen and serving an apprenticeship with an established practitioner. Among the semi-trained "physics," surgeons, and healers, the occasional "doctoress" was fully accepted and frequently well rewarded. County records of all the colonies contain references to the work of the female physicians. There was even a female Army surgeon, a Mrs. Allyn, who served during King Philip's war. Plantation records mention by name several slave women who were granted special privileges because of their useful service as midwives and "doctoresses."

The period of the professionalization of American medicine dates from 1765, when Dr. William Shippen began his lectures on midwifery in Philadelphia. The founding of medical faculties in several colleges, the standardization of training requirements, and the proliferation of medical societies intensified during the last quarter of the 18th century. The American Revolution dramatized the need for trained medical personnel, afforded first-hand battlefield experience to a number of surgeons and brought increasing numbers of semi-trained practitioners in contact with the handful of European-trained surgeons working in the military hospitals. This was an experience from which women were excluded. The resulting interest in improved medical training, the gradual appearance of graduates of medical colleges, and the efforts of medical societies led to licensing legislation. In 1801 Maryland required all medical practitioners to be licensed; in 1806 New York enacted a similar law, followed by all but three states. This trend was reversed in the 1830s and 40s when most states repealed their licensure requirements. This was due to pressure from eclectic, homeopathic practitioners, the public's dissatisfaction with the "heroic medicine" then practiced by licensed physicians, and to the distrust of state regulation, which was widespread during the Age of Jackson. Licensure as prime proof of qualification for the practice of medicine was reinstituted in the 1870s.

In the middle of the 19th century it was not so much a license of an M.D. which marked the professional physician as it was graduation from an approved medical college, admission to hospital practice and to a network of referrals through other physicians. In 1800 there were four medical schools, in 1850, forty-two. Almost all of them excluded women from admission. Not surprisingly, women turned to eclectic schools for training. Harriot Hunt, a Boston physician, was trained by apprenticeship with a husband and wife team of homeopathic physicians. After more than twenty years of practice she attempted to enter Harvard Medical school and was repeatedly rebuffed. Elizabeth Blackwell received her M.D. from Geneva (New York) Medical College, an eclectic school. Sarah Adamson found all regular medical schools closed against her and earned an M.D. in 1851 from Central College at Syracuse, an eclectic institution. Clemence Lozier graduated from the same school two years later and went on to found the New York Medical College and Hospital for women in 1862, a homeopathic institution which was later absorbed into the Flower-Fifth Avenue Hospital.

Another way in which professionalization worked to the detriment of women can be seen in the cases of Drs. Elizabeth and Emily Blackwell, Marie Zakrzewska, and Ann Preston, who despite their M.D.s and excellent training were denied access to hospitals, were refused recognition by county medical societies, and were denied customary referrals by male colleagues. Their experiences were similar to those of most of the pioneer women physicians. Such discrimination caused the formation of alternate institutions for the training of women physicians and for hospitals in which they might treat their patients. The point here is not so much that any one aspect of the process of professionalization excluded women but that the process, which took place over the span of almost a century, proceeded in such a way as to institutionalize an exclusion of women, which had earlier been accomplished irregularly, inconsistently, and mostly by means of social pressure. The end result was an *absolute* lowering of status for all women in the medical profession and a *relative* loss. As the professional status of all physicians advanced, the status differential between male and female practitioners was more obviously disadvantageous and underscored women's marginality. Their vital exclusion from the most prestigious and lucrative branches of the profession and their concentration in specializations relating to women and children made such disadvantaging more obvious by the end of the 19th century.

This process of pre-emption of knowledge, of institutionalization of the profession, and of legitimation of its claims by law and public acceptance is standard for the professionalization of the sciences, as George Daniels has pointed out. It inevitably results in the elimination of fringe elements from the profession. It is interesting to note that women had been pushed out of the medical profession in 16th century Europe by a similar process. Once the public had come to accept licensing and college training as guarantees of up-to-date practice, the outsider, no matter how well qualified by years of experience, stood no chance in the competition. Women were the casualties of medical professionalization.

In the field of midwifery the results were similar, but the process was more complicated. Women had held a virtual monopoly in the profession in colonial America. In 1646 a man was prosecuted in Maine for practicing as a midwife. There are many records of well-trained midwives with diplomas from European institutions working in the colonies. In most of the colonies midwives were licensed, registered, and required to pass an examination before a board. When Dr. Shippen announced his pioneering lectures on midwifery, he did it to "combat the widespread popular prejudice against the man-midwife" and because he considered most midwives ignorant and improperly trained.

Yet he invited "those women who love virtue enough, to own their Ignorance, and apply for instruction" to attend his lectures, offering as an inducement the assurance that female pupils would be taught privately. It is not known if any midwives availed themselves of the opportunity.

Technological advances, as well as scientific, worked against the interests of female midwives. In 16th-century Europe the invention and use of obstetrical forceps had for three generations been the well-kept secret of the Chamberlen family and had greatly enhanced their medical practice. Hugh Chamberlen was forced by circumstances to sell the secret to the Medical College in Amsterdam, which in turn transmitted the precious knowledge to licensed physicians only. By the time the use of the instrument became widespread, it had become associated with male physicians and male midwives. Similarly in America, introduction of the obstetrical forceps was associated with the practice of male midwives and served to their advantage. By the end of the 18th century a number of male physicians advertised their practice of midwifery. Shortly thereafter female midwives also resorted to advertising, probably in an effort to meet the competition. By the early 19th century male physicians had virtually monopolized the practice of midwifery on the Eastern seaboard. True to the generally delayed economic development in the Western frontier regions, female midwives continued to work on the frontier until a much later period. It is interesting to note that the concepts of "propriety" shifted with the prevalent practice. In 17th-century Maine the attempt of a man to act as a midwife was considered outrageous and illegal; in mid-19th-century America the suggestion that women should train as midwives and physicians was considered equally outrageous and improper.

Professionalization, similar to that in medicine with the elimination of women from the upgraded profession, occurred in the field of law. Before 1750, when law suits were commonly brought to the courts by the plaintiffs themselves or by deputies without specialized legal training, women as well as men could and did act as "attorneys-in-fact." When the law became a paid profession and trained lawyers took over litigation, women disappeared from the court scene for over a century.

A similar process of shrinking opportunities for women developed in business and in the retail trades. There were fewer female storekeepers and business women in the 1830s than there had been in colonial days. There was also a noticeable shift in the kind of merchandise handled by them. Where previously women could be found running almost every kind of retail shop, after 1830 they were mostly found in businesses which served women only.

The only fields in which professionalization did not result in the elimination of women from the upgraded profession were nursing and teaching. Both were characterized by a severe shortage of labor. Nursing lies outside the field of this inquiry, since it did not become an organized profession until after the Civil War. Before then, it was regarded peculiarly as a woman's occupation, although some of the hospitals and the Army during wars employed male nurses. These bore the stigma of low skill, low status, and low pay. Generally, nursing was regarded as simply an extension of the unpaid services performed by the housewife—a characteristic attitude that haunts the profession to this day.

Education seems, at first glance, to offer an entirely opposite pattern from that of the other professions. In colonial days women had taught "Dame schools" and grade schools during summer sessions. Gradually, as educational opportunities for girls expanded, they advanced just a step ahead of their students. Professionalization of teaching occurred between 1820 and 1860, a period marked by a sharp increase in the number of women teachers. The spread of female seminaries, academies, and normal schools provided new opportunities for the training and employment of female teachers.

This trend, which runs counter to that found in the other professions, can be accounted for by the fact that women filled a desperate need created by the challenge of the common schools, the ever-increasing size of the student body, and the westward growth of the nation. America was committed to educating its children in public schools, but it was insistent on doing so as cheaply as possible. Women were available in great numbers, and they were willing to work cheaply. The result was another ideological adaptation: in the very period when the gospel of the home as woman's only proper sphere was preached most loudly, it was discovered that women were the natural teachers of youth, could do the job better than men, and were to be preferred for such employment. This was always provided, of course, that they would work at the proper wage differential—30 to 50 per cent of the wages paid male teachers was considered appropriate. The result was that in 1888 in the country as a whole 63 per cent of all teachers were women, while the figure for the cities only was 90.04 per cent.

It appeared in the teaching field, as it would in industry, that role expectations were adaptable provided the inferior status group filled a social need. The inconsistent and peculiar patterns of employment of black labor in the present-day market bear out the validity of this generalization.

There was another field in which the labor of women was appreciated and which they were urged to enter—industry. From Alexander Hamilton to Matthew Carey and Tench Coxe, advocates of industrialization sang the praises of the working girl and advanced arguments in favor of her employment. The social benefits of female labor particularly stressed were those bestowed upon her family, who now no longer had to support her. Working girls were "thus happily preserved from idleness and its attendant vices and crimes," and the whole community benefitted from their increased purchasing power.

American industrialization, which occurred in an underdeveloped economy with a shortage of labor, depended on the labor of women and children. Men were occupied with agricultural work and were not available or were unwilling to enter the factories. This accounts for the special features of the early development of the New England textile industry: the relatively high wages, the respectability of the job and relatively high status of the mill girls, the patriarchal character of the model factory towns, and the temporary mobility of women workers from farm to factory and back again to farm. All this was characteristic only of a limited area and of a period of about two decades. By the late 1830s the romance had worn off: immigration had supplied a strongly competitive, permanent work force willing to work for subsistence wages; early efforts at trade union organization had been shattered, and mechanization had turned semi-skilled factory labor into unskilled labor. The process led to the replacement of the New England-born farm girls by immigrants in the mills and was accompanied by a loss of status and respectability for female workers.

The lack of organized social services during periods of depression drove ever greater numbers of women into the labor market. At first, inside the factories distinctions between men's and women's jobs were blurred. Men and women were assigned to machinery on the basis of local need. But as more women entered industry the limited number of occupations open to them tended to increase competition among them, thus lowering pay standards. Generally, women regarded their work as temporary and hesitated to invest in apprenticeship training, because they expected to marry and raise families. Thus they remained untrained, casual labor and were soon, by custom, relegated to the lowest paid, least skilled jobs. Long hours, overwork, and poor working conditions would characterize women's work in industry for almost a century.

Another result of industrialization was in increasing differences in life styles between women of different classes. When female occupations, such as carding, spinning, and weaving, were transferred from home to factory, the poorer women followed their traditional work and became industrial workers. The women of the middle and upper classes could use their newly gained time for leisure pursuits: they became ladies. And a small but significant group among them chose to prepare themselves for professional careers by advanced education. This group would prove to be the most vocal and troublesome in the near future.

As class distinctions sharpened, social attitudes toward women became polarized. The image of "the lady" was elevated to the accepted ideal of femininity toward which all women would strive. In this formulation of values, lower-class women were simply ignored. The actual lady was, of course, nothing new on the American scene; she had been present ever since colonial days. What was new in the 1830s was the cult of the lady, her elevation to a status symbol. The advancing prosperity of the early 19th century made it possible for middle-class women to aspire to the status formerly reserved for upper-class women. The "cult of true womanhood" of the 1830s became a vehicle for such aspirations. Mass circulation newspapers and magazines made it possible to teach every woman how to elevate the status of her family by setting "proper" standards of behavior, dress, and literary tastes. *Godey's Lady's Book* and innumerable gift books and tracts of the period all preach the same gospel of "true womanhood"—piety, purity, domesticity. Those unable to reach the goal of becoming ladies were to be satisfied with the lesser goal—acceptance of their "proper place" in the home.

It is no accident that the slogan "woman's place is in the home" took on a certain aggressiveness and shrillness precisely at the time when increasing numbers of poorer women *left* their homes to become factory workers. Working women were not a fit subject for the concern of publishers and mass media writers. Idleness, once a disgrace in the eyes of society, had become a status symbol. Thorstein Veblen, one of the earliest and sharpest commentators on the subject, observed that it had become almost the sole social function of the lady "to put in evidence her economic unit's ability to pay." She was "a means of conspicuously unproductive expenditure," devoted to displaying her husband's wealth. Just as the cult of white womanhood in the South served to preserve a labor and social system based on race distinctions, so did the cult of the lady in an egalitarian society serve as a means of preserving class distinctions. Where class distinctions were not so great, as on the frontier, the position of women was closer to what it had been in colonial days; their economic contribution was more highly valued, their opportunities were less restricted, and their positive participation in community life was taken for granted.

In the urbanized and industrialized Northeast the life experience of middle-class women was different in almost every respect from that of the lower-class women. But there was one thing the society lady and the mill girl had in common—they were equally disfranchised and isolated from the vital centers of power. Yet the political status of women had not actually deteriorated. With very few exceptions women had neither voted nor stood for office during the colonial period. Yet the spread of the franchise to ever wider groups of white males during the Jacksonian age, the removal of property restrictions, the increasing numbers of immigrants who acquired access to the franchise, made the gap between these new enfranchised voters and the disfranchised women more obvious. Quite naturally, educated and propertied women felt this deprivation more keenly. Their own career expectations had been encouraged by widening educational opportunities; their consciousness of their own abilities and of their potential for power had been enhanced by their activities in the reform movements of the 1830s; the general spirit of upward mobility and venturesome entrepreneurship that pervaded the Jacksonian era was infectious. But in the late 1840s a sense of acute frustration enveloped these educated and highly spirited women. Their rising expectations had met with frustration, their hopes had been shattered; they were bitterly conscious of a relative lowering of status and a loss of position. This sense of frustration led them to action; it was one of the main factors in the rise of the woman's rights movement.

The women, who at the first woman's rights convention at Seneca Falls, New York, in 1848 declared boldly and with considerable exaggeration that "the history of mankind is a history of repeated injuries and usurpations on the part of man toward woman, having in direct object the establishment of an absolute tyranny over her," did not speak for the truly exploited and abused working woman. As a matter of fact, they were largely ignorant of her condition and, with the notable exception of Susan B. Anthony, indifferent to her fate. But they judged from the realities of their own life experience. Like most revolutionaries, they were not the most downtrodden but rather the most status-deprived group. Their frustrations and traditional isolation from political power funneled their discontent into fairly utopian declarations and immature organizational means. They would learn better in the long, hard decades of practical struggle. Yet it is their initial emphasis on the legal and political "disabilities" of women which has provided the framework for most of the historical work on women.* For almost a hundred years sympathetic historians have told the story of women in America

---

*To the date of the first printing of this article (1969).

by deriving from the position of middle-class women a generalization concerning all American women. To avoid distortion, any valid generalization concerning American women after the 1830s should reflect a recognition of class stratification.

For lower-class women the changes brought by industrialization were actually advantageous, offering income and advancement opportunities, however limited, and a chance for participation in the ranks of organized labor.* They, by and large, tended to join men in their struggle for economic advancement and became increasingly concerned with economic gains and protective labor legislation. Middle- and upper-class women, on the other hand, reacted to actual and fancied status deprivation by increasing militancy and the formation of organizations for woman's rights, by which they meant especially legal and property rights.

The four decades preceding the Seneca Falls Convention were decisive in the history of American women. They brought an actual deterioration in the economic opportunities open to women, a relative deterioration in their political status, and a rising level of expectation and subsequent frustration in a privileged elite group of educated women. It was in these decades that the values and beliefs that clustered around the assertion "Woman's place is in the home" changed from being descriptive of an existing reality to becoming an ideology. "The cult of true womanhood" extolled woman's predominance in the domestic sphere, while it tried to justify women's exclusion from the public domain, from equal education, and from participation in the political process by claims to tradition, universality, and a history dating back to antiquity, or at least to the *Mayflower*. In a century of modernization and industrialization, women alone were to remain unchanging, embodying in their behavior and attitudes the longing of men and women caught in rapid social change for a mythical archaic past of agrarian family self-sufficiency. In preindustrial America the home was indeed the workplace for both men and women, although the self-sufficiency of the American yeoman, whose economic well-being depended on a network of international trade and mercantilism, was even then more apparent than real. In the 19th and 20th centuries, the home was turned into the realm of woman, while the workplace became the public domain of men. The ideology of "woman's sphere" sought to upgrade women's domestic function by elaborating the role of mother, turning the domestic drudge into a "homemaker" and charging her with elevating her family's status by her exercise of consumer functions and by her display of her own and her family's social graces. These prescribed roles never *were* a reality. In the 1950s Betty Friedan would describe this ideology and rename it "the feminine mystique," but it was no other than the myth of "woman's proper sphere" created in the 1840s and updated by consumerism and the misunderstood dicta of Freudian psychology.

The decades 1800–1840 also provide the clues to an understanding of the institutional shape of the later women's organizations. These would be led by middle-class women whose self-image, life experience, and ideology had largely been fashioned and influenced by these early, transitional years. The concerns of middle-class women—property rights, the franchise, and moral uplift—would

---

*In 1979, I would not agree with this optimistic generalization.

dominate the woman's rights movement. But side by side with it, and at times co-operating with it, would grow a number of organizations serving the needs of working women.

American women were the largest disfranchised group in the nation's history, and they retained this position longer than any other group. Although they found ways of making their influence felt continuously, not only as individuals but as organized groups, power eluded them. The mill girl and the lady, both born in the age of Jackson, would not gain access to power until they learned to cooperate, each for her own separate interests. It would take almost six decades before they would find common ground. The issue around which they finally would unite and push their movement to victory was the "impractical and utopian" demand raised at Seneca Falls—the means to power in American society—female suffrage.

Robert L. Griswold

Domestic Ideology in the West

When nineteenth-century Anglo women left their homes in New England, the South, or the Midwest to live in the West, they took with them more than the material items necessary for survival. They also took a set of values, assumptions, and ideals that enabled them to make sense of their lives. Although the content of this ideological baggage is not altogether clear, very likely these women subscribed to some variant of domestic ideology. Most undoubtedly believed that women's chief responsibilities were homemaking and child rearing, that females represented the moral foundation of the family and society, and that a commitment to family preceded and took precedence over a commitment to self. As a corollary, they also likely believed that women deserved respect and consideration commensurate with their high moral influence both inside and outside the home.

Yet, the key word is variant. Much of the confusion about women's roles and self-perceptions in the West stems from an overly rigid conception of domestic ideology: as a consequence, the historical debate too often turns on whether or not women slavishly adhered to a narrowly conceived conception of domesticity. Were or were not women submissive, pure, domestic, and pious? Did they or did they not subscribe to the cult of true womanhood? But if ideology is understood less narrowly, if ideology is perceived as a cultural system and not as a cult, such questions disappear and a more complex picture emerges of western Anglo women who were both brave and timid, resourceful and dependent, aggressive and retiring. In short, domestic ideology in the West was less a rigid set of assumptions than a supple perspective about gender ideals, less a well-defined "cult of true womanhood" than a way common women made sense of everyday existence. Antonio Gramsci, the Italian Marxist, had this conception of ideology in mind when he wrote that "Most men [sic] are philosophers in as much as they operate on the practical level and in their practice (in the controlling pattern of their conduct) have a conception of the world, a philosophy that is implicit." Thus, the domestic ideal existed as both a relatively formal ideology enunciated by middle-class moralists like Catharine Beecher and Sarah Hale and as a collection of half-seen, inchoate, imperfectly realized assumptions and values that enabled Anglo western women to interpret reality.

The key, then, to understanding the ideology of western Anglo women is to focus on the regularities and patterns, the popular languages and signs—the *mentalité*—that comprised their belief system. These beliefs helped the emigrants perceive and shape their culture, and this culture, this structure of thought, both decoded reality and defined and set limits on women's actions. Culture, in fact, gives meaning to action and defines and delimits such action: "This collective cultural system that we have assimilated, consciously or unconsciously," writes Gordon Wood, "suffuses all parts of our mind and in effect creates our behavior. It does so by forcing us to describe that behavior in its terms." Actions are circumscribed by the ways we can make them meaningful, and they are meaningful "only publicly, only with respect to an inherited system of social rules, conventions, and values." In short, the cultural system brings order to reality and simultaneously sets limits on individual thought, and hence action, at any particular moment.

This view of ideology as a cultural system permits exploration of the mental world of western women without looking for the carefully articulated world view of eastern moralists. It also helps us understand why depressed farm wives, intrepid frontier women, temperance reformers, suffragists, and the wives of socialist miners might all describe their lives in terms of the cultural symbols of domesticity. The patterns, the language, the cultural signs of domesticity had broad appeal to women from a wide variety of backgrounds and temperaments. Moreover, it meant different things to different women: a lonely, passive, sad-eyed rancher's wife and a fiery, determined Montana temperance reformer might both pledge allegiance to domesticity. To complicate matters further, an individual woman might exhibit behavior and attitudes that simultaneously confirmed and seemingly contradicted the ideology of domesticity. The staunch believer in a single woman's ability to homestead or the woman who went west for the adventure might also insist that wifehood and motherhood were women's ultimate callings. Her ideology might incorporate both traditional and proto-feminist assumptions about womanhood: depending on circumstances, she could well occupy a virtually limitless number of positions between these two poles, pushed and pulled along the continuum according to changing demands of family, community, and self.

This less rigid definition of ideology allows suspension of the debate on whether or not western Anglo women actually adhered to eastern moralists' conceptions of ideal womanhood. This is not the issue. Instead of conceiving of ideology as the pietistic desiderata of eastern urbanites, analysis should center on what James Henretta has called a phenomenological approach to social history, an approach focusing on the individual's act of "perceiving, judging, experiencing, and willing." Or as Elizabeth Jameson has suggested, "We need to approach western women's history not through the filters of prescriptive literature or concepts of frontier liberation and oppression, but through the experiences of the people who lived the history." Western Anglo women inherited an ideology that arose in the East, but it was an ideology that was fluid, elastic, and complex: women explained their own action by its assumptions, sometimes wrestled to align behavior with diverse perceptions of its tenets, and modified it to meet changing realities. In so doing, these migrants became creators as well as preservers of ideology.

The fact that domesticity arose in the East as part of the complex shift from a corporate household economy to a nascent urban, industrial economy would suggest that domestic ideology might have had trouble establishing firm roots in the West; moreover, eastern domesticity arose in conjunction with the separation of men's and women's worlds into two separate spheres, a separation that was virtually impossible to establish on the plains and in the mining towns of the West. Yet domestic ideology—in particular the valorization of motherhood and the emphasis on women's moral responsibilities to their families and communities—was central to the world view of Anglo women in the West. Although the spheres may have overlapped, the cultural values of domestic ideology had a powerful appeal to female settlers: they gave meaning to women's domestic work, made the blurring of sex roles culturally intelligible, helped confirm women's self-worth, offered a sense of stability in an inherently unstable world, and fostered bonds of friendship with other women. Domestic ideology, furthermore, legitimated women's efforts to "civilize" the West and provided a vocabulary with which to redefine the nature of manhood.

Domesticity for western Anglo women cannot be divorced from the productive labor they performed within the home. While some eastern urban women and a few elite westerners may have done little such work, most Anglo women contributed mightily to the economic survival of their families. The lives of all but wealthy women were characterized by hard work, work given cultural meaning by the ideology of domesticity. After all, the physical and moral well-being of the family stood at the core of nineteenth-century domestic social theory, and while a few privileged women could concentrate exclusively on the latter, most nineteenth-century wives, especially western wives, had to direct much of their energies to the former. But domesticity was never a theory of idleness: it always underscored the importance of productive labor, hence Catharine Beecher's efforts to increase the productivity and efficiency of housewives. And though western women, like their eastern counterparts, observed a gender-based division of labor, the spheres overlapped as women often performed labor generally reserved for men and as men occasionally did the reverse.

The labor of farm wives, for example, was indispensable to the success of the family venture. With her labor she produced the goods necessary for survival and often earned what little cash the family could claim by selling produce. Miners' wives likewise performed a seemingly endless number of tasks essential for their families' survival: they cooked, cleaned, hauled water, gardened, cared for livestock, chopped wood, sewed, canned, slaughtered, cured meat, made candles and soap and, if poor, washed, sewed, and cooked for single men. Despite this numbing work load, "the underlying social ideology of the Victorian era," writes Elliot West, "survived largely intact among Western miners' wives." A virtuous woman used her labor and talents to establish and maintain a proper home, a sphere that would be a refuge for her husband "and a school of strength and virtue for her children." To be successful, West concluded, women had to be assertive, resourceful, dynamic and skillful. This variant of domesticity had no room for passivity. To what extent such economic indispensability translated into power within the family is unclear, but the variety of work done by women both stretched and confirmed the fundamental belief that women's first responsibilities were to her family and home. When a wife made clothes, took in laundry, slaughtered livestock, mended fences, or harvested wheat, she did so because her family needed her labor.

The private writings of western women reveal that domestic tasks and the ideology that made cultural sense of these tasks validated women's self-worth. Frontier women described their first homes with affection and wrote with pride of their own innovativeness and resourcefulness in maintaining a home. One Iowa frontierswoman could not contain her pride or excitement as she and her family prepared to move into their new home: "It seems real nice to have the whole control of my house; can say I am monarch of all I survey and none to dispute my right." So, too, miners' wives improvised to make their homes comport with Victorian standards of taste and often moved a few cherished belongings from mine to mine in an effort to secure symbolically the domestic stability their peripatetic lives so clearly lacked. Many women seemed to gain an artisan's satisfaction from their domestic duties and regarded their work as a craft. Women took understandable pride in pies well-baked, shirts well-made, and children well-tended. Here was a healthy, instrumental, republican brand of domesticity free of the ornamental parasitism that allegedly plagued elite urban women.

Although the satisfaction women gained from their domestic work should not be overestimated—after all, many women also complained of the drudgery of their lives—work within the home may have also seemed relatively desirable given the alternatives outside the home. In other words, just as factory work confirmed conventional life expectations for eastern women at the turn of the century, the even more narrow job choices for western women likely did the same thing. In light of their high cultural status, wifehood and motherhood were very appealing in comparison to life as an unmarried domestic, seamstress, or laundress. Teaching was probably the most appealing occupation, in part because teachers combined aspects of domestic ideology with some prospects of autonomy and advancement, but in most towns, life as a teacher required life without marriage and children. That was a sacrifice few women willingly made. Finally, the slow development of industrialization in the West left women there with even fewer job possibilities than in the East.

Given the low level of industrialization, women in far western cities worked primarily in domestic service. For young single working women, this universally despised occupation undoubtedly helped propel them into marriage. The fact that most single working women lived at home also made marriage seem inviting: it was a way to chart an independent course from parents, no matter how illusory the independence might actually be. Thus, for every adventuresome, single, female homesteader, there were scores of overworked and underpaid domestics, sales clerks, and non-industrial manufacturers for whom marriage and family represented a genuine hope for a better life.

The significance of domesticity, of course, went far beyond the nature of the work itself. Domesticity represented ties with community, and migration disrupted those ties. Most wives dutifully followed their husbands on the arduous and dangerous trail west. En route, women encountered the sickness and death, hardship and heartache that accompanied almost every overland expedition. But though a woman might have to leave her home, she did not leave behind the thoughts that filled that home. Domestic ideology was a tie to the past, a way one connected new surroundings to older roots. Amidst the uncertainties and upheavals characteristic of life in a new land, domesticity offered a familiar way to describe one's basic attitudes and hopes. Mothers were especially concerned that their daughters receive the lessons of domesticity, thereby validating the mothers' past and providing a sense of continuity between the two generations. External conditions might change without altering, so mothers hoped, the great lessons of life. The bonds of womanhood between mother and daughter, the complex web of obedience and obligation inherent in that relationship, served to mitigate the upheaval beyond the home.

A shared set of ideas about woman's place also bound non-related women to each other. Frontier women missed the company of other women, urged friends from home to migrate, promised repeatedly to visit female friends in the East, and made determined efforts to establish new friendships as quickly as possible. The cement of these bonds was comprised, in part, of a shared belief about women's duties, responsibilities, and prerogatives. Thus, women sought out other virtuous women for company and shunned those who violated the principles of nineteenth-century womanhood. Whether or not domestic ideology was prevalent among working-class women is debatable—evidence from Mormon women, black women, California divorcees, and miners' wives suggest that it was not restricted to the white middle-class—but domestic ideology strengthened the bonds of sisterhood among women. It did so by offering women a cultural system of social rules, conventions, and values—a moral vocabulary of discourse—that gave meaning to their daily behavior and to their friendships with other women.

Domestic ideology brought western Anglo women together in another way as well. Fired by the moral message of domesticity, women united to "civilize" the West. This effort should not be confused with the influence of ethereal "madonnas in sunbonnets" or bloodless "gentle tamers" who allegedly worked wonders by the sheer force of their pious, self-sacrificing example. These images of western women are useless stereotypes that obscure the real relations between men and women and blind us to women's prolonged battle over what the West was to become, a battle that often brought women into conflict with entrenched male interests. If women were civilizers, they civilized for their families, for themselves, and for their gender: their quest was not to establish a lofty, other-worldly abstraction called *civilization* but to create the institutions—the schools, churches, charity associations, reforms—that would check male inspired disorder, assist the victims and losers of the male dominated society, and secure a social order within which domestic virtues and family life could flourish.

Sexual struggle was at the core of this quest, a struggle predicated on the fact that western men and women had different conceptions of social order. Where womenless men dominated the West, prostitution and drinking were not only tolerated but were integral parts of the service structure of the community. Men without families in mining camps and cowtowns had little interest in schools and even less in charity associations, benevolent societies, temperance reforms, and churches. "Competitive opportunism" underlay their enterprise, a search for individual gain that often led to sharp clashes and factionalization within the Western communities. This male-inspired, competitive, acquisitive ethos created an inhospitable climate for social reform. Most western mining camps, for example, were places of brief but intense economic exploitation occupied by highly transient males who showed open disdain for the domestic morality of the East. These men came for money, not for righteousness, and the laws they passed generally focused on economic matters and practical needs. Only with the arrival of families did the more stable western mining towns witness the emergence of the appurtenances of civilization.

Men on the prairies shared many characteristics with men in the mining camps. They, too, were highly transient; they, too, came to exploit the land or to make money from those who did. These men fought over the location of the railroad and the county seat and shamelessly boosted the attributes of their own communities at the expense of their rivals. The fraternal orders they established symbolized not so much small town camaraderie as the ethnic and class tensions that accompanied rapid town development. The straightforward emphasis on economic development left few men, either of the elite or of the working class, particularly interested in moral reform. In the cowtowns of Kansas, "those who defined the business community consensus," writes historian Robert Dykstra, "viewed the brothel, the dance house, the gaming room, and the saloon as necessary adjuncts to the cattle trade." If they supported moral reform, they did so cautiously and hesitantly and justified such reforms in economic terms. To these men, prostitution was not the target, only the wide-open bawdy house that gave the town a bad name to visitors and future settlers; gambling per se was not evil, only gamblers who cheated naive outsiders of their money, thereby discrediting the town and hurting future economic growth. When reformers did make headway, it occurred only as the cattle trade died out and the cowtowns became farming and ranching centers for respectable middle-class farmers.

To the farmers and merchants who succeeded the cowboy, brothels, saloons, and gambling dens were open affronts to middle-class economic order based upon hard work and self-restraint: such evils hurt business, or at least the kinds of businesses middle-class entrepreneurs hoped to establish. Brothels and saloons might appeal to lonely cowboys, rowdy cattlemen, and hard luck miners, but the future of the towns lay with solid farmers, craftsmen, merchants, and their families. Thus, law, order, morality, and economic prosperity stood lined against the get-rich-quick immorality of the booming cowtowns and mining camps. Men's support for reform, then, stemmed from a conception of morality inextricably linked to bourgeois economic respectability, rather than from a sense that men were primarily responsible for the moral purity of their communities or that frontier vices subverted their ability to rear proper children: hence men's willingness to compromise and to allow other men to pursue their fortunes and pleasures.

The wives of these men, however, likely had a different perception of social order. Entrusted with primary child-rearing responsibilities, intent on protecting and enhancing the morality of their families, women's opposition to frontier vice had roots deep within their own perceptions of self, family, and society. To protect morality, to build churches and schools, to see that sons and daughters grew up morally straight, these were important goals of many, if not most, Anglo western women. For them, compromise with vice—with the sinful indulgences of men—was unacceptable. Building a decent society required the efforts of both men and women, but women had the greater moral leverage to accomplish the needed reforms. They were the gender entrusted with the moral welfare of their home and community, and to protect their homes, middle-class women had to weave domestic morality into the fabric of society. After all, a pious, peaceful, domestic sphere might somehow survive amidst immoral conditions but would flourish only in an environment suffused with Christian morality. Thus women's diaries and letters record their efforts to establish schools, churches, Sunday school classes, benevolent associations, and charities. Some single females, in fact, came to the West intent on rescuing the region from barbarity: hundreds of unmarried female teachers from New England and upper New York state, for example, tried with mixed success to redeem the West with a blend of pietism and pedagogy.

These school teachers were, however, the exception. Most women had simply accompanied their husbands or fathers to the West and equated civilization with certain institutions and values. Imbued with an ideology that emphasized women's moral natures, these women instituted reforms and created agencies that simultaneously expressed and promoted their visions of domesticity. Men might dominate church hierarchies, but women dominated the pews and the auxiliaries that sustained the church on a day-to-day basis. Sunday schools, benevolent associations, prayer meetings, and church socials were all dominated by women. So, too, were the special organizations that brought at least a veneer of eastern civilization to the West. Inspired by a belief in women's civilizing mission, western women formed reading clubs, debating societies, amateur musical and dramatic groups, libraries, maternal societies, and moral reform organizations. Rather than merely preserving civilization, western women, as Julie Roy Jeffrey has written, became the creators, a role that must have had a powerful appeal to women: "Women were extolled as mothers, wives, and civilizers. Their confrontation with the wilderness reaffirmed their image as molders of civilizations, through church, school, and social activities."

Civilizing the West meant, above all, civilizing men, and nowhere was the clash between male and female cultures more vivid than in the western settlements. To change male behavior and to define the nature of disorder and moral impropriety, women turned to the assumptions of domesticity. They did so not only because the domestic ideal elevated women's status within the family but because it also legitimated the call for a new style of masculine behavior both inside and outside the family. Thus, in building schools, churches, and charities, women recreated eastern civilization and checked a certain style of western masculinity that tolerated drinking, violence, gambling, and whoring. With the arrival of mothers and daughters, a struggle between women and men over masculine identity ensued, a struggle involving the sexual double standard, religious commitment, temperance, gambling, men's psychological commitment to their wives and children, and male and female prerogatives within the family. Domesticity's reforming power lay in its ability to dramatize the social importance of a home-inspired morality and to insist that men and women adhere to a single standard of conduct, and a feminine one at that.

For women the choice was clear: either descend to the level of a male culture that tolerated vice—an unthinkable prospect—or align with righteous women and men and destroy these appurtenances of undomesticated masculinity. Thus, it was women who dominated the ranks of those opposed to drink, gambling, and prostitution. Antiprostitution, temperance, and reform campaigns in Kansas illustrate the reform process at work. In the early booming years of the cow-towns, for example, local newspapers viewed prostitution with amused tolerance, and ordinances against the practice simply served to fill the town coffers with collected fines. Local authorities considered prostitution a necessary social service. The arrival of families, however, challenged this vision of prostitution. With the advent of more even sex ratios, a sharp increase in the number of children, and the rise of respectable, middle-class occupations, women (and some men) called for the strict regulation or abolition of brothels. After all, prostitution was an affront to women's moral sensibilities and to Victorian ideas about sexual exclusivity, emotional intimacy, the sanctity of motherhood, and the importance of domestic life. To virtuous women, prostitution degraded men and women and threatened the sexual integrity of husbands and sons.

· Nor did Kansas women limit themselves to antiprostitution campaigns. Helped by connections with eastern organizations (a Lawrence, Kansas study club, for example, evolved directly from a group in Quincy, Illinois) Kansas women settlers in the late nineteenth century established a host of organizations to civilize the new state. Within a year of settlement, both Wichita and Dodge City witnessed the birth of women's benevolent societies. Organizations like the Woman's Relief Corps, the American Association of University Women, the PEO, the Kansas Federation of Women's Clubs, and the Woman's Christian Temperance Union "affirmed the women's sense of the validity and importance of their own values." The meetings helped break down the isolation many women undoubtedly felt, created complex networks among women reformers, offered women useful instruction on frontier living, and, perhaps most importantly, provided a way for women to translate the moral lessons of domesticity into direct social action. One women's club, for example, ran a successful day nursery for working mothers; another group founded the Home for Friendless Women in Leavenworth; a third helped to start what became the Girls' Industrial School in Beloit. Still other women tried to help prostitutes, poor older women and widows, or concentrated on school reforms, including scholarships for poor girls and an end to gender-based teacher pay inequities. Whether fighting for these reforms or for temperance legislation, the right of wives to refuse intercourse with drunken husbands, or protection and relief for female victims of a male-run economy, the women's groups of Kansas offered an implicit and sometimes explicit critique of a social order dominated by men.

Women's efforts at church formation and temperance, antiprostitution, and gambling reforms were public efforts that protected women's families and fostered in women a collective sense of identity and accomplishment. But the female effort to change male behavior also reverberated within the private lives of western women. Here, too, a battle of sorts was being waged. Domestic ideology made sense to Anglo women not only because it offered a moral basis for social reform but because it gave wives, within the privacy of the home, the right to expect, even demand, behavior from husbands commensurate with women's moral position within the family. Thus, a paradox emerges: domesticity was an ideology of social order, a "cultural rationalization for a specific social ordering of the relations between men and women" that helped legitimate male monopolization of economic, political, educational, and legal life. Yet, domestic ideology contained within it elements of a powerful critique of male behavior and prerogatives that could, if pursued far enough, break up the family, the very foundation of Victorian social order. Civilizing men included civilizing the man who headed the household, and if he could not be reconstructed, increasing numbers of western women simply filed for divorce.

Evidence from California divorce courts from 1850 to 1890 suggests that domestic ideology, however vague and imperfectly realized, shaped the ongoing debate on gender by providing a language that checked traditional male prerogatives and called for both intimacy and mutual respect within the family. Helped by California's wide ranging grounds for divorce and expansive interpretations of marital cruelty by the state supreme court, female divorce seekers could use the leverage afforded by domestic ideology to break free of ties with cold, aloof, insensitive, and domineering husbands. Wives took pains to describe their own allegiance to the domestic ideal and to show how their husbands' cruel behavior made the establishment of peaceful, respectable homes impossible. As home guardians and moral exemplars, women deserved better treatment. Thus, a wife might complain about an overbearing husband "who treated me as a slave" or about one who insisted that his wife follow his every command. Other wives demanded respect and complained of husbands' selfishness and of husbands who tried to restrict their wives' contacts outside the home; wives also criticized husbands who meddled in their personal correspondence, who ignored them with a "brutal silence," who unfairly denied them credit with local merchants, or who ignored their physical limitations. While such male behavior might have been objectionable in the first half of the nineteenth century, only in the second half do such complaints by women gain standing in divorce suits. Although these particular complaints might not bring a divorce in and of themselves—California law demanded proof of extreme cruelty—they did bolster cruelty complaints and helped to prove that a man's general behavior did not comport with social expectations for husbands.

When husbands brought suit or defended themselves against complaints, they, too, tried to establish their allegiance to the canons of domestic morality.

Lawyers and friendly witnesses described these husbands as kind, affectionate, and attentive to their wives, and the husbands in their own defense underscored their allegiance to visions of domesticated manhood. Although many men's actual behavior surely did not comport with these publicly articulated ideals—some men were undoubtedly more aloof, authoritarian, unemotional, and patriarchal than their testimony would indicate—the vocabulary they used to describe their behavior indicates how thoroughly domestic assumptions pervaded private life.

If the divorce rate is an accurate barometer of rising marital expectations, women's claims on men were clearly rising in the second half of the nineteenth century. Women brought almost 70 percent of the suits, and courts showed little inclination to stem the tide of divorce. These trends were especially pronounced in the West, the region with the highest divorce rate, the most expansive statutes, and the most liberal judicial interpretations of matrimonial cruelty in the nation. In fact, California was a leader in this regard—from 1867 to 1906, over seven thousand California wives sued successfully for divorce on the ground of cruelty—and in the late nineteenth century, California courts redefined the nature of marital cruelty to include mental anguish, a definition with far more latitude than traditional interpretations had permitted.

Why western courts adopted such expansive positions is not altogether clear: perhaps women's claims had special appeal in the West where an overwhelmingly male culture (at least initially) met with female demands for a different cultural ethos. This clash of men's and women's conceptions of social order may have lent considerable weight to women's desires to break free of cruel husbands. Far from home and kin and bereft of familiar institutions, harshly treated women likely made strong claims on the sensibility of middle-class jurists. Thus, judges in rural California listened sympathetically to wives who complained about husbands' brutish sexual demands or about husbands who ignored their sick or pregnant wives, who spent too much time away from the domestic hearth, or who were heartless toward the children. With such behavior, husbands stood opposed to women's civilizing influence, thereby threatening to stop the moral progress so necessary to middle-class perceptions of settlement in the West. By their actions, they lost their right to be husbands. The moral leverage of domesticity asked men to reshape their behavior and to treat the opposite sex with more respect, and when men failed to do so, women increasingly turned to divorce courts for relief.

The value of the divorce evidence lies in its access to the private lives of Westerners, specifically to the underlying marital tensions between husbands and wives. These tensions often developed because men did not meet women's expectations of appropriate male behavior, expectations shaped largely by corollaries of domestic ideology. Thus, domesticity lay at the heart of the nineteenth-century definition of gender roles for both men and women. Domesticity empowered women to demand of men respect, consideration, emotional commitment, and even a measure of deference to their better moral judgment. If men refused such recognition, women showed a willingness to organize with other women (and with sympathetic men) against the misguided behavior of irreligious, habitually absent, sexually abusive, adulterous, and alcoholic males. Others, like the Californians in divorce court, simply decided to end their marriage when a husband's insensitivity and cruelty became unbearable.

Despite its origins in the East, domestic ideology established a powerful hold on the lives of western Anglo women. En route, and once settled, women kept alive the basic assumptions of domesticity, helped, no doubt, by frontier schoolbooks, newspapers, and magazines that underscored women's duties as childrearers, housewives, and moral guardians of family and community. The advice was general and vague but also ubiquitous and constant, and the effect was to preempt competing visions of womanhood. A woman who opposed domestic ideology for whatever reasons likely lacked even the language to express alternative views.

Moreover, the very suppleness of the concepts, the fact that domestic ideology was less a cult or a rigid orthodoxy and more a flexible vocabulary about gender ideals, meant that most Anglo women could turn to its values to make sense of their own lives. For most women, western migration was a family enterprise, and their commitment to their families defined their sense of self. What gave cultural meaning to these family responsibilities was the ideology of domesticity, an elastic and resilient set of ideas which supplied a much needed sense of stability, community, and generational continuity in a new region and provided an effective critique of immoral, undomesticated men. The last point is especially important. Given the masculine ethos of the early West, domesticity may have been especially appealing to western Anglo women who found in the ideology a powerful counterpoint to male assumptions about family and community life.

SUGGESTIONS FOR FURTHER READING

After years of neglect the field of women in American history is now booming; every month new titles come from the publishers. Several scholarly journals devoted to women's studies have made their appearance: *Feminist Studies, Signs,* and *Women's Studies* are three examples. In addition, the traditional scholarly journals now publish women's history regularly.

A number of fine general studies will introduce the beginner to this new and growing field: Mary P. Ryan, *Womanhood in America: From Colonial Times to the Present,* 3rd ed. (New York, 1983); Carol Ruth Berkin and Mary Beth Norton, *Women in America: A History* (Boston, 1979); Carl Degler, *At Odds: Women and the Family in America from the Revolution to the Present* (New York, 1980); Sara M. Evans, *Born for Liberty: A History of Women in America* (New York 1989); and Glenna Mathews, *Just a Housewife: The Rise and Fall of Domesticity in America* (New York, 1987).

Three books of documents, each with perceptive introductions, are especially recommended: Nancy F. Cott, *Root of Bitterness: Documents of the Social History of American Women* (New York, 1972) publishes material concerning women of all classes and describes the condition of women as well as their rebellion against that condition; Alice S. Rossi, *The Feminist Papers: From Adams to de Beauvoir* (New York, 1973) reprints some of the most important documents from the women's movement and provides introductions that fit the documents into the social context; Gerda Lerner, *Black Women in*

*Available in paperback edition.

White America: A Documentary History (New York, 1973) reprints documents that illustrate the special problems faced by black women.

Some of the recent work has been collected in easily available readers: Nancy F. Cott and Elizabeth H. Pleck, *A Heritage of Her Own* (New York, 1979); Jean E. Friedman and William G. Shade, *Our American Sisters: Women in American Life and Thought* (Lexington, 1982); and Linda K. Kerber and Jane De Hart, eds., *Women's America: Refocusing the Past* (New York, 1995). A collection of theoretical articles is Berenice A. Carroll, *Liberating Women's History: Theoretical and Critical Essays* (Urbana, Ill., 1976). Vicki L. Ruiz and Ellen Carol Dubois, eds., *Unequal Sisters* (New York, 1994) is an anthology of recent scholarship that deals with gender but also with race and class.

In one sense, much of this work emphasizes conflict, describing the legal, political, and ideological restraints upon women, the efforts of some to overcome or to adapt to these restraints in one way or another, and the effects these attempts had on women themselves and on the society.

Studies of the fight for women's rights and especially the right to vote are Eleanor Flexner, *Century of Struggle: The Woman's Rights Movement in the United States* (Cambridge, Mass., 1959) and Ellen Carol Dubois, *Feminism and Suffrage: The Emergence of an Independent Women's Movement* (Ithaca, N.Y., 1978). Black women were sometimes welcomed into the women's rights movement, but more often they were excluded, argues Rosalyn Terborg-Penn in "Discrimination Against Afro-American Women in the Woman's Movement, 1830–1920," in Sharon Harley and Rosalyn Terborg-Penn, eds., *The Afro-American Woman: Struggles and Images* (Port Washington, N.Y., 1978), 17–27, 121–22. Readers of these studies will find that this struggle was primarily, although not exclusively, an effort of middle-class women.

Similar emphasis on middle-class women may be found in Nancy F. Cott, *The Bonds of Womanhood: Woman's Sphere in New England, 1780–1835* (New Haven, Conn., 1977); Cott provides a detailed extension of Barbara Welter's thesis. Ann Douglas, *The Feminization of American Culture* (New York, 1977) uses a variety of sources including fiction to argue that middle-class women and liberal clergymen created a feminine consensus. Working-class women were usually less concerned with political and status rights than they were with employment opportunities, wages, working conditions, and the other problems they faced on the job. Although they shared such concerns with men, women often found themselves in competition and conflict with their fellow male workers as well as with their employers. Karen V. Hansen, *A Very Special Time: Crafting Community in Antebellum New England* (Berkeley, 1994) denies the concept of separate spheres and stresses community and consensus across gender lines.

The experiences of working women during the pre–Civil War years may be studied in Thomas Dublin, *Women at Work: The Transformation of Work and Community in Lowell, Massachusetts, 1826–1860* (New York, 1979) and in Alice Kessler-Harris, *Out to Work: A History of Wage-Earning Women in the United States* (New York, 1982). Sharon Harley, "Northern Black Female Workers: Jacksonian Era," in Sharon Harley and Rosalyn Terborg-Penn, eds., *The Afro-American Woman: Struggles and Images* (Port Washington, N.Y., 1978), 5–16, 119–21, considers some of the special problems of black women workers.

Race and regional differences affected women in different ways. Varying views of slaveowning women, including their attitudes towards and relationships with their slaves, may be found in Anne Firor Scott, *The Southern Lady: From Pedestal to Politics, 1830–1930* (Chicago, 1970), part 1; Catherine Clinton, *The Plantation Mistress: Woman's World in the Old South* (New York, 1982); Elizabeth Fox-Genovese, *Within the Plantation Household: Black and White Women of the Old South* (Chapel Hill, N.C.,

1988); and Suzanne Lebsock, *The Free Women of Petersburg: Status and Culture in a Southern Town: 1784–1860* (New York, 1984). Herbert G. Gutman, *The Black Family in Slavery and Freedom, 1750–1925* (New York, 1976) discusses kinship relations among slaves and free blacks. Although the westward movement is usually viewed as primarily a male enterprise, several recent studies show that the movement was primarily a family affair, that the work of the women was indispensable, and that the division of labor between men and women often broke down during the long and arduous trip: John Mack Faragher, *Women and Men on the Overland Trail* (New Haven, Conn., 1979); Julie Roy Jeffrey, *Frontier Women: The Trans-Mississippi West, 1840–1880* (New York, 1979); and Lillian Schlissel, Vicki L. Ruiz, and Janice Monk, *Western Women: Their Land, Their Lives* (Albuquerque, 1988).

Recent studies of farm women are Joan M. Jensen, *Loosening the Bonds: Mid-Atlantic Farm Women, 1750–1850* (New Haven, Conn., 1986); Rachel Ann Rosenfeld, *Farm Women: Work, Farm, and Family in the United States* (Chapel Hill, N.C., 1985); and Carolyn E. Sachs, *The Invisible Farmers: Women in Agricultural Production* (Totowa, N.J., 1983). The experiences of northern urban women are considered in Christine Stansell, *City of Women: Sex and Class in New York, 1789–1860* (New York, 1986).

7

The Black Response
to Slavery

The first blacks in the English mainland colonies of North America arrived in 1619; John Rolfe recorded that, in that year, there "came in a dutch man of warre that sold us twenty Negars." While there is some dispute about when the institution of slavery was actually established—these early arrivals were probably indentured servants with limited terms of servitude—it is quite clear that by 1660 the black had become a slave. Servitude had become permanent, and children of slave mothers, according to law, themselves became slaves. In the years that followed, slaves increased in numbers, gradually displacing indentured servants as the primary form of labor on Southern plantations. Declining profits in tobacco culture in the late eighteenth century, combined with the nagging contradiction between human bondage and colonial proclamations of liberty and human rights, led some Americans to foresee an early end to slavery. These expectations dissolved, however, when Eli Whitney invented the cotton gin in 1793 and made commercial cotton growing economically feasible. Suddenly, Southern planters found a new and profitable use for their slaves.

In the North, slavery gradually disappeared, but in the South, the number of slaves grew rapidly, and slavery expanded as planters and farmers took their slaves to the West to carve plantations and farms out of the wilderness. By 1860, the nation had some four million slaves, most of them living in the cotton-growing areas from Virginia to Texas. Slavery had become the South's "peculiar institution."

The existence of slavery in the South produced political and social conflicts throughout the nation. The holding of human beings as property offended the religious and moral scruples and the democratic inclinations of many, and often such people became militant abolitionists. Others considered slavery a menace to free labor, and they fought the extension of slavery into new territories. Some, including nonslaveholding Southerners, charged that servile labor stifled economic development and consigned the South to poverty. And still others charged that the slave system created an arrogant and dangerous ruling group of slaveowners who used their considerable political power in the federal government to support the slaveowners' needs at the expense of the nation as a whole.

But perhaps the most potent of the conflicts generated by slavery were those between slaves and their owners. Slaves were restricted in their movements, forced to work for little more than subsistence, subjected to corporal punishment, and afforded little or no legal redress for grievances. It might be expected that such conditions in the midst of an essentially democratic society would have induced longings for freedom as well as resentments provoking servile insurrections. Slaves who escaped from the South often wrote of their experiences in slavery in just such terms; and the elaborate precautions Southerners took to prevent revolt reflected their concern.

Yet even as they spoke of the dangers of slave revolts, Southerners attempted to deny their concern by insisting that the slaves were happy in their servitude. On the one hand, proslavery advocates insisted that slaves were better treated than abolitionist and antislavery proponents charged; indeed, black slaves received far better treatment than the white "wage slaves" of the North. On the other hand, defenders of slavery also insisted that blacks could never be freed and treated like whites because they were innately incapable of understanding and appreciating freedom; blacks had to be forced to work under the direction of whites in order to survive.

Thus the debate on the blacks' response to slavery is as old as the peculiar institution itself. And, until relatively recently, most historians have discussed the matter in much the same way as did the pro- and antislavery advocates of the antebellum years, drawing most of their evidence from the whites who participated in the antebellum debate and left their observations of slavery.

Modern historians, however, have shifted the emphasis significantly. Some have found more evidence of organized opposition and revolt among slaves than had previous historians. Others deny that the blacks' response to servitude must be seen as either docile acceptance or militant opposition. Some note that slaves effectively resisted in ways short of armed rebellion, while others argue that even within the restricted confines of a barbaric system, slaves found ways to protect themselves, to maintain their cultural identity, and to mitigate at least some of the rigors of their servitude. Much of this new work draws upon evidence left by the blacks themselves, evidence that earlier historians had simply ignored.

Although this shift in emphasis and the use of new sources have provided important new insights, they have not stilled the debate, as the following selections make clear.

Kenneth M. Stampp finds the slaves restive under their bondage, seeking always to lessen its restraints, willing to chance punishment in order to escape, and at times even attempting outright rebellion. Implicit in his approach to the black in this selection is a point of view that he expresses explicitly in the preface of the book from which the selection is taken: "I have assumed that the slaves were merely ordinary human beings, that innately Negroes are, after all, only white men with black skins, nothing more, nothing less." Blacks, in other words, could be expected to—and did—act the way whites, had they been enslaved, would have acted.

In the next selection, Robert William Fogel and Stanley L. Engerman argue that the slaves were efficient and productive workers largely because of the effective organization of plantation work, which was very often directed by the slaves themselves. The slaves were successful workers not because they were happy with their lot but because this course was the best available to them: ". . . though they longed for freedom, slaves could strive to develop and improve themselves in the only way that was open to them."

Eugene D. Genovese argues that the work rhythms of the slaves were those of the preindustrial system in which they lived. Moreover, he continues, the slaves, within the limitations imposed by a barbaric system, were able to develop their own work ethic, which was a part of the unique black culture that they were able to carve out for themselves under slavery. For Genovese blacks under slavery were able to forge a culture that provided them with living space within the system, a culture that remains the property of blacks today.

As these selections make clear, the response of blacks to slavery cannot be assessed simply by counting the numbers of armed revolts. We must look more deeply into the problem of how the experience of slavery affected the blacks themselves. Did the slaves respond to a system that they were powerless to alter by becoming highly motivated and efficient workers in hopes that this would mitigate the rigors of the system? Did the conditions of slavery produce resentments, frustrations, and a will to resist that led to day-to-day resistance and, when the possibility arose, to armed conflict and rebellion? Did the conflict between master and slave create an identifiable black identity and culture that became the means for black resistance to servitude?

Are the answers to these questions necessarily mutually exclusive? In what ways might resentment that sometimes led to revolt or to reluctant accommodation become the basis for the development of a unique black culture under slavery?

KENNETH M. STAMPP

A Troublesome Property

Slaves apparently thought of the South's peculiar institution chiefly as a system of labor extortion. Of course they felt its impact in other ways—in their social status, their legal status, and their private lives—but they felt it most acutely in their lack of control over their own time and labor. If discontented with bondage, they could be expected to direct their protests principally against the master's claim to their work. Whether the majority were satisfied with their lot, whether they willingly obeyed the master's commands, has long been a controversial question.

It may be a little presumptuous of one who has never been a slave to pretend to know how slaves felt; yet defenders of slavery did not hesitate to assert that most of them were quite content with servitude. Bondsmen generally were cheerful and acquiescent—so the argument went—because they were treated with kindness and relieved of all responsibilities; having known no other condition, they unthinkingly accepted bondage as their natural status. "They find themselves first existing in this state," observed a Northerner who had resided in Mississippi, "and pass through life without questioning the justice of their allotment, which, if they think at all, they suppose a natural one." Presumably they acquiesced, too, because of innate racial traits, because of the "genius of African temperament," the Negro being "instinctively . . . contented" and "quick to respond to the stimulus of joy, quick to forget his grief." Except in rare instances when he was cruelly treated, his "peaceful frame of mind was not greatly disturbed by the mere condition of slavery."

Though sometimes asserted with such assurance, it was never proved that the great majority of bondsmen had no concept of freedom and were therefore contented. It was always based upon inference. Most masters believed they understood their slaves, and most slaves apparently made no attempt to discourage this belief. Instead, they said the things they thought their masters wanted to

From *The Peculiar Institution*, by Kenneth M. Stampp. Copyright © 1956 by Kenneth M. Stampp. Reprinted by permission of Alfred A. Knopf, Inc.

hear, and they conformed with the rituals that signified their subservience. Rare, no doubt, was the master who never heard any of his humble, smiling bondsmen affirm their loyalty and contentment. When visitors in the South asked a slave whether he wished to be free, he usually replied: "No massa, me no want to be free, have good massa, take care of me when I sick, never 'buse nigger; no, me no want to be free."

This was dubious evidence, as some slaveholders knew and others learned. (They would have acknowledged the validity of an affirmation later to be made by a post-bellum South Carolinian: "the white man does not know the Negro so well as he thinks he does.") A Virginia master believed that slaves had their faculties "sharpened by constant exercise" and that their perceptions were "extremely fine and acute." An overseer decided that a man who "put his confidence in a Negro . . . was simply a Damned Fool." A Georgia planter concluded: "So deceitful is the Negro that as far as my own experience extends I could never in a single instance decipher his character. . . . We planters could never get at the truth." When advertising for runaways, masters repeatedly confirmed these opinions by describing them as being "very artful," as acting and conversing in a way "calculated to deceive almost any one," and (most frequently) as possessing a "pretty glib and plausible tongue." Yet proslavery writers swallowed whole the assurances of contentment which these glib-tongued "scoundrels" gave them.

Since there are few reliable records of what went on in the minds of slaves, one can only infer their thoughts and feelings from their behavior, that of their masters, and the logic of their situation. That they had no understanding of freedom, and therefore accepted bondage as their natural condition, is hard to believe. They had only to observe their masters and the other free men about them to obtain a very distinct idea of the meaning and advantages of freedom. All knew that some Negroes had been emancipated; they knew that freedom was a *possible* condition for any of them. They "continually have before their eyes, persons of the same color, many of whom they have known in slavery . . . freed from the control of masters, working where they please, going whither they please, and expending their money how they please." So declared a group of Charleston whites who petitioned the legislature to expel all free persons of color from South Carolina.

Untutored slaves seldom speculated about freedom as an abstraction. They naturally focused their interest upon such immediate and practical benefits as escaping severe discipline and getting increased compensation for less labor. An ex-slave explained simply what freedom meant to her: "I am now my own mistress, and need not work when I am sick. I can do my own thinkings, without having any to think for me,—to tell me when to come, what to do, and to sell me when they get ready." Though she may never have heard of the doctrine of natural rights, her concept of freedom surely embraced more than its incidental aspects.

If slaves had some understanding of the pragmatic benefits of freedom, no doubt most of them desired to enjoy these benefits. Some, perhaps the majority, had no more than a vague, unarticulated yearning for escape from burdens and restraints. They submitted, but submission did not necessarily mean enjoyment or even contentment. And some slaves felt more than a vague longing, felt a sharp pang and saw a clear objective. They struggled toward it against imposing obstacles, expressing their discontent through positive action.

Were these, the actively discontented, to be found only among slaves exposed to great physical cruelty? Apparently not. Slaves of gentle masters might seek freedom as eagerly as those of cruel ones. Frederick Douglass, the most famous refugee from slavery, testified: "Beat and cuff your slave, keep him hungry and spiritless, and he will follow the chain of his master like a dog; but feed and clothe him well,—work him moderately—surround him with physical comfort,—and dreams of freedom intrude. Give him a *bad* master, and he aspires to a *good* master; give him a good master, and he wishes to become his *own* master." Here was a problem confronting conscientious slaveholders. One confessed that slave-ownership subjected "the man of care and feeling to more dilemmas than perhaps any other vocation he could follow. . . . To moralize and induce the slave to assimilate with the master and his interest, has been and is, the great desideratum aimed at; but I am sorry to say I have long since desponded in the completion of this task." Another slaveholder who vaguely affirmed that his bondsmen were "as contented as their nature will permit" was in reality agreeing with what a white man once bluntly stated before the Louisiana Supreme Court: The desire for freedom "exists in the bosom of every slave—whether the recent captive, or him to whom bondage has become a habit."

Slaves showed great eagerness to get some—if they could not get all—of the advantages of freedom. They liked to hire their own time, or to work in tobacco factories, or for the Tredegar Iron Company, because they were then under less restraint than in the fields, and they had greater opportunities to earn money for themselves. They seized the chance to make their condition approximate that of freemen.

But they were not satisfied with a mere loosening of the bonds. Former slaves affirmed that one had to "know the *heart* of the poor slave—learn his secret thoughts—thoughts he dare not utter in the hearing of the white man," to understand this. "A man who has been in slavery knows, and no one else can know, the yearnings to be free, and the fear of making the attempt." While he was still in bondage Douglass wondered how white people knew that God had made black people to be slaves. "Did they go up in the sky and learn it? or, did He come down and tell them so?" A slave on a Louisiana sugar plantation assured Olmsted that slaves did desire freedom, that they talked about it among themselves, and that they speculated about what they would do if they were emancipated. When a traveler in Georgia told a slave he understood his people did not wish to be free, "His only answer was a short, contemptuous laugh."

If slaves yielded to authority most of the time, they did so because they usually saw no other practical choice. Yet few went through life without expressing discontent somehow, some time. Even the most passive slaves usually before they reached middle age, flared up in protests now and then. The majority, as they grew older, lost hope and spirit. Some, however, never quite gave in, never stopped fighting back in one way or another. The "bad character" of this "insolent," "surly," and "unruly" sort made them a liability to those who owned them, for a slave's value was measured by his disposition as much as by his strength and skills. Such rebels seldom won legal freedom, yet they never quite admitted they were slaves.

Slave resistance, whether bold and persistent or mild and sporadic, created for all slaveholders a serious problem of discipline. As authors or as readers they saw the problem discussed in numberless essays with such titles as "The Management of Negroes," essays which filled the pages of southern agricultural periodicals. Many masters had reason to agree with the owner of a hundred slaves who complained that he possessed "just 100 troubles," or with the North Carolina planter who said that slaves were "a troublesome property."

The record of slave resistance forms a chapter in the story of the endless struggle to give dignity to human life. Though the history of southern bondage reveals that men can be enslaved under certain conditions, it also demonstrates that their love of freedom is hard to crush. The subtle expressions of this spirit, no less than the daring thrusts for liberty, comprise one of the richest gifts the slaves have left to posterity. In making themselves "troublesome property," they provide reassuring evidence that slaves seldom wear their shackles lightly.

The record of the minority who waged ceaseless and open warfare against their bondage makes an inspiring chapter, also, in the history of Americans of African descent. True, these rebels were exceptional men, but the historian of any group properly devotes much attention to those members who did extraordinary things, men in whose lives the problems of their age found focus, men who voiced the feelings and aspirations of the more timid and less articulate masses. As the American Revolution produced folk heroes, so also did southern slavery—heroes who, in both cases, gave much for the cause of human freedom. . . .

The masses of slaves, for whom freedom could have been little more than an idle dream, found countless ways to exasperate their masters—and thus saw to it that bondage as a labor system had its limitations as well as its advantages. Many slaves were doubtless pulled by conflicting impulses: a desire for the personal satisfaction gained from doing a piece of work well, as against a desire to resist or outwit the master by doing it badly or not at all. Which impulse dominated a given slave at a given time depended upon many things, but the latter one was bound to control him at least part of the time. Whether the master was humane or cruel, whether he owned a small farm or a large plantation, did not seem to be crucial considerations, for almost all slaveholders had trouble in managing this kind of labor.

Not that every malingering or intractable bondsman was pursuing a course calculated to lead toward freedom for his people, or at least for himself. He was not always even making a conscious protest against bondage. Some of his "misdeeds" were merely unconscious reflections of the character that slavery had given him—evidence, as one planter explained, that slavery tended to render him "callous to the ideas of honor and even honesty" (as the master class understood those terms). "Come day, go day, God send Sunday," eloquently expressed the indifference of the "heedless, thoughtless," slave.

But the element of conscious resistance was often present too; whether or not it was the predominant one the master usually had no way of knowing. In any case, he was likely to be distressed by his inability to persuade his slaves to "assimilate" their interest with his. "We all know," complained one slaveholder, that the slave's feeling of obligation to his master "is of so flimsy a character that none of us rely upon it."

Slaveholders disagreed as to whether "smart" Negroes or "stupid" ones caused them the greater trouble. A Mississippian told Olmstead that the "smart" ones were "rascally" and constantly "getting into scrapes," and a Louisianian confessed that his slave Lucy was "the greatest rascal" and the "smartest negro of her age" he had ever known. On the other hand, many masters were annoyed by the seeming stupidity of some of their slaves, by their unwillingness to "think for themselves." A Negro recently imported from Africa was said to be especially prone to this kind of stubborn obtuseness: "let a hundred men shew him how to hoe, or drive a wheelbarrow, he'll still take the one by the Bottom and the other by the Wheel."

According to a former slave, the bondsmen had good reason for encouraging their master to underrate their intelligence. Ignorance was "a high virtue in a human chattel," he suggested, and since it was the master's purpose to keep his bondsmen in this state, they were shrewd enough to make him think he succeeded. A Virginia planter concluded from his own long experience that many slaveholders were victimized by the "sagacity" of Negroes whom they mistakenly thought they understood so well. He was convinced that the slaves, "under the cloak of great stupidity," made "dupes" of their masters: "The most general defect in the character of the negro, is hypocrisy; and this hypocrisy frequently makes him pretend to more ignorance than he possesses; and if his master treats him as a fool, he will be sure to act the fool's part. This is a very convenient trait, as it frequently serves as an apology for awkwardness and neglect of duty."

Slaveowners generally took it as a matter of course that a laborer would shirk when he could and perform no more work than he had to. They knew that, in most cases, the only way to keep him "in the straight path of duty" was to watch him "with an eye that never slumbers." They frequently used such terms as "slow," "lazy," "wants pushing," "an eye servant," and "a trifling negro" when they made private appraisals of their slaves. "Hands won't work unless I am in sight," a small Virginia planter once wrote angrily in his diary. "I left the Field at 12 [with] all going on well, but very little done after [that]." Olmsted, watching an overseer riding among the slaves on a South Carolina plantation, observed that he was "constantly directing and encouraging them, but . . . as often as he visited one end of the line of operations, the hands at the other end would discontinue their labor, until he turned to ride towards them again." Other visitors in the South also noticed "the furtive cessation from toil that invariably took place, as the overseer's eye was turned from them."

Slaves sought to limit the quantity of their services in many different ways. At cotton picking time they carried cotton from the gin house to the field in the morning to be weighed with the day's picking at night. They concealed dirt or rocks in their cotton baskets to escape punishment for loafing. They fixed their own work quotas, and masters had to adopt stern measures to persuade them that they had been unduly presumptuous. Where the task system was used, they stubbornly resisted any attempt to increase the size of the daily tasks fixed by custom. Athletic and muscular slaves, as Frederick Douglass recalled, were in-

clined to be proud of their capacity for labor, and the master often sought to promote rivalry among them; but they knew that this "was not likely to pay," for
"if, by extraordinary exertion, a large quantity of work was done in one day, the
fact becoming known to the master, might lead him to require the same amount
every day." Some refused to become skilled craftsmen, for, as one of them explained, he would gain nothing by learning a craft. Few seemed to feel any personal shame when dubbed "eye servants."

Slaves retaliated as best they could against those who treated them severely,
and sometimes their reprisals were at least partly successful. Experience taught
many slaveholders "that every attempt to force a slave beyond the limit that he
fixes himself as a sufficient amount of labor to render his master, instead of ex-
torting more work, only tends to make him unprofitable, unmanageable, a vexa-
tion and a curse. If you protract his regular hours of labor, his movements become proportionally slower." The use of force might cause him to work still more
slowly until he fell "into a state of impassivity" in which he became "insensible and
indifferent to punishment, or even to life." After a slave was punished in the Richmond tobacco factories, the other hands, "gave neither song nor careless shout for
days, while the bosses fretted at slackened production."

Besides slowing down, many slaves bedeviled the master by doing careless
work and by damaging property. They did much of this out of sheer irresponsi-
bility, but they did at least part of it deliberately, as more than one master suspected. A Louisiana doctor, Samuel W. Cartwright, attributed their work habit to
a disease, peculiar to Negroes, which he called *Dysaethesia Æthiopica* and which
overseers "erroneously" called "rascality." An African who suffered from this
exotic affliction was "apt to do much mischief" which appeared "as if intentional." He destroyed or wasted everything he touched, abused the livestock, and
injured the crops. When he was driven to his labor he performed his tasks "in a
headlong, careless manner, treading down with his feet or cutting with his hoe
the plants" he was supposed to cultivate, breaking his tools, and "spoiling everything." This, wrote the doctor soberly, was entirely due to "the stupidness of
mind and insensibility of the nerves induced by the disease."

But slaveowners ignored this clinical analysis and persisted in diagnosing the
disease as nothing but "rascality." To overcome it, they had to supervise the
work closely. They searched for methods to prevent slaves from abusing horses
and mules, plowing and hoeing "badly," damaging tools, killing young plants,
and picking "trashy cotton." James H. Hammond noted in his diary: "I find
[hoe-hands] chopping up cotton dreadfully and begin to think that my stand has
every year been ruined in this way." A Louisiana sugar planter advised his son to
turn to cotton production, because it was "trouble enough to have to manage negroes in the simplest way, without having to overlook them in the manufacture of
sugar and management of Machinery." "Rascality" was also a major problem for
those who employed slaves in factories.

Olmsted found slaveholders fretting about this problem everywhere in the
South. In Texas an angry mistress complained that her domestics constantly
tracked mud through the house: "What do they care? They'd just as lief clean
the mud after themselves as [do] anything else—*their time isn't any value to
themselves.*" A Virginia planter said that he grew only the coarser and cheaper

tobaccos, because the finer varieties "required more pains-taking and discretion than it was possible to make a large gang of negroes use." Another Virginian complained that slaves were "excessively careless and wasteful, and, in various ways . . . subject us to very annoying losses." Some masters used only crude, clumsy tools, because they were afraid to give their hands better ones. One slaveholder felt aggrieved when he saw that the small patches which his Negroes cultivated for themselves were better cared for and more productive than his own fields.

Masters were also troubled by the slave who idled in quarters because of an alleged illness or disability. They often suspected that they were being victimized, for feigning illness was a favorite method of avoiding labor. Olmsted found one or more bondsmen "complaining" on almost every plantation he visited, and the proprietor frequently expressed "his suspicion that the invalid was really as well able to work as anyone else." Some masters and overseers believed that they could tell when a slave was deceiving them, but others were afraid to risk permanent injury to their human property. According to one overseer, trying to detect those who were "shamming illness" was "the most disagreeable duty he had to perform. Negroes were famous for it."

Slave women had great success with this stratagem. The overseer on Pierce Butler's Georgia plantation reported that they were constantly "shamming themselves into the family-way in order to obtain a diminution of their labor." One female enjoyed a "protracted pseudo-pregnancy" during which she "continued to reap increased rations as the reward of her expectation, till she finally had to disappoint and receive a flogging." A Virginian asserted that a slave woman was a less profitable worker after reaching the "breeding age," because she so often pretended to be suffering from what were delicately called "female complaints." "You have to take her word for it . . . and you dare not set her to work; and so she will lay up till she feels like taking the air again, and plays the lady at your expense."

Almost every slaveholder discovered at one time or another that a bondsman had outwitted him by "playing possum" or by some ingenious subterfuge. One Negro spread powdered mustard on his tongue to give it a foul appearance before he was examined by a doctor. Another convinced his owner that he was totally disabled by rheumatism, until one day he was discovered vigorously rowing a boat. A master found two of his slaves "grunting" (a common term), one affecting a partial paralysis and the other declaring that he could not walk; but he soon learned that they "used their limbs very well when they chose to do so." For many years a slave on a Mississippi plantation escaped work by persuading his master that he was nearly blind. After the Civil War, however, he produced "no less than eighteen good crops for himself" and became one of "the best farmers in the country."

In these and other ways a seemingly docile gang of slaves drove an inefficient manager well nigh to distraction. They probed for his weaknesses, matched their wits against his, and constantly contrived to disrupt the work routine. An efficient manager took cognizance of the fact that many of his bondsmen were "shrewd and cunning," ever ready to "disregard all reasonable restraints," and eager "to practice upon the old maxim of 'give an inch and take an ell.' " This was the reason why the owner of a small cotton plantation rejoiced when at last he could afford to employ an overseer: "I feel greatly relieved at the idea of getting a lazy trifling set of negroes off my hands. . . . They have wearied out all the patience I had with them.". . .

For the most part the slaves who thus provoked masters and overseers were the meek, smiling ones whom many thought were contented though irresponsible. They were not reckless rebels who risked their lives for freedom; if the thought of rebellion crossed their minds, the odds against success seemed too overwhelming to attempt it. But the inevitability of their bondage made it none the more attractive. And so, when they could, they protested by shirking their duties, injuring the crops, feigning illness, and disrupting the routine. These acts were, in part, an unspectacular kind of "day to day resistance to slavery."

According to Dr. Cartwright, there was a . . . disease peculiar to Negroes which he called *Drapetomania:* "the disease causing negroes to run away." Cartwright believed that it was a "disease of the mind" and that with "proper medical advice" it could be cured. The first symptom was a "sulky and dissatisfied" attitude. To forestall the full onset of the disease, the cause of discontent must be determined and removed. If there were no ascertainable cause, then "whipping the devil out of them" was the proper "preventive measure against absconding."

Though Cartwright's dissertations on Negro diseases are mere curiosities of medical history, the problem he dealt with was a real and urgent one to nearly every slaveholder. Olmsted met few planters, large or small, who were not more or less troubled by runaways. A Mississippian realized that his record was most unusual when he wrote in his diary: "Harry ran away; *the first* negro that ever ran from me." Another slaveholder betrayed his concern when he avowed that he would "rather a negro would do anything Else than run away."

The number of runaways was not large enough to threaten the survival of the peculiar institution, because slaveholders took precautions to prevent the problem from growing to such proportions. But their measures were never entirely successful, as the advertisements for fugitives in southern newspapers made abundantly clear. Actually, the problem was much greater than these newspapers suggested, because many owners did not advertise for their absconding property. (When an owner did advertise, he usually waited until his slave had been missing for several weeks.) In any case, fugitive slaves were numbered in the thousands every year. It was an important form of protest against bondage.

Who were the runaways? They were generally young slaves, most of them under thirty, but occasionally masters searched for fugitives who were more than sixty years old. The majority of them were males, though female runaways were by no means uncommon. It is not true that most of them were mulattoes or of predominantly white ancestry. While this group was well represented among the fugitives, they were outnumbered by slaves who were described as "black" or of seemingly "pure" African ancestry. Domestics and skilled artisans—the ones who supposedly had the most intimate ties with the master class—ran away as well as common field-hands. . . .

"His look is impudent and insolent, and he holds himself straight and walks well." So a Louisiana master described James, a runaway slave. There were always bondsmen like James. In 1669, a Virginia statute referred to "the obstinacy of many of them"; in 1802, a South Carolina judge declared that they were "in general a headstrong, stubborn race of people"; and in 1859, a committee of a South Carolina agricultural society complained of the "insolence of disposition to which, as a race, they were remarkably liable." An overseer on a Louisiana plantation wrote nervously about the many "outrageous acts" recently committed by slaves in his locality and insisted that he scarcely had time to eat and sleep: "The truth is no man can begin to attend to Such a business with any Set of negroes, without the Strictest vigilance on his part." It was the minority of slaves whom his discipline could not humble (the "insolent," "surly," and "unruly" ones) that worried this overseer—and slaveholders generally. These were the slaves whose discontent drove them to drastic measures.

Legally the offenses of the rebels ranged from petty misdemeanors to capital crimes, and they were punished accordingly. The master class looked upon any offense as more reprehensible (and therefore subject to more severe penalties) when committed by a slave than when committed by a free white. But how can one determine the proper ethical standards for identifying undesirable or even criminal behavior among slaves? How distinguish a "good" from a "bad" slave? Was the "good" slave the one who was courteous and loyal to his master, and who did his work faithfully and cheerfully? Was the "bad" slave the one who would not submit to his master, and who defiantly fought back? What were the limits, if any, to which a man deprived of his freedom could properly go in resisting bondage? How accountable was a slave to a legal code which gave him more penalties than protection and was itself a bulwark of slavery? This much at least can be said: many slaves rejected the answers which their masters gave to questions such as these. The slaves did not thereby repudiate law and morality: rather, they formulated legal and moral codes of their own.

The white man's laws against theft, for example, were not supported by the slave's code. In demonstrating the "absence of moral principle" among bondsmen, one master observed: "To steal and not to be detected is a merit among them." Let a master turn his back, wrote another, and some "cunning fellow" would appropriate part of his goods. No slave would betray another, for an informer was held "in greater detestation than the most notorious thief."

If slaveholders are to be believed, petty theft was an almost universal "vice"; slaves would take anything that was not under lock and key. Field-hands killed hogs and robbed the corn crib. House servants helped themselves to wines, whiskey, jewelry, trinkets, and whatever else was lying about. Fugitives sometimes gained from their master unwilling help in financing the journey to freedom, the advertisements often indicating that they absconded with money, clothing, and a horse or mule. Thefts were not necessarily confined to the master's goods: any white man might be considered fair game.

Some bondsmen engaged in theft on more than a casual and petty basis. They made a business of it and thus sought to obtain comforts and luxuries which were usually denied them. A South Carolina master learned his house servants had been regularly looting his wine cellar and that one of them was involved in an elaborate "system of roguery." A planter in North Carolina found that three of his slaves had "for some months been carrying on a robbery" of meat and lard, the leader being "a young carpenter, remarkable for smartness . . . and no less worthy for his lamentable deficiency in common honesty."

If the stolen goods were not consumed directly, they were traded to whites or to free Negroes. This illegal trade caused masters endless trouble, for slaves were always willing to exchange plantation products for tobacco, liquor, or small sums of money. Southern courts were kept busy handling the resulting prosecutions. One slaveholder discovered that his bondsmen had long been engaged in an extensive trade in corn. "Strict vigilance," he concluded, was necessary "to prevent them from theft; particularly when dishonesty is inherent, as is probably the case with some of them." Dishonesty, as the master understood the term, indeed seemed to be a common if not an inherent trait of southern slaves.

The slaves, however, had a somewhat different definition of dishonesty in their own code, to which they were reasonably faithful. For appropriating their master's goods they might be punished and denounced by him, but they were not likely to be disgraced among their associates in the slave quarters, who made a distinction between "stealing" and "taking." Appropriating things from the master meant simply taking part of his property for the benefit of another part or, as Frederick Douglass phrased it, "taking his meat out of one tub, and putting it in another." Thus a female domestic who had been scolded for the theft of some trinkets was reported to have replied: "Law, mam, don't say I's wicked; ole Aunt Ann says its allers right for us poor colored people to 'popiate whatever of de wite folk's blessings de Lord puts in our way." Stealing, on the other hand, meant appropriating something that belonged to another slave, and this was an offense which slaves did not condone.

The prevalence of theft was a clear sign that slaves were discontented, at least with the standard of living imposed upon them. They stole food to increase or enrich their diets or to trade for other coveted commodities. Quite obviously they learned from their masters the pleasures that could be derived from the possession of worldly goods; and when the opportunity presented itself, they "took" what was denied them as slaves.

Next to theft, arson was the most common slave "crime," one which slaveholders dreaded almost constantly. Fire was a favorite means for aggrieved slaves to even the score with their master. Reports emanated periodically from some region or other that there was an "epidemic" of gin-house burnings, or that some bondsman had taken his revenge by burning the slave quarters or other farm buildings. More than one planter thus saw the better part of a year's harvest go up in flames. Southern newspapers and court records are filled with illustrations of this offense, and with evidence of the severe penalties inflicted upon those found guilty of committing it.

Another "crime" was what might be called self-sabotage, a slave deliberately unfitting himself to labor for his master. An Arkansas slave, "at any time to save an hour's work," could "throw his left shoulder out of place." A Kentucky slave made himself unserviceable by downing medicines from his master's dispensary (thus showing a better understanding of the value of these nostrums than his owner). A slave woman was treated as an invalid because of "swillings in her arms"—until it was discovered that she produced this condition by thrusting her arms periodically into a beehive. Yellow Jacob, according to his master's plantation journal, "had a kick from a mule and when nearly well would bruise it and by that means kept from work." Another Negro, after being punished by his owner, retaliated by cutting off his right hand; still another cut off the fingers of one hand to avoid being sold to the Deep South.

A few desperate slaves carried this form of resistance to the extreme of self-destruction. Those freshly imported from Africa and those sold away from friends and relatives were especially prone to suicide. London, a slave on a Georgia rice plantation, ran to the river and drowned himself after being threatened with a whipping. His overseer gave orders to leave the corpse untouched "to let the [other] negroes see [that] when a negro takes his own life they will be treated in this manner." A Texas planter bewailed the loss of a slave woman who hanged herself after two unsuccessful breaks for freedom: "I had been offered $900.00 for her not two months ago, but damn her . . . I would not have had it happened for twice her value. *The fates pursue me.*"

Some runaways seemed determined to make their recapture as costly as possible and even resisted at the risk of their own lives. One advertisement, typical of many, warned that an escaped slave was a "resolute fellow" who would probably not be taken without a "show of competent force." When, after a day-long chase, three South Carolina fugitives were cornered, they "fought desperately," inflicted numerous wounds upon their pursuers with a barrage of rocks, and "refused to surrender until a force of about forty-five or fifty men arrived." In southern court records there are numerous cases of runaway slaves who killed whites or were themselves killed in their frantic efforts to gain freedom.

In one dramatic case, a Louisiana fugitive was detected working as a free Negro on a Mississippi River flatboat. His pursuers, trailing him with a pack of "Negro dogs," finally found him "standing at bay upon the outer edge of a large raft of drift wood, armed with a club and pistol." He threatened to kill anyone who got near him. "Finding him obstinately determined not to surrender, one of his pursuers shot him. He fell at the third fire, and so determined was he not to be captured, that when an effort was made to rescue him from drowning he made battle with his club, and sunk waving his weapon in angry defiance."

An effort to break up an organized gang of runaways was a dangerous business, because they were often unwilling to surrender without a fight. The fugitives in one well-armed band in Alabama were building a fort at the time they were discovered. Their camp was destroyed after a "smart skirmish" during which three of them were killed. Such encounters did not always end in defeat for the slaves; some runaway bands successfully resisted all attempts at capture and remained at large for years.

Ante-bellum records are replete with acts of violence committed by individual slaves upon masters, overseers, and other whites. A Texan complained, in 1853, that cases of slaves murdering white men were becoming "painfully frequent." "Within the last year or two many murders have taken place, by negroes upon their owners," reported a Louisiana newspaper. And a Florida editor once wrote: "It is our painful duty to record another instance of the destruction of the life of a white man by a slave."

Many masters owned one or more bondsmen whom they feared as potential murderers. A Georgia planter remembered Jack, his plantation carpenter, "the most notoriously bad character and worst Negro of the place." Jack "was the only Negro ever in our possession who I considered capable of Murdering me, or burning my dwelling at night, or capable of committing any act."

Slaves like Jack could be watched closely; but others appeared to be submissive until suddenly they turned on their masters. Even trusted house servants might give violent expression to long pent up feelings. One "first rate" female domestic, while being punished, abruptly attacked her mistress, "threw her down, and beat her unmercifully on the head and face." A "favorite body servant" of a "humane master who rarely or never punished his slaves" one day became insolent. Unwilling to be disciplined, this slave waylaid his owner, "knocked him down with a whiteoak club, and beat his head to a pumice." Here was another reason why it seemed foolish for a master to put his "confidence in a Negro."

At times these acts of violence appeared to be for "no cause"—that is, they resulted from a slave's "bad disposition" rather than from a particular grievance. But more often they resulted from a clash of personalities, or from some specific incident. For example, a slave who had been promised freedom in his master's will, poisoned his master to hasten the day of liberation. A South Carolina bondsman was killed during a fight with an overseer who had whipped his son. In North Carolina a slave intervened while the overseer was whipping his wife, and in the ensuing battle the overseer met his death.

The most common provocation to violence was the attempt of a master or overseer either to work or to punish slaves severely. An Alabama bondsman confessed killing the overseer because "he was a hard down man on him, and said he was going to be harder." Six Louisiana slaves together killed an overseer and explained in their confession that they found it impossible to satisfy him. Three North Carolina slaves killed their master when they decided that "the old man was too hard on them, and they must get rid of him." During one of these crises an overseer called upon his hands to help him punish an "unmanageable" slave: "not one of them paid the least attention to me but kept on at their work." These encounters did not always lead to death, but few plantations escaped without at least one that might easily have ended in tragedy. "Things move on here in the old Style except that now and then a refractory negro has to be taken care of," was the offhand comment of a planter.

Sometimes a slave who showed sufficient determination to resist punishment managed to get the best of his owner or overseer. A proud bondsman might vow that, regardless of the consequences, he would permit no one to whip him. An overseer thought twice before precipitating a major crisis with a strong-willed slave; he might even overlook minor infractions of discipline.

But an impasse such as this was decidedly unusual; if it had not been, slavery itself would have stood in jeopardy. Ordinarily these clashes between master and slave were fought out to a final settlement, and thus a thread of violence was woven into the pattern of southern bondage. Violence, indeed, was the method of resistance adopted by the boldest and most discontented slaves. Its usual reward, however, was not liberty but death!

No ante-bellum Southerner could ever forget Nat Turner. The career of this man made an impact upon the people of this section as great as that of John C. Calhoun or Jefferson Davis. Yet Turner was only a slave in Southampton County,

Virginia—and during most of his life a rather unimpressive one at that. He was a pious man, a Baptist exhorter by avocation, apparently as humble and docile as a slave was expected to be. There is no evidence that he was underfed, overworked, or treated with special cruelty. If Nat Turner could not be trusted, what slave could? That was what made his sudden deed so frightening.

Somehow Turner came to believe that he had been divinely chosen to deliver his people from bondage, and he persuaded several other slaves to assist him. In due time he saw the sign for which he had waited, and early in the morning of August 22, 1831, he and his followers rose in rebellion. They began by killing the family to whom Turner belonged. As they marched through the Southampton countryside they gained additional recruits, making a total of about seventy. (Others seemed ready to join if the rebels came their way. The slave Jacob, for example, proclaimed "that if they came by he would join them and assist in killing all the white people.") Within two days they killed nearly sixty whites. They could have killed more. They left undisturbed at least one poor white family, "because they thought no better of themselves than they did of the negroes." To justify the killings, members of Turner's band declared that they had had enough of punishment, or that they now intended to be as rich as their masters. One rebel demonstrated his new status by walking off in his late owner's shoes and socks.

The Nat Turner rebellion lasted only forty-eight hours. Swiftly mobilizing in overwhelming strength, the whites easily dispersed the rebels. Then followed a massacre during which not only the insurrectionists but scores of innocent bondsmen were slaughtered. Others, charged with "feloniously consulting, advising and conspiring . . . to rebel . . . and making insurrection and taking the lives of divers free white persons of this Commonwealth," were tried before a court of oyer and terminer during the months of September and October. Some were executed, others transported. Most of those transported had not actively participated in the rebellion; they had merely expressed sympathy for the rebels.

Nat Turner himself was not captured until October 30, more than two months after the uprising. He was brought to trial on November 5, convicted the same day, and hanged six days later. Thus ended an event which produced in the South something resembling a mass trauma, from which the whites had not recovered three decades later. The danger that other Nat Turners might emerge, that an even more serious insurrection might some day occur, became an enduring concern as long as the peculiar institution survived. Proslavery writers boldly asserted that Southerners did not fear their slaves, that a rebellion of the laboring class was more likely to transpire in the North than in the South; but the fear of rebellion, sometimes vague, sometimes acute, was with them always.

Though it was the most disastrous (for both slaves and masters), Nat Turner's was not the first insurrection. Several earlier conspiracies, which narrowly missed being carried into execution, might easily have precipitated rebellions much more extensive than that of Turner. These uprisings and conspiracies began as early as the seventeenth century and kept Southerners apprehensive throughout the colonial period. The preamble to the South Carolina statute of 1740 defining the duties of slave patrols stated that many "horrible and barbarous massacres" had been committed or plotted by the slaves who were "generally prone to such cruel practices." On the eve of the American Revolution a

Charlestonian wrote about a "disturbance" among the bondsmen who had "mimicked their betters in crying *Liberty*." In 1785, a West Florida slaveholder was dismayed to learn that several of his slaves were involved in an insurrection plot: "Of what avail is kindness and good usage when rewarded by such ingratitude . . . [?]" Such incidents set the pattern for the nineteenth century.

The new century opened with the Gabriel Conspiracy (August, 1800) in Henrico County, Virginia, in which at least a thousand slaves were implicated. The warnings of two bondsmen and a severe storm enabled the whites to forestall a projected march upon Richmond. A decade later some five hundred slaves in St. John the Baptist Parish, Louisiana, armed with cane knives and other crude weapons, advanced toward New Orleans. But the planters and a strong detachment of troops put them to flight. In 1822, Denmark Vesey, a free Negro in Charleston, planned a vast conspiracy which came to nothing after it was given away by a slave. These and other plots were invariably followed by severe reprisals, including the indiscriminate killing of slaves as well as mass executions after regular trials. The heads of sixteen Louisiana rebels were stuck upon poles along the Mississippi River as a grim warning to other slaves. After the Vesey conspiracy, Charlestonians expressed disillusionment with the idea that by generous treatment the slaves "would become more satisfied with their condition and more attached to the whites."

The shock of Nat Turner caused Southerners to take preventive measures, but these never eliminated their apprehensions or the actual danger. Hardly a year passed without some kind of alarming disturbance somewhere in the South. When no real conspiracy existed, wild rumors often agitated the whites and at times came close to creating an insurrection panic. The rumors might be entirely unfounded, or they might grow out of some local incident which was magnified by exaggeration. Even the historian cannot always distinguish between the rumors and the facts. Most of the stories seem to have had a foundation in at least a minor disturbance, limited perhaps to a single plantation where the slaves suddenly became insubordinate, or to a whole neighborhood where they showed signs of becoming restive. Whether caused by rumor or fact, the rebellion often troubled the sleep of the master class.

The Turner rebellion itself produced an insurrection panic that swept the entire South. A Richmond editor wondered whether the southern press was trying to give the slaves "false conceptions of their numbers and capacity, by exhibiting the terror and confusion of the whites, and to induce them to think that practicable, which they see is so much feared by their superiors." In eastern North Carolina the panic caused the arrest of scores of slaves and the execution of more than a dozen. A South Carolinian reported that there was "considerable alarm" in his state too and that some slaves were hanged to prevent a rumored uprising. The excitement spread into the Southwest where it was feared that bondsmen would become "troublesome." A Mississippian, confessing "great apprehension," noted that "within 4 hours march of Natchez" there were "2200 able bodied male slaves." He warned: "It behooves [us] to be vigilant—but silent."

Similar insurrection panics developed from time to time thereafter. In 1835, one of these frightful disturbances centered in Mississippi and Louisiana; before it subsided, numerous bondsmen had been legally or extralegally executed. This panic even spread into Roane County in East Tennessee, though that county contained a very small slave population. There was "a great deal of talk and some dread of the negroes rising at Christmas or new year," reported a local slaveholder. "I can not say that I have had much fear of their rising here, but have thought it right to be careful and watchful. It is a disagreeable state of living to be ever suspicious of those with whom we live." This point was illustrated by a not uncommon incident in a small village on the Eastern Shore of Virginia. One night in 1849, the firing of guns "alarmed the people very much. They at once thought that the Slaves had risen to murder the white people. Many immediately left their houses and fled to the woods. . . . But it was afterwards ascertained that it was a false alarm." This was indeed a "disagreeable state of living"!

The most acute and widespread insurrection panics, after the Turner rebellion, occurred in 1856 and 1860, each of them resulting in part from the rise of the Republican party and the exciting political campaigns. On both occasions alarming stories of huge conspiracies spread through every slave state, stories frequently mentioning "unscrupulous" white men (presumably abolitionist emissaries like John Brown) who were "tampering" with the Negroes and encouraging them to rebel. "All at once, in Kentucky, Tennessee, Missouri, Arkansas, Louisiana and Texas, it is discovered that the slaves are meditating schemes of insurrection," proclaimed a Richmond newspaper in a hysterical editorial. "From almost every point in the Southwest, rumors of insurrectionary movements among the negroes come upon us with more or less distinct and authentic detail." In Virginia, as a slaveholder noted, "reports of negro plots" had "induced proper measures of vigilance." A South Carolinian observed privately that there was "a good deal of anxiety," but little was being said about it, "as every one felt it should not be the subject of general talk." In Texas, one of the principal centers of these insurrection panics, vigilance committees were hastily formed to deal with the expected emergency. On these occasions, as on others, there was some substance to the rumors, however much they were exaggerated. In 1856 slave unrest did increase noticeably in certain areas, including Texas, where there was at least one well authenticated conspiracy.

Sometimes rebellions took odd forms. The Seminole War in Florida was in part a slave revolt, for many fugitive Negroes fought alongside the Indian warriors. In 1841, a group of slaves being carried from Virginia to New Orleans on the brig *Creole* rose in rebellion, seized the ship, and sailed it to the Bermudas. In 1848, about seventy-five slaves from Fayette County, Kentucky, led by a white man, made a break for the Ohio River. They waged a brisk battle with their pursuers before they were forced to surrender. More than forty of them were tried for "most wickedly, seditiously, and rebelliously" making a "public insurrection." Three of the slaves were executed, and their white leader was sentenced to twenty years in prison.

One of the last ante-bellum slave conspiracies occurred in October, 1860, in the neighborhood of Plymouth, in eastern North Carolina. It began when a score of slaves met in a swamp to plan an insurrection. Their plan was to persuade several hundred bondsmen to join them in a march on Plymouth; they would kill all the whites they met on the road, burn the town, take money and weapons, and escape by ship through Albemarle Sound. The plot was betrayed by a slave, and once again panic spread throughout the neighborhood. "When I reached Plymouth," wrote a local planter, "the town was in the greatest of commotion, and, as even calm persons thought, with some reason." The country people were "so much excited and alarmed as to vow themselves as ready to slaughter the negroes indiscriminately." This planter believed that during an insurrection panic "the negroes are in much more danger from the non slave holding whites than the whites are from the negroes." He was probably right, though the slaveholders were hardly less inclined, on that account, to be ruthless whenever rumors of rebellion swept through the land.

That there was no slave conspiracy comparable to Denmark Vesey's and no rebellion comparable to Nat Turner's, during the three decades before the Civil War, has been explained in many ways. The explanations, however, do not sufficiently emphasize the impact which the Turner rebellion had on the slaves themselves. The speed with which it was crushed and the massacre that followed were facts soon known, doubtless, to every slave in Virginia and, before long, to almost every slave in the South. Among the Negroes everywhere, news generally spread so far and so fast as to amaze the whites. The Turner story was not likely to encourage slaves to make new attempts to win their freedom by fighting for it. They now realized that they would face a united white community, well armed and quite willing to annihilate as much of the black population as might seem necessary.

In truth, no slave uprising ever had a chance of ultimate success, even though it might have cost the master class heavy casualties. The great majority of the disarmed and outnumbered slaves, knowing the futility of rebellion, refused to join in any of the numerous plots. Most slaves had to express their desire for freedom in less dramatic ways. They rarely went beyond disorganized individual action—which, to be sure, caused their masters no little annoyance. The bondsmen themselves lacked the power to destroy the web of bondage. They would have to have the aid of free men inside or outside the South.

The survival of slavery, then, cannot be explained as due to the contentment of slaves or their failure to comprehend the advantages of freedom. They longed for liberty and resisted bondage as much as any people could have done in their circumstances, but their longing and their resistance were not enough even to render the institution unprofitable to most masters. The masters had power and, as will be seen, they developed an elaborate technique of slave control. Their very preoccupation with this technique was, in itself, a striking refutation of the myth that slavery survived because of the cheerful acquiescence of the slaves.

ROBERT WILLIAM FOGEL
AND STANLEY L. ENGERMAN

The Quality of Slave Labor and Racism

Perhaps the most important technological advance within the agricultural
sector of the South after 1800 was in the realm of management, particularly
in the development of organizational methods which permitted southern planters
to capture the potential benefits of economies of large-scale operation. It must be
remembered that the shift from the production of grain and tobacco to cotton,
sugar, and rice coincided with a substantial increase in the average size of slaveholdings. The optimal farm size appears to have differed by crop. There is little
evidence of economies of scale in grain production; and economies of scale appear to have been fairly limited in tobacco production. Thus, farms located in
counties specializing in these crops grew little between 1790 and 1860. On the
eve of the Civil War the average size of Virginia slaveholdings was still only 18.8,
while the county averages in the alluvial regions of short-staple cotton production ranged as high as one hundred and twenty-five slaves per holding. By the last
decade prior to the Civil War the optimal size (minimum size of the most efficient
farms) had increased to approximately fifty slaves in the cotton lands of the black
belt and to over two hundred slaves in counties of the alluvial lands along the
Mississippi. Indeed by the last decade of the slave era, the ability to provide efficient management appears to have become the main constraint on the optimal
size of plantations.

One should not leap to the conclusion that this finding supports the stereotype of planters as a class of "idlers" who lacked "steady habits and frugal instincts," and who usually entrusted the primary management of their plantations
to inept, cruel overseers while they indulged their taste for pleasure in various
cities of the South, the North, or of Europe. No doubt such planters existed. But
they were a distinct minority. Among moderate-sized holdings (sixteen to fifty

---

slaves) less than one out of every six plantations used a white overseer. On large slaveholdings (over fifty slaves) only one out of every four owners used white overseers. Even on estates with more than one hundred slaves, the proportion with white overseers was just 30 percent, and on many of these the planters were usually in residence.

The continual discussions of problems of plantation management in the agricultural journals of the South were not evidence of the failure of southern planters but of the earnestness with which they approached their tasks. Far from being cavalier fops, the leading planters were, on the whole, a highly self-conscious class of entrepreneurs who generally approached their governmental responsibilities with deliberation and gravity—a manner which accorded with their self-image. They strove to become steeped in the scientific agricultural literature of the day; they organized agricultural societies as a means of disseminating information on the "best practices" in various aspects of farming, and in order to encourage experimentation in animal husbandry, agronomy, horticulture, and related matters; and they established journals in which they could report their findings as well as debate the full range of problems that they encountered in plantation management.

No question was treated with more gravity than that of labor management. Planters recognized that this was the critical issue. Economic success rode or fell with it. No aspect of slave management was considered too trivial to be omitted from consideration or debate. Details of housing, diet, medical care, marriage, child rearing, holidays, incentives and punishments, alternative methods of organizing field labor, the duties of managerial personnel, and even the manner or air to be assumed by a planter in his relationship with his slaves were all deemed worthy of debate. Discussions of diet included such matters as the balance between meat, vegetables, grains, and dairy products, and virtues of fat versus lean meats, and the optimum method of food distribution and preparation. With respect to housing, planters debated the respective merits of single- and multi-family dwellings, the benefits and costs of various types of building materials, the design of chimneys, and the optimum spatial distribution of slave houses and other buildings. On marriage and the family, the debate included such issues as whether or not slaves should be permitted to marry across plantations, and the latitude to be allowed to drivers and overseers in the mediation of intra- as well as interfamily disputes. Debates around the incentive structure turned on such matters as the relative advantages of gifts or cash bonuses versus allotments of plots of land, the types of crops that slaves could grow on their individual plots, whether or not slaves should be permitted to have quasi-property rights in the small livestock, and whether slaves should be permitted to market their own crops and livestock or should be required to sell them to the planter at prevailing market prices.

Whatever the differences among planters in the resolution of these particular issues, there was widespread agreement that the ultimate objective of slave management was the creation of a highly disciplined, highly specialized, and well-coordinated labor force. Specialization and interdependence were the hallmarks of the medium- and large-sized plantations. On family-sized farms, each worker had to fulfill a multiplicity of duties according to a pace and pattern which were quite flexible and largely independent of the activities of others. On plantations, the hands were as rigidly organized as in a factory. Each hand was assigned to a set of tasks which occupied him throughout the year, or at least through particular seasons of the year. There were drivers, plowmen, hoe hands, harrowers, seed sowers, coverers, sorters, ginners, packers, milkmaids, stock minders, carpenters, blacksmiths, nurses, and cooks—to give only a partial listing.

With respect to field labor, the various hands were formed into gangs or teams in which the interdependence of labor was a crucial element. During the planting period the interdependence arose largely from within each gang. A planting gang consisted of five types of hands who followed one another in a fixed procession. Leading off the procession were plowmen who ridged up the unbroken earth; then came harrowers who broke up the clods; then drillers who created the holes to receive the seeds, each hole a prescribed distance apart from the next one; then droppers who planted the seeds in the holes; and finally rakers who covered up the holes. The intensity of the pace of these gangs was maintained in three ways.

First, by choosing as the plowmen and harrowers who led off the planting operation the strongest and ablest hands.

Second, by the interdependence of each type of hand on the other. (For as on an assembly line, this interdependence generated a pressure on all those who worked in the gang to keep up with the pace of the leaders.)

Third, by assigning drivers or foremen who exhorted the leaders, threatened the laggards, and did whatever was necessary to ensure both the pace and the quality of each gang's labor.

During the period of cultivation, this interdependence, and the productive tension which it created, stemmed to a considerable extent from the interaction between gangs. Field hands were divided into two groups; the hoe gang and the plow gang. The hoe hands chopped out the weeds which surrounded the cotton plants as well as excessive sprouts of cotton plants. The plow gangs followed behind, stirring the soil near the rows of cotton plants and tossing it back around the plants. Thus the hoe and plow gangs each put the other under an assembly-line type of pressure. The hoeing had to be completed in time to permit the plow hands to carry out their tasks. At the same time the progress of the hoeing, which entailed lighter labor than plowing, set a pace for the plow gang. The drivers or overseers moved back and forth between the two gangs, exhorting and prodding each to keep up with the pace of the other, as well as inspecting the quality of the work.

This feature of plantation life—the organization of slaves into highly disciplined, interdependent teams capable of maintaining a steady and intense rhythm of work—appears to be the crux of the superior efficiency of large-scale operations on plantations, at least as far as fieldwork was concerned. It is certainly the factor which slaveowners themselves frequently singled out as the key to the superiority of the plantation system of organization. Although Olmsted repeatedly reported that planters preferred slave labor to white labor because slaves "could be driven," the significance of these statements completely eluded him. White men, said one planter, "are not used to steady labour, they work reluctantly, and will not bear driving; they cannot be worked to advantage with slaves, and it is inconvenient to look after them, if you work them separately." A slaveholder who listened to Olmsted's report of his conversation with Griscom, the Northerner who claimed that slave laborers produced only one fourth as much output per day as northern laborers, responded that these slaves "could not have been well 'driven.' " Another reported that "he would never have white people at ordinary work, because he couldn't drive them." Still another said: "You never could depend on white men, and you couldn't *drive* them any; they wouldn't stand it. Slaves were the only reliable laborers. . . ." The conclusion that Olmsted drew from such reports was not that slave labor in the plantation context was of a superior quality, but that southern free laborers must have been extremely lazy, inept, and of low quality compared to northern laborers.

Even on those few occasions when Olmsted actually witnessed gangs working in the field, he failed to appreciate the significance of slave team-work, coordination, and intensity of effort, although he faithfully recorded these features of their work. The hoe gang, he reported on one of these instances, "numbered nearly two hundred hands (for the force of two plantations was working together), moving across the field in parallel lines, with a considerable degree of precision. I repeatedly rode through the lines at a canter, with other horsemen, often coming upon them suddenly, without producing the smallest change or interruption in the dogged action of the labourers, or causing one of them, so far as I could see, to lift an eye from the ground." What conclusion did Olmsted draw from this experience? Did he view it as a remarkable demonstration of the teamwork of black laborers and of the intensity of their concentration on the task at hand? The "stupid, plodding, machine-like manner in which they labour," said Olmsted, "is painful to witness." While Olmsted was willing to concede that these slave hands probably worked "harder, and more unremittingly," than northern laborers, he still doubted that "they accomplish as much in the same time as agricultural labourers at the North usually do."

Harvest operations in cotton do not appear to have offered the opportunities for division of labor and specialization that existed during the planting and cultivation seasons (although such opportunities do appear to have existed in sugar harvesting). In the absence of an interdependence that could be exploited to promote an intense rhythm of work, planters attempted to achieve the same objective by dividing harvest hands into competing groups. There were daily as well as weekly races, with prizes (bonuses) offered to the winning team and to the leading individual picker. There were daily weigh-ins of the cotton picked, and those who did not respond to the positive incentive had to face the abuse, verbal or physical, of the driver, if they fell too far below the expected pace.

The so-called "task method" was still another means of promoting the intensity of labor during the harvest season. Under this method, slaves were assigned given plots of land which were to be picked each day. Intensity of labor was promoted by permitting the slave to use his time for his own purposes when the task was completed. One way of ensuring that the work was done well under this system was to reassign the same plot to the same slave in each of the successive rounds of picking. Daily weighing of cotton also served as a check on performance.

Specialization and division of labor were not limited to fieldwork. They carried over into domestic aspects of plantation life. Certain domestic tasks were socialized to a considerable extent. This was true of child rearing and, to a lesser extent, of the production of clothing and of cooking. It was women, predominantly, who specialized in these employments. Most large plantations maintained nurseries. These were supervised by one or more of the older women, depending on the size of the plantation, who generally were assisted by older children. Women who worked in the fields, or at other assignments, deposited their children in the morning and picked them up in the evening. Nursing mothers returned to the nursery three or four times per day for feedings.

The production of clothing was, in varying degrees, carried out on most plantations. Some had loom houses in which most of the cloth consumed on plantations was woven. Others limited production to the sewing of purchased cloth. Sometimes these tasks were carried out by women in their own houses, when the weather was inclement or during slack seasons. In other cases, a permanent staff was assigned to a special building. Olmsted described the loom-house staff on one very large plantation. Of the dozen hands so employed, one "was insane, and most of the others were crippled, invalids with chronic complaints, or unfitted by age, or some infirmity, for field work."

Olmsted's description points to another aspect of the efficiency of plantations—the extraordinarily high labor-force participation rate (share of the population in the labor force). In the free economy—North and South—approximately one third of the population was in the labor force. Among slaves, the labor-force participation rate was two thirds. Virtually every slave capable of being in the labor force was in it. This was due largely to the inability of slaves, particularly women and children, to choose leisure, education, or work at home, if they preferred it, to work in fields or other assigned tasks. It was partly due to institutional arrangements which permitted plantations to find methods of employing those who would, to a large extent, be unemployable in free societies, particularly in free urban societies—the mentally retarded, the crippled, the aged.

Plantations not only brought a larger share of the population into the labor force, but they were also able to move closer to "full-capacity" utilization of the labor potential than was true of the free economy. This was not because slaves worked more hours per day or more days per week than free farmers. The best available evidence is that both slaves and free farmers averaged approximately 70–75 hours of work per week during the peak labor periods of planting, cultivation, and harvesting. Nor does it appear that slaves worked more days per year. In addition to having Sundays off, slaves had all or part of half of their Saturdays free, most of these being concentrated in the off-peak periods of farming. There was also up to a week or so of additional holidays, some at predesignated times, as during Christmas or in the interstice between the end of cultivation and the beginning of the harvest, some as unscheduled rewards for work well done. About a dozen days per year were lost due to illness. Thus the work year appears to have consisted of roughly 265–275 days.

The higher rate of the utilization of labor capacity was partly due to what was, by the usual standards of farmers, an extraordinary intensity of labor. Far from being "ordinary peasants" unused to "pre-industrial rhythms of work," black plantation agriculturalists labored under a regimen that was more like a modern assembly line than was true of the routine in many of the factories of the antebellum era. It was often easier for factory workers to regulate the pace of machines to their accustomed rhythm than for slaves to regulate the pace set by drivers. For much of antebellum manufacturing was still operated on the work patterns of the handicrafts. Division of labor was still at relatively low levels and interdependence of operations was still limited. Just as the great plantations were the first large, scientifically managed business enterprises, and as planters were the first group to engage in large-scale, scientific personnel management, so, too, black slaves were the first group of workers to be trained in the work rhythms which later became characteristic of industrial society. It was not the slaves but men like Olmsted who retained a "pre-industrial peasant mentality," who viewed the team-work, coordination, and intensity of effort achieved by black field hands as "stupid, plodding, machine-like," and "painful to witness." While Olmsted's revulsion is quite understandable, he was nevertheless wrong in concluding that the gang system was inefficient, and his belittling of the quality of slave labor was unwarranted. . . .

The large slave plantations were about 34 percent more efficient than free southern farms. This advantage was not due to some special way in which land or machinery was used, but to the special quality of plantation labor. It is true that large plantations used more land and equipment (by value) per worker than small plantations. However, this feature was taken into account in computing the efficiency indexes. In other words, even after one adjusts for the fact that on large plantations slaves generally worked on better land than free southern farmers and had more equipment, large plantations were still some 34 percent more efficient than free farms.

The advantage of plantations, at least that part which has been measured thus far, was due to the combination of the superior management of planters and the superior quality of black labor. In a certain sense, all, or nearly all, of the advantage is attributable to the high quality of slave labor, for the main thrust of management was directed at improving the quality of labor. How much of the success of this effort was due to the management, and how much to the responsiveness of the workers is an imperative question, but its resolution lies beyond the range of current techniques and available data.

Whatever the contribution of management, however, it should not all be assigned to white planters and overseers. For blacks—though slaves, though severely limited in the extent to which they could climb the economic ladder of antebellum society—were a vital part of the management of plantations and, in this capacity, of the economic success of the plantation.

Slaves entered into plantation management at two levels. As drivers or gang foremen they were ubiquitous on medium and large plantations. In the fields the drivers were responsible for ensuring that each gang achieved its daily objectives and, if the gang was operating on the task system, for determining the daily tasks of particular hands. Gang objectives were sometimes established either by the plantation owner or overseer. In other instances the establishment of these objectives was left to the discretion of the drivers.

Slaves also operated at the highest level of plantation supervision, short of actual ownership, as overseers or general managers. When acting as overseers, slaves were responsible not only for the overall direction of the labor force but for various entrepreneurial decisions, including the scheduling of the particular field operations and the purchasing of supplies. In such cases the burden of the success or failure of the entire production side of plantation operations rested on these slaves. Much of the attention of owners was directed to the commercial aspects of operations—the marketing of the crops, the purchase of equipment, the acquisition of new lands, the construction of new buildings, the negotiation of loans—or to other nonagricultural enterprises in which they were engaged.

Various scholars have recognized that slaves sometimes acted as overseers or general managers. But it has been assumed that this was rare, that on most large plantations the general management of *production* was in the hands of white overseers. The white overseer is assumed to have been a ubiquitous figure, present on virtually all plantations of one hundred or more slaves and on the majority of those with fifty to one hundred slaves. As pointed out previously, data in the census manuscripts clearly invalidates this assumption. Only 30 percent of plantations with one hundred or more slaves employed white overseers. On smaller plantations the proportion was even lower.

It might be thought that on many of the large plantations sons of planters took over the functions of the overseer. The data in the manuscript schedules of the census rules this possibility out in most cases. Among large plantations without overseers, 61 percent had only one adult male over age nineteen in the planter's family. In these cases the planter was the only adult male in his family who was in residence, or else the father was absent or dead and his only resident son was running the plantation. In any event there was no second male family member to take up the duties of the overseer. On 6 percent of the large plantations there were two adults over age nineteen, but the second of these persons was at least seventy years of age, and hence was probably too old to be actively involved in the business affairs of the plantation. Another 9 percent of the plantations had no male at all over age nineteen in residence. Thus, for 75 percent of the plantations without overseers there were no sons or other males who could have assumed the duties of the overseer. The conclusion indicated by these findings is startling: On a majority of the large plantations, the top nonownership management was black.

The question that begs to be explained is how so many scholars could have been so badly misled on this issue? Part of the explanation turns on a methodological consideration. To a considerable extent, the views of historians regarding the nature of plantation management are based on inferences from correspondence between owners and overseers. However, such correspondence (including instructions to overseers) was most likely to arise when owners did not reside on their plantations. Thus, previous historians based their conclusions on a biased sample of evidence, on a relatively small group of plantations which were unrepresentative of the whole. It is probable that absentee owners relied on white overseers to a much greater extent than did resident owners, among other reasons, because laws made it illegal to leave slaves exclusively under their own supervision.

Part of the explanation also turns on the way in which many historians have accepted the arguments of the authors of the economic indictment of slavery. One would hardly expect a system in which even the masters were cavalier fops and idlers to produce a high-quality class of slave managers. Nor was a mass of blacks "incapable of all but the rudest forms of labour," "evasive," incapable of maintaining "a steady routine," "incorrigibly indolent," "wanting in versatility," and unsuited for any activity that requires "the slightest care, forethought, or dexterity" likely to throw up any considerable number of able managers. If one accepts the premise that the system crushed all opportunity for the personal and intellectual development of slaves, mere consistency requires one also to expect to find that slaves were debarred from virtually all positions of responsibility.

Interestingly enough, Olmsted did not show such consistency of mind. Despite his low opinion of the quality of the black masses, he had a high opinion of the quality of blacks who functioned as drivers.

In the selection of drivers, regard seems to be had to size and strength—at least, nearly all the drivers I have seen are tall and strong men—but a great deal of judgment, requiring greater capacity of mind than the ordinary slave is often supposed to be possessed of, is certainly needed in them. A good driver is very valuable and usually holds office for life. His authority is not limited to the direction of labour in the field, but extends to the general deportment of the negroes. He is made to do the duties of policeman, and even of police magistrate. It is his duty, for instance, on Mr. X's estate, to keep order in the settlement, and, if two persons, men or women, are fighting, it is his duty to immediately separate them, and then to "whip them both."

Before any field of work is entered upon by a gang, the driver who is to superintend them has to measure and stake off the tasks. To do this at all accurately, in irregular-shaped fields, must require considerable powers of calculation. A driver with a boy to set the stakes, I was told, would accurately lay out forty acres a day, in half-acre tasks. The only instrument used is a five-foot measuring rod. When the gang comes to the field, he points out to each person his or her duty for the day, and then walks about among them, looking out that each proceeds properly. If, after a hard day's labour, he sees that the gang has been overtasked, owing to a miscalculation of the difficulty of the work, he may excuse the completion of the tasks; but he is not allowed to extend them. In the case of uncompleted tasks, the body of the gang begin new tasks the next day, and only a sufficient number are detailed from it to complete, during the day, the unfinished tasks of the day before. The relation of the driver to the working hands seems to be similar to that of the boatswain to the seamen in the navy, or of the sergeant to the privates in the army.

Having generally had long experience on the plantation, the advice of the drivers is commonly taken in nearly all the administration, and frequently they are, de facto, the managers. Orders on important points of the plantation economy, I have heard given by the proprietor directly to them, without the overseer's being consulted or informed of them; and it is often left with them to decide when and how long to flow the rice-grounds—the proprietor and overseer deferring to their more experienced judgment. Where the drivers are discrete, experienced, and trusty, the overseer is frequently employed merely as a matter of form, to comply with the laws requiring the superintendence or presence of a white man among every body of slaves; and his duty is rather to inspect and report than to govern. Mr. X considers his overseer an uncommonly efficient and faithful one, but he would not employ him, even during the summer, when he is absent for several months, if the law did not require it. He has sometimes left his plantation in care of one of the drivers for a considerable length of time, after having discharged an overseer; and he thinks it has then been quite as well conducted as ever. His overseer consults the drivers on all important points, and is governed by their advice.

"Mr. X" was not the only planter who frequently consulted with his slave managers and who deferred to their judgment, or insisted that his overseers do so. Nor was Olmsted the only one to note the high quality of black managers. When McBride, the owner of the Hickory Hill plantation, left on a long trip, he wrote detailed instructions to his overseer on the method of planting and cultivating various crops. In the case of rice, however, McBride said he was too ill-informed on that crop to offer advice and suggested that the overseer consult the driver who was "an old rice planter." Similarly, Charles Manigault instructed his overseer to "be careful not to interfere too much with the beating and management of the Rice Mill" since "the Negroes in charge have much experience therein." Indirect testimony of their slave drivers and other lower echelon personnel comes from the frequent complaints of white overseers that direct consultations between planters and drivers or other respected slaves were undermining their authority. No doubt some drivers deliberately provoked tests of strength between themselves and the overseers. In many such instances they were successful, and the overseer was fired or left of his own volition. On many of those plantations which did make use of white overseers, the turnover rate of overseers was quite high.

That the quality of slaves, both as ordinary workers and as managers, could have been so completely misrepresented by the antebellum critics of slavery is testimony to the extent of their racist myopia. What bitter irony it is that the false stereotype of black labor, a stereotype which still plagues blacks today, was fashioned not primarily by the oppressors who strove to keep their chattel wrapped in the chains of bondage, but by the most ardent opponents of slavery, by those who worked most diligently to destroy the chains of bondage.

While keenly aware of the torment which these false stereotypes of incompetence have helped to impose on blacks for more than a century, we are, as social scientists, impressed by this exceptional demonstration of the power of ideology to obliterate reality, and we view it as an unparalleled opportunity to investigate the complex interrelationships between ideas and the material circumstances of life. What is at issue here is not only how these false stereotypes regarding blacks came into being, but how they could have persisted for so long. Resolution of the first issue involves consideration of the intricate ways in which variations of racist viewpoints among critics and defenders of slavery, among northern and southern whites—for with very few exceptions they were all racists—interacted with each other to create an almost indestructible image of black incompetence. Resolution of the second issue involves consideration of why it has been so difficult for the many historians and social scientists who have studied slave society to penetrate this image and to discover the reality which it hid.

Much as we desire to do so, we cannot settle these issues—not merely because they lie beyond the scope of this book, or even because they require skills which go beyond our special areas of expertise, but because much research is still required before the various aspects of these questions can be treated adequately. Nevertheless, we cannot resist the opportunity to suggest some considerations which we believe ought to enter into the ultimate resolution.

One point on which there can be little doubt is that the belief in Negro incompetence was given a powerful fillip by the racial theories that came into prominence during the first half of the nineteenth century. These theories were embraced by Northerners as well as Southerners, by critics of slavery as well as its defenders. The theories asserted that blacks and whites were of different species or at least that blacks were an "inferior variety" of the human species. The African origins of blacks were thought to have contributed to the biological defects. Some attributed the racial differences to geographic factors. Thus, Negroes had "a dull torpid brain," a feature thought to be characteristic of "inhabitants of the warmer climates." Others saw Negro backwardness as being rooted in their savage ancestry. Whatever the cause, the innate inferiority of the Negro race was said to manifest itself in laziness, limited intellectual capacity, a childlike simplicity, docility, sensuousness, and tempestuousness. It is important to stress that these racist views were not embraced merely in popular thought. They were the reigning tenets of mid-nineteenth-century anthropology, in Europe as well as in the United States.

Although both critics and defenders of slavery believed in the innate inferiority of Negroes, there were important differences between them in assessing the effect of slavery on the natural endowments of Negroes. Critics of slavery believed that bondage had not only retarded the development of blacks but had exacerbated the baser features of their nature. Slavery had encouraged blacks to be slovenly, to prefer indolence to industry, to be evasive, to lie, and to steal. Abolitionists believed that slavery retarded black development because it was incapable of recognizing individual accomplishment and rewarding it, because it relied on the lash to elicit effort, thus identifying labor with pain. They also believed that the plantation form of organization kept blacks relatively isolated from contacts with whites and hindered their capacity to assimilate the higher white culture. Hence they drew a distinction between house servants and field hands, assuming the former were more highly developed intellectually and culturally because of their more intimate association with whites.

Defenders of slavery argued that their system not only had a beneficial development on blacks but was, indeed, pushing them to the outer limits of their capacity. Despite the fact that they were of an inferior race, under the slave system of labor organization blacks were induced to work harder and produce more than white labor. Not only was the natural indolence of blacks thus thwarted, but the most talented of their number were trained in the handicrafts and in other higher arts, thus achieving a status under slavery which was not only "elevated from the condition in which God first created them" but was clearly more lofty than anything that might be obtained under freedom. For everybody knew that slave labor was "vastly more efficient and productive than the labor of free blacks."

Obviously a debate cast along the lines just described could only serve to reinforce the stereotype of Negro incompetence. For neither side ever called the alleged natural incompetence of the Negro into question. Quite the contrary—each new round of debate served to raise the proposition of natural incompetence to the status of an axiomatic truth. Critics of slavery emphasized the failings of southern production, attributing these to a system which was not only based on an inferior variety of human labor but which degraded all labor, reducing in quality not only the effort of blacks but of whites as well. Defenders of slavery attributed outstanding accomplishments in production not to the high quality of black labor but to the success of the system of slavery which enabled the South to achieve as much as it did from what was basically inferior human material.

That Olmsted fully accepted the racial views of his day is clearly evident in his books. The Germans appear as the only whites in the South capable of resisting the degrading effects of slavery on white labor. They are invariably portrayed as industrious and efficient—the very models of enterprising, thrifty, and ambitious small proprietors. On the other hand, the only Jews that Olmsted encountered in the South were moneylenders "of no character" who charged extortionate interest rates ("often . . not less than 25 percent per annum"), who lived in squalid homes, and who engaged "in an unlawful trade with the simple negroes." Similarly, the Irish were "dumb Paddies" who easily succumbed to the degrading southern attitude toward labor and usually fell to a level that made their labor even less desirable than that of slaves. Olmsted's northern chauvinism came to the fore whenever he compared the quality of northern and southern laborers. Few northern employers would have recognized their employees from his description of them. Northern workers were almost invariably portrayed as highly motivated, diligent, self-propelled, and polite, even when being fired for some infraction of their normally high standards of behavior. There can be little doubt that Olmsted's jaundiced views of black relative to white labor, and of southern relative to northern labor, were influenced by the racial presuppositions that he brought with him on his travels through the South.

But to leave the matter there is to grossly oversimplify the issue. For whatever his prejudices, Olmsted was an extremely keen and diligent observer who was striving to discover those characteristics which distinguished the system of slave labor and which differentiated it from the system of free labor. While his prejudices undoubtedly predisposed him toward misinterpreting what he in fact observed, or had reported to him, it is not likely that he would have fallen into these errors if there had not been mitigating circumstances that made his misinterpretations plausible—if there had not been substantial elements which lent support, or at least appeared to lend support, to his conclusions. . . .

The issue which probably confused Olmsted more than any other one came to the fore during his very first visit to a slave plantation—a wheat farm in Maryland which he examined on December 14, 1852. The slaves he saw there were not engaged in the fields but were at work in the neighborhood of the plantation buildings. The owner of the plantation told Olmsted that while he had employed white laborers on several occasions for digging ditches, he would not think of using whites "for common farm-labor, and made light of their coming in competition with slaves. Negroes at hoeing and any steady field work, he assured me, would 'do two to their one'. . . ."

Olmsted did not press the planter further. He clearly did not accept such a high appraisal of the quality of the planter's black labor force. Olmsted characterized the slaves on this farm as "stupid and dilatory in executing any orders given to them." "Those I saw at work," he said, "appeared to me to move very slowly and awkwardly, as did also those engaged in the stable."

This Maryland wheat plantation was not a run-down, piddling farm operated by a "mean white." It was, in Olmsted's words, a "fine farm," over two thousand acres in extent, run under "excellent management," with a main house which had "somewhat the look of an old French chateau," with "well-secured, wire fences," with a "nicely graveled and rolled" road, with "thorough-bred Shorthorns" as the milking stock ("I have seldom seen a better lot of milkers," said Olmsted), and with drains on the farm's lowlands that were so well built that they lasted "twenty years without failing." The planter's experiments with fertilizers so impressed Olmsted that he singled them out. How could so keen a planter, a man whose excellence in farm management had won him "a national reputation," have deceived himself so badly about the quality of his laborers? And how had he been able to prosper with workers who were "stupid and dilatory," who moved "very slowly" and who "must" have been "very difficult to direct efficiently"?

The mistake was Olmsted's. What he observed on this plantation was the easy-going rhythm of slaves during the winter interstice. The planting of winter wheat had been completed more than a month before Olmsted's arrival and the fall harvesting of other crops, such as corn, had also been completed well before his visit. This was a period for putting things in order—repairing fences, thoroughly cleaning stables, rerolling of roads—important tasks all, but not the type that called for intensive effort. The high-pressure tasks of planting, cultivating, and harvesting were either over, or not yet at hand. As we have previously stated, Olmsted's itinerary during his first trip kept him squarely in the interstice between harvesting and planting. As he moved south and westward into cotton country, he generally moved toward both later completion of the harvest and later resumption of the date of planting. By the time he arrived in Georgia, Alabama, and Louisiana, states in which he might still have observed the picking of cotton in mid-December, he was already into February. He left Louisiana well before the onset of the new planting season, which began during the last days of March or early in April.

Thus, Olmsted's opinion of the typical work rhythms of slaves, an opinion in which he gained more and more confidence as he traveled through the "Seaboard States," was once again based on an unrepresentative sample of evidence. Olmsted appears to have made the mistake of assuming that the leisurely work pace of slaves during the southern agricultural interstice prevailed throughout the balance of the year. In his subsequent two trips, Olmsted did, of course, witness the typical rhythms of planting and cultivating. But by then he had become so convinced that the pace he had observed during his first trip was the norm, that he invariably classified his later encounters with intense labor as exceptions.

Toward an Explanation for the Persistence of the Myth of Black Incompetence

The principal cause of the persistence of the myth of black incompetence in American historiography is racism. Perhaps no single history book written during the twentieth century has had a greater impact on the interpretation of slave life than U. B. Phillips's *American Negro Slavery*. To point out that this volume was deeply marred by its author's adherence to the proposition that Negroes were racially inferior to whites would hardly evoke controversy among historians today. This point is now emphasized not only by the critics of Phillips but also his defenders.

How different the situation was when *American Negro Slavery* was published in 1918. Of the principal reviewers of the book, only two attacked Phillips's treatment of Negroes—and they were not in the mainstream of the historical profession as it was then constituted. One of these reviewers was W. E. B. Du Bois, the director of publicity and research for the N.A.A.C.P. and the editor of its journal, *Crisis*. Du Bois found *American Negro Slavery* "curiously incomplete and unfortunately biased."

The Negro as a responsible human being has no place in the book. To be sure individual Negroes are treated here and there but mainly as exceptional or as illustrative facts for purposes outside themselves. Nowhere is there any adequate conception of "darkies," "niggers" and "negroes" (words liberally used throughout the book) as making a living mass of humanity with all the usual human reactions. . . .

Mr. Phillips recurs again and again to this inborn character of Negroes: they are "submissive," "light-hearted" and "ingratiating" (p. 342), very "fond of display" (pp. 1, 291), with a "proneness to superstition" and "acceptance of subordination" (p. 291); "chaffing, and chattering" (p. 292) with "humble nonchalance and a freedom from carking care" (p. 416). From the fourteenth to the twentieth century Mr. Phillips sees no essential change in these predominant characteristics of the mass of Negroes; and while he is finishing his book in a Y.M.C.A. army hut in the South all he sees in the Negro soldier is the "same easy-going amiable serio-comic obedience," and all he hears is the throwing of dice (pp. viii, ix). This Negro nature is, to Mr. Phillips, fixed and unchangeable. A generation of freedom has brought little change (p. ix). Even the few exceptional Negroes whom he mentions are of interest mainly because of their unexpected "ambition" and not for any especial accomplishment (p. 432). The fighting black maroons were overcome by "fright" (p. 466), and the Negroes' part in the public movements like the Revolution was "barely appreciable" (p. 116); indeed his main picture is of "inert Negroes, the majority of whom are as yet perhaps less efficient in freedom than their forbears were as slaves" (p. 396)!

Brilliant as it was, Du Bois's critique fell largely on deaf ears. It could hardly have been otherwise during an era when the pseudoscientific racial theories which still dominated anthropology were widely accepted in scholarly circles. Indeed, more than two decades elapsed before scholars in the mainstream of the history profession began to press the theme enunciated by Du Bois.

While not unanticipated by others, the flag of general revolt against the Phillips school was raised by Richard Hofstadter in a 1944 paper entitled "U. B. Phillips and the Plantation Legend." Hofstadter attacked Phillips for exaggerating the paternalistic impulses of the planter, for painting too "rosy" a portrait of the material conditions of slave life, and for depicting the Negro as "a singularly contented and docile 'serio-comic' creature." The real nature of the treatment of slaves, said Hofstadter, was far more cruel than admitted by Phillips, slave health was much poorer than Phillips admitted, and slaves were more often left to the mercy of harsh overseers by their absentee owners than Phillips admitted. Hofstadter also charged Phillips with having underestimated the extent, and having distorted the nature of, "the slave's resistance to slavery." He chided Phillips for stressing a benign type of "give-and-take process between master and slave," for failing to appreciate "the extent to which the easement of the slave's condition came not from the master's benevolence but from the slave's resistance." Hofstadter ended his essay with a call for the rewriting of the history of slavery from the "viewpoint of modern cultural anthropology"; by this he meant the new view on race, pioneered by Franz Boas, which held that racial factors were unimportant in determining intellectual capacity.

Hofstadter's rebellion was far less sweeping than might appear. Hofstadter did not challenge Phillips on the general profitability and viability of slavery. Neither did he take issue with him on the quality of slave labor, on the economic efficiency of slavery, or on the effect of slavery on southern economic growth. Indeed, Hofstadter confined his attack to just four of the twenty-three chapters of *American Negro Slavery,* specifically excluding from consideration those which dealt with the issues of profitability, efficiency, and growth.

The limited nature of Hofstadter's attack on Phillips is not difficult to explain. Like so many others, Hofstadter's conception of slavery was developed largely from his reading of Olmsted. Hofstadter excoriated Phillips for not having made greater use of the work of his witness and critic. "Olmsted was not only an honest but an unusually acute observer," said Hofstadter, "and I believe that a fuller and more accurate knowledge of the late antebellum South can be obtained from the volumes of Olmsted than from Professor Phillips's own writings." But Phillips, despite his mistrust for the man, had read Olmsted with care and made great use of him. On the issues of the profitability and efficiency of slavery, as well as on the quality of slave labor and the effect of slavery on southern economic growth, Phillips was pure Olmsted. And on some of these issues Phillips merely paraphrased Olmsted. (Olmsted: "Slaves thus get a fictitious value like stocks 'in a corner.' " Phillips: "When the supply [of slaves] was 'cornered' it was unavoidable that the price should be bid up to the point of overvaluation.")

Despite Phillips's pretensions to a revolutionary break with James Ford Rhodes, the dominant historian in the interpretation of southern slavery at the time Phillips was a graduate student, and despite Hofstadter's claims to a revolutionary break with Phillips, all three men—and the schools of historical writing on the antebellum South which they symbolize—were adherents to what we have termed the "traditional interpretation" of the slave economy. That interpretation is the one which emerged from the economic indictment of slavery. . . . It consists of five main propositions. These are: 1, that slavery was generally an unprofitable investment, or depended on a trade in slaves to be profitable, except on new, highly fertile land; 2, that slavery was economically moribund; 3, that slave labor, and agricultural production based on slave labor, was economically inefficient; 4, that slavery caused the economy of the South to stagnate, or at least retarded its growth, during the antebellum era; 5, that slavery provided extremely harsh material conditions of life for the typical slave.

Phillips accepted all of these propositions except the last. When he claimed he was revolutionizing the interpretation of the antebellum South, he was referring only to point five, the harsh treatment of slaves, and to the shadow which that treatment cast on the character of slaveholders. Phillips did not have to overturn Rhodes on the character of blacks and the quality of their labor. Rhodes's views on the character of slaves and on the quality of their labor were fully congenial to Phillips. Rhodes described slaves as "indolent and filthy"; their expression was "besotted and generally repulsive"; on their "brute-like countenances . . . were painted stupidity, indolence, duplicity, and sensuality"; their labor was "stupid, plodding, machine-like"; licentiousness and indifference to chastity were "a natural inclination of the African race" which was further fostered by slavery; as women displayed "an entire lack of chastity," the men displayed "an entire lack of honesty"; and slave women yielded "without objection, except in isolated cases, to the passion of their master." In Rhodes's view the error of southern apologists was not in the claim that blacks were inferior, but in the manner in which they sought to cope with the problem created by this inferiority. "So long as Southern reasoners maintained that the negro race was inferior to the Caucasian, their basis was scientific truth, although their inference that this fact justified slavery was cruel as well as illogical."

The irony of Hofstadter's call for a rejection of the Phillips position on treatment, without a simultaneous attack on the other four points, is that it led in the direction of the re-establishment of the pre-Phillips or "pure" version of the traditional interpretation of the economics of slavery. As long as historians remained locked in combat on the issue of treatment, explicitly accepting all other aspects of the economic indictment of slavery, the myth of Negro incompetence continued to reign supreme—just as it had in the antebellum era when critics of slavery and apologists debated over whether slavery had exacerbated or ameliorated the "natural" inferiority of blacks.

We do not mean that Hofstadter, or that scholars who responded to his call, aimed to re-establish the theories of the racial inferiority of Negroes as they existed in Rhodes or as in Clay, Helper, and Olmsted. Quite the contrary, as both Hofstadter and those who rallied to his banner have made clear, their aim was the unequivocal and complete rout of the racist myths that lingered on in the historiography of the antebellum South. What they failed to appreciate was that these racist myths drew sustenance not merely from one of the five points in the traditional interpretation of slavery but from each of them.

This was true even of Kenneth Stampp who . . . went further than any other post-Phillips scholar, except perhaps Lewis C. Gray, in rejecting the traditional interpretation of slavery. In *The Peculiar Institution,* Stampp argued that investments in slaves were quite generally profitable, indeed, highly profitable for most planters. He also rejected the contention that economic forces would by themselves have led to the demise of slavery, even in the upper South. Nor did Stampp find any evidence to support the claim that slavery prevented industrialization and economic growth. He pointed to "innumerable experiments" which "demonstrated that slaves could be employed profitably in factories," arguing that slaveholders preferred to operate in agriculture because, for the South, agriculture "seemed to be the surest avenue to financial success."

Stampp even expressed doubts about the fourth proposition in the traditional interpretation—that slavery was less efficient than an economic system based on free labor. "Slavery's economic critics overlooked the fact," he said, "that physical coercion, or the threat of it, proved to be a rather effective incentive, and that the system did not prevent masters from offering tempting rewards for the satisfactory performance of assigned tasks."

At this point, however, Stampp faltered. He hesitated to go on to the conclusion that slaves were equal to free men in the efficiency of their labor. He conceded that slave productivity was sharply reduced by "the slave's customary attitude of indifference toward his work, together with the numerous methods he devised to resist his enslavement." Stampp was able to hold on to his contention that slavery was profitable only by arguing that there were other "advantages" which "more than compensated for whatever superiority free labor had in efficiency." These "advantages," included longer hours of work, more complete exploitation of women and children, and lower real wages for slaves than for free men.

Why did Stampp, who broke with so much of the traditional interpretation and who came so close to rejecting the myth of the incompetence of slave labor, fail to do so? Why did he, as it were, pull back just as he seemed about to do so?

The answer lies in Stampp's preoccupation with the refutation of Phillips on point five, the nature of the treatment of slaves. Surely Phillips's idyllic portrait needed correction. In reacting against the Rhodes treatment of plantations as houses of immorality and unmitigated terror run by men who were not only brutal but corrupt, Phillips substituted a near-paradise—at least as much of a paradise on earth as was reasonable to expect from a "primitive" race whose "savage" instincts had to be kept in check and which had to be trained to overcome a "natural ineptitude" and "indolence." In Phillips's reconstruction, planters emerged not merely as good men but, to use Du Bois's word, as supermen. Slavery became "less a business than a life." The objective of planters was not so much to make a profit as to make men.

Recoiling from such apologetics, Stampp provided testimony that cruelty was indeed an ingrained feature of the treatment of slaves. The cases of cruelty which Phillips regarded as unusual, as outside the unwritten rules of the master class, emerged as a common pattern of white behavior in *The Peculiar Institution*. Cruelty, Stampp said, "was endemic in all slaveholding communities"; even those "who were concerned about the welfare of slaves found it difficult to draw a sharp line between acts of cruelty and such measures of physical force as were an inextricable part of slavery." For Stampp, cruelty arose not because of the malevolent nature of the slaveholders but because of the malevolent nature of the system—because a master could brook nothing less from his slave than "perfect" submission. To achieve that goal masters were impelled, regardless of their humanity in other respects, to develop in the Negro "a paralyzing fear of white men," to "impress upon him his innate inferiority," and to "instill in him a sense of complete dependence." While Stampp did not employ the concentration camp analogy later set forth by Stanley Elkins, his plantation strongly suggested a prison with cruel wardens.

From this point the argument could have gone—and did in fact go—in two directions. One was the direction taken by Elkins, who argued that a system as cruel as the one described by Stampp must have had a devastating impact on the personality of slaves. No one could live under so brutal a regime without succumbing to it. Negroes were not supermen, any more than were the Jews in Hitler's concentration camps. Although plantations were not concentration camps, the masters who ran the plantations had as much absolute power over slaves as Hitler's gauleiters had over the Jews, and as much determination to crush their spirit. What emerged from the process was "Sambo, the typical plantation slave . . . docile but irresponsible, loyal but lazy, humble but chronically given to lying and stealing." Sambo's "behavior was full of infantile silliness" and his "relationship with his master was one of utter dependence and childlike attachment."

Stampp decided to move in a direction that, on the surface, appears quite different from the one Elkins chose. He argued that slaves did not succumb; they resisted. Resistance did not generally take the form of revolution or strikes. Such open forms of resistance were sheer suicide. There were no rebellions among U.S. slaves comparable to those in Jamaica or Brazil; there was no protracted guerrilla warfare. Resistance in the U.S. took a much more subtle form; it came in guises so innocent that masters and overseers failed even to recognize it. The participants in this resistance movement "were the meek, smiling ones whom many thought were contented though irresponsible."

They were not reckless rebels who risked their lives for freedom; if the thought of rebellion crossed their minds, the odds against success seemed too overwhelming to attempt it. But the inevitability of their bondage made it none the more attractive. And so, when they could, they protested by shirking their duties, injuring the crops, feigning illness, and disrupting the routine. These acts were, in part, an unspectacular kind of "day to day resistance to slavery."

What, of course, is common to both Stampp and Elkins is agreement on the characteristic of slave behavior: slaves lie, steal, feign illness, behave childishly, and shirk their duties. Indeed, this characterization has been one of the enduring constants in the literature on slavery. By whatever path they moved, writers on slavery usually returned to the theme of the inferiority of slave labor. To Olmsted, Rhodes, and Phillips the inferiority was due to racial factors. To Cairnes, inferiority was sociological in origin. To Elkins, the cause was psychological. To Stampp, the inferiority was due to "day to day resistance." Paradoxically, it was the slaveholders who were least inhibited in acknowledging that blacks were better workers than whites, although they attributed this superiority to themselves rather than to their bondsmen.

Stampp hesitated to make the leap required to recognize the superior quality of slave labor because he remained too enmeshed in the debate between the critics of slavery and the apologists, and he overestimated the cruelty of the slave system. The logic of this position made it difficult to acknowledge that ordinary slaves could be diligent workers, imbued like their masters with a Protestant ethic, or that, even though they longed for freedom, slaves could strive to develop and improve themselves in the only way that was open to them.

EUGENE D. GENOVESE

The Black Work Ethic

It goes without saying that "niggers are lazy": the planters always said so, as did the "poor white trash," whose own famous commitment to hard and steady work doubtless assured their entrance into John Calvin's Kingdom of Heaven. Some of the refrain may be dismissed as obvious ideological rationalization and self-serving cant or a distorted interpretation of the effects of a lack of adequate incentives. Yet much more needs to be said, for the slaves themselves sang at their work:

> Nigger mighty happy when he layin' by the corn,
> Nigger mighty happy when he hear dat dinner horn;
> But he more happy when de night come on,
> Dat sun's a slantin', as sho's you born!
> Dat old cow's a shakin' dat great big bell,
> And de frogs tunin' up 'cause de dew's done fell.

"The white men," Johann David Schoepf observed on his travels during the 1780s, "are all the time complaining that the blacks will not work, and they themselves do nothing." Virginia's great humorist, George W. Bagby, once reflected on the complacency and self-satisfaction of antebellum life: "Time was abundant in those days. It was made for slaves, and we had the slaves."

The slaveholders presided over a plantation system that constituted a half-way house between peasant and factory cultures. The tobacco and cotton plantations, which dominated the slave economy in the United States, ranged closer to the peasant than the factory model, in contradistinction to the great sugar plantations of the Caribbean, which in some respects resembled factories in the field; but even the small holders pushed their laborers toward modern work discipline.

The planters' problem came to this: How could they themselves preserve as much as possible of that older way of life to which they aspired and yet convince their slaves to repudiate it? How could they instill factorylike discipline into a working population engaged in a rural system that, for all its tendencies toward modern discipline, remained bound to the rhythms of nature and to traditional ideas of work, time, and leisure?

They succeeded in overcoming this contradiction only to the extent that they got enough work out of their slaves to make the system pay at a level necessary to their survival as a slaveholding class in a capitalist world market. But they failed in deeper ways that cast a shadow over the long-range prospects for that very survival and over the future of both blacks and whites in American society. Too often they fell back on the whip and thereby taught and learned little. When they went to other incentives, as fortunately most tried to do, they did get satisfactory economic results, but at the same time they reinforced traditional attitudes and values instead of replacing them with more advanced ones.

The black work ethic grew up within a wide Protestant Euro-American community with a work ethic of its own. The black ethic represented at once a defense against an enforced system of economic exploitation and an autonomous assertion of values generally associated with preindustrial peoples. As such, it formed part of a more general southern work ethic, which developed in antagonism to that of the wider American society. A Euro-American, basically Anglo-Saxon work ethic helped shape that of southerners in general and slaves in particular and yet, simultaneously, generated a profound antithesis. . . .

The setting remained rural, and the rhythm of work followed seasonal fluctuations. Nature remained the temporal reference point for the slaves. However much the slaveholders might have wished to transform their slaves into clock-punchers, they could not, for in a variety of senses both literal and metaphoric, there were no clocks to punch. The planters, especially the resident planters of the United States and Brazil but even the typical West Indian agents of absentee owners, hardly lived in a factory world themselves and at best could only preach what the most docile or stupid slave knew very well they did not and could not practice. Since the plantation economy required extraordinary exertion at critical points of the year, notably the harvest, it required measures to capitalize on the slaves' willingness to work in spurts rather than steadily. The slaveholders turned the inclinations of the slaves to their own advantage, but simultaneously they made far greater concessions to the value system and collective sensibility of the quarters than they intended.

The slaveholders, as usual, had their way but paid a price. The slaves, as usual, fell victim to the demands of their exploiters but had some success in pressing their own advantage. Thus, the plantation system served as a halfway house for Africans between their agricultural past and their imposed industrial future. But, it froze them into a position that allowed for their exploitation on the margins of industrial society. The advantage of this compromise, from the black point of view, lay in the protection it provided for their rich community life and its cultural consolidation. The disadvantage lay in its encouragement of a way of life that, however admirable intrinsically, ill prepared black people to compete in the economic world into which they would be catapulted by emancipation. . . .

The black view of time, conditioned by the plantation slave experience, has provided a great source of strength for a people at bay, as one of Bishop A. G. Dunston's sermons makes clear:

You know, that's the way God does it. Same as you can't hurry God—so why don't you wait, just wait. Everybody's ripping and racing and rushing. And God is taking his time. Because he knows that it isn't hurtin' neary so bad as you and I think it's hurtin'—and that is the way he wants us to go. But by and by he brings relief. . . .

Black people, in short, learned to take the blow and to parry it as best they could. They found themselves shut out by white racism from part of the dominant culture's value system, and they simultaneously resisted that system both by historically developed sensibility and by necessity. Accordingly, they developed their own values as a force for community cohesion and survival, but in so doing they widened the cultural gap and exposed themselves to even harder blows from a white nation that could neither understand their behavior nor respect its moral foundations. . . .

The slaves' world outlook, as manifested in their attitude toward work, has usually been treated as a mechanism of resistance to labor or to the demoralization occasioned by an especially oppressive labor system. Older and openly racist writers like Ulrich Bonnell Phillips or A. H. Stone accounted for it primarily by reference to "Negro traits." Ironically, W. E. B. Du Bois, the one scholar who attacked the question without bias and with sympathetic care, came out closer to the white racists than to the liberals, for he too proclaimed profound cultural differences; but he simultaneously stripped away the racists' distortions and, as it were, turned their arguments back on them. Any consideration of this question—indeed, any consideration of any question concerning slave life—must begin with a careful reconsideration of Dr. Du Bois's great work.

Perhaps Dr. Du Bois's best discussion of the black work ethic is the one in *The Gift of Black Folk:*

The black slave brought into common labor certain new spiritual values not yet fully realized. As a tropical product with a sensuous receptivity to the beauty of the world, he was not as easily reduced to be the mechanical draft-horse which the northern European laborer became. He was not easily brought to recognize any ethical sanctions in work as such but tended to work as the results pleased him and refused to work or sought to refuse when he did not find the spiritual returns adequate, thus he was easily accused of laziness and driven as a slave when in truth he brought to modern manual labor a renewed valuation of life.

And again:

Many a northern manager has seen the contradiction when, facing the apparent laziness of Negro hands, he has attempted to drive them and found out that he could not and at the same time has afterward seen someone used to Negro labor get a tremendous amount of work out of the same gangs. The explanation of all this is clear and simple: the Negro laborer has not been trained in modern organized industry but rather in a quite different school.

Dr. Du Bois located the difference in the attitudes of Euro-American and Afro-American workers in the difference between the bourgeois social system of the one and the ostensibly "communistic" social system of the other. The white worker worked hard not only to avoid starvation but to avoid disgracing himself and his family, whereas the black worker "looked upon work as a necessary evil and maintained his right to balance the relative allurements of leisure and satisfaction at any particular day, hour, or season." Ever alert to complexities, Dr. Du Bois suggested that the white worker brought to America the habit of regular toil as a great moral duty and used it to make America rich, whereas the black worker brought the idea of work as a necessary evil and could, if allowed, use it to make America happy.

There is much that is wise as well as humane in Dr. Du Bois's point of view, and it seems incomprehensible that it should so long have been ignored, if only because it raises so many questions of a kind that now threaten to tear the country apart generationally as well as racially. Santayana, with whom Dr. Du Bois studied at Harvard, once wrote: "Certain moralists, without meaning to be satirical, often say that the sovereign cure for unhappiness is work. Unhappily, the work they recommend is better fitted to dull pain than to remove its cause. It occupies the faculties without rationalising the life." Notwithstanding the great merit of Dr. Du Bois's interpretation, its historical specifics cannot go unchallenged. The blacks may indeed be seen as "a tropical product with a sensuous receptivity to the beauty of the world." Despite appearances, there is nothing mystical here—merely a proper concern for the impact of physical environment on the historically developed, collective sensibilities of peoples. But, Dr. Du Bois made a costly error in assuming that white European workers came to the United States after having internalized the Puritan work ethic, and he thereby drew attention away from the central character of the slave experience and moved it to the African experience, which was only a special case in the general immigrant experience.

The immigrants who filled the ranks of the unskilled labor force during the nineteenth century came, to a great extent, from peasant societies with a rural work ethic reinforced by Roman Catholicism. The Sicilians and East Europeans who followed did not bring the maxims of Benjamin Franklin with them. Each wave of immigrants had to undergo a process of acculturation that meant a harsh struggle to break down an established set of values and the slow inculcation of those values we associate with specifically industrial discipline. Moreover, as E. P. Thompson has so well demonstrated, the English working class itself had arisen from the countryside amidst the bitter contention of rival value systems in general and work ethics in particular. Thus, the contribution of Africa came not from some supposed communistic tradition but from its particular participation in a much broader tradition that we associate with most agrarian peoples. But whereas the Europeans found themselves drawn into an industrial system that slowly transformed them into suitable industrial workers, the Africans found themselves drawn into a plantation system that, despite certain similarities to an industrial setting, immensely reinforced traditional values and also added elements of corruption and degradation.

The African tradition, like the European peasant tradition, stressed hard work and condemned and derided laziness in any form. Not hard work but steady, routinized work as moral duty was discounted. In this attitude African agriculturalists resembled preindustrial peoples in general, including urban peoples. The familiar assertion that certain people would work only long enough to earn the money they needed to live was leveled not only against day laborers but against the finest and most prestigious artisans in early modern Europe.

Olmsted reported that the slaves could be and often were driven into hard, unremitting toil but that they responded with a dull, stupid, plodding effort which severely reduced their productive contribution. The slaves, he added, "are far less adapted for steady, uninterrupted labor than we are, but excel us in feats demanding agility and tempestuous energy." Olmsted's argument became standard among postbellum employers who were trying to rebuild with a labor force of freedmen. As one farmer in North Carolina told John Richard Dennett in 1865, "You know how it is with them—for about three days it's work as if they'd break everything to pieces; but after that it's go out late and come in soon." Ironically, this distinction parallels precisely the one made by proslavery ideologues who wished to describe the cultural differences between themselves and the Yankees. It is also the distinction made by scholars in describing the position of southern blacks who went north to cities like Chicago during the twentieth century.

What did the blacks themselves say? Isaac Adams, who had been a slave on a big plantation in Louisiana, recalled that most of the blacks remained there when the Yankees emancipated them. "But," he added, "they didn't do very much work. Just enough to take care of themselves and their white folks." Frank Smith, an ex-slave who went north from Alabama to Illinois, complained: "I didn't lak de Yankees. Dey wanted you to wuk *all de time,* and dat's sump'n I hadn't been brung up to do." Colin Clark and Margaret Haswell may have a point when they argue, in *The Ecomomics of Subsistence Agriculture,* that subsistence laborers will overcome their attachment to leisure and work steadily once they have been brought into contact with communities and values strong enough to stimulate their wants. But powerful cultural resistance to any such tendency must be overcome, and the projected outcome of such a confrontation is not inevitable. In part the outcome must depend on the extent to which the more traditional group has organized itself into a community rather than continuing as a conglomerate of individuals and on the extent to which assimilation to the more economically advanced community is blocked by discrimination.

The slaves' willingness to work extraordinarily hard and yet to resist the discipline of regularity accompanied certain desires and expectations. During Reconstruction the blacks sought their own land, worked it conscientiously when they could get it; resisted being forced back into anything resembling gang labor for the white man; and had to be terrorized, swindled, and murdered to prevent their working for themselves. This story was prefigured in antebellum times when slaves were often allowed garden plots for their families and willingly worked them late at night or on Sundays in order to provide extra food or clothing. The men did not generally let their families subsist on the usual allotments of pork and corn. In addition to working with their wives in the gardens, they fished and hunted and trapped animals. In these and other ways they demonstrated considerable concern for the welfare of their families and a strong desire to take care of them. But in such instances they were working for themselves and at their own pace. Less frequently, slaves received permission to hire out their own time after having completed the week's assigned tasks. They were lured, not by some internal pressure to work steadily, but by the opportunity to work for themselves and their families in their own way.

Many slaves voluntarily worked for their masters on Sundays or holidays in return for money or goods. This arrangement demonstrated how far the notion of the slaves' "right" to a certain amount of time had been accepted by the masters; how readily the slaves would work for themselves; and how far the notion of reciprocity had entered the thinking of both masters and slaves.

The slaves responded to moral as well as economic incentives. They often took pride in their work, but not necessarily in the ways most important to their masters. Solomon Northup designed a better way to transport lumber only to find himself ridiculed by the overseer. In this case it was in the master's interest to intervene, and he did. He praised Northup and adopted the plan. Northup comments: "I was not insensible to the praise bestowed upon me, and enjoyed especially, my triumph over Taydem [the overseer], whose half-malicious ridicule had stung my pride."

From colonial days onward plantation slaves, as well as those in industry, mining, and town services, received payments in money and goods as part of a wider system of social control. These payments served either as incentive bonuses designed to stimulate productivity, or more frequently, as a return for work done during the time recognized as the slaves' own. Many planters, including those who most clearly got the best results, used such incentives. Bennet H. Barrow of Louisiana provides a noteworthy illustration, for he was not a man to spare the whip. Yet his system of rewards included frequent holidays and dinners, as well as cash bonuses and presents for outstanding work. In Hinds County, Mississippi, Thomas Dabney gave small cash prizes—a few cents, really—to his best pickers and then smaller prizes to others who worked diligently even if they could not match the output of the leaders. In Perry County, Alabama, Hugh Davis divided his workers into rival teams and had them compete for prizes. He supplemented this collective competition with individual contests. In North Carolina at the end of the eighteenth century Charles Pettigrew, like many others before and after him, paid slaves for superior or extra work.

The amounts sometimes reached substantial proportions. Captain Frederick Marryat complained that in Lexington, Kentucky, during the late 1830s a gentleman could not rent a carriage on Sundays because slaves with ready money invariably rented them first for their own pleasure. Occasionally, plantation records reported surprising figures. One slave in Georgia earned fifty to sixty dollars per year by attending to pine trees in his off hours. Others earned money by applying particular skills or by doing jobs that had to be done individually and carefully without supervision. Amounts in the tens and even hundreds of dollars, although not common, caused no astonishment.

The more significant features of these practices, for the society as a whole if not for the economy in particular, was the regularity—almost the institutionalization—of payments for work on Sundays or holidays. Apart from occasional assignments of Sunday or holiday work as punishment and apart from self-defeating greed, not to say stupidity, which led a few masters to violate the social norm, Sunday was the slaves' day by custom as well as law. The collective agreement of the slaveholders on these measures had its origin in a concern for social peace and reflected a sensible attitude toward economic efficiency. But once the practice took root, with or without legal sanction, the slaves transformed it into a "right." So successfully did they do so that the Supreme Court of Louisiana ruled in 1836: "According to . . . law, slaves are entitled to the produce of their labor on Sunday; even the master is bound to remunerate them, if he employs them." Here again the slaves turned the paternalist doctrine of reciprocity to advantage while demonstrating the extent to which that doctrine dominated the lives of both masters and slaves.

Ralph Ellison writes of his experience as a boy: "Those trips to the cotton patch seemed to me an enviable experience because the kids came back with such wonderful stories. And it wasn't the hard work which they stressed, but the communion, the playing, the eating, the dancing and the singing." A leading theme in the blues tradition of black "soul" music is "Do your best." The emphasis in both performance and lyrics rests not on the degree of success but on the extent and especially the sincerity of effort. Underlying black resistance to prevailing white values, then, has been a set of particular ideas concerning individual and community responsibility. It is often asserted that blacks spend rather than save as someone else thinks they should. But the considerable evidence for this assertion must be qualified by the no less considerable evidence of the heartbreaking scraping together of nickels and dimes to pay for such things as the education of children, which will generally draw Anglo-Saxon applause, and the provision of elaborate funerals, which generally will not but which for many peoples besides blacks constitutes a necessary measure of respect for the living as well as the dead.

The slaves could, when they chose, astonish the whites by their worktime élan and expenditure of energy. The demands of corn shucking, hog killing, logrolling, cotton picking, and especially sugar grinding confronted the slaves with particularly heavy burdens and yet drew from them particularly positive responses.

With the exception of the Christmas holiday—and not always that—former slaves recalled having looked forward to corn shucking most of all. Sam Colquitt of Alabama explained:

Next to our dances, de most fun was corn-shucking. Marsa would have de corn hauled up to de crib, and piled as a house. Den he would invite de hands 'round to come and hope shuck it. Us had two leaders or generals and choose up two sides. Den us see which side would win first and holler and sing. . . . Marsa would pass de jug around too. Den dey sho' could work and dat pile'd just vanish.

Some ex-slaves remembered corn shuckings as their only good time, but many more said simply that they were the best. Occasionally a sour note appeared, as when Jenny Proctor of Alabama said, "We had some co'n shuckin's sometimes but de white folks gits de fun and de nigger gits de work." For the vast majority, however, they were "de big times."

The descriptions that have been preserved provide essential clues for an understanding of plantation life and its work rhythms. According to Robert Shepherd of Kentucky:

Dem corn shuckin's was sure 'nough big times. When us got all de corn gathered up and put in great long piles, den de gettin' ready started. Why, dem womans cooked for days, and de mens would get de shoats ready to barbecue. Master would send us out to get de slaves from de farms round about dere. De place was all lit up with light-wood knot torches and bonfires, and dere was 'citement a-plenty when all niggers get to singin' and shoutin' as dey made de shucks fly.

An ex-slave from Georgia recalled:

In corn shucking time no padderollers would ever bother you. We would have a big time at corn shuckings. They would call up the crowd and line the men up and give them a drink. I was a corn general—would stand out high above everybody, giving out corn songs and throwing down corn to them. There would be two sides of them, one side trying to outshuck the other. Such times we have.

White contemporaries provided comments that complement those of former slaves. Fredrika Bremer, one of the more astute and thoughtful travelers to the South, wrote that corn shuckings "are to the negroes what the harvest-home is to our [Swedish] peasants."

Certainly, the slaves had some material incentives. The best shuckers would get a dollar or a suit of clothes, as might those who found a red ear. But these incentives do not look impressive and do not loom large in the testimony. Those plantations on which the prize for finding a red ear consisted of a dollar do not seem to have done any better than those on which the prize consisted of an extra swig of whiskey or a chance to kiss the prettiest girl. The shucking was generally night work—overtime, as it were—and one might have expected the slaves to resent it and to consider the modest material incentives, which came to a special dinner and dance and a lot of whiskey, to be inadequate.

The most important feature of these occasions and the most important incentive to these long hours of extra work was the community life they called forth. They were gala affairs. The jug passed freely, although drunkenness was discouraged; the work went on amidst singing and dancing, friends and acquaintances congregated from several plantations and farms; the house slaves joined the field slaves in common labor; and the work was followed by an all-night dinner and ball at which inhibitions, especially those of class and race, were lowered as far as anyone dared.

Slavery, a particularly savage system of oppression and exploitation, made its slaves victims. But the human beings it made victims did not consent to be just that; they struggled to make life bearable and to find as much joy in it as they could. Up to a point even the harshest of masters had to help them do so. The logic of slavery pushed the masters to try to break their slaves' spirit and to reconstruct it as an unthinking and unfeeling extension of their own will, but the slaves' own resistance to dehumanization compelled the masters to compromise in order to get an adequate level of work out of them.

The combination of festive spirit and joint effort appears to have engaged the attention of the slaves more than anything else. Gus Brown, an ex-slave from Alabama, said simply, "On those occasions we all got together and had a regular good time." The heightened sense of fellowship with their masters also drew much comment. Even big slaveholders would join in the work, as well as in the festivities and the drinking, albeit not without the customary patriarchal qualifications. They would demand that the slaves sing, and the slaves would respond boisterously. Visitors expressed wonder at the spontaneity and improvisation the slaves displayed. The songs, often made up on the spot, bristled with sharp wit, both malicious and gentle. The slaves sang of their courtships and their lovers' quarrels; sometimes the songs got bawdy, and the children had to be hustled off to bed. They sang of their setbacks in love:

> When I'se here you calls me honey.
> When I'se gone you honies everybody.

They sang of their defeats in competition:

> You jumped and I jumped;
> Swear by God you outjumped me,
> Huh, huh, round de corn, Sally.

and of their victories:

> Pull de husk, break de ear
> Whoa, I'se got de red ear here.

But the songs also turned to satire. White participation in these festivals was always condescending and self-serving, and the slaves' acceptance of it displayed something other than childlike gratitude for small favors. They turned their wit and incredible talent for improvisation into social criticism. Occasionally they risked a direct, if muted, thrust in their "corn songs," as they came to be called.

> Massa in the great house, counting out his money,
> Oh, shuck that corn and throw it in the barn.
> Mistis in the parlor, eating bread and honey,
> Oh, shuck that corn and throw it in the barn.

More often, they used a simpler and safer technique. Ole Massa was always God's gift to humanity, the salt of the earth, de bestest massa in de whole wide worl'. But somehow, one or more of his neighbors was mighty bad buckra.

I

Massa's niggers am slick and fat,
  Oh! Oh! Oh!
Shine jes like a new beaver hat,
  Oh! Oh! Oh!

Refrain: Turn out here and shuck dis corn.
  Oh! Oh! Oh!
Biggest pile o' corn since I was born,
  Oh! Oh! Oh!

II

Jones' niggers am lean an po'
  Oh! Oh! Oh!
Don't know whether they git 'nough ter eat or no,
  Oh! Oh! Oh!

Blacks—any blacks—were not supposed to sass whites—any whites; slaves—any slaves—were not supposed to sit in judgment on masters—any masters. By the device of a little flattery and by taking advantage of the looseness of the occasion, they asserted their personalities and made their judgments.

A curious sexual division of labor marked the corn shuckings. Only occasionally did women participate in the shucking. The reason for the exclusion is by no means clear. Field women matched the men in hard work, not only in picking cotton but in rolling logs, chopping wood, and plowing. Yet at corn shuckings they divided their time between preparing an elaborate spread for the dinner and taking part in quilting bees and the like. As a result, the corn shuckings took on a peculiarly male tone, replete with raucous songs and jokes not normally told in front of women, as well as with those manifestations of boyish prancing associated with what is called—as if by some delightful Freudian slip—a "man's man."

The vigor with which the men worked and the insistence on a rigid sexual separation raise the central question of the slaves' attitude toward work in its relationship to their sense of family and community. The sense of community established by bringing together house and field slaves and especially slaves from several plantations undoubtedly underlay much of the slaves' positive response, and recalled the festivities, ceremonials, and rituals of traditional societies in a way no office Christmas party in an industrial firm has ever done. And corn shucking, like hog killing, had a special meaning, for at these times the slaves were literally working for themselves. The corn and pork fed them and their families; completion of these tasks carried a special satisfaction.

From this point of view the sexual division of labor, whatever its origins, takes on new meaning. In a limited way it strengthened that role of direct provider to which the men laid claim by hunting and fishing to supplement the family diet. Even the less attractive features of the evening in effect reinforced this male self-image. Nor did the women show signs of resentment. On the contrary, they seem to have grasped the opportunity to underscore a division of labor and authority in the family and to support the pretensions of their men. Slavery represented a terrible onslaught on the personalities and spirit of the slaves, and whatever unfairness manifested itself in this sexual bias, the efforts of male and female slaves to create and support their separate roles provided a weapon for joint resistance to dehumanization.

Hog-killing time rivaled corn shucking as a grand occasion. Consider two accounts from Virginia—one from J. S. Wise's well-known memoir, *The End of an Era,* and the other from Joseph Holmes's account of his life as a slave. First, Wise:

Then there was hog-killing time, when long before day, the whole plantation force was up with knives for killing, and seething cauldrons for scalding, and great doors for scraping, and long racks for cooling the slaughtered swine. Out to the farmyard rallied all the farm hands. Into the pens dashed the boldest and most active. Harrowing was the squealing of the victims, quick was the stroke that slew them, and quicker the sousing of the dead hog into the scalding water; busy the scraping of his hair away; strong the arms that bore him to the beams, and hung him there head downward to cool; clumsy the old woman who brought tubs to place under him; deft the strong hands that disemboweled him.

And now, Joseph Holmes:

Dat was de time of times. For weeks de mens would haul wood an' big rocks, an' pile 'em together as high as dis house, an' den have several piles, lak dat 'roun' a big hole in de groun' what has been filled wid water. Den jus' a little atter midnight, de boss would blow de ole hawn, an' all de mens would git up an' git in dem big pens. Den dey would sot dat pile of wood on fire an' den start knockin' dem hogs in de haid. Us neber shot a hog lak us does now; us always used an axe to kill 'em wid. Atter knockin' de hog in de haid, dey would tie a rope on his leg an' atter de water got to de right heat, fum dose red-hot rocks de hog would be throwed in an' drug aroun' a while, den taken out an' cleaned. Atter he was cleaned he was cut up into sections an' hung up in de smoke house. Lawsie lady, dey don't cure meat dese days; dey jus' uses some kind of liquid to bresh over it. We useta have sho' nuff meat.

The slaves enjoyed a special and delightful inducement here, for they could eat as they worked and could display pride in their individual skills within the totality of a community effort. As in corn shucking, they did this work for themselves and poured enthusiasm into it.

Logrollings called forth some of the same festive spirit but came less frequently. They had some direct reference to the slaves' own life when they contributed to building the quarters. Women worked along with the men, and teams competed against each other. In other respects the event had the same style as the corn shuckings. As Frank Gill, an ex-slave from Alabama, recalled:

Talkin' 'bout log rollin', dem was great times, 'ca'se if some ob dem neighborin' plantations wanated to get up a house, dey would invite all de slaves, men and women, to come wid dere masters. De women would help wit de cookin' an' you may be shore dey had something to cook. Dey would kill a cow, or three or four hogs, and den hab peas, cabbage, an' everything lack grows on de farm.

The evidence from the sugar plantations is especially instructive. Louisiana's sugar planters reputedly drove their slaves harder than any others in the slave states. Such reputations are by no means to be accepted at face value, but they certainly drove them hard during the grinding season. Yet, slaves took to the woods as limited and local runaways more often during the spring and summer months than during the autumn grinding season, when the work reached a peak of intensity and when the time for rest and sleep contracted sharply. Once again, the small material incentives cannot account for the slaves' behavior.

The slaves brought to their labor a gaiety and élan that perplexed observers, who saw them work at night with hardly a moment to catch their breath. Many, perhaps most, found themselves with special tasks to perform and special demands upon them; by all accounts they strained to rise to the occasion. The planters, knowing that the season lasted too long to sustain a fever pitch of effort, tried to break it up with parties and barbecues and at the very least promised and delivered a gala dinner and ball at the end. Ellen Betts, an ex-slave from Texas, recalled: "Massa sho' good to dem gals and bucks what cuttin' de cane. Whey dey git done makin' sugar, he give a drink called 'Peach 'n' Honey' to de women folk and whiskey and brandy to de men." Another ex-slave, William Stone of Alabama, said that the slaves were "happy" to work during the sugar harvest " 'cause we knowed it mean us have plenty 'lasses in winter."

Still, the demands of the sugar crop meant the sacrifice of some Sundays and even the Christmas holiday. The slaves showed no resentment at the postponement of the holiday. It would come in due time, usually in mid-January, and the greater their sacrifices, the longer and fuller the holiday would likely be. For the slaves on the sugar plantations Christmas did not mean December 25; it meant the great holiday that honored the Lord's birth, brought joy to His children, and properly fell at the end of the productive season.

Cotton picking was another matter. One ex-slave recalled cotton-picking parties along with corn-shucking parties but added, "Dere wasn't so much foolishness at cotton pickin' time." The slaves missed, in particular, the fellowship of slaves from other plantations. An exchange of labor forces on a crash basis sometimes occurred, and ex-slaves remembered precisely those times warmly. The planters had to have their cotton picked at about the same time and could not easily exchange labor forces. But the neighborly tradition was too strong to be denied entirely, and when a planter fell dangerously behind, others would come to his aid. Unable to take time away from their own work unless well ahead of schedule, friendly planters had to send their slaves after hours to pick by moonlight. The slaves, instead of becoming indignant over the imposition, responded with enthusiasm and extra effort. Many of them later recalled this grueling all-night work as "big times," for they were helping their own friends and combining the work with festivity. Bonuses, parties, and relaxed discipline rewarded their cooperation. Scattered evidence suggests less whipping and harsh driving during the cotton-picking season on some plantations but the opposite on others.

Some planters congratulated themselves on their success in getting a good response during the critical cotton harvest. Virginia Clay visited Governor Hammond's noteworthy plantation in South Carolina and enthusiastically reported on the magnificent singing and general spirit of the slaves, and Kate Stone was sure that "the Negroes really seemed to like the cotton picking best of all." Henry William Ravenel, in his private journal, made an interesting observation that provides a better clue to the slaves' attitude. Writing in 1865, immediately after their emancipation, he declared that the slaves had always disliked planting and cultivating cotton and would now prefer almost any alternative labor. The picking season must have struck the slaves as a mixed affair. It meant hard and distasteful work and sometimes punishment for failure to meet quotas, but also the end of a tough season, prizes for good performances, and the prelude to relaxation and a big celebration. Yet, the special spirit of the season was not strong enough to carry the slaves through the rigors of labor; the whip remained the indispensable spur.

Some anthropologists and cultural historians, noting the tradition of collective work among West Africans, have suggested its continuing influence among Afro-Americans. The Yoruba, for example, ingeniously combine community spirit and individual initiative by organizing hoeing in a line, so that everyone works alongside someone else and yet has his own task. But evidence of direct influence remains elusive, and, as William R. Bascom points out, collective patterns of work abounded in medieval Europe too. Whatever the origins of the slaves' strong preference for collective work, it drew the attention of their masters, who knew that they would have to come to terms with it. Edmund Ruffin, the South's great soil chemist and authority on plantation agriculture, complained that the pinewoods of North Carolina were set afire every spring by inconsiderate poor whites who cared nothing for the damage they did in order to provide grazing land for their few cows. He added that the slaves also set many fires because they intensely disliked collecting turpentine from the trees. This work was light and easy in Ruffin's estimation, but the slaves resisted it anyway because it had to be performed in isolation. "A negro," Ruffin explained from long experience, "cannot abide being alone and will prefer work of much exposure and severe toil, in company, to any lighter work, without any company."

This preference for work in company manifested itself in a readiness to help each other in field labor. Richard Mack, among others, recalled that he could finish a given task quickly and would then help others so that they would avoid punishment. This attitude, by no means rare, led another ex-slave, Sylvia Durant of South Carolina, to protest in the 1930s, "Peoples used to help one another out more en didn't somebody be tryin' to pull you down all de time."

Mrs. Durant's lament, common in the testimony of ex-slaves, hints at an anomaly reminiscent of the attitude of the Russian peasants who left the *mir*. The powerful community spirit and preference for collective patterns of working and living had their antithesis in an equally powerful individualism, manifested most attractively during and after Reconstruction in an attempt to transform themselves into peasant proprietors. This particular kind of individualism has also had less attractive manifestations, from the creation of the ghetto hustler and the devil-take-the-hindmost predator to the creation of a set of attitudes that many blacks hold responsible for a chronic lack of political unity. Certainly, the old collective spirit remains powerful, as the very notion of a black "brotherhood" demonstrates, but it does rest on a contradictory historical base. The work ethic of the slaves provided a firm defense against the excesses of an oppressive labor system, but like the religious tradition on which it rested, it did not easily lend itself to counterattack. Once the worst features of the old regime fell away, the ethic itself began to dissolve into its component parts. Even today we witness the depressing effects of this dissolution in a futile and pathetic caricature of bourgeois individualism, manifested both in the frustrated aspirations so angrily depicted in E. Franklin Frazier's *Black Bourgeoisie* and in violent, antisocial nihilism. But we also witness the continued power of a collective sensibility regarded by some as "race pride" and by others as a developing black national consciousness.

The slaves expressed their attitude in song. The masters encouraged quick-time singing among their field slaves, but the slaves proved themselves masters of slowing down the songs and the work. They willingly sang at work, as well as going to work, coming from work, and at almost any time. While assembling for field work they might sing individually.

> Saturday night and Sunday too
> Young gals on my mind.
> Monday morning 'way 'fore day,
> Old master's got me gwine.
> Peggy, does you love me now?

But whenever possible they sang collectively, in ways derived from Africa but rooted in their own experience. When they had to work alone or when they felt alone even in a group, they "hollered." Imamu Amiri Baraka's extraordinary analysis of the historical development of black music, however controversial, speculative, and tentative it may be judged, remains the indispensable introduction to the subject. He remarks on the roots of the blues: "The shouts and hollers were strident laments, more than anything. They were also chronicles but of such a mean kind of existence that they could not assume the universality any lasting musical form must have." Imamu Baraka traces the spread of hollers during and after Reconstruction when work patterns fragmented; but even during slavery a large portion of the slaves worked in isolation on small farms. Their hollers provided a counterpart to plantation work songs, but ranged beyond a direct concern with labor to a concern with the most personal expressions of life's travail. As such, they created a piercing history of the impact of hardship and sorrow on solitary black men. Their power notwithstanding, they represented a burning negative statement of the blacks' desire for community in labor as well as in life generally. As positive expression, both in themselves and in the legacy they left for blues singers to come, they contributed to the collective in a strikingly dialectical way, for they provided a form for a highly individualistic self-expression among a people whose very collectivity desperately required methods of individual self-assertion in order to combat the debilitating thrust of slavery's paternalistic aggression.

SUGGESTIONS FOR FURTHER READING

The first systematic study of slavery by an American scholar is Ulrich B. Phillips, *American Negro Slavery* (New York, 1918; paperback edition, Baton Rouge, La., 1966). Phillips's work was informed by his overtly racist assumption that blacks were innately inferior to whites. Although critical of the economic effects of slavery on the South, he argued that slaves were usually well treated and were generally happy with their lot; he explained instances of slave unrest simply as criminal behavior. Phillips had an enormous influence on later scholarship; his interpretation dominated the history of slavery as presented in school books and college texts. His critics, primarily blacks such as W. E. B. Du Bois (see Du Bois's review in *American Political Science Review,* 12 [November 1918], 722–26), were simply ignored by most historians.

Sustained criticism of Phillips by white scholars did not begin until the World War II years, when a repudiation of his racist assumption and a reexamination of his evidence resulted in widespread revision of his interpretation. In the years that followed, almost every aspect of the slave experience and its effects on African-Americans came under scrutiny by historians and other scholars.

A significant early contribution to the criticism and reinterpretation of the views of Phillips is Kenneth M. Stampp's *The Peculiar Institution* (New York, 1956), a portion of which is reprinted here. Using many of the same sources used by Phillips but eschewing his racism, Stampp came to very different conclusions. Instead of finding slaves well treated and satisfied, Stampp found them restive and rebellious, a view presented earlier in Herbert Aptheker's pioneering work *American Negro Slave Revolts* (New York, 1943, 1987).

Stanley M. Elkins, *Slavery* (Chicago, 1959, 1976) presents a very different view of the response of blacks to servitude. Elkins described slavery as a total, closed, repressive system that had devastating effects on the black personality and effectively destroyed any indigenous black culture, an interpretation that other scholars sharply attacked. John W. Blassingame, *The Slave Community,* rev. ed. (New York, 1979); George P. Rawick, *From Sundown to Sunup* (Westport, Conn., 1972); Eugene D. Genovese, *Roll, Jordan, Roll: The World the Slaves Made* (New York, 1974), a portion of which is reprinted here; Leslie Howard Owens, *This Species of Property: Slave Life and Culture in the Old South* (New York, 1976); and Nathan Irvin Huggins, *Black Odyssey: The Afro-American Ordeal in Slavery* (New York, 1977)—all find evidence of a viable black culture developing under slave conditions, although all are not in agreement as to the nature of that culture. Herbert G. Gutman, *The Black Family in Slavery and Freedom, 1750–1925* (New York, 1976) argues that blacks under slavery developed a unique family and kinship structure that, like much else in their culture, was not simply a reflection of the dominant white culture. Gutman's study is an attempt at a direct historical refutation of Daniel P. Moynihan's *The Negro Family in America: The Case for National Action,* printed in Lee Rainwater and William L. Yancey, *The Moynihan Report and the Politics of Controversy* (Cambridge, Mass., 1967), and E. Franklin Frazier, *The Negro Family in the United States* (Chicago, 1939). Lawrence W. Levine, *Black Culture and Black Consciousness: Afro-American Folk Thought from Slavery to Freedom* (New York, 1977) and Albert J. Raboteau, *Slave Religion: The 'Invisible Institution' in the Antebellum South* (New York, 1978) are important studies of particular aspects of slave culture. Robert W. Fogel and Stanley L. Engerman, *Time on the Cross* (Boston, 1974), a portion of which is reprinted here, is a general revisionist study of the whole question of the economics of black slavery. The Fogel and Engerman book stirred an enormous controversy, a taste of

---

*Available in paperback edition.

which may be seen in Paul A. David et al., *Reckoning with Slavery* (New York, 1976). Fogel's response to the criticism, along with much more, is his recent * Without Consent or Contract: The Rise and Fall of American Slavery* (New York, 1989).

Genovese's views on the nature of Southern society may be followed in his *The Political Economy of Slavery* (New York, 1965) and *The World the Slaveholders Made* (New York, 1969). For Genovese's views of Fogel and Engerman as well as of some of their critics, see chapters 5 and 6 of Elizabeth Fox-Genovese and Eugene D. Genovese, *Fruits of Merchant Capital* (New York, 1983). A view contrary to that of Genovese and similar to that of Stampp is James Oakes, *The Ruling Race* (New York, 1982). For important investigations of the effects of slavery on particular aspects of Southern society see Richard C. Wade, *Slavery in the Cities* (New York, 1964) and Robert S. Starobin, *Industrial Slavery in the Old South* (New York, 1970). Not all Southern blacks were slaves; for a fine study of those who were not, see Ira Berlin, *Slaves Without Masters: The Free Negro in the Antebellum South* (New York, 1974). Outstanding studies of the responses of western Europeans and Americans to black slavery are two volumes by David Brion Davis: *The Problem of Slavery in Western Culture* (Ithaca, N.Y., 1966) and *The Problem of Slavery in the Age of Revolution* (Ithaca, N.Y., 1975).

Much of the more recent work uses long available but previously seldom used black sources. Two convenient collections of some of these sources are Willie Lee Rose, ed., *A Documentary History of Slavery in North America* (New York, 1976) and John W. Blassingame, ed., *Slave Testimony* (Baton Rouge, La., 1977).

The literature on slavery is extensive. A good review of recent work is Charles B. Dew, "The Slavery Experience," in John B. Boles and Evelyn Thomas Nolen, *Interpreting Southern History: Historiographical Essays in Honor of Sanford W. Higginbotham* (Baton Rouge, La., 1987), 120–61.

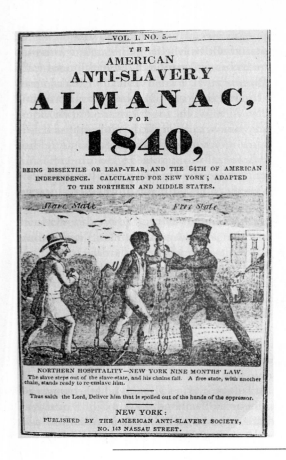

VOL. I. NO. 5.—

THE

AMERICAN

ANTI-SLAVERY

ALMANAC,

FOR

1840,

BEING BISSEXTILE OR LEAP-YEAR, AND THE 64TH OF AMERICAN
INDEPENDENCE. CALCULATED FOR NEW YORK ; ADAPTED
TO THE NORTHERN AND MIDDLE STATES.

NORTHERN HOSPITALITY—NEW YORK NINE MONTHS' LAW.
The slave steps out of the slave-state, and his chains fall. A free state, with another
chain, stands ready to re-enslave him.

Thus saith the Lord, Deliver him that is spoiled out of the hands of the oppressor.

NEW YORK:
PUBLISHED BY THE AMERICAN ANTI-SLAVERY SOCIETY,
NO. 143 NASSAU STREET.

8

Antebellum Reform

The age of Jackson was also an age of reform. If it was a time of optimism, intellectual ferment, and growing nationalism, it was also a time when a large number of men and women discovered that America had many problems. A religious revival (The Second Great Awakening), led by ministers like Charles Grandison Finney, spread across the land, leaving in its wake an army of converts ready to drive sin from the face of the earth. But not all reformers were motivated by religious zeal; some were influenced by a rational belief that men could improve their world. Like most Americans these reformers had faith in progress, and they were confident that they could speed the way toward a perfect social order.

The reform impulse took many forms. Some reformers founded utopian communities, such as Brook Farm near Boston, in order to experiment with new ways of organizing society. Perhaps these utopians were trying to escape the complicated problems of a country just beginning to be transformed by the revolutions in industry and transportation, but they sincerely believed that they were forerunners of a new order and that the world would follow their lead. Although there were a few eccentrics like Sylvester Graham, who was confident that he could change the world by getting everyone to eat "Graham Crackers," most were sincere men and women who set out to promote peace, to improve education, to secure the more humane treatment of prisoners, to win more opportunities and more rights for women, and to prohibit the use of alcoholic beverages. But the greatest reform of all was the crusade against slavery.

There had been opposition to slavery before the 1830s. The Quakers had been one of the few groups that had consistently opposed slavery in the colonial period; but the Revolution, with its emphasis on the rights of "life, liberty and the pursuit of happiness" for all men, initiated a more general movement that resulted by 1804 in the end of slavery, or provision for its abolition, in all Northern states. Even in the South there were many who favored gradual emancipation or who supported the American Colonization Society (organized 1817), which projected an eventual solution to the problem by shipping freed slaves to Africa.

The antislavery movement changed dramatically in about 1830 with the emergence of a small group of abolitionists led by William Lloyd Garrison, Theodore Weld, and other militant radicals who denounced slavery as a crime and demanded immediate emancipation. They were willing to disrupt the Union and to incite riot and even war to get rid of human bondage. The abolitionists, always in the minority, often did not agree among themselves, but they uniformly spoke the language of conflict. "I do not wish to think or speak or write with moderation," Garrison announced. "I will not retreat a single inch, and I will be heard."

The abolitionists were promptly labeled dangerous radicals and fanatics who overemphasized the evils of slavery, ignored the progress being made toward reform, and stirred up passions that endangered the Union. They responded that the system of human bondage was shameful and criminal, that organizations such as the American Colonization Society were really attempts to avoid, rather than face, the problem, and that a Union with slavery was a union with the devil.

Controversial in their own time, the abolitionists have continued to arouse disagreement among historians who have tried to determine who the abolitionists were, what motivated them to risk life and limb, and what effects they had. The selections that follow show some of the disagreements historians have in dealing with a group of militant agitators who believed in conflict—or at least were willing to accept it—in order to eradicate evil.

In the first selection, James Brewer Stewart describes the general religious and secular reformist sentiments in New England that gave birth to abolitionism. He depicts the abolitionists as a small band of "holy warriors," confident that they had discovered a religious truth and determined to eliminate the sin of slavery once and for all. United by a "romantic faith that God would put all things right," the abolitionists persisted in their efforts and willingly faced opposition, even physical danger. The abolitionists, Stewart concludes, considered themselves to be reformers, not revolutionaries, but their agitation generated considerable opposition, even among nonslaveholders. Religious leaders feared that the agitation would divide the churches; politicians worried that the political parties would split on the issue; and businessmen were dismayed by the danger of disruption of business relations with the South.

Martin Duberman, in the second selection, argues that the abolitionists were not mere reformers. In their militant attack on slavery as a social evil with which there could be no compromise, the abolitionists became radicals who questioned basic American values. Even though most Northerners opposed slavery, they would not accept the "extremism" of the abolitionists. Americans, Duberman insists, feared a "radical attack on social problems" because it "would compromise the national optimism," a fear that nineteenth-century opponents of the abolitionists share with twentieth-century opponents of real reforms. Duberman also strikes out at those historians who argue that any individual who protests strongly against social injustice is disturbed or fanatical. Those who fail to protest strongly against an institution as inhuman as slavery are the real "neurotics," he suggests.

Many of the abolitionists were active participants in other mid-nineteenth-century reform movements. In the final selection, Blanche Glassman Hersh describes how many of the middle-class women who became involved in the abolitionist movement became feminists and fighters for women's rights, usually less by design than by necessity. Many abolitionist women accepted the cult of true womanhood and used it to justify their reform activities in opposition to slavery. But as these women became involved in the abolitionist struggle they found themselves in conflict not only with opponents of abolitionism but also with some of the male abolitionists as well. Thus, for women the two reform movements became inextricably combined as they found it necessary to fight for their own rights as part of their battle against slavery.

Perhaps it is incorrect to term abolitionism a reform. The abolitionists sought an immediate end to slavery, which would have meant, in effect, the confiscation of millions of dollars worth of property owned by whites in the South. In this sense, then, abolitionists were radicals who sought a revolutionary social and economic change in the South. This may explain the opposition to abolitionism in the South, but why were so many Northerners so adamantly opposed to abolitionism? Did Northerners fear that the attack on slave property in the South might spread to become a general attack on private property elsewhere in the nation? If so, why did many Northerners who opposed the abolitionists become "free soilers" who opposed the expansion of slavery into the new territories in the West but were willing to let slavery remain untouched in the South? The free-soil movement would seem to be just as revolutionary as abolitionism in that it would deprive slaveowners of their property rights outside of the South, a limitation, Southerners were quick to point out, that no other property owners had to face.

Perhaps the Northerners' opposition to the abolitionists reflected their indifference to the plight of the blacks. If blacks remained enslaved and if slavery were confined to the South, Northern workers could avoid competition from freed blacks and farmers could avoid the competition from slaveowning Southern planters in the newly opened lands in the West. What, then, induced some to become abolitionists and regularly to face angry mobs of opponents in an effort to end slavery?

Evaluating the goals and methods of the abolitionists and the attitudes of those who opposed them raises general questions about the problem of reform in American society. Does successful reform always require a willingness to act within established institutions, to avoid extremism, and to be willing to accept compromise?

JAMES BREWER STEWART

The Abolitionists: Holy Warriors

American society in the late 1820's presented the pious, well-informed Yankee with tremendous challenges. For the better part of a decade, Protestant spokesmen had warned him against the nation's all-absorbing interest in material wealth, geographic expansion, and party politics. Infidelity, he was told, flourished on the Western and Southern frontiers; vice reigned supreme in the burgeoning Eastern cities. In politics, he was exhorted to combat atheist demagogues called Jacksonians who insisted on popular rule and further demanded that the clerical establishment be divorced from government. Urban workingmen and frontier pioneers, morally numbed by alcoholism and illiteracy, were being duped in massive numbers by the blandishments of these greedy politicos. America, he was assured, faced moral bankruptcy and the total destruction of its Christian identity. Exaggerated as such claims may seem, they had some grounding in reality. Yankee Protestantism was indeed facing immense new challenges from a society in the throes of massive social change. As Protestants struggled to overcome these adversities, the abolitionists' crusade for immediate emancipation also took form.

By the end of the 1820's, America was in the midst of unparalleled economic growth. Powerful commercial networks were coming to link all sections of the country; canals, mass-circulation newspapers, and (soon) railroads reinforced this thrust toward regional interdependency. Northern business depended as never before on trade with the South. The "cotton revolution" which swept the Mississippi-Alabama-Georgia frontier in turn stimulated textile manufacturing and shipping in the Northeast. In the Northwest, yet another economic boom took shape as businessmen and farmers in Ohio, Indiana, and Illinois developed lucrative relationships with the Eastern seaboard, and the population of North-

---

ern cities grew apace. Politicians organized party machines which catered to these new interests and to the "common man's" mundane preferences.

The cosmopolitan forces of economic interdependence, urbanization, democratic politics, and mass communication all posed major challenges to provincial New England culture. The Protestant response, in John L. Thomas's apt phrase, was "to fight democratic excess with democratic remedies." Throughout the 1820's New Englanders mounted an impressive counterattack against the forces of "immorality" by commandeering the tools of their secular opponents: the printing press, the rally, and the efficiently managed bureaucratic agency. With the hope of renovating American religious life, the American Tract Society spewed forth thousands of pamphlets which exhorted readers to repent. The Temperance Union carried a similar message to the nation's innumerable hard drinkers. Various missionary societies sent witnesses to back-country settlements, the waterfront haunts of Boston's seamen, the bordellos of New York City. These societies envisioned a reassertion of traditional New England values on a national scale. At the same time, although unintentionally, these programs for Christian restoration were stimulating in pious young men and women stirrings of spiritual revolt.

All of these reform enterprises drew their vitality from revivalistic religion. Once again, social discontent and political alienation found widespread expression through the conversion experience; the Great Revivals announced the Protestant resurgence of the 1820's. Like their eighteenth-century predecessors, powerful evangelists such as Charles G. Finney and Lyman Beecher urged their audiences that man, though a sinner, should nonetheless strive for holiness and choose a new life of sanctification. Free will once again took precedence over original sin, which was again redefined as voluntary selfishness. As in the 1750's, God was pictured as insisting that the "saved" perform acts of benevolence, expand the boundaries of Christ's kingdom, and recognize a personal responsibility to improve society. Men and women again saw themselves playing dynamic roles in their own salvation and preparing society for the millennium. By the thousands they flocked to the Tract Society, the Sunday School Union, the temperance and peace organizations, and the Colonization Society. Seeking prevention, certainly not revolution, evangelicals thus dreamed of a glorious era of national reform: rid of liquor, prostitution, atheism, and popular politics, the redeemed masses of America would gladly submit to the leadership of Christian statesmen. So blessed, Americans would no longer fall prey to the blandishments of that hard-drinking gambler, duelist, and unchurched slaveowner, President Andrew Jackson.

From this defensive setting sprang New England's crusade against slavery. Indeed, radical reformers of all varieties, not just abolitionists, traced their activism to the revivals of the 1820's. As we have seen, revivalism had also given powerful impetus to abolitionism in the eighteenth century. History was hardly repeating itself, however. The revivals of the Revolutionary era had not generated sustained movements for radical change. By contrast, the evangelical outbursts of the 1820's fostered alienation and rebellion among thousands of young men and women. The result was a bewildering variety of projects for reform.

Several factors help to explain this difference. For one thing, the revivalists of the 1820's found it impossible to define specific sources for the immorality that so disturbed them. There was no tyrannical king or corrupt Parliament to focus upon. There was also no glorious political brotherhood to join, such as the Sons of Liberty, no exalted goal to achieve, such as permanent independence from England. In short, the evangelical crusaders of the 1820's had few stable points of reference upon which to fix. Few institutions or popular leaders commanded their loyalties. Lacking these, revivalists sensed that infidelity could issue from any source, that corruption crowded in from all quarters. Their own dedication was all that stood between a sinning nation and God's all-consuming retribution. Here was a temperament which urged a lifetime of intense Christian struggle and a searching reexamination of accepted American institutions. The potential for radical commitment was indeed enormous.

While revivalism's ambiguities stimulated anxiety in the 1820's, its network of benevolent agencies opened opportunities for young Americans which their eighteenth-century counterparts could never have foreseen. The missionary agencies and even the revivals themselves were organized along complex bureaucratic lines. Volunteers were always needed to drum up donations or to organize meetings. New careers were also created. For the first time in American history, young people could regard social activism as a legitimate profession. Earnest ministerial candidates began accepting full-time positions as circuit riders, regional agents, newspaper editors, and schoolteachers, with salaries underwritten by the various benevolent agencies. One important abolitionist-to-be, Joshua Leavitt, spent his first years after seminary editing the *Seaman's Friend,* an evangelical periodical for sailors. Another, Elizur Wright, Jr., was employed by the American Tract Society.

Most important to abolitionism was the effect of revivalism on the ministry itself. Once open to only an elite, the ministry had by the 1820's become a common profession. Spurred by expanding geography, seminaries increased their enrollments as they attracted young New Englanders who burned to aid in America's regeneration. Included were some destined to number among abolitionism's dominant figures: Samuel J. May, Amos A. Phelps, Theodore D. Weld, Joshua Leavitt, and Stephen S. Foster, to name only a few. First as seminarians, then as volunteers, paid agents, clergymen, and teachers, many pious young Americans dedicated themselves to fighting sin and disbelief. Given the intensity of the evangelical temperament, the results of such experiences were to suggest, to some, far more radical courses of action, and there can be no question that these abolitionists-to-be took their responsibilities in deadly earnest.

There is some persuasive evidence that family background and upbringing predisposed young New Englanders toward a radical outlook. Over twenty years ago, David Donald gathered information which suggests the influence of parental guidance on abolitionism's most prominent spokesmen. Abolitionism, he reported, was a revolt of youth raised by old New England families of farmers, teachers, ministers, and businessmen. The parents of abolitionists were usually well-educated Presbyterians, Congregationalists, Quakers, and Unitarians who participated heavily in revivalism and its attendant benevolent projects. Many scholars have effectively criticized Donald's methods and have raised serious questions about the reliability of his evidence regarding the movement's rank-and-file. Donald also erred in concluding that commitments to abolitionism were reactions to a loss of social status to nouveau riche neighbors. Actually, abolitionism flourished among groups with rising social prospects during the 1830's. Nevertheless, Donald's findings remain extremely suggestive as to the influence of parental guidance on abolitionism's most prominent leaders.

In such families, as numerous biographers have since attested, a stern emphasis on moral uprightness and social responsibility generally prevailed. In the words of Bertram Wyatt-Brown, young men and women "learned that integrity came not from conformity to the ways of the world, but to the principles by which the family tried to live." Parents were usually eager to inculcate a high degree of religious and social conscience. In their reminiscences, abolitionists commonly paid homage to strong-minded mothers or fathers whose intense religious fervor dominated their households. In his early years, Wendell Phillips constantly turned to his mother for instruction, and after her death he confessed that "whatever good is in me, she is responsible for." Thomas Wentworth Higginson, Arthur and Lewis Tappan, and William Lloyd Garrison became, like Phillips, leading abolitionists and also internalized the religious dictates of dominating mothers. Sidney Howard Gay, James G. Birney, Elizur Wright, Jr., and Elijah P. Lovejoy are examples of abolitionists who modeled their early lives to fit the intentions of exacting fathers. Young women who were to enter the movement usually sought the advice of their fathers, as in the cases of Elizabeth Cady Stanton and Maria Weston Chapman. Yet whatever the child's focus, the expectations of parents seldom varied. Displays of conscience and upright behavior brought the rewards of parental love and approval.

Children also learned that sexual self-control was a vital part of righteous living. Parents stressed prayer and benevolent deeds as substitutes for "carnal thoughts" and intimacy; they associated sexual sublimation with family stability and personal redemption. During his years at boarding school and later at Harvard, Wendell Phillips strove to satisfy his mother on all these counts. Lewis Tappan, too, remembered how hard he had worked "to be one of the best scholars, often a favorite with the masters, and a leader among the boys in our plays." When he was twenty and living away from home, Tappan still received admonitions from his mother about the pitfalls of sex. Recalling a dream, she wrote, "Methought you had, by frequenting the theatre, been drawn into the society of lewd women, and had contracted a disease that was preying upon your constitution." For his part, Tappan had already sworn to "enjoy a sound mind and body, untainted by vice." A strong sense of their individuality, a deadly earnestness about moral issues, confidence in their ability to master themselves and to improve the world—these were the qualities which so often marked abolitionists in their early years. Above all, these future reformers believed in their own superiority and fully expected to become leaders.

Of course, not all children of morally assertive New England parents became radical abolitionists. William Lloyd Garrison's brother, for example, emerged from his mother's tutelage and lapsed into alcoholism. Still, the predisposition to rebellion remains hard to dismiss. Alienation and self-doubt certainly ran especially deep among these sensitive, socially conscious young people. Besides,

America in the 1820's appeared to many a complex and bewildering place. Certain social realities were soon to seem disturbingly at variance with their high expectations and fixed moral codes.

These future abolitionists entered young adulthood at a time when rapid mobility, technological advance, and dizzying geographic expansion were transforming traditional institutions. Those who took up pastorates, seminary study, or positions in benevolent agencies were shocked to discover that the Protestant establishment was hardly free from the acquisitive taint and bureaucratic selfishness that they had been brought up to disdain. Expecting to lead communities of godfearing, Christian families, young ministers like Amos A. Phelps, Elizur Wright, Jr., and Charles T. Torrey confronted instead a fragmented society of entrepreneurs. Theodore Dwight Weld, for example, wrote critically to the great evangelist Charles G. Finney that "*revivals* are fast becoming with you a sort of trade, to be worked at so many hours a day." Promoters of colonization, such as James G. Birney and Joshua Leavitt, became increasingly disturbed that many of their co-workers were far less interested in Christian benevolence than in ridding the nation of inferior blacks. In politics, Lewis Tappan, William Jay, and William Lloyd Garrison searched desperately and without success for a truly Christian leader, an alternative to impious Andrew Jackson and the godless party he led.

Predictably, misgiving became ever more frequent among young evangelicals. They began to question their abilities, to rethink their choices of career, and to doubt the Christianity of the churches, seminaries, and benevolent societies. Just possibly, the nation was far more deeply mired in sin than anyone had imagined. Just possibly, parental formulas for godly reformation were fatally compromised. And, most disturbing of all, just possibly the idealist-reformer himself needed reforming—a new relationship with God, a new vision of his responsibility as a Christian American.

The powerful combination in the 1820's of Yankee conservatism, revivalist benevolence, New England upbringing, and social unrest was leading young evangelicals toward a genuinely radical vision. Given this setting, it hardly seems surprising that a militant abolitionist movement began to take shape. Opposition to slavery certainly constituted a dramatic affirmation of one's Christian identity and commitment to a life of Protestant purity. Economic exploitation, sexual license, gambling, drinking and dueling, disregard for family ties—all traits associated with slaveowning—could easily be set in bold contrast with the pure ideals of Yankee evangelicalism.

There were a few militant antislavery spokesmen in the upper South in the 1820's, but their influence on young New Englanders was negligible. The manumission societies organized largely by evangelical Quakers and Moravian Brethren in Tennessee, Kentucky, and other border areas were already collapsing at the start of New England's crusade for immediate emancipation. The Southern antislavery movement's chief spokesman, editor Benjamin Lundy, had retreated northward from Tennessee. By 1829 he was living in Baltimore and had hired a zealous young editorial assistant from Newburyport, Massachusetts: William Lloyd Garrison.

The sudden emergence of immediate abolitionism in New England thus cannot be explained as a predictable offshoot of Yankee revivalism or a legacy from the upper South. Instead, one must emphasize the interaction between the rebellious feelings of these religious men and women and the events of the early 1830's. As the 1830's opened in an atmosphere of crisis, their attentions became intensely fixed on slavery. As in the early 1820's, the nation was again beset by black rebellions and threats of southern secession. Concurrently, events in England and in its sugar islands empire seemed to confirm the necessity of demanding the immediate emancipation of all slaves, everywhere. An unprecedented array of circumstances and jarring events suddenly converged on these anxious young people and launched them upon the lifetime task of abolishing slavery.

By far the most alarming was the ominous note of black militancy on which the new decade opened. In Boston in 1829, an ex-slave from North Carolina, David Walker, published the first edition of his famous *Appeal*. A landmark in black protest literature, Walker's *Appeal* condemned colonization as a white supremacist hoax, excoriated members of his own race for their passivity, and called, as a last resort, for armed resistance. "I do declare," wrote Walker, "that one good black man can put to death six white men." Whites had never hesitated to kill blacks, he advised, so "if you commence . . . do not trifle, for they will not trifle with you." Other events, even more shocking, were to follow. In 1831, William Lloyd Garrison, now living in Boston, issued a call for immediate emancipation in the *Liberator*. Soon after, Southampton County, Virginia, erupted in the bloody Nat Turner insurrection, the largest slave revolt in antebellum America. Still another massive slave rebellion broke out in British Jamaica in 1831. Coinciding with these racial traumas was the Nullification Crisis of 1831–32, a confrontation ignited by South Carolina's opposition to national tariff policy and by the deeper fear that the federal government might someday abolish slavery. Intent on preserving state sovereignty and hence slavery, South Carolina politicians led by John C. Calhoun temporarily defied national authority, threatened secession, and risked occupation by federal troops.

As these frightening events unfolded, young evangelicals cast aside their self-doubt. Unfocused discontent gave way to soul-wrenching commitments to eradicating the sin of slavery. The combined actions of Nat Turner, the South Carolina "Nullifiers," and David Walker suggested with dramatic force that slavery was the fundamental cause of society's degraded state. As Theodore D. Weld observed, the abolitionist cause "not only *overshadows* all others, but . . . absorbs them into itself. Revivals, moral Reform etc. will remain stationary until the temple is cleansed." The step-by-step solutions advocated by their parents suddenly appeared to invite only God's retribution. Like Garrison, Arthur Tappan, and many others, James G. Birney sealed his commitment to immediate abolition by decrying colonization. The Colonization Society, Birney charged, acted as "an opiate to the consciences" of those who would otherwise "feel deeply and keenly the sin of slavery."

In one sense, these sudden espousals of immediate abolition can be understood as a strategic innovation developed because of the manifest failures of gradualism. Slaveholders had certainly shown no sympathy to moderate schemes. In England, too, where immediatism was also gaining followers, the general public had remained unmoved by gradualist proposals. Demands for "immediate, unconditional, uncompensated emancipation" thus appealed to young American idealists—at least the slogan was free of moral qualifications. Indeed, in 1831 the British government, responding to immediatist demands, enacted a massive program of gradual, compensated emancipation in the West Indies. But, even more important, by dedicating themselves to immediatism, the young reformers performed acts of self-liberation akin to the experience of conversion.

By freeing themselves from the shackles of gradualism, American abolitionists had finally triumphed over their feelings of selfishness, unworthiness, and alienation. Now they were morally fit to take God's side in the struggle against all the worldliness, license, cruelty, and selfishness that slaveowning had come to embody. Immediatists sensed themselves involved in a cosmic drama, a righteous war to redeem a fallen nation. They now felt ready to make supreme sacrifices and prove their fitness in their new religion of antislavery. "Never were men called on to die in a holier cause," wrote Amos A. Phelps in 1835, as he began his first tour as an abolitionist lecturer. It was far better, he thought, to die "as the negro's plighted friend" than to "sit in silken security, the consentor to & abettor of the manstealer's sin."

The campaign for Protestant reassertion had thus brought forth a vibrant romantic radicalism. Orthodox evangelicals quite rightly recoiled in fear. Abolitionists now put their faith entirely in the individual's ability to recognize and redeem himself from sin. No stifling traditions, no restrictive loyalties to institutions, no timorous concern for moderation or self-interest should be allowed to inhibit the free reign of Christian conscience. In its fullest sense, the phrase "immediate emancipation" described a transformed state of mind dominated by God and wholly at war with slavery. "The doctrine," wrote Elizur Wright, Jr., in 1833, "may be thus briefly stated":

It is the duty of the holders of slaves to restore them to their liberty, and to extend to them the full protection of the law . . . to restore to them the profits of their labors, . . . to employ them as voluntary laborers on equitable wages. Also it is the duty of all men . . . to proclaim this doctrine, to urge upon slaveholders immediate emancipation, so long as there is a slave—to agitate the consciences of tyrants, so long as there is a tyrant on the globe.

Embedded in this statement was a vision of a new America, a daring affirmation that people of both races could reestablish their relationships on the basis of justice and Christian brotherhood. Like many other Americans who took up the burdens of reform, abolitionists envisioned their cause as leading to a society reborn in Christian brotherhood. Emancipation, like temperance, women's rights and communitarianism, became synonymous with the redemption of mankind and the opening of a purer phase of human history.

Abolitionists constantly tried to explain that they were not expecting some sudden Day of Jubilee when, with a shudder of collective remorse, the entire planter class would abruptly strike the shackles from all two million slaves and beg their forgiveness. Emancipation, they expected, would be achieved gradually; still it must be immediately begun. Immediatists were also forced to rebut the recurring charge that their demands promoted emancipation by rebellion on the plantations. "Our objects are to save life, not destroy it," Garrison exclaimed in

1831. "Make the slave free and every inducement to revolt is taken away." Few Americans believed these disclaimers. Instead, most suspected that immediate emancipation would suddenly create a large and mobile free population of inferior blacks. Most in the North were quite content to discriminate harshly against their black neighbors while the slaves remained at a safe distance on far-away plantations. According to Alexis de Tocqueville, the unusually acute foreign observer of antebellum society of the early 1830's: "Race prejudice seems stronger in those states that have abolished slavery than in those where it still exists, and nowhere is it more intolerant than in those states where it has never been known." White supremacy and support for slavery were thus inextricably bound up with all phases of American political, economic, and religious life. Immediatist agitation was bound to provoke hostility from nearly every part of the social order.

As we have seen, by the 1830's the Northeast and Midwest enjoyed a thriving trade with the South, and the nation's economic well-being had become firmly tied to slave labor. Powerful financial considerations could thus dictate that abolitionism be harshly suppressed. Religious denominations were also deeply enmeshed in slavery, for Southerners were influential among the Methodists, Presbyterians, Anglicans, and Baptists. Little wonder that most clergymen vigorously rejected demands that their churches declare slaveholders in shocking violation of God's Law.

But by far the most consistent opponents of the abolitionist crusade were found in politics. Young reformers had long ago come to abhor what they saw as the hollow demagoguery and secularism of Jacksonian mass politics. By 1830 they were fully justified in adding the politician's unstinting support of slavery to their bill of particulars. As Richard H. Brown has shown, Jackson's Democratic Party was deliberately designed to uphold the planters' interests. Jacksonian ideology soon became synonymous with racism and anti-abolition. In the North, men who aspired to careers in Democratic Party politics had to solicit the approval of slaveholding party chiefs like Amos Kendall, John C. Calhoun, and Jackson himself. When anti-Jacksonian dissidents finally coalesced into the Whig Party during the 1830's, they, too, relied upon this formula for getting votes and recruiting leaders. Obviously, neither party dared to alienate proslavery interests in the South or racist supporters in the North. Moreover, as the Missouri and Nullification controversies had shown, political debates about slavery caused party allegiances to break ominously along sectional lines. For these reasons, party loyalty meant the suppression of all discussions of slavery.

The challenges which the abolitionists faced as they began their crusade were thus enormous. So was their own capability for disruption, although they were hardly aware of it at first. The ending of slavery whether peacefully or violently would require great changes in American life. Yet, if immediate emancipation provoked fear and violent hostility, it was nevertheless a doctrine appropriate to the age. The evangelical outlook with its rejection of tradition and expedience both embodied and challenged the culture that had created it. In retrospect, moderate approaches to the problem of slavery hardly seemed possible in Jacksonian America.

As a result, immediatist goals were anything but limited. Abolitionists now proposed to transform hundreds of millions of dollars worth of slaves into millions of black citizens by eradicating two centuries of American racism. Nevertheless, they sincerely felt that they promoted a conservative enterprise, and in certain respects this was an understandable (if misleading) self-assessment. Their unqualified attacks on slavery were, as they understood them, simply emulations of well-established evangelical methods. The Temperance Society's assault on liquor and the revivalist's denunciation of unbelief had hardly been characterized by restraint. Besides, immediatists were simply proposing an ideal by which all Christians were to measure themselves. They were not planning bloody revolution. They relied solely on voluntary conversion and rejected violence. As agitators, they defined their task as restoring time-honored American freedoms to an unjustly deprived people. Except for their opposition to racism, they offered no criticism of ordinary Protestant values. Was it anarchy, they wondered, to urge that pure Christian morality replace what they believed was the sexual abandon of the slave quarters? "Are we then fanatics," Garrison asked, "because we cry, *Do not rob! Do not murder!?*"

In their own eyes, then, abolitionists were hardly behaving like incendiaries as they opened their crusade. In slaveholding they discovered the ultimate source of the moral collapse which so deeply disturbed them. The race violence of Nat Turner and the secession threats of the "Nullifiers" constituted evidence that the nation had jettisoned all her moral ballasts. But immediate abolition seemed to hold forth the promise of Christian reconciliation between races, sections, and individuals. All motive for race revolt, all reason for political strife, and all inducement for moral degeneracy would be swept away. Indeed, the alternative of silence only invited the further spread of anarchy in a nation which Garrison described in 1831 as already "full of the blood of innocent men, women and babies—full of adultery and concupiscence—full of blasphemy, darkness and woeful rebellion against God—full of wounds and bruises and putrefying sores." Abolitionists were thus filled "with burning earnestness" when they insisted, as Elizur Wright did, that "the instant abolition of the whole slave system is safe." Most other Americans remained firm in their suspicions to the contrary.

Nevertheless, the abolitionists launched their crusade on a note of glowing optimism. Armed with moral certitude, they were also completely naïve politically. "The whole system of slavery will fall to pieces with a rapidity which will astonish," wrote Samuel E. Sewall, one of the first adherents to immediatism. Weld predicted in 1834 that complete equality for all blacks in the upper South was but two years away, and that "scores of clergymen in the slaveholding states . . . *are really with us.*" Anxious for the millennium, abolitionists had wholly misjudged the depth of Northern racism, not to mention the extent of Southern tolerance.

All the same, there was wisdom in the naïveté. Without this romantic faith that God would put all things right, abolitionists would have lacked the incentive and creative stamina necessary for sustained assaults against slavery. Moreover, by stressing intuition as a sure guide to reality, abolitionists made an unprecedented attempt to establish empathy with the slave. One result, to be sure, was racist sentimentalism, a not surprising outcome considering the gulf which separated a Mississippi field hand from an independently wealthy Boston abolitionist. Yet the abolitionists were trying hard to imagine what it was like to be stripped of one's autonomy, prevented from protecting one's family, and deprived of legal safeguards and the rewards of one's own labor. This view of slavery made piecemeal reform completely unacceptable. To give slaves better food, fewer whippings, and some education was not enough. They deserved immediate justice, not charity. So convinced, and certain of ultimate victory, abolitionists set out to induce each American citizen to repent the sin of slavery.

The Northern Response to Slavery

The abolitionist movement never became the major channel of Northern antislavery sentiment. It remained in 1860 what it had been in 1830: the small but not still voice of radical reform. An important analytical problem thus arises: why did most Northerners who disapproved of slavery become "nonextensionists" rather than abolitionists? Why did they prefer to attack slavery indirectly, by limiting its spread, rather than directly, by seeking to destroy it wherever it existed?

On a broad level, the answer involves certain traits in the national character. In our society of abundance, prosperity has been the actual condition—or the plausible aspiration—of the majority. Most Americans have been too absorbed in the enjoyment or pursuit of possessions to take much notice of the exactions of the system. Even when inequalities have become too pronounced or too inclusive any longer to be comfortably ignored, efforts at relief have usually been of a partial and half-hearted kind. Any radical attack on social problems would compromise the national optimism; it would suggest fundamental defects, rather than occasional malfunctions. And so the majority has generally found it necessary to label "extreme" any measures which call for large-scale readjustment. No one reasonably contented welcomes extensive dislocation; what seems peculiarly American is the disbelief, under *all* circumstances, in the necessity of such dislocation.

Our traditional recoil from "extremism" can be defended. Complex problems, it might be said, require complex solutions; or, to be more precise, complex problems have no solutions—at best, they can be but partially adjusted. If even this much is to be possible, the approach must be flexible, piecemeal, pragmatic. The clear-cut blueprint for reform, with its utopian demand for total solution, intensifies rather than ameliorates disorder.

There is much to be said for this defense of the American way—in the abstract. The trouble is that the theory of gradualism and the practice of it have not been the same. Too often Americans have used the gradualist argument as a technique of evasion rather than as a tool for change, not as a way of dealing with difficult problems slowly and carefully, but as an excuse for not dealing with them at all. We do not want time for working out our problems—we do not want problems, and we will use the argument of time as a way of not facing them. As a chosen people, we are meant only to have problems which are self-liquidating. All of which is symptomatic of our conviction that history is the story of inevitable progress, that every day in every way we *will* get better and better even though we make no positive efforts toward that end.

Before 1845, the Northern attitude toward slavery rested on this comfortable belief in the benevolence of history. Earlier, during the 1830's, the abolitionists had managed to excite a certain amount of uneasiness about the institution by invoking the authority of the Bible and the Declaration of Independence against it. Alarm spread still further when mobs began to prevent abolitionists from speaking their minds or publishing their opinions, and when the national government interfered with the mails and the right of petition. Was it possible, men began to ask, that the abolitionists were right in contending that slavery, if left alone, would not die out but expand, would become more not less vital to the country's interests? Was it possible that slavery might even end by infecting free institutions themselves?

The apathetic majority was shaken, but not yet profoundly aroused; the groundwork for widespread antislavery protest was laid, but its flowering awaited further developments. The real watershed came in 1845, when Texas was annexed to the Union, and war with Mexico followed. The prospect now loomed of a whole series of new slave states. It finally seemed clear that the mere passage of time would not bring a solution; if slavery was ever to be destroyed, more active resistance would be necessary. For the first time large numbers of Northerners prepared to challenge the dogma that slavery was a local matter in which the free states had no concern. A new era of widespread, positive resistance to slavery had opened.

Yet such new resolve as had been found was not channeled into a heightened demand for the abolition of the institution, but only into a demand that its further extension be prevented. By 1845 Northerners may have lost partial, but not total confidence in "Natural Benevolence"; they were now wiser Americans perhaps, but Americans nonetheless. More positive action against slavery, they seemed to be saying, was indeed required, but nothing too positive. Containing the institution would, in the long run, be tantamount to destroying it; a more direct assault was unnecessary. In this sense, the doctrine of nonextension was but a more sophisticated version of the standard faith in "time."

One need not question the sincerity of those who believed that nonextension would ultimately destroy slavery, in order to recognize that such a belief partook of wishful thinking. Even if slavery was contained, there remained large areas in the Southern states into which the institution could still expand; even without further expansion, there was no guarantee that slavery would cease to be profitable; and finally, even should slavery cease to be profitable, there was no certainty that the South, psychologically, would feel able to abandon it. Nonextension, in short, was hardly a fool-proof formula. Yet many Northerners chose to so regard it. And thus the question remains: why did not an aroused antislavery conscience turn to more certain measures and demand more unequivocal action?

To have adopted the path of direct abolition, first of all, might have meant risking individual respectability. The unsavory reputation of those already associated with abolitionism was not likely to encourage converts to it. Still, if that doctrine had been really appealing, the disrepute of its earlier adherents could not alone have kept men from embracing it. Association with the "fanatics" could have been smoothed simply by rehabilitating their reputations; their notoriety, it could have been said, had earlier been exaggerated—it had been the convenient invention of an apathetic majority to justify its own indifference to slavery. When, after 1861, public opinion did finally demand a new image of the abolitionists, it was readily enough produced. The mere reputation of abolitionism, therefore, would not have been sufficient to repel men from joining its ranks. Hostility to the movement had to be grounded in a deeper source—fear of the doctrine of "immediatism" itself.

Immediatism challenged the Northern hierarchy of values. To many, a direct assault on slavery meant a direct assault on private property and the Union as well. Fear for these values clearly inhibited antislavery fervor (though possibly a reverse trend operated as well—concern for property and Union may have been stressed in order to justify the convenience of "going slow" on slavery).

As devout Lockeans, Americans did believe that the sanctity of private property constituted the essential cornerstone for all other liberties. If property could not be protected in a nation, neither could life nor liberty. And the Constitution, so many felt, had upheld the legitimacy of holding property in men. True, the Constitution had not mentioned slavery by name, and had not overtly declared in its favor, but in giving the institution certain indirect guarantees (the three-fifths clause; non-interference for twenty-one years with the slave trade; the fugitive slave proviso), the Constitution had seemed to sanction it. At any rate no one could be sure. The intentions of the Founding Fathers remained uncertain, and one of the standing debates of the antebellum generation was whether the Constitution had been meant by them to be a pro- or an antislavery document. Since the issue was unresolved, Northerners remained uneasy, uncertain how far they could go in attacking slavery without at the same time attacking property.

Fear for property rights was underscored by fear for the Union. The South had many times warned that if her rights and interests were not heeded, she would leave the Union and form a separate confederation. The tocsin had been sounded with enough regularity so that to some it had begun to sound like hollow bluster. But there was always the chance that if the South felt sufficiently provoked she might yet carry out the threat.

It is difficult today fully to appreciate the horror with which most Northerners regarded the potential breakup of the Union. The mystical qualities which surrounded "Union" were no less real for being in part irrational. Lincoln struck a deep chord for his generation when he spoke of the Union as the "last best hope of earth"; that the American experiment was thought the "best" hope may have been arrogant, a hope at all, naïve, but such it was to the average American, convinced of his own superiority and the possibility of the world learning by example. Today, more concerned with survival than improvement, we are bemused (when we are not cynical) about "standing examples for mankind," and having seen the ghastly deeds done in the name of patriotism, we are impatient at signs of national fervor. But 100 years ago, the world saw less danger in nationalism, and Americans, enamored with their own extraordinary success story, were especially prone to look on love of country as some of the noblest of human sentiments. Even those Southerners who had ceased to love the Union had not ceased to love the idea of nationhood; they merely wished to transfer allegiance to a more worthy object.

Those who wanted to preserve the old Union acted from a variety of motives: the Lincolns, who seem primarily to have valued its spiritual potential, were joined by those more concerned with maintaining its power potential; the Union was symbol of man's quest for a benevolent society—and for dominion. But if Northerners valued their government for differing reasons, they generally agreed on the necessity for preserving it. Even so, their devotion to the Union had its oscillations. In 1861 Lincoln and his party, in rejecting the Crittenden Compromise, seemed willing to jeopardize Union rather than risk the further expansion of slavery (perhaps because they never believed secession would really follow, though this complacency, in turn, might only have been a way of convincing themselves that a strong antislavery stand would not necessarily destroy the Union). After war broke out the value stress once more shifted: Lincoln's party now loudly insisted that the war was indeed being fought to preserve the Union, not to free the slaves. Thus did the coexisting values of Union and antislavery tear the Northern mind and confuse its allegiance.

The tension was compounded by the North's ambivalent attitude toward the Negro. The Northern majority, unlike most of the abolitionists, did not believe in the equality of races. The Bible (and the new science of anthropology) seemed to suggest that the Negro had been a separate, inferior creation meant for a position of servitude. Where there was doubt on the doctrine of racial equality, its advocacy by the distrusted abolitionists helped to settle the matter in the negative.

It was possible, of course, to disbelieve in Negro equality, and yet disapprove of Negro slavery. Negroes were obviously men, even if an inferior sort, and as men they could not in conscience (the Christian-Democratic version) be denied the right to control their own souls and bodies. But if anti-Negro and antislavery sentiments were not actually incompatible, they were not mutually supportive either. Doubt of the Negro's capacity for citizenship continually blunted the edge of antislavery fervor. If God had intended the Negro for some subordinate role in society, perhaps a kind of benevolent slavery was, after all, the most suitable arrangement; so long as there was uncertainty, it might be better to await the slow unfolding of His intentions in His good time.

And so the average Northerner, even after he came actively to disapprove of slavery, continued to be hamstrung in his opposition to it by the competitive pull of other values. Should prime consideration be given to freeing the slaves, even though in the process the rights of property and the preservation of the Union were threatened? Should the future of the superior race be endangered in order to improve the lot of a people seemingly marked by Nature for a degraded station? Ideally, the North would have liked to satisfy its conscience about slavery and at the same time preserve the rest of its value system intact—to free the Negro and yet do so without threatening property rights or dislocating the Union. This struggle to achieve the best of all possible worlds runs like a forlorn hope throughout the ante-bellum period—the sad, almost plaintive quest by the American Adam for the perfect world he considered his birthright.

The formula of nonextension did seem, for a time, the perfect device for balancing these multiple needs. Nonextension would put slavery in the course of ultimate extinction without producing excessive dislocation; since slavery would not be attacked directly, nor its existence immediately threatened, the South would not be unduly fearful for her property rights, the Union would not be needlessly jeopardized, and a mass of free Negroes would not be precipitously thrust upon an unprepared public. Nonextension, in short, seemed a panacea, a formula which promised in time to do everything while for the present risking nothing. But like all panaceas, it ignored certain hard realities: would containment really lead to the extinction of slavery? would the South accept even a gradual dissolution of her peculiar institution? would it be right to sacrifice two or three more generations of Negroes in the name of uncertain future possibilities? Alas for the American Adam, so soon to be expelled from Eden.

The abolitionists, unlike most Northerners, were not willing to rely on future intangibles. Though often called impractical romantics, they were in some ways the most tough-minded of Americans. They had no easy faith in the benevolent workings of time or in the inevitable triumphs of gradualism. If change was to come, they argued, it would be the result of man's effort to produce it; patience and inactivity had never yet helped the world's ills. Persistently, sometimes harshly, the abolitionists denounced delay and those who advocated it; they were tired, they said, of men using the councils of moderation to perpetuate injustice.

In their own day, and ever since, the abolitionists have faced a hostile majority; their policies have been ridiculed, their personalities reviled. Yet ridicule, like its opposite, adoration, is usually not the result of analysis but a substitute for it. Historians have for so long been absorbed in denouncing the abolitionists, that they have had scant energy left over for understanding them. The result is that we still know surprisingly little about the movement, and certainly not enough to warrant the general assumptions so long current in the historical profession.

Historians have assumed that the abolitionists were unified in their advocacy of certain broad policies—immediate emancipation, without compensation—and also unified in refusing to spell out details for implementing these policies. To some extent this traditional view is warranted. The abolitionists did agree almost unanimously (Gerrit Smith was one of the few exceptions) that slaveholders must not be compensated. One does not pay a man, they argued, for ceasing to commit a sin. Besides, the slaveholder had already been paid many times over in labor for which he had never given wages. Defensible though this position may have been in logic or morals, the abolitionists should perhaps have realized that public opinion would never support the confiscation of property, and should have modified their stand accordingly. But they saw themselves as prophets, not politicians; they were concerned with what was "right," not with what was possible, though they hoped that if men were once made aware of the right, they would find some practical way of implementing it.

The abolitionists were far less united on the doctrine of immediate emancipation—at least in the 1830's, before Southern intransigence and British experience in the West Indies convinced almost all of them that gradualism was hopeless. But during the 1830's, there was a considerable spectrum of opinion as to when and how to emancipate the slave. Contrary to common myth, some of the abolitionists did advocate a period of prior education and training before the granting of full freedom. Men like Weld, Birney, and the Tappans, stressing the debasing experience of slavery, insisted only that gradual emancipation be immediately begun, not that emancipation itself be at once achieved. This range of opinion has never been fully appreciated. It has been convenient, then and now, to believe that all abolitionists always advocated instantaneous freedom, for it thus became possible to denounce any call for emancipation as "patently impractical."

By 1840, however, most abolitionists had become immediatists, and that position, "practical" or not, did have a compelling moral urgency. Men learned how to be free, the immediatists argued, only by being free; slavery, no matter how attenuated, was by its very nature incapable of preparing men for those independent decisions necessary to adult responsibility. Besides, they insisted, the Negro, though perhaps debased by slavery, was no more incapacitated for citizenship than were many poor whites, whose rights no one seriously suggested curtailing.

The immediatist position was not free of contradiction. If slavery had been as horrendous as the abolitionists claimed, it was logical to expect that its victims would bear deep personality scars—greater than any disabilities borne by a poor white, no matter how degraded his position. Either slavery had not been this deadly, or, if it had, those recently freed from its toils could not be expected to move at once into the responsibilities of freedom. This contradiction was apparent to some immediatists, but there was reason for refusing to resolve it. Ordinarily, they said, a system of apprenticeship might be desirable, but if conditions to emancipation were once established, they could be used as a standing rationale for postponement; the Negro could be kept in a condition of semislavery by the self-perpetuating argument that he was not yet ready for his freedom.

Moreover, any intermediary stage before full freedom would require the spelling out of precise "plans," and these would give the enemies of emancipation an opportunity to pick away at the impracticality of this or that detail. They would have an excuse for disavowing the broader policy under the guise of disagreeing with the specific means for achieving it. Better to concentrate on the larger issue and force men to take sides on that alone, the abolitionists argued, than to give them a chance to hide their opposition behind some supposed disapproval of detail. Wendell Phillips, for one, saw the abolitionists' role as exclusively that of agitating the broader question. Their primary job, Phillips insisted, was to arouse the country's conscience rather than to spell out to it precise plans and formulas. After that conscience had been aroused, it would be time to talk of specific proposals; let the moral urgency of the problem be recognized, let the country be brought to a determination to rid itself of slavery, and ways and means to accomplish that purpose would be readily enough found.

No tactical position could really have saved the abolitionists from the denunciation of those hostile to their basic goal. If the abolitionists spelled out a program for emancipation, their enemies would have a chance to pick at details; if they did not spell out a program, they could then be accused of vagueness and impracticality. Hostility can always find its own justification.

A second mode of attack on the abolitionists has centered on their personalities rather than their policies. The stereotype which long had currency sees the abolitionist as a disturbed fanatic, a man self-righteous and self-deceived, motivated not by concern for the Negro, as he may have believed, but by an unconscious drive to gratify certain needs of his own. Seeking to discharge either individual anxieties or those frustrations which came from membership in a "displaced élite," his antislavery protest was, in any case, a mere disguise for personal anguish.

A broad assumption underlies this analysis which has never been made explicit—namely, that strong protest by an individual against social injustice is ipso facto proof of his disturbance. Injustice itself, in this view, is apparently never sufficient to arouse unusual ire in "normal" men, for normal men, so goes the canon, are always cautious, discreet, circumspect. Those who hold to this model of human behavior seem rarely to suspect that it may tell us more about their hierarchy of values than about the reform impulse it pretends to describe. Argued in another context, the inadequacies of the stereotype become more apparent: if normal people do not protest "excessively" against injustice, then we should be forced to condemn as neurotic all those who protested with passion against the Nazi persecution of the Jews.

Some of the abolitionists, it is true, were palpable neurotics, men who were not comfortable within themselves and therefore not comfortable with others, men whose "reality-testing" was poor, whose life styles were pronouncedly compulsive, whose relationships were unusual compounds of demand and phantasy. Such neurotics *were* in the abolitionist movement—the Parker Pillsburys, Stephen Fosters, Abby Folsoms. Yet even here we must be cautious, for our diagnostic accuracy can be blurred if the life style under evaluation is sharply different from our own. Many of the traits of the abolitionists which today "put us off" were not peculiar to them, but rather to their age—the declamatory style, the abstraction and idealization of issues, the tone of righteous certainty, the religious context of argumentation. Thus the evangelical rhetoric of the movement, with its thunderous emphasis on sin and retribution, can sound downright "queer" (and thus "neurotic") to the 20th century skeptic, though in its day common enough to abolitionists and nonabolitionists alike.

Then, too, even when dealing with the "obvious" neurotics, we must be careful in the link we establish between their pathology and their protest activity. It is one thing to demonstrate an individual's "disturbance" and quite another then to explain all of his behavior in terms of it. Let us suppose, for example, that Mr. Jones is a reformer; he is also demonstrably "insecure." The two may seem logically related (that is, if one's mind automatically links "protest" with "neurosis"), but we all know that many things can be logical without being true.

Even if we establish the neurotic behavior of certain members of a group, we have not, thereby, established the neurotic behavior of *all* members of that group. The tendency to leap from the particular to the general is always tempting, but because we have caught one benighted monsignor with a boy scout does not mean we have conclusively proved that all priests are pederasts. Some members of every group are disturbed; put the local police force, the Medal of Honor winners, or the faculty of a university under the Freudian microscope, and the number of cases of "palpable disturbance" would probably be disconcertingly high. But what *precisely* does their disturbance tell us about the common activities of the group to which they belong—let alone about the activities of the disturbed individuals themselves?

Actually, behavioral patterns for many abolitionists do *not* seem notably eccentric. Men like Birney, Weld, Lowell, Quincy—abolitionists all—formed good relationships, saw themselves in perspective, played and worked with zest and spontaneity, developed their talents, were aware of worlds beyond their own private horizons. They all had their tics and their traumas—as who does not—but the evidence of health is abundant and predominant. Yet most historians have preferred to ignore such men when discussing the abolitionist movement. And the reason, I believe, is that such men conform less well than do the Garrisons to the assumption that those who become deeply involved in social protest are necessarily those who are deeply disturbed.

To evaluate this assumption further, some effort must be made to understand current findings in the theory of human motivation. This is difficult terrain for the historian, not made more inviting by the sharp disagreements which exist among psychologists themselves (though these disagreements do help to make us aware of the complexities involved). Recent motivational research, though not conclusive, throws some useful new perspectives on "reformers."

A reaction has currently set in among psychologists against the older behaviorist model of human conduct. The behaviorists told us that men's actions were determined by the nature of the stimulus exerted upon them, and that their actions always pointed towards the goal of "tension reduction." There was little room in behaviorist theory for freedom of choice, for rationality, or for complex motives involving abstract ideas as well as instinctive drives.

Without denying the tension-reducing motives of certain kinds of human behavior, a number of psychologists are now insisting on making room for another order of motivation, involving more than the mere "restoration of equilibrium." Mature people, they believe—that is, those who have a realistic sense of self—*can* act with deliberation and *can* exercise control over their actions. This new view presumes an active intellect, an intellect capable of interpreting sensory data in a purposive way. The power of reflection, of self-objectification, makes possible a dynamic as opposed to a merely instinctive life. Men, in short, need not be wholly driven by habit and reflex; they need not be mere automatons who respond in predictable ways to given stimuli. Rather, they can be reasoning organisms capable of decision and choice. Among the rational choices mature men may make is to commit themselves to a certain set of ethical values. They are not necessarily forced to such a commitment by personal or social tensions (of which they are usually unaware), but may come to that commitment deliberately, after reflective consideration.

The new psychology goes even one step further. It suggests that the very definition of maturity may be the ability to commit oneself to abstract ideas, to get beyond the selfish, egocentric world of children. This does not mean that every man who reaches outward does so from mature motives; external involvement may also be a way of acting out sick phantasies. The point is only that "commitment" need not be a symptom of personality disturbance. It is just as likely to be a symptom of maturity and health.

It does not follow, of course, that all abolitionists protested against slavery out of mature motives; some may have been, indeed were, "childish neurotics." But if we agree that slavery was a fearful injustice, and if motivational theory now suggests that injustice will bring forth protest from mature men, it seems reasonable to conclude that at least some of those who protested strongly against slavery must have done so from "healthy" motives.

The hostile critic will say that the abolitionists protested *too* strongly to have been maturely motivated. But when is a protest *too* strong? For a defender of the status quo, the answer (though never stated in these terms) would be: when it succeeds. For those not dedicated to the current status, the answer is likely to be: a protest is too strong when it is out of all proportion to the injustice it indicts. Could any verbal protest have been too strong against holding fellow human beings as property? From a moral point of view, certainly not, though from a practical point of view, perhaps. That is, the abolitionist protest might have been *too* strong if it somehow jeopardized the very goal it sought to achieve—the destruction of human slavery. But no one has yet shown this to have been the case.

At any rate, current findings in motivational theory suggest that at the very least we must cease dealing in blanket indictments, in simple-minded categorizing and elementary stereotyping. Such exercises may satisfy our present-day hostility to "reformers," but they do not satisfy the complex demands of historical truth. We need an awareness of the wide variety of human beings who became involved in the abolitionist movement, and an awareness of the complexity of human motivation sufficient to save us from summing up men and movements in two or three unexamined adjectives.

Surely there is now evidence enough to suggest that commitment and concern need not be aberrations; they may represent the profoundest elements of our humanity. Surely there are grounds for believing that those who protested strongly against slavery were not all misguided fanatics or frustrated neurotics—though by so believing it becomes easier to ignore the injustice against which they protested. Perhaps it is time to ask whether the abolitionists, in insisting that slavery be ended, were indeed those men of their generation furthest removed from reality, or whether that description should be reserved for those Northerners who remained indifferent to the institution, and those Southerners who defended it as a "positive good." From the point of view of these men, the abolitionists were indeed mad, but it is time we questioned the sanity of the point of view.

Those Northerners who were not indifferent to slavery—a large number after 1845—were nonetheless prone to view the abolitionist protest as "excessive," for it threatened the cherished values of private property and Union. The average Northerner may have found slavery disturbing, but convinced as he was that the Negro was an inferior, he did not find slavery monstrous. Certainly he did not think it an evil sufficiently profound to risk, by "precipitous action," the nation's present wealth or its future power. The abolitionists were willing to risk both. They thought it tragic that men should weigh human lives in the *same* scale as material possessions and abstractions of government. It is no less tragic that we continue to do so.

Abolitionist Beginnings

Abby Kelley Foster, writing her reminiscences in 1886, described the work of the early antislavery women. No other women did so much, she said; "they 'scorned delights and lived laborious days.' " No burden was too heavy and no work too revolting, "yet we were standing against the whole world on the woman question."

These women who "stood against the whole world" in the 1830's were not only abolitionists, but also the first feminists. Motivated to work against slavery by the same moral indignation as men, they found themselves outside women's traditional sphere and were faced with cries of "unsexed women." Though their primary commitment was to abolitionism, they moved surely and inevitably toward the realization that human enslavement took many forms. As deeply religious people, they felt that divine will placed them in a position to fight for the emancipation of women as well as slaves, and they responded to what they considered a sacred obligation. The resulting controversy, which divided the antislavery movement, produced the first public discussion of women's rights.

The actions of Abby Kelley Foster and other abolitionist women constituted the vital link between abolitionism and feminism. Their efforts to gain support from other antislavery women in the 1830's was essentially a "pre-movement" which led directly to the first attempts to organize for women's rights in the 1840's and 1850's. The arguments the female reformers used to defend their unpopular position as public antislavery agents would become the basis for a feminist ideology. Though at this early date they could not anticipate the full-fledged women's movement, they were remarkably prescient in articulating the issues around which it would be organized.

The abolitionist women prepared the way for the feminist movement in another equally significant but more subtle way. By venturing into the male domain of antislavery work, they set precedents for future feminists and became the cutting edge for the creation of new social roles for women. In defending woman's domestic role but demanding that she have equal access to a broader sphere, they foreshadowed the basic spirit of nineteenth-century feminism. By expanding their own spheres to include the dual roles of wife-mother and reformer, they provided models for other women eager to free themselves from old patterns in order to exert an influence on the world around them. In ideology, personality, and lifestyle, they were prototypes for a whole generation of women's rights leaders. In a broader sense, they set the example for a new type of nineteenth-century woman who was both a private and a public person.

Though the "woman question" did not burst into public view until William Lloyd Garrison launched his radical crusade for immediate emancipation in the 1830's, intimations of the issue appeared earlier, in the writings of Elizabeth Chandler. A little-known reformer whose extraordinary career was cut short by her early death, Chandler was a serious and scholarly writer; she was raised in Philadelphia by her Quaker grandmother and began her antislavery work in 1826, at nineteen, by sending contributions to Benjamin Lundy's weekly, *The Genius of Universal Emancipation*. . . .

Elizabeth Chandler, so modest that she left her articles unsigned, had nevertheless assumed a daring role for a woman. Though she was not consciously a feminist, Chandler's writings suggested many of the themes that would become important in the antebellum women's movement. She saw her main function as agitator, with her goal the arousal of American women to their special moral duty, as women, to oppose slavery. In her first column, "An Appeal to the Ladies of the United States," she exhorted: "By all the holy charities of life is *woman* called upon to lend her sympathy and her aid. . . . Will Christian sisters and wives and mothers stand coldly inert, while those of their own sex are daily exposed, not only to the threats and revilings, but to the very *lash* of a stern unfeeling taskmaster?"

Here were two themes that would appear regularly in the rhetoric of the feminist-abolitionists: women, as the more sensitive and sympathetic sex, were the natural foes of slavery; furthermore, they had a special obligation because members of their own sex were in bondage. . . .

Chandler became the first antislavery woman called upon to defend her right, as a woman, to speak out against slavery. Shortly after she became an editor for the *Genius,* she was rebuked by a New England woman who questioned the propriety of females becoming public advocates of emancipation, taking over a "man's work." Chandler denied that she was acting improperly: "To plead for the miserable . . . can never be unfeminine or unbefitting the delicacy of woman." She was not advocating emancipation for political (i.e., "male") reasons, but because slavery was "an outrage against *humanity* and *morality and religion* . . . and because a great number of *her own sex* are among its victims." Woman was not seeking to share a political role with man; rather, she was only pleading that he "lift the iron foot of despotism from the neck of her sisterhood."

This work, she argued, was "not only quite within the sphere of her privileges, but also of her positive duties.". . .

The controversy over the "woman question," only hinted at in Chandler's experience, came to a head in the late 1830's. Although these events have been detailed in antislavery studies, they need to be reexamined here from a new perspective. For the abolitionist movement, the internal dispute over women's role was a serious, divisive blow. However, this same controversy sparked an increased feminist consciousness and the beginnings of an important and continuing debate over women's rights. It also led to an expanded role for women in the radical wing of the movement.

William Lloyd Garrison was the catalyst who changed the nature of the antislavery movement and helped to transform women's role in it. In the first issue of his *Liberator,* published in Boston in 1831, Garrison renounced all gradualist solutions to the problem of slavery. Declaring that there could be no compromise with sin, he called for immediate and unconditional emancipation. By focusing dramatically on the moral issue and hammering away at it week after week, he launched a religious crusade which drew the hostility of most of New England and eventually of the nation. He also attracted a small band of dedicated followers, most of whom had been raised with a Puritan sense of moral duty and took this obligation seriously. A large number of these followers were women. They were incensed by the injustice of slavery, as Chandler had been; similarly, they had talent and energy to contribute to the cause. Many also enjoyed the benefits of education, leisure, and money by virtue of their positions in the middle and upper classes.

Garrison made a special effort to appeal to women and to arouse their indignation and sympathy for the cause. His early issues contained a "Ladies Department" headed by a picture of a kneeling slave woman in chains and captioned with the entreaty "Am I Not a Woman and a Sister?" He implored his female readers to take note of the one million enslaved women "exposed to all the violence of lust and passion—and treated with more indelicacy and cruelty than cattle," and he urged them to work for immediate emancipation. He continued to pound away at this theme in articles, speeches, and letters: "Women of New England . . . if my heart bleeds over the degraded and insufferable condition of a large portion of your sex, how ought you, whose sensibility is more susceptible than the windharp, to weep, and speak, and act, in their behalf?"

The majority of New England women, like their male counterparts, were indifferent or hostile to Garrison's appeal. A few unusual Boston women, however, responded enthusiastically and became his staunch supporters. The abolitionist cause changed their lives drastically, moving them from positions of status and respectability to places among the outcasts and the martyrs of their society. They, in turn, transformed the traditional auxiliary role of women in antislavery into a more active, independent force in the next decade.

Maria Weston Chapman was one of the first to respond to Garrison's appeal; she became so important in his campaign that she was known as "Garrison's chief lieutenant." Born to one of the first families of Boston and educated in England, Chapman was a strong-minded and elegant young matron; her friend Harriet Martineau, the English writer and reformer, called her the most beautiful woman in Boston. Self-confident, with a strong consciousness of class as well as pride in her sex, she was a controversial, heroic type worshiped by friends and vilified by enemies. Her domineering manner earned her the furtive title "Captain Chapman" even among admiring co-workers. Her grandson, the critic and writer John Jay Chapman, recalled her as an imposing figure who looked like a cameo but was a "doughty swordswoman" in conversation. Antislavery memoirs frequently include an account of her dramatic stand at an 1835 meeting (which ended with a mob dragging Garrison through the streets at the end of a rope). Confronted by a hostile mayor who tried to disperse the group, Chapman resisted with the true fervor of the revolutionary: "If this is the last bulwark of freedom, we may as well die here as anywhere."

In 1832, Maria Weston Chapman and three of her sisters organized the Boston Female Anti-Slavery Society to serve as an auxiliary to Garrison's newly formed New England Anti-Slavery Society, an all-male group. They were supported in their work by Maria's husband, Henry Chapman, a wealthy merchant, and by the entire Weston and Chapman families. As the moving force of the female society, Maria Chapman concentrated initially on fund-raising, which became the main task of all the women's groups. She organized yearly antislavery fairs which became models for fairs in other cities, and she edited the *Liberty Bell,* a gift book containing articles and poems by well-known abolitionists.

From this relatively conventional start, Maria Chapman subsequently moved to the more "male" role of propagandist and agitator, intitiating petition campaigns and publishing the annual report of the Society as a propaganda vehicle. Increasingly she took on aspects of Garrison's job, editing the *Liberator,* for example, when he was busy elsewhere. When the American Anti-Slavery Society was formed in 1833 as a national organization, she became, in effect, its general manager. In the next decade she applied her enormous talent and energy to a wider circle of activities and became an organizer and spokeswoman for many radical causes of the day.

Garrison's crusade for immediate emancipation changed the life of another well-known Boston woman, Lydia Maria Child, who met him following her marriage in 1828 to one of his disciples, David Lee Child. In the 1820's she was a popular author of romantic novels, the editor of the first periodical for children, *Juvenile Miscellany,* and a versatile writer. Her book *The Frugal Housewife,* published in 1829, was a cookbook which also gave abundant practical advice on living in a thrifty and industrious manner. It was so successful that it went through thirty-three editions.

Child herself was a temperamental romantic who was more interesting and complex than most feminist-abolitionists. Portraits show her plain, square face as kindly but determined; however, her warm, motherly exterior hid a soul in conflict. She was torn throughout her life between her desire to retreat from the public sphere into the world of music and literature, and her strong sense of moral obligation to work in the broader world and help reform it. Her "savage love of freedom," she explained, compelled her to aid in the emancipation of slaves and women. She was also a self-styled "free spirit" who felt oppressed by the "machinery" of societies and conventions. Except for a brief stint as an anti-slavery editor, she solved this dilemma by contributing her name and her words to both causes, but withholding her person.

Lydia Maria Child's name and words proved to be formidable weapons. She later recalled how Garrison had gotten hold of the strings of her conscience and pulled her into reform: "It is of no use to imagine what might have been if I had never met him. Old dreams vanished, old associates departed, and all things became new." He inspired her to write *An Appeal on Behalf of That Class of Americans Called Africans* (1833), the first antislavery work to be published in book form in this country, and an influential tract that had a strong impact on distinguished Bostonians such as Charles Sumner, Wendell Phillips, and William Ellery Channing. Basically a call for immediate emancipation, it is also notable for its condemnation of racial prejudice in the North, an important Garrisonian theme. Child documented her attack by compiling facts on the treatment of free blacks in the schools, churches, and public accommodations, as well as on the illegality of interracial marriages. She concluded with the prediction that "public opinion is on the verge of a great change." She felt that antislavery reformers would be successful because "God and truth is on their side."

The *Appeal* was a turning point in Child's career, antagonizing Boston's literary circles with its controversial and unwelcome subject, and bringing a sharp halt to her popularity with the general public. Anticipating this reaction, she had explained in the text that duty and conscience compelled her to write the tract, at the risk of displeasing all classes. Her courage in taking this step is especially noteworthy, since Child disliked controversy more than any of her contemporaries. When she had published her first novel in 1824, she had been warned that female writers were considered "unsexed," but at that time she had chosen not to take issue with her critics. Now, too, she preferred to stay in the background and let her words speak. In spite of herself, she became a symbol of independent, defiant womanhood.

Though individual women were challenging the traditional female role, in the early 1830's the issue of women's rights was still far from the minds even of abolitionists. Events of the first national convention in 1833 confirmed this fact. In December, male antislavery workers from New England and New York joined their co-workers in Philadelphia for a three-day meeting at which the American Anti-Slavery Society was organized. On the second day, apparently as an afterthought, an invitation was sent to the Philadelphia antislavery women. Lucretia Mott, accompanied by her mother, her daughter, and two sisters, joined the group of about sixty men. All the women were Quakers—as were seventeen of the men—and were accustomed to speaking in mixed assemblages. Mrs. Mott, tiny but with a commanding presence, was a Friends minister who, with her husband, James, had been involved with antislavery since the 1820's. Their home was a focal point of the Underground Railroad which helped fugitive slaves, and it became the Philadelphia outpost of Garrisonian abolitionism.

The other women who attended this first convention left no record, but Lucretia Mott's contribution was reported by abolitionist J. Miller McKim. When the crucial first session of the day was delayed because two prominent men failed to appear, causing doubt and confusion, Mrs. Mott rallied the group by reminding them that "right principles are stronger than great names." She also helped in lesser ways. When a "Declaration of Sentiments and Purposes" was drafted, she suggested that it would sound better if its key sentences were transposed. Later she recalled "one of the younger members turning to see what woman there was there who knew what the word 'transpose' meant."

Though Lucretia Mott helped to draft this historic document, it did not occur to her, or to any other member of the convention, that the women present should also sign it. Instead, they were rewarded with a resolution of thanks "to our female friends, for the deep interest they have manifested in the cause of antislavery." The fact that the women present were not invited to add their signatures, and did not expect to be so invited, reveals the state of feminist consciousness even among the more independent and outspoken women in 1833. Samuel J. May, a Unitarian minister and beloved elder statesman of the feminist-abolitionist group, wrote many years later that his pride in recalling this convention "will be forever associated [with] the mortifying fact, that we *men* were then so blind, so obtuse, that we did not recognize those women as members of our Convention. . . ."

Following this convention, the women organized a meeting of female abolitionists. The group, which was biracial and consisted mostly of Friends, like the parent body, became the Philadelphia Female Anti-Slavery Society. (Even an experienced speaker like Lucretia Mott hesitated to take on the "male" role of chairing this meeting, and a black male friend was called upon for the job. Mrs. Mott later recalled the irony of the situation: "You know that at the time, even to the present day, Negroes, idiots and women were in legal documents classed together; so that we were very glad to get one of our own class to come and aid in forming that Society.") This group of Quaker women functioned as the core of an important female network that offered support and a home base for feminist-abolitionist women for the remainder of the century.

Lucretia Coffin Mott was the pivotal person among antislavery women in Philadelphia, just as Maria Weston Chapman was in Boston. However, Mrs. Mott's role in the development of a women's movement was even greater; indeed, her stature and influence among the feminist-abolitionists was unparalleled. In 1833 she was forty, about ten years older than Chapman and Child; already she had behind her a career as minister, reformer, and scholar, as well as accomplished housewife and mother of five. She had been a precocious child, taking to serious literature and Bible study "as a cat laps milk" (and also falling into the common error, her sister recalled, of "judging other people's minds by her own"). She continued her systematic and scholarly study of the Bible throughout her life, but found in it "a wholly different construction of the text from that which was forced upon our acceptance." Early in life she decided that much of it belonged to "a past, barbarous age."

An important part of Lucretia Mott's enormous influence among the feminist-abolitionists involved moving them from orthodox religious dogma to her special brand of intellectual liberalism, built upon Quaker beliefs but extending beyond them. Extraordinarily open and tolerant of nonconforming ideas, she carried on a lifetime crusade for freedom of religion and liked to say of this effort, "Call me a radical of the radicals." She prided herself on always placing fidelity to conscience above external strictures and relied on her favorite motto in speeches and sermons: "Truth for authority, not authority for truth." The superiority of practical Christianity over ceremonial religion was a favorite theme, and she was a steadfast critic of narrow dogmatism and petty sectarianism. Garrison described Mott's influence precisely when he wrote that he felt indebted to her (and her husband) for helping his mind to burst the bonds of theological dogmas and to interpret the Scriptures so that, instead of being "killed by the letter," he had been "made alive by the spirit."

Lucretia Mott was an especially influential teacher and model for the younger women in the antislavery movement. Elizabeth Cady Stanton, her most important protégée, later recalled that Mrs. Mott was the first woman she had ever met who was progressive in her religious beliefs as well as in her concept of woman's role. She described her friend as having a magnetic presence: "The amount of will force and intelligent power in her small body was enough to direct the universe." To her young admirers, Lucretia Mott was the ideal woman, both consummate reformer and perfect wife and mother. Her marriage to James Mott was the model union to which all aspired; her success in balancing family and reform work was an example which all tried to emulate.

This kind of leadership—by women who rejected traditional social roles as well as orthodox religious beliefs—inspired the small groups of abolitionist women in Boston and Philadelphia to organize in their separate female societies and later to think about challenging the accepted pattern of segregation and male dominance. (The women in antislavery circles in New York City, with close ties to evangelicalism, were not sympathetic to feminism.) In the years following the 1833 national meeting, the women busied themselves with circulating petitions, raising funds, and organizing new groups. The movement was expanding in an exciting manner—in 1838, the Massachusetts society alone recorded 183 local chapters including 41 female and 13 juvenile auxiliaries, with memberships ranging from fewer than twenty to more than three hundred. Though abolitionists were still a tiny minority, their success in this period undoubtedly raised some women's sights in the direction of greater participation.

By 1837 there were intimations that abolitionist women were feeling hampered in their auxiliary role. Their first attempt at national organization, the Anti-Slavery Convention of American Women, met in May, with about one hundred delegates from ten states attending the three-day meeting. Lucretia Mott, recalling the mood of the group, noted that one of their first resolutions proclaimed it time for "woman to act in the sphere which Providence had assigned her, and no longer to rest satisfied with the circumscribed limits in which corrupt custom and a perverted application of the Scriptures had encircled her." Mary S. Parker of Boston, president of the convention and sister of the Unitarian minister and reformer Theodore Parker, was authorized to send a circular to all female antislavery societies of the country. In it she urged action on current petitions and gave the women some feminist advice: they should follow their own consciences, not the wills of their husbands—women could be "very obstinate concerning a gay party, a projected journey, or a new service of china; but when great *principles* were at stake, they very promptly sacrificed them to earn the reputation of meek and submissive wives."

The question of woman's proper role in the antislavery movement was finally raised publicly later in 1837, and the women's rights issue was never quiescent thereafter. The central figures in the first stage of the controversy were Angelina and Sarah Grimké. Born in South Carolina and reared in an aristocratic, slaveholding family, they were unlikely additions to the New England-dominated movement. Angelina was thirty-two; Sarah, her sister and godmother (Angelina called her "sister mother"), was forty-five. Both were unmarried. As young women they had become alienated from their proslavery environment, and in the 1820's they had moved to Philadelphia. Looking for something that would give their lives meaning, they found a sense of purpose first in Quakerism and, more lastingly, in antislavery work. Caught up in the enthusiasm of Garrison's crusade, the Grimkés became active in the Philadelphia Female Anti-Slavery Society.

Like all abolitionists, the Grimkés felt they were doing God's work in battling slavery; this sense of divine mission would enable them to endure the even greater public censure and private criticism heaped on them when they became active feminists. Angelina especially exhibited a self-assurance that came from feeling "called" to the work of reform. Responding only to the demands of an inner voice, she seemed naturally endowed with the kind of protective shield that other reformers worked hard to acquire. She had displayed an awesome sense of duty at an early age—a sister recalled her single-minded "devotion to an idea" as a girl. As a young woman of twenty-three, preparing to leave South Carolina, she wrote in her diary, "I feel that I am called with a high and heavy calling, and that I ought to be peculiar, and cannot be too zealous." Wendell Phillips described her as a woman "morally sufficient to herself" who reminded him of "the spotless dove in the tempest." Although this image of innocence amid the storm of abuse and controversy would fit others as well—they were shielded by righteousness and moral certainty from knowledge of the complex realities that surrounded the evils they opposed—it applies best to Angelina Grimké.

In 1836 Angelina came to public attention by writing *An Appeal to the Christian Women of the South,* in which she urged her southern sisters to influence husbands and brothers to act against slavery. In explaining her bold action she wrote: "God has shown me what I can do . . . to speak to them in such tones that they *must* hear me, and through me, the voice of justice and humanity." Her pamphlet was published by the American Anti-Slavery Society and circulated widely in the North. In the South it coincided with a swell of anti-abolitionist activity and was publicly burned by the postmaster in Charleston, making its author an outlaw in her home state.

Angelina followed this *Appeal* with an eloquent address to the convention of antislavery women in 1837, challenging the "Women of the Nominally Free States" to break their own bonds to aid those of their sex who were in slavery. Published as a seventy-page pamphlet by the convention, it served to enhance the reputation of both sisters among the abolitionists. Following this convention, they were invited by Maria Weston Chapman to address the Boston Female Anti-Slavery Society. The Grimkés were especially desirable as speakers because of their unique experience with slavery. They went on from Boston to speak to other women's groups in the area. Prim and plain in their Quaker bonnets, they impressed their audiences with their intense devotion to their cause. In addition,

Angelina was becoming known as an eloquent orator. For all of these reasons, churches and meeting halls were filled to overflowing when the Grimkés lectured. They found themselves addressing mixed audiences, a situation which abolitionist women had not faced before. Even staunch antislavery people doubted the wisdom of defying convention to this extent. The Reverend Samuel J. May, for example, was hesitant about allowing Angelina to speak from his pulpit before a mixed congregation, but he was won over completely by the force of her address and became her ardent supporter.

The Grimkés' speaking tour lasted about six months and included over sixty New England towns. They addressed an estimated 40,500 people and may have been influential in the formation of six new societies during this period. Though they successfully gained attention for their cause, they also brought down upon themselves the wrath of the orthodox clergy of Massachusetts. This body was already hostile to the Garrisonians, who constantly attacked the church for its complicity with slavery. The action of the Grimkés in defying much-hallowed custom, in addition to preaching radical abolitionism, was more than the clerics could tolerate. The General Association of Congregationalist Ministers issued an edict to all its member churches, in effect condemning the Grimkés (without specifically mentioning them) for the unfeminine act of addressing "promiscuous" or mixed audiences.

The pastoral letter attacking the Grimkés triggered the first extended public controversy over women's rights because it spoke directly to the question of women's proper sphere, an issue that would dominate the nineteenth-century movement. Its language clearly revealed the boundaries of acceptable female behavior in 1837. Citing the New Testament as its authority, the letter emphasized that woman's power lay in her dependence. Likening her to a vine "whose strength and beauty is to lean upon the trellis-work," it warned that the vine which "thinks to assume the independence and the overshadowing nature of the elm" not only would cease to bear fruit, but also would "fall in shame and dishonor into the dust." The character of the woman who "assumes the place and tone of man as a public reformer . . . becomes unnatural." The action of the sisters, according to the clergy, presented dangers which threatened the female character with "permanent injury" and opened the way for "degeneracy and ruin."

This harsh public attack on the Grimkés served as a warning to other women who might dare to venture outside their prescribed sphere. To withstand such statements the sisters could rely on their own piety, an important weapon in the battle as well as a source of strength for them personally. Frances Wright, a Scottish radical reformer, had lectured on women's rights in 1828–29 but, as a "notorious" advocate of free love, she was not taken seriously. The Grimkés were so obviously pious and respectable that their defiance of social custom forced many people to rethink the question of woman's proper sphere.

Their own state of mind is revealed in the large correspondence which the Grimkés carried on during the ensuing controversy, each letter closing with "Thy sister in the bonds of woman and the slave." To Henry C. Wright, their most loyal supporter, Sarah wrote that Angelina was troubled about the clerical uproar, "but the Lord knows that we did not come to forward our own interests but in simple obedience to his commands." In another letter she reiterated their determination to resist intimidation. "If in calling us thus publicly to advocate the cause of the downtrodden slave, God has unexpectedly placed us in the forefront of the battle which is to be waged against the rights and duties and responsibilities of woman, it would ill become us to shrink from such a contest."

Though their critics initiated the controversy, the abolitionist women were not entirely unprepared for it. At the start of their New England tour the Grimkés had spent a social evening at the Chapman home and discussed their situation with "the brethren" (a term they, like their contemporaries, used to denote sisters as well as brothers). Angelina's comments on this meeting, written in a letter to a friend, are significant: "I had a long talk with the brethren on the rights of women, and found a very general sentiment prevailing that it is time our fetters were broken. L. M. Child and Maria Chapman strongly supported this view; indeed, very many seem to think a new order of things is very desirable in this respect . . . I feel it is not only the cause of the slave we plead but the cause of woman as a moral, responsible being. . . ."

The most immediate issue for the women was the right to continue their public antislavery work. The question of women's equal participation in the work of the American Anti-Slavery Society was not made explicit at this point, but emerged naturally from the initial debate. Other basic grievances were also brought to mind by the controversy: the denial of legal rights to married women, the lack of opportunity for higher education and dignified employment, and a host of other inequalities and indignities. The cause of the slave opened a Pandora's box of grievances and demands on behalf of women.

Many abolitionist women were not ready for the Grimkés' "new order of things." Instead, they felt comfortable in their separate female auxiliaries and useful in their work of gathering petitions and holding fund-raising affairs. Sharing the prevalent view of woman's sphere, they were content to allow their men to represent them in public and make the decisions for the national organization. Although radical in their defense of the slave, they had not made the connection, as the Grimkés had, between the rights of slaves and the rights of women. The controversy over the sisters' public speaking forced them to become involved in this "woman question."

Anne Warren Weston, sister of Maria Weston Chapman, was one of those who attempted to gain support for the Grimkés' right to speak. Addressing the Boston Female Anti-Slavery Society, she used many of the principal arguments of the feminist-abolitionist cause. The very theologians who had used the Scriptures to justify slavery were now "perverting the same sainted oracles" to sanction woman's inferiority and subordination. "Will you," she demanded, "allow those men who have been for years unmindful of their own most solemn duties to prescribe you yours?" Those who considered women as goods and chattels were not fit judges of the sphere women should occupy; they had not objected that the slave woman in the rice fields was "out of her sphere," nor the southern woman who held her fellow creature as property. Weston concluded that the Grimkés, working for the slave, were "in the very sphere to which God has appointed every Christian."

The Grimkés also stood firm in their own defense, claiming that men and women had the same moral right and duty to oppose slavery. They were clearly sensitive to the broader implications of the controversy and made a conscious decision to speak for all women, calling on the broad doctrine of human rights, rather than merely claiming rights for themselves. At stake was the right of women not merely to an equal role in antislavery, but to an equal position in all areas of society. The sisters were defending not only their right to speak publicly, but also the right of all women to be as free as men to develop their talents and to enjoy lives of usefulness, respect, and independence. The arguments they had used to defend slave women merged easily and logically with their own defense to become an ideology espousing equality for all women.

A high degree of feminist consciousness was revealed in their correspondence in this period. "The whole land seems aroused to discussion on the province of woman," Angelina noted defiantly in 1837, "and I am glad of it. We are willing to bear the brunt of the storm, if we can only be the means of making a break in that wall of public opinion which lies right in the way of woman's rights, true dignity, honor and usefulness." She had a strong sense of the importance of their role and understood that the question, once raised, could not be suppressed. To Anne Warren Weston she confided, "It is causing deep searchings of heart and revealing the secrets of the soul." She also displayed a keen insight into the basic nature of the opposition. In a letter written during her speaking tour, she admitted to scolding "most terribly" while lecturing on slavery, and noted that many of the men in the audience "look at me in utter amazement." "I am not at all surprized," she wrote, "they are afraid lest such a woman should usurp authority over the men." Sarah later revealed a similarly sophisticated understanding of the power struggle between the sexes.

Because Angelina was more in demand as a speaker, Sarah Grimké took on the job of publicly defending their position in a series of "Letters on the Province of Woman" which ran in the *New England Spectator* beginning in July, 1837. The publication of these letters caused the sisters difficulty with friends who had not opposed their speaking but who feared that a public defense would stir unnecessary controversy and injure the antislavery cause. John Greenleaf Whittier, the noted poet and abolitionist, asked whether their aggressiveness was really necessary: "Is it not forgetting the great and dreadful wrongs of the slave in a selfish crusade against some paltry grievance of our own?" Theodore Weld, their close co-worker who was to become Angelina's husband, took their cause more seriously and, in fact, was a solid "woman's rights man." But even he, for purely tactical reasons, opposed "agitating the question" and advised them to go on with their lecturing "without making any ado about 'attacks' and 'invasions' and 'oppositions' "; their example alone would be the most convincing argument for women's rights and duties.

To the sisters, the issue of women's rights was not "a paltry grievance." As Angelina explained in a letter to Whittier and Weld, "We *must establish this right* for if we do not, it will be impossible for us to go *on with the work of Emancipation.*" She pleaded with them: "Can you not see that woman *could* do, and *would* do a hundred times more for the slave if she were not fettered?" Responding to the charge that the time was not right, she wrote to Weld: "I think this must be the Lord's time and therefore the *best* time, for it seems to have been brought about by a concatenation of circumstances over which we had no control." After much debate, a compromise was effected: Sarah's letters were continued in the press, but the subject was not discussed in their talks. Angelina gave up her idea of a series of lectures on women's rights.

Sarah's letters, published in 1838 as *Letters on the Equality of the Sexes, and the Condition of Woman,* constituted the first serious discussion of women's rights by an American woman, preceding Margaret Fuller's *Woman in the Nineteenth Century* by seven years. Lucretia Mott called it "the best work after Mary Wollstonecraft's *Vindication of the Rights of Woman*"—no small praise from a feminist who kept the earlier revolutionary work on the center table in her home for forty years, lending it "when she could find readers."

In her *Letters,* Sarah Grimké made an important contribution to the development of a nineteenth-century feminist ideology by basing her defense of woman on the Scriptures, thus challenging her critics on their ground. Starting from her belief that the Bible had been falsely translated by men, she developed her thesis that men and women had been created in perfect equality, subject only to God; as human beings, they had the same responsibilities and the same rights. Adam and Eve fell from innocence, *but not from equality,* since their guilt was shared. This argument remained at the heart of much of the debate over women in the next decades.

The controversy that followed the pastoral letter served to heighten all abolitionist women's awareness of the obstacles they faced because of their sex. It also intensified the feminist sensitivities of some not yet in the movement. Lucy Stone, who in the 1840's became the first abolitionist to lecture solely on women's rights, heard the pastoral letter read in the Congregationalist Church in North Brookfield, where she was teaching. Only nineteen years old, she was already sensitive to her inferior position as a woman. Her church had refused to permit her to vote or join in its discussions, and her father adamantly objected to her plea to follow her brothers to college. The low pay she received as a teacher, compared with male salaries, undoubtedly added to her mortification. All these resentments were intensified as she heard the condemnation of the Grimkés. She later described her feeling of rebelliousness: "If I had felt bound to silence before by interpretation of Scriptures, or believed that equal rights did not belong to woman, that 'pastoral letter' broke my bonds." The orthodox church became anathema to Lucy Stone, as to most feminist-abolitionists, because of its proslavery stance as well as its antifeminism.

More significant even than the pastoral letter was the condemnation of "women out of their sphere" by clergymen *within* the antislavery movement. What began in 1837 as a confrontation with forces which were anti-abolitionist as well as antifeminist, became an internecine conflict which lasted from 1838 to 1840 and eventually contributed to the division of the entire abolitionist movement. The focal point of this controversy was the right of women to vote and participate in the business of the "male" antislavery societies. The final division in the movement came in 1840, when Abby Kelley was appointed to a committee of the American Anti-Slavery Society—Whittier called her "the bomb-shell that *exploded* the society." Garrison and his supporters defended her, while their opponents in the organization demanded her resignation. Kelley refused to resign and, like the Grimkés, defended her position on the ground that men and women had the same moral rights and duties. The impasse over her appointment split the national society. The group of New York abolitionists who opposed her—the Garrisonians called them "New Organization men"—seceded to form a second organization.

Abby Kelley was the appropriate person to stand firmly at the center of the explosion over the woman question. An intense young Quaker whose attractive features were set against a severe hairdo and plain dress, she was among the most radical and uncompromising Garrisonians. While the Grimkés' role in the limelight was brief, Abby Kelley's public stand in 1840 was only the beginning of her long and arduous service in defense of the rights of slaves and women. When the sisters retired to the sidelines after Angelina's marriage to Theodore Weld in 1838, the role they had created as female antislavery lecturers was taken over by the younger Abby Kelley.

Like the Grimkés, Kelley was driven by a desire to rid the world of evil, a religious perfectionism that was shared by all the Garrisonians. As a young teacher in Massachusetts, she had circulated petitions and solicited funds for her local antislavery society. She saw her father's death in 1836 as a sign of God's will and threw herself even further into reform work, contributing her small inheritance to the cause and selling some of her clothing to obtain additional funds. A family letter written the following year reveals her ingenuous optimism: " 'Tis a great joy to see the world grow better in anything—Indeed I think endeavors to improve mankind is the only object worth living for."

Abby Kelley gave her first public speech at the second Anti-Slavery Convention of American Women in May, 1838, a meeting which coincided with the Grimké-Weld wedding. This convention was a traumatic one for all concerned, and a dramatic beginning to Kelley's career. The abolitionists were attacked by a stone-throwing mob on the first day and saw their newly built Pennsylvania Hall burned to the ground on the second. Maria Weston Chapman became so distraught that she suffered a temporary mental breakdown.

In spite of the threatening crowd outside, Abby Kelley's speech had been so eloquent that Theodore Weld assured her that God meant her to take up the antislavery mission: "Abby, if you don't, God will smite you." She spent the next year in intense soul-searching, confessing in a letter to the Weld-Grimké family that she was praying most earnestly "that this cup might pass from me." They responded that the Lord was trying her faith and advised her "to wait for *him* to make a way where there seems now to be no way." In 1839 she decided to go ahead, after seeing divine confirmation for her "call" in this scriptural passage: "But God hath chosen the foolish things of the world to confound the wise. . . ." She gave up her teaching job to become an antislavery agent. A year later she was at the center of the culminating controversy over women in the movement.

The "woman question" was the more explosive of the two issues dividing the abolitionists in 1840. The other conflict, more tactical and less ideological, was over the value of political action. The radical Boston group, which defended women's equal participation, chose to continue using moral suasion as their chief antislavery tactic. These Garrisonians were "come-outers" who opposed any association with institutions tainted by slavery, which included the government as well as the established churches. The New York group, led by Lewis Tappan,

James G. Birney, Henry B. Stanton, and others, favored broadening the base of the movement by political activity and coalition tactics, and many of them went on to form the Liberty party. They accused the Garrisonians of dragging in "extraneous questions," like the women's rights issue, which they feared would antagonize possible supporters and hurt the antislavery cause. They sensed that women's rights was an even more controversial issue than abolition.

While some "New Organization" men wished to suppress the women's rights issue purely for tactical reasons, their leaders included a core of evangelical clergymen who, like their proslavery counterparts, saw the "woman question" as a social threat. One of this group expressed "grief and astonishment" that this issue was forced upon the antislavery cause. Women's rights principles, if carried out, "would strike a death blow at the purest and *loveliest* social condition of man" and tear up the "foundations of human virtue and *happiness.*" This group was already antagonistic to Garrison because of his head-on assault on the churches, as well as his espousal of nonresistance and other ultraist causes. The Garrisonians' defense of women's rights was the final insult.

The Garrisonians accused their opponents of sectarianism and argued that women's rights, like antislavery, constituted only one aspect of the broad struggle for human rights. James Mott commented in a letter to Anne Weston: "Verily some of our northern gentlemen are as jealous of any interference in rights they have long considered as belonging to them exclusively as the southern slaveholder is in the right of holding his slaves—both are to be broken up, *human* rights alone recognized." Maria Weston Chapman viewed the woman's rights controversy as an inevitable development of the antislavery struggle. She summed it up tersely: "Freedom begets freedom." Lydia Maria Child accused the New Organization men of harboring the "proslavery spirit in new disguise," although she acknowledged that many were sincere abolitionists who were "frightened at new and bold views." Summing up the Garrisonian philosophy, she wrote to Lucretia Mott: "It requires great faith to trust truth to take care of itself in all encounters." Though the Garrisonians exhibited the righteousness of true believers by claiming a monopoly on the truth, in practice their philosophy often meant that they were open to new ideas and supported a variety of reforms, like women's rights, believing "all good causes help one another."

The women received some support from political abolitionists who were not antifeminists. Joseph C. Hathaway, antislavery agent in western New York, could not remain silent while the rights of women were "rudely trampled upon by a corrupt clergy" who thought that "woman was made for the slave of man, instead of a *helpmeet* for him." "What earthly objection can there be to her standing on the same platform with us," he asked. "Are we afraid that the overflowing exuberance of her sympathizing heart will eclipse us?"

Regardless of their stand on political action, virtually all of the antislavery women who were feminists remained with the Garrisonians; only there were they accepted on an equal basis with men. Many women were not sympathetic to the feminist cause, however, and chose to maintain their traditional role in maledominated organizations. One of Maria Chapman's associates described a New Organization meeting where the women dutifully left when the men got down to business. She deeply regretted "that they can find any 'sisters' who will allow themselves to be dismissed for I feel that if Woman would not consent to her own degradation her Emancipation would be sure."

Maria Weston Chapman and her sisters themselves resisted an attempt by anti-Garrisonian women to dissolve the Boston Female Anti-Slavery Society. Chapman was a fierce protagonist in the controversy, condemning her opponents as traitors and tools of the clergy and citing their "hypocrisy as abolitionists" and "want of integrity as women." When her opponents withdrew from the organization to form the Massachusetts Female Emancipation Society, Chapman wrote a friend that the group would continue without the defectors and with "more vigour than ever." She only regretted not being able to change the name to one she far preferred: "Anti-Slavery Society of Boston Women." ("Women" had a rebellious connotation: "female" was the more proper term.) This unwillingness of many women to be "emancipated" would remain, of course, one of the major obstacles in the women's movement.

Following the fight over the woman question in this country, the Garrisonians shortly faced a similar challenge at the World's Anti-Slavery Convention in London in 1840. This meeting became another direct link between abolitionism and feminism. The controversy at home had been so traumatic and so destructive of antislavery unity that even the most dedicated feminist-abolitionists felt ambivalence about further harming the movement. Sarah Grimké wrote to a friend that she hoped women would not present themselves as delegates in London. Ironically, in claiming that such action would "divert the attention of the meeting from the great subject of human liberty," she was using the same argument that had been used against her in 1837.

Lucretia Mott and the other women delegates from the United States did, however, stand on principle and demand to be seated in spite of intense opposition. (Though the Motts' liberal Quaker views were also anathema to the orthodox Friends who organized the convention, it was Mrs. Mott's sex that was crucial; James Mott had no difficulty being seated.) In a heated debate reminiscent of the exchange between the Grimkés and the Massachusetts clergy, members of the English clergy cited the Scriptures as the authority for relegating women to their "God-ordained" sphere. To give the vote to females, they argued, was to act in opposition to the word of God. They also called upon the powerful source of custom which prevented them from subjecting the "shrinking nature of woman" to the indelicacies involved in a discussion of slavery.

The ultimate decision was to adhere to custom. The women were compelled to view the proceedings from a screened-off area; they were accompanied there by Garrison and a few other male supporters. Among the women was Elizabeth Cady Stanton, then a young bride who had chosen to accompany her husband to this meeting as a honeymoon trip. Henry Brewster Stanton, a delegate and leader of the New Organization faction, voted with the women. Though undoubtedly antagonizing most of his co-workers, fresh from the same battle at home, he got his marriage off to a good start.

The rejection of the women delegates was an important feminist experience for Elizabeth Cady Stanton, who would become the major thinker and propagandist of nineteenth-century feminism. Her long talks with Lucretia Mott made an even more lasting impression on her. Hearing Mrs. Mott deliver a sermon in a

Unitarian church in London was to her "like the realization of an oft-repeated, happy dream." Out of the meeting of these two came the idea to organize women to take action in their own defense. The Seneca Falls meeting would be that logical fruition of the "woman question" controversy.

In the period following the split in the movement and the London meeting, the Garrisonian women merged their societies with the male groups which remained in the American Anti-Slavery Society. They were now able to work with greater freedom and to expand their activities. Child, Chapman, and Mott served on the executive committee of the national society; Child became editor of their newspaper, the *National Anti-Slavery Standard;* Abby Kelley lectured and organized in the West. Maria Chapman insisted that they were stronger for the defection because women "who were not easily discouraged" were more valuable to the cause than men "whose dignity forbade them to be fellow-laborers with women." This rhetoric notwithstanding, the movement as a whole was weakened by the division and never again achieved the strength and unity which it had possessed in the 1830's. The New Organization abolitionists moved into the broader stream of political antislavery, while the Garrisonians continued their "no-government" moral crusade. However, the decade had been a productive one for radical reform. Not only had the question of the immediate emancipation of the slaves been raised, but the possibility of the future emancipation of women had also been initiated.

The Garrisonian women—the Grimkés, Mott, Chapman, Child, Kelley, and their supporters—were actually playing two kinds of roles on two separate but overlapping stages. The more visible drama revolved about their part in antislavery. On the larger stage, a more subtle kind of action was occurring: a new dialogue for women was being shaped, and new images were being created that would endure long after antislavery action ended. Although the women were propelled into this dual action by circumstances they had not controlled, they were fully aware of the implications for the future.

Angelina Grimké, spectacularly capping her brief public career by appearing before a committee of the Massachusetts legislature in 1838, typified this new image and feminist awareness. Accompanied by Chapman, Child, and other friends, she presented antislavery petitions on behalf of 20,000 women. Child later recalled Grimké's pale face and trembling, frail frame as she faced her audience: "The feminine shrinking was soon overcome by her sense of the duty before her, and her words flowed forth free, forcible, and well-arranged." Arguing for the right of women to have an equal voice in political decisions, and clearly anticipating the later demand for suffrage, Grimké declared: "Are we aliens, because we are women? Are we bereft of citizenship because we are mothers, wives and daughters of a mighty people?" Excited by her triumph, she wrote to a friend: "We Abolition Women are turning the world upside down. . . ."

While "turning the world upside down" was more hyperbole than fact, Grimké and others were setting important precedents and helping to raise the feminist consciousnesses of future leaders. Mary Livermore, who would become a leading suffragist, ran away from school for the day to hear Angelina Grimké address the legislature. She later recalled that the experience forever fixed in her mind the conviction that women ought to be free to do whatever their powers enabled them to do well.

The early feminist-abolitionists were not only sources of inspiration for the later movement; they were also role models for a new type of woman. They served this purpose by challenging their society's view of woman's proper sphere and expanding their own roles to include public work as well as private duties. With the support of their feminist-abolitionist husbands, they became antislavery agents, lecturers, editors, agitators—a blasphemous violation of their society's code of behavior for well-bred ladies. Not incidentally, they also created precedents for a radically new kind of marriage involving shared responsibility and shared public work, a partnership in which the woman was viewed as an equal and autonomous member.

In the process of expanding and reshaping female roles, the abolitionist women also set precedents for different styles of feminist leadership. Maria Weston Chapman and Abby Kelley were boldly aggressive, willing to take on "male" roles and choosing agitation and direct confrontation as their tactics. They were archetypal leaders of the radical, uncompromising sort whose positions move the mainstream into action, albeit reluctantly, and force public discussion of issues which other more moderate types could then negotiate and attempt to resolve.

Lydia Maria Child preferred a softer, more private way, using her pen rather than her voice and putting a high value on setting an example for others. When criticized for not being more zealous in defense of the Grimkés, she explained her position in the *Liberator:* "It is best not to *talk* about our rights, but simply go forward and *do* whatsoever we deem a duty. In toiling for the freedom of others, we shall find our own." Through her writings she exerted her greatest influence in the women's movement. Her *History of the Condition of Women*, written in 1835 as a pioneer effort to uncover the origins of women's inequality, was an important source for Sarah Grimké's *Letters* as well as for later feminists. An early novel, *The Rebels* (1825), embodied a protest against the position of women in eighteenth-century society. *Good Wives*, written between 1832 and 1835, was a collection of biographies of women (significantly, wives) who had achieved fame in earlier times.

Lydia Maria Child departed from her preferred style only once when she agreed, in 1841, to take on a "male" role as editor of the new *National Anti-Slavery Standard*, despite her aversion to controversy and organizations. Her first editorial revealed her cautious ambivalence. She wrote of the woman question: "A budding conscience must struggle for human rights," but added that she herself preferred "quietly and unobtrusively to take her freedom without disputing it." Her attempt to follow a middle course on antislavery as well as on the woman question caused her difficulty with her more radical co-workers; she left after three years, determined "never to work in harness again." Wendell Phillips criticized the mildness of her editorial tone in the *Standard*, declaring the paper was "but a holiday banner compared with the real black pirate flag of Abby Kelley." Much later, however, he praised her for her gentle, "feminine" manner and eulogized her as "the kind of woman one would choose to represent woman's entrance into broader life."

Probably the most effective style of leadership was displayed by Lucretia Mott, whom historian Mary Beard perceptively described as "a genuine radical with balance." Her practical brand of idealism enabled her to work with, and be accepted by, all of the factions in abolitionism and feminism, and to act as a bridge between the two movements. While Kelley and others were rigid and uncompromising in their perfectionism, Mott was able to combine her radical vision of the future with a realistic assessment of what was possible in the here and now. Though she appreciated the importance of a few women leading the way, for example, she understood that centuries of custom and indoctrination could not be swept aside overnight. During the storm over women speaking to mixed audiences, she encouraged those who wished to take this step to "act in accordance with the light they have." There was no better way of preparing the public for "Christian equality, without distinction of sex." Meanwhile, she suggested, other women might go on meeting by themselves "without compromise of the principle of equality" until they were ready for "more public and general exercise of their rights." Like Child, she put a high value on the creation of models and new female roles, but she was also unwilling to force women into those new roles until they were ready.

All of the women were keenly aware of the responsibility, as well as the difficulties, of taking on "male" roles. Child, working as a "first" woman editor, had come to New York alone and left her husband to pursue his own antislavery activities in Massachusetts. To Maria Chapman she wrote: "You may well suppose that a woman is obliged to take more pains than a man would do. . . ." She also complained to friends that, in addition to the work which male editors had to perform, she was obliged to do her own washing and ironing, as well as cleaning and mending for her husband on her periodic trips home. Nevertheless, she managed both jobs successfully enough for Lucretia Mott to write to Ann Weston, "I rejoice with thee that L. M. Child is doing so much for the cause and for woman by acquitting herself so nobly in the editorial chair. It is one of the best things we have done."

The double heresy of acting both as abolitionist and as public woman was committed by such leaders at immense personal cost. Maria Weston Chapman told friends of the total loss of social prestige and the personal indignities she suffered. She was afraid to walk on Boston streets alone, she wrote, because clerks came out of their shops to shout insults at her. Criticism of her "unfeminine" behavior came from antislavery people as well. Her private mail contained this typical rebuke: "For the sake of the honor of the sex to which you belong, strive to put on the garb of modesty, which you are at present so totally destitute of. . . ." This critic went on to condemn her for pursuing a course "which God and nature never intended" and advised her, if she must do something charitable, to help the poor in Massachusetts.

As a counter to this kind of criticism, the women were sustained and comforted by their close-knit circle of sister abolitionists. They were also encouraged by the Garrisonian men, who functioned as family and support in the early years and continued to do so, both literally and in a broader sense, throughout the antebellum period. The sympathy and help of such husbands made it possible for their wives to defy convention and pursue unorthodox careers. At a time when women were legally subservient to their husbands, male approval was necessary and crucial. Henry Chapman, David Lee Child, James Mott, Theodore Weld, and Stephen Symonds Foster (who married Abby Kelley in 1845) all believed in the right of women to equality and to independence in marriage. This belief made them initiators of the early women's movement and models for later feminists.

As co-workers, the Garrisonians provided the feminists with the psychological and material resources that families customarily offer to fledglings. The feeling of being "kindred spirits" extended over the entire antislavery movement but was particularly strong among the feminist-abolitionists, who were carrying a double burden of unpopular causes. The parent body served a vital function as a reference group, providing the social approval and reinforcement of values that made it easier for the women to defy social mores. Abby Kelley received this kind of support from the Grimkés and from Theodore Weld; in turn, the sisters themselves had been bolstered by the encouragement of Garrison and his friend Henry C. Wright. Sarah Grimké wrote with great emotion, in 1838, of the blessings that would "come upon those of our brethren who have been willing to stand by us, notwithstanding the contumely and ridicule and reproach to which it has subjected them."

As a group, the abolitionist women had other important strengths which helped them endure constant criticism and harassment. Brighter and better educated than average, they were also "strong-minded," with a sturdy consciousness of self and a keen sensitivity to all infringements on personal liberty. Most significant was the strength of their religious beliefs. Though they rejected the orthodox tenets and formal trappings of Protestantism, their personal perfectionism and sense of moral duty and "calling" sustained them through difficult trials. In all these ways, they were prototypes for future feminist leaders.

There was still another important link with the future: by defending their own right to speak publicly, the early women helped to establish the same right for those who followed. At Abby Kelley's death in 1887, Lucy Stone noted that Kelley's greatest service had been to earn "for all of us the right of free speech." Mary Livermore similarly observed that "all the women of today" were in Kelley's debt. Kelley herself recognized her unique contribution in preparing the way for the acceptance of women as public lecturers and reformers. She addressed the first national women's rights convention in 1850 with these words: "Sisters, bloody feet have worn smooth the path by which you came up here." Though she and the others played only a peripheral role in the postwar suffrage movement, they were its legendary heroines.

In the 1830's there was as yet no women's rights "movement"—it would begin in the next decade with lecturers, newspapers, political campaigns, and the first conventions. Significant beginnings had occurred during these early years, however, and the important bond between abolitionism and feminism had been forged. The two movements were linked in crucial ways: by the antislavery events and controversies, which proved to be feminist consciousness-raising experiences; by the feminist-abolitionist people, whose leadership spanned both movements; and by the belief in human rights, which provided the ideological underpinning for both causes.

The controversy over woman's role in antislavery had been the important catalyst, moving a few independent-minded abolitionist women to take action in defense of women's rights. Stirred to a realization of their own enslavement in "woman's sphere," feminism became for those women a necessary adjunct to abolitionism. Abby Kelley expressed this fact best when she noted, in 1838, that women had good cause to be grateful to the slave "for the benefit we have received to *ourselves* in working for *him*." "In striving to strike his irons off," she continued, "we found most surely that *we* were manacled *ourselves*. . . ." In order to free the slaves, women were forced to free themselves.

In this early period an important start was also made in laying the groundwork for a feminist ideology. Forced to justify their "unfeminine" behavior, the abolitionist women articulated arguments that were repeated through the entire movement: the equal moral rights and responsibilities of men and women as sanctioned by the Bible; the special obligation of women to aid their oppressed sisters; the need of women for independence, self-respect, and a serious purpose in life. Much of their rhetoric was patterned after antislavery language. The parallel between the status of woman and slave came naturally out of a common belief in human rights, expressed in both secular and religious form.

Abolitionism also bequeathed to feminism the basic philosophy which sustained all radical reform: the idea that all good causes are linked together. "Truth is like a strong cable," as Maria Weston Chapman expressed it. The belief in fundamental principles would lead inevitably to the emancipation of *all* people from bondage—not only slaves, but also "women from the subjugation of men," and people oppressed by poverty, religion, and government. In short, Chapman wrote of emancipation "of the whole earth from sin and suffering." With this belief, the women who began their antislavery work with the plea "Am I Not a Woman and a Sister?" went on to speak in the name of a sisterhood which included not just slave women, but all women.

SUGGESTIONS FOR FURTHER READING

Abolitionism was only one of many mid-nineteenth-century reform movements. An older, but still valuable, general study of antebellum reform is Alice Felt Tyler, *Freedom's Ferment* (Minneapolis, 1944). Ronald G. Walters, *American Reforms, 1815–1860* (New York, 1978) is a brief, more recent survey. Steven Mintz, *Moralists and Modernizers: America's Pre–Civil War Reformers* (Baltimore, 1995) uses recent research to draw portraits of a fascinating array of reformers. David Brion Davis has assembled a variety of interpretations, along with a valuable bibliography, in *Ante-Bellum Reform* (New York, 1967).

The historical literature on abolitionism is extensive and filled with controversy. Some historians are sharply critical of the abolitionists and of the tactics they adopted. Avery Craven, *The Coming of the Civil War* (Chicago, 1957) argues that the abolitionists were maladjusted, misguided fanatics who provoked a conflict that was unnecessary and tragic. David Donald, "Toward a Reconsideration of Abolitionists," in Donald, *Lincoln*

---

*Available in paperback edition.

Reconsidered, 2nd ed. (New York, 1961), 19–36, argues that abolitionist leaders became militant reformers because they were "an elite without function," suffering because the industrial revolution had displaced them from their positions of leadership in society.

Other historians, although less critical of the abolitionists, differ in emphasis and interpretation. Louis Filler, *The Crusade Against Slavery* (New York, 1960) makes connections between the abolitionists and other reforms of the period. Gerda Lerner, *The Grimké Sisters from South Carolina* (New York, 1971) traces the relationship between abolitionism and the struggle for women's rights. Gilbert H. Barnes, *The Anti-Slavery Impulse, 1830–1844* (New York, 1933) emphasizes the importance of religious revivalism and especially the leadership of Theodore Weld for the movement, while Aileen S. Kraditor, *Means and Ends in American Abolitionism* (New York, 1976) emphasizes tactics and the role of Garrison. Two good studies of the role of blacks in the abolitionist movement are Benjamin Quarles. *Black Abolitionists* (New York, 1969) and William H. and Jane H. Pease, *They Who Would be Free: Blacks Search for Freedom, 1830–1861* (New York, 1974).

Among the more recent evaluations of the abolitionists are Lawrence J. Friedman, *Gregarious Saints: Self and Community in American Abolitionism, 1830–1870* (New York, 1982); Louis S. Gerteis, *Morality and Utility in American Antislavery Reform* (Chapel Hill, N.C., 1987); and Edward Magdol, *The Antislavery Rank and File: A Social Profile of the Abolitionists' Constituency* (New York, 1986).

A number of good studies deal with aspects of the opposition to abolitionism. Leon I. Litwack, *North of Slavery: The Negro in the Free States, 1790–1860* (Chicago, 1961) shows that Northern racism was pervasive, even affecting many abolitionists. On this matter see also William H. and Jane H. Pease, "Antislavery Ambivalence: Immediatism, Expediency, Race," *American Quarterly,* 17 (Winter 1965), 682–95. Leonard L. Richards, *Gentlemen of Property and Standing: Anti-Abolition Mobs in Jacksonian America* (New York, 1970) describes some of the conflict and violence directed against the abolitionists.

Those seeking to learn more about the relationship between abolitionism and the women's movement should see Jean Fagen Yellin, *Women and Sisters: The Antislavery Feminists in American Culture* (New Haven, 1989), and the collection of essays, Jean Fagen Yellin and John C. Van Horne, eds., *The Abolitionist Sisterhood: Women's Political Culture in Antebellum America* (Ithaca, N.Y., 1995).

Convenient collections of essays showing different interpretations of abolitionism are Richard O. Curry, *The Abolitionists: Reformers or Fanatics?* (New York, 1965); Martin Duberman, *The Antislavery Vanguard: New Essays on the Abolitionists* (Princeton, N.J., 1965); and Lewis Perry and Michael Fellman, *Antislavery Reconsidered: New Perspectives on the Abolitionists* (Baton Rouge, La., 1979). Selections from the writings of the abolitionists themselves may be found in William H. and Jane H. Pease, *The Anti-Slavery Argument* (New York, 1965) and Louis Ruchames, *The Abolitionists: A Collection of Their Writings* (New York, 1963). Frederick Douglass, *Life and Times of Frederick Douglass* (Hartford, Conn., 1882) is the autobiography of the best-known black abolitionist.

The Civil War

mericans have found their Civil War to be more interesting than any other event in their history. Even the Revolution that marked the birth of the republic cannot compete in popularity with the bloody fratricidal conflict of 1861–1865. The popular imagination has been fed by thousands of books and articles, movies, and television performances. Civil War roundtables and other discussion groups, composed of both professional and amateur historians, meet regularly to discuss various aspects of the war. Commemorative monuments, museums, and cemeteries dot every state that saw battle. The sites of major battles have become carefully preserved national, state, and local parks, and no skirmish, however minor, lacks at least a historical marker to remind visitors of the event. State and local historical societies in states that participated in the war carefully preserve and exhibit its mementos—flags, uniforms, guns, and letters from soldiers to their families and friends. And until death claimed the last of them, old veterans regularly appeared at anniversary commemorations to recount their experiences—real and imagined—in the war.

Historians have not been immune to this fascination with our Civil War. They have recounted the battles many times over and have described, defended, and attacked the actions of the important actors (and many not so important) on both sides of the conflict.

One million casualties, including a half million deaths, and millions of dollars in destroyed property are ample evidence that the Civil War marked a sharp conflict in American history. But how significant were the differences that led to war between North and South in 1861? In October 1858 William H. Seward, a prominent New York Republican leader, declared that the struggle over slavery dividing North and South was "an irrepressible conflict." Earlier that same year an Illinois Republican politician, Abraham Lincoln, had enunciated similar beliefs: "A house divided against itself cannot stand. I believe this government cannot endure permanently, half-slave and half-free."

Some historians, taking their lead from such statements, argue that the Civil War revealed fundamental differences in American society. The gulf separating the sections had become so wide that a bridge of consensus could not be built, leaving war as the only way to resolve the differences. Therefore, many of these scholars argue, the defeat and subjugation of the South marked a fundamental turning point in American history. Military victory by the North became a victory for the Northern point of view; compromise, which had been impossible, now had become unnecessary. Those who hold this general view, however, do not all agree about the source of the fundamental differences that divided North and South. Some insist that slavery was at the root of the problem, although they often disagree among themselves about the precise role that slavery played. Others give little or no emphasis to slavery and instead see the war as a result of a fundamental conflict between an industrial North and an agrarian South for control of the Union.

Another group of historians, however, dispute any interpretation that stresses irreconcilable differences between North and South. The nation had lived with slavery for many generations, they argue; and, when disputes arose between the sections, they had repeatedly been resolved through compromise. While Lincoln made it clear that he did not like slavery, he also made it clear that he would not interfere with it in the South. War was not inevitable; on the contrary it could have been prevented. That it was not prevented was not the result of fundamental differences between North and South, but rather the result of what one historian has called the failures of a "blundering generation."

Some of this debate may be seen in the selections that follow. For Charles and Mary Beard, in the first selection, the Civil War was a struggle for political power waged by representatives of two economic systems. The war was an "irrepressible conflict" between the industrial North and the agricultural South; the prize for which they contended was political domination of the nation. When the North won on the battlefields, the industrialists won in Congress. The domination of the country by the agricultural interests was at an end; and thus, the Beards conclude, the Civil War was "a Second American Revolution." Note that slavery plays an important but secondary role in the Beards' interpretation. The slavery question serves to divide the agrarians, separating the Southern farmers from those in the West, thereby paving the way for the triumph of the industrial interests.

James M. McPherson, in the second selection, also writes of "revolution," but he puts far more emphasis on slavery than do the Beards. Southerners who led their states out of the Union compared themselves to the revolutionaries in 1776 who were defending their "rights and liberties." But the rights they sought to protect, McPherson argues, were the rights to own slaves and to have their slave property protected wherever they chose to take it. Fearing that the election of Lincoln signaled the onset of a revolution that would destroy their slave system, Southerners decided to leave the Union, a move McPherson terms a "counterrevolution," which actually preceded and, indeed, "provoked the very revolution it sought to preempt."

In the third selection, Daniel J. Boorstin views the Civil War from a very different perspective and finds neither revolution nor counterrevolution. His analysis of the political ideology of the North and the South reveals what he considers to be the essential "continuity" in American thought—North and South—throughout the period of the Civil War. He finds both sides more alike than different in their arguments about institutions and politics, and he argues that despite the long years of bloody conflict, the defeat of the South "did not significantly interrupt the continuity of our thinking about institutions."

It would seem that the American people would turn to war as a way of settling their differences only after every other means of settlement had proved ineffective. Can we say, then, that the Civil War arose because the differences between North and South were so great and so fundamental that compromise had become impossible? If so, what were these differences? Why were they so great that they could not be compromised and had instead to be settled on the battlefield? Why did the Constitution, which since 1787 had proved to be such an effective instrument to forge unity in the nation, become so ineffective when, under the provisions of that Constitution, Abraham Lincoln was duly elected in 1860?

One possible answer to these questions is that earlier compromises simply papered over and therefore failed to settle irreconcilable differences between the North and South, differences that finally led to war. On the other hand, few modern social scientists would deny the role of irrational factors in motivating human behavior. Can such factors explain the Civil War? Were Americans, North and South, so blinded by irrational emotionalism that they lost sight of their common interests and of the compromise and accommodation available to them and utilized by them many times before 1861? Clearly, a bloody civil war is a national tragedy. But when such a war could have been avoided had the participants acted more wisely, the tragedy is compounded.

The Second American Revolution

Had the economic systems of the North and the South remained static or changed slowly without effecting immense dislocations in the social structure, the balance of power might have been maintained indefinitely by repeating the compensatory tactics of 1787, 1820, 1833, and 1850; keeping in this manner the inherent antagonisms within the bounds of diplomacy. But nothing was stable in the economy of the United States or in the moral sentiments associated with its diversities.

Within each section of the country, the necessities of the productive system were generating portentous results. The periphery of the industrial vortex of the Northeast was daily enlarging, agriculture in the Northwest was being steadily supplemented by manufacturing, and the area of virgin soil open to exploitation by planters was diminishing with rhythmic regularity—shifting with mechanical precision the weights which statesmen had to adjust in their efforts to maintain the equilibrium of peace. Within each of the three sections also occurred an increasing intensity of social concentration as railways, the telegraph, and the press made travel and communication cheap and almost instantaneous, facilitating the centripetal process that was drawing people of similar economic status and parallel opinions into cooperative activities. Finally the intellectual energies released by accumulating wealth and growing leisure—stimulated by the expansion of the reading public and the literary market—developed with deepened accuracy the word-patterns of the current social persuasions, contributing with galvanic effect to the consolidation of identical groupings.

As the years passed, the planting leaders of Jefferson's agricultural party insisted with mounting fervor that the opposition, first of the Whigs and then of the Republicans, was at bottom an association of interests formed for the pur-

The Rise of American Civilization, Vol. II by Beard/Beard, © 1927. Reprinted by permission of Prentice-Hall, Inc., Upper Saddle River, NJ.

pose of plundering productive management and labor on the land. And with steadfast insistence they declared that in the insatiable greed of their political foes lay the source of the dissensions which were tearing the country asunder.

"There is not a pursuit in which man is engaged (agriculture excepted)," exclaimed Reuben Davis of Mississippi in 1860,

which is not demanding legislative aid to enable it to enlarge its profits and all at the expense of the primary pursuit of man—agriculture. . . . Those interests, having a common purpose of plunder, have united and combined to use the government as the instrument of their operation and have thus virtually converted it into a consolidated empire. Now this combined host of interests stands arrayed against the agricultural states; and this is the reason of the conflict which like an earthquake is shaking our political fabric to its foundation.

The furor over slavery is a mere subterfuge to cover other purposes. "Relentless avarice stands firm with its iron heel upon the Constitution." This creature, "incorporated avarice," has chained "the agricultural states to the northern rock" and lives like a vulture upon their prosperity. It is the effort of Prometheus to burst his manacles that provokes the assault on slavery. "These states struggle like a giant," continued Davis, "and alarm these incorporated interests, lest they may break the chain that binds them to usurpation; and therefore they are making this fierce onslaught upon the slave property of the southern states."

The fact that free-soil advocates waged war only on slavery in the territories was to Jefferson Davis conclusive proof of an underlying conspiracy against agriculture. He professed more respect for the abolitionist than for the free-soiler. The former, he said, is dominated by an honest conviction that slavery is wrong everywhere and that all men ought to be free; the latter does not assail slavery in the states—he merely wishes to abolish it in the territories that are in due course to be admitted to the Union.

With challenging directness, Davis turned upon his opponents in the Senate and charged them with using slavery as a blind to delude the unwary:

What do you propose, gentlemen of the Free-Soil party? Do you propose to better the condition of the slave? Not at all. What then do you propose? You say you are opposed to the expansion of slavery. . . . Is the slave to be benefited by it? Not at all. It is not humanity that influences you in the position which you now occupy before the country. . . . It is that you may have an opportunity of cheating us that you want to limit slave territory within circumscribed bounds. It is that you may have a majority in the Congress of the United States and convert the Government into an engine of northern aggrandizement. It is that your section may grow in power and prosperity upon treasures unjustly taken from the South, like the vampire bloated and gorged with the blood which it has secretly sucked from its victim. . . . You desire to weaken the political power of the southern states; and why? Because you want, by an unjust system of legislation, to promote the industry of the New England states, at the expense of the people of the South and their industry.

Such in the mind of Jefferson Davis, fated to be president of the Confederacy, was the real purpose of the party which sought to prohibit slavery in the territories; that party did not declare slavery to be a moral disease calling for the severe remedy of the surgeon; it merely sought to keep bondage out of the new states as they came into the Union—with one fundamental aim in view, namely, to gain political ascendancy in the government of the United States and fasten upon the country an economic policy that meant the exploitation of the South for the benefit of northern capitalism.

But the planters were after all fighting against the census returns, as the phrase of the day ran current. The amazing growth of northern industries, the rapid extension of railways, the swift expansion of foreign trade to the ends of the earth, the attachment of the farming regions of the West to the centers of manufacture and finance through transportation and credit, the destruction of state consciousness by migration, the alien invasion, the erection of new commonwealths in the Valley of Democracy, the nationalistic drive of interstate commerce, the increase of population in the North, and the southward pressure of the capitalistic glacier all conspired to assure the ultimate triumph of what the orators were fond of calling "the free labor system." This was a dynamic thrust far too powerful for planters operating in a limited territory with incompetent labor on soil of diminishing fertility. Those who swept forward with it, exulting in the approaching triumph of machine industry, warned the planters of their ultimate subjection.

To statesmen of the invincible forces recorded in the census returns, the planting opposition was a huge, compact, and self-conscious economic association bent upon political objects—the possession of the government of the United States, the protection of its interests against adverse legislation, dominion over the territories, and enforcement of the national fugitive slave law throughout the length and breadth of the land. No phrase was more often on the lips of northern statesmen than "the slave power." The pages of the Congressional Globe bristled with references to "the slave system" and its influence over the government of the country. But it was left for William H. Seward of New York to describe it with a fullness of familiar knowledge that made his characterization a classic.

Seward knew from experience that a political party was no mere platonic society engaged in discussing abstractions. "A party," he said, "is in one sense a joint stock association, in which those who contribute most direct the action and management of the concern. The slaveholders contributing in an overwhelming proportion to the capital strength of the Democratic party, they necessarily dictate and prescribe its policy. The inevitable caucus system enables them to do this with a show of fairness and justice." This class of slaveholders, consisting of only three hundred and forty-seven thousand persons, Seward went on to say, was spread from the banks of the Delaware to the banks of the Rio Grande; it possessed nearly all the real estate in that section, owned more than three million other "persons" who were denied all civil and political rights, and inhibited "freedom of speech, freedom of press, freedom of the ballot box, freedom of education, freedom of literature, and freedom of popular assemblies. . . . The slaveholding class has become the governing power in each of the slaveholding states and it practically chooses thirty of the sixty-two members of the Senate, ninety of the two hundred and thirty-three members of the House of Representatives, and one hundred and five of the two hundred and ninety-five electors of the President and Vice-President of the United States."

Becoming still more concrete, Seward accused the President of being "a confessed apologist of the slave-property class." Examining the composition of the Senate, he found the slave-owning group in possession of all the important committees. Peering into the House of Representatives he discovered no impregnable bulwark of freedom there. Nor did respect for judicial ermine compel him to spare the Supreme Court. With irony he exclaimed:

How fitting does the proclamation of its opening close with the invocation: "God save the United States and this honorable court.". . . The court consists of a chief justice and eight associate justices. Of these five were called from slave states and four from free states. The opinions and bias of each of them were carefully considered by the President and Senate when he was appointed. Not one of them was found wanting in soundness of politics, according to the slaveholder's exposition of the Constitution, and those who were called from the free states were even more distinguished in that respect than their brethren from the slaveholding states.

Seward then analyzed the civil service of the national government and could descry not a single person among the thousands employed in the post office, the treasury, and other great departments who was "false to the slaveholding interest." Under the spoils system, the dominion of the slavocracy extended into all branches of the federal administration. "The customs-houses and the public lands pour forth two golden streams—one into the elections to procure votes for the slaveholding class; and the other into the treasury to be enjoyed by those whom it shall see fit to reward with places in the public service." Even in the North, religion, learning, and the press were under the spell of this masterful class, frightened lest they incur its wrath.

Having described the gigantic operating structure of the slavocracy, Seward drew with equal power a picture of the opposing system founded on "free labor." He surveyed the course of economy in the North—the growth of industry, the spread of railways, the swelling tide of European immigration, and the westward roll of free farmers—rounding out the country, knitting it together, bringing "these antagonistic systems" continually into closer contact. Then he uttered those fateful words which startled conservative citizens from Maine to California—words of prophecy which proved to be brutally true—"the irrepressible conflict."

This inexorable clash, he said, was not "accidental, unnecessary, the work of interested or fanatical agitators and therefore ephemeral." No. "It is an irrepressible conflict between opposing and enduring forces." The hopes of those who sought peace by appealing to slave owners to reform themselves were as chaff in a storm. "How long and with what success have you waited already for that reformation? Did any property class ever so reform itself? Did the patricians in old Rome, the noblesse or clergy in France? The landholders in Ireland? The landed aristocracy in England? Does the slaveholding class even seek to beguile you with such a hope? Has it not become rapacious, arrogant, defiant?" All attempts at compromise were "vain and ephemeral." There was accordingly but one supreme task before the people of the United States—the task of confounding and over-throwing "by one decisive blow the betrayers of the Constitution and freedom forever." In uttering this indictment, this prophecy soon to be fulfilled with such appalling accuracy, Seward stepped beyond the bounds of cautious politics and read himself out of the little group of men who were eligible for the Republican nomination in 1860. Frantic efforts to soften his words by explanations and ad-ditions could not appease his critics.

Given an irrepressible conflict which could be symbolized in such unmistak-able patterns by competent interpreters of opposing factions, a transfer of the is-sues from the forum to the field, from the conciliation of diplomacy to the deci-sion of arms was bound to come. Each side, obdurately bent upon its designs and convinced of its rectitude, by the fulfillment of its wishes precipitated events and effected distributions of power that culminated finally in the tragedy foretold by Seward. Those Democrats who operated on historic knowledge rather than on prophetic insight, recalling how many times the party of Hamilton had been crushed at elections, remembering how the Whigs had never been able to carry the country on a cleancut Webster-Clay program, and counting upon the contin-ued support of a huge array of farmers and mechanics marshaled behind the planters, imagined apparently that politics—viewed as the science of ballot enu-meration—could resolve the problems of power raised by the maintenance of the Union.

And in this opinion they were confirmed by the outcome of the presidential campaign in 1852, when the Whigs, with General Winfield Scott, a hero of the Mexican war, at their head, were thoroughly routed by the Democratic candi-date, General Franklin Pierce of New Hampshire. Indeed the verdict of the peo-ple was almost savage, for Pierce carried every state but four, receiving 254 out of 296 electoral votes. The Free-Soil party that branded slavery as a crime and called for its prohibition in the territories scarcely made a ripple, polling only 156,000 out of more than three million votes, a figure below the record set in the previous campaign.

With the Whigs beaten and the Free-Soilers evidently a dwindling handful of negligible critics, exultant Democrats took possession of the Executive offices and Congress, inspired by a firm belief that their tenure was secure. Having won an overwhelming victory on a definite tariff for revenue and pro-slavery pro-gram, they acted as if the party of Hamilton was for all practical purposes as powerless as the little band of abolitionist agitators. At the succeeding election in 1856 they again swept the country—this time with James Buchanan of Pennsyl-vania as their candidate. Though his triumph was not as magisterial as that of Pierce it was great enough to warrant a conviction that the supremacy of the Democratic party could not be broken at the polls.

During these eight years of tenure, a series of events occurred under Demo-cratic auspices, which clinched the grasp of the planting interest upon the coun-try and produced a correlative consolidation of the opposition. One line of devel-opment indicated an indefinite extension of the slave area; another the positive withdrawal of all government support from industrial and commercial enter-

prise. The first evidence of the new course came in the year immediately following the inauguration of Pierce. In 1854, Congress defiantly repealed the Missouri
Compromise and threw open to slavery the vast section of the Louisiana Purchase which had been closed to it by the covenant adopted more than three
decades before. On the instant came a rush of slavery champions from Missouri
into Kansas determined to bring it into the southern sphere of influence. Not
content with the conquest of the forbidden West, filibustering parties under proslavery leaders attempted to seize Cuba and Nicaragua and three American ministers abroad flung out to the world a flaming proclamation, known as the "Os-
tend Manifesto," which declared that the United States would be justified in
wresting Cuba from Spain by force—acts of imperial aggression which even the
Democratic administration in Washington felt constrained to repudiate.

Crowning the repeal of the Missouri Compromise came two decisions of the
Supreme Court giving sanction to the expansion of slavery in America and assuring high protection for that peculiar institution even in the North. In the Dred
Scott case decided in March, 1857, Chief Justice Taney declared in effect that the
Missouri Compromise had been void from the beginning and that Congress had
no power under the Constitution to prohibit slavery in the territories of the
United States anywhere at any time. This legal triumph for the planting interest
was followed in 1859 by another decision in which the Supreme Court upheld
the fugitive slave law and all the drastic procedures provided for its enforcement.
To the frightened abolitionists it seemed that only one more step was needed to
make freedom unconstitutional throughout the country.

These extraordinary measures on behalf of slavery were accompanied by
others that touched far more vitally economic interests in the North. In 1859, the
last of the subsidies for trans-Atlantic steamship companies was ordered discon-
tinued by Congress. In 1857, the tariff was again reduced, betraying an unmistakable drift of the nation toward free trade. In support of this action, the representatives of the South and Southwest were almost unanimous and they gathered
into their fold a large number of New England congressmen on condition that no
material reductions should be made in duties on cotton goods. On the other
hand, the Middle States and the West offered a large majority against tariff reduction so that the division was symptomatic.

Immediately after the new revenue law went into effect an industrial panic
burst upon the country, spreading distress among business men and free laborers.
While that tempest was running high, the paper money anarchy let loose by the
Democrats reached the acme of virulence as the notes of wildcat banks flooded the
West and South and financial institutions crashed in every direction, fifty-one failing in Indiana alone within a period of five years. Since all hope of reviving Hamilton's system of finance had been buried, those who believed that a sound currency
was essential to national prosperity were driven to the verge of desperation. On top
of these economic calamities came Buchanan's veto of the Homestead bill which
the impatient agrarians had succeeded in getting through Congress in a compromise form—an act of presidential independence which angered the farmers and
mechanics who regarded the national domain as their own inheritance. . . .

The amazing acts of mastery—legislative, executive, judicial—committed by
the federal government in the decade between 1850 and 1860 changed the whole

political climate of America. They betrayed a growing consolidation in the planting group, its increased dominance in the Democratic party, and an evident determination to realize its economic interests and protect its labor system at all hazards. In a kind of doom, they seemed to mark the final supremacy of the political army which had swept into office with Andrew Jackson. During the thirty-two years between that event and the inauguration of Lincoln, the Democrats controlled the Presidency and the Senate for twenty-four years, the Supreme Court for twenty-six years, and the House of Representatives for twenty-two years. By the end of the period, the old farmer-labor party organized by Jackson had passed under the dominion of the planting interest and the farming wing of the North was confronted with the alternative of surrender or secession.

In this shift of power the Whigs of the South, discovering the tendencies of the popular balloting, moved steadily over into the Democratic camp. Though unavoidable, the transfer was painful; the planting Whigs, being rich and influential, had little affection for the white farmers who rallied around the Jacksonian banner. According to the estimate of a southern newspaper in 1850, the Whigs owned at least three-fourths of all the slaves in the country and it was a matter of common knowledge that leaders among them disliked wildcat banking as much as they hated high duties on the manufactured goods they bought. Indeed to a southern gentleman of the old school the radical agrarianism of Andrew Jackson was probably more odious than the tariff schedules devised by Daniel Webster. It was said that one of them, when asked whether a gentleman could be a Democrat, snapped back the tart reply: "Well, he is not apt to be; but if he is, he is in damned bad company."

But the rich planters were relatively few in numbers and virtue was subject to the law of necessity; the populace had the votes, northern manufacturers were demanding protection, abolitionists were agitating, and in the end all but the most conservative remnant of the southern Whigs had to go over to the party that professed the dangerous doctrines of Jackson. The achievements of the years that lay between 1850 and 1860 seemed to justify the sacrifice.

Though the drift toward the irrepressible conflict was steady and strong, as events revealed, the politics of the decade had the outward semblances of dissolution. The abolitionists and free-soilers, while a mere minority as we have seen, were able to worry the politicians of both parties in the North. Largely deserted by their southern cohorts, the Whigs, whose organization had always been tenuous at best, could discover no way of mustering a majority of votes on the bare economic policies of Hamilton and Webster. Their two victories—in 1840 and 1848—had been dubious and their only hope for a triumph at the polls lay in a combination with other factors. . . .

The signal for a general realignment of factions and parties was given by the passage of the Kansas-Nebraska bill of 1854 repealing the Missouri Compromise. In fact, while that measure was pending in Congress a coalescing movement was to be observed: northern Whigs persuaded that their old party was moribund, Democrats weary of planting dominance, and free-soilers eager to exclude slavery from the territories began to draw together to resist the advance of the planting power. In February of that year, a number of Whigs and Democrats assembled at Ripon, Wisconsin, and resolved that a new party must be formed if the bill passed.

When the expected event occurred, the Ripon insurgents created a fusion committee and chose the name "Republican" as the title of their young political association. In July, a Michigan convention composed of kindred elements demanded the repeal of the Kansas-Nebraska act, the repeal of the fugitive slave law, and the abolition of slavery in the District of Columbia. This convention also agreed to postpone all differences "with regard to political economy or administrative policy" and stay in the field as a "Republican" party until the struggle against slavery extension was finished. All over the country similar meetings were mustered and the local cells of the new national party rose into being. Meanwhile the old Whigs who wanted peace and prosperity were floating about looking for any drifting wreckage that might hold them above the waves. . . .

"The Government has fallen into the hands of the Slave Power completely," wrote Wendell Phillips in 1854.

So far as national politics are concerned, we are beaten—there's no hope. We shall have Cuba in a year or two, Mexico in five, and I should not wonder if efforts were made to revive the slave trade, though perhaps unsuccessfully, as the northern slave states, which live by the export of slaves, would help us in opposing that. Events hurry forward with amazing rapidity; we live fast here. The future seems to unfold a vast slave empire united with Brazil and darkening the whole West. I hope I may be a false prophet, but the sky was never so dark.

Three years later, when the inauguration of Buchanan had turned discouragement into despair, the only strategic stroke that Phillips and his colleagues could invent was to hold an abolition convention in Massachusetts and adopt a solemn slogan calling for the disruption of the Union with the slave states. And the events of the swiftly flowing months that followed, as we have already indicated, merely seemed to confirm the belief of Phillips in the supremacy of the Democratic party led by the indomitable planting interest; events such as the downward revision of the tariff, the withdrawal of the ship subsidies, and the Dred Scott decision opening the territories to slavery.

All the while the conflict was growing more furious. Advocates of protection, taking advantage of the panic which followed the tariff revision, organized a stirring campaign to wean workingmen from their allegiance to a free-trade Democracy. Advocates of a sound currency protested against the depreciated notes and the wildcat banks that spread ruin through all sections of the land. The abolitionists maintained their fusillade, Garrison and Phillips, despite their pessimism, resting neither day nor night. Going beyond the bounds of mere agitation, the slavery faction of Missouri in its grim determination to conquer Kansas for bondage and northern abolitionists in their equally firm resolve to seize it for freedom convulsed the country by bloody deeds and then by bloody reprisals. In a powerful oration, "The Crime against Kansas," done in classical style but bristling with abuse of the slavery party, Charles Sumner threw Congress into a tumult in 1856 and provided a text for the free-soilers laboring to wrest the government from the planting interest. Before the public excitement caused by this speech had died away, the attention of the nation was arrested by a series of debates between Lincoln and Douglas held in Illinois in 1858—debates which set forth in clear and logical form the program for excluding slavery from the territories and the squatter-sovereignty scheme for letting the inhabitants decide the issue for themselves.

Then came the appalling climax in 1859 when John Brown, after a stormy career in Kansas, tried to kindle a servile insurrection in the South. In the spring of that year, Brown attended an anti-slavery convention from which he went away muttering: "These men are all talk; what we need is action—action!" Collecting a few daring comrades he made a raid into Harpers Ferry for the purpose of starting a slave rebellion. Though his efforts failed, though he was quickly executed as a "traitor to Virginia," the act of violence rocked the continent from sea to sea.

In vain did the Republicans try to treat it as the mere work of a fanatic and denounce it as "among the gravest of crimes." In vain did Lincoln attempt to minimize it as an absurd adventure that resulted in nothing noteworthy except the death of Brown. It resounded through the land with the clangor of an alarm bell, aggravating the jangling nerves of a people already excited by fears of a race war and continued disturbances over the seizure of slaves under the fugitive slave act—disorders which sometimes assumed the form of menacing riots.

The turmoil in the country naturally found sharp echoes in the halls of Congress. Buchanan's policy of aiding the slavery party in its efforts to get possession of Kansas and the taunting action of the free-soilers in their determination to save it for liberty, gave abundant occasions for debates that grew more and more acrimonious. Indeed the factions in Congress were now almost at swords' points, passion in argument and gesture becoming the commonplace of the day.

When Senator Sumner made a vehement verbal attack on Senator Butler of South Carolina in 1856, Preston Brooks, a Representative from the same state and a relative of the latter, replied in terms of physical force, catching Sumner unawares and beating his victim senseless with a heavy cane. Though the act was not strictly chivalrous—for Sumner, wedged between his chair and his desk, could not defend himself—admiring South Carolinians gave Brooks a grand banquet and presented him with a new cane bearing the words: "Use knockdown arguments." On both sides of the Senate chamber all the arts of diplomacy were discarded, and the meanest weapons of personal abuse brought into play. Douglas called Sumner a perjurer who spat forth malignity upon his colleagues. The prim, proud Senator from Massachusetts, conscious of possessing a mellow culture, replied by likening Douglas to a "noisome, squat and nameless animal" that filled the Senate with an offensive odor.

Things were even worse in the lower house. Again and again debate was on the verge of physical combat, for which members equipped themselves with knives and revolvers. A Representative from Pennsylvania and another from North Carolina had to be put under bonds to keep the peace. A general mêlée occurred in the spring of 1860 when Lovejoy, whose brother had been shot by a pro-slavery mob in Illinois, made an unbridled attack on slave owners and

Democrats, advanced to their side of the house shaking his fists in a terrible rage, and threw the whole chamber into such a confusion that all the resources of experienced leaders were needed to prevent bloodshed then and there. Without exaggeration did Jefferson Davis exclaim that members of Congress were more like the agents of belligerent states than men assembled in the interest of common welfare—an utterance that was startlingly accurate—born of prophetic certainty. After a few fleeting days, the irrepressible conflict that had so long been raging was actually to pass from the forum to the battlefield, to that court where the only argument was the sword and where the one answer that admitted of no appeal was death.

Every shocking incident on the one side only consolidated the forces on the other. By 1860 leaders of the planting interest had worked out in great detail their economic and political scheme—their ultimatum to the serried opposition—and embodied it in many official documents. The economic elements were those made familiar to the country through twenty years of agitation: no high protective tariffs, no ship subsidies, no national banking and currency system; in short, none of the measures which business enterprise deemed essential to its progress. The remaining problem before the planting interest, namely, how to clinch its grip and prevent a return to the Hamilton-Webster policy as the industrial North rapidly advanced in wealth and population, was faced with the same penchant for definition.

Plans for accomplishing that purpose were mapped out by able spokesmen from the South in a set of Senate resolutions adopted on May 24–25, 1860: slavery is lawful in all the territories under the Constitution; neither Congress nor a local legislature can abolish it there; the federal government is in duty bound to protect slave owners as well as the holders of other forms of property in the territories; it is a violation of the Constitution for any state or any combination of citizens to intermeddle with the domestic institutions of any other state "on any pretext whatever, political, moral, or religious, with a view to their disturbance or subversion"; open or covert attacks on slavery are contrary to the solemn pledges given by the states on entering the Union to protect and defend one another; the inhabitants of a territory on their admission to the Union may decide whether or not they will sanction slavery thereafter; the strict enforcement of the fugitive slave law is required by good faith and the principles of the Constitution.

In brief, the federal government was to do nothing for business enterprise while the planting interest was to be assured the possession of enough political power to guarantee it against the reenactment of the Hamilton-Webster program. Incidentally the labor system of the planting interest was not to be criticized and all runaway property was to be returned. Anything short of this was, in the view of the planting statesmen, "subversive of the Constitution."

The meaning of the ultimatum was not to be mistaken. It was a demand upon the majority of the people to surrender unconditionally for all time to the minority stockholders under the Constitution. It offered nothing to capitalism but capitulation; to the old Whigs of the South nothing but submission. Finally— and this was its revolutionary phase—it called upon the farmers and mechanics who had formed the bulk of Jacksonian Democracy in the North to acknowledge the absolute sovereignty of the planting interest. Besides driving a wedge into the nation, the conditions laid down by the planters also split the Democratic party itself into two factions.

Soon after the Democratic convention assembled at Charleston in April, 1860, this fundamental division became manifest. The northern wing, while entirely willing to indorse the general economic program of the planters, absolutely refused to guarantee them sovereignty in the party and throughout the country. Rejecting the proposal of the southern members to make slavery obligatory in the territories, it would merely offer to "abide by the decisions of the Supreme Court on all questions of constitutional law." Since the Dred Scott case had opened all the territories to slavery, that tender seemed generous enough but the intransigent representatives of the planting interest would not accept it as adequate. Unable to overcome the majority commanded in the convention by the northern group, they withdrew from the assembly, spurning the pleas of their colleagues not to break up the union of hearts on "a mere theory" and countering all arguments with a declaration of finality: "Go your way and we will go ours."

After balloting for a time on candidates without reaching a decision under the two-thirds rule, the remaining members of the Charleston conference adjourned to meet again at Baltimore. When they reassembled, they nominated Stephen A. Douglas of Illinois, the apostle of "squatter sovereignty," who was ready to open the territories to slavery but not to guarantee the planting interest unconditional supremacy in the Democratic party and the Union. Determined to pursue their separate course to the bitter end, the Charleston seceders adopted the platform rejected by the Douglas faction and chose as their candidate, John C. Breckinridge of Kentucky, an unyielding champion of planting aristocracy and its labor system. The union of farmers and slave owners was thus severed: the Republicans had carried off one large fragment of the northern farmers in 1856; Douglas was now carrying off another.

During the confusion in the Democratic ranks, the Republicans, in high glee over the quarrels of the opposition, held their convention in Chicago—a sectional gathering except for representatives from five slave states. Among its delegates the spirit of opposition to slavery extension, which had inspired the party assembly four years before, was still evident but enthusiasm on that ticklish subject was neutralized by the prudence of the practical politicians who, sniffing victory in the air, had rushed to the new tent. Whigs, whose affections were centered on Hamilton's program rather than on Garrison's scheme of salvation, were to be seen on the floor. Advocates of a high protective tariff and friends of free homesteads for mechanics and farmers now mingled with the ardent opponents of slavery in the territories. With their minds fixed on the substance of things sought for, the partisans of caution were almost able to prevent the convention from indorsing the Declaration of Independence. Still they were in favor of restricting the area of slavery; they had no love for the institution and its spread helped to fasten the grip of the planting interest on the government at Washington. So the Republican convention went on record in favor of liberty for the territories, free homesteads for farmers, a protective tariff, and a Pacific railway. As the platform was read, the cheering became especially loud and prolonged when the homestead and tariff planks were reached. Such at least is the testimony of the stenographic report.

Since this declaration of principles was well fitted to work a union of forces, it was essential that the candidate should not divide them. The protective plank would doubtless line up the good old Whigs of the East but tender consideration had to be shown to the Ohio Valley, original home of Jacksonian Democracy, where national banks, tariffs, and other "abominations" still frightened the wary. Without Ohio, Indiana, and Illinois, the Republican managers could not hope to win and they knew that the lower counties of these states were filled with settlers from the slave belt who had no love for the "money power," abolition, or anything that savored of them. In such circumstances Seward, idol of the Whig wing, was no man to offer that section; he was too radical on the slavery issue and too closely associated with "high finance" in addition. "If you do not nominate Seward, where will you get your money?" was the blunt question put by Seward's loyal supporters at Chicago. The question was pertinent but not fatal.

Given this confluence of problems, a man close to the soil of the West was better suited to the requirements of the hour than a New York lawyer with somewhat fastidious tastes, obviously backed by fat purses. The available candidate was Abraham Lincoln of Illinois. Born in Kentucky, he was of southern origin. A son of poor frontier parents, self-educated, a pioneer who in his youth had labored in field and forest, he appealed to the voters of the backwoods. Still by an uncanny genius for practical affairs, he had forged his way to the front as a shrewd lawyer and politician. In his debates with Douglas he had shown himself able to cope with one of the foremost leaders in the Democratic party. On the tariff, bank, currency, and homestead issues he was sound. A local railway attorney, he was trusted among business men.

On the slavery question Lincoln's attitude was firm but conservative. He disliked slavery and frankly said so; yet he was not an abolitionist and he saw no way in which the institution could be uprooted. On the contrary, he favored enforcing the fugitive slave law and he was not prepared to urge even the abolition of slavery in the District of Columbia. His declaration that a house divided against itself could not stand had been counterbalanced by an assertion that the country would become all free or all slave—a creed which any southern planter could have indorsed. Seward's radical doctrine that there was a "higher law" than the Constitution, dedicating the territories to freedom, received from the Illinois lawyer disapproval, not commendation.

Nevertheless Lincoln was definite and positive in his opinion that slavery should not be permitted in the territories. That was necessary to satisfy the minimum demands of the anti-slavery faction and incidentally it pleased those Whigs of the North who at last realized that no Hamiltonian program could be pushed through Congress if the planting interest secured a supremacy, or indeed held an equal share of power, in the Union. Evidently Lincoln was the man of the hour: his heritage was correct, his principles were sound, his sincerity was unquestioned, and his ability as a speaker commanded the minds and hearts of his auditors. He sent word to his friends at Chicago that, although he did not indorse

Seward's higher-law doctrine, he agreed with him on the irrepressible conflict. The next day Lincoln was nominated amid huzzas from ten thousand lusty throats.

A large fraction of Whigs and some fragments of the Know Nothing, or American, party, foreseeing calamity in the existing array of interests, tried to save the day by an appeal to lofty sentiments without any definitions. Assuming the name of Constitutional Unionists and boasting that they represented the "intelligence and respectability of the South" as well as the lovers of the national idea everywhere, they held a convention at Baltimore and nominated John Bell of Tennessee and Edward Everett of Massachusetts for President and Vice-President. In the platform they invited their countrymen to forget all divisions and "support the Constitution of the country, the union of the states, and the enforcement of the laws." It was an overture of old men—men who had known and loved Webster and Clay and who shrank with horror from agitations that threatened to end in bloodshed and revolution—a plea for the maintenance of the status quo against the whims of a swiftly changing world.

A spirited campaign followed the nomination of these four candidates for the presidency on four different platforms. Huge campaign funds were raised and spent. Beside pursuing the usual strategy of education, the Republicans resorted to parades and the other spectacular features that had distinguished the log-cabin crusade of General Harrison's year. Emulating the discretion of the Hero of Tippecanoe, Lincoln maintained a judicious silence at Springfield while his champions waged his battles for him, naturally tempering their orations to the requirements of diverse interests. They were fully conscious, as a Republican paper in Philadelphia put it, that "Frémont had tried running on the slavery issue and lost." So while they laid stress on it in many sections, they widened their appeal.

In the West, a particular emphasis was placed on free homesteads and the Pacific railway. With a keen eye for competent strategy, Carl Schurz carried the campaign into Missouri where he protested with eloquence against the action of the slave power in denying "the laboring man the right to acquire property in the soil by his labor" and made a special plea for the German vote on the ground that the free land was to be opened to aliens who declared their intention of becoming American citizens. Discovering that the homestead question was "the greatest issue in the West," Horace Greeley used it to win votes in the East. Agrarians and labor reformers renewed the slogan: "Vote yourself a farm."

In Pennsylvania and New Jersey, protection for iron and steel was the great subject of discussion. Curtin, the Republican candidate for governor in the former state, said not a word about abolishing slavery in his ratification speech but spoke with feeling on "the vast heavings of the heart of Pennsylvania whose sons are pining for protection to their labor and their dearest interests." Warming to his theme, he exclaimed: "This is a contest involving protection and the rights of labor. . . . If you desire to become vast and great, protect the manufacturers of Philadelphia. . . . All hail, liberty! All hail, freedom! Freedom to the white man! All hail freedom general as the air we breathe!" In a fashion after Curtin's own heart, the editor of the Philadelphia *American* and *Gazette,* surveying the canvass at the finish, repudiated the idea that "any sectional aspect of the slavery question" was up for decision and declared that the great issues were protection for industry, "economy in the conduct of the government, homesteads for settlers on the public domain, retrenchment and accountability in the public expenditures, appropriation for rivers and harbors, a Pacific railroad, the admission of Kansas, and a radical reform in the government."

With a kindred appreciation of practical matters, Seward bore the standard through the North and West. Fully conversant with the Webster policy of commercial expansion in the Pacific and knowing well the political appeal of Manifest Destiny, he proclaimed the future of the American empire—assuring his auditors that in due time American outposts would be pushed along the northwest coast to the Arctic Ocean, that Canada would be gathered into our glorious Union, that the Latin-American republics reorganized under our benign influence would become parts of this magnificent confederation, that the ancient Aztec metropolis, Mexico City, would eventually become the capital of the United States, and that America and Russia, breaking their old friendship, would come to grips in the Far East—"in regions where civilization first began." All this was involved in the election of Lincoln and the triumph of the Republican party. Webster and Cushing and Perry had not wrought in vain.

The three candidates opposed to Lincoln scored points wherever they could. Douglas took the stump with his usual vigor and declaimed to throngs in nearly every state. Orators of the Breckinridge camp, believing that their extreme views were sound everywhere, invaded the North. Bell's champions spoke with dignity and warmth about the dangers inherent in all unwise departures from the past, about the perils of the sectional quarrel. When at length the ballots were cast and counted, it was found that the foes of slavery agitation had carried the country by an overwhelming majority. Their combined vote was a million ahead of Lincoln's total; the two Democratic factions alone, to say nothing of Bell's six hundred thousand followers, outnumbered the Republican army. But in the division and uproar of the campaign Lincoln, even so, had won the Presidency; he was the choice of a minority—a sectional minority at that—but under the terms of the Constitution, he was entitled to the scepter at Washington.

From what has just been said it must be apparent that the forces which produced the irrepressible conflict were very complex in nature and yet the momentous struggle has been so often reduced by historians to simple terms that a reexamination of the traditional thesis has become one of the tasks of the modern age. On the part of northern writers it was long the fashion to declare that slavery was the cause of the conflict between the states. Such for example was the position taken by James Ford Rhodes and made the starting point of his monumental work.

Assuming for the moment that this assertion is correct in a general sense, it will be easily observed even on a superficial investigation that "slavery" was no simple, isolated phenomenon. In itself it was intricate and it had filaments through the whole body economic. It was a labor system, the basis of planting, and the foundation of the southern aristocracy. The aristocracy, in turn, owing to the nature of its economic operations, resorted to public policies that were opposed to capitalism, sought to dominate the federal government, and, with the help of free farmers also engaged in agriculture, did at last dominate it. In the course of that political conquest, all the plans of commerce and industry for federal protection and subvention were overborne. It took more than a finite eye to discern where slavery as an ethical question left off and economics—the struggle over the distribution of wealth—began.

On the other hand, the early historians of the southern school, chagrined by defeat and compelled to face the adverse judgment of brutal fact, made the "rights of states"—something nobler than economics or the enslavement of Negroes—the issue for which the Confederacy fought and bled. That too like slavery seems simple until subjected to a little scrutiny. What is a state? At bottom it is a majority or perhaps a mere plurality of persons engaged in the quest of something supposed to be beneficial, or at all events not injurious, to the pursuers. And what are rights? Abstract, intangible moral values having neither substance nor form? The party debates over the economic issues of the middle period answer with an emphatic negative. If the southern planters had been content to grant tariffs, bounties, subsidies, and preferences to northern commerce and industry, it is not probable that they would have been molested in their most imperious proclamations of sovereignty.

But their theories and their acts involved interests more ponderable than political rhetoric. They threatened the country with secession first in defying the tariff of abominations and when they did secede thirty years later it was in response to the victory of a tariff and homestead party that proposed nothing more dangerous to slavery itself than the mere exclusion of the institution from the territories. It took more than a finite eye to discern where their opposition to the economic system of Hamilton left off and their affection for the rights of states began. The modern reader tossed about in a contrariety of opinions can only take his bearings by examining a few indubitable realities.

With reference to the popular northern view of the conflict, there stands the stubborn fact that at no time during the long gathering of the storm did Garrison's abolition creed rise to the dignity of a first-rate political issue in the North. Nobody but agitators, beneath the contempt of the towering statesmen of the age, ever dared to advocate it. No great political organization even gave it the most casual indorsement.

When the abolitionists launched the Liberty party in the campaign of 1844 to work for emancipation, as we have noted, the voters answered their plea for "the restoration of equality of political rights among men" in a manner that demonstrated the invincible opposition of the American people. Out of more than two and a half million ballots cast in the election, only sixty-five thousand were recorded in favor of the Liberty candidate. That was America's answer to the call for abolition; and the advocates of that policy never again ventured to appeal to the electorate by presenting candidates on such a radical platform.

No other party organized between that time and the clash of arms attempted to do more than demand the exclusion of slavery from the territories and not until the Democrats by repealing the Missouri Compromise threatened to extend slavery throughout the West did any party poll more than a handful of votes on that issue. It is true that Van Buren on a free-soil platform received nearly three hundred thousand votes in 1848 but that was evidently due to personal influence, because his successor on a similar ticket four years afterward dropped into an insignificant place.

Even the Republican party, in the campaign of 1856, coming hard on the act of defiance which swept away the Missouri compact, won little more than one-third the active voters to the cause of restricting the slavery area. When transformed after four more years into a homestead and high tariff party pledged merely to liberty in the territories, the Republicans polled a million votes fewer than the number cast for the opposing factions and rode into power on account of the divided ranks of the enemy. Such was the nation's reply to the anti-slavery agitation from the beginning of the disturbance until the cannon shot at Sumter opened a revolution.

Moreover not a single responsible statesman of the middle period committed himself to the doctrine of immediate and unconditional abolition to be achieved by independent political action. John Quincy Adams, ousted from the Presidency by Jacksonian Democracy but returned to Washington as the Representative of a Massachusetts district in Congress, did declare that it was the duty of every free American to work directly for the abolition of slavery and with uncanny vision foresaw that the knot might be cut with the sword. But Adams was regarded by astute party managers as a foolish and embittered old man and his prophecy as a dangerous delusion.

Practical politicians who felt the iron hand of the planters at Washington—politicians who saw how deeply intertwined with the whole economic order the institution of slavery really was—could discover nothing tangible in immediate and unconditional abolition that appealed to reason or came within the range of common sense. Lincoln was emphatic in assuring the slaveholders that no Republican had ever been detected in any attempt to disturb them. "We must not interfere with the institution of slavery in the states where it exists," he urged, "because the Constitution forbids it and the general welfare does not require us to do so."

Since, therefore, the abolition of slavery never appeared in the platform of any great political party, since the only appeal ever made to the electorate on that issue was scornfully repulsed, since the spokesman of the Republicans emphatically declared that his party never intended to interfere with slavery in the states in any shape or form, it seems reasonable to assume that the institution of slavery was not the fundamental issue during the epoch preceding the bombardment of Fort Sumter.

Nor can it be truthfully said, as southern writers were fond of having it, that a tender and consistent regard for the rights of states and for a strict construction of the Constitution was the prime element in the dispute that long divided the country. As a matter of record, from the foundation of the republic, all factions were for high nationalism or low provincialism upon occasion according to their desires at the moment, according to turns in the balance of power. New England nullified federal law when her commerce was affected by the War of 1812 and came out staunchly for liberty and union, one and inseparable, now and forever, in 1833 when South Carolina attempted to nullify a tariff act. Not long afterward, the legislature of Massachusetts, dreading the overweening strength of the Southwest, protested warmly against the annexation of Texas and resolved that "such an act of admission would have no binding force whatever on the people of Massachusetts."

Equally willing to bend theory to practical considerations, the party of the slavocracy argued that the Constitution was to be strictly and narrowly construed whenever tariff and bank measures were up for debate; but no such piddling concept of the grand document was to be held when a bill providing for the prompt and efficient return of fugitive slaves was on the carpet. Less than twenty years after South Carolina prepared to resist by arms federal officers engaged in collecting customs duties, the champions of slavery and states' rights greeted with applause a fugitive slave law which flouted the precious limitations prescribed in the first ten Amendments to the Constitution—a law which provided for the use of all the powers of the national government to assist masters in getting possession of their elusive property—which denied to the alleged slave, who might perchance be a freeman in spite of his color, the right to have a jury trial or even to testify in his own behalf. In other words, it was "constitutional" to employ the engines of the federal authority in catching slaves wherever they might be found in any northern community and to ignore utterly the elementary safeguards of liberty plainly and specifically imposed on Congress by language that admitted of no double interpretation.

On this very issue of personal liberty, historic positions on states' rights were again reversed. Following the example of South Carolina on the tariff, Wisconsin resisted the fugitive slave law as an invasion of her reserved rights—as a violation of the Constitution. Alarmed by this action, Chief Justice Taney answered the disobedient state in a ringing judicial decision announcing a high nationalism that would have delighted the heart of John Marshall, informing the recalcitrant Wisconsin that the Constitution and laws enacted under it were supreme; that the fugitive slave law was fully authorized by the Constitution; and that the Supreme Court was the final arbiter in all controversies over the respective powers of the states and the United States. "If such an arbiter had not been provided in our complicated system of government, internal tranquility could not have been preserved and if such controversies were left to the arbitrament of physical force, our Government, State and National, would cease to be a government of laws, and revolution by force of arms would take the place of courts of justice and judicial decisions." No nullification here; no right of a state to judge for itself respecting infractions of the Constitution by the federal government; federal law is binding everywhere and the Supreme Court, a branch of the national government, is the final judge.

And in what language did Wisconsin reply? The legislature of the state, in a solemn resolution, declared that the decision of the Supreme Court of the United States in the case in question was in direct conflict with the Constitution. It vowed that the essential principles of the Kentucky doctrine of nullification were sound. Then it closed with the rebel fling: "that the several states . . . being sovereign and independent, have the unquestionable right to judge of its [the Constitution's] infraction and that a positive defiance by those sovereignties of all unauthorized acts done or attempted to be done under color of that instrument is the rightful remedy."

That was in 1859. Within two years, men who had voted for that resolution and cheered its adoption were marching off in martial array to vindicate on southern battlefields the supremacy of the Union and the sovereignty of the nation. By that fateful hour the southern politicians who had applauded Taney's declaration that the Supreme Court was the final arbiter in controversies between the states and the national government had come to the solemn conclusion that the states themselves were the arbiters. Such words and events being facts, there can be but one judgment in the court of history; namely, that major premises respecting the nature of the Constitution and deductions made logically from them with masterly eloquence were minor factors in the grand dispute as compared with the interests, desires, and passions that lay deep in the hearts and minds of the contestants.

Indeed, honorable men who held diametrically opposite views found warrant for each in the Constitution. All parties and all individuals, save the extreme abolitionists, protested in an unbroken chant their devotion to the national covenant and to the principles and memory of the inspired men who framed it. As the Bible was sometimes taken as a guide for theologians traveling in opposite directions, so the Constitution was the beacon that lighted the way of statesmen who differed utterly on the issues of the middle period. . . .

When the modern student examines all the verbal disputes over the nature of the Union—the arguments employed by the parties which operated and opposed the federal government between the adoption of the Constitution and the opening of the Civil War—he can hardly do otherwise than conclude that the linguistic devices used first on one side and then on the other were not derived from inherently necessary concepts concerning the intimate essence of the federal system. The roots of the controversy lay elsewhere—in social groupings founded on differences in climate, soil, industries, and labor systems, in divergent social forces, rather than varying degrees of righteousness and wisdom, or what romantic historians call "the magnetism of great personalities."

In the spring of 1861 the full force of the irrepressible conflict burst upon the hesitant and bewildered nation and for four long years the clash of arms filled the land with its brazen clangor. For four long years the anguish, the calamities, and the shocks of the struggle absorbed the energies of the multitudes, blared in the headlines of the newspapers, and loomed impressively in the minds of the men and women who lived and suffered in that age.

Naturally, therefore, all who wrote of the conflict used the terms of war. In its records, the government of the United States officially referred to the contest as the War of the Rebellion, thus by implication setting the stigma of treason on those who served under the Stars and Bars. Repudiating this brand and taking for his shield the righteousness of legitimacy, one of the leading southern statesmen, Alexander H. Stephens, in his great history of the conflict, called it the War between the States. This, too, no less than the title chosen by the federal government, is open to objections; apart from the large assumptions involved, it is not strictly accurate for, in the border states, the armed struggle was a guerrilla war and in Virginia the domestic strife ended in the separation of several counties, under the aegis of a new state constitution, as West Virginia. More recently a distinguished historian, Edward Channing, entitled a volume dealing with the period *The War for Southern Independence*—a characterization which, though fairly precise, suffers a little perhaps from abstraction.

As a matter of fact all these symbols are misleading in that they overemphasize the element of military force in the grand denouement. War there was unquestionably immense, wide-sweeping, indubitable, as Carlyle would say. For years the agony of it hung like a pall over the land. And yet with strange swiftness the cloud was lifted and blown away. Merciful grass spread its green mantle over the cruel scars and the gleaming red splotches sank into the hospitable earth.

It was then that the economist and lawyer, looking more calmly on the scene, discovered that the armed conflict had been only one phase of the cataclysm, a transitory phase; that at bottom the so-called Civil War, or the War between the States, in the light of Roman analogy, was a social war, ending in the unquestioned establishment of a new power in the government, making vast changes in the arrangement of classes, in the accumulation and distribution of wealth, in the course of industrial development, and in the Constitution inherited from the Fathers. Merely by the accidents of climate, soil, and geography was it a sectional struggle. If the planting interest had been scattered evenly throughout the industrial region, had there been a horizontal rather than a perpendicular cleavage, the irrepressible conflict would have been resolved by other methods and accompanied by other logical defense mechanisms.

In any event neither accident nor rhetoric should be allowed to obscure the intrinsic character of that struggle. If the operations by which the middle classes of England broke the power of the king and the aristocracy are to be known collectively as the Puritan Revolution, if the series of acts by which the bourgeois and peasants of France overthrew the king, nobility, and clergy is to be called the French Revolution, then accuracy compels us to characterize by the same term the social cataclysm in which the capitalists, laborers, and farmers of the North and West drove from power in the national government the planting aristocracy of the South. Viewed under the light of universal history, the fighting was a fleeting incident; the social revolution was the essential, portentous outcome.

To be sure the battles and campaigns of the epoch are significant to the military strategist; the tragedy and heroism of the contest furnish inspiration to patriots and romance to the makers of epics. But the core of the vortex lay elsewhere. It was in the flowing substance of things limned by statistical reports on finance, commerce, capital, industry, railways, and agriculture, by provisions of constitutional law, and by the pages of statute books—prosaic muniments which show that the so-called civil war was in reality a Second American Revolution and in a strict sense, the First.

James M. McPherson

The Counterrevolution of 1861

I

The second Continental Congress had deliberated fourteen months before declaring American independence in 1776. To produce the United States Constitution and put the new government into operation required nearly two years. In contrast, the Confederate States of America organized itself, drafted a constitution, and set up shop in Montgomery, Alabama, within three months of Lincoln's election.

The South moved so swiftly because, in seeming paradox, secession proceeded on a state-by-state basis rather than by collective action. Remembering the lesson of 1850, when the Nashville Convention had turned into a forum of caution and delay, fire-eaters determined this time to eschew a convention of states until the secession of several of them had become a *fait accompli*. And because the ground had long since been plowed and planted, the harvest of disunion came quickly after the thunderstorm of Lincoln's election.

Not surprisingly, South Carolina acted first. "There is nothing in all the dark caves of human passion so cruel and deadly as the hatred the South Carolinians profess for the Yankees," wrote the correspondent of the London *Times* from Charleston. The enmity of Greek for Turk was child's play "compared to the animosity evinced by the 'gentry' of South Carolina for the 'rabble of the North.'. . . 'The State of South Carolina was,' I am told, 'founded by gentlemen. . . . Nothing on earth shall ever induce us to submit to any union with the brutal, bigoted blackguards of the New England states!' " In this mood the South Carolina legislature called a convention to consider secession. Amid extraordinary scenes of marching bands, fireworks, displays, militia calling themselves Minute Men, and huge rallies of citizens waving palmetto flags and shouting slogans of southern rights, the convention by a vote of 169–0 enacted on December 20 an "ordinance" dissolving "the union now subsisting between South Carolina and other States."

As fire-eaters had hoped, this bold step triggered a chain reaction by conventions in other lower-South states. After the Christmas holidays—celebrated this year with a certain ambivalence toward the teachings of the Prince of Peace—Mississippi adopted a similar ordinance on January 9, 1861, followed by Florida on January 10, Alabama on January 11, Georgia on January 19, Louisiana on January 26, and Texas on February 1. Although none of these conventions exhibited the unity of South Carolina's, their average vote in favor of secession was 80 percent. This figure was probably a fair reflection of white opinion in those six states. Except in Texas, the conventions did not submit their ordinances to the voters for ratification. This led to charges that a disunion conspiracy acted against the will of the people. But in fact the main reason for non-submission was a desire to avoid delay. The voters had just elected delegates who had made their positions clear in public statements; another election seemed superfluous. The Constitution of 1787 had been ratified by state conventions, not by popular vote; withdrawal of that ratification by similar conventions satisfied a wish for legality and symmetry. In Texas the voters endorsed secession by a margin of three to one; there is little reason to believe that the result would have been different in any of the other six states.

Divisions in the lower South occurred mainly over tactics and timing, not goals. A majority favored the domino tactics of individual state secession followed by a convention of independent states to form a new confederacy. But a significant minority, especially in Alabama, Georgia, and Louisiana, desired some sort of cooperative action *preceding* secession to ensure unity among at least the cotton-South states. These "cooperationists," however, did not fully agree among themselves. At the radical end of their spectrum were cooperative secessionists, who professed as much ardor for southern independence as immediate secessionists but argued that a united South could present a stronger front than could a few independent states. But they were undercut by the swiftness of events, which produced a league of a half-dozen seceded states within six weeks of South Carolina's secession. As a Georgia cooperationist admitted ruefully in mid-January, four states "*have* already seceded. . . . In order to *act* with them, we must secede with them."

At the center of the cooperationist spectrum stood a group that might be labeled "ultimatumists." They urged a convention of southern states to draw up a list of demands for presentation to the incoming Lincoln administration—including enforcement of the fugitive slave law, repeal of personal liberty laws, guarantees against interference with slavery in the District of Columbia or with the interstate slave trade, and protection of slavery in the territories, at least those south of 36°30'. If Republicans refused this ultimatum, then a united South would go out. Since Republicans seemed unlikely to promise all of these concessions and most southerners would not trust them even if they did, the ultimatumists commanded little support in secession conventions.

The third and most conservative group of cooperationists were conditional unionists, who asked fellow southerners to give Lincoln a chance to prove his moderate intentions. Only if Republicans committed some "overt act" against southern rights should the South resort to the drastic step of secession. But while the ranks of conditional unionists contained influential men like Alexander Stephens, they too were swept along by the pace of events. "The prudent and conservative men South," wrote Senator Judah P. Benjamin of Louisiana, who counted himself one of them, were not "able to stem the wild torrent of passion which is carrying everything before it. . . . It is a revolution . . . of the most intense character . . . and it can no more be checked by human effort, for the time, than a prairie fire by a gardener's watering pot."

Other southerners used similar metaphors to describe the phenomenon. "It is a complete landsturm. . . . People are wild. . . . You might as well attempt to control a tornado as to attempt to stop them." Secession was an unequivocal act which relieved the unbearable tension that had been building for years. It was a catharsis for pent-up fears and hostilities. It was a *joyful* act that caused people literally to dance in the streets. Their fierce gaiety anticipated the celebratory crowds that gathered along the Champs-Elysées and the Unter den Linden and at Piccadilly Circus in that similarly innocent world of August 1914. Not that the flag-waving, singing crowds in Charleston and Savannah and New Orleans wanted or expected war; on the contrary, they believed that "the Yankees were cowards and would not fight"—or said they did, to assure the timid that there was no danger. "So far as civil war is concerned," remarked an Atlanta newspaper blithely in January 1861, "we have no fears of that in Atlanta." A rural editor thought that women and children armed with popguns firing "Connecticut wooden nutmegs" could deal with every Yankee likely to appear in Georgia. Senator James Chestnut of South Carolina offered to drink all the blood shed as a consequence of secession. It became a common saying in the South during the secession winter that "a lady's thimble will hold all the blood that will be shed."

Cooperationists were not so sure about this. "War I look for as almost certain," wrote Alexander Stephens, who also warned that "revolutions are much easier started than controlled, and the men who begin them [often] . . . themselves become the victims." But Stephens's prescient warning was lost in the wind, and he joined the revolution himself when his state went out. Before that happened, however, the cooperationists had demonstrated considerable strength in each state except South Carolina and Texas. In elections for convention delegates, candidates representing some kind of cooperationist position polled at least 40 percent of the vote in those five states. Many eligible voters had not gone to the polls in these elections, leading to a belief that the potential cooperationist electorate was even larger. In Alabama and Georgia, 39 and 30 percent respectively of the delegates voted against the final resolution of secession despite the enormous pressures brought on them to go along with the majority.

This caused many northerners and some historians to exaggerate the strength of unionism in the lower South. As late as July 1861, Lincoln expressed doubt "whether there is, to-day, a majority of the legally qualified voters of any State, except perhaps South Carolina, in favor of disunion." A century later several historians echoed this faith in a silent majority of southern unionists. "It can hardly be said that a majority of the South's white people deliberately chose to dissolve the Union in 1861," wrote one. "Secession was not basically desired even by a majority in the lower South," concluded another, "and the secessionists succeeded less because of the intrinsic popularity of their program than because of the extreme skill with which they utilized an emergency psychology."

Though an emergency psychology certainly existed, the belief in a repressed unionist majority rests on a misunderstanding of southern unionism. As a Mississippi "unionist" explained after Lincoln's election, he was no longer "a Union man in the sense in which the North is Union." His unionism was conditional; the North had violated the condition by electing Lincoln. Cooperationists in Alabama who voted against secession cautioned outsiders not to "misconstrue" their action. "We scorn the Black Republicans," they declared. "The State of Alabama cannot and will not submit to the Administration of Lincoln. . . . We intend to resist . . . but our resistance is based upon . . . unity of action, with the other slave states." Or as a Mississippi cooperationist put it: "Cooperation before secession was the first object of my desire. Failing this I am willing to take the next best, subsequent cooperation or cooperation after succession." This was the position of most delegates who initially opposed immediate secession. It was a weak foundation on which to build a faith in southern unionism.

Was secession constitutional? Or was it an act of revolution? The Constitution is silent on this question. But most secessionists believed in the legality of their action. State sovereignty, they insisted, had preceded national sovereignty. When they had ratified the Constitution, states delegated some of the functions of sovereignty to a federal government but did not yield its functional attributes. Having ratified the Constitution by a convention, a state could reassert total sovereignty in the same manner. This theory presented a slight problem for states (five of the seven) that had come into the Union after 1789. But they, too, despite the appearance of being creatures rather than creators of the Union, could assert the prior sovereignty of their states, for each had formed a state constitution (or in the case of Texas, a national constitution) *before* petitioning Congress for admission to the Union.

Those southerners (mostly conditional unionists) who found this theory a bit hard to swallow could fall back on the right of revolution. Senator Alfred Iverson of Georgia conceded that while no state had a constitutional right to secede "each State has the right of revolution. . . . The secession of a State is an act of revolution." The mayor of Vicksburg described secession as "a mighty political revolution which [will] result in placing the Confederate States among the Independent nations of the earth." A Confederate army officer declared that he had "never believed the Constitution recognized the right of secession. I took up arms, sir, upon a broader ground—the right of revolution. We were wronged. Our properties and liberties were about to be taken from us. It was a sacred duty to rebel."

Sporting blue cockades (the symbol of secession), some of these enthusiastic revolutionaries even sang "The Southern Marseillaise" in the streets of Charleston and New Orleans. Ex-Governor Henry Wise of Virginia, who urged the formation of committees of public safety, gloried in his reputation as the "Danton of the Secession Movement in Virginia." Carried away by an excess of Robespierrian zeal, a Georgia disunionist warned cooperationists that "we will go for revolution, and if you . . . oppose us . . . we will brand you as traitors, and chop off your heads."

But the American Revolution, not the French, was the preferred model for secessionists. *Liberté* they sought, but not *égalité* or *fraternité*. Were not "the men of 1776 . . . Secessionists?" asked an Alabamian. If we remain in the Union, said a Florida slaveholder, "we will be deprived of that right for which our fathers fought in the battles of the revolution." From "the high and solemn motive of defending and protecting the rights . . . which our fathers bequeathed to us," declared Jefferson Davis, let us "renew such sacrifices as our fathers made to the holy cause of constitutional liberty."

What were these rights and liberties for which Confederates contended? The right to own slaves; the liberty to take this property into the territories; freedom from the coercive powers of a centralized government. Black Republican rule in Washington threatened republican freedoms as the South understood them. The ideology for which the fathers had fought in 1776 posited an eternal struggle between liberty and power. Because the Union after March 4, 1861, would no longer be controlled by southerners, the South could protect its liberty from the assaults of hostile power only by going out of the Union. "On the 4th of March, 1861," declared a Georgia secessionist, "we are either *slaves in the Union or freemen out of it.*" The question, agreed Jefferson Davis and a fellow Mississippian, was " 'Will you be slaves or will [you] be independent?'. . . Will you consent to be robbed of your property" or will you "strike bravely for liberty, property, honor and life?" Submission to Black Republicans would mean "the loss of liberty, property, home, country—everything that makes life worth having," proclaimed a South Carolinian. "I am engaged in the glorious cause of liberty and justice," wrote a Confederate soldier, "fighting for the rights of man—fighting for all that we of the South hold dear."

What stake did nonslaveholding whites have in this crusade for the freedom of planters to own slaves? Some secessionists worried a great deal about this question. What if Hinton Rowan Helper was right? What if nonslaveowners were potential Black Republicans? "The great lever by which the abolitionists hope to extirpate slavery in the States is the aid of non-slaveholding citizens in the South," fretted a Kentucky editor. How would they ply this lever? By using the patronage to build up a cadre of Republican officeholders among nonslaveowners—first in the border states and upcountry where slavery was most vulnerable, and then in the heart of the cotton kingdom itself. Governor Joseph E. Brown of Georgia feared that some whites would be "bribed into treachery to their own section, by the allurements of office." When Republicans organized their "Abolition party . . . of Southern men," echoed the *Charleston Mercury,* "the contest for slavery will no longer be one between the North and the South. It will be in the South, between the people of the South."

The elections of delegates to secession conventions seemed to confirm this fear. Many upcountry districts with few slaves sent cooperationist delegates. In the conventions, delegates supporting delay or cooperation owned, on the average, less wealth and fewer slaves than immediate secessionists. The implications of these data should not be pushed too far. A good many low-slaveholding Democratic counties voted for immediate secession, while numerous high-slaveholding Whig counties backed cooperation. And of course cooperationism did not necessarily mean unionism. Nevertheless, the partial correlation of cooperationism with low slaveholding caused concern among secessionists.

So they undertook a campaign to convince nonslaveholders that they too had a stake in disunion. The stake was white supremacy. In this view, the Black Republican program of abolition was the first step toward racial equality and amalgamation. Georgia's Governor Brown carried this message to his native uplands of north Georgia whose voters idolized him. Slavery "is the poor man's best Government," said Brown. "Among us the poor white laborer . . . does not belong to the menial class. The negro is in no sense his equal. . . . He belongs to the only true aristocracy, the race of *white men*." Thus yeoman farmers "will never consent to submit to abolition rule," for they "know that in the event of the abolition of slavery, they would be greater sufferers than the rich, who would be able to protect themselves. . . . When it becomes necessary to defend our rights against so foul a domination, I would call upon the mountain boys as well as the people of the lowlands, and they would come down like an avalanche and swarm around the flag of Georgia."

Much secessionist rhetoric played variations on this theme. The election of Lincoln, declared an Alabama newspaper, "shows that the North [intends] to free the negroes and force amalgamation between them and the children of the poor men of the South." "Do you love your mother, your wife, your sister, your daughter?" a Georgia secessionist asked nonslaveholders. If Georgia remained in a Union "ruled by Lincoln and his crew . . . in TEN years or less our CHILDREN will be the *slaves* of negroes." "If you are tame enough to submit," declaimed South Carolina's Baptist clergyman James Furman, "Abolition preachers will be at hand to consummate the marriage of your daughters to black husbands." No! No! came an answering shout from Alabama. "Submit to have our wives and daughters choose between death and gratifying the hellish lust of the negro!! . . . Better ten thousand deaths than submission to Black Republicanism."

To defend their wives and daughters, presumably, yeoman whites therefore joined planters in "rallying to the standard of Liberty and Equality for white men" against "our Abolition enemies who are pledged to prostrate the white freemen of the South down to equality with negroes." Most southern whites could agree that "democratic liberty exists solely because we have black slaves" whose presence "promotes equality among the free." Hence "freedom is not possible without slavery."

This Orwellian definition of liberty as slavery provoked ridicule north of the Potomac. For disunionists to compare themselves to the Revolutionary fathers "is a libel upon the whole character and conduct of the men of '76," declared William Cullen Bryant's *New York Evening Post*. The founders fought "to establish the rights of man . . . and principles of universal liberty." The South was rebelling "not in the interest of general humanity, but of a domestic despotism. . . . Their motto is not liberty, but slavery." Thomas Jefferson's Declaration of Independence spoke for "Natural Rights against Established Institutions," added the

New York Tribune, while "Mr. Jeff Davis's caricature thereof is made in the interest of an unjust, outgrown, decaying Institution against the apprehended encroachments of Natural Human Rights." It was, in short, not a revolution for liberty but a counterrevolution "reversing the wheels of progress . . . to hurl everything backward into deepest darkness . . . despotism and oppression."

Without assenting to the rhetoric of this analysis, a good many disunionists in effect endorsed its substance. The signers of the Declaration of Independence were wrong if they meant to include Negroes among "all men," said Alexander Stephens after he had become vice president of the Confederacy. "Our new government is founded upon exactly the opposite idea; its foundations are laid, its cornerstone rests, upon the great truth that the negro is not equal to the white man; that slavery . . . is his natural and normal condition. This, our new government, is the first in the history of the world based upon this great physical, philosophical, and moral truth." Black Republicans were the real revolutionaries. They subscribed to "tenets as radical and revolutionary" as those of the abolitionists, declared a New Orleans newspaper. These "revolutionary dogmas," echoed numerous southerners, were "active and bristling with terrible designs and as ready for bloody and forcible realities as ever characterized the idea of the French revolution." Therefore it was "an abuse of language" to call secession a revolution, said Jefferson Davis. We left the Union "to save ourselves from a revolution" that threatened to make "property in slaves so insecure as to be comparatively worthless." In 1861 the Confederate secretary of state advised foreign governments that southern states had formed a new nation "to preserve their old institutions" from "a revolution [that] threatened to destroy their social system."

This is the language of counterrevolution. But in one respect the Confederacy departed from the classic pattern of the genre. Most counterrevolutions seek to restore the *ancien régime*. The counterrevolutionaries of 1861 made their move before the revolutionaries had done anything—indeed, several months before Lincoln even took office. In this regard, secession fit the model of "pre-emptive counterrevolution" developed by historian Arno Mayer. Rather than trying to restore the old order, a pre-emptive counterrevolution strikes first to protect the status quo before the revolutionary threat can materialize. "Conjuring up the dangers of leaving revolutionaries the time to prepare their forces and plans for an assault on *their* terms," writes Mayer, "counterrevolutionary leaders urge a preventive thrust." To mobilize support for it, they "intentionally exaggerate the magnitude and imminence of the revolutionary threat."

Though Mayer was writing about Europe in the twentieth century, his words also describe the immediate secessionists of 1860. They exaggerated the Republican threat and urged pre-emptive action to forestall the dangers they conjured up. The South could not afford to wait for an "overt act" by Lincoln against southern rights, they insisted. "If I find a coiled rattlesnake in my path," asked an Alabama editor, "do I wait for his 'overt act' or do I smite him in his coil?" When conditional unionists tell us "that it will be several years before Lincoln will have control of the sword and the purse through the instrumentality of Congress," observed a Mississippian, that only "furnishes additional argument for action

NOW. Let us rally . . . before the enemy can make good his promise to over-whelm us. . . . Delay is dangerous. Now is the time to strike."

II

Seldom in history has a counterrevolution so quickly provoked the very revolution it sought to pre-empt. This happened because most northerners refused to condone disunion. On that matter, if on little else, the outgoing and incoming presidents of the United States agreed.

In his final message to Congress, on December 3, 1860, James Buchanan surprised some of his southern allies with a firm denial of the right of secession. The Union was not "a mere voluntary association of States, to be dissolved at pleasure by any one of the contracting parties," said Buchanan. "We the People" had adopted the Constitution to form "a *more* perfect Union" than the one existing under the Articles of Confederation, which had stated that "the Union shall be perpetual." The framers of the national government "never intended to implant in its bosom the seeds of its own destruction, nor were they guilty of the absurdity of providing for its own dissolution." State sovereignty was *not* superior to national sovereignty, Buchanan insisted. The Constitution bestowed the highest attributes of sovereignty exclusively on the federal government: national defense; foreign policy; regulation of foreign and interstate commerce; coinage of money. "This Constitution," stated that document, "and the laws of the United States . . . shall be the supreme law of the land . . . any thing in the constitution or laws of any State to the contrary notwithstanding." If secession was legitimate, warned the president, the Union became "a rope of sand" and "our thirty-three States may resolve themselves into as many petty, jarring, and hostile republics. . . . By such a dread catastrophe the hopes of the friends of freedom throughout the world would be destroyed. . . . Our example for more than eighty years would not only be lost, but it would be quoted as a conclusive proof that man is unfit for self-government."

Thousands of northern editorials and speeches echoed these themes. Fears of a domino effect were especially pervasive. "A successful rebellion by a few States now," ran an editorial typical of hundreds, "will be followed by a new rebellion or secession a few years hence." This was not mere alarmism. Some Americans were already speculating about a division of the country into three or four "confederacies" with an independent Pacific coast republic thrown in for good measure. Several New York merchants and Democrats with ties to the South were talking of setting up as a free city. A prominent New York lawyer secretly informed railroad president George B. McClellan in December 1860 that "when secession is fairly inaugurated at the South, we mean to do a little of the same business here & cut loose from the fanatics of New England & of the North generally, including most of our own State." In January 1861 Mayor Fernando Wood brought this matter into the open with a message to the aldermen advocating the secession of New York City. The project went nowhere, but it did plant seeds of copperheadism that germinated a couple of years later.

"The doctrine of secession is anarchy," declared a Cincinnati newspaper. "If any minority have the right to break up the Government at pleasure, because they have not had their way, there is an end of all government." Lincoln too considered secession the "essence of anarchy." He branded state sovereignty a "sophism." "The Union is older than any of the States," Lincoln asserted, "and, in fact, it created them as States." The Declaration of Independence transformed the "United Colonies" into the United States; without this union then, there would never have been any "free and independent States." "Having never been States, either in substance, or in name, *outside* the Union," asked Lincoln, "whence this magical omnipotence of 'State rights,' asserting a claim of power to lawfully destroy the Union itself?" Perpetuity was "the fundamental law of all national governments." No government "ever had provision in its organic law for its own termination. . . . No State, upon its own mere motion, can lawfully get out of the Union. . . . They can only do so against law, and by revolution."

Neither Lincoln nor any other northerner denied the right of revolution. After all, Yankees shared the legacy of 1776. But there was no "right of revolution at *pleasure*," declared a Philadelphia newspaper. Revolution was "a moral right, when exercised for a morally justifiable cause," wrote Lincoln. But "when exercised without such a cause revolution is no right, but simply a wicked exercise of physical power." The South had no just cause. The event that precipitated secession was the election of a president by a constitutional majority. The "central idea" of the Union cause, said Lincoln, "is the necessity of proving that popular government is not an absurdity. We must settle this question now, whether in a free government the minority have the right to break up the government whenever they choose."

But how was it to be settled? This problem was compounded by the lame-duck syndrome in the American constitutional system. During the four-month interval between Lincoln's election and inauguration, Buchanan had the executive power but felt little responsibility for the crisis, while Lincoln had responsibility but little power. The Congress elected in 1860 would not meet in regular session for thirteen months, while the Congress that did meet in December 1860 experienced an erosion of authority as members from the lower South resigned when their states seceded. Buchanan's forceful denial of the legality of disunion ended with a lame confession of impotence to do anything about it. Although the Constitution gave no state the right to withdraw, said the president, it also gave the national government no power "to coerce a State into submission which is attempting to withdraw."

Republicans ridiculed this reasoning. Buchanan had demonstrated that "no state has the right to secede unless it wishes to," jibed Seward, and that "it is the President's duty to enforce the laws, unless somebody opposes him." But Republicans seemed unable to come up with any better alternative. Several options presented themselves: coercion, compromise, or allowing "the erring sisters to depart in peace." Although various Republican leaders sanctioned each of these approaches at one time or another, none of the options commanded a majority before April 1861. Instead, a rather vague fourth alternative emerged—described as "masterly inactivity" or a "Fabian policy"—a position of watchful waiting, of making no major concessions but at the same time avoiding needless provocation, in the hope that the disunion fever would run its course and the presumed legions of southern unionists would bring the South back to its senses.

When Congress convened in December several Republicans, especially from the Old Northwest, "swore by everything in the Heavens above and the Earth beneath that they would convert the rebel States into a wilderness." "Without a little blood-letting," wrote Michigan's radical, coarse-grained Senator Zachariah Chandler, "this Union will not . . . be worth a rush." The danger of losing access to the lower Mississippi valley may have accounted for the bellicosity of many midwesterners. The people of the Northwest, said the *Chicago Tribune,* would never negotiate for free navigation of the river. "It is *their right,* and they will assert it to the extremity of blotting Louisiana out of the map.". . .

In six days the delegates [to the Confederate convention] at Montgomery drafted a temporary constitution, turned themselves into a provisional Congress for the new government, elected a provisional president and vice president, and then spent a more leisurely month fashioning a permanent constitution and setting the machinery of government in motion. Elections for a bicameral Congress and for a president and vice president to serve the single six-year term prescribed by the Constitution were to be held in November 1861.

Although Barnwell Rhett and a few other fire-eaters came to Montgomery as delegates, they took a back seat at a convention that did its best to project a moderate image to the upper South. Befitting the new Confederacy's claim to represent the true principles of the U.S. Constitution which the North had trampled upon, most of the provisional constitution was copied verbatim from that venerable document. The same was true of the permanent Confederate Constitution, adopted a month later, though some of its departures from the original were significant. The preamble omitted the general welfare clause and the phrase "a more perfect Union," and added a clause after We the People: "each State acting in its sovereign and independent character." Instead of the U.S. Constitution's evasions on slavery ("persons held to service or labor"), the Confederate version called a slave a slave. It guaranteed the protection of bondage in any new territory the Confederacy might acquire. The Constitution did forbid the importation of slaves from abroad, to avoid alienating Britain and especially the upper South, whose economy benefitted from its monopoly on export of slaves to the lower South. The Constitution permitted a tariff for revenue but not for protection of domestic industries, though what this distinction meant was unclear since the clause did not define it. Another clause forbade government aid for internal improvements. The Constitution also nurtured states' rights by empowering legislatures to impeach Confederate officials whose duties lay wholly within a state. After weakening the executive by limiting the president to a single six-year term, the Constitution strengthened that branch by giving the president a line-item veto of appropriations and granting cabinet officers a potential non-voting seat on the floor of Congress (this was never put into effect).

Most interest at Montgomery focused on the choice of a provisional president. There as no shortage of aspirants, but the final nod went to a West Point graduate who would have preferred to become commander of the Confederacy's army. As the most prominent of the original secessionists, Rhett and Yancey had a strong claim for preference. But conditional unionists north of the 35th parallel, especially in Virginia, regarded them as no less responsible than the blackest of Republicans for the tragic division of the country that was forcing them to choose sides. Since the new Confederacy—containing scarcely 10 percent of the country's white population and 5 percent of its industrial capacity—desperately needed the allegiance of the upper South, Yancey and Rhett were ruled out. Toombs, Stephens, and Howell Cobb, all from Georgia, seemed to fit the bill better. But the Georgia delegation could not unite on one of them. Moreover, as a conditional unionist until the last minute, Stephens was suspect in the eyes of original secessionists, while Toombs, a former Whig, suffered a similar handicap among the long-time Democrats who predominated at Montgomery. Toombs's heavy drinking—he appeared at a party falling-down drunk two nights before the balloting for president—also hurt his chances. Word from Richmond that Virginia's pro-secession senators Mason and Hunter favored Jefferson Davis proved decisive. Austere, able, experienced in government as a senator and former secretary of war, a Democrat and a secessionist but no fire-eater, Davis was the ideal candidate. Though he had not sought the job and did not really want it, the delegates elected him unanimously on February 9. His sense of duty—and destiny—bid him accept. To console Georgia and strengthen the Confederacy's moderate image, one-time Whig and more recently Douglas Democrat Alexander Stephens received the vice presidency. To satisfy geographical balance, Davis apportioned the six cabinet posts among each state of the Confederacy except his own Mississippi, with the top position of secretary of state going to the sulking Toombs.

"The man and the hour have met!" So said a genial William L. Yancey as he introduced Jefferson Davis to a cheering crowd in Montgomery on February 16. It was on this occasion that "Dixie" began its career as the unofficial Confederate anthem. Perhaps inspired by the music, Davis made a brief, bellicose speech. "The time for compromise has now passed," he said. "The South is determined to maintain her position, and make all who oppose her smell Southern powder and feel Southern steel." His inaugural address two days later was more pacific. He assured everyone that the Confederacy wished to live in peace and extended a warm invitation to any states that "may seek to unite their fortunes to ours." Davis then settled down to the heavy responsibilities of organizing a new nation—and of enlarging its borders.

Abraham Lincoln's chief concern was to prevent that enlargement. And part of the energy expended in building *his* cabinet was directed to that end. Putting together a cabinet gave Lincoln no end of trouble. The infant Republican party was still a loose coalition of several previous parties, of down-east Yankees and frontiersmen, radicals and conservatives, ideologues and pragmatists, of upper North and lower North and border-state tycoons like the Blairs of Maryland, of strong leaders several of whom still considered themselves better qualified for the presidency than the man who won it. Lincoln had to satisfy all of these interests with his seven cabinet appointments, which would also indicate the direction of his policy toward the South.

With an aplomb unparalleled in American political history, the president-elect appointed his four main rivals for the nomination to cabinet posts. Lincoln did not hesitate in his choices of Seward for secretary of state and Bates for attorney general. Cameron represented a more formidable problem. The Pennsylvanian believed that he had a commitment from Lincoln's convention managers. In any case, to leave him out would cause disaffection. But putting him in provoked an outcry when word leaked that Lincoln had offered Cameron the treasury. Many Republicans considered the "Winnebago Chief"—a derisive nickname Cameron had acquired years earlier when he had allegedly cheated an Indian tribe in a supply contract—to be "a man destitute of honor and integrity." Taken aback, Lincoln withdrew the offer, whereupon Cameron's friends mobilized a campaign in his behalf that distracted the party as the inauguration neared. Lincoln finally settled the matter—but not the controversy—by giving Cameron the war department. The treasury went to Chase, who had become a leader of the "iron-back" Republicans opposed to any hint of concession to the South. Chase's appointment so offended Seward that he withdrew his acceptance as secretary of state—an obvious attempt to make Lincoln dump Chase. This was the first test of Seward's ambition to be "premier" of the administration. "I can't afford to let Seward take the first trick," Lincoln told his private secretary. The president-elect persuaded Seward to back down and remain in the cabinet with Chase—though one more confrontation lay ahead before Seward was convinced that Lincoln intended to be his own premier.

Paying a debt to Indiana for early support of his nomination, Lincoln named Caleb Smith secretary of the interior. The fussy, bewigged Connecticut Yankee Gideon Welles received the navy department. Lincoln wanted to appoint a non-Republican from the upper South as a gesture of good will to hold this region in the Union. He offered a portfolio to Congressman John Gilmer of North Carolina. But to join a Black Republican administration was too much of a political risk, so Gilmer turned down the offer on grounds that Lincoln's refusal to compromise on slavery in the territories made it impossible for him to accept. Lincoln thereupon rounded out his cabinet with Montgomery Blair as postmaster general. Though a resident of Maryland, Blair was a Republican and an "iron-back."

Even more important than the cabinet as a sign of future policy would be Lincoln's inaugural address. Knowing that the fate of the upper South, and of hopes for voluntary reconstruction of the lower South, might rest on what he said on March 4, Lincoln devoted great care to every phrase of the address. It went through several drafts after consultation with various Republican leaders, especially Seward. This process began in Springfield two months before the inauguration and continued through Lincoln's twelve-day roundabout trip by rail to Washington, during which he made dozens of speeches to trackside crowds and official receptions. The president-elect felt an obligation to greet the multitudes who lined his route to catch a glimpse of their new leader. In effect, Lincoln was making a whistle-stop tour *after* his election, even to the point of climbing down from the train to kiss the eleven-year-old girl in upstate New York who had suggested that he grow the beard which was now filling out on his face.

This tour may have been a mistake in two respects. Not wishing by a careless remark or slip of the tongue to inflame the crisis further, Lincoln often indulged in platitudes and trivia in his attempts to say nothing controversial. This produced an unfavorable impression on those who were already disposed to regard the ungainly president-elect as a commonplace prairie lawyer. Second, Lincoln's mail and the national press had for weeks been full of threats and rumors of assassination. A public journey of this sort with all stops announced in advance greatly increased the risk of violence. Two days before he was scheduled to travel through Baltimore, a city rife with secession sympathizers and notorious for political riots, Lincoln's party got wind of a plot to assassinate him as he changed trains there. Indeed, warnings came from two independent sources—a Pinkerton detective force employed by the railroad and an agent of the war department— both of which had infiltrated Baltimore's political gangs. Lincoln reluctantly consented to a change in his schedule which took him secretly through Baltimore in the middle of the night. An assassination plot probably did exist; the danger was real. But Lincoln thereafter regretted the decision to creep into Washington "like a thief in the night." It embarrassed many of his supporters and enabled opposition cartoonists to ridicule him. The whole affair started his administration off on the wrong foot at a time when it needed the appearance of firmness and command.

Lincoln put the finishing touches on his inaugural address during these first days in Washington. While he had been composing it, seven states were not only seceding but were also seizing federal property within their borders—customs-houses, arsenals, mints, and forts. The first draft of the inaugural therefore had one theme and two variations. The theme was Lincoln's determination to preserve an undivided Union. The variations contrapuntally offered a sword and an olive branch. The sword was an intention to use "all the powers at my disposal" to "reclaim the public property and places which have fallen; to hold, occupy, and possess these, and all other property and places belonging to the government, and to collect the duties on imports." The olive branch was a reiteration of his oft-repeated pledge not "to interfere with the institution of slavery where it exists" and to enforce the constitutional injunction for the return of fugitive slaves. Lincoln also promised the South that "the government will not assail *you, unless you *first* assail *it.*"

Seward and Lincoln's Illinois confidant Orville Browning found the sword too prominent in this draft. The upper South, not to mention the Confederate government, was sure to regard any attempt to "reclaim" forts and other property as "coercion." And even the promise not to assail these states unless they first assailed the government contained a veiled threat. Seward persuaded Lincoln to delete "unless you *first* assail *it*" and to soften a few other phrases. He also drafted a peroration appealing to the historic patriotism of southern people. The president-elect added a passage assuring southerners that whenever "in any interior locality" the hostility to the United States was "so great and so universal, as to prevent competent resident citizens from holding the Federal offices," he would suspend government activities "for the time." Most significantly, perhaps, Browning prevailed on Lincoln to drop his threat to *reclaim* federal property, so that the final version of the address vowed only to "hold, occupy, and possess" such property and to "collect duties and imposts."

These phrases were ambiguous. How would the duties be collected? By naval vessels stationed offshore? Would this be coercion? How could the government "hold, occupy and possess" property that was under control of Confederate forces? The only remaining property in Union hands were two obscure forts in the Florida Keys along with Fort Pickens on an island at the mouth of Pensacola

Bay and Fort Sumter on an island in Charleston harbor. Fort Sumter had become a commanding symbol of national sovereignty in the very cradle of secession, a symbol that the Confederate government could not tolerate if it wished its own sovereignty to be recognized by the world. Would Lincoln use force to defend Sumter? The ambiguity was intentional. Hoping to avoid provocation, Lincoln and Seward did not wish to reveal whether the velvet glove enclosed an iron fist.

There was no ambiguity about the peroration, revised and much improved from Seward's draft. "I am loth to close," said Lincoln. "We are not enemies, but friends. We must not be enemies. Though passion may have strained, it must not break our bonds of affection. The mystic chords of memory, stretching from every battlefield, and patriot grave, to every living heart and hearthstone, all over this broad land, will yet swell the chorus of the Union, when again touched, as surely they will be, by the better angels of our nature."

Contemporaries read into the inaugural address what they wished or expected to see. Republicans were generally satisfied with its "firmness" and "moderation." Confederates and their sympathizers branded it a "Declaration of War." Douglas Democrats in the North and conditional unionists in the south formed the constituencies that Lincoln most wanted and needed to reach. From these quarters the verdict was mixed but encouraging. "I am with him," said Douglas. Influential Tennesseans commended the "temperance and conservatism" of the address. And John Gilmer of North Carolina, though he had been unwilling to join Lincoln's cabinet, approved the president's first act in office. "What more does any reasonable Southern man expect or desire?" Gilmer asked.

Lincoln had hoped to cool passions and buy time with his inaugural address—time to organize his administration, to prove his pacific intent, to allow the seeds of voluntary reconstruction to sprout. But when the new president went to his office for the first time on the morning after the inauguration, he received a jolt. On his desk lay a dispatch from Major Robert Anderson, commander of the Union garrison at Fort Sumter. Anderson reported that his supplies would last only a few more weeks. Time was running out.

The Civil War and
the Spirit of Compromise

As the American Revolution had been a struggle within a long-established colonial framework, so the Civil War was a struggle within a working federal system. The two events were to have analogous consequences in hedging in our political reflection, and in identifying the special institutions of this country with the normal conditions of life on this continent. Whatever theoretical debate went on, with few exceptions, was concerned not with the nature of governments but rather with the nature of this particular government.

That the Civil War was a federal conflict, like the colonial character of our Revolution, seems, perhaps, too obvious to require elaboration. But some of our ablest recent historians have given currency to an emphasis which has tended to obscure, or even to displace, the obvious.

In their brilliant *Rise of American Civilization*, Charles A. and Mary R. Beard christened the Civil War "The Second American Revolution." The phrase and the idea have had wide appeal. It has suited our current attitudes to suspect that the actual subject of debate was not the real cause of the conflict. The battle itself, supposedly, was but a symptom of deeper forces: "the social cataclysm in which the capitalists, laborers, and farmers of the North and West drove from power in the national government the planting aristocracy of the South . . . the social revolution was the essential, portentous outcome." Without denying that such a social revolution was taking place, we can recall that there was another side to the conflict. If we turn our attention from inevitable forces to human debate, we must look primarily at a different aspect of the struggle. This is only appropriate, since we are concerned with the place of theory in our conscious political life.

The name "The Second American Revolution" given by the Beards and their disciples, is misleading. They (and others who find the center of change in economic events) would thus emphasize the *dis*continuity of our history: the Civil War as a hiatus in our development, a gulf between an agricultural-commercial and an industrial society. But to those students who, like me, are impressed by the extraordinary continuity of our history, such an emphasis seems distortion. As we all know, the great economic developments are slow, evolutionary, and sometimes imperceptible; their triumphs are not self-announced in manifestoes. The Industrial Revolution was a matter of centuries, and the kind of revolution to which the Beards refer must also have been a matter of decades.

But *political* history (such events as go by the name of "revolution" and "civil war") has the abruptness of mutation. It is therefore in this area that it would be especially significant to note that what is called a great gulf in our history may not be so great as has been supposed. One of the remarkable characteristics of our Civil War, as contrasted with civil wars of recent European history (excepting possibly the English Civil War), is that ours did not significantly interrupt the continuity of our thinking about institutions.

From the point of view of political and constitutional thought, we might do better to call our Civil War "The Second War of Independence." I have already mentioned Guizot's remark that the English Revolution succeeded twice, once in England in the seventeenth century and a second time in America in the eighteenth. We must go further and say that, from the point of view of constitutional law and political theory, the Revolution occurred a third time, namely, in the middle of the nineteenth century. For the relation of the ancient rights of Englishmen to federalism, which was only partly redefined in the course of the American Revolution, was more extensively explored and settled during the Civil War.

That continuity of our political thought which, as we have seen, had been expressed in the legalistic character of the American Revolutionary debate was also expressed later in much of the argument over the Civil War. There is even less evidence here for the pattern which Carl Becker saw in the Revolution. The main current did not seem to rise above the "provincial" level of constitutionalism to the more "cosmopolitan" atmosphere of natural law. Indeed, we find something of the opposite of what Becker remarks as the increasing abstractness of Revolutionary debate. In the South at least, as the crisis proceeded the debate seemed to become more and more legalistic, reaching its climax actually after the war was over. The legal debate never rose to the realm of natural law, not even to the extent found in the American Revolution.

The North and the South each considered that it was fighting primarily for its legal rights under the sacred federal Constitution. A man like Thoreau probably stood only for himself and a few fire-eating abolitionists. On neither side do we hear much of the sort of argument familiar in European civil wars: that the existing federal constitution was bad and ought to be changed, and that was what one should fight for. On the contrary, each side purported to represent the authentic original doctrine, to be *defending* the Constitution.

Calhoun, who was by far the most profound of the southern writers on the subject, shows this peculiarity. His major theoretical work, not published until after his death in 1850, consists of two parts: "A Disquisition on Government" and "A Discourse on the Constitution and Government of the United States." It is on these that his growing reputation as a political philosopher largely depends.

These works taken together (as Calhoun intended that they should be) admirably illustrate the point of view I have been describing.

The "Disquisition," an essay of about a hundred pages, though starting from some general principles of psychology and political theory, is primarily a defense of Calhoun's principle of the "concurrent majority" and an exposition of his objections to governments based on the "numerical majority." In a closely reasoned argument, Calhoun points out the dangers of uncontrolled majority rule. The only safeguard, he insists, is a system of constitutionalism which will allow each separate interest a veto on all legislation to which it objects. Such a system, he urges, results in moderation and compromise and still can leave government strong enough to combat enemies from without. He supports his argument by the experience of Rome, Poland, and Great Britain.

"A Discourse on the Constitution and Government of the United States," a work about three times the length of the "Disquisition," is the sequel. In it Calhoun tries to show that

> *it was the object of the framers of the constitution, in organizing the government, to give to the two elements [the states as units and the voting population], of which it is composed, separate, but concurrent action; and, consequently, a veto on each other, whenever the organization of the department, or the nature of the power would admit: and when this could not be done, so to blend the two, as to make as near an approach to it, in effect, as possible. It is, also, apparent, that the government, regarded apart from the constitution, is the government of the concurrent, and not of the numerical majority* [Works, I, 181].

By reference to the proceedings of the Philadelphia convention and of the ratifying conventions, Calhoun demonstrates that, through a happy coincidence, the true and original conception of the federal Constitution was actually nothing but a design for the attainment of his ideal government. The departure from his ideal, the gradual growth of a consolidated national government, and the development of means by which one section could dominate another were all to be explained as departures from the true intent of the Framers.

> *To the one, or to the other,—to monarchy, or disunion it must come, if not prevented by strenuous and timely efforts. And this brings up the question—How is it to be prevented? How can these sad alternatives be averted? For this purpose, it is indispensable that the government of the United States should be restored to its federal character. Nothing short of a perfect restoration, as it came from the hands of its framers, can avert them* [Works, I, 381].

This restoration was to be effected by getting rid of certain perversions which had been introduced after the adoption of the Constitution. Calhoun urges, for example, the repeal of Section 25 of the Judiciary Act of 1789, and of the Act of 1833; "the repeal of all acts by which the money power is carried beyond its constitutional limits"; the confining of the president to those powers expressly conferred on him by the Constitution and by acts of Congress; the return in practice to the original way of electing the president and vice-president.

Such means as these—together with a few reforms like the introduction of a plural executive—would, in Calhoun's phrase, "complete the work of restoration." We are never allowed to forget that what Calhoun aims at is not revolution but *restoration.*

A Conflict of Orthodoxies

Here, once again, was a competition between constitutional orthodoxies. As often in American history, a great political conflict was taking the form not of a struggle between essentially different political theories but between differences of constitutional emphasis. There was a striking, if obvious, parallel to the epoch of the Revolution. But the South was now even more conservative than the Revolutionaries had been. It found no reason to issue a Declaration of Independence. The colonists had set themselves up as defenders of the British constitution and contended that it was not they but the parliament who were actually the revolutionaries. So now, champions of the South could—and did—argue that it was not they, but the northerners, who were, properly speaking, the revolutionaries. Each accused the other of seeking to overthrow the established doctrine of the federal Constitution, the ideas of the Founding Fathers.

The Civil War secessionist argument—like that of the Revolution—could be carried on in such a conservative vocabulary because both events were, theoretically speaking, only surface breaches in a firm federal framework. Because of this, they both implied, win or lose, the continued acceptance of the existing structure of local government. Thus in the Civil War southern partisans, like the Americans in the Revolution, could continue to profess loyalty to the theory of the Union. As a New Yorker championing the Southern cause declared in 1860:

The South views the matter in the spirit of Patrick Henry. "The object is now, indeed, small, but the shadow is large enough to darken all this fair land." They can have no faith in men who profess what they think a great moral principle, and deny that they intend to act upon it. It was the principle of taxation without representation that the colonies resisted, and it is the principle of the "irrepressible conflict," based avowedly on a "higher law," that the South resists. She is now in the position of the Colonies eighty-four years ago, and is adopting the same measures that they adopted. . . . A prompt retreat from this dangerous agitation within the shadow of the Constitution, is the only means of realizing the rich future, which will be the reward only of harmony, good faith, and loyalty to the Constitution [Thomas P. Kettell, Southern Wealth and Northern Profits *(New York, 1860), p. 5].*

On the other side, Lincoln, in nearly every one of his principal speeches, appealed to the authentic Revolutionary tradition. His most succinct statement was, of course, in the familiar opening of the Gettysburg Address, to which I have already referred in another connection. But he rang all the rhetorical changes on this appeal, as, for example, in his speech at Peoria in 1854:

Our republican robe is soiled and trailed in the dust. Let us repurify it. Let us turn and wash it white in the spirit, if not the blood, of the Revolution. Let us turn slavery from its claims of "moral right" back upon its existing legal rights and its argument of "necessity." Let us turn it to the position our fathers gave it, and there let it rest in peace. Let us readopt the Declaration of Independence, and with it the practices and policy which harmonize with it.

Statesmen of the North were perhaps more inclined to appeal to the Declaration of Independence, while those of the South leaned more heavily on the Constitution. But both had in common the assumption that the pretty homogeneous philosophy of the Founding Fathers was what they were being called upon to vindicate. Fitzhugh did, to be sure, characterize the Declaration as "exuberantly false, and arborescently fallacious." Yet even the Declaration of Independence was by no means generally rejected by southern advocates. Some southerners, for example, Chief Justice Taney in the Dred Scott decision, even argued that their position had been well stated in the Declaration. They adduced historical proof (in my opinion convincing) that the authors of the sacred document had intended that Negroes be excluded from their professions of "equality." Another remarkable feature of the Dred Scott decision for us is the frankness with which it takes a preformation or a static view of the Constitution. Chief Justice Taney seemed to assume that the legal question of Negro status could be resolved by accurate historical definition of the original meaning of the Declaration of Independence and the Constitution, considered together.

Few documents could be more interesting in this connection than one which nowadays is almost never read. For there is probably no more authentic index to the theoretical conservatism of the "rebel" cause than the Constitution of the Confederate States of America. President Jefferson Davis boasted that the document proved the "conservative" temper of the people of the Confederate States. Alexander Stephens, his vice-president, declared that the form of the document showed that "their only leading object was to sustain, uphold, and perpetuate the fundamental principles of the Constitution of the United States." Closely following the original in organization, the Confederate constitution is almost a verbatim copy of the federal Constitution.

Its differences consist mainly in that it incorporates into the body of the document some of the principal amendments to the federal Constitution (the Bill of Rights, for example, being absorbed into Art. I, sec. 9); and it explicitly resolves certain ambiguities (for example, those concerning slavery and the federal principle generally) in the sense which the South believed to have been the original intent of the authors. The Preamble, for examples, reads:

We, the People of the Confederate States, each State acting in its sovereign and independent character, in order to form a permanent Federal Government, establish justice, insure domestic tranquility, and secure the blessings of liberty to ourselves and our posterity—invoking the favor and guidance of Almighty God—do ordain and establish this Constitution for the Confederate States of America.

It is of great significance that in our bloody Civil War the so-called "rebel" side produced, through two of its best minds, treatises on the origin and nature of our Constitution which deserve to stand, alongside *The Federalist* and Adams' *Defence of the Constitutions,* on the small shelf of basic books about the American political system. The first, of course, is Calhoun's "Discourse on the Constitution and Government of the United States" (1851), which I have already described. The second is Alexander H. Stephens' *Constitutional View of the Late War between the States* (1868–70).

We cannot be surprised that the South, weaker in economy and in arms, found an incentive to be stronger in legal debate. But it remains a curiosity of political thought, as well as a pregnant fact of American history, that the principal theoretical defense of the southern position should have been a treatise on the origin of the federal Constitution, produced actually *after* the South had lost the last battle. Stephens' work was dedicated to "All true friends of the Union under the Constitution of the United States, throughout their entire limits, without regard to present or past party associations." The conflict, Stephens emphasized, was not basically over slavery but over two "different and opposing ideas as to the nature of what is known as the General Government. The contest was between those who held it to be strictly Federal in its character, and those who maintained that it was thoroughly National." The work is historical: a documented demonstration that the Constitution was intended to set up a *federal* government.

We can begin to grasp the true proportions of what I have called the continuity of the history of the United States, as contrasted with that of the countries of western Europe, if we try to imagine the leader of a defeated party in any of the recent European civil wars producing a heavy scholarly treatise proving that he had been in the right *strictly from the point of view of constitutional theory.* George Fitzhugh in 1857 and Jefferson Davis in 1881 both earnestly wished for the "strength and perpetuity" of the Union.

In virtually every one of the recent domestic struggles in Europe, the conflict has been so basic that only one side could conceivably have set itself up as the champion of existing legal institutions. The other has proudly stood for a new concept of goverment, for a new constitution, and another basis of law. Hitler's cynicism toward the German constitution is typical of this frame of mind. Yet in the American Civil War, after hundreds of thousands of lives had been lost, both sides were still thinking on similar constitutional assumptions. An intelligent and realistic critic like Alexander Stephens still after the war considered it possible that his image of the original doctrine (that the Union was a federal and not a national government) might eventually prevail. This hope would have been hardly conceivable, had not both parties to the conflict accepted the same premises of political theory, had they not preserved a common devotion to a hypothetically perfect original theory. This is what I mean by the idea of "preformation."

For the reasons which I have mentioned, the legacy of the Civil War to American thought has been one of sectionalism and constitutional debate rather than of dogmatic nationalism and "return to fundamentals." The tendency of sectionalism has been to reinforce our awareness of variety within our national culture and of the desirability and inevitability of preserving it. The tendency of the continuous constitutional tradition has been to give the defeated cause, the South, a legitimate theoretical position within the federal system.

The South, except in its romantic literature of chivalry and mint juleps, is now no champion of a different concept of life but rather of a different constitutional emphasis. The South remains, as it is desirable that someone should always be, champion of the states'-rights, local-autonomy principle of our federal Constitution. The South can still debate about what it once gave its lives to defend, for it has never lost essential devotion to the constitutional spirit and its pure original image. What Lincoln called "the spirit of concession and compromise, that spirit which has never failed us in past perils, and which may be safely trusted for all the future"—that spirit can survive precisely because the Civil War was poor in political theory. Notwithstanding the abolitionists and people like Garrison who wished to burn the Constitution, the war did not represent a quest for a general redefinition of political values.

Whatever the crimes, the senseless bitterness, that were visited on the South in the era of reconstruction, they were committed in a vindictive or narrowly provincial spirit. The triumph of the national emphasis in the federal structure did not carry with it victory of a nationalist philosophy. In Lincoln's phrase, "the Union"—not any self-conscious national culture—was what was to be preserved. This distinguished him sharply from his contemporaries like Bismarck and Cavour. The remarkable reintegration of the South into our constitutional system is the best evidence of the community of certain assumptions. The Civil War emerged, then, as a struggle over complicated matters, on which everyone knew there had been a long series of compromises, beginning with the Declaration of Independence and the Constitution themselves. Such controversy could have happened only within the framework of going federal institutions.

Not the least remarkable feature of the Civil War—apart from the fact that it occurred at all—is that it was so unproductive of political theory. This, the bloodiest single civil war of the nineteenth century, was also perhaps the least theoretical. The sectional character of the conflict had tended to make sociology—the description of things as they were—take the place of the uncharted exploration of things as they ought to be. It also prevented the crisis from propagating panaceas. This was another example of the recurrent tendency in American history to identify the "is" with the "ought," to think of values and a theory of society as implicit in facts about society. The era was strikingly lacking in romanticism of the Rousseauistic brand. The romantics of the day were the Thaddeus Stevenses—the bearers of fire and sword.

At the same time, the federal character of the struggle, the fact that it took place within a functioning federal order, confined much of the theoretical discussion within the area of constitutional law, of the search for the true original image of the Constitution. This, too, discouraged American thinkers of the age (excepting a vagrant Thoreau) from making confusion in the market place an excuse for going off into the solitude of the woods to rethink the whole problem of institutions. The sense of "givenness" was reinforced. In this case it meant the empirical tradition, the reliance on constitutionalism, and an unwillingness to remake institutions out of whole cloth.

The continuity of American political thought—which included the American way of *not* philosophizing about politics—was to stay. The mere fact that the nation had survived the ordeal of civil war seemed itself to prove the strength of the thread which bound the present to the past and to confirm the common destiny of the nation.

SUGGESTIONS FOR FURTHER READING

Charles and Mary Beard's description of the Civil War as a "revolution" is supported by Louis M. Hacker, *The Triumph of American Capitalism* (New York, 1940). Arthur C. Cole finds the Civil War to be *The Irrepressible Conflict, 1850–1865* (New York, 1934), and Robert R. Russel describes some Southern economic grievances in his *Economic Aspects of Southern Sectionalism, 1840–61* (Urbana, Ill., 1924).

Arthur M. Schlesinger, Jr., "The Causes of the Civil War: A Note on Historical Sentimentalism," *Partisan Review,* 16 (October 1949), 969–81, argues that slavery was a fundamental moral issue of dividing the sections, an issue that could not be compromised. In two important books, *The Political Economy of Slavery* (New York, 1965) and *The World the Slaveholders Made* (New York, 1969), Eugene D. Genovese argues that slavery created a premodern society in the South with an ideology and systems of law, morality, and social relations that differed sharply from the bourgeois, capitalist society in the North. Eric Foner, *Free Soil, Free Labor, Free Men: The Ideology of the Republican Party Before the Civil War* (New York, 1970) describes the ideology of free labor in the North that put it into sharp conflict with slave society ideology. Richard H. Sewell, *A House Divided: Sectionalism and the Civil War, 1848–1865* (Baltimore, 1988) argues that slavery created the political, economic, and moral conflicts that finally led to civil war. Roger L. Ransom, *Conflict and Compromise: The Political Economy of Slavery, Emancipation, and the American Civil War* (Cambridge, Eng., 1989) emphasizes economic history in making much the same point.

A number of scholars have found the Civil War to be repressible, or at least not the inevitable outcome of economic and social forces. James G. Randall is critical of the politicians who failed to achieve the compromise that would have averted war in "The Blundering Generation," *Mississippi Valley Historical Review,* 27 (June 1940), 3–28. Avery Craven in *An Historian and the Civil War* (Chicago, 1964) and *The Coming of the Civil War* (Chicago, 1957) argues that prejudices, misconceptions, and emotionalism led Americans to transform political issues into moral absolutes, making compromise impossible. David Donald has argued perceptively against both Craven's and the Beards' points of view, finding the drift to war to be the result of a social crisis arising from the lack of traditional values and norms in "An Excess of Democracy: The American Civil War and the Social Process," chapter 11 of his *Lincoln Reconsidered,* 2nd ed. (New York, 1961). Donald spells out this interpretation in richer detail in *Liberty and Union: The Crisis of Popular Government* (Boston, 1978). David M. Potter, *The Impending Crisis, 1848–1861* (New York, 1976) is a fine, balanced survey of the coming of the Civil War that emphasizes Northern and Southern nationalism as a significant source of the conflict.

No subject has received more attention than the Civil War. Geoffrey C. Ward, *The Civil War: An Illustrated History* (New York, 1990), written to supplement a recent, very

---

*Available in paperback edition.

successful documentary television series, is an indication that the Civil War still fascinates Americans of all ages. James M. McPherson, *Battle Cry of Freedom* (New York, 1988), a portion of which is reprinted here, is a recent, one-volume scholarly treatment of the background and causes of the war as well as its political and military history. McPherson's notes and bibliography will take the interested reader more deeply into the literature on all aspects of the Civil War. Recent surveys are Eric Foner, "The Causes of the American Civil War: Recent Interpretations and New Directions," *Civil War History,* 20 (September 1974), 197–214, and Kenneth M. Stampp, "The Irrepressible Conflict," chapter 7 of his *The Imperiled Union: Essays on the Background of the Civil War* (New York, 1980). A beautifully written scholarly new biography is David Herbert Donald's *Lincoln* (New York, 1995).

10

Reconstruction

The civil war has had an endless fascination for Americans, who usually see it as a time of great heroism and idealism on the part of both sides in the conflict. But no such rosy aura surrounds the years after the war, the years when an attempt was made to reconstruct the nation and heal the wounds of war. If the Civil War made heroes, Reconstruction produced villains; if the war was marked by tragic idealism, Reconstruction was characterized by venal corruption. Even those historians who find much that was beneficial in Reconstruction conclude that the period ended in dismal failure.

The basic problem facing Northern leaders after the war was how to restore national unity after a bitter and bloody sectional conflict. But there was sharp disagreement as to the best approach. Should the Confederacy be treated as a conquered province, or should the Southern states be welcomed back into the Union as wayward but repentant members of the family? What kinds of changes should the former Confederate states accept before being allowed to participate once again in the political process?

Even during the war there was disagreement between President Lincoln, who favored treating the seceded states leniently, and some congressional leaders, who argued for harsher peace terms. This executive-legislative battle continued after the assassination of Lincoln, but the mid-term elections of 1866, favorable to the so-called radicals, made it possible for Congress to pass legislation concerning the South over the opposition and vetoes of President Andrew Johnson. Congress quickly passed the Civil Rights Act, the Freedman's Bureau Act, and, finally, the Reconstruction Acts of 1867. The Southern states were put under military rule until they approved new constitutions guaranteeing black suffrage, ratified the Fourteenth Amendment, and in other ways satisfied the radical majority in Congress.

Only after each Southern state organized a new government under congressional tutelage was it declared reconstructed and its representatives and senators admitted to Congress. For the first time, blacks voted and held state and local office; some even served as their states' senators and representatives in Congress. The new Republican-dominated state governments were often marked by corruption and inefficiency, but in this they differed little from state legislatures elsewhere in the nation and, indeed, from the national government. But radical Southern state legislatures also instituted significant and needed reforms in education and welfare for blacks and whites alike. These reforms, along with the resentment many Southern whites felt toward being ruled by governments in which blacks participated, elicited sharp and often violent opposition, and one by one the radical Republican governments fell from power. The victors termed themselves "redeemers," because they promised to redeem the states and return them to those who, they said, had the necessary talent and education and, therefore, deserved to rule. None of the radical governments remained when the last Federal troops were removed from the South in 1877.

The conflicts of the Reconstruction era were a continuation of the bitter antebellum struggles made even more bitter by the Northern victory and emancipation. Slavery may not have been the cause of the Civil War, as some have argued, but emancipation was clearly its key result. And emancipation raised a myriad of social, economic, and political questions, the answers to which would have profound effects on the future of the blacks, the South, and the entire nation. What exactly did freedom mean for the blacks? Did freedom carry with it the rights that free whites in the country enjoyed—the right to vote, to hold office, to own property, to use all public facilities, for example? Did the nation have any obligations to the former slaves—for example, to compensate them for the two centuries in which they were enslaved by granting them land and equipment to help them gain economic independence to match their freedom?

The answers given to these questions obviously affected Southern whites. Were those who had participated in rebellion to be punished by having their land confiscated and distributed to former slaves? Were whites who had ruled the

South to be allowed to continue to do so, or were they to be forced to share political power with enfranchised blacks?

The answers to these questions would, of course, affect the future of the nation. Were Southern political and economic interests to be subordinated to those of the North?

These were the questions that politicians and the people hotly debated. As blacks sought to give meaning to their newly won freedom, their former masters sought to limit their losses and maintain as much of their political and economic power as they could. As Republican politicians and those who supported the Republican economic and political programs sought to maintain their dominance, Democrats and those who supported their programs saw the return of the South to the Union as an opportunity to increase their following.

Invariably the debate centered on the future of the blacks. For former abolitionists and those who came to see the Civil War as a moral crusade to rid the nation of slavery and for former slaves seeking to become free citizens, granting civil and economic rights to blacks became crucial. Conversely, for those who reluctantly accepted emancipation and continued to believe that the blacks were innately inferior and incapable of assuming the rights and obligations of a free people, limiting the civil and political rights of blacks became necessary. Even those who cared little about the blacks but were concerned mainly with national politics and future legislation could not avoid the debate on the future of the blacks because granting or denying civil and economic rights to blacks would affect the outcome of elections and, therefore, votes in Congress.

This furious debate among contemporaries and the answers that finally emerged have sharply influenced historians' interpretations of Reconstruction and its results. No period has evoked more impassioned and opinionated historical writing. Some historians, seeing the South as victim, have called it a "tragic era," a period during which the defeated South was "put to the torture" by a vindictive conqueror. Others, sensitive to the position and aspirations of the black population, have depicted Reconstruction as a time of real opportunity to right the wrongs of generations of slavery, and they see the end of Reconstruction as a betrayal by opportunistic Northerners who abandoned the blacks to racist violence and a life of discrimination and fear that lasted for a century.

Some of this debate among contemporaries and among modern historians who consider this debate in their interpretations may be seen in the selections that follow. In the first selection, Eric Foner writes that for the newly emancipated slaves freedom meant more than simply the absence of slavery. The freedmen's efforts to order their own lives, to determine their own religious practices, family life, and work regimes, and their efforts to enter politics all reflected their "desire for independence from white control, for autonomy both as individuals and as members of a community being transformed by emancipation." The freedmen's aspirations for equality as individuals and as a community met with violent opposition from Southern whites who refused to accept those rights that blacks deemed essential to make their newly won freedom meaningful.

In the second selection, Thomas C. Holt compares the emancipation experience in the British West Indies with that in the United States and concentrates on the transformation of slaves into free workers. He shows that freedom had very different meanings for former slaves, for former slaveowners, and for emancipa-tors, and, as a result, each group looked to a different kind of free labor system in the future. The differing views of the meaning of freedom led to sharp conflicts among the three groups. In the end, Holt concludes that repression, buttressed by racism, forced the blacks into a free labor system producing commercial crops for the market.

La Wanda Cox, in the third selection, centers her attention on the national policymakers. She argues that one of their goals was to guarantee civil rights for the freed slaves, and she considers some of the possible alternatives open to the politicians attempting to reach that goal. She finds that some actions, such as the distribution of land to former slaves, would not have had the desired results. She notes that there were some realistic opportunities available that the politicians ig-nored, but argues that historical conditions set limits to what could be accom-plished. To assume that Reconstruction following the Civil War could have achieved the consensus that the civil rights movement of the 1960s achieved, she concludes, is to ignore the political realities of the time.

The Reconstruction era witnessed sharp political conflict that often turned into physical violence as the Ku Klux Klan and other groups intimidated, ha-rassed, beat, and killed blacks. Obviously, former slaveholders and their support-ers used such tactics in their attempt to maintain their accustomed control, and, just as obviously, such actions often met determined and armed resistance by blacks, many of them former Federal soldiers, who sought to give meaning to their newly won freedom. Less obvious are the reasons that the victorious North permitted this violence and then allowed the conflict in the South to be resolved in a manner so detrimental to the former slaves. What were the victorious Northern-ers trying to achieve in the South? If preservation of the Union, emancipation, and a return to the commercial production of the South's staple crops were their goals, then the North succeeded, and the way in which Reconstruction ended revealed a large measure of consensus, at least among the nation's white population.

But if, as some have argued, civil rights for the emancipated blacks was also a Northern goal, then why did Northerners abandon that goal? Did they lack the power? The will? Or did they face problems that really could not be solved in the mid-nineteenth century? In short, did racism create a new consensus that led most whites to accept the subordination of blacks? How did blacks respond to the conditions in which they found themselves? Did they continue their struggle to make freedom real? In what ways?

All decisions made in the past affect the future in one way or another. But the settlement made during Reconstruction had repercussions that have lasted to this day, as all of the selections suggest. What have been some of those effects? And how might a different settlement have affected the course of history in the United States?

The Meaning of Freedom

Freedom came in different ways to different parts of the South. In large areas, slavery had disintegrated long before Lee's surrender, but elsewhere, far from the presence of federal troops, blacks did not learn of its irrevocable end until the spring of 1865. Despite the many disappointments that followed, this generation of blacks would always regard the moment when "de freedom sun shine out" as the great watershed of their lives. Houston H. Holloway, who had been sold three times before he reached the age of twenty in 1865, later recalled with vivid clarity the day emancipation came to his section of Georgia: "I felt like a bird out of a cage. Amen. Amen. Amen. I could hardly ask to feel any better than I did that day. . . . The week passed off in a blaze of glory."

"Freedom," said a black minister, "burned in the black heart long before freedom was born." But what did "freedom" mean? "It is necessary to define that word," Freedmen's Bureau Commissioner O. O. Howard told a black audience in 1865, "for it is most apt to be misunderstood." Howard assumed a straightforward definition existed. But "freedom" itself became a terrain of conflict, its substance open to different and sometimes contradictory interpretations, its content changing for whites as well as blacks in the aftermath of the Civil War.

Blacks carried out of bondage an understanding of their new condition shaped both by their experience as slaves and by observation of the free society around them. What one planter called their "wild notions of rights and freedom" encompassed, first of all, an end to the myriad injustices associated with slavery. Some, like black minister Henry M. Turner, stressed that freedom meant the enjoyment of "our rights in common with other men." "If I cannot do like a white man I am not free," Henry Adams told his former master in 1865. "I see how the poor white people do. I ought to do so too, or else I am a slave."

But underpinning the specific aspirations lay a broader theme: a desire for independence from white control, for autonomy both as individuals and as members of a community being transformed by emancipation. Before the war, free blacks had created churches, schools, and mutual benefit societies, while slaves had forged a culture centered on the family and church. With freedom, these institutions were consolidated, expanded, and liberated from white supervision, and new ones—particularly political organizations—joined them as focal points of black life. In stabilizing their families, seizing control of their churches, greatly expanding their schools and benevolent societies, staking a claim to economic independence, and forging a political culture, blacks during Reconstruction laid the foundation for the modern black community, whose roots lay deep in slavery but whose structure and values reflected the consequences of emancipation.

From Slavery to Freedom

Long after the end of the Civil War, the experience of bondage remained deeply etched in blacks' collective memory. The freedmen resented not only the brutal incidents of slavery but the fact of having been held as slaves at all. During a visit to Richmond, Scottish minister David Macrae was surprised to hear a former slave complain of past mistreatment, while acknowledging he had never been whipped. "How were you cruelly treated then?" asked Macrae. "I was cruelly treated," answered the freedman, "because I was kept in slavery."

In countless ways, the newly freed slaves sought to overturn the real and symbolic authority whites had exercised over every aspect of their lives. Blacks relished opportunities to flaunt their liberation from the innumerable regulations, significant and trivial, associated with slavery. Freedmen held mass meetings and religious services unrestrained by white surveillance, acquired previously forbidden dogs, guns, and liquor, and refused to yield the sidewalks to whites. They dressed as they pleased, black women sometimes wearing gaudy finery, carrying parasols, and replacing the slave kerchief with colorful hats and veils. Whites complained of "insolence" and "insubordination" among the freedmen, by which they meant any departure from the deference and obedience expected under slavery. On the Bradford plantation in Florida, one untoward incident followed another. First, the family cook told Mrs. Bradford "if she want any dinner she kin cook it herself." Then the former slaves went off to a meeting with Northern soldiers to discuss "our freedom." Told that she and her daughter could not attend, one woman replied "they were now free and if she saw fit to take her daughter into that crowd it was nobody's business." "Never before had I a word of impudence from any of our black folk," recorded nineteen-year-old Susan Bradford, "but they are not ours any longer."

Among the most resented of slavery's restrictions was the rule, enforced by patrols, that no black could travel without a pass. With emancipation, it seemed that half the South's black population took to the roads. Southern towns and cities experienced an especially large influx of freedmen during and immediately after the Civil War. In the cities, many blacks believed, "freedom was free-er." Here were schools, churches, and fraternal societies, as well as the army (including, in 1865, black soldiers) and the Freedmen's Bureau, offering protection from the violence so pervasive in much of the rural South. Between 1865 and 1870, the black population of the South's ten largest cities doubled, while the number of white residents rose by only ten percent. Smaller towns, from which blacks had often been excluded as slaves, experienced even more dramatic increases.

Black migrants who hoped to find urban employment often encountered severe disappointment. The influx from the countryside flooded the labor market, consigning most urban blacks to low-wage, menial employment. Unable to obtain decent housing, black migrants lived in squalid shantytowns on the outskirts of Southern cities, where the incidence of disease and death far exceeded that among white city dwellers. The result was a striking change in Southern urban living patterns. Before the war, blacks and whites had lived scattered throughout Southern cities. Reconstruction witnessed the rise of a new, segregated, urban geography.

No aspect of black mobility was more poignant than the effort to reunite families separated during slavery. "In their eyes," wrote a Freedmen's Bureau agent, "the work of emancipation was incomplete until the families which had been dispersed by slavery were reunited." One freedman, writing from Texas, asked the Bureau's aid in locating "my own dearest relatives," providing a long list of sisters, nieces, nephews, uncles, and in-laws, none of whom he had seen since his sale in Virginia twenty-four years before. A typical plea for help appeared in the Nashville *Colored Tennessean:*

During the year 1849, Thomas Sample carried away from this city, as his slaves, our daughter, Polly, and son. . . . We will give $100 each for them to any person who will assist them . . . to get to Nashville, or get word to us of their where-abouts.

Although vulnerable to disruption, strong family ties had existed under slavery. Emancipation allowed blacks to solidify their family connections, and most freedmen seized the opportunity. Many families, in addition, adopted the children of deceased relatives and friends rather than see them apprenticed to white masters or placed in Freedmen's Bureau orphanages. By 1870, a large majority of blacks lived in two-parent households.

But while emancipation strengthened the preexisting black family, it also transformed the roles of its members and relations among them. One common, significant change was that slave families, separated because their members belonged to different owners, could now live together. More widely noticed by white observers in early Reconstruction was the withdrawal of black women from field labor.

Beginning in 1865, and for years thereafter, Southern whites throughout the South complained of the difficulty of obtaining female field laborers. Planters, Freedmen's Bureau officials, and Northern visitors all ridiculed the black "female aristocracy" for "acting the *lady*" or mimicking the family patterns of middle-class whites. White employers also resented their inability to force black children to labor in the fields, especially after the spread of schools in rural areas. Contemporaries appeared uncertain whether black women, black men, or both were responsible for the withdrawal of females from agricultural labor. There is no question that many black men considered it manly to have their wives work at home and believed that, as head of the family, the male should decide how its labor was organized. But many black women desired to devote more time than under slavery to caring for their children and to domestic responsibilities like cooking, sewing, and laundering.

The shift of black female labor from the fields to the home proved a temporary phenomenon. The rise of renting and sharecropping, which made each family responsible for its own plot of land, placed a premium on the labor of all family members. The dire poverty of many black families, deepened by the depression of the 1870s, made it essential for both women and men to contribute to the family's income. Throughout this period, a far higher percentage of black than white women and children worked for wages outside their homes. Where women continued to concentrate on domestic tasks, and children attended school, they frequently engaged in seasonal field labor. Thus, emancipation did not eliminate labor outside the home by black women and children, but it fundamentally altered control over their labor. Now blacks themselves, rather than a white owner or overseer, decided where and when black women and children worked.

For blacks, liberating their families from the authority of whites was an indispensable element of freedom. But the family itself was in some ways transformed by emancipation. Although historians no longer view the slave family as matriarchal, it is true that slave men did not function as economic breadwinners and that their masters wielded authority within the household. In a sense, slavery had imposed on black men and women the rough "equality" of powerlessness. With freedom came developments that strengthened patriarchy within the black family and consigned men and women to separate spheres.

Outside events strongly influenced this development. Service in the Union Army enabled black men to participate more directly than women in the struggle for freedom. The Freedmen's Bureau designated the husband as head of the black household, insisting that men sign contracts for the labor of their entire families and establishing lower wage scales for women. After 1867 black men could serve on juries, vote, hold office, and rise to leadership in the Republican party, while black women, like their white counterparts, could not. And black preachers, editors, and politicians emphasized women's responsibility for making the home "a place of peace and comfort" for men and urged them to submit to their husbands' authority.

Not all black women placidly accepted the increasingly patriarchal quality of black family life. Indeed, many proved more than willing to bring family disputes before public authorities. The records of the Freedmen's Bureau contain hundreds of complaints by black women of beatings, infidelity, and lack of child support. Some black women objected to their husbands signing labor contracts for them, demanded separate payment of their wages, and refused to be liable for their husbands' debts at country stores. Yet if emancipation not only institutionalized the black family but also spawned tensions within it, black men and women shared a passionate commitment to the stability of family life as the solid foundation upon which a new black community could flourish.

Building the Black Community

Second only to the family as a focal point of black life stood the church. And, as in the case of the family, Reconstruction was a time of consolidation and transformation for black religion. With the death of slavery, urban blacks seized control of their own churches, while the "invisible institution" of the rural slave church emerged into the light of day. The creation of an independent black religious life proved to be a momentous and irreversible consequence of emancipation.

In antebellum Southern Protestant congregations, slaves and free blacks had enjoyed a kind of associate membership. Subject to the same rules and discipline as whites, they were required to sit in the back of the church or in the gallery during services and were excluded from Sabbath schools and a role in church governance. In the larger cities, the number of black members often justified the organization of wholly black congregations and the construction of separate churches, although these were legally required to have white pastors. In the aftermath of emancipation, the wholesale withdrawal of blacks from biracial congregations redrew the religious map of the South. Two causes combined to produce the independent black church: the refusal of whites to offer blacks an equal place within their congregations and the black quest for self-determination.

Throughout the South, blacks emerging from slavery pooled their resources to purchase land and erect their own churches. Before the buildings were completed, they held services in structures as diverse as a railroad boxcar, where Atlanta's First Baptist Church gathered, or an outdoor "bush arbor," where the First Baptist Church of Memphis congregated in 1865. The first new building to rise amid Charleston's ruins was a black church on Calhoun Street; by 1866 ten more had been constructed. In the countryside, a community would often build a single church, used in rotation by the various black denominations. By the end of Reconstruction in 1877, the vast majority of Southern blacks had withdrawn from churches dominated by whites. On the eve of the war, 42,000 black Methodists worshipped in biracial South Carolina churches; by the 1870s, only 600 remained.

The church was "the first social institution fully controlled by black men in America," and its multiple functions testified to its centrality in the black community. Churches housed schools, social events, and political gatherings. In rural areas, church picnics, festivals, and excursions often provided the only opportunity for fellowship and recreation. The church served as an "Ecclesiastical Court House," promoting moral values, adjudicating family disputes, and disciplining individuals for adultery and other illicit behavior. In every black community, ministers were among the most respected individuals, esteemed for their speaking ability, organizational talents, and good judgment on matters both public and private.

Inevitably, too, preachers played a central role in Reconstruction black politics. Many agreed with Rev. Charles H. Pearce, who held several Reconstruction offices in Florida, that it was "impossible" to separate religion and politics: "A man in this State cannot do his whole duty as a minister except he looks out for the political interests of his people." Even those preachers who lacked ambition for political position sometimes found it thrust upon them. Often among the few literate blacks in a community, they were called on to serve as election registrars and candidates for office. Over 100 black ministers, hailing from North and South, from free and slave backgrounds, and from every black denomination from African Methodist Episcopal to Primitive Baptist, would be elected to legislative seats during Reconstruction.

Throughout Reconstruction, religious convictions shaped blacks' understanding of the momentous events around them, the language in which they voiced aspirations for justice and autonomy. Blacks inherited from slavery a distinctive version of Christian faith, in which Jesus appeared as a personal redeemer offering solace in the face of misfortune, while the Old Testament suggested that they were a chosen people, analogous to the Jews in Egypt, whom God, in the fullness of time, would deliver from bondage. "There is no part of the Bible with which they are so familiar as the story of the deliverance of the Children of Israel," a white army chaplain reported in 1866.

Emancipation and the defeat of the Confederacy strongly reinforced this messianic vision of history. Even nonclerics used secular and religious vocabulary interchangeably, as in one 1867 speech recorded by a North Carolina justice of the peace:

He said it was not now like it used to be, that . . . the negro was about to get his equal rights. . . . That the negroes owed their freedom to the courage of the negro soldiers and to God. . . . He made frequent references to the II and IV chapters of Joshua for a full accomplishment of the principles and destiny of the race. It was concluded that the race have a destiny in view similar to the Children of Israel.

The rise of the independent black church was accompanied by the creation of a host of fraternal, benevolent, and mutual aid societies. In early Reconstruction, blacks created literally thousands of such organizations; a partial list includes burial societies, debating clubs, Masonic lodges, fire companies, drama societies, trade associations, temperance clubs, and equal rights leagues. Offering social fellowship, sickness and funeral benefits, and, most of all, a chance to manage their own affairs, these voluntary associations embodied a spirit of collective self-improvement. Robert G. Fitzgerald, who had been born free in Delaware, served in both the U.S. Army and Navy, and came to Virginia to teach in 1866, was delighted to see rural blacks establishing churches, lyceums, and schools. "They tell me," he recorded in his diary, "before Mr. Lincoln made them free they had nothing to work for, to look up to, now they have everything, and will, by God's help, make the best of it." Moreover, the spirit of mutual self-help extended outward from the societies to embrace destitute nonmembers. In 1865 and 1866, blacks in Nashville, Jackson, New Orleans, and Atlanta, as well as in many rural areas, raised money to establish orphanages, soup kitchens, employment agencies, and poor relief funds.

Perhaps the most striking illustration of the freedmen's quest for self-improvement was their seemingly unquenchable thirst for education. Before the war, every Southern state except Tennessee had prohibited the instruction of slaves, and although many free blacks had attended school and a number of slaves became literate through their own efforts or the aid of sympathetic masters, over ninety percent of the South's adult black population was illiterate in 1860. Access to education for themselves and their children was, for blacks, central to the meaning of freedom, and white contemporaries were astonished by their "avidity for learning." Adults as well as children thronged the schools. A Northern teacher in Florida reported how one sixty-year-old woman, "just beginning to spell, seems as if she could not think of any thing but her book, says she spells her lesson all the evening, then she dreams about it, and wakes up thinking about it."

Northern benevolent societies, the Freedmen's Bureau, and, after 1868, state governments provided most of the funding for black education during Reconstruction. But the initiative often lay with blacks themselves. Urban blacks took immediate steps to set up schools, sometimes holding classes temporarily in abandoned warehouses, billiards rooms, or, in New Orleans and Savannah, former slave markets. In rural areas, Freedmen's Bureau officials repeatedly expressed surprise at discovering classes organized by blacks already meeting in churches, basements, or private homes. And everywhere there were children teaching their parents the alphabet at home, laborers on lunch breaks "poring over the elementary pages," and the "wayside schools" described by a Bureau officer:

A negro riding on a loaded wagon, or sitting on a hack waiting for a train, or by the cabin door, is often seen, book in hand delving after the rudiments of knowledge. A group on the platform of a depot, after carefully conning an old spelling book, resolves itself into a class.

Throughout the South, blacks in 1865 and 1866 raised money to purchase land, build schoolhouses, and pay teachers' salaries. Some communities voluntarily taxed themselves; in others black schools charged tuition, while allowing a number of the poorest families to enroll their children free of charge. Black artisans donated their labor to construct schoolhouses, and black families offered room and board to teachers to supplement their salaries. By 1870, blacks had expended over $1 million on education, a fact that long remained a point of collective pride. "Whoever may hereafter lay claim to the honor of 'establishing' . . . schools," wrote a black resident of Selma in 1867, "I trust the fact will never be ignored that Miss Lucy Lee, one of the emancipated, was the pioneer teacher of the colored children, . . . without the aid of Northern societies."

Inevitably, the first black teachers appeared incompetent in Northern eyes, for a smattering of education might place an individual in front of a class. One poignantly explained, "I never had the chance of goen to school for I was a slave until freedom. . . . I am the only teacher because we can not doe better now." Yet even an imperfect literacy, coupled with the courage often required to establish a rural school in the face of local white opposition, marked these teachers as community leaders. Black teachers played numerous roles apart from education, assisting freedmen in contract disputes, engaging in church work, and drafting petitions to the Freedmen's Bureau, state officials, and Congress. Like the ministry, teaching frequently became a springboard to political office. At least seventy black teachers served in state legislatures during Reconstruction. And many black politicians were linked in other ways to the quest for learning, like Alabama Congressman Benjamin S. Turner, an ex-slave "destitute of education," who financed a Selma school.

Not surprisingly, the majority of black teachers who held political office during Reconstruction had been free before the Civil War. Indeed the schools, like the entire institutional structure established by blacks during Reconstruction, symbolized the emergence of a community that united the free and the freed, and Northern and Southern blacks. The process occurred most smoothly in the Upper South, where the cultural and economic gap between free blacks and slaves had always been less pronounced than in the urban Deep South. While generally lighter in color than slaves, most Upper South free blacks were poor urban workers or farm laborers, often tied to the slave community through marriage and church membership. In cities like New Orleans, Mobile, Savannah, and Charleston, however, affluent mulatto elites responded with deep ambivalence to the new situation created by emancipation. Even in New Orleans, where politically conscious free blacks had already moved to make common cause with the freedmen, a sense of exclusivity survived the end of slavery. The Freedmen's Bureau found many free blacks reluctant to send their children to school with former slaves.

After New Orleans, the South's largest and wealthiest community of free blacks resided in Charleston, although the free elite there was neither as rich nor as culturally distinct as its Louisiana counterpart. Arriving in Charleston in November 1865, Northern journalist John R. Dennett found some members of the free elite cultivating their old exclusiveness. Others, however, took the lead in organizing assistance for destitute freedmen and in teaching the former slaves. Sons and daughters of prominent free families, mostly young people in their twenties, fanned out into the South Carolina countryside as teachers and missionaries. Several thereby acquired positions of local political leadership and later returned to Charleston as constitutional convention delegates and legislators. Thus the children of the Charleston elite cast their lot with the freedmen, bringing, as they saw it, modern culture to the former slaves. This encounter was not without its tensions. But in the long run it hastened the emergence of a black community stratified by class rather than color, in which the former free elite took its place as one element of a new black bourgeoisie, instead of existing as a separate caste as in the antebellum port cities.

In the severing of ties that had bound black and white families and churches to one another under slavery, the coming together of blacks in an explosion of institution building, and the political and cultural fusion of former free blacks and former slaves, Reconstruction witnessed the birth of the modern black community. All in all, the months following the end of the Civil War were a period of remarkable accomplishment for Southern blacks. Looking back in January 1866, the Philadelphia-born black missionary, Jonathan C. Gibbs could only exclaim: "we have progressed a century in a year."

The Economics of Freedom

Nowhere were blacks' efforts to define their freedom more explosive for the entire society than in the economy. Freedmen brought out of slavery a conception of themselves as a "Working Class of People" who had been unjustly deprived of the fruits of their labor. To white predictions that they would not work, blacks responded that if any class could be characterized as lazy, it was the planters, who had "lived in idleness all their lives on stolen labor." It is certainly true that many blacks expected to labor less as free men and women than they had as slaves, an understandable aim considering the conditions they had previously known. "Whence comes the assertion that the 'nigger won't work'?" asked an Alabama freedman. "It comes from this fact: . . . the freedman refuses to be driven out into the field two hours before day, and work until 9 or 10 o'clock in the night, as was the case in the days of slavery."

Yet freedom meant more than shorter hours and payment of wages. Freedmen sought to control the conditions under which they labored, end their subordination to white authority, and carve out the greatest measure of economic autonomy. These aims led them to prefer tenancy to wage labor, and leasing land for a fixed rent to sharecropping. Above all, they inspired the quest for land. Owning land, the freedmen believed, would "complete their independence."

To those familiar with the experience of other postemancipation societies, blacks' "mania for owning a small piece of land" did not appear surprising. Freedmen in Haiti, the British and Spanish Caribbean, and Brazil all saw ownership of land as crucial to economic independence, and everywhere former slaves sought to avoid returning to plantation labor. Unlike freedmen in other countries, however, American blacks emerged from slavery convinced that the federal government had committed itself to land distribution. Belief in an imminent division of land was most pervasive in the South Carolina and Georgia lowcountry, but the idea was shared in other parts of the South as well, including counties that had never been occupied by federal troops. Blacks insisted that their past labor entitled them to at least a portion of their owners' estates. As an Alabama black convention put it: "The property which they hold was nearly all earned by the sweat of *our* brows."

In some parts of the South, blacks in 1865 did more than argue the merits of their case. Hundreds of freedmen refused either to sign labor contracts or to leave the plantations, insisting that the land belonged to them. On the property of a Tennessee planter, former slaves not only claimed to be "joint heirs" to the estate but, the owner complained, abandoned the slave quarters and took up residence "in the rooms of my house." Few freedmen were able to maintain control of land seized in this manner. A small number did, however, obtain property through other means, squatting on unoccupied land in sparsely populated states like Florida and Texas, buying tiny city plots, or cooperatively purchasing farms and plantations. Most blacks, however, emerged from slavery unable to purchase land even at the depressed prices of early Reconstruction and confronted by a white community unwilling to advance credit or sell them property. Thus, they entered the world of free labor as wage or share workers on land owned by whites. The adjustment to a new social order in which their persons were removed from the market but their labor was bought and sold like any other commodity proved in many respects difficult. For it required them to adapt to the logic of the economic market, where the impersonal laws of supply and demand and the balance of power between employer and employee determine a laborer's material circumstances.

Most freedmen welcomed the demise of the paternalism and mutual obligations of slavery and embraced many aspects of the free market. They patronized the stores that sprang up throughout the rural South, purchasing "luxuries" ranging from sardines, cheese, and sugar to new clothing. They saved money to build and support churches and educate their children. And they quickly learned to use and influence the market for their own ends. The early years of Reconstruction witnessed strikes or petitions for higher wages by black urban laborers, including Richmond factory workers, Jackson washerwomen, New Orleans and Savannah stevedores, and mechanics in Columbus, Georgia. In rural areas, too, plantation freedmen sometimes bargained collectively over contract terms, organized strikes, and occasionally even attempted to establish wage schedules for an entire area. Blacks exploited competition between planters and nonagricultural employers, seeking work on railroad construction crews and at turpentine mills and other enterprises offering pay far higher than on the plantations.

Slavery, however, did not produce workers fully socialized to the virtues of economic accumulation. Despite the profits possible in early postwar cotton farming, many freedmen strongly resisted growing the "slave crop." "If ole massa want to grow cotton," said one Georgia freedman, "let him plant it himself." Many freedmen preferred to concentrate on food crops and only secondarily on cotton or other staples to obtain ready cash. Rather than choose irrevocably between self-sufficiency and market farming, they hoped to avoid a complete dependence on either while taking advantage of the opportunities each could offer. As A. Warren Kelsey, a representative of Northern cotton manufacturers, shrewdly observed:

The sole ambition of the freedmen at the present time appears to be to become the owner of a little piece of land, there to erect a humble home, and to dwell in peace and security at his own free will and pleasure. If he wishes, to cultivate the ground in cotton on his own account, to be able to do so without anyone to dictate to him hours or system of labor, if he wishes instead to plant corn or sweet potatoes—to be able to do that free from any outside control. . . . That is their idea, their desire and their hope.

Historical experience and modern scholarship suggest that acquiring small plots of land would hardly, by itself, have solved the economic plight of black families. Without control of credit and access to markets, land reform can often be a hollow victory. And where political power rests in hostile hands, small landowners often find themselves subjected to oppressive taxation and other state policies that severely limit their economic prospects. In such circumstances, the autonomy offered by land ownership tends to be defensive, rather than the springboard for sustained economic advancement. Yet while hardly an economic panacea, land redistribution would have had profound consequences for Southern society, weakening the land-based economic and political power of the old ruling class, offering blacks a measure of choice as to whether, when, and under what circumstances to enter the labor market, and affecting the former slaves' conception of themselves.

Blacks' quest for economic independence not only threatened the foundations of the Southern political economy, it put the freedmen at odds with both former owners seeking to restore plantation labor discipline and Northerners committed to reinvigorating staple crop production. But as part of the broad quest for individual and collective autonomy, it remained central to the black community's effort to define the meaning of freedom. Indeed, the fulfillment of other aspirations, from family autonomy to the creation of schools and churches, all greatly depended on success in winning control of their working lives and gaining access to the economic resources of the South.

Origins of Black Politics

If the goal of autonomy inspired blacks to withdraw from religious and social institutions controlled by whites and to attempt to work out their economic destinies for themselves, in the polity, "freedom" meant inclusion rather than separation. Recognition of their equal rights as citizens quickly emerged as the animating impulse of Reconstruction black politics. In the spring and summer of 1865, blacks organized a seemingly unending series of mass meetings, parades, and petitions demanding civil equality and suffrage as indispensable corollaries of emancipation. By midsummer, "secret political Radical Associations" had been formed in Virginia's major cities. Richmond blacks first organized politically to protest the army's rounding up of "vagrants" for plantation labor, but soon expanded their demands to include the right to vote and the removal of the "Rebel-controlled" local government.

Statewide conventions held throughout the South in 1865 and early 1866 offered the most visible evidence of black political organization. Several hundred delegates attended these gatherings, some selected by local meetings, others by churches, fraternal societies, Union Leagues, and black army units, still others simply appointed by themselves. The delegates "ranged all colors and apparently all conditions," but urban free mulattoes took the most prominent roles, and former slaves were almost entirely absent from leadership positions. But other groups also came to the fore in 1865. In Mississippi, a state with few free blacks before the war, ex-slave army veterans and their relatives comprised the majority of the delegates. Alabama and Georgia had a heavy representation of black ministers, and all the conventions included numerous skilled artisans.

The prominence of free blacks, ministers, artisans, and former soldiers in these early conventions foreshadowed black politics for much of Reconstruction. From among these delegates emerged such prominent officeholders as Alabama Congressman James T. Rapier and Mississippi Secretary of State James D. Lynch.

In general, however, what is striking is how few of these early leaders went on to positions of prominence. In most states, political mobilization had advanced far more rapidly in cities and in rural areas occupied by federal troops during the war than in the bulk of the plantation counties, where the majority of the former slaves lived. The free blacks of Louisiana and South Carolina who stepped to the fore in 1865 remained at the helm of black politics throughout Reconstruction; elsewhere, however, a new group of leaders, many of them freedmen from the black belt, soon superseded those who took the lead in 1865.

The debates at these conventions illuminated conflicting currents of black public life in the immediate aftermath of emancipation. Tensions within the black community occasionally rose to the surface. One delegate voiced resentment that a Northern black had been chosen president of North Carolina's convention. By and large, however, the proceedings proved harmonious, the delegates devoting most of their time to issues that united blacks rather than divided them. South Carolina's convention demanded access to all the opportunities and privileges enjoyed by whites, from education to the right to bear arms, serve on juries, establish newspapers, assemble peacefully, and "enter upon all the avenues of agriculture, commerce, [and] trade."

The delegates' central preoccupation, however, was equality before the law and the suffrage. In justifying their demand for the vote, the delegates invoked America's republican traditions, especially the Declaration of Independence—"the broadest, the deepest, the most comprehensive and truthful definition of human freedom that was ever given to the world." The North Carolina freedmen's convention portrayed the Civil War and emancipation as chapters in the onward march of "progressive civilization," embodiments of "the fundamental truths laid down in the great charter of Republican liberty, the Declaration of Independence." Such language was not confined to the convention delegates. Eleven Alabama blacks, who complained of contract frauds, injustice before the courts, and other abuses, concluded their petition with a revealing masterpiece of understatement: "This is not the persuit of happiness."

Like their Northern counterparts during the Civil War, Southern blacks proclaimed their identification with the nation's history, destiny, and political system. The abundance of letters and petitions addressed by black gatherings and ordinary freedmen to military officials, the Freedmen's Bureau, and state and federal authorities, as well as the decision of a number of conventions to send representatives to Washington to lobby for black rights, revealed a belief that the political order was at least partially open to their influence. "We are Americans," declared a meeting of Norfolk blacks, "we know no other country, we love the land of our birth." Their address reminded white Virginians that in 1619, "our fathers as well as yours were toiling in the plantations on James River" and that a black man, Crispus Attucks, had shed "the first blood" in the American Revolution. And, of course, blacks had fought and died to save the Union. America, resolved one meeting, was "now *our* country—made emphatically so by the blood of our brethren."

Despite the insistence on equal rights, the convention resolutions and public addresses generally adopted a moderate tone, offering "the right hand of fellowship" to Southern whites. Even the South Carolina convention, forthright in claiming civil and political equality and in identifying its demand with "the cause of millions of oppressed men" throughout the world, took pains to assure the state's white minority of blacks' "spirit of meekness," their consciousness of "your wealth and greatness, and our poverty and weakness."

To some extent, this cautious tone reflected a realistic assessment of the political situation at a time when Southern whites had been restored to local power by President Johnson and Congress had not yet launched its own Reconstruction policy. But the blend of radicalism and conciliation also mirrored the indecision of an emerging black political leadership still finding its own voice in 1865 and 1866 and dominated by urban free blacks, ministers, and others who had in the past enjoyed harmonious relations with at least some local whites and did not always feel the bitter resentments of rural freedmen.

Nor did a coherent economic program emerge from these assemblies. Demands for land did surface at local meetings that chose convention delegates. Yet such views were rarely expressed among the conventions' leadership. By and large, economic concerns figured only marginally in the proceedings, and the addresses and resolutions offered no economic program apart from stressing the "mutual interest" of capital and labor and urging self-improvement as the route to personal advancement. The ferment rippling through the Southern countryside found little echo at the state conventions of 1865, reflecting the paucity of representation from plantation counties and the prominence of political leaders more attuned to political equality and self-help formulas than to rural freedmen's thirst for land.

Nonetheless, these early black conventions both reflected and advanced the process of political mobilization. Some Tennessee delegates, for example, took to heart their convention's instruction to "look after the welfare" of their constituents. After returning home, they actively promoted black education, protested to civil authorities and the Freedmen's Bureau about violence and contract frauds, and struggled against unequal odds to secure blacks a modicum of justice in local courts. Chapters of the Georgia Equal Rights and Educational Association, established at the state's January 1866 convention, became "schools in which the colored citizens learn their rights." Spreading into fifty counties by the end of the year, the Association's local meetings attracted as many as 2,000 freedmen, who listened to speeches on issues of the day and readings from Republican newspapers.

All in all, the most striking characteristic of this initial phase of black political mobilization was unevenness. In some states, organization proceeded steadily in 1865 and 1866; in others, such as Mississippi, little activity occurred between an initial flurry in the summer of 1865 and the advent of black suffrage two years later. Large parts of the black belt remained untouched by organized politics, but many blacks were aware of Congressional debates on Reconstruction policy and quickly employed on their own behalf the Civil Rights Act of 1866. "The negro of today," remarked a correspondent of the New Orleans *Tribune* in September 1866, "is not the same as he was six years ago. . . . He has been told of his rights, which have long been robbed." Only in 1867 would blacks enter the "political nation," but in organization, leadership, and an ideology that drew on America's republican heritage to demand an equal place as citizens, the seeds that flowered then were planted in the first years of freedom.

Violence and Everyday Life

The black community's religious, social, and political mobilization was all the more remarkable for occurring in the face of a wave of violence that raged almost unchecked in large parts of the postwar South. In the vast majority of cases freedmen were the victims and whites the aggressors.

In some areas, violence against blacks reached staggering proportions in the immediate aftermath of the war. "I saw white men whipping colored men just the same as they did before the war," testified ex-slave Henry Adams, who claimed that "over two thousand colored people" were murdered in 1865 in the area around Shreveport, Louisiana. In some cases, whites wreaked horrible vengeance for offenses real or imagined. In 1866, after "some kind of dispute with some freedmen," a group near Pine Bluff, Arkansas, set fire to a black settlement and rounded up the inhabitants. A man who visited the scene the following morning found "a sight that apald me 24 Negro men women and children were hanging to trees all round the Cabbins."

The pervasiveness of violence reflected whites' determination to define in their own way the meaning of freedom and to resist black efforts to establish their autonomy, whether in matters of family, church, labor, or personal demeanor. Georgia freedman James Jeter was beaten "for claiming the right of whipping his own child instead of allowing his employer and former master to do so." Black schools, churches, and political meetings also became targets. Conduct deemed manly or dignified on the part of whites became examples of "insolence" and "insubordination" in the case of blacks. One North Carolina planter complained bitterly to a Union officer that a black soldier had "bowed to me and said good morning," insisting blacks must never address whites unless spoken to first. In Texas, Bureau records listed the "reasons" for some of the 1,000 murders of blacks by whites between 1865 and 1868: One victim "did not remove his hat"; another "wouldn't give up his whiskey flask"; a white man "wanted to thin out the niggers a little"; another wanted "to see a d—d nigger kick." Gender offered no protection—one black woman was beaten by her employer for "using insolent language," another for refusing to "call him master," a third "for crying because he whipped my mother." Probably the largest number of violent acts stemmed from disputes arising from blacks' efforts to assert their freedom from control by their former masters. Freedmen were assaulted and murdered for attempting to leave plantations, disputing contract settlements, not laboring in the manner desired by their employers, attempting to buy or rent land, and resisting whippings.

The pervasive violence underscored what might be called the politicization of everyday life that followed the demise of slavery. A seemingly insignificant incident reported to the state's governor in 1869 by black North Carolinian A. D. Lewis graphically illustrates this development:

Please allow me to call your kine attention to a transaction which occured to day between me and Dr. A. H. Jones. . . . I was in my field at my own work and this Jones came by me and drove up to a man's gate that live close by . . . and ordered my child to come there and open that gate for him`. . . while there was children in the yard at the same time not more than twenty yards from him and jest because they were white and mine black he wood not call them to open the gate. . . . I spoke gently to him that [the white children] would open the gate. . . . He got out of his buggy . . . and walked nearly hundred yards rite into my field where I was at my own work and double his fist and strick me in the face three times . . . cursed me [as] a dum old Ratical. . . . Now governor I wants you to please rite to me how to bring this man to jestus.

No record exists of the disposition of this complaint, but Lewis's letter conveys worlds of meaning about Reconstruction: his powerful sense of place, his quiet dignity in the face of assault, his refusal to allow his son to be treated differently from white children or to let a stranger's authority be imposed on his family, the way an everyday encounter rapidly descended into violence and acquired political meaning, and Lewis's assumption (reflecting the situation after 1867) that blacks could expect justice from the government under which they lived. Most of all, it illustrates how day-to-day encounters between the races became infused with the tension inevitable when a social order, with its established power relations and commonly understood rules of conduct, has been swept away and a new one has not yet come into being. As David L. Swain, former governor of North Carolina, remarked in 1865, "With reference to emancipation, we are at the beginning of the war."

Thomas C. Holt

Emancipation, Race, and Ideology

The first half of the nineteenth century was preeminently an era of revolutions—in social and political thought, in social and economic relations. We now know that the problem of slavery was a vital nexus for the ideological transformation of the era and that slave emancipation figured prominently in its political and military upheavals. Beginning with Haiti at the turn of the century and ending with Cuba and Brazil during its final decades, slave-labor systems in the Western Hemisphere were eroded and finally swept away in successive waves of slave revolt, wars of national liberation, and internal conflicts between social classes. Concurrent with and linked to the dramatic transition from slavery to free labor was the maturing of industrial capitalism and the liberal democratic ideology that purported to explain and justify the new bourgeois economic order.

But while antislavery agitation was closely intertwined with the rise of bourgeois ideology in the early decades of the century, actual emancipation exposed the difficulty of applying that ideology to radical transformations in the social relations of culturally different populations. In the wake of these developments, the late nineteenth century witnessed the rise of an explicitly racist ideology that gained a hitherto unprecedented intellectual and social legitimacy, clashed with critical premises of liberal democratic thought, and undermined the promise of black emancipation. Indeed, there appear to have been subtle relationships and interactions between the social transformations occasioned by slave emancipation and this subsequent racist reaction. Early social reformers had posed the problem of slavery in a way that justified a particular concept of freedom in the emerging capitalist social order; by the late nineteenth century what one might call "the problem of freedom" in former slave societies confronted many of these same thinkers with difficulties inherent in liberal democratic thought. Racism appears to have been, in part, a means of evading that confrontation.

The confrontation was most compelling in the British and the American emancipation experiences. In ideological as well as diplomatic terms, abolition in the British West Indies and in the southern United States were major turning points in the international antislavery struggle. The emancipation of approximately three-quarters of a million British West Indian and four million American blacks eliminated well over half the entire slave population in the Western Hemisphere. Furthermore, only in Haiti was the emancipation process more rapid than that under British and American auspices; in both places the process was completed over a four-year period. Of course, in the British West Indies this "gradualism" was by design, while in the United States it was caused by the vicissitudes of war. Hundreds of thousands of American slaves fled to Union lines from the commencement of the Civil War in 1861; their quest for freedom was accelerated by the Emancipation Proclamation in 1863 and completed with the Thirteenth Amendment in 1865. British West Indian planters, however, were paid compensation totaling £20 million sterling for their slave property and enjoyed an official four-year transition period between the abolition of legal slavery on August 1, 1834, and the complete emancipation of their workers on August 1, 1838. During this so-called apprenticeship period, the freedmen were required to remain on the plantations and to work much as they had before. They could not be subjected to corporal punishment by their former masters, however, and part of their week was reserved for their own use, preferably to work for wages. Special magistrates, whose duties and recruitment were similar to those of the American Freedmen's Bureau agents, were appointed to supervise the transition and to protect the freedmen from abuse; however, they could and did order physical punishment to force recalcitrant freedmen to work.

It was not simply the size and political significance of emancipation in the British possessions and the United States that affected other slaveholding powers; American and British policy debates shaped the terms of discussion if not the actual policies pursued elsewhere. For example, in July 1839, Alexis de Tocqueville completed a study of the British West Indian experience and recommended an emancipation plan for the French islands to the Chamber of Deputies. Following the British precedent, he suggested that a special transition period separate the ending of formal slavery and complete emancipation. This period, he thought, was "the most favorable moment to found that empire over the minds and habits of the black population" that was essential to preserving social order. Moreover, he proposed that during this transition period the French must be prepared, if necessary, to "compel the laborious and manly habits of liberty." Drawing attention to Tocqueville's remarks, C. Vann Woodward has observed that the problem of reconciling force with freedom, and liberty with necessity, represented a "paradox that lay at the heart of the problem of emancipations and reconstructions everywhere in the world."

The political systems of Great Britain and the United States differed radically, and the British West Indies and the American South were politically, economically, and demographically distinct. Nevertheless, policymakers at the White House and in Whitehall posed the problem of emancipation in strikingly similar political and philosophical terms and wrestled with the same paradoxical issues. These similarities exist no doubt because the terms of their policy discussions were derived from the broader ideological presuppositions that British and American policymakers shared. The task of compelling the "voluntary" transformation of slaves into wage laborers, the crux of the problem of formulating emancipation policy everywhere, found precedents in the ongoing transformation of white agricultural workers into an industrial working class. Yet, the fact that such a transformation would pose an intellectual "problem" is comprehensible only in the context of the prevailing liberal democratic ideology of the emancipators, that is, the paradoxical situation of having to compel people to be "free" was rooted in the character of the "freedom" espoused.

Defining freedom was the beginning of the difficulty. David Brion Davis has revealed how social reformers used slavery as a curious negative referent with which to define the otherwise elusive concept of freedom. For none was this difficulty more poignant than for English Quakers, the vanguard of British industrial development as well as of the abolitionist movement. For them slavery helped define the meaning of freedom within a capitalist economy and a liberal political state. Slavery, being clearcut and concrete, could be used to symbolize "all the forces that threatened the true destiny of man." Freedom, being abstract and liable to misuse, was more difficult to define in substance. Thus slavery helped locate the outer boundaries of freedom; it was the antithesis of freedom. Slavery meant subordination to the physical coercion and personal dominion of an arbitrary master; freedom meant submission only to the impersonal forces of the marketplace and to the rational and uniform constraints of law. Slavery meant involuntary labor for the master's benefit; freedom meant voluntary contracts determined by mutual consent, which theoretically should guarantee that one received the value of one's labor. Slavery meant little, if any, legal protection of property, person, or family; freedom meant equal protection of the laws. Historians might empirically determine that slavery and capitalism were compatible, but to contemporaries of the reform era, slavery was logically synonymous with irrational monopoly power in both labor markets and commodity markets. The power of the abolition movement in this era derived in large part from the fact that slavery was such a convenient foil for free markets, free labor, and free men.

Moreover, the abolitionists and those men who fashioned and implemented emancipation policies were all heirs to a historically unique set of concepts about human behavior, about the sources of social action, and about the nature of political and economic justice. First, there was a materialist assumption regarding man's nature: man is a creature of insatiable material appetites, and all humans share an innate desire for self-improvement and personal gain. Second, it was assumed that in general men have a natural aversion to labor and that therefore material incentives are necessary to make them work. From these unquestioned assumptions was deduced a coherent view of political economy. Its key axiom was the notion C. B. Macpherson has called "possessive individualism"— namely, that society consists of an aggregation of individuals each of whom is proprietor of his own person and capacities, for which he owes nothing to society. Consequently, social action (at least beyond the bounds of the family) is reducible to exchange relations between these individual proprietors. The mainspring of the entire socioeconomic and political system is "that men do calculate their most profitable courses and do employ their labour, skill, and resources as that calculation dictates." Political order exists merely as "a calculated device for the protection of this property and for the maintenance of an orderly relation of exchange." In such a social order human freedom is defined as autonomy from the will of others, except in relations entered into voluntarily with a view to one's own interest, that is, self-interested contractual relations. But autonomy also means that whether one eats or starves depends solely on one's individual will and capacities. In the liberal democratic state, social relations—in their political as well as their economic dimensions—are ultimately self-regulating, impersonal, and therefore just.

The efforts of British and American policymakers to define a framework for the transition from slavery to freedom reveal the force of these ideas. The essential difference between freedom and slavery, as Viscount Howick lectured the members of Parliament during the debate on British West Indian emancipation in 1833, was that free men worked "because they are convinced that it is in their interest to do so." Theirs was a rational calculation of the relative advantages to be gained from industry over the privation to be expected if they "indulge in their natural inclination for repose." Slaves worked out of fear of punishment and for the benefit of others.

Three decades later, Americans echoed Howick's sentiments. "The incentive to faithful labor," advised the Boston *Advertiser* in 1865, "is self-interest." This pithy rule confirmed sentiments articulated earlier by the men and women who had gathered at Port Royal, South Carolina, to conduct the first experiment with black free labor in the American South. One of them, William Gannett, declared, "Let all the natural laws of labor, wages, competition, &c come into play—and the sooner will habits of responsibility, industry, self-dependence & manliness be developed." His colleague Edward Philbrick added, "Negro labor has got to be employed, if at all, because it is *profitable,* and it has got to come into the market like everything else, subject to the supply and demand." Upon returning from Port Royal in May 1862, John Murray Forbes, a pre–Civil War abolitionist and postwar investor in Southern cotton, assessed the South Carolina situation for readers of the Boston *Advertiser*: "All those engaged in the experiment will testify that the negro has the same selfish element in him which induces other men to labor, and that with a fair prospect of benefit . . . he will work like other human beings." Elsewhere Forbes put the matter more bluntly: "The necessity of getting a living is the great secret of providing for sheep, negroes and humans generally."

It was not so simple as all that, however. While it was true that "sheep, negroes and humans generally" work to keep from starving, it did not follow that freedmen would apply themselves to the production of plantation staples or that their labor would be disciplined and reliable. The problem was not merely to make ex-slaves work, but to make them into a working class, that is, a class that would submit to the market because it adhered to the *values* of a bourgeois society: regularity, punctuality, sobriety, frugality, and economic rationality.

One of the more thoughtful examinations of this central problem of freedom, from the liberal point of view, was written in 1833 by Henry Taylor, a middle-level bureaucrat in the British Colonial Office. In colonies like Jamaica, wrote Taylor, where the population density was low and large areas of the interior had not been devoted to plantation staples, the problem of getting the freedmen to work on the sugar estates would be formidable. Jamaican planters had encouraged their slaves to grow foodstuffs on interior lands to supplement their weekly rations of salt fish and corn. They allocated garden plots either on the plantation itself or on land leased from others. By custom, Jamaican slaves had come to treat these so-called provision grounds as their private property. They sold their surplus produce in the weekend markets of nearby villages and towns and retained the profits for themselves. Taylor noted that testimony before the House of Commons had shown conclusively that freedmen could earn their accustomed subsistence needs by working these provision grounds for little better than one day a week. The key question, therefore, was "What, except compulsion, shall make them work six?"

Taylor brushed aside abolitionist testimony that the slaves' industry on their provision grounds showed they would continue to work on plantations after emancipation. Slaves who worked one or two days to purchase necessities would not necessarily work five or six more days for superfluous luxuries. They could be expected to expand their workweek sixfold only if their needs and wants were likewise expanded; this was an "extremely improbable" occurrence in the foreseeable future. "It is true that the wants and desires of mankind are indefinitely expansive," wrote Taylor, echoing a basic premise of Adam Smith's *Wealth of Nations,* "but when the habits of a whole population are concerned, the expansion must be necessarily gradual. Their habits cannot be suddenly changed." For the moment, one had to expect that the freedmen would strive merely for the possessions they were accustomed to, or for those which persons of slightly higher status—that is, the black headmen and estate artisans—possessed. It would be reasonable to assume that "it will only be in the long course of years and progress of society that their wants will creep up the scale of luxury, and be characterized by that exigency in the higher degrees of it which might suffice to animate and prolong their labours."

Taylor thought that the dangers implicit in the proposed West Indian emancipation and the subsequent needs of the colonial economy would not permit such delay. It was necessary that industrious habits be inculcated in some manner; work discipline must be internalized by the freedmen without the normal spur of necessity or desire. The problem, therefore, was to overcome the legacy of slavery. "The state of slavery if it implies much injustice, implies also much ignorance and want of moral cultivation," Taylor concluded. Being "ignorant, destitute of moral cultivation, and . . . habituated to dependence," slaves required "both a sense of subordination in themselves, and the exercise by others over them of a strict and daily discipline." But there was reason to believe that under "disinterested instructors" they would advance in civilization. Once it had been thought that blacks were intellectually inferior, but the preponderant evidence presented to Parliament revealed striking cultural progress. Under the tutelage of missionaries, the slaves showed a strong desire to learn and were "a quick and intelligent race of people." Of course, some racial differences remained. Taylor rejected one witness's testimony that the blacks possessed "shrewd" intellects; he thought their mental character might be better described as rash, volatile, and somewhat shallow, "the intelligence, in short, of minds which had neither discipline nor cultivation, and nothing but natural vivacity to enlighten them."

Given their character and the absence of sufficient incentives to work for wages, freedmen were likely to relapse "into a barbarous indolence" if suddenly or completely emancipated. Experience showed that where population density was low, people have a "strong propensity to scatter themselves" and to live in the wild as hunter-gatherers. A society must be "condensed" to be civilized, otherwise a situation develops wherein "capitalists [will be] shorn of their profits by the want of labour, and . . . those who *should be* labourers, turning squatters and idlers, and living like beasts in the woods.". . .

The problem that Taylor's memorandum highlights is that the necessity that leads men to work is culturally defined and therefore varies from culture to culture. Thus Taylor recognized that the remaking of slaves into a working class involved remaking the slaves' culture. As long as the freedmen limited their material aspirations to goods they had received as slaves, their interest in working for wages would be insufficient to maintain the production of plantation staples. Therefore, the physical coercion of slavery must be replaced by more subtle stimuli. Those insatiable material appetites that all humans were alleged to be blessed with needed to be awakened in the freed slaves. . . .

Americans were also aware of the connection between black consumer desires and the larger economic and social order. John Miller McKim returned to Philadelphia in 1862 from Port Royal, waxing eloquent about the greatly expanded market for Northern goods in the South in the postwar period. "They [the Negroes] begin to demand articles of household use also such as pots, kettles, pans, brushes, brooms, knives, forks, spoons, soap, candles, combs, Yankee clocks, etc." In 1866 the New York *Herald* praised the role of business-minded people in managing freedmen's affairs in the South and made explicit the links between material consumption, education, and the preservation of social order. "Negroes will unquestionably be made better members of society, less subject to the influences of the enemies of social order, more industrious, because more ambitious to have the comforts and luxuries of life, if they can be thoroughly educated, than if they were allowed to remain in ignorance. A negro with no needs beyond a slave's allowance and a couple of suits of osnaburg a year, has far less motive to exert himself than one who sports a gold watch and fine clothes." The New York *Independent* expanded upon this theme. "Families that once fed out of the pot in which their hominy was cooked—the pot being their only utensil, and the hominy the only article of food—now breakfast, dine and sup as do other people, sitting down at a table, with food before them varying in character and decently served.". . .

The state papers produced by Americans—though generally less full or articulate than Taylor's memorandum—expressed identical propositions about human behavior, the principles of social action, and the significance of race. In the spring of 1863, Secretary of War Edwin M. Stanton assigned three social reformers—Robert Dale Owen, Samuel Gridley Howe, and James McKaye—the task of studying the problems involved in the transition from slavery to free labor and recommending appropriate policies and programs. The report of this Freedmen's

Inquiry Commission formed the basis for the establishment two years later of the U.S. Freedmen's Bureau, which like the British Special Magistracy was charged with overseeing the immediate transition from slavery.

Although the commissioners specifically rejected the unsuccessful British apprenticeship system as a model for American policy, they strongly recommended a very similar "guided" transition from slavery to free labor, during which the federal government would act as the temporary guardian, protector, and educator of the freedmen. In the first instance, they felt, the freedmen had to be taught that "emancipation means neither idleness nor gratuitous work, but fair labor for fair wages." The commissioners urged that the freedmen be given "a fair chance," but no more than that. There should be no compulsory contracts to labor, no statutory rate of wages, no interference between the hirer and the hired, and, except for antivagrancy legislation, no regulation of workers' movements. Thus freedom was defined in terms of wage labor, and wage labor meant competition in a market regulated only by "the natural laws of supply and demand."

Freedom to compete did not imply equality, however. The commissioners were confident that "the African race . . . lacks no essential aptitude for civilization," but they did not expect blacks in general to equal whites in the race of life. Like Henry Taylor, they found blacks intelligent but different. They were "a knowing rather than a thinking race"; their intelligence was that of "quick observation rather than comprehensive views or strong sense." It was not, the commissioners felt, "a race that will ever take a lead in the material improvement of the world; but it will make for itself, whenever it has fair play, respectable positions, [and] comfortable homes." The freedman would become "a useful member of the great industrial family of nations. Once released from the disabilities of bondage, he will somewhere find, and will maintain, his own appropriate social position."

The commissioners made clear that freedom of opportunity was not expected to lead to equality of condition, and they made racist assessments of black character and ability. But these should not distract us from the essential thrust of their report. Blacks were judged to have the same innate nature and potential desires and appetites as whites and were expected, therefore, to respond to the same market incentives. Consequently, they required neither perpetual guardianship nor special privileges. The import of such propositions and the subtlety of the distinctions were not lost on George King, a South Carolina freedman. "The Master he says we are all free, but it don't mean we is white. And it don't mean we is equal. Just equal for to work and earn our living and not depend on him for no more meat and clothes."

The Freedman's Bureau was established to implement the policy recommendations of the Inquiry Commissioners. Bureau officials carefully instructed freedmen and planters alike in the principles of a market economy. First of all, labor power—rather than the laborer—was now the commodity to be exchanged for wages. The rates of exchange would vary solely according to supply and demand. Neither the bureau nor combinations of planters would be allowed to set wage prices artificially. Accordingly, General Clinton B. Fisk, the Bureau Commissioner for Tennessee, declared in a circular that labor would be "free to compete with other commodities in an open market." Similarly in Florida, T. W. Osborn, in later years a radical Republican politician, declared that "labor is a commodity in the market and that the possessor of it is entitled to the highest market value."

Other Bureau officials expressed confidence in the freedmen's successful adoption of market values. Wages would induce thrift, J. W. Alvord, the Bureau's inspector of schools, assured General Oliver O. Howard. "The wants and opportunities of freedom show the worth of money, and what can be done with it." The South Carolina Bureau commissioner Rufus Saxton, after urging the freedmen to grow more cotton, the "regal crop," explained in phrases reminiscent of Special Magistrate Chamberlain the transformation he expected to observe in them. "In slavery you only thought of to-day. Having nothing to hope for beyond the present, you did not think of the future, but, like the ox and horse, thought only of food and work for the day. In freedom you must have an eye to the future, and have a plan and object in life."

But it was clear to British and American authorities that the re-education and resocialization of the freedmen would require more formal institutions than the Freedmen's Bureau or the British Special Magistracy. In both instances religious and secular missionaries seemed best suited to achieve the desired transformation in ex-slave cultures and characters. Education seemed to offer the paradoxical possibility of encouraging greater material and moral aspirations as well as inculcating social restraint and acceptance of the status quo in social relations. "It was education which made us free, progressive, and conservative," declared the Boston cotton merchant Edward Atkinson in 1861, "and it is education alone which can keep us so." In a field report to President Andrew Johnson, Carl Schurz reiterated the conservative role of education. "The education of the lower orders is the only reliable basis of the civilization as well as of the prosperity of a people." Moreover, it was "the true ground upon which the efficiency and the successes of free labor society grows"; it was the means for making the freedman "an intelligent cooperator in the general movements of society." Similarly, a special magistrate reporting to the Jamaican governor insisted that "in infant schools we at once get over the obstacle to regulated thought and action in the negro's cottage.". . .

Thus it was that missionaries and schoolmasters were dispatched to the British West Indies and the defeated Confederacy. Ex-slaves had to be taught to internalize the discipline and materialist psychology required in a free, but not equal, society. One should not lose sight of the fact, however, that fundamental to these emancipation policies was the belief that blacks shared the innate nature, desires, and psychology of white men. This is not to say that the emancipators were without racial bias; the point is that those biases were less salient in shaping their policies than were other propositions about human behavior which constituted their larger ideological commitments.

Ideally the freedmen would have access to economic, political, and social opportunities on the same basis as whites, as long as they conformed to the behavior patterns of whites. Should they fail to imbibe these cultural values and adhere to these norms, should education, religion, and consumerism fail to take, the freedmen would be remanded to the same types of social institutions used to discipline white deviants. In the harsh words of Henry Taylor, those who did not conform to the new order would be considered "an idle and spendthrift residue, whose liberation from arbitrary control would be duly retarded." In the liberal democratic state, when the market failed to achieve the appropriate discipline, these "arbitrary controls" were exercised by penal and reformatory institutions in various guises—workhouses, asylums, poorhouses, and penitentiaries.

Of course, the emancipators assumed that such deviance would be the exception rather than the rule and that these institutions would act not simply to coerce but to reform their inmates. They were prepared for the fact that slavery had unfitted both the planter and the freedmen for the roles they would have to play in the new economy, and they anticipated the need to re-educate the master as well as the slave. But nowhere were they prepared for the depth and breadth of the resistance actually encountered from both former masters and ex-slaves.

A major obstacle to the attempt to transform slave societies into liberal states was the planter. In his 1865 tour of the Southern states, Carl Schurz found uniform and pervasive among white Southerners the belief that blacks would not work without physical compulsion. The planters rejected the free-labor system, one student of the period concludes, "not because it had been tried and failed, but because it contradicted fundamental assumptions." Clearly, the defense of slavery had left a legacy of racism that would not be easily surrendered. A Southern planter summarized the viewpoint of his class succinctly: "Northern laborers are like other men, [but] southern laborers are nothing but niggers, and you can't make anything else out of them. They're not controlled by the same motives as white men, and unless you have power to compel them, they'll only work when they can't beg or steal enough to keep from starving." A Louisiana planter declared that "the nature of the negro cannot be changed by the offer of more or less money, all he desires is to eat, drink and sleep, and perform the least possible amount of labor." The Alabamian Hugh J. Davis, Jr., declared, "Negroes will not work for pay, the lash is all I feel that will make them."

That the planters clung to racist views of their black work force is clear, but the extent to which racial perceptions as opposed to perceptions of the requirements of the plantation regime governed their behavior is yet unclear. Putative racial deficiencies provided a justification for maintaining a highly coercive labor discipline, but the crux of the problem was the need for labor discipline regardless of the racial character of the work force. "Authority and control," George Beckford reminds us, "are inherent in the plantation system." After all, the raison d'être of slavery in the first place was the plantation's need for a docile, subservient, and immobile labor force. Arguing against free labor, Hugh W. Pugh, a Louisiana sugar planter, insisted that he needed "thorough control of ample and continuous labor." During the Civil War, planters in Union-occupied Jefferson Parish, Louisiana, expressed their willingness to accept "free" labor but wanted one or two military guards stationed on each plantation to "compel the negroes to work." Alabama planters meeting in 1867 resolved "that when we hire freedmen they concede to us the right to control their labor as our time and convenience requires." Historian Lawrence Powell has observed with appropriate sarcasm that "when the old masters talked of free labor, they really meant slave labor, only hired not bought."

The freedmen also proved reluctant to accept the new economic order as defined by the emancipators. In the British West Indies as well as in the American

South, most blacks had been born into slavery and few had experienced freedom. Nevertheless, ex-slaves had their own ideas about the meaning of freedom. They shared with their emancipators the notion that freedom involved some measure of personal autonomy, the ability to make choices about one's life and destiny. Initially, autonomy and control seemed to refer primarily to limitations on white action against them. They wished to be free from physical abuse, especially whipping. They wished to maintain the integrity of their families against forced separation by slave owners. In Jamaica and America freed women and children abandoned field labor for other economic endeavors and education, respectively. It was of such matters as these that they sang during the days of jubilee: no more "peck o'corn," "no more mistress' call," no more stocks and chains, no more driver's lash, no more auction block. But the act of singing itself points up the fact that autonomy was not simply personal, that it embraced familial and community relationships as well. In the American South freedmen withdrew from white churches and formed their own; in Jamaica they expanded their Christian congregations but returned to African rituals and beliefs.

But the freedmen clearly recognized the bearing that economic relationships had on other social arrangements. When informed that the federal government would return to the planters lands temporarily confiscated during the war, a Georgia freedman declared, "Damn such freedom as that." After the war Southern freedmen everywhere resisted the Union policy of evicting them from those confiscated plantations, even when resistance brought them musket to musket against veteran federal troops. Freedmen in Edisto Island, South Carolina, expressed their incredulity at a government policy that rewarded its erstwhile enemies and punished its loyal supporters; in the process they also revealed their understanding of the essence of freedom.

[W]e are at the mercy of those who are combined to prevent us from getting land enough to lay our Fathers bones upon. We Have property In Horses, cattle, carriages, & articles of furniture, but we are landless and homeless, from the Homes we Have lived In In the past we can only do one of three things Step Into the public road or the sea or remain on them working as In former time and subject to their will as then. We can not resist It In any way without being driven out Homeless upon the road. You will see this Is not the condition of really freemen[.]

Other Afro-Americans and Afro-Jamaicans were jealous of their rights as they understood them and quick to defend against any infringement of those rights, even when defense required violence against planters and legal authorities. For example, efforts by planters and special magistrates in Jamaica to impose extra work on the apprentices or to reduce their compensation were met by determined resistance. There were work stoppages, sit-down strikes, and arson on Jamaican plantations. Likewise, in Louisiana during the Civil War, General Nathaniel Banks's forced-labor policies were resisted with strikes and work stoppages by black field hands.

In certain ways the freedmen learned their new economic roles too well, in the view of some whites. They learned to bargain with and to discriminate among potential employers. They learned quickly to place a money value on their time and to demand overtime pay for work beyond normal hours. As one exasperated planter described the situation, "If he goes to the house for an axe he is to be paid extra for it. It's well enough to pay a man for all he does, but who can carry on a farm in such a way as that?" Jamaican planters voiced similar complaints about the freedmen's allegedly overscrupulous attention to the monetary value of time.

The dramatic increase in market activity and thrift among Jamaican and American freedmen immediately following emancipation encouraged missionaries, Bureau officials, and special magistrates to report favorably on their apparent adjustment to the new order. As one American Missionary Association agent reported from the South Carolina Sea Islands: "In temporal things, the colored people of these islands, are mainly doing well. I do not think it would be for their good, at the present time, to increcis [sic] their facilities for getting money. Most of them have ample means for gaining property fast, by their industry & shrewdness; they have become owners of land to a considerable extent, & are raizing [sic] cotton, as they say for 'old nigger himself,' & not fo 'massa.' "

Despite this evidence, however, metropolitan authorities were disturbed by the tendency of freedmen everywhere to devote themselves to economic activities other than the cultivation of plantation staples. Both in Jamaica and in the American South many blacks showed a preference for raising food crops rather than cotton or sugar, just as Henry Taylor had feared they might. No doubt this was due in part to the fact that the labor requirements were much less rigorous for food gardening than for staples, especially for sugar. And on occasion, particularly in Jamaica, provision crops could be more remunerative than plantation wages. But there probably existed more profound causes than these. Jamaicans were not averse to growing sugar, and American blacks grew cotton—on their own account. It was not the crop but the mode of labor organization that they seemed to object to. In both societies freedmen strongly resisted working for wages, preferring task systems and tenant arrangements that left them in apparent, and sometimes substantial, control of their labor.

Of course, the freedmen's views of political economy are less accessible than are those of their emancipators and the planters; we can only infer their "ideology" or world view from their behavior. But one might begin with the hypothesis that because they issued from a radically different set of social relations, they embraced a radically different vision of what man, work, and society should be. In both the British West Indies and the American South many slaves had participated in a market economy, hiring their "own time" and keeping part of the proceeds of their labor, raising and marketing food crops, and so forth. In Jamaica, slave provision grounds fed an extensive and well-developed internal marketing system. But this market experience had to be very different from that envisioned by classical economists, simply because slaves were not subject to the market's full rigor. One needs to distinguish between mere participation in exchange relationships, as in the case of peasants and small landowners who sell their surpluses to buy "luxuries," and complete absorption in and loss of autonomy to the market, as in the case of planters, wage workers, and others whose *primary* purpose is to produce for exchange.

In an attempt to clarify the inherent difficulties in liberal democratic thought, C. B. Macpherson describes a hypothetical simple market society, which he contrasts with a possessive market society like that of nineteenth-century Britain and America. In the former there is an exchange of goods and services that is regulated by the market (supply and demand, etc.), but labor itself is not a commodity. It is presumed that productive resources, such as land, are available to all in such a society. All members of the society retain control over their own resources, including their labor, and exchange only goods and services; consequently no person's gain comes at the expense of another. No person can accumulate more than he produces with his own hand. Although there can be a division of labor in a simple market economy and people are motivated by gain, according to Macpherson one maximizes gains only by greater exertion and more product exchanges and not by converting another man's labor power to one's own use. The difference between what one would earn as a dependent wage laborer and one's earnings as an independent producer—raising subsistence crops and selling the surplus in the market—is likely to be less than "the satisfaction of retaining control of one's labour," that is, one's autonomy. Presumably any inequities that might develop in such a society arise only because of differences in individual will and effort and not because of an unequal distribution of productive resources.

Macpherson defines a possessive market society as one in which labor itself is a commodity. One man's conversion of another's labor power to his own use quickly leads to a society divided by class—one group controlling the means of production and another left without resources. Ultimately such a division undercuts the ostensible benefits of a free economy and liberal democratic political order, argues Macpherson, as one class loses its "powers" and its freedom of action not only in the marketplace but in political and social spheres as well.

It would appear that the ex-slaves, by their own lights, of course, recognized this danger. In Jamaica many withdrew into the hills and raised food crops, laboring on the sugar estates only during the time they could spare from their provision grounds or when natural and man-made disasters forced them back to the plantations. In the American South, given the relative lack of access to land, freedmen made the best deal they could to avoid the wage system—sharecropping. In retrospect, of course, we recognize that sharecropping degenerated into a system of in-kind wages, but this was not self-evident as the system evolved. Indeed, such a development was probably less the result of inevitable economic tendencies than a consequence of the collapse of black political power.

In whatever way one might interpret the freedmen's behavior, it is clear that it disappointed many of the emancipation advocates and played an as yet uncharted role in the racial backlash of the late nineteenth century. It was not so simple a matter as racist ideas appearing where there had been none before. Racist ideas had been there all along; what was new was the willingness to express them, the use to which they were put, and the policies they appeared to justify. People like Henry Taylor, Carl Schurz, and Samuel Gridley Howe had always believed that blacks were inferior to whites in some respects, but their somewhat contradictory belief that blacks had the same basic innate character as whites had leeched their racism of many of its most poisonous consequences. But when released from slavery, blacks did not appear to respond in the ways predicted by the emancipators' other, more powerful ideas about human behavior. Thus racial explanations of the freedmen's behavior—by placing them in a different category of humankind—allowed the reformers to maintain their faith in their liberal democratic ideology which justified the bourgeois world they had created.

The irony, of course, is that the ex-slaves' response to freedom was in accord with many of the tenets of the liberal reformers as to "rational" self-interested behavior. Freedmen were motivated by gain. They worked hard, saved their money, built churches and schools, and tried to improve themselves materially and morally. But as long as they had choices—and possession of or access to land was the major factor creating choice—freedmen resisted working for wages on the plantations. It could be argued, of course, that higher pay, better working conditions, and greater security could have overcome this resistance (or as economists would put it, their "high reserve price" for plantation work). But plantations have traditionally, if not inherently, required cheap and docile labor forces. In any case, to improve conditions was not the way most planters dealt with the situation. American cotton planters adopted sharecropping, which along with crop liens and political coercion helped insure a subservient labor force. Sugar planters turned to indentured workers and mechanization. Where they monopolized the land and controlled the political system, the retooling of their industry proceeded without undue strain on themselves and often with indirect subsidies from their laborers.

The pattern of events following emancipation, then, should have alerted the emancipators to the inconsistencies in their own ideology—namely, that inequality was a precondition for the economic and social system they envisioned. Given their three centuries of experience, the planter class saw this clearly. As long as they were unable to monopolize resources and alternatives, especially land, plantations required slavery or something very much like it. To give, sell, or allow freedmen to squat on land to any significant degree was to surrender the whole plantation system. Furthermore, conceding effective political power to ex-slaves, whereby they might redirect society's resources, threatened a similar disaster. . . .

By the late 1860s and 1870s disillusionment with the progress of the freedmen was pervasive among emancipation advocates and policymakers of the preceding decades. The sighs of despair of an A.M.A. missionary in Jamaica, reflecting on the poverty and irreligion of his congregants, summed up the sentiments of many of his British and American colleagues:

In speaking thus of the straitened circumstances of our people, I cannot in truthfulness attribute it to causes altogether independent of themselves. For while they are not given to vicious habits which tend to impoverish those who indulge them, yet they lack qualities of heart & mind which are essential to success in undertakings of any kind. They are not indolent, yet they are not industrious after the manner of our countrymen, making the most of precious time. They are not extravagant, but neither are they wisely economical. They lack forethought, reflection & practical wisdom in the management of their affairs. They possess little or nothing of the spirit of enterprise & are especially lacking in that indomitable

pluck which grapples with difficulties & scorns to succumb to adverse circum-
stances. . . .

In America many of the liberal reformers of the 1860s formed the core of the
Liberal Republican movement in the 1870s and the Mugwumps of the 1880s and
1890s. Having urged a thorough reconstruction of Southern society earlier, one
including civil and political rights for blacks, they came to revise their assessments of blacks and of the policies to be pursued. They now expressed disappointment with black progress since emancipation, opposed legislation favorable
to the civil and political rights of blacks, and urged that such matters be returned
to the control and discretion of Southern whites.

One could interpret these reversals of racial attitudes as mere expressions of
personal idiosyncrasies or group pathologies. But the strange ideological career
of British and American emancipators suggests a different interpretation. Their
racial attitudes and beliefs were not autonomous, discrete entities unrelated to
other ideas and events; during the emancipation era racial attitudes were shaped
by events even as they shaped events in turn. Thus these beliefs must be treated as
a part of, and not abstracted from, the broader ideological and historical context
in which they occurred.

Perhaps there are implications here for the general treatment of race and
racism in American history. Historians often tend to treat racism as more or less
constant in effect over time, undifferentiated in content, and disconnected from
other developments—in short, as unresponsive to the processes and forces of history itself. Given such treatment, racism becomes a phenomenon that is *a*historical or, as another author has written, "*trans*historical." As such, racial phenomena are almost beyond the scope of historical analysis. It might be more fruitful
to approach such ideas as integral to the larger world view of the protagonists we
study and to evaluate them in the context of their ideas about human behavior
generally.

And, perhaps, it is precisely at this juncture that contemporary historians
confront the difficulty that we are also heirs to the broader nineteenth-century
ideology, even if not necessarily to its particular racist component. Our notions
of the responsibilities of freedom and of appropriate human behavior are no less
experientially and historically unique than were those of the nineteenth-century
emancipators. Most of us would have difficulty defining innate human character
and aspirations in other than our own Western cultural terms. The question of
what terms ex-slaves would have used—their world view—is yet to be fully explored. But while we await that exploration, we must recognize the nature and
limitations of our own presuppositions and resist imposing them upon people
whose experience was by definition quite different. We are heirs of nineteenth-
century liberal democratic thought; often we are its prisoners as well.

Reflections on the Limits
of the Possible

The victory for equal civil and political rights inaugurated by national legislation and the southern state conventions of 1868 was tragically temporary, but it should not be deprecated. Opportunities were opened to former slaves and antebellum free blacks for participation in political power, opportunities they pursued with vigor. However brief and episodic their role in political decision-making and their enjoyment of public facilities formerly denied them, free blacks had defied old taboos and left an imprint upon the institutions of the South—political, social, and economic—which the resurgence of white supremacy never completely annihilated. Some native white southerners not only had supported them out of expediency or loyalty to the Union but had come to accept as valid concepts of racial equity alien to their own past. Yet there can be no question but that the equality of citizenship embodied in national and state law during the 1860s lay shattered and apparently unmendable as the South entered the twentieth century. Most former slaves and their children still lived in agrarian dependence and poverty, poorly educated, increasingly disfranchised and segregated, with little protection against a new surge of white violence.

All accounts of Reconstruction recognize the intensity of white southern resistance to the new status of blacks imposed by Republicans upon the defeated South. Curiously, in explaining the outcome, generally characterized by modern historians as the failure of Reconstruction (though with qualification and some dissent), they tend to place major responsibility not upon the South but upon "the North." By "the North" they usually mean the Republican party, which held national political power, and sometimes say as much. Their explanation is not free of moral stricture, often patently implicit when not expressly stated. Since the mid-1960s there has seldom been missing from accounts of the "First

Reconstruction" the pejorative term "betrayal." Present-day scholars do not indulge in "moral discourse" on black slavery, for as David Donald observed "in the middle of the twentieth century there are some things that do not need to be said." Even less likely is an echo of antebellum abolitionist strictures upon slaveholders as "sinners," though there has been lively debate as to whether or not planters harbored a sense of guilt about their peculiar institution. In terms of the moral judgment of history, the vanquished hold an advantage over the victors. Little restraint or understanding has been extended to the latter. Yet few historians would question the statement that those who won the military contest lost the peace. They have not considered the implications. To lose a battle is not to betray a cause; to retreat in the face of a seemingly weak but relentless and resourceful foe is not the equivalent of treachery; to put an end to a bruising fight that has been lost is not without a certain moral justification of its own. In a self-governing nation the will to persevere indefinitely in a just cause, subordinating all else both of interest and conviction, is beyond the realm of reasonable expectation. If Republican politicians and their constituencies of the 1860s and '70s have received little charity, the one professionally acceptable defense of the opprobrium cast upon them is that the political leaders had viable alternatives—viable in the sense that other policies would have changed the outcome, viable also in the sense that such measures could have been perceived and implemented. . . .

If the success of Republicans in reconstructing the South rested upon the precondition of an absence of race prejudice, the limits of the possible were so narrow as to have foreordained failure. Modern scholarship has recognized and amply documented the pervasiveness and persistence of racial prejudice. In some form it contaminated almost all white Americans. Had mid-nineteenth-century America constituted a society utopian in its freedom from "racism," the obstacles to successful reordering of southern society would have been immensely lessened, though European experience suggests that they would not have been completely removed. It does not follow, however, that race prejudice precluded an equality of civil and political rights. Differences in the quality and priority of prejudice, not only between individuals but between the two major parties, provided a significant opening for political action. By the 1860s many northerners who did not find objectionable discrimination against blacks in private and social relationships had come to view an unacceptable discrimination against blacks in public matters. Most of them were Republicans. Prejudices existed among Republicans, but they did not prevent the party from making equal citizenship the law of the land. To explain the breakdown of that law by pointing to the racial bias of Republicans is unconvincing unless one assumes that a commitment to civil and political equality can be met only by men who accept and seek to realize the more far-reaching twentieth-century concept of racial equality, a highly questionable premise.

Neither can it be taken for granted that a racism so strong as to reject an equality of basic rights is impervious to change. There is no question but that racial attitudes affect behavior, but it is also recognized that behavior affects racial attitudes, though more slowly. Furthermore, a belief in racial inferiority or an emotional revulsion against accepting one of a different race as an equal does not necessarily result in discriminatory action. That may be held in check by a whole range of countervailing forces—by self-interest or a common goal, by institutions such as law with courts that enforce the law, by a perception of discrimination as unwarranted because it conflicts with other norms of societal behavior. And the experience gained by foregoing discrimination can result in changed views and changed emotional responses. Even when it does not, nondiscriminatory practices may continue. Logically, equality may be indivisible; in practice, it has never been a seamless web.

Failure to enforce black civil and political rights in the South is often attributed to a lack of will on the part of Republican leaders and their constituencies due to their racial views. The explanation may not be susceptible of definite disproof, but it has not been proven and probably cannot be. Many factors entered into the abandonment of the cause of the black man in the South, and Republicans gave up neither quickly or easily. The voting record of regular Republicans in Congress through 1891 remained remarkably consistent and cohesive behind efforts to strengthen federal enforcement of Reconstruction legislation. Democratic party obstruction was equally consistent and created a major roadblock. Republicans enacted a drastic enforcement law in 1870 and another in 1871. For most of the twenty years after the elections of 1870 they did not have the power in Congress to pass additional legislation supportive of black rights but they kept the issue alive. It is true that as early as 1872 some Republicans, notably those who joined the Liberal Republican movement, broke with the policy of national action in support of black rights. But race prejudice was neither a conscious nor a major determinant of their new attitude toward federal intervention in the South. Indeed, the Liberal Republican platform of 1872 tried to reconcile a policy of national retreat with loyalty to the Reconstruction amendments. When Republicans regained control of both houses of Congress in 1890–1891 by only a narrow margin, they passed in the House an enforcement bill to protect black voters but narrowly lost it in the Senate by the perfidy of a few who broke ranks to gain support for silver legislation. On the local front in the northern states, in keeping with party tradition, the Republican record on black rights remained better than that of their opponents.

In 1877 when President Hayes withdrew federal troops and acquiesced to "home rule" for the South, racism was not the key to presidential decision. No critical causal connection has been established between the "betrayal" and race attitudes. There is no doubt but that Hayes' action was related to a general lessening of northern support for intervention in the South. The erosion had been going on for several years, and for that there were a number of reasons. The will to continue the battle was undermined by growing doubt of the wisdom of immediate universal black enfranchisement, increasingly seen as the source of corruption. There was revulsion against the turmoil of disputed elections and the force used to settle them. Many Republicans were discouraged as state after state came under "Redeemer" control, or distracted by the pressure of problems closer at home. There was a general desire in the North for the peace and national reconciliation that Grant had invoked but could not attain as president. Whatever part race prejudice played in weakening Republican support for continuing military intervention, its role was peripheral rather than central. . . .

Race prejudice played a larger role in the obstructionist tactics of northern Democrats than in weakening the will of Republicans. During and after the Civil War, appeal to the race prejudice of their constituencies was a standard procedure in election battles. Yet when it failed to yield decisive political profit, northern Democratic leaders changed tactics. By the mid-1870s they had retreated from public avowals to overturn Reconstruction. By the 1880s in northern states they were wooing black voters by helping to enact local civil rights laws and by giving blacks recognition in patronage appointments. Prejudice had bowed to political advantage. Within little more than a decade, an equal right to the ballot was accepted and institutionalized in both northern parties. Continuing support by northern Democrats in Congress for their southern colleagues in opposing federal enforcement of the right to vote rested upon party advantage in maintaining solidarity with the Democratic South.

Racism linked to southern resistance was more politically formidable. As events developed after Congress repudiated Johnsonian Reconstruction and prescribed its own plan, the appeal to white prejudice was critically important. It enabled Democrats to recapture political ascendancy and to cripple the projected operational arm of congressional policy, the Republican party in the South, as an effective contestant for political power. To attain victory the "Redeemers" mobilized a racism whose many faces were evident about them—conviction that white superiority and black incapacity were nature's law, revulsion against accepting the black man on an equal basis in any capacity as both distasteful and insulting, umbrage at being confronted with violations of the race etiquette to which whites had been conditioned by slavery. Racial hostility was used to organize and to justify terror, intimidation, and fraud, particularly in election contests but also in more mundane activities when freedom led blacks beyond "their place."

Even so, racism alone does not explain southern intransigence. It was strongly reinforced by other factors—by the psychological need of white southerners to avoid "dishonor" in defeat, by fears of economic chaos and race warfare, by shock and outrage at the congressional peace terms of 1867, by a perception of Republican demand for black civil and political equality as punitive. Increased taxation at a time of economic stress helped inflame emotions. The result was resistance, sometimes open and sometimes covert, often violent but also subtle. A guerrilla warfare outmaneuvered and overwhelmed Republican forces in the South and gave way before federal military force only to regroup and strike again. It was a resistance strengthened by a sense of right in safeguarding a social order in which blacks were subordinate to whites. If racism was a crucial element in the failure to establish securely black civil and political rights, it was not because racial prejudice permeated both sections, both parties, and all classes. It was because prejudice in the South was deeply rooted, intrinsic to the social and economic structure, and effectively mobilized for political combat. To induce a change in southern white racial behavior to the extent of accepting the black man as an equal in the courts and at the ballot box and as a free laborer entitled to choose, to move about, to better his condition—that task was not in theory beyond the power of Congress and president but it was an uncertain undertaking that would have tested the political skill of any party and president. Fortuitous circumstances, both political and economic, may well have precluded success.

Lincoln's assassination changed the direction of presidential policy, and the downward slide of the postbellum cotton economy of the South reinforced white resistance to change.

A critical question needs to be addressed. Could a greater use of force have brought white southerners to accept civil and political rights for blacks? Neither history nor theory can answer this question with certainty. A number of historians have implied that direct coercion could have effected a fundamental change, that Reconstruction was the nation's great missed opportunity. Few would go so far as Eugene Genovese, who has written that there was no prospect of a better future for blacks unless several thousand leaders of the Lost Cause had been summarily killed. Michael Perman would have had the political and economic power of the southern elite eliminated by means less Draconian and more nearly representative of recent historiographic opinion. He suggests an immediate "edict of the conqueror" enforced by occupying troops to exclude the elite from political power, give suffrage to blacks, confiscate plantations, and divide their lands among the freedmen. Far too good an historian to argue that such an edict had been a practical postwar possibility, he nonetheless believes that had it been possible, it would have worked. William Gillette has taken a more historically realistic approach to the problem. Recognizing that Republicans were not in a position to enforce their Reconstruction program until 1869 when they obtained control of the presidency as well as of Congress, he examines closely the southern record of the Grant years. While he comes to the conclusion that Republicans might have succeeded, or at least achieved a great deal, his analysis of the requirements for success is not reassuring. The skill he sees lacking but needed by Grant might have overtaxed even a Lincoln. According to Gillette, Grant should have been cautious where he was bold, bold where he was timid. He had to be both master politician and resolute soldier. The situation required his effective direction of an expert bureaucracy and an overwhelming military muscle, neither of which was at his disposal. Grant should have overpowered militarily southern white resistance yet come to terms with the fact that "in the long run coercion could not replace a sanctioned consensus." Given the nation's traditional commitment to civilian control and majority rule, "the use of force was self-defeating."

Force *and* consent, how to achieve the one by use of the other, posed a dilemma which by the 1870s strained the bounds of the possible. The outcome would have been only a little less problematic had Reconstruction been formulated in early 1865 and backed by force, i.e., by force alone. Particularly vulnerable is the assumption that by eliminating the power of the landed aristocracy, resistance would have been broken and a new order of equal rights for blacks securely established. There would still have remained for the South as a whole a white majority with prejudices and interests inimical to the advancement of blacks. A stunned acceptance in the despondency of defeat of such peace terms as Perman has outlined would have been no guarantee of their permanent observance by white southerners. Here theory is of some help to speculation. It lends support to Gillette's perception of the need to reconcile the seemingly irreconcilable. Historians have tended to approach the concepts of coercion/consent, or conflict/consensus, as coercion vs. consent or conflict vs. consensus, and not without precedent in political and sociological thought. There exist, however, theoretical analyses that see coercion and consensus as compatible, even complementary. They suggest that the problem, both in theory and practice, is one of interrelationship. Even theorists identified with the view that conflict and coercion are essential to the creation of a new and better social order seldom argue that force alone is sufficient to bring about the change desired. Nor do they overlook the danger that coercion can be self-defeating. The more consensus oriented see force as unable to operate alone over any length of time. The concern to identify "authority," to examine the sources of its "legitimacy," to distinguish authority from "power," to establish the noncoercive forms of power and the nonphysical forms of coercion—these continuing efforts indicate the importance attached to means other than direct force in effecting and maintaining social change. And there is a long tradition of political thought that admonishes caution in trying to force change contrary to traditional convictions lest it provoke deep and bitter reaction. From an approach either through theory or history, it would seem reasonable to conclude that a policy of force *plus* some form and degree of consent—even if the consent, to borrow from P. H. Partridge, were only "a patchwork of divergent and loosely adjusted values, norms, and objectives"—would have had a better chance of success in reordering the South than force alone. Lincoln was capable of a "patchwork" design in implementing policy.

Certainly by the mid-1870s the use of coercion had intensified a deep and bitter reaction. Instead of passive resignation, coercion led to a "negative consensus" that rejected the legitimacy of national authority over the status of blacks, fed resistance, and united white southerners to an unprecedented degree. It is well to be reminded that the coercion used had been considerable. Whatever the formality of consent in the ratification of the Fourteenth Amendment, Congress had left the recalcitrant secession states no effective choice. In the initial enfranchisement of blacks, white southerners were allowed not even the formality of consenting; enfranchisement was mandated by Congress and implemented by military authority and presence. The military also intervened in the reorganization of the South's labor system and in the operation of its local courts. The presence of an occupying army preceded the interim period of military rule set up by Congress in 1867 and did not disappear with the restoration of state authority. Violent resistance to the new order was answered not only by the passage of drastic congressional legislation in 1870 and 1871 but also by the use under these laws of federal armed forces, notably in Mississippi, South Carolina, North Carolina, and Alabama. Troops helped make arrests, guarded prisoners, protected court proceedings, and maintained order at the polls. Over a thousand military arrests were made in three counties of South Carolina in 1871–1872. Federal attorneys obtained 540 criminal convictions in Mississippi in 1872–1873 and 263 in North Carolina in 1873. The district attorney for the northern and middle districts of Alabama obtained indictments of more than 350 persons from two grand juries, one in the fall of 1871 and the other in the spring of 1872. From 1870, when the first enforcement law was passed, through 1874, 3,382 cases under the acts were adjudicated in federal courts in the southern states. In addition, under Grant's direction federal troops in effect decided disputes over who rightfully held elective office in Louisiana, Arkansas, and Mississippi.

The force employed in the 1870s was grossly insufficient for the task at hand. Too often local officials and courts sidestepped justice for blacks without interference. Troops stationed in the South were woefully inadequate in number to contain violent resistance wherever it erupted. Relatively few of the men arrested in South Carolina were brought to trial. In general, indictments were difficult to obtain and even in the federal courts many cases were dismissed. By the end of 1874 little vitality was left in the federal enforcement program. Southern resistance turned increasingly to intimidation and more subtle, less legally vulnerable means than the earlier violence. Democratic power in Congress deprived the executive of resources needed to enforce the laws and prevented legislative action to strengthen them.

Nonetheless, the direct coercion mobilized by the national government in the 1860s and 1870s was substantial, far greater than any similar action in support of desegregation and black voting in the 1950s and '60s. It was large enough to give strong support to the contention that a century ago the amount of force necessary to realize equal civil and political rights in the South was impossible to sustain in a nation whose democratic tradition and constitutional structure limited the use of power, exalted the rule of law, and embodied the concept of government by the consent of the governed. Neither national institutions nor public opinion could be expected to have sustained a military intervention of indefinite length and of sufficient strength to crush all local resistance. And by the mid-1870s, the issue at stake no longer appeared clear-cut, even to northern Republicans. Popular government at the South seemed to have become "nothing but a sham."

Assumptions regarding the potency of national power to effect social change, largely valid for the "Second Reconstruction," may inadvertently have biased historical judgment concerning the earlier period. By the 1950s the capacity for resistance in the South, although still strong, was markedly less than in the post–Civil War decades. Race prejudice remained formidable, but in the wake of Hitler's holocaust and advances in the social sciences, psychology, and biology, prejudice could no longer command arguments of scientific or moral respectability. Despite shocking episodes of violence, white terror never reached the epidemic proportions of the 1860s and '70s. Apparently it was no longer condoned by majority white opinion in the South. Moreover, in the 1950s and '60s not Congress but the judiciary took the initiative in forcing change and remained a vital mechanism for implementing it. The aura of legitimacy created by supportive judicial decisions, lacking in the earlier period, greatly lessened the necessity for direct physical coercion. With a few exceptions, notably at Little Rock in 1957, federal enforcement of court decisions and civil rights legislation proceeded without a show of force. Nor were federal criminal prosecutions numerous. A total of only 323 criminal cases were filed by the newly established civil rights division of the Justice Department from 1958 through mid-1972, only a tenth of the number that had been brought by the attorney general's office in the first five years of the 1870s. Other methods of coercion were available, both more effective and more consonant with the traditional primacy of civil over military authority, or persuasion over force. Civil cases initiated or assisted by the Justice Department far outnumbered criminal ones, and the department was active in negotiating voluntary agreements of compliance and in community counseling. With the great increase in the functions undertaken by the federal government to meet the needs of a mature industrial society, there were at hand powerful monetary and administrative sanctions, and a bureaucracy to use them.

In contrast to the 1870s, during the "Second Reconstruction" votes and time were available to pass a whole array of acts, progressively more comprehensive in scope and more resourceful in their enforcement provisions. What made this achievement possible, according to authorities in the field, was the existence of a national consensus. Although it did not encompass majority white opinion in the South, elsewhere it found support in both major parties, quite unlike the situation in the Civil War era when consensus, on a much more limited program of black rights, existed only within the Republican party. Presidential leadership by the second President Johnson, in contrast to that of the first, was exerted to expand civil rights. In the creation of the national consensus of the 1950s blacks themselves played a key role beyond that open to them a century earlier. Their political influence in the North was considerable because of the numbers who had moved out of the South to fill northern labor needs. The distance from slavery allowed their leaders, South as well as North, to operate with formidable resources, skills, and organization and to present a case that could no longer be evaded by a show of scientific or social justification. They made inescapably visible to white America the injustices piled high during the postemancipation decades.

In short, the "Second Reconstruction" is a false model from which to project in retrospect the limits of the possible a century earlier. As an analogy, however, it suggests the need for far more than direct force to attain success. Its loss of momentum by the 1970s also indicates the difficulty of sustaining a national moral purpose, even with a task recognized as unfinished. In November 1971, the United States Commission on Civil Rights wrote "that the American people have grown somewhat weary, that the national sense of injustice, which was the foundation on which the legislative victories of the 1960s were built, has dimmed." And a few years later other informed analysts agreed. They attributed the fuel for the engine of change during the two previous decades in part to the deceptive clarity of the problems seen through the lens of the New Frontier and the New Society. There had been a naive public faith that new programs of government intervention would quickly bear fruit. Results failed to meet expectations. Advance slowed as injustices were reduced to ones less shockingly visible, as moral issues became clouded by the complexity of problems, as economic conditions turned less favorable, and as conflicts of interest intensified. Analysts concluded that the future was not sanguine. The circumstances of the 1960s had been unusually conducive to change and were not apt to be duplicated. . . .

A fatal weakness of Reconstruction, constitutional historians have argued, arose from the constitutional conservatism of Republican lawmakers, particularly their deference to the traditional federal structure embodied in the Constitution. This led them to preserve the primacy of state responsibility for the rights of citizens, thereby denying to the national government effective power to protect the rights of blacks. It has been contended that Reconstruction required "a major constitutional upheaval," that it "could have been effected only by a revolutionary destruction of the states and the substitution of a unitary constitutional system." Part of the argument is unassailable. The new scholarship has demolished the old stereotype of Republican leaders as constitutional revolutionaries. They had, indeed, been waging a war for constitution as well as for nation with every intent of maintaining both. And the concern of Republicans for state and local government was no superficial adulation of the constitution; it was deeply rooted in their commitment to self-government. Yet unlike Democrats who denounced as unconstitutional any amendment to the constitution that enlarged federal authority at the expense of the states, Republicans did not uphold state rights federalism without qualification. They believed that they had found a way to protect freedmen in their new citizenship status by modifying, rather than destroying, the traditional federal structure. . . .

Similarly circumscribed was any potential role for Lincoln in helping shape economic developments to assure freedmen an escape from poverty and dependence. No explanation for the tragic outcome of the postwar decades for black America has been more generally accepted in modern scholarship than that Reconstruction failed because the national government did not provide land for the freedmen. The thesis has been sharply challenged, and the challenge has not been met. The work of historians and economists in exploring afresh the roots of poverty, particularly of black poverty, in the postbellum South afford some relevant perspectives. Between 1974 and 1979 six book-length studies appeared with significant bearing on the problem of black poverty, and others were in progress; conference papers and published articles also reflected the vigor of scholarly interest in the question.

No consensus has developed either as explanation for the continuing dependence and poverty of southern blacks or as an analysis of the potential economic effect of land distribution. However, four of five econometricians who addressed the latter question concluded that grants of land, while desirable and beneficial, would not have solved the predicament of the freedmen and their children. Robert Higgs has written that "historians have no doubt exaggerated the economic impact of such a grant." Gavin Wright holds that "the tenancy systems of the South cannot be assigned primary blame for Southern poverty," that a more equitable distribution of land "would not have produced dramatic improvements in living standards" or "generated sustained progress." In their book, *One Kind of Freedom*, Roger Ransom and Richard Sutch appear to accept what Heman Belz has characterized as the "new orthodoxy" of the historians, but they dramatically qualified that position in a subsequent paper. They argued that confiscation and redistribution would have resulted in little improvement in the postbellum situation, which they characterize as one of economic stagnation and exploitation, unless accompanied by federally funded compensation for landowners thereby providing liquid capital for reinvigorating agriculture and possibly developing manufactures. This retrospective prescription is restrained as compared to the requirements outlined by twentieth-century experts who seek land distribution as an avenue out of rural poverty. They see successful land reform as requiring supplementary government programs providing credit, seed and fertilizer distribution, marketing facilities, rural and feeder transportation, pricing mechanisms affecting both what the farmer buys and what he sells, technical research, and agricultural education.

More than a land program was needed to insure the freedman's economic future. Although areas of land with high fertility prospered, it seems doubtful that income from cotton between the close of the war and the turn of the century, even if equitably distributed, could have sustained much beyond a marginal level of existence for those who worked the cotton fields whether as wage earner, cropper, tenant, or small owner. And the lower South because of its soils and climate, as Julius Rubin has convincingly shown, had no viable alternative to cotton as a commercial crop until the scientific and technological advances of the twentieth century. Nor could nonmarket subsistence farming offer much by way of material reward. The "more" that was needed can be envisaged in retrospect, and was glimpsed by contemporaries, but it is not clear how it could have been achieved. Gavin Wright has concluded that the postbellum South "required either a massive migration away from the region or a massive Southern industrial revolution." Both in the North and the South there was enthusiasm for promoting southern industry, but only the future could reveal how elusive would be that "New South" of ever-renewed expectations. Despite scholarship, new and old, there is no certain explanation of why the South failed to catch up with the North. If historians and economists should agree upon a diagnosis, it is unlikely that they will uncover a remedy that could have been recognized and implemented a century ago. The heritage of slavery most certainly will be part of the diagnosis. It left behind an underdeveloped, overwhelming rural economy tied to the world market and bereft of adequate foundations for rapid economic growth. Recovery and growth had to be attempted in a period of initial crop disasters, of disadvantage for primary products in terms of world trade, and by the mid-1870s of prolonged and recurrent economic crises. There were high hopes for southern industrialization in the 1880s, but the effort substantially failed. With opportunity drastically limited in the South and industry expanding in the North, there was yet no great out-migration of blacks until the twentieth century. The reasons for this also are not altogether clear. Neither the restraints placed on southern agricultural labor by law and custom nor the discrimination blacks faced in the North is sufficient explanation. The ways in which European immigrants blocked black advance deserve further study, as does the attitude of blacks themselves both toward leaving the South and toward the unskilled, menial labor which alone might have afforded them large-scale entry into the northern labor market. . . .

There were limits to the possible. Yet the dismal outcome for southern blacks as the nation entered the twentieth century need not have been as unrelieved as it was in fact. More than a land program, the civil and political rights Republicans established in law, had they been secured in practice, could have mitigated the discrimination that worsened their condition and constricted whatever opportunities might otherwise have existed for escape from poverty. Moreover, the extraordinary effort black men made to vote—and to vote independently in the face of white cajolery, intimidation, and economic pressure—strongly suggests that for the emancipated to cast a ballot was to affirm the reality of freedom and the dignity of black manhood.

The priority Republicans gave to civil and political rights in their fight to establish a meaningful new status for ex-slaves has been too readily discounted by

historians. Small landholdings could not have protected blacks from intimidation, or even from many forms of economic coercion. They would not have
brought economic power. In the face of overwhelming white opposition, they
could not have safeguarded the new equality of civil and political status. Where
blacks voted freely, on the other hand, there was always the potential for sharing
political power and using it as a means to protect and advance their interests.
There is considerable evidence that this did happen. Local officials elected by
black votes during the years of Republican control upheld blacks against planters, state legislators repealed Black Codes, shifted the burden of taxation from
the poor, granted agriculture laborers a first lien on crops, increased expenditures
for education. Eric Foner has concluded that at least in some areas Republican
Reconstruction resulted in subtle but significant changes that protected black labor and prevented planters from using the state to bolster their position. Harold
D. Woodman's study of state laws affecting agriculture confirms the generalization that a legislative priority of the Redeemer governments was passage of measures to give landowners greater control over the labor force. By the end of the
century legal bonds had been so tightened that as prosperity returned to cotton
culture neither cropper nor renter but only their employer was in a position to
profit. In a study of rural Edgefield County, South Carolina, Vernon Burton has
found that black voting made possible real gains in economic position and social
status between 1867 and 1877. Howard Rabinowitz's examination of the urban
South discloses that Republican city governments brought blacks a greater share
of elected and appointed offices, more jobs in construction work, in fire and police departments. And beyond immediate gains, black votes meant support for
educational facilities through which blacks could acquire the literacy and skills
essential for advancement.

Security for black civil and political rights required acceptance by white
southerners. An acquiescence induced by a judicious combination of force and
consent needed for its perpetuation reinforcement by self-interest. The most effective vehicle of self-interest would have been a Union-Republican party able to
command substantial continuing support from native whites. The Republican
party that gained temporary dominance through the congressional legislation of
1867 enfranchising blacks failed to meet the test of substantial white support.
Despite a strong white following in a few states, its scalawag component from
the start was too limited to offset the opposition's attack on it as the party of the
black man and the Yankee. And white participation diminished as appeals to race
prejudice and sectional animosity intensified.

The potential for a major second party among southern whites existed in the
aftermath of Confederate defeat. The Democratic party was in disarray, discred-
ited for having led the South out of the Union and having lost the war. Old Whig
loyalists subsumed by the slavery issue had nonetheless endured; southern unionism had survived in varying degrees from wartime adherence to the Union to reluctant support of the Confederacy. Opposition to Jefferson Davis's leadership
and willingness to accept northern peace terms had grown as the hope for southern victory diminished. Such sources of Democratic opposition overlapped with
the potential for ready recruits to Union-Republicanism from urban dwellers,
from men whose origins had been abroad or in the North, from those whose

class or intrasectional interests created hostility to the dominant planter leadership of the Democracy. A "New South" of enterprise and industry presented an attractive vision to many a native son. And there were always those who looked to the loaves and the fishes dispensed from Washington.

Had party recruitment and organization, with full presidential support, begun at the end of hostilities and escaped the period of confusion and bitterness that thinned the ranks of the willing during the conflict between Johnson and Congress, the result could have been promising. Greater white support and the accession of black voters by increments might have eased racial tension and lessened deadly factionalism within the party. Lincoln's political skill and Whig background would certainly have served party-building well, as would the perception of presidential policy as one of moderation and reconciliation. The extent to which southern whites did in fact support the Republican party after 1867 despite its image as Radical, alien, and black-dominated, an image that stigmatized and often ostracized them, suggests the potency of a common goal, or a common enmity, in bridging the chasm between the races.

Even under the guidance of a Lincoln, the building of a permanent biracial major party in the South was by no means assured. A broad enduring coalition of disparate elements would face the necessity of reconciling sharply divergent economic interests. Agricultural workers sought maximum autonomy, more than bare necessities, and an opportunity for land ownership while planter-merchants strove to control labor and maximize profit. The burden of increased taxation to meet essential but unaccustomed social services, particularly for blacks, meant an inescapable clash of class and racial interests. Concessions by the more privileged were especially difficult in a South of limited available resources and credit, impoverished by war and enmeshed in inflated costs, crop disasters, and falling cotton prices. By the mid-1870s a nationwide depression intensified regional problems. Efforts to promote a more varied and vigorous economy by state favor, credit, and appropriation became a political liability as the primary effect appeared to be the proliferation of civic corruption and entrepreneurial plunder.

Outside the South a vigorous Republican party and two-party system managed to endure despite the clash of intraparty economic interests. A similar development in the South faced the additional and more intractable conflict inherent in the new black-white relationship. Within the Republican party that took shape after 1867, factionalism often cut between blacks and carpetbaggers, on the one hand, and scalawags on the other; but there was also a considerable amount of accommodation, not all of it from blacks. A study of the voting record of 87 Republicans, 52 of them native whites, who served in the North Carolina House of Representatives in the 1868 to 1870 session shows scalawags trailing carpetbaggers and blacks in voting on issues of Negro rights and support for public schools, yet compiling a positive overall record, a score of 61.2 and 55.9 respectively. On the few desegregation questions that came to a roll call, however, only a small minority of native whites voted favorably. In Mississippi when the black-carpetbagger faction gained control, they quietly ignored the platform calling for school integration even though black legislators were sufficiently numerous and powerful to have pressed the issue. Black office-holding was a similar matter where fair treatment held danger, and black leaders often showed restraint. Such issues were explosive. They not only threatened the unity of the party but undermined its ability to attract white votes or minimize opposition demagoguery and violence. A Lincolnian approach to building an interracial party would have diminished the racial hazard, but could hardly have eliminated it.

The years of political Reconstruction, to borrow an apt phrase from Thomas B. Alexander's study of Tennessee, offered no "narrowly missed opportunities to leap a century forward in reform." Not even a Lincoln could have wrought such a miracle. To have secured something less, yet something substantially more than blacks had gained by the end of the nineteenth century, did not lie beyond the limits of the possible given a president who at war's end would have joined party in an effort to realize "as nearly as we can" the fullness of freedom for blacks.

SUGGESTIONS FOR FURTHER READING

Howard K. Beale, *The Critical Year: A Study of Andrew Johnson and Reconstruction* (Baton Rouge, La., 1947) and William B. Hesseltine, "Economic Factors in the Abandonment of Reconstruction," *Mississippi Valley Historical Review,* 22 (September 1935), 191–220, argue that Radical Republicans were primarily concerned with efforts to perpetuate Republican political control and to advance the economic interests of the Northern industrialists. Claude G. Bowers, *The Tragic Era: The Revolution After Lincoln* (Boston, 1929) argues that during Reconstruction "the Southern people literally were put to the torture" by a "brutal, hypocritical, and corrupt" leadership in the North. E. Merton Coulter argues along much the same lines in *The South During Reconstruction* (Baton Rouge, La., 1947). The "father" of the antiradical school is William A. Dunning. See, especially, his *Reconstruction, Political and Economic* (New York, 1907).

W. E. B. Du Bois, *Black Reconstruction in America* (New York, 1935) is a vigorous direct attack on the position taken by Dunning and his many students, which dominated work on Reconstruction for a half-century. Where Dunning found only unrelieved corruption and evil in the Radical Republican state governments in the South, Du Bois points to their many accomplishments. Du Bois was the first of those historians who have been termed "revisionists"—that is, those who have sought to revise the uniformly negative picture of Reconstruction painted by Dunning and his followers. But it took a quarter-century before the new interpretation suggested by Du Bois became widely accepted. Among the many important revisionist interpretations are the following: John Hope Franklin, *Reconstruction After the Civil War* (Chicago, 1961); Kenneth M. Stampp, *The Era of Reconstruction* (New York, 1965); James M. McPherson, *The Struggle for Equality: Abolitionists and the Negro in the Civil War and Reconstruction* (Princeton, N.J., 1964); Willie Lee Rose, *Rehearsal for Reconstruction: The Port Royal Experiment* (Indianapolis, 1964); Leon Litwack, *Been in the Storm So Long: The Aftermath of Slavery* (New York, 1979); Michael Perman, *Emancipation and Reconstruction, 1862–1879* (Arlington Heights, Ill., 1987); and Eric Foner, *Reconstruction: America's Unfinished Revolution, 1863–1877* (New York, 1988), a portion of which is reprinted here. These works not only give a more positive picture of radical governments in the South; they also avoid the unconcealed racism in the work of Dunning and many of his students.

---

*Available in paperback edition.

Although C. Vann Woodward's monumental study, *The Origins of the New South, 1877–1913* (Baton Rouge, La., 1951, 1971) deals with the post-Reconstruction years in the South, it offers important insights into the meaning of Reconstruction and has exerted an enormous influence on studies of what may be called economic and social Reconstruction in the South, the effects of emancipation and the postwar settlement on the life and labor of the Southern landlords, the yeomen, and the freed slaves. Woodward argues that the Civil War and emancipation marked a fundamental turning point in Southern history. Woodward writes of "new men" taking control and creating a new South on the ruins of the old. This view, when applied more generally, is in line with the "second American revolution" interpretation of Charles and Mary Beard in the previous chapter.

Studies that tend to offer support for Woodward's argument include Michael Wayne, *The Reshaping of Plantation Society: The Natchez District, 1860–1880* (Baton Rouge, La., 1983); Ronald L. F. Davis, *Good and Faithful Labor: From Slavery to Sharecropping in the Natchez District, 1860–1890* (Westport, Conn., 1982); Willie Lee Rose, *Slavery and Freedom* (New York, 1982); and Thavolia Glymph and John J. Kushma, eds., *Essays on the Postbellum Southern Economy* (College Station, Tex., 1985).

Other studies tend to disagree with Woodward and see considerable continuity in Southern history although they disagree with one another in substantial ways: Jonathan M. Wiener, *Social Origins of the New South: Alabama, 1860–1885* (Baton Rouge, La., 1978); Jay R. Mandle, *The Roots of Black Poverty* (Durham, N.C., 1978); Roger L. Ransom and Richard Sutch, *One Kind of Freedom* (Cambridge, Eng., 1977); Robert Higgs, *Competition and Coercion* (Cambridge, Eng., 1977); Gerald David Jaynes, *Branches Without Roots: Genesis of the Black Working Class in the American South, 1862–1882* (New York, 1986); and Gavin Wright, *Old South, New South: Revolutions in the Southern Economy Since the Civil War* (New York, 1986). A broader study that emphasizes continuity and includes a valuable discussion of the literature is Carl Degler, *Place over Time: The Continuity of Southern Distinctiveness* (Baton Rouge, La., 1977). J. Morgan Kousser and James M. McPherson, eds., *Region, Race, and Reconstruction: Essays in Honor of C. Vann Woodward* (New York, 1982) contains a number of important essays reflecting the most recent scholarship (the Holt essay reprinted here is taken from this book). The essays are all by Woodward's former students, but not all agree with his emphasis on discontinuity.

In recent years historians have attempted to provide fuller explanations of how the freedpersons understood the meaning of freedom and their efforts to set goals for the future that gave meaning to their perceptions. Important examples of this work are Julie Saville, *The Work of Reconstruction: From Slave to Wage Laborer in South Carolina, 1860–1870* (Cambridge, Eng., 1994) and Barbara Jeanne Fields, *Slavery and Freedom on the Middle Ground: Maryland During the Nineteenth Century* (New Haven, Conn., 1985).

Studies of the life and policies of Andrew Johnson reveal some of the controversy among historians. He has been depicted as a racist who worked to block equal rights for blacks, as a Jacksonian democrat who despised the planter aristocracy as much as he hated the thought of black equality, and as an inept politician who unnecessarily fomented radical opposition. For examples of studies of Johnson, see Eric McKitrick, *Andrew Johnson and Reconstruction* (Chicago, 1960); Hans L. Trefousse, *Andrew Johnson: A Biography* (New York, 1989); and David Warren Bowen, *Andrew Johnson and the Negro* (Knoxville, Tenn., 1989).

The bitter conflicts over Reconstruction policy left little room for moderate middle-of-the-roaders. A recent study that shows the difficulties faced by moderate Southerners attempting to lead the reconstruction of their states immediately after the Civil War is Dan T. Carter, *When the War Was Over: The Failure of Self-Reconstruction in the South,*

1865–1867 (Baton Rouge, La., 1985). The moderate position, Carter argues, could not survive the conflicts generated by the goals and attitudes of blacks, the masses of former Confederates, and the political aims of the Republicans. Political conflicts among radicals, conservatives, and moderates on the national level may be followed in books by Franklin and Stampp noted above and in David Herbert Donald, *The Politics of Reconstruction, 1863–67* (Baton Rouge, La., 1965); Michael Les Benedict, *A Compromise of Principle: Congressional Republicans and Reconstruction, 1865–69* (New York, 1974); and William Gillette, *Retreat from Reconstruction, 1869–1879* (Baton Rouge, La., 1979).

The literature on Reconstruction is enormous and varied. Students who desire to follow changing interpretations or to find books and articles relating to any aspect of the period might look into the following surveys of the historical literature: Bernard A. Weisberger, "The Dark and Bloody Ground of Reconstruction Historiography," *Journal of Southern History,* 25 (November 1959), 427–47; Richard O. Curry, "The Civil War and Reconstruction, 1861–1877: A Critical Overview of Recent Trends and Interpretations," *Civil War History,* 20 (September 1974), 215–28; Eric Foner, "Reconstruction Revisited," *Reviews in American History,* 10 (November 1982), 82–100; and La Wanda Cox, "From Emancipation to Segregation: National Policy and Southern Blacks" and Harold D. Woodman, "Economic Reconstruction and the Rise of the New South, 1865–1900," both in John B. Boles and Evelyn Thomas Nolen, eds., *Interpreting Southern History: Historiographical Essays in Honor of Sanford W. Higginbotham* (Baton Rouge, La., 1987), 199–253 and 254–307.

An outstanding collection of documents from the Freedmen's Bureau papers and other records in the National Archives, along with splendid introductions and bibliographic references, is the series of volumes appearing under the general title *Freedom: A Documentary History of Emancipation, 1861–1867,* edited by Ira Berlin et al. (Cambridge, Eng., 1982, 1985, 1991). Several volumes are already published, and more are under way.